Public Policy Toward Disabled Workers

Public Policy Toward Disabled Workers

CROSS-NATIONAL ANALYSES OF ECONOMIC IMPACTS

Robert H. Haveman
University of Wisconsin-Madison

Victor Halberstadt
Leyden University

Richard V. Burkhauser
Vanderbilt University

Cornell University Press

Ithaca and London

First published 1984 by Cornell University Press.
Published in the United Kingdom by
Cornell University Press Ltd., London.

International Standard Book Number 0-8014-1626-4
Library of Congress Catalog Card Number 83-7115
Printed in the United States of America
Librarians: Library of Congress cataloging information appears on the last page of the book.

The paper in this book is acid-free and meets the guidelines for permanence and durability of the Committee on Production Guidelines for Book Longevity of the Council on Library Resources.

Contents

Preface

Since the late 1960s the growth in the number of people receiving disability benefits—and the costs of public disability programs—have shown a phenomenal increase in highly industrialized countries. By the 1980s, total expenditures on these programs had grown to a substantial share of total public spending, ranging up to 25 percent. A number of reasons may explain this growth. They include the growing generosity of disability benefit levels; generally deteriorating employment prospects, especially for older workers and those with some work-limiting impairment; liberalized eligibility standards of disability programs; and increases in the population covered by disability programs. The relative importance of these various factors is not known within any single country.

As interest in the growth of disability programs and the use of them as an instrument of social and economic policies has increased, so have the controversies surrounding them. This twin development is largely due to a lack of information on several issues: What are the benefits and costs of disability programs and of program growth? How do the economic effects of the growth of disability programs compare with alternative policy strategies in the context of low economic growth? How are general economic conditions influenced by these programs and their specific design, and vice versa?

In order to examine these issues, the United States Social Security Administration awarded a grant to the first two authors of this volume to support a cross-national study of the recent pattern of evolution and growth in public programs toward disabled workers in eight industrialized countries. These countries were selected on the basis of both the degree of development of their disability programs and the availability of information on the programs during the 1960s and 1970s. Late in 1978, the project was started with a meeting at the Organization for Economic Cooperation and Development (OECD) in Paris, at which the economists chosen to write the eight country papers were present. The purpose of the meeting was to discuss the outlines of the national reports, and to develop a uniform outline and approach for preparing each of the papers. In mid-1979, first drafts of all the country papers were discussed at a second meeting, held at Leyden University, in the Netherlands. Revised drafts of the papers along with an overview paper were presented at a conference in Washington, D.C., in the autumn of 1980. Following this meeting, each of the papers underwent extensive and time-consuming revision and elaboration.

While completing this project, we felt that the insights gained deserved more attention than the publication of the separate country papers and some overview reports and papers would afford.* Encouraged by reactions from academic colleagues and from policymakers, we prepared a synthesis study which organized the insights and information in the eight country papers and placed them in a cross-national and economic context. That synthesis forms Part One of this volume. Richard Burkhauser, who is co-author of the U.S. paper, which was published separately,† joined us in preparing this part. The country papers, apart from that of the United States, form Part Two of this volume.

The goal of this book is to provide a readily accessible exploration of both general economic and specific program issues surrounding public policies toward disabled persons of working age. As such it is a tentative and first step which provides a much-needed cross-national source of information. The available data are of varying quality and accessibility over countries and must therefore be used with great caution. Also, while many of the data in Part One are drawn from the country papers in Part Two, other data are from supplemental sources, and hence rely on program definitions and time periods not reported in the country papers. The focus in Part One is on the 1968-78 period, the most extensive period covered by all the country papers. The data in the volume extend beyond 1978 only where necessary because of program changes. While many developments in disability policy have occurred since 1978, the issues discussed here have only increased in relevance.

The authors of this book are especially grateful to Martin Pfaff and Walter Huber (Federal Republic of Germany), Beatrice Majnoni d'Intignano and Jacqueline Repellin (France), Jack Habib, Haim Factor, and Vincent Mor (Israel), Lucia Vitali (Italy), Han Emanuel and Carel

*Earlier reports on the cross-national findings from the project include V. Halberstadt, R. H. Haveman, K. P. Goudswaard, and B. L. Wolfe, "The Economics of Disability Policy in Selected European Community Countries," in F. A. J. van den Bosch and C. Petersen, eds., *Economic and Arbeidsongeschiktheid* (Deventer, The Netherlands: Kluwer, 1983), and R. H. Haveman and V. Halberstadt, "Public Income Support to Disabled Workers: Issues of Program Growth, Costs, and Labor Supply in a Cross-National Context," in Martin Pfaff, ed., *Effizienz und Effektivität Staatlicher Transferpolitik in der Wirtschaftskrise* (Berlin: Duncker und Humblot, 1983).

†R. V. Burkhauser and R. H. Haveman, *Disability and Work: The Economics of American Policy* (Baltimore: Johns Hopkins Press, 1982).

Petersen (the Netherlands), Eskil Wadensjö (Sweden), and Michael J. McCrostie and Alan Peacock (United Kingdom), who, with us, struggled mightily to trace data and information for their country papers. In several countries, information of the sort contained in the papers had never before been assembled. Assistance in organizing the project was given by Terence F. Kelly (then with OECD), Aaron Krute and Mordechai Lando of the U.S. Social Security Administration, and Leo Crijns (then with the Commission of the European Communities). Able research assistance was given by George Parsons and Kees Goudswaard; and secretarial and administrative assistance by Virginia Martens, Saskia ten Asbroek, and Bonnie Hayward. Helpful comments and suggestions for revision and extension were offered by Barbara Wolfe, and they are gratefully acknowledged. Part One of the manuscript was edited for publication by Elizabeth Evanson; Part Two by Jan Blakeslee, Elizabeth Evanson, and Judith Kirkwood.

The production process for this volume was unique. Making use of the University of Wisconsin-Madison computing facility, the typed manuscript went directly from word processor discs to typeset pages. Todd Hill, Jack Sorenson, and Elizabeth Evanson were crucial in implementing this process and refining the computer programs and techniques necessary for it to succeed. Marie Goodman, Bonnie Hayward, Nancy Rortvedt, and Anne Kremers typed the manuscript and tables with great skill.

Financial support for this project was provided primarily by the U.S. Social Security Administration. A wide variety of other organizations also made the research possible, including the Institute for Research on Poverty at the University of Wisconsin, the Center for Research in Public Economics of the University of Leyden, the German Marshall Fund, the Rockefeller Foundation, the Commission of the European Communities, the Organization for Economic Cooperation and Development (OECD), the Netherlands Social Security Council, and the Swedish Institute for Social Research.

Clearly, the views expressed in the volume are only those of the authors.

October 1983

Robert Haveman
Victor Halberstadt
Richard Burkhauser

Part One

Public Policy Toward Disabled Workers: An Overview

Chapter 1

The Economics of Disability Policy Toward Those of Working Age: An Introduction

Disability programs that are sponsored by governments form an important component of social policies in most industrialized countries. In 1968, among the eight countries included in our study—the Federal Republic of Germany, France, Israel, Italy, the Netherlands, Sweden, the United Kingdom, and the United States[1]—the mean share of national government expenditure committed to the working-aged disabled was just under 7 percent. One decade later it stood at nearly 10 percent, with a high of 25 percent in Italy.[2] This reflects a mean average real increase of about 10 percent per year over the period of our study, and thus represents a substantial and rapidly increasing share of public sector revenues. Indeed, these figures clearly underestimate the degree to which the social commitment is made. They fail to reflect either the ultimate benefits to, or the costs borne directly by, the private sector in adjusting to the expanded network of "right to work" and "equal access" regulations created to integrate the working-age disabled population into an able-bodied society.

The configuration of programs and regulations which has evolved from disability policy in the eight countries over the past two decades reflects a number of social responses and objectives. Some of these are *ameliorative* in nature: they seek to ease the burden of impairments on and the loss of income by handicapped people. Others are *corrective*: they seek to alter either the productivity of handicapped workers or the economic environment in which they function. Still others seek to prevent the onset of disabilities, and involve health and safety regulations and other incentives for accident avoidance and health maintenance.

The ameliorative and corrective disability policy responses undertaken by industrialized countries are the subject of this volume; we exclude the discussion of preventive responses. The income support, labor market, and "equal access" policies which form the ameliorative and corrective strategies for disability policy have a number of characteristics in common, and require joint treatment. First, both types of responses are targeted on disabled persons; both seek to ease the economic burden which the handicapped bear. Second, in most industrialized countries the programs generated by these social responses have experienced rapid growth over the postwar period, and especially in the 1970s. This growth has had costly economic side effects, involving constraints on economic growth and reduced incentives for work effort. These costs have called into question the nature and size of the programs, and have done so with increasing intensity in economies confronted with growing unemployment and little if any expansion. Third, these responses are interrelated. It may make little sense to undertake corrective measures of training and rehabilitation when liberal income transfers make working less attractive than benefit recipiency. In high-unemployment economies, it may or may not be effective to expand corrective measures designed to return disabled people to the labor market relative to ameliorative income support efforts. It is likely that corrective measures in the form of public employment, "equal access," and employment quotas for disabled people may not be cost-effective when even able-bodied workers are unable to find work.

These issues, and others like them, are being increasingly addressed in industrialized nations, and they have motivated this study. Indeed, it was the rapid growth in the budgetary costs and the number of recipients in these programs in several countries that first brought the issues to our attention. The potential efficiency costs of these measures—reduced work effort in the form of early retirement, the displacement of more productive, able-bodied workers by the mandated employment of handicapped workers, the large resource costs associated with training the handicapped and assuring their equal access to employment and mobility—are large, and pose impediments to economic growth which can be especially burdensome in economies plagued by high unemployment, economic stagnation, and high tax burdens. Continuation of these programs at unchanged eligibility requirements and benefit levels without considering the full efficiency costs and other implications of this growth seems unwise, at best.

In principle, the costs and other implications of rapid growth in ameliorative and corrective disability policies can best be, and have been, studied in a single country. We judge, however, that variations in program growth, program structure, and economic performance among industrialized nations provide a richer basis for studying the efficiency and equity trade-offs implicit in the formation of disability policy. This cross-national approach was encouraged by the United States Social Security Administration, and the subsequent research effort resulted in the detailed study of the economic issues underlying disability policy in eight industrialized countries with developed disability policies.[3]

This volume reports the results of that research. The individual studies of the nature and effects of disability policy in seven of the eight countries form the research detail of the volume, and are presented in Part Two. Part One attempts to integrate the material from those country studies with that from the United States study.[4] For this reason, many of the data, research summaries, and illustrations in Part One refer to the situation in the United States. Data and research from the United States are emphasized in Part One because the available data and analyses from that country are both more comprehensive and up to date than elsewhere. Nevertheless, the emphasis in Part One is on the lessons to be learned from a cross-national perspective.

We would stress the unique character of the study. To our knowledge, it is the first time that the *economics* of a major *social policy area* has been addressed in a *cross-national* context. While results and implications are found throughout the volume, it is in Chapter 8 that we develop these lessons fully. We do so by discussing what appear to us to be the major disability policy issues to be confronted over the next decade in all of the countries. If a few sentences had to be used to describe the main conclusion we reach, they would run something as follows:

> Public provision of increasingly adequate income support, training and rehabilitation services to disabled people of working age, and greater efforts to assure them equal access to employment and mobility have yielded substantial social benefits. But achieving these ameliorative and corrective responses to the disabled population has entailed substantial costs—in the form of reductions in work effort and economic growth, in the form of resource diversion from other activities, and in the form of the displacement of more productive resources by those with lower productivity. These costs are the more burdensome in a period of stagnation and low economic growth than when employment is full and incomes are growing rapidly. If, in fact, the prospects for growth over the next decade are relatively poor, these costs must be explicitly recognized and accounted for if an optimal balance between equity and efficiency is to be attained in disability policy.

This conclusion, however, contains no explicit policy recommendations. This is consistent with the entire body of research contained in the volume, which stresses economic approaches to choosing policy options rather than arguing for specific policies.

Our effort is a tentative and first step. The insights developed tell more about the issues that future research should address than they do about the immediate policy changes which should be implemented.

In Chapter 2, we describe the extent and character of the disabled working-age population in the eight countries studied. Data for the United States are used for illustrative purposes, but the patterns described hold for the remaining countries as well. The emphasis in this chapter (and in the remainder of the book) is on the working-age population—especially the older members of that population. It is with respect to this group that the primary policy issues lie. Most of the data analyzed are for the 1968-78 period, for which information was available in all eight countries.

Chapter 3 addresses a most basic economic issue in this area: Why should governments intervene to share or reduce the costs of disability in a society? Three justifications for collective action are presented. The first is a traditional, neoclassical rationale, and rests on a variety of market failures including spillovers, public goods, information problems, and incomplete markets. The second rationale rests on the recognition that numerous constraints—some imposed by government, such as the minimum wage or mandated costs to the employer—inhibit the performance of labor markets, and that these constraints are not likely to be reduced or eliminated. This rationale, then, leads to the search for policy instruments which can offset the adverse effects of these constraints. It is a second-best rationale. The third rationale is a radical one and emphasizes the need for policies to change the economy—indeed, the society—to accommodate the disabled, rather than policies designed to assist or to train the disabled.

Chapter 4 describes the nature of disability policy in the United States as an illustration of those in a number of developed countries. The structure, eligibility criteria, benefit levels, and growth of the primary programs in the system are described within the context of their ameliorative (disability cost-sharing) and corrective (work-enhancing) responses to the disabled population. The character of this system is compared with that in the seven other countries studied through a series of thumbnail sketches of the policy approaches taken in these other countries.

The generosity of and government expenditures on ameliorative programs—as well as the number of disability transfer recipients—have grown very rapidly in several of the eight countries studied. The nature and sources of this liberalization and growth, and their impact on benefit acceptance and work effort, are the subjects of Chapter 5. We present a simple economic model of how government programs affect the choices which individuals make, and analyze the empirical evidence of their effect on the labor supply of older workers.

Chapter 6 looks at another impact of ameliorative programs; it measures the extent to which disability programs replace lost income and prevent those with impairments from falling into poverty. It is the "adequacy" of disability programs which is the issue in this chapter.

Chapter 7 turns from ameliorative to corrective programs and describes and evaluates the work-enhancement programs—sheltered workshops, vocational rehabilitation, subsidized employment, and equal access programs—in the eight countries. The efficiency of these programs is the issue. Are resources productively employed in these activities, or is the effort to generate or guarantee employment to this basically lower-productivity group ill-advised from an efficiency point of view?

Finally, Chapter 8 discusses the primary disability policy issues confronting industrialized countries with mature social welfare programs. These include the tension between the use of disability income transfer policies as instruments of income redistribution as opposed to insurance programs, the orientation of the system toward income support or rehabilitation and employment provision, and the costs and benefits of assuring equal access of disabled people to employment, mobility, and public facilities.

Notes

1. The country studies were prepared by Martin Pfaff and Walter Huber (Federal Republic of Germany), Beatrice Majnoni d'Intignano and Jacqueline Repellin (France), Jack Habib, Haim Factor, and Vincent Mor (Israel), Lucia Vitali (Italy), Han Emanuel, Victor Halberstadt, and Carel Petersen (the Netherlands), Eskil Wadensjö (Sweden), Michael J. McCrostie and Alan Peacock (United Kingdom), and Richard Burkhauser and Robert Haveman (United States).

2. The figure for Italy includes expenditures for disabled people above retirement age.

3. The primary financial support for this study was from the U.S. Social Security Administration. A wide variety of other organizations also contributed to the research, including the Institute for Research on Poverty at the University of Wisconsin, the Center for Research in Public Economics of the University of Leyden (the Netherlands), the German Marshall Fund, the Rockefeller Foundation, the Commission of the European Communities, the Organization for Economic Cooperation and Development (OECD), the Netherlands Social Security Council, and the Swedish Institute for Social Research.

4. The complete study of disability policy in the United States is given in Burkhauser and Haveman (1982).

Chapter 2

The Extent and Character of Measured Disability among the Working-Age Population

Any discussion of the economic and policy issues affecting those who are disabled must rest on some common understanding of what the term "disability" means, and some notion of the extent of the disabled population and its demographic and economic composition. In this chapter, we focus first on defining disability and then on measuring the size of this population and delineating its demographic and economic characteristics. Our definition of disability will remain constant throughout the chapter, and some effort will be made to present measures of the extent and composition of disability across countries. However, because countries use varying definitions in their statistics and programs, comparisons are difficult. It must be emphasized that in this study we are only concerned with the *working-age population*.

Defining Disability and Measuring Its Extent

It takes little reflection to realize the difficulty of establishing a meaningful definition of disability. At the limit, any personal characteristic which reduces a person's proficiency in performing some worthwhile function could be described as a handicap or disabling condition. Hence, if two otherwise identical and normally functioning people differ only in the average amount of sleep they require per night, the person requiring more sleep is handicapped relative to the person requiring less. Yet few would define the former person to be disabled. If two otherwise identical people differ only in that one is able to work cooperatively with others while the other is not, is the latter to be considered disabled? In standard economic (as opposed to medical) definitions of disability, the *characteristics* admitted to the definition involve mental and physical characteristics—

traits of personality, taste, and appearance have been excluded. And those physical or mental characteristics which have been admitted are those which either constrain normal daily activities or cause a substantial reduction in productivity on the job. Hence, the individual who has difficulty cooperating may well be classified as disabled if this characteristic results in emotional difficulties which cause reduced productivity or an inability to obtain or retain employment.[1]

Having identified those individual characteristics on which the judgment concerning disability status will focus, a *norm* or standard must be set in order to decide whether or not a disabling condition is present and, if so, its extent. Clearly, setting as a norm the completing of a marathon race in less than four hours would leave the overwhelming majority of the working-age population classified as disabled. For those of working age, the norm most commonly adopted concerns the ability to carry out the tasks of a commonly accepted occupation—in short, the ability to engage in work that is sufficient to earn a living. In the United States, for example, the definition tends to revolve around the ability of the person to engage in "substantial gainful activity." Reference is also made to a somewhat less demanding norm—a norm which concerns the ability of a person to live independently, carrying out standard housekeeping and personal maintenance functions without assistance. In both of these cases, it is not the personal or mental characteristics which are observed, but rather the outcome of these characteristics. The criterion is a performance criterion, and not a structural one. Having said that, however, it should be noted that in practice certain structural characteristics are accepted as proof that performance cannot be adequate. Thus, a quadraplegic is typically classified as disabled, even though he or she may have perfectly adequate labor market performance and earnings.

The focus on performance seems appropriate, given the multidimensional character of physical or mental conditions, the difficulty of accurately measuring many of them, and the complex ways in which they relate to the demands of the labor market. In a world in which a paraplegic can operate more successfully in the labor market and in self-care than a person of equal age and education with a combination of varicose veins, back problems, and low level of education, the identification of disability through the scrutiny of physical and mental characteristics seems far less satisfactory than observing performance directly.

This focus on performance, however, raises a crucial issue. If one could reliably determine the extent to which a person is constrained in earning a living or living independently by comparing physical or mental characteristics to items on a medical listing, medical or psychological personnel could make objective determinations. And yet the gap between such determinations and actual performance is a substantial one. But, while one is more likely to gain an accurate assessment of the extent of disability by focusing on performance, the door is left open for abuse. It is easier to alter behavior or performance in order to be classified as eligible for support than it is to alter more objectively defined mental or physical characteristics. At least some of what is gained by using a performance norm is sacrificed by the conscious alteration of performance to meet the implicit standard.

Setting a norm, however, does not resolve the issue. The third issue in defining disability is how great a *deviation from the norm* is required before a person is classified as disabled. If it is labor market performance which is to serve as the criterion, how poor does an individual's actual or potential performance have to be before the person is to be classified as disabled? Is poor performance to be measured in terms of the number of hours per week that a person can work relative to, say, 40 hours per week, or is the wage rate which can be earned also a consideration? Is the standard of comparison to be the person's former performance or some average performance of persons of his or her age and education cohort? And how far below this norm is a person to be before he or she is classified as disabled? Even if the norm was based on the presence of disabling physical or mental characteristics—a medical definition of disability—there is an issue of deviation. Nearly all such conditions involve a continuum, and a decision is required on the extent to which the severity of the condition warrants the declaration that a disability exists.

This brief excursion through a few of the issues surrounding the definition and measurement of disability is sufficient to convey the multidimensional character of disability—and this discussion has focused only on the two-category classification of disabled versus not disabled. Additional problems arise when one attempts to identify various degrees of disablement. Just as there is no reliable guide as to where the line should be drawn between disabled and not disabled, there is no clear way of distinguishing the severely disabled from those who are disabled but not severely. Clearly, some judgment regarding the deviation from a norm must be made, but the extent to which that judgment should reflect the temporary or permanent character of the condition—or the age or education of the person, or the condition of the labor market in which he or she operates—is not clear. And it is at this point that societal judgments enter the definition. Different societies, or the same society at different points in time, have quite different expectations regarding the level of performance of an individual that would qualify the individual as being disabled. Indeed, some authors have viewed the definition of disability as, ultimately, a subjective judgment.[2]

Irrespective of this need for judgment, some estimate of the magnitude and composition of the disabled working-age population is essential in developing effective disability policies. Such estimates establish the domain of the policy problem and give a rough notion of the economic, demographic, and social circumstances of those who occupy that domain.

For example, if the number of disabled individuals was small, the provision of rehabilitation and training services would seem to be more appropriate than the provision of income transfers. While the definitions and measurement techniques adopted by the countries with developed disability systems vary widely, in each case the size and composition of the working-age population with disabilities have been identified.

Among the countries studied, two primary measurement techniques have been employed: the self-assessment of disability status through surveys, and the use of actual disability determinations in social assistance programs. Clearly, these techniques are likely to yield quite different estimates—the strengths of one are precisely the weaknesses of the other. While survey methods can obtain full coverage of the population, the self-assessment procedure can lead to substantial and unknown biases.[3] While program eligibility determinations have a more objective basis, the coverage of the population is far from comprehensive, even in those countries with developed and universal social security programs.

Table 2.1 provides a sketch of the nature of the definitions of disability used by the eight countries studied, and a brief description of how these countries have measured the size and composition of the working-age disabled population. While nearly all of the countries explicitly include some limitation on work or earnings capacity as part of the definition, the degree to which this factor is relevant varies widely. Neither the Netherlands nor the United Kingdom focuses on this work-capacity criterion, relying rather on a reduction in functional or self-care abilities. Nearly all of the countries include mental as well as physical limitations, but there are some exceptions here as well. The Netherlands has adopted a definition which focuses on physical handicaps; to some extent, this is true for the Federal Republic of Germany as well.

Table 2.1. The Definition and Measurement of the Disabled Working-Age Population in Eight Countries, 1978

	Definition of Disability	Measurement of the Disabled Population
Federal Republic of Germany	Permanent or indefinite loss or reduction in ability to pursue gainful employment caused by congenital or occupational disease, work accidents, or injuries due to political events. In the survey, those who declare themselves handicapped and recipients of a disability pension are considered disabled.	Supplemental survey to the micro-census of 1976.
France	The definition has varied significantly over survey measurement efforts, but some notion of work and self-care capability is the central focus. Alterna-	Census-type studies in 1962 and 1964 with disability self-defined. Reliance on data on program benefit recipients for distinguishing severely disabled.

Table 2.1. (cont.)

	Definition of Disability	Measurement of the Disabled Population
	tive definition is based on program eligibility determinations.	Updated by assuming constant incidence rates within demographic group.
Israel	The definition relates to "sickness or disability" as the *primary* cause of work restriction, when fewer than 35 hours per week or 40 weeks per year were observed.	1974 Income and Labor Force Survey, in which effort was undertaken to determine causes of part-time or part-year work.
Italy	The definition—established in 1939 as part of the disability pension program—stipulates a reduction of two-thirds in earnings capacity in occupations suited to ability due to illness or physical or mental impairment. *Capacity* refers to a "general adequacy" to provide an income through work. *Impairment* refers to a permanent condition, and *illness* refers to a long-term condition. *Suitable occupation* refers to positions consistent with training, age, strength.	Data on number and composition of public program budget recipients. Official program assessment of disability status depends on (1) an objective medical test, (2) judgment of working skills, and (3) evaluation of social and economic environment, leading to judgment of the reduction in earning capacity.
The Netherlands	The definition used in the survey concerns only physical handicaps, thought of as a permanent functional limitation. For purposes of program eligibiity, the law defines as disabled, wholly or partially, "he who as a consequence of illness or infirmity, fully or partly, is unable to gain—with labor which is commensurate to his force and capabilities and which, in view of his training and previous profession, he can reasonably be asked to perform at the place where he works or worked last or at a similar place—what physically and mentally healthy persons of the same kind and similar training at such a place usually gain through labor." The degree of disability is distinguished by 7 classes from 15 to 100 percent.	A 1971-72 mail survey of 70,000 persons, asked to self-report disability. Respondents reporting some handicap were visited to verify handicap, and to ascertain its severity. Updated by assuming constant incidence rates within demographic groups.
Sweden	The presence of a long-standing illness or ailments caused by an accident, handicap, or other weakness (or the need for regular medication) *and* a reduction in working capacity caused by the long-standing condition.	Annual surveys of living conditions.
United Kingdom	The definition used in the survey of the impaired population is as follows: "the absence of all or some part of a limb, or the presence of a defective limb, organ, or mechanism of the body." Severity of impairment dis-	A 1968-69 national survey updated by assuming constant incidence rates within demographic groups.

	Definition of Disability	Measurement of the Disabled Population
	tinguished by 8 categories relating to the ability to provide self-care. To determine eligibility for official registration as disabled, a person is regarded as disabled "if he/she is one who on account of injury, disease, or congenital deformity is substantially handicapped in obtaining or keeping employment—or in undertaking work on his own account of a kind which, apart from that injury, disease or deformity, would be suited to his age, experience and qualifications."	
United States	Limitation in the kind or amount of work (or housework) resulting from a chronic health condition or impairment lasting 3 or more months. Severely disabled implies an inability to work altogether or regularly.	Household surveys in 1966 and 1972, with follow-ups in 1970 and 1974. Household survey in 1978 (by Social Security Administration).

In most of the countries, estimation of the size of the disabled population is by means of a survey in which self-reporting and, to some extent, self-definition are required. The surveys, however, are often outdated and extrapolation to obtain current estimates requires the application of constant incidence rates to demographic groups whose size changes over time. In one country, Italy, no survey data are available and estimates have to rely on data on the number of recipients of program benefits. Because of the extensiveness of the disability system in Italy, however, these estimates are likely to convey a reasonable picture of the size and composition of the disabled population.

The Size of the Working-Age Population: A Cross-National Comparison

Table 2.2 presents estimates of the size of the disabled working-age population in 1978 in the eight countries studied, stated as a percentage of the total population of working age. Where possible, the composition of the disabled working-age population by severity of the disabling condition is also shown. The primary source of data for the incidence estimates is from surveys in which health status is self-reported. The definitions of disability indicated in Table 2.1 are reflected in the surveys. As a result, the estimates in this table must be interpreted with great caution.[4]

The two countries with the highest incidence are Sweden and the United States, with 17.7 and 14.6 percent, respectively. While the statistics in these countries are perhaps the most accurate among the countries studied, the

Table 2.2. Incidence of Disability in the Working-Age Population, 1978

	Percentage of Working-Age Population		
	Severely Disabled	Disabled, but Not Severely	Total
Federal Republic of Germany[a]	NA	NA	7.3
France[b]	1.7	1.7	3.4
Israel[c]	NA	NA	4.5
Italy[d]	NA	NA	9.3 (20.0)
The Netherlands[e]	NA	NA	8.2
Sweden[f]	7.9	9.8	17.7
United Kingdom[g]	1.0	2.6	3.6
United States[h]	7.3	7.3	14.6

[a]The disabled population aged 15-64 as a percentage of the total population aged 15-64. The disabled population includes those who self-report themselves to be disabled in a 1976 "micro-census" *plus* all recipients of a disability pension who did not report themselves to be disabled.

[b]The disabled of working age as a percentage of the working-age (18-64) population. Estimates made from a combination of self-reported, self-defined census-type information from 1962 (assuming constant prevalence rates among demographic groups) and institutional data from agencies providing assistance to the handicapped.

[c]The number of nonaged disabled (with health-related work limitations) as a percentage of the working age (18-64) population. [Note: The numerator is likely to understate the appropriate total because it includes only those who give health status as a *primary* reason for less than full-time, full-year work and hence understates the female total.]

[d]The number of disabled receiving benefits who are below pensionable age (60 years for men, 55 for women) as a percentage of the labor force. The figure in parentheses (20.0) includes those receiving a disability pension who are above pensionable age. After subtracting an estimate of the number of disability pensioners who would not be disabled from a medical point of view (based on a comparison of regional differences) the two figures become, respectively, 7.9 percent and 16.1 percent.

[e]The number of physically handicapped aged 20-64 as a percentage of the age 20-64 population. The data are based on a 1971-72 survey. [Note: The numerator includes only the physically handicapped, and thus understates the total. The denominator is the correct concept—the working-age population.]

[f]The number of disabled aged 16-64 as a percentage of the age 16-64 population. Disability is self-reported in the 1978 level-of-living survey, and those considered to be disabled report the presence of a long-standing illness or handicap which causes a reduction in earnings capacity. [Note: The definition of disability appears to be somewhat less restrictive than that for other countries.]

[g]The disabled population aged 16-64 as a percentage of the age 16-64 population. Disability was self-reported in a 1968-69 national survey and updated to 1978 by assuming that disability incidence within age groups is constant. The definition of disability is closely related to the nature of a physical impairment, rather than the loss of functional ability. Perhaps this definition—especially the lack of emphasis on mental problems—accounts for the low incidence reported in the survey.

[h]The disabled population aged 20-64 as a percentage of the age 20-64 population. The presence and severity of disability is self-reported in the 1972 Survey of Disabled and Non-Disabled Adults. The 1978 estimate is obtained by assuming a constant incidence of disability within demographic groups. The "disabled, but not severely" group includes the occupationally disabled and those with secondary work limitations.

high percentages are likely to be in part attributable to the inclusion of substantial numbers of nonpermanently disabled. In Sweden, the condition simply had to be "long-standing," whereas a three-month duration was stipulated in the U.S. survey. The indefinite character of the "long-standing" designation in the Swedish case would seem to yield an exaggerated estimate. The two countries with the lowest incidence are France and the United Kingdom, with 3.4 and 3.6 percent, respectively. The statistical basis of the estimate in both of these countries is among the weakest of the countries studied. The estimate for France is especially poor. The estimate for the United Kingdom appears biased downward owing to the focus on physical—rather than physical and mental—impairments in the definition employed. This restriction of the definition to physical handicaps also plagues the estimate for the Netherlands.[5]

Given these weaknesses in the data, a good deal of judgment must be exercised before reaching any general conclusion regarding the extent of disability among the working-age population, and its variation across the eight countries. If a definition of disability which emphasizes both the permanence of the condition *and* its effect in seriously reducing work or earnings capacity were applied consistently over all countries, it seems likely that from 5 to 10 percent of the total working-age population in the countries studied would be classified as disabled. The variation in this percentage across the countries would be substantial, however. Given the biases which have been observed, it seems likely that the "true" incidence of disability would be higher in Israel, Italy, the Netherlands, and the United States (and, perhaps, Sweden) than in France, the United Kingdom, and the Federal Republic of Germany. Because of the inherent weaknesses in the data, these should be regarded as best estimates offered on the basis of available information.

The Characteristics of the Disabled Working-Age Population

From information which is fairly complete in some of the countries but fragmentary in others, it appears that for the period 1968-78 the demographic characteristics of the disabled population are quite similar across countries. Among those of working age, older people are far more likely to report being disabled than younger people. Similarly, those with less education have a higher incidence of self-reported disability than those with more education. To some extent, this is caused by the concentration of workers with less education in the more dangerous occupations and industries. The direction of causality may also run the other way, however. Those with congenital disabilities or those who have become disabled while young may not find it economically worthwhile to pursue extensive education. Conversely, some may seek additional education in an effort to offset the adverse effects of a handicap.

Countries with racial (or foreign) minorities find higher rates of self-reported disability among these groups than among racial majorities (or native citizens). To some unknown extent, this may be because of the relationship between education and disability, as the foreign minority may tend to be of lower than average education and in less-skilled occupations. In most of the countries, the female population shows a somewhat higher incidence of disability than does the male population. Presumably this is caused by the longer average length of life of women relative to men. As a result, women outnumber men in the upper age ranges of the working-age population. Offsetting this are the aftereffects of war and the greater participation of men in the work force, and hence in occupations which are physically dangerous. Finally, disabled workers work less and earn less than others in the working population and, even with government programs, they have less total income.

Because detailed statistics on these patterns among working-age people who report disability are not available in systematic form for most of the countries studied, we will illustrate these patterns with data for the United States. The general patterns shown there are representative of those in the other countries. Special circumstances in some of the countries will be mentioned after these data are described.

The demographic composition of the self-reported disabled members of the working-age population for 1978 is shown in Table 2.3. It is based largely on the Social Security Administration's *Survey of Disability and Work*. This survey is based on household interviews in which individuals were asked to classify themselves in terms of the extensiveness of their impairment.[6] These statistics indicate that disability prevalence was greater among women than among men (17.7 percent of women had some degree of disability compared to 15.8 percent of men), and that the disparity was even greater between men and women who classify themselves as severely disabled. The composition of the disabled is also heavily weighted toward older people. While 35 percent of the population aged 18-64 was 45 years old or more, 72 percent of the severely disabled group was older than 45 years. This is reflected in the median age of the severely disabled and the nondisabled—the former group has a median age which is 15 years greater than the latter group.

The data in Table 2.3 also show that blacks and other nonwhites are more heavily represented among the disabled than among the general population. Nonwhites composed 12 percent of the total working-age population, but accounted for 16 percent of the disabled population and over 18 percent of the severely disabled population.

As with sex, age, and race, the composition of the disabled population is heavily weighted toward individuals with low educational attainment.

Table 2.3. The Composition of the Disabled Working-Age (18-64) Population in the United States, 1978

Characteristic	Total U.S. Working-Age Population (millions)	Disabled and Nondisabled as Percentages of Total: Severely Disabled: 10.8 million (%)	Disabled, but Not Severely: 10.5 million (%)	Nondisabled: 105.8 million (%)
Total population	127.1	8.5	8.3	83.2
Race				
White	111.2	7.9	8.3	83.7
Nonwhite	15.9	12.3	8.0	79.7
Sex				
Men	63.1	7.3	8.5	84.2
Women	64.0	9.6	8.1	82.3
Age				
18-34	58.2	2.6	5.5	91.9
35-44	24.9	6.4	8.1	85.5
45-54	23.7	11.3	12.3	76.4
55-64	20.3	24.8	11.7	63.5
Marital Status				
Married	86.3	7.8	8.8	83.4
Widowed	3.7	30.5	6.9	62.6
Divorced, separated	10.9	15.3	10.7	74.0
Never married	26.0	4.6	5.9	89.5
Education				
8 years or less	14.6	24.8	11.0	64.2
High School	68.4	8.3	8.8	82.9
College	43.5	3.2	6.5	90.3
Region				
Northeast	30.4	6.9	7.6	85.5
North Central	34.9	7.2	9.0	83.8
South	40.2	10.7	7.5	81.8
West	21.6	8.6	9.5	81.8
Urbanization				
Rural[a]	17.6	10.2	7.9	81.9
Urban, under 100,000	45.1	6.4	7.9	85.6
City, 100,000 or more	29.1	7.6	7.3	85.1
Suburb	10.0	4.8	5.0	90.2

Sources: 1978 data from Lando, Cutler, and Gamber (1982); 1972 data (area and size of community) from Allan (1976, p. 20).

[a]The data for area and size of community (rural, urban, city, and suburb) are for 1972.

While only 9 percent within the nondisabled population had 8 or fewer years of education, more than 34 percent within the severely disabled group had not attended high school. Of course, part of the compositional effect is explained by the relationship between age and disability, as older people also tend to have less education. However, as noted above, the nature of causality between education and disability status is not well understood.

The composition of the disabled also has a regional and a rural-urban dimension. As Table 2.3 shows, the South is substantially more heavily represented in the disabled population than in the population as a whole. While 32 percent of the nation's population resides in the South, 40 percent of the nation's severely disabled population is located in that region. Again, because of the relative concentration of blacks in the South, the relationship between race and disability is likely to account for some of this regional disparity.

Finally, the disabled population—in particular, the severely disabled group—is composed of unmarried individuals to a larger extent than in the nondisabled population. While about 68 percent of the nondisabled population is married, only about 63 percent of those in the severely disabled population are married. Consistent with this pattern, the disabled population is more heavily composed of divorced and widowed individuals than is the nondisabled population. This high concentration of widows or widowers among the disabled is, in part, explained by the older average age of the disabled group.

From the evidence available, these basic patterns appear to be replicated in the other countries studied. These countries, however, often have special circumstances which give the demographic composition of their disabled population a unique character. A few of these deserve mention. In the Federal Republic of Germany, the aftereffects of World War II are seen in the sex composition of its working-age disabled population. In 1960, nearly 80 percent of the disabled were male; by 1978, the proportion had fallen to about 50, as many of the war injured had died or reached retirement age. In Israel, the pattern that persisted earlier in the Federal Republic of Germany still exists. In the 1974 survey in Israel, the incidence of health-related work limitations among men was 170 percent of that for women. For the population aged 55-64, the male incidence was more than 220 percent that of the female population. While some of this disparity is war-related, the survey questionnaire, by inquiring into the primary reason for not working, was biased against the inclusion of women. Housewives who have disabilities may well have other reasons—such as child care responsibilities—which serve as the primary reasons for not working.

The regional variation in the incidence of disability which was seen in the United States is also observed in the other countries. Indeed, in three of the countries studied—United Kingdom, Italy, and Sweden—this regional variation was very pronounced. In the United Kingdom, the incidence of the impaired population in the southwestern region was 50 percent greater than that of the region which includes Greater London.[7] In Italy, as we will see, the disability pension program is explicitly used as an instrument to support those who are underemployed or who have experienced long-term unemployment. As a result, the number of those receiving disability pensions as a percentage of the labor force in the poor, high-unemployment, largely agricultural southern region (the Mezzogiorno), was nearly 150 percent of that in the industrialized northwestern region.[8] For Sweden, it is the northern, sparsely populated regions which showed the highest incidence of disability—about 130 percent of that of the total population.[9]

Disabled Workers, the Labor Market, and Economic Status

Consistent with economic theory, the wage earnings of two individuals with the same tastes for work and employed in the same labor market will differ depending upon the productivity of the two individuals as perceived by employing businesses. Productivity, in turn, depends on a host of other characteristics of the individual—education, age, sex, job experience, and so on. In addition to productivity, other factors can also influence individual earnings. For example, labor market discrimination may make it more difficult for women than for men (or blacks than for whites) to obtain and keep jobs, or to move up internal job ladders. Moreover, unemployment rates in depressed or slowly growing regions will cause average earnings in these regions to be lower than elsewhere.

Leaving aside considerations of health status, we have observed that disabled individuals have productivity characteristics which would imply relatively low incomes. Disabled people tend to be older workers and to have relatively low levels of education. Moreover, to the extent that women and other minorities are disproportionately represented in the disabled population (as is true in many of the countries studied), labor market characteristics may tend further to constrain their realized earnings.

By definition, however, disabled individuals are impaired, although with varying degrees of severity. As a result, observed earnings for them are likely to be even lower than would be expected from their adverse demographic and other economic characteristics. In some sense, then, they are "doubly disadvantaged" in their expected labor market performance.

As with the discussion of the demographic characteristics of the disabled, we will illustrate the general patterns of economic status with data for the United States. Again, among most of the countries studied, data of this sort vary widely in detail and quality, and in some of the countries only fragmentary data exist. After the discussion of the U.S. data, patterns of labor market and economic status peculiar to the other countries studied will be described.

To look more closely at work characteristics of the disabled population, we rely on U.S. Census Bureau data for 1977 from the Current Population Survey (CPS).[10] While this survey of 50,000 families is not designed to yield estimates of the disabled population, it is possible to use information on the CPS microdata file concerning reasons for work limitation, program participation, and wage rates to estimate the size and composition of the disabled, noninstitutionalized population aged 20-64.

Table 2.4 presents data on the labor force participation of the disabled and the nondisabled. A far higher proportion of the disabled than of the nondisabled do not work, and of those who do work, many fewer work full time. This pattern is not surprising, since disabled people tend to be older

Table 2.4. Labor Force Participation of Disabled and Nondisabled in the United States, by Sex, 1977 (percentages)

	Men		Women	
	Disabled	Nondisabled	Disabled	Nondisabled
Do not work	36.2	4.1	47.2	35.6
Work part time, all year	3.0	2.3	5.5	7.4
Work full time, part year	25.9	16.5	23.0	13.6
Work part time, part year	4.7	3.1	13.7	10.4
Work full time	30.3	74.0	10.7	33.0

Source: Wolfe (1979).

workers and those with relatively low levels of education. In addition, the disabled population has a disproportionate share of women and blacks, who have traditionally found it difficult to succeed in the job market. We would expect lower earnings from such a group even if health were not a problem. But add to this the adverse effect on productivity of poor health status, the availability of government income support to disabled people which requires that reported earnings be very low, and the discrimination of employers against disabled workers, and the result is substantially less work effort by the disabled than the nondisabled.

Given these constraints and incentives, what is surprising is the substantial amount of work effort which is reported by the disabled. As can be seen in Table 2.4, over 30 percent of the men work full time, full year, and another 25 percent work full time for at least part of the year. This level of work effort exceeds that of the nondisabled female population.[11]

Table 2.5 presents data on the wage rates reported by the disabled and the nondisabled. For every educational level, the average wage rate of the disabled is below that of the nondisabled. When only full-time workers are considered, the average wage rate for both disabled and nondisabled rises substantially, and that of the disabled rises more than that of the nondisabled. Hence, the disabled-nondisabled wage rate gap is smaller for

Table 2.5. Average Wage Rate and Percentage with Wage Rates Greater Than or Equal to $4 per Hour among Disabled and Nondisabled Populations in the United States, by Education, 1977

	Disabled		Nondisabled	
Years of Education	Average Wage Rate	Percentage Earning $4 or More	Average Wage Rate	Percentage Earning $4 or More
Less than 8	$1.08	8.6	$2.85	26.8
8	1.79	16.1	3.18	34.7
9-11	1.87	18.2	3.24	33.9
12	2.93	29.4	3.86	42.1
13-15	3.64	38.3	4.43	46.8
16 or more	5.07	47.8	6.73	70.0
All	$2.57	25.1%	$4.27	45.3%

Source: Wolfe (1979).

full-time than non-full-time workers. When these results are further disaggregated by race, the black-white wage gap among the disabled is substantial, leading to the speculation that labor market disadvantages—e.g., handicaps and race—interact to cause low wage rates.

These data indicate that, in terms of labor market performance, the disabled are at a serious disadvantage relative to the nondisabled. They are less likely to work, and when they do are more likely to be part-time workers than is the case with the nondisabled. In addition, their average wage rates are only 60 percent of those of the nondisabled.

A full appraisal of the economic status of the disabled must, however, reflect the total income of the living unit in which disabled people reside, and not simply their own earnings. This total income includes not only the earnings of the disabled person, but also the earnings of his or her spouse and any other adults in the unit. In addition, income from public and private transfer programs, and income such as interests, dividends, and rent must be included. Because of their loss of earnings or of the ability to earn, disabled individuals are often eligible for a number of transfer benefits. These benefits tend to replace income "lost" from the earnings reduction due to disablement.

Table 2.6 gives some indication of the extent of this income replacement from income transfers and other sources. While earned income accounts for 90 percent of total income for the living units of the nondisabled, it contributes 59 percent of the income of households which contain a severely disabled adult of working age. Conversely, income from public and private income support programs contributes a substantially larger share of the income of households with a severely disabled working-age adult than of those with no disabled member. Indeed, government income support payments account for about 30 percent of income for households of the severely disabled, as compared to less than 5 percent for households with no disabled adult.

Table 2.6. Income Sources of U.S. Households with Disabled and Nondisabled Members, 1978 (percentages)

Income Source	Total Population	Severely Disabled	Disabled, but Not Severely	Non-disabled
Earnings	87.9	59.4	84.2	90.1
Assets	3.6	4.2	3.8	3.5
Transfer payments[a]	5.9	29.7	8.3	4.2
Other and not reported	2.6	6.6	3.6	2.2
Total	100.0	100.0	100.0	100.0
Median 1978 annual income	$16,425	$9,128	$14,000	$17,246

Source: Lando, Cutler, and Gamber (1982).

[a]Transfer payments include Social Security, veterans' payments, government pensions, public assistance, and private pensions.

Table 2.7 compares the median household income of the disabled and nondisabled, and income among various family types within each category. For the total groups, the disabled—even with income transfers and spouses' earnings—have only about two-thirds of the total income of the nondisabled. This disparity is substantially less for the households of the disabled who are married men—their incomes are about three-fourths of the family incomes of the households of nondisabled men. For the nonmarried, however, the gap is much larger—for example, disabled previously married men have incomes which are only about 40 to 45 percent of that of their nondisabled counterparts.

Table 2.7. Estimated Median Family Income of the Disabled and Nondisabled in the United States, Aged 18-64, by Household Type, 1979

Category	Total Population	Disabled	Non-disabled
Total	$16,907	$11,798	$17,848
Married men	18,492	14,194	19,132
Married women	18,641	14,321	19,473
Prevously married men	14,565	7,178	16,639
Previously married women	7,522	5,005	8,555
Never-married men	15,137	9,495	16,316
Never-married women	13,130	7,426	13,859

Source: Lando, Cutler, and Gamber (1982).

Finally, in Table 2.8, the patterns of poverty incidence between the disabled and nondisabled are shown for various demographic groups. In spite of the contribution of government transfer programs, the incidence of poverty is much higher for the disabled than for the nondisabled. This is especially true for older, nonwhite, single individuals, suggesting a strong interaction between disability and other socioeconomic characteristics associated with low income. Overall, the family of a disabled working-age person is more than twice as likely to be in poverty than the family of a nondisabled person.[12]

In terms of labor market performance, then, the disabled in the United States—especially the severely disabled—are at a serious disadvantage relative to the nondisabled. They work fewer hours per year than the nondisabled. They work at low-status, lower-paying jobs, and as a consequence earn far less than do the nondisabled. Because of income support policies and the earnings of other household members, the income position of the households within which the disabled live is more favorable than their relative earnings position. Nevertheless, the economic status of the disabled is well below that of the nondisabled, and those with severe impairments are especially disadvantaged. These disparities are reflected in the incidence of poverty among the various groups.

With respect to labor market performance, how does the experience of

Table 2.8. Incidence of Poverty of Families of Disabled and Nondisabled Working-Age People in the United States, by Age, Race, and Marital Status, 1978 (percentages)

Characteristics	Disabled	Nondisabled	All
Age			
18-34	14.2	7.2	7.8
35-44	17.8	5.5	7.4
45-54	14.2	7.5	9.1
55-64	14.7	4.9	8.5
Race			
White	12.3	5.5	6.6
Black	31.4	17.1	20.3
Other	14.5	6.7	8.0
Marital Status			
Married	9.4	4.5	5.3
Single	26.4	11.2	13.9
All	15.0	6.7	8.1

Source: Lando, Cutler, and Gamber (1982).

the other countries studied compare with that of the United States? In general, the situation in the other countries resembles quite closely the patterns described in Tables 2.4 and 2.5 for the United States. The disabled are less likely to be employed, and when working are in low-skill occupations earning substantially less per hour and per year than the nondisabled. While there are undoubtedly some differences in employment, occupation, and earnings patterns among the countries, the differences in data and definitions among them preclude any comprehensive comparison including all of the countries.

However, the differences in household economic status—taking into account income support programs—are sufficiently large to warrant a rough comparison. The conclusion from such a comparison is that the disabled population in those countries with generous income support policies (e.g., the Netherlands and Sweden) and a relatively high proportion of the working-age population in the labor force (e.g., Sweden) tend to be relatively better off than those in countries without these characteristics. Table 2.9 presents this comparison for the United States and Sweden, the latter country having a relatively generous income support system, a strong commitment to employment, and a very large and progressive income tax. In Sweden, the median income of the severely disabled is 81 percent of the nondisabled median; in the United States it is about 60 percent of the Swedish value. For those not severely disabled, the figures for the two countries are far more comparable.

One other comparison is relevant. For most of the countries studied, the unemployment rate of the disabled is not significantly different from that of the nondisabled. This is not the case for the United Kingdom, however. There the unemployment rate for the disabled is about three times that of the rest of the population, and the expected duration of unemployment is

Table 2.9. Relative Economic Status of the Disabled Population, United States and Sweden, 1978

	Median Household Income of the Disabled as a Percentage of That of the Nondisabled	
	Severely Disabled	Disabled, but Not Severely
Sweden	81.0	92.3
United States	47.2	84.8

Note: For Sweden, the income concept is disposable family income. For the United States, it is total pretax household income. Because the income tax system in the United States is progressive, the comparison overstates the difference between the countries to some extent.

substantially longer for the disabled. While some of this difference may result from the close tie of disability policy to the employment registration system, this linkage is unlikely to explain a large part of the difference.

Summary and Conclusions

Measuring the extent and character of disability among the working-age population is an elusive enterprise. Nevertheless, some idea of how many severely work-impaired individuals exist in a country, and who they are, is essential to forming sound policy to assist them. As a result, estimates of the size and character of this population have been attempted for all of the countries studied.

Measurements of the size of this population vary substantially among the countries, in large part because of differences in the definition of disability used and in the procedures for ascertaining the disability status of individuals. After allowing for the differences in definition and measurement procedures, a reasonable, if rough, estimate, is that working-age individuals with sufficiently long-standing work impairments to warrant their being called disabled form from 5 to 10 percent of the working-age population in the countries covered by this study.

The characteristics of the disabled population—however defined—are easier to identify and are more uniform across the countries. Age is the most significant demographic variable: older workers show a much higher incidence of disability than do younger workers. The disabled population is also characterized by relatively low educational level and occupational status. When a country has racial or national minority groups, these workers tend to have a significantly higher incidence of disability than majority groups or national citizens. Except for populations reflecting the aftereffects of war, women tend to have a higher incidence of disability than do men. Disabled individuals also tend to be unmarried and to live alone more often than is true of the remainder of the working-age population.

Because of their handicaps and lower productivity, disabled workers—especially those who are severely disabled—work less than the nondisabled, and earn less when they do work. They are concentrated in low-status occupations and are probably subject to some labor market discrimination, which depresses their earnings below those expected from their disability alone. Income transfer programs and increased work effort on the part of spouses compensate to some extent for these low earnings. Nevertheless, disabled workers have substantially lower net household incomes than nondisabled workers—again, the severely disabled and the disabled who are not married are especially disadvantaged. These groups, as well, have the highest incidence of poverty.

From this survey, it is clear that the disabled population represents an important policy problem. Because of the size of this population—5 to 10 percent of the working-age group—their impairments represent a substantial amount of lost productivity. Given that the disabled are older and less well educated than the average person of working age, the output loss from disability as a percentage of national income will be less than the estimate of 5 to 10 percent—say, approximately 3 to 7 percent. This estimate accounts for both the lost work time and the effectiveness of the disabled, and the lost productivity at the margin from the resource reallocations which occur as disabled individuals compete for positions which would be held by nondisabled workers. It does not, however, reflect either the lost productivity from resources diverted to provide them training or other services or the reductions in work effort of those required to finance the income transfers or service provision attributable to the labor supply incentives implicit in tax programs. And it does imply the existence of relatively full employment of labor resources.

All in all, it is reasonable to speculate that in most industrialized countries the efficiency losses from (1) disabling conditions among working-age citizens, (2) the diversion of medical and training resources designed to assist the disabled of working age, and (3) the labor supply effects of public transfer programs targeted on disabled workers (and the taxes required to finance them) could total as much as 6 to 8 percent of national income. And this loss, it should be noted, does not include any estimate of the sociopsychological losses in well-being experienced by the disabled themselves, or others who are related to or concerned about those with impairments.

Notes

1. This economic approach to defining disability, it should be noted, is a functional and practical one which emphasizes the interactions of a person's

limitation with a variety of nonmedical characteristics of that person, such as age, occupation, and work experience. Its focus is on the ability of persons with physical or mental limitations to adjust to their work environment. This definition is based on what is referred to as the impairment-limitation disability model, as opposed to the medical model of disability. See Berkowitz, Johnson, and Murphy (1976) and Nagi (1979). The definition is employed to facilitate measurement of the extent and nature of disability status in a sociey. As such, it says nothing about the welfare of individuals who are categorized as disabled relative to those who are not.

2. See, for example, Culyer (1974).

3. The issue of the potential bias in self-reported disability measures is widely debated. For example, Parsons (1980a) has claimed that self-reported disability measures are endogenous, serving as an ex post justification for not working. On the other hand, Waldron, Herald, and Dunn (1982) have indicated that, for women, self-reported assessments do not exaggerate true health status.

4. Data collection methods and the definition of both the numerator and the denominator of the ratio vary across countries, and the data on which the incidence of extrapolation for 1978 are based come from different years. Moreover, in one case (the Federal Republic of Germany) the survey data are supplemented by information on benefit recipients. In a second case (Italy), recipient data are the only bases for estimating incidence.

5. Moreover, if the growth of disability in the Netherlands since the 1971-72 survey parallels the growth in those receiving disability transfers, the estimate will be seriously biased downward. Other anomalies also exist in the data. For example, in the case of the Federal Republic of Germany, the numerator includes all recipients of aid for the disabled who do not classify themselves as disabled. Some members of this group may be younger than 15 or older than 64, in which case the 7.3 percent estimate would be biased upward. The estimates for Italy have several problems. First, the number of disabled people of working age is taken from program recipient data. To the extent that disabled people are not covered by the programs, the incidence of working-age disability will be understated. Second, the denominator is stated as the labor force and not the working-age population. Because the former group is smaller than the latter, the incidence estimate will tend to be biased upward. The extent to which the implicit biases in the numerator and denominator offset each other is unknown. However, given the extensiveness of the coverage of public programs in Italy, it seems likely that the estimated numerator is closer to the true figure than is the denominator. Hence, the percentage estimate is likely to be biased downward.

6. Disability was defined as "a limitation in the kind or amount of work (or housework) resulting from a chronic health condition or impairment lasting three or more months." This definition, it should be noted, differs from that employed by the Social Security Administration for establishing eligibility for Disability Insurance or Supplemental Security Income-Disability benefits. In using this definition, we are able to distinguish among various work-related degrees of impairment in estimating a disabled population. *Severely disabled* implies an inability to work altogether or regularly. *Occupationally disabled* indicates an inability to do the same work as before the onset of disability, or an inability to work full time. *Secondary work limitations* indicate limitations in the performance of work, even if full time and regular work of the same type occurs. See Allan (1976, pp. 19, 35) and Riley and Nagi (1970, p. 1).

7. Because the data used in this case included those over 65, a portion of this enormous variation is due to a higher incidence of older people in the southwestern region.

8. Recall from Table 2.1 that the number of public disability program recipients is used to estimate the size and the composition of the disabled working-age population in Italy.

9. The higher incidence of foreign minorities in Sweden forms an interesting pattern. Some groups composed mainly of foreign workers (nearly 5 percent of the population is not Swedish) show rates of disability incidence up to 170 percent that of the Swedish population, after adjusting for age and sex differences. This pattern is largely caused by the fact that most of the immigrants are low-skill workers who tend to be employed in relatively dangerous occupations. Moreover, the stress of being an immigrant without family or meaningful work can lead to illnesses or deteriorating health.

10. Many of the data in this section are from Wolfe (1979). In her study, Wolfe used several criteria by which to identify disabled individuals of working age. First, the criterion based on program participation in the Disability Insurance, Supplemental Security Income, Railroad Disability, Workers' Compensation, and Veterans' Disability programs resulted in identification of 6 percent of the working-age, noninstitutionalized population as disabled—9 percent of the men and 5 percent of the women. The second criterion, that of work limitation, yielded another 6.9 percent of the population—7.5 percent of men and 6.3 percent of women. The third criterion draws on the minimum wage exemption for some sheltered workshops which employ disabled people, and counts as disabled any individual aged 20-64 whose wage rate is less than $1.00 per hour and whose occupation is included in the list of sheltered workshop occupations. This criterion yields 1.5 percent of the population as disabled. After eliminating doublecounting, 12.3 percent of the working-age population was designated as disabled, slightly below the 16.8 percent shown in Table 2.3.

The disabled identified in the Wolfe study have a composition similar to those of the Social Security Survey data. This disabled population is older, less likely to work, has less education, less likely to be married, and is "less white" than the nondisabled population. Its members also work less than the nondisabled population, and at lower wages —even after controlling for education.

11. These data on labor force participation should be interpreted with caution. Because one of the criteria chosen for defining the disabled population is the limitation on work due to illness or disability, the resulting estimates of labor force participation are likely to be biased downward. The defense for presenting them is that labor force participation patterns are simply one relevant characteristic of that population which has been identified as "disabled."

12. These poverty incidence calculations are based on the official income poverty lines. Those lines reflect the needs of families of various sizes and regions; they do not reflect the special, larger needs of disabled people. Hence, the "true" poverty incidence of the disabled based on a poverty line which reflected their needs would be greater than that depicted here, as would the disparity between the disabled and the nondisabled. Offsetting this, however, is the fact that in-kind government benefits, a number of which are targeted on disabled people, are not included in the definition of income.

Chapter 3

An Economic View of Disability and Disability Policy

In Chapter 2, we described the economic concept of disability—based on the work-impairment disability model rather than the medical model—and indicated the extent and composition of the disabled population in the countries studied. It is for this working-age, disabled population that each of the countries have constructed a welter of policy measures. Some policies transfer cash to disabled people according to a fixed benefit schedule; others transfer cash in relationship to the seriousness of the individual's impairment or his or her loss in earning capacity attributable to the impairment; still others provide in-kind support such as medical care, pharmaceuticals, or appliances. Another set of policy strategies is designed to reduce the seriousness of impairments or to provide rehabilitation or job training or other means to "work around" the problem. Finally, a variety of policies exist which impose regulations on or provide subsidies to third parties to induce treatment of disabled people as if they did not have impairments. There appears to be no obvious rationale for this diverse and disparate set of approaches. While some of the programs appear complementary to each other (e.g., rehabilitation and employment subsidies), others appear to work at cross-purposes (e.g., earnings limits in income support programs and job training programs).

The purpose of this chapter is to provide some logic or structure to this complex network of approaches before they are described and evaluated in succeeding chapters. The discussion is presented from the perspective of the economist. In the first section, an economic view of the meaning and implications of disability is presented. The essence of this view is that the presence of an impairment represents a loss of economic well-being—a *social* cost—which must be borne by someone. This welfare loss, however, is difficult to measure; some idealized state in which no impairments exist must be accepted as the counterfactual or baseline prior to any measurement. Determining how this cost should be shared by the disabled person, his or her immediate family, his or her employer, or the rest of society is one of the functions of disability policy. A second function of disability policy is undertaking activities to reduce the total volume of disability costs which society incurs. The second section delineates considerations guiding these cost-bearing and cost-reducing decisions by society. The characteristics of disability which warrant intervention by the public sector into this area are discussed, and three economic and political rationales for collective action are identified. Finally, on the basis of these considerations, we present a description of the wide range of options open to policy-makers, each of which are based on one or more of the rationales and each of which contribute in some unique way to these cost-sharing or cost-reducing functions.[1]

An Economic View of Disability

The purpose of this section is to set the problem of disability within an economic framework. Only with such a framework is it possible to see clearly the potential role of disability policy, and to discern what options are available to society in fulfilling this role. Disability is viewed as an economic problem because its existence generates social costs; this section seeks to define these costs and to identify their sources.

Consider an individual seriously impaired in an automobile accident, unable to work and to travel unassisted owing to the impairment. Because of the accident, aggregate social welfare has decreased. This reduction in aggregate welfare is appropriately viewed as a social cost. That cost, however, is made up of a large number of components.

Assume for a moment that neither society at large nor the impaired person's family are affected by the individual's impairment or take action in response to it. In this case, the full cost of the handicap falls on the disabled person. These costs take a variety of forms: (1) medical care costs attributable to the impairment, (2) the loss of labor market earnings and other sources of productivity attributable to the impairment, (3) the cost of special aids (appliances, nurses, assistants) required for performing standard (or, in some cases, minimal) daily functions, and (4) the loss of social and psychological well-being experienced by the impaired person.

From an economic perspective, an important question in framing policy is: What is the total social value of these disability-related losses? Presumably, the policy response would differ if the aggregate cost of disability totaled .01 percent of GNP as opposed to 10 percent of GNP. Standard welfare economics has long been concerned with questions such as this, and several ways of valuing individually borne losses have been developed. Unfortunately, these various concepts do not always give consistent answers. Consider the following two questions, each of which represents a defensible basis for valuing the welfare loss attributable to disability:

1. What is the *minimum* sum of money the impaired individual would require to return him or her to the level of economic welfare prior to the impairment?
2. What is the *maximum* amount the individual would be willing to pay to eliminate the consequences of the disabling condition?

The values generated by these two questions will generally not be the same, even though they both involve compensation to the individual. The first value may well be infinite—is there any price that could persuade someone to, say, forego the loss of an otherwise healthy arm? On the other hand, once one has lost an arm, the price that one would be willing to pay for a perfectly functioning artificial arm or arm graft is likely to be less than the total sum of the person's present and future expected wealth.

Leaving aside the question of which measure to choose—and both have some claim to being the correct measure—the impaired person's willingness to pay value is the total cost suffered by society because of the impairment, assuming no one else is affected by the impairment.

Let us now complicate the issue somewhat. First, what if the impairment was not caused by an accident, as above, but rather represents a congenital condition of the individual? With this complication, it is no longer clear what it means to "return the individual to his level of economic welfare prior to the impairment" or to "eliminate the consequences of the disabling condition." In the absence of the congenital disability, what would be the individual's earning capacity, or medical care requirements, or education, or sociopsychological status? There is no longer a clear benchmark or a counterfactual.

This complication, of course, immediately returns us to the basic question of how to define "disability." If there is no clear counterfactual, some more or less arbitrary norm must be established, and it is in the setting of that norm that social judgments enter. The need for such judgments is consistent with the work-impairment disability model which we have adopted in defining disability.[2] And, if the definition of disability rests on a social judgment, the costs associated with an impairment will also reflect that judgment.

If, now, we complicate that case still further, the difficulty of objectively assessing the costs of disability becomes even more severe. Let us assume that the impaired person's family, friends, and acquaintances suffer some loss of economic well-being simply by knowing of or observing the impaired person's situation. These losses are, in effect, what economists define as external or "spillover" costs—those which are imposed on others and for which no market exists or no compensation is paid. And, clearly, there is no market that reflects the collective compassion felt for one whose impairments deny him or her the opportunities for a "normal" life.

Where such collective compassion or other spillover effects are present, an additional component of the aggregate social cost of disability must be introduced. In concept, these external (to the handicapped person) costs can also be defined, and again the two questions posed above form the basis for assessing this willingness to pay. If people other than the disabled person are affected by the impairment, the potential compensations of all of these individuals—at the limit, all of the members of society—must be measured and aggregated. This component of the costs of an impairment must be added to the direct costs borne by the impaired individual. The difficulty of obtaining information of the value of these spillover losses again suggests the need for a social judgment.

From this discussion, then, we have established a number of propositions regarding the cost which an impairment or a disability imposes on society.

1. The presence of an impairment generates costs in the form of losses of economic welfare. These losses are experienced by both the disabled person and those who are, somehow, affected by his or her impairment. The total cost of disability is the sum of the welfare losses experienced by all of the members of society in response to the stock of impairments present in society.
2. Both the definition of an impairment or a handicap, and the costs attributable to it, ultimately rest on a social judgment as to the appropriate benchmark or counterfactual.
3. The private costs of an impairment—those borne by the impaired person—are subjective, and two compensation principles can be relied on to capture these costs. However, different cost estimates are likely to flow from the two principles.
4. The existence of a disabled person generates external or spillover costs in the form of what we have labeled "collective compassion." These costs, which are to be added to the private costs of disability, stem from the individual valuations made by all relevant members of society and are also subjective.

In this economic view of the problem of disability, then, mental or physical impairments which cause limitations can be thought of in the same way as other problems whose existence imposes social costs on individuals. The range of such problems is large and includes acts of God (floods, bad harvests, or earthquakes), environmental pollution, or recessions.[3] With this formulation, the stage is set for a discussion of disability policy. Is there an economic basis for collective action to deal with the problem of disability? If so, what objectives should policy seek to achieve? What are the available options with which to achieve these objectives?

The Economic Rationale for Disability Policy

Having established disability as an economic problem, it does not directly follow that government has a role to play. Numerous events impose costs on individuals without establishing a need or rationale for public policy. For example, individual prices rise or fall daily, and losers and gainers are established with each change. Yet few would argue a role for government to either constrain such price changes or to compensate losers or to extract the benefits from winners. Similarly, business failures or job changes with positive and negative side effects occur daily, and imply no role for government action. What is there, then, about the costs associated with disability which creates a role for collective action?

In this section, we will discuss three approaches to establishing an economic rationale for collective, or government, policy in the disability area. The first is a standard economic perspective for discussing government intervention as it applies to disability policy. This "neoclassical" approach is often cited to justify traditional income support interventions or labor supply measures such as job training and rehabilitation. The second approach has been used to justify more recent interventions into the market on behalf of disabled workers—the attempt directly to create jobs, often public sector jobs. This intervention supplements the traditional approach and rests on a quite different economic rationale. The third approach is a "radical" rationale for government intervention. It is based on the proposition that society should accommodate the presence of handicapped citizens by causing changes in social and economic arrangements designed to guarantee the disabled "equal access" to employment, education, and mobility.

Spillovers and "Public Goods": The Standard Basis for Public Interventions

The presence of uncompensated spillover or external costs associated with a disabling condition provides an important clue as to why governments intervene to share or reduce the costs of disability. When no market exists to enable compensation for spillover costs (or when the market is seriously imperfect), individuals are confronted with signals which only partly reflect true social values. As a result, their decisions are likely to be erroneous ones—perhaps right for themselves but surely wrong from society's point of view. For example, when the costs of an impairment are only partly borne by an individual, he or she is likely to take fewer precautions to avoid becoming impaired than is socially optimal. As a result of these erroneous signals and nonoptimal decisions, the aggregate level of impairments—and, hence, the total cost of disability—is likely to be larger than is optimal. Collective action is required to correct such erroneous signals; in the economist's jargon, to "internalize externalities."

While this spillover phenomenon provides one basis for collective action, a second rationale is also related to the existence of an externality. The source of the spillover, however, is somewhat different in this case. As we have noted, individuals in society may experience "collective compassion" costs because of the existence of a disabled individual. As a result of these costs, individuals generally would be willing to contribute something, however small, to assist an impaired individual. While the option of individual, one-on-one charity is available, the amount each individual would be willing to contribute is likely to depend on the existence of others who are also contributing. An individual's voluntary contributions to charity are likely to be larger if one realizes that his or her contribution is being made jointly with those of numerous other people. Charitable giving, that is to say, has "public goods" characteristics—I benefit by my own gifts but also by the charitable contributions which others make.

If this is the case, an optimal level of contributions can be attained only if all beneficiaries of the reduction in "collective compassion" costs are jointly contributing to the reduction. Again, there is a potential role for the public sector. In this case, the optimal level of provision of support to disabled individuals requires some form of collective action. In the process, the disability-related costs of impaired individuals are shared more widely, as nondisabled individuals—donors—secure an efficient mechanism for expressing "collective compassion."

A third aspect of this standard economic rationale for collective action stems from the same sort of externality. Activities can be undertaken to reduce the privately borne costs of an impairment. Consider, for example, the provision of rehabilitation services, appliances, or job retraining services. These activities have all of the characteristics of an investment—resources are spent currently, and the benefits in the form of increased earnings and productivity are experienced over a long period of time. Because of both constraints on the ability of a disabled person to finance these investments,[4] and the fact that some benefits of these investments spill over onto individuals other than the impaired person, the level of voluntary investment by disabled people is likely to be less than optimal. Again, collective action, presumably in the form of government subsidies or direct provision of services, is required in order to achieve an efficient level of such cost-reducing investments.

A final potential role for public sector efforts to share or reduce disability costs stems from a pure equity or humanitarian motive. Even if, through collective action, the optimal incentives for precautionary activities are generated, the optimal sharing of aggregate disability costs is achieved, and the optimal level of investment in reducing the effects or the level of disability is attained, there may be social benefits achievable by transferring income from nondisabled to disabled people. Even with optimal, efficiency-based collective action, disabled individuals may be at the bottom of the income distribution. In this case, income support for disabled people may convey social benefits, but the benefits in this case stem from income distribution objectives rather than any disability-related characteristics of the beneficiaries. Again, government intervention may be necessary to accomplish such redistribution.[5]

These four aspects of the standard economic rationale—three rooted in efficiency considerations and one related to an equity goal—form the case for public cost-sharing or cost-reducing interventions when aggregate disability costs exist. It is possible, however, that other institutions—namely, the legal system or private insurance markets—could satisfy at least some of these functions, hence reducing or eliminating the need for government action. Let us consider some of these possibilities.

The Potential Role of Nongovernmental Institutions

If impairments and handicaps are allocated among citizens through some probabilistic mechanism, is it not possible for individuals to secure private insurance which provides them protection against income and other losses stemming from disability? The answer, of course, is that it would be possible to privately insure if impairments were randomly assigned, or if the nonrandom character of their distribution were known. But that is only a part of the story. If insurance markets were perfect (or were relatively smoothly functioning), *and* if it could be assumed that all citizens would have the information and financial means necessary to voluntarily provide themselves coverage, *and* if the impairments occurred after, say, adulthood (as opposed to being congenital), the availability of private insurance would go far toward reducing the need for collective intervention.

In fact, however, none of these conditions are fulfilled. Private insurance markets for disability coverage are notoriously partial and seriously deficient. Coverage for the full private costs of disablement—including social and psychological costs—is simply unavailable. In addition, individuals would appear to lack full information on the insurance available and on the relationship of risk to insurance costs. Even if this information were possessed, some individuals would not purchase insurance coverage because of financial constraints, and coverage among low-income families would likely be low. Perhaps most important, the incidence of impairments is not simply the outcome of some probabilistic mechanism. Some impairments accompany an individual from birth; others are induced by carelessness and risk-taking behavior. Finally, given the spillover costs associated with individual impairments, even a fully informed individual operating in a perfect insurance market would not purchase the optimal level of coverage. Hence, while the sheer existence of private disability markets does blunt the four components of the standard basis for collective action, it does not eliminate them.

A second question involves the role of the legal system. Is it not conceivable that the legal system could assign full liability to an individual whose negligence or other activities result in some other individual becoming disabled? In concept, one can imagine that full compensation of private disability costs might be awarded in cases where legal liability is determined. In such cases, public intervention would not be required. In reality, however, the number of such cases relative to the total volume of impairments is small; moreover, as many legal scholars point out, the legal system is not equipped to assign damages efficiently, and in fact does so in relatively few cases. In addition, the damages actually awarded may bear little relationship to the full social costs of the disability. For example, liability rights are often limited by some judgment regarding the liable party's "ability to pay." The availability of some legal compensation—like the private insurance possibility—does not void the case for public intervention based on the four arguments we have discussed.

The Primary Functions of Disability Policy: Sharing and Reducing Costs

The standard economic rationale suggests two primary functions for government policy in the disability area—establishing mechanisms to achieve the appropriate *sharing* of the costs of impairments, and sponsoring programs to achieve an optimal *reduction* in the aggregate cost of disability. The former of these functions—cost-sharing—has both an equity and an efficiency basis. Public income transfers to disabled people reduce the "collective compassion" costs of disability borne by the nondisabled. The potential increase in well-being of the nondisabled through such compensation forms the efficiency basis for such a public policy. And, as we have described, even after efficiency has been attained, additional compensation might be warranted because of income distribution concerns—the equity motive. The basis for public programs to reduce aggregate disability costs through, say, rehabilitation or training is more firmly rooted in efficiency concerns.

Let us consider first the role of government in securing socially desirable institutions by which to *share* the costs of disability. In performing this function, public intervention can take a wide variety of forms. At one extreme, the public sector could attempt to create a more comprehensive and accessible private insurance market for disability. This could be done, for example, by regulating the private insurance industry, by providing information, by mandating insurance purchases, or by any combination of these. Alternatively, to ensure comprehensive coverage, the government could establish its own disability insurance system, a social insurance system. In principle, government action could achieve both efficiency and equity goals through either a privately run system—with appropriate taxes, subsidies, and regulations—or a publicly sponsored and operated system. The choice, ultimately, rests on an appraisal of the resource allocation efficiency which could be achieved through each approach. Were a social insurance system to be adopted, impairments could be insured at any level of severity deemed desirable by society. The covered population could include all citizens, only workers, or any other group. And either pure insurance benefits (i.e., benefits related only to the true social costs of the impairments) or benefits that attempted to redistribute income could be provided. Similarly, the costs of the system could be raised by premiums or fees of a wide variety of types, or through taxation. This form of public disability policy would rely on some assessment of the collective probabilities of impairment and would, simultaneously, be based on collective contributions.

An alternative approach, though complementary to social disability insurance, would impose liability for some impairments on a specific group. A common variant of this approach recognizes that many impairments are job-related and that, in the absence of liability (or an efficient system with which to assign liability), employers have little incentive to reduce the probability of accidents and other dangers in the workplace. In such a workers' compensation approach, benefits are provided to workers for impairments experienced on the job, with the financial liability for these costs falling on employers. This mechanism contributes to the cost-sharing objective and, simultaneously, provides employers with incentives to undertake actions which will reduce the number of impairments and the associated cost of disability.[6]

An additional cost-sharing mechanism—one which is complementary to both social insurance and workers' compensation—would seek to guarantee a minimum level of income support to disabled individuals. Such a program could be targeted explicitly on disabled people, if they are—because of, say, collective compassion—judged to be entitled to special assistance. A program designed to achieve this objective would be largely equity-based and have little if any insurance character. It would be a welfare program for disabled people.

In addition to these insurance or welfare-based compensation arrangements, society might choose to single out special groups who, for reasons of national policy, have been required to bear high risks of impairment. Persons in the military, especially in time of war, are such a group. Programs to provide compensation to them for the impairments experienced in these high-risk activities could be established, with society at large contributing to the financing of the costs.

All of these approaches involve cash compensation to disabled persons. Public intervention might, however, choose to provide compensation in another form. For example, instead of providing compensation for the medical expenses actually incurred by an impaired individual, society might choose directly to provide medical services. Such in-kind provision could also be made for other components of private disability costs—for example, pharmaceuticals, appliances, adapted automobiles, or nursing care.

In addition to providing a basis for policies to share the costs of disability, the standard economic rationale can be used to justify government actions to *reduce* the aggregate costs of existing impairments. The provision of job or skill training or the provision of rehabilitation services are examples of such activities. These interventions, it should be noted, have the character of standard public investments, and are justified on the same market-failure grounds. Expenditures are undertaken in the near term for the purpose of securing future reductions in the cost of disability (for example, reductions in earnings losses or social and psychological costs). The efficiency of such public cost-reducing investments can be appraised by means of standard benefit-cost analysis techniques.

These cost-sharing and cost-reducing options, then, form the menu of potential public sector interventions designed to correct the externality, public good, and informational problems surrounding disability, and to achieve equity goals. Choice among these options must ultimately be a social choice resting on a wide variety of considerations. Among the primary considerations are the costs of various impairments, the breakdown of these costs among those impaired and other citizens affected by impairments, the extent to which nonimpaired citizens wish to undertake compensation of the direct costs of disability, the feasibility, administrative costs, and incentive effects of the various options, and the tastes of members of society for providing income assistance to the disabled population. While the assessment of the total costs of disability do have an objective welfare basis, measurement of them is highly problematic. Moreover, all of the other considerations mentioned reflect social judgments and tastes and have but a small chance of being objectively appraised by standard criteria. Ultimately, then, in a democratic society, political leaders must somehow reflect these social tastes and reconcile competing interests in choosing a system of public interventions in the disability area. Anthony Culyer (1974) has perhaps stated this best with regard to the choice among cost-sharing policies:

> The collective judgment as to what should be paid [in the form of disability benefits] . . . is properly taken, in my view, by persons with collective responsibility. These may be the officials of charitable organizations or, alternatively, the government, for these are the ways in which collective values get themselves expressed. I do not think that . . . even the most inventive benefit-cost analyst could devise a shadow price for "collective compassion." Part of the job of governments is, of course, precisely to give expression to such collective urges.

Direct Labor Market Interventions: A "Second-Best" Rationale

The standard economic bases for government intervention in the private sector provide a rationale for income support programs or traditional interventions on the supply side of the labor market—job training and rehabilitation. The relatively new governmental interventions in the labor market designed to create jobs for disadvantaged workers rest on a quite different rationale. These direct job creation interventions include employment subsidies for disabled workers, the subsidization of enterprises established for the purpose of employing handicapped workers (i.e., sheltered workshops), the subsidization of workplace adaptation costs, the imposition of quotas for the hiring of disabled workers on individual enterprises, or the direct provision of public employment.

The primary rationale offered for direct job creation measures is a political one, arising from dissatisfaction with the growth in the income support system. The substantial postwar increase in education, training, and income transfer expenditures has tended to generate opposition from those who pay the taxes required to finance the welfare state. In this opposition, the failures of that system are emphasized, work disincentives cited, and the absence of substantial reductions in poverty and unemployment noted. Income transfer and social policy are viewed as encumbering the economy, restraining initiative, investment, and growth. This opposition also suggests that the strategy of "giveaways" is ill-advised and counterproductive. Little can be expected from a system of money or food or housing or medical care gifts in which no quid pro quo in the form of effort is required or expected, and in which the gift is withdrawn as effort increases. The remedy is clear—provision of income support should be granted only as a payment for work provided. The direct creation of jobs for the employment handicapped—including those with physical and mental impairments—meets this concern. Unfortunately, what is required to satisfy the political need for a quid pro quo is the presence of an individual in a job slot—an input—and not the value of the output which his or her services yield.

This political rationale for direct job creation has been buttressed by arguments concerning the self-esteem associated with work as opposed to welfare, the value of work experience, and the outputs produced. Moreover, it is suggested that the provision of employment would reduce a primary constraint on the success of training programs—the lack of jobs—and offset whatever work disincentives are created by standard transfer programs.

These arguments, in turn, find support in the economic analysis of labor market performance. The economic rationale for direct job creation starts from a perception of the adverse economic effects of existing legal and institutional constraints on the operation of the labor market. Because of these constraints—minimum wage laws, government regulations, employer discriminatory behavior, union power and influence, supply disincentives caused by income transfer and income and payroll tax programs, and the demand disincentives caused by unemployment insurance and payroll taxes—labor markets do not respond quickly to changes in labor supply or demand, and a wedge is created between the gross wage paid by employers and the net wage received by workers. Employer-borne gross wage costs are increased relative to the perceived marginal product of low-skill workers, and the net wage received by workers is reduced relative to the supply price of labor for these workers; the market-clearing effect of flexible wages is not permitted to operate. In this context, high unemployment among groups of low-skill workers—handicapped, youth, minorities—is inevitable, as is the persistence of income poverty among these same groups.

Two basic approaches are possible to correct these labor market distortions—many of which are created by government policies, often in other areas and for other purposes. The most direct approach would involve the direct elimination of the constraints—reducing the minimum wage and the disincentives of income-conditioned transfer programs and eliminating restrictive employer union practices. An alternative approach is a second-best solution to ameliorate or offset the adverse side effects of these policies and practices—side effects in the form of wedges between employer-borne gross wages and the perceived marginal product of low-wage workers and between the net wage received by labor and the supply price of his or her working. It is precisely the reduction of these wedges which is accomplished by direct job creation programs. To employers, the program reduces the wage costs of hiring low-wage workers, while to those workers, the program increases the possibility of finding and the rewards to holding a job. In short, this rationale suggests that well-designed direct job creation programs can serve to offset the adverse side effects of labor market constraints, and in so doing lead to increased employment and earnings of disabled and other low-wage workers, and to increased output and aggregate employment with little or no inflationary pressure. The numerous programs involving employment subsidies targeted on disabled and other hard-to-employ workers, publicly sponsored or supported sheltered workshops, employment quotas imposed on private employers, and direct public service employment all rest on some variant of this second-best economic rationale.

Guaranteeing "Equal Access" to a New Minority: A Radical Rationale

A third justification for government intervention on behalf of disabled people is the analog of the efforts in the 1960s and 1970s to end employment and housing discrimination against racial minorities, especially in the United States. In the historic U.S. civil rights legislation of the 1960s, government intervention was justified as a means of guaranteeing equal justice, equal opportunity, and equal access to citizens regardless of color. During the 1970s that commitment led to major public interventions in the private sector designed to redress discrimination. Affirmative action programs were the principal tools used to integrate racial minorities into white society. The major changes in U.S. government policy toward the disabled which occurred in the 1970s are based on a commitment by society to use these same techniques in order to integrate handicapped people into an able-bodied society. The implementation of that commitment—both then and now—is controversial.

Recall that in the work-impairment disability approach to defining disability it is the wide variation in the physical and mental attributes of individuals which is the crucial phenomenon. Assuming that it is possible to rank these attributes (i.e., running speed, eye-hand coordination, etc.) with some degree of accuracy, those below some threshold level are considered by society as having functional limitations, and hence, being disabled. This approach, however, rests on an appraisal of limitations which depends on the existing network of relationships that link individuals to one another.

A work-disabled person is defined as one whose functional limitations are such that they lead to "job impairments." That is, they affect a person's ability to perform in a job. But clearly such a disability is a function of *both* an individual's condition *and* the structure of the job as it has developed in the economy. According to this perspective, functional limitations alone do not limit individual productivity. For instance, if the rules of basketball were such that the game is to be played by people who sit in chairs with wheels, paraplegics would probably be high-productivity workers.

The major shift in public disability policy in the 1970s was marked by the acceptance of the position that the handicapped represent a distinct minority group subject to economic discrimination, in the same way that blacks and women are considered minority groups. That is, handicapped people possess characteristics which distinguish them from other members of society, and based on these characteristics they are "discriminated" against. Government's responsibility, then, is to reduce or eliminate this discrimination. The crucial implication of this justification for public intervention is that just as one does not cure racial discrimination by making blacks white, the cure to the disability problem does not lie in reducing the functional limitations of the disabled. Nor does it lie in overcoming these limitations through traditional programs which share the cost of disability through income maintenance, or counteract it with increased training. Rather, it means compelling society to change the network of private relationships which prevent this social minority of handicapped persons from being fully integrated into all aspects of society.

This view of the world gives recognition to the belief that the handicapped are members of an oppressed minority whose ability to compete with able-bodied workers is impaired by the physical structure of the work environment and existing work practices—or whose entrance into the work force is prevented altogether because of these factors. This special discrimination against the handicapped is in addition to the more traditional forms of stigma and prejudice jointly suffered by blacks and women.

Consistent with this view, it has been argued that it was not so much the defective biology of the handicapped which condemns them to a life outside normal society as it is an unwillingness of society to redefine normality. Gliedman and Roth (1980, p. 266) express this view best: "'handicapped' is not simply the residual category into which society places individuals whom it believes incapable of assuming adult roles; it is also a political classification—a label that can be used to deny the rights of any legitimate political group on medical grounds." The solution to this discrimination problem by those relying on this rationale parallels, the authors state, that of civil rights activists: "a grass-roots disability civil rights movement is essential—a movement that uses every weapon in the political arsenal to compel the integration of disabled people into the mainstream." The policy implication of this view is that the government should enact tough antidiscrimination laws for the disabled worker, using the same language of a decade earlier to provide similar protection to racial minorities and women. Guaranteeing equal access to employment, education, and mobility is the objective.

It is noteworthy that this new and radical view of the rights of handicapped people looks dimly on the more traditional treatment of the handicapped. Scott (1969) for instance, argues that the network of established agencies for the handicapped have socialized the handicapped into a passive and dependent role. Workers classified as "severely work-disabled" often enter this economic category not because of their impairment but because of a set of beliefs about the abilities of the impaired drummed into them when they were "rehabilitated" by a private social agency for the disabled. Gliedman and Roth view sheltered workshops as the economic equivalent of custodial institutions and chronic care wards.

Thus, rather than emphasize income maintenance or traditional work-related programs, advocates of this civil rights rationale argue that government guarantee of true access to a job is the best method of allowing handicapped people to enter the world of the able-bodied. In addition, the advocates of this rationale suggest that even if all physical barriers to mobility were removed, there is no reason to believe that the number of disabled adults who can find work or the job options open to those already employed will increase substantially. Handicapped people's claim to a fair share of jobs and income will be satisifed only when the patterns of discrimination against disabled individuals in given plants, companies, or industries are exposed and government-enforced affirmative action plans imposed.

This view leads not only to compulsory structural social change but also to increased intervention by government in the marketplace. As opposed to ner two rationales discussed, economic efficiency and cost considera- play little if any role in this civil rights justification for government ention on behalf of the handicapped. Economic and social changes are expected to be made if they are "feasible"; considerations of cost-effectiveness or of the benefits produced relative to the costs imposed are not admitted.

Summary and Conclusions

In this chapter, we have attempted to give economic content to the concept of disability. The concept of the social cost imposed by disability became the key concept in viewing disability as an economic problem.

This economic view of disability provides the basis for considering the reasons why government policies toward the disabled might, on economic grounds, be justified. We presented three types of economic justification: a standard one based on welfare economics concepts, a "second-best" justification, and a civil rights justification. Each of these rationales underlies a particular form of government intervention; respectively, traditional income support and training or rehabilitation, direct job creation, and guarantees of "equal access."

These policy strategies will be discussed in the remainder of the volume. After describing each of the strategies as implemented in the countries studied, we attempt to assess the economic implications of each. The nature of the next decade's debate over disability policy will focus on the advantages and disadvantages of each of these approaches, and we will, in a final chapter, also discuss the economic issues which are likely to pervade this debate.

Notes

1. A thoughtful discussion of some of the economic issues involved in formulating social policy toward disabled workers is found in Culyer (1974).

2. The role of social judgments in the work-impairment disability framework can be thought of as follows. There is a social and economic environment in which we all live. Some of us function well in this environment, others less well. When the physical or mental characteristics of a person are such as to dictate that his or her options, or life chances, or potential economic performance is "substantially" lower than that of some "normal" or "median" person, society labels that person as disabled.

In this framework, disability is properly considered as a matter of degree. Once having set the norm, individuals can be placed either above the norm (the gifted) or below the norm (the disabled). An analogy here is with the issue of income poverty—some people have incomes which are above some threshold which reflects a social minimum; others are below that threshold. In both cases, public concern is related to one's deviation from the norm—those who are two standard deviations below the norm would be given more assistance than those that are but one standard deviation. Indeed, some poverty-related income support programs work in just this way (e.g., the negative income tax).

3. This approach neglects one important issue in the economics of disability as well as in many of the other areas, such as natural disasters, in which social costs are the issue. In many cases, the origin or cause of the social cost rests on the choices made by individuals, e.g., the decision to live or build on a floodplain or a fault line or to engage in dangerous activities. In such cases, the responsibility for generating the social cost may well lie with the harmed individual. Society may (or may not) respond differently to such assignable losses based on individual choices than to those which are unavoidable.

4. Such constraints can, in fact, be viewed as capital market imperfections, and as such yet another economic rationale for collective action.

5. The case for aiding the disabled stemming from this objective is no different than the case of assisting any poor individual. Because disabled people have a far higher probability of being poor than other people, however, this issue is explicitly introduced here.

6. If workers and employers both had full information on the risks associated with various jobs of each employer, one would expect that the wage rates for risky jobs would, holding all else constant, be higher than for safe jobs. In this case, employers would automatically face incentives to undertake safety measures. The absence of such full information on such risks is pervasive.

Chapter 4

Approaches to Disability Policy: The United States System in a Comparative Assessment with Other Industrialized Nations

The level of employment, output, and economic well-being in each country reflects both previous and existing levels of physical and mental capabilities of the population. Each of these indicators of economic performance would increase substantially were, at the stroke of a pen, all those with impairments restored to nondisabled status. Conceptually, the difference between these two levels of economic well-being represents the aggregate cost of disability, and includes the foregone contribution to output of the disabled, the medical care, appliances, and other services which the disabled utilize, and the social and psychological losses of the disabled and the family, friends, and employers who relate to them. For the nonhandicapped individuals in a society, the presence of disabled individuals implies higher taxes (or contributions in some form) to sustain the income level of the disabled person and to provide medical care and other services. And, for some nonhandicapped individuals, the presence of handicapped persons entails especially large burdens, involving the provision of care in the home and, in some cases, the sacrifice of a job or career in order to provide this care. Undoubtedly, a major cost is in the loss of well-being of the handicapped person as an individual. The loss of mobility, social contacts, employment opportunities, and the satisfaction of full participation in society often lead to the development of a grim set of attitudes and outlooks.

In this chapter, we first catalogue the set of options available to society in dealing with the costs of disability. Then we discuss the selection of such options chosen by each of the countries studied. Our purpose is to present an overview of the policy approaches in a wide variety of industrialized economies.

A Catalogue of Policy Approaches

Societies have numerous ways of responding to the aggregate costs of disability. As we suggested in the previous chapter, some responses follow directly from the rationale for public intervention on which they are based. Income support and rehabilitation, for example, are rather natural responses to the spillover and public goods phenomena associated with disability which motivate cost-sharing and cost-reducing activities. Similarly, direct job creation programs primarily emerge from the labor market rationale, and affirmative action regulations follow from the "equal access civil rights" rationale for disability policy. The catalogue of approaches presented here is more descriptive and less theoretical, though it overlaps substantially with the earlier discussion of the rationale for government policy. In this section, policy approaches are described as being either ameliorative—providing income support—or corrective—work-enhancing—in their relationship to the presence of disability costs.

Ameliorative Responses

Undoubtedly, the most common ameliorative response to the presence of a disabled person is care by the family. In nearly all societies, even those with well-developed public social welfare systems, the direct and indirect support of disabled people via *intrafamily cash* and *in-kind support* is pervasive. The provision of housing and food is perhaps the most common, and is associated with living arrangements and lifestyles designed to accommodate the handicapped person. Increasingly, however, industrialized societies have assigned social responsibility for assisting the disabled to the state, which commonly provides this assistance through a wide variety of income transfer policies. Here the effort is to ensure that the handicapped individuals and their dependents have access to a minimum level of consumption. Typically, this provision is made through both a disability pension and social welfare programs, which guarantee some minimal level of living.

Often partial provision of this minimum is made through *in-kind transfers* in addition to cash income transfers. Special housing allowances and subsidized health care are among the most common, although a wide variety of other programs are also observed. They include subsidized mass transit fares and automobile purchases, subsidized educational opportunities, and subsidized entry fees to public performances or facilities.

In many in-kind programs, handicapped individuals are given special conditions of access to commonly consumed goods and services (e.g., food and medical care). Another form of in-kind transfer recognizes that disabled individuals often have *special needs*, and provides subsidies to meet these needs. Free or subsidized provision of special appliances, such as wheelchairs, is an example of such an ameliorative policy. The list of these special needs is a long one, and includes home care and home nurse subsidies, adaptation devices for homes (e.g., stair elevators) and places of employment, especially designed housing, home care and cleaning, home-delivered meals, and special library or reading materials.

While some of these public provisions may have a "corrective" aspect to them (e.g., special appliances), by and large they are designed to either ease the plight of the handicapped or to stabilize the degree of handicap. As such they afford access to commonly consumed goods or services or by recognizing that special consumption needs of the handicapped must be met if minimally acceptable living standards are to be guaranteed. All of these ameliorative responses can be viewed as efforts to share the total costs of disability among citizens in general, hence reducing the costs borne by the disabled.

Corrective Responses

A second approach to the problem of handicapped individuals involves efforts to reduce or remove the effects of the handicapped. Some corrective policies focus on the disabled person and his or her characteristics. Others seek to reduce the effects of the handicap by altering the milieu and institutional framework within which—and, hence, the conditions under which—the handicapped person functions.

While the subsidization of health care was classified as an ameliorative response, the provision of *rehabilitation services* is clearly an effort to reduce the effect of the impairment on mobility or employment activities. The goal of most rehabilitation programs is to promote a return to work, and therefore an increase in work time or productivity. As such, these programs focus on the dual problems of lost output and the loss of well-being of the disabled who are deprived of the opportunity to work, and seek to reduce this component of the economic cost of disability.

A somewhat different approach is directed toward the provision of an alternative activity in which the disabled person can engage, rather than correcting the effects of the handicap itself. While often a part of a rehabilitation program, these activities are more in the vein of *providing skills and training*—working around, rather than directly reducing, the disabling condition. Here the goal is to define an activity in which the handicapped person can engage, and then to provide the training required for that activity.

These efforts, it is worth noting, are all targeted on the supply side of the labor market in which disabled workers operate. They can appropriately be viewed as human capital investments designed to increase the supply of labor. Their effectiveness is likely to depend heavily on the conditions of demand in these labor markets. With high unemployment, rehabilitation and training efforts are likely to have little corrective payoff, at least in the short run.

Closely aligned with rehabilitation and job-training activities are *job-adaptation* programs. Rather than focusing on the characteristics of the person, these programs emphasize the workplace. They endeavor to alter the nature of the tasks and environment associated with any given job so as to match the capabilities of a particular worker. In some of the eight countries studied, such programs are mainly directed at public sector jobs; other countries provide subsidies to private firms for job-adaptation activities.

An analog to job-adaptation programs in the mobility area is the *adaptation of vehicles*—automobiles, buses, subways. The allocation of public monies to this purpose is based on (at least) implicit acceptance of the proposition that there is a collective responsibility to alter the environment in which disabled people function so as to assure them employment and mobility possibilities equivalent to those of the nondisabled.

It is this rationale which also underlies more recent efforts to ensure *equal access* for disabled people to all commonly used facilities—offices, shops, theaters, etc.—and to employment. The drive for equal access to facilities involves the architectural design (or redesign) of private and public buildings and public places (e.g., sidewalks) to ensure improved access by the disabled. This regulatory approach to assuring the disabled a larger role in the general activities of an able-bodied society runs parallel with a view held strongly in many Western European countries that all workers have a "right to work." In several of the countries studied, the attempts to establish a "right to work" have led to the establishment of both public and private sector quotas for hiring the disabled and attempts to equalize the burden of unemployment during economic downturns. The corrective action in this case amounts to either a fundamental change in institutions designed to ensure equality of opportunity for the handicapped population, or in the operation of the labor market to more equitably distribute the burden of the business cycle.

In a very real sense, the establishment of *sheltered workshops* or the provision of *employment subsidies* to private employers for hiring disabled workers can be viewed similarly—as collective efforts by the public sector to alter the institutional environment in which handicapped people operate. In this case, the effect of the policy is on the demand side of the labor market. The objective is directly to stimulate employment opportunities for the disabled, in hopes that such demand policies will complement supply efforts involving rehabilitation and training.

Policy Issues and Policy Choices across Eight Countries

Within each country studied, public policy toward disabled working-age people includes measures with ameliorative and corrective objectives. In the next two sections, the mix of these strategies across the eight countries is assessed in some detail. As we will see, the patterns vary widely. We first note some of these patterns, and do so in a very impressionistic fashion. Their wide variation raises the question of which factors determine the structure of policy approaches in each country. Why, among countries with relatively similar levels of development, should the range of approaches to this social problem be so wide? The list of questions which affect the ultimate choice is a long one, and we attempt to convey some sense of its diversity.

While all of the countries provide an array of income transfers to working-age disabled people, the differences in the nature and generosity of these transfer programs across the countries are large. In terms of access and generosity, the Netherlands would appear to be in a class by itself. This is reflected in both the very large number of pension recipients relative to the working population and the level of income support expenditures, statistics which are reviewed in Chapter 5. At the opposite end of the spectrum is France. Income tranfer programs in this country appear not to be well developed, and collective (or government) responsibility for the support of disabled people has only recently replaced the presumption of family responsibility.

Reliance on in-kind transfers to the disabled appears to be the heaviest in Israel and the United Kingdom. Both of these countries provide a wide variety of such transfers, emphasizing medical care, housing, and mobility, but including a range of other programs designed to meet the special needs of the disabled. The United States is at the opposite end of this spectrum, providing some income-conditioned medical care support, virtually no special provisions for housing assistance for the disabled, and a limited amount of support for special needs.

Among the countries studied, Sweden and the Federal Republic of Germany appear to place the heaviest reliance on the "work option." This objective is consistent with the active labor market policies adopted in these countries, and is reflected in the high level of state expenditures designed to assure disabled persons the option of participating in productive activities. As a result, corrective policies aimed at individual workers—testing and training, rehabilitation, and direct work provision —are heavily emphasized. While the relative emphasis given these programs is not as great in Israel as in these countries, its system of rehabilitation and training activities appears to be among the most well integrated of the systems studied. Similarly, the very substantial Social Employment program in the Netherlands is justified on the grounds that the disabled have as great a "right to work" as do those without impairment. While the United States has a substantial rehabilitation effort which also includes some training activities, there is no organized program of assisting or sponsoring sheltered employment or the subsidization of employment of the disabled in the private sector. Like the United States, the United Kingdom also has no integrated public program for corrective action. Much of the rehabilitation activity there is carried out by voluntary and charitable organizations. Neither Italy nor France have well-developed public systems for rehabilitation and training activities.

In terms of adapting workplaces to meet the needs of disabled workers, or changing the operation of the labor market, Sweden and Israel rank high. These countries, along with some of the other Western European countries, have also imposed employment quotas on private employers. The United States appears to rank at the bottom in terms of imposing such employment standards on employers and in sponsoring programs designed to adapt workplaces to meet the needs of individual disabled workers.

On the other hand, the United States has proceeded the most rapidly—and perhaps the farthest—in imposing equal-access provisions on public buildings and transportation facilities. Similarly, the occupational health and safety requirements imposed by the U.S. government on the private sector appear to be among the most far-reaching. In all of the countries, industrial injury programs financed by private employers—and often experience-rated—exist, though they vary widely in their adequacy and structure. In most cases, these were among the first public programs targeted on the disabled.

While this brief description gives some sense of the diversity in the mix of public policies toward working-age individuals among the countries, it does not provide an overview of the structure of disability policy for any particular country. Nor does it yield any insight into the determinants of the various policy strategies across countries.

The question of which factors determine policy choice is an extremely complex one. The list of possible factors which can bend policy in one direction or another is very long, and the weight given any particular factor in any particular country is difficult to discern. Here we provide a catalogue of the primary issues on which choices must be made. Some of the issues are ideological or ethical in nature, while others are more narrow issues of program design. The nature of the choices made by any country with respect to these issues determines the ultimate mix of policies adopted toward disabled working-age people.

- Can public policies be designed to encourage optimal levels of individual insurance against liability for impairment? Is compulsory private insurance combined with no-fault compensation for a wide range of potential negligence a means of encouraging optimal insurance and negligence prevention? If so, can public programs be viewed as playing a residual role?
- If compulsory insurance is adopted, what is the optimal role of the state? Should it only regulate the insurance activity or should subsidization or direct provision also be undertaken? Is the loss from

disability an inherently difficult risk against which to insure (because of, say, disincentive effects), and hence is public provision or subsidization required?

- Should society, as opposed to the family of the person, accept responsibility for assisting working-age disabled individuals? Is there an economic basis for considering the problem a collective responsibility? If income support is viewed as a collective responsibility, should a full-fledged social insurance system be adopted for the country, and if so, which conditions of disablement should be insured against?
- Should the benefits provided to disabled working-age people be based on a strict insurance principle, in which preimpairment premiums or wages are the primary determinants, or should the system incorporate income redistribution goals as well? In the latter case, should the benefit structure be tilted in favor of lower-earning individuals or those with smaller contributions?
- Should the disability benefits provided within a social insurance system be based on the expected effects of the impairment or on the actual effects? Should the benefits be earnings- or income-conditioned, or should an earnings test (a cap on earnings) be made a part of the system?
- Should the benefits provided a disabled poor person exceed those provided an equally poor nondisabled individual receiving, for example, unemployment benefits?
- Should disability benefits recognize the family size of the recipient, or the number of individuals dependent on him or her? And related to that, should nonearners (e.g., nonworking spouses) be included in the program?
- Should eligibility for benefits be limited to the totally disabled or should those with partial disabilities also be included? Similarly, should individuals whose impairment is likely to be temporary be eligible for social insurance benefits?
- What criteria for eligibility should be adopted? To what extent should vocational considerations or labor market conditions be admitted as eligibility criteria?
- To what extent should the program be used to encourage early retirement, or to provide implicit unemployment benefits for older workers or those who are otherwise difficult to employ?
- At what level of wage replacement should the program be targeted? If a high replacement rate is chosen, what policy should be adopted to minimize voluntary labor supply reductions?
- How can the benefits and financing of industrial accident benefits be structured so as to induce socially optimal risk-taking and insuring on the part of the workers, and optimal safety and injury prevention activities on the part of employers?

- Should the benefits in industrial injury programs be viewed as compensation to victims and, hence, be awarded as a lump-sum payment? Or should the compensation be in the form of an annuity or pension? Should individual effort or motivation which determine postdisability economic status be considered in the award?
- Should participation in industrial injury programs be compulsory or voluntary? Should benefit (compensation) levels be subject to collective bargaining?
- Does compulsory imposition of risk-taking, such as military service, impose an obligation for a special or more generous level of social compensation in case of disablement than do impairments experienced from other sources?
- Given that impairment generates special needs, should these needs be met by public programs? If so, how does one distinguish the appropriate level of special needs so as to ensure horizontal equity among the disabled? Should assistance for special needs aim at restoring to the disabled person the ability to engage in activities equivalent to those available prior to disablement? Should the expected contribution of family and others be considered in the determination of special needs awards?
- Should in-kind assistance of basic medical care, housing, and mobility needs be provided in addition to income support? What is the basis for viewing income and in-kind support as substitutes?
- Given the occurrence of disability, what is the appropriate role of the state in correcting the effects of the impairment? Should rehabilitation and training be provided beyond a socially efficient level, in recognition of the moral commitment to provide meaningful work to all who desire it? Should disabled individuals be required to share in the costs of the rehabilitation and training services provided?
- To what extent should policy measures emphasize employment in the public sector relative to subsidies to private employers for hiring the disabled? Should the former be guaranteed if the latter fail to generate employment offers?
- To what extent should policy toward disabled working-age people reflect the unemployment conditions in the economy? Should policymakers acknowledge that, in the absence of sufficient economic activity to generate full employment, it is the disabled or other lower-productivity workers who should be excluded from the labor force? Or, do the disabled have a "right-to-work" claim that is as viable as that of the nondisabled?
- Aside from work, what is the appropriate role of the state in affording disabled workers access to mobility, facilities, and activities equivalent to those enjoyed prior to disablement or equal to those enjoyed by the nondisabled? If the principle of "equal access" (or "equivalent

access'') is adopted, should the cost of providing such access be a consideration?
- If the structure of insurance arrangements does not induce an optimal level of ''negligence avoidance,'' what policies should be adopted to increase safety measures? Is the imposition of direct and detailed health and safety regulations an efficient strategy for inducing responsible behavior?

As this list of questions suggests, there is no clear set of principles on which to structure an efficient and equitable set of policies toward disabled workers. To the extent that values differ regarding the efficiency consequences of a pure insurance approach *or* the desirability of achieving horizontal and vertical equity goals through policy measures *or* the obligation to ''make whole'' the productivity of the disabled person *or* the desire to place a high social value on the work activity of even those with low productivity, the structure of disability policies will vary. In addition to such ''taste'' factors, countries also differ with respect to the resources available to support the level of living of the disabled. Moreover, as we have seen, the extent of the disability problem varies among countries. As a result, even with identical tastes and resources, the levels of program adequacy would also vary.

Disentangling these various taste, resource, and demand considerations is extremely difficult. With our listing of the primary factors which appear to determine policy choices within countries, we now describe the main characteristics of the policy outcome which has been chosen in each of the eight countries in this study. The next section outlines the nature of policy in the United States; the following section describes the structure of disability policy in the remaining countries.

Public Policy toward the Disabled in the United States

Programs targeted on the disabled population are numerous, and expenditures on them by the federal government are growing. While the list of programs is long, they in no sense provide an integrated system based on a simple objective. They are administered by a variety of government agencies with greatly varying standards of eligibility, and they have different and sometimes conflicting goals which have changed substantially over the last decade. The major thrust of U.S. disability policy is income support. Most programs are ameliorative in nature, designed to share the costs of handicaps widely among the population. The programs are many, and their interrelationships are complex. They have grown rapidly, and accounted for about 17 percent of federal expenditures in 1980. With the exception of vocational rehabilitation, whose goal is corrective in nature, all of the programs identified in Table 4.1 are ameliorative. As the table indicates, expenditures on income programs have grown rapidly, from $5 billion in 1960, to $26 billion in 1970, to over $80 billion in 1978. As we shall see in a later chapter, corrective programs whose costs are not easily estimated also increased rapidly in the 1970s, so that the overall expenditures on the handicapped population were well over $100 billion at the close of the decade.

Elsewhere (Burkhauser and Haveman, 1982) we discussed in greater detail the characteristics of the United States disability system. In this section, we provide a brief description of the set of programs which make up this system. For each program, we describe its objectives, the definition of disability which it either implicitly or explicitly accepts, and its size as indicated by number of beneficiaries and public expenditure costs.

Ameliorative Programs

The Social Security Disability Insurance Program

The Disability Insurance (DI) program is an integral part of the Old Age, Survivors, Disability and Hospital Insurance (OASDHI)—or Social Security—system in the United States. Social Security is a compromise between an insurance program and an income redistribution program. Unlike private insurance or annuity systems, Social Security does not directly relate a worker's potential benefits to that worker's contributions into the system. The creation of DI within this system indicated that it too would try to satisfy both these goals. As a result, it is neither a perfect substitute for private disability insurance nor a means-tested welfare system. A wage tax is used to collect revenues, and benefits are based on the worker's past wage history. However, the benefit formula is tilted toward lower-income wage earners.

A few of the characteristics of this program are of particular note. First, the definition of disability in the program is a very narrow one—the worker must be found to be so severely impaired that he or she is unable to engage in substantial gainful activity (SGA) for a period lasting at least 12 months. Second, even though this criterion is a stringent one, a number of tests are employed to determine eligibility, some of which give attention to the vocational characteristics of the applicant. Third, as can be seen in Table 4.1, program expenditure growth has been very rapid, and expenditures were almost $15 billion in 1980. Average annual growth in the number of recipients was 7.6 percent between 1968 and 1978. Finally, the program rules severely limit the earnings of workers. During a trial work period of 12 months, earnings above $300 per month are allowed, with no reduction in benefits. Upon completion of the trial work period, earnings in excess of the limit are considered proof of recovery, and result in termination from the program.

Table 4.1. Annual Expenditures on Major Disability Programs in the United States, 1955-1980 (in millions of dollars)

Year	1955	1960	1965	1970	1972	1974	1975	1976	1977	1978	1979	1980
Disability Insurance	—	568	1,573	3,067	4,473	6,903	8,414	9,966	11,463	12,513	13,428	14,899
Supplemental Security Income[a]	135	236	417	976	1,393	2,602	3,142	3,422	3,709	3,966	4,372	5,012
Workers' Compensation	916	1,295	1,814	2,921	3,494	4,820	5,595	6,535	7,657	8,712	10,060	NA
Black Lung	0	0	0	110	554	951	957	980	967	1,023	1,712	1,840
Veterans' Programs	1,982	2,530	3,026	3,930	4,498	5,141	5,583	6,147	6,709	7,000[b]	7,700[b]	8,100[b]
Railroad and Government Employee Disability Programs	510	696	941	1,587	2,012	2,670	3,153	3,606	4,029	4,520[b]	5,080[b]	5,650[b]
Medicaid	0	0	0	5,507	8,709	11,476	14,177	15,543	17,721	19,812	22,867	26,827
Medicare	0	0	0	7,149	8,819	11,348	14,781	17,777	21,543	25,189	29,155	35,000
Vocational Rehabilitation	42	96	211	722	905	1,022	1,127	1,279	1,344	1,298	1,309	NA
Total	3,585	5,421	7,982	25,969	34,857	46,933	56,929	65,255	75,142	84,033	95,683	

Sources: Program data in various publications of U.S. Department of Health, Education, and Welfare, Social Security Administration, and Department of Labor Employment, Employment Labor Standards. Additional data are from McMillan and Bixby (1980), p. 5.

[a]Prior to 1974, SSI data are payments to disabled under the Aid to Permanently Disabled and Totally Disabled program.

[b]= Estimated by authors from incomplete data.

The Supplemental Security Income Program

Dating back to the 1930s, welfare programs aimed at the Aged, Blind, and Disabled have been an important part of this country's income support policy. In 1974, these welfare programs were made into a separate federal program, Supplemental Security Income (SSI), and a standard federal benefit schedule was established. States, however, are permitted to supplement these federal benefits.

As a means-tested welfare program, SSI has totally removed the link between contributions and benefits. It neither requires a given amount of previous work nor bases benefits on past earnings experience. However, it retains the same strict health eligibility criteria as in the DI program. Its monies come from general revenues. Table 4.1 documents the growth in expenditures, which in 1980 were $5 billion. Growth in recipients averaged 11.9 percent per year between 1968 and 1978.

The Workers' Compensation Program

The development of the Social Security program paralleled a related development at the state government level. By 1978, over 90 percent of the labor force was covered by programs which would compensate for work-related injuries. The presumption in these statutes was that employers are liable for compensation at some level, but with no presumption of fault. By the mid-1970s, all state programs also contained specific provisions for occupational diseases.

Typically, benefits are paid to covered workers who are temporarily disabled, whether partially or totally, and to those whose impairments are permanent, whether partial or total, but the basis for determining the amount of compensation varies widely across the states. In some, payments are determined by fixed tables relating well-defined impairments (e.g., loss of the right hand) to compensated amounts. In others, compensation is determined as some fraction of estimated wage loss. The remaining states employ variants of both methods. In some cases, compensation is made by periodic payments over some time period; for other cases, lump-sum payments are made. Expenditures in 1978 were in excess of $8 billion. Average annual growth in number of recipients between 1968 and 1978 was 3.7 percent.

The Federal Black Lung Program

In 1969, the federal government inaugurated a special program providing benefits to coal workers with the symptoms of pneumoconiosis. Although it was envisioned as a relatively small program, by 1980 payments for benefits grew to almost $2 billion. Table 4.1 summarizes the growth in federal benefit expenditures for this program from 1970 to 1980. Pressure for similar programs to provide earmarked benefits to other occupationally distinguishable illnesses has been building, but none has been started.

Veterans' Disability Programs

A very large component of the set of ameliorative programs aiding disabled persons is targeted toward veterans. The Veterans' Compensation program provides direct payments for service-connected impairments, and the benefit level is based on the estimated loss in earning capacity attributable to the impairment. The program parallels Workers' Compensation in that only those veterans with an established service-connected impairment are eligible. Cash benefits varying widely by the extent of the impairment were paid to about 2.3 million veterans in 1977. In addition, benefits are paid for over 600,000 dependents of veterans with more than a 50 percent disability.

The U.S. Veterans Administration also administers a means-tested program which provides assistance to veterans with war records who are permanently and totally disabled, irrespective of cause. All *aged* veterans with war service are assumed to be totally and permanently disabled, for the purpose of this program. Benefit rates vary widely, depending on other income and the number of dependents. In 1977, one million veterans and 800,000 dependents received benefits from this program.

In addition to these two cash benefit programs, the Department of Defense administers a Military Disability Retirement program for career military personnel with over 20 years of service or a service-connected disability rated at 30 percent or more, if the impairment causes the person to be unfit to perform the duties of his pay grade. In 1977, 152,000 military persons received benefits totaling $980 million.

Medicare and Medicaid

Medicare and Medicaid are the two primary federal health care support programs. The Medicare program provides payment for hospitalization and medical care costs of persons over 65 and those persons who have received DI benefits for more than two years. In 1978, the costs of this program totaled $7.3 billion for physician and outpatient care and $17.9 billion for hospital and skilled nursing home care, and bills were paid on behalf of approximately 15 million persons. The Medicaid program pays the medical care costs of public assistance recipients and other medically needy individuals. In 1978, total costs in the program were $18 billion, about $10 billion of which was borne by the federal government. Over 24 million people received benefits.

It is difficult to make the case that all of these expenditures provide assistance to disabled people. However, because most of the expenditures are for hospitalization, nursing home care, or physician services, it is clear that the bulk of them are for individuals who at the time of receipt have some nontrivial impairment. A Rutgers University study (Berkowitz and Rubin, 1977, p. 34) suggests that 85 to 90 percent of such expenditures should be allocated to the disabled. It should be noted, however, that many—and perhaps most—of the benefits are not paid on behalf of working-age disabled people. This is particularly true of the Medicare program, which is targeted on the aged. An alternative estimate made by the Health Care Financing Administration suggested that 50 percent of Medicaid and 12 percent of Medicare expenses were appropriately allocated to the working-age disabled.

Corrective Programs

Vocational Rehabilitation

From a very narrowly defined vocational guidance and training program started in the 1920s, the Vocational Rehabilitation program in 1980 had a budget of about $1.3 billion, serves over one million clients each year, and claims to have rehabilitated nearly 280,000 people per year. Its scope of services includes extended medical care, education, social and personal development, placement in sheltered workshops, special projects in industry, and independent living. The client base of the program has expanded to include individuals with "social" handicaps so that, in addition to the physically and mentally handicapped, others disadvantaged by reason of age, youth, low educational attainment, ethnic differentiation, or other factors are now eligible for services.

Sheltered Employment

Regular sheltered workshops have as their primary purpose the provision of *transitional* employment for the handicapped. Their objective is to supply clients with short-term income and with evaluation and adjustment services to facilitate their transition into competitive employment. Skill training is not emphasized, in the belief that private sector employers will provide the skill training required if the workshop can produce a dependable person with some work experience. In the 1970s, special "work activities" centers were created. They provide *permanent* employment to disabled persons whose impairment is so severe as to make their productive capacity very small. The great majority of these workshops are operated as private nonprofit enterprises, the remainder being publicly owned, usually by local communities. Both types are heavily subsidized by government.

In 1950, there were about 400 shops in existence, serving approximately 35,000 clients daily. By 1976, however, there were more than 3,000 shops, and the daily clientele had grown to about 155,000 disabled persons. A reasonable guess of the total subsidy by governments to these workshops in 1980 would be $150 million.

Employment Subsidies

The budgets of the major programs targeted on disabled people as shown in Table 4.1 understate the real level of the government commitment, since they do not include expenditures for programs which provide employment for disabled workers. In the 1970s, changes in government policy greatly increased the public resources that went into employment creation efforts. Much of this activity is based on the labor market rationale that we outlined in the preceding chapter.

One method of achieving this goal was through direct public sector employment of disadvantaged groups (including the employment handicapped). The most important program of this nature was the Comprehensive Employment and Training Act—CETA. In 1979, 43 percent of the nearly 700,000 CETA jobs were being performed by structurally unemployed workers; by 1980 this had increased to about 55 percent. Beginning in 1981, the CETA program was phased out as part of the Reagan administration's budget control program.

The other method was indirect, through government tax policy which subsidized the hiring of certain earmarked workers (again including the employment handicapped). The major private sector program designed to increase the demand for low wage labor was the New Jobs Tax Credit (NJTC), enacted in 1977. It provided a tax credit equal to 50 percent of the first $6,000 of wages paid workers hired in a firm above 102 percent of the firm's previous year employment level. In 1979 it was replaced by the Targeted Jobs Tax Credit (TJTC) which provided a two-year subsidy to designated target groups, including disabled workers.

"Equal Access" Programs

The primary legislation of this sort is the Rehabilitation Act of 1973 (PL93-112). It requires "affirmative action programs" for hiring handicapped workers in government and in private firms doing business with the government. In addition it requires any organization receiving federal financial assistance to be accessible to the handicapped.

The objective of this set of regulations is to provide handicapped people with equal access or equal opportunities in three aspects of their lives—employment, education, and mobility. The strategy here is to change the organization and functioning of the economy and society so that the attributes of the handicapped—e.g., lower earning capacity and relative immobility—are ignored or compensated for in the economic and social arrangements by which society functions. Once again the costs of these arrangements are not counted in Table 4.1, since they are rule-making policies, whose costs are not reflected in public expenditures and whose benefits are not measured in the numbers of people being supported or provided services.

The potential of this legislation for imposing major cost increases on private business and government agencies is substantial. Information on the costs of the legislation is sparse; first, because the legislation is only now being implemented and, second, because most of the real burden of regulatory legislation of this type is borne by those who must comply with it. One study commissioned by the Department of Health, Education, and Welfare found that affected institutions estimated that it would cost them between $4 and $6 billion for the one-time structural modifications required by section 504 of the act (Smith, 1980). HEW's own experts argued that the real costs would be between $1 and $2 billion. A second study looked at costs of modifying the public transportation sector to comply with Department of Transportation regulations. Over the next 30 years it was estimated that $6.8 billion would be necessary to implement these regulations (Smith, 1980).

Overall Costs of Disability Programs

In addition to the programs discussed above, there are many other programs of assistance or service provisions to the disabled. Elsewhere (Burkhauser and Haveman, 1982, Appendix B) we presented a comprehensive list of these other programs and estimated that expenditures on behalf of the disabled in those programs totaled $23 billion in 1977. When this amount is added to the $74 billion of expenditures on the disabled in the programs shown in Table 4.1, aggregate public expenditures on behalf of the disabled in 1977 were $97 billion. If it is assumed that a reasonable estimate of the proportions of Medicaid and Medicare expenditures targeted on the working-age disabled are 50 percent and 12 percent, respectively (as suggested by the Health Care Financing Administration), this total falls to $70.4 billion.

In Chapter 2, it was estimated that there were about 21.3 million disabled working-age people in the United States in 1978, of which 10.8 million were severely disabled. Another 4.7 million were estimated to be occupationally disabled, meaning not able to work in their normal occupation. If it is assumed that $70 billion of public expenditures provided assistance only to the 21.3 million disabled people, the per person expenditure would be $3,286.[1] It is clear, however, that those disabled with but secondary work limitations (i.e., able to perform work to some degree) do not receive substantial income support. If it is assumed that the total expenditures of $70 billion only provide support to the 15.5 million severely and occupationally disabled, the per person expenditure is $4,516. If each such worker has one dependent, the per person support figure falls to $2,258. Finally, on the assumption that the support is limited to the 10.8 million severely disabled individuals, the per person expenditures are $6,481 with no dependents and $3,241 if it is assumed that each recipient has one dependent. Given the strict definition of disability employed in the DI program—one which excludes nearly one-half of all applicants—it would seem reasonable to estimate that per person public expenditures on those disabled people who are assisted is likely to be in the range of $6,000 to $10,000.[2]

Policy Approaches and Recent Developments Elsewhere

The previous section described the nature of the U.S. system of disability income support policies toward working-age individuals. The system was seen to be disjointed, composed of several disparate programs, and experiencing rapid growth in both expenditures and recipients. In this section, we concentrate on the policy approaches taken by a range of other countries with relatively mature economies and income transfer systems. The countries to be surveyed are, as before, the Federal Republic of Germany, France, Israel, Italy, the Netherlands, Sweden, and the United Kingdom. Rather than proceed seriatim through a description of policy approaches in these countries, we will deal with them in two categories—the more mature systems with relatively well-integrated transfer, rehabilitation, and work programs, and those less developed systems with relatively uncoordinated programs. Disability policy in Sweden, the Netherlands, and the Federal Republic of Germany falls in the first category; Italy, France, and Israel fall into the second category. For reasons outlined below, we will discuss the case of the United Kingdom in the second category as well.

Disability Policy within Mature Income Transfer Systems

The central characteristic of the structure of disability policies in Sweden, the Netherlands, and the Federal Republic of Germany is the relatively integrated nature of the several components of the system, and their ties with the remainder of the income transfer system and with social policy in general. By and large, these systems have rather well-defined income support, work, and rehabilitation goals, and the programs implementing these goals are designed to fit well with each other. In addition to the integrated nature of these systems, the adequacy of their income support provisions distinguishes them from systems in the other countries.

Sweden

The basic principle guiding disability policy in Sweden is that of medical rehabilitation. This focus is consistent with, and an integral part of, an active labor market policy. In implementing this principle, an early determination is made of the potential for return to work of a disabled working-age person, and guidance toward a track consistent with this determination is then made.

Consider, for example, a 30-year-old worker who becomes sufficiently sick or disabled to be unable to continue working. The first entry to the system will be a temporary one which involves access to benefits from three programs: (1) *sickness benefits*, providing 90 percent of the income loss from the disability, up to a very high maximum; (2) *social assistance*, providing base income support to those workers with very low incomes or who were without work prior to the disablement; and (3) *medical care benefits*, providing 100 percent coverage of all medical care costs, through a county-based plan financed by a proportional income tax.

After this initial entry to the disability system, a determination is made concerning the appropriate track for the disabled worker. For workers with the most severe handicaps a permanent severance from the work force is accepted. In such cases, a *regular (permanent) disability pension* is awarded. Three pension amounts are available—full, two-thirds, and one-half, depending on the extent of lost earning capacity. These percentages determine the amount of the basic pension which is awarded. This rather low basic pension is then supplemented with a formula-based *supplementary disability pension* in which the supplement depends on the number of years worked, the income earned during those work years, and (for persons aged 30 years or more) the expected income during the remaining years of working life if the individual had not been disabled. The regular (base) pension and the supplement are paid together. Eligibility for this regular disability pension is based on a medical determination, but with an explicit (and increasing) consideration of labor market conditions for older workers. Both the basic benefit and the supplement are indexed, and both are taxed. Neither, however, is subject to taxation if they together form the only source of income of the recipient.

This track, it must be emphasized, is for those who will be permanently out of the work force—primarily older workers. Nearly all of these workers are granted a full disability pension award, and nearly two-thirds of all disabled recipients (and a far higher proportion of new recipients) receive a supplementary pension.[3] A quite different track is available for those whose severance from the work force is expected to be *temporary*. Most of the younger disabled workers are initially placed in this temporary track (irrespective of the severity of the disability). The same eligibility rules and percentage award conditions hold for these workers as well, and they too are eligible for the supplementary pension. For them, however, participation in a wide variety of work or training programs is expected, depending on their chances of being productive. These programs—skill training, public relief work, sheltered employment, and "work with wage subsidy" (employment subsidies to the private sector)—are administered by the Labor Market Administration. Depending on the results of their rehabilitation, training, or work experience, workers may be reclassified from the temporary to the regular pension scheme or be placed in a regular work situation.

These work programs constitute an important part of national disability policy. Over one-third of those classified as temporarily disabled are in a training program, and the sheltered workshop and "work with wage subsidy" programs are of substantial size as well. The wage paid in these programs is the same as that negotiated by the trade unions and private employees.

In addition to the pension programs integrated with work options, Sweden also has had since 1977 an *Employment Injury Insurance* program, providing support for industrial worker injuries incurred at, or in traveling to or from, work. This program covers medical care costs and income losses after the first 90 days (which are automatically covered) and until permanent disability status is established. It also provides an annuity for the permanent loss of earning capacity, which can be used to supplement the disability pension.

A number of other supplementary programs should be mentioned. Among the largest is the *municipal housing subsidy*. It is income-tested, and the benefits also depend on the cost of the dwelling (though varying rather widely across municipalities). Since a part of the supplementary disability pension is not counted as income, nearly one-half of all disability pensioners have a municipal housing subsidy. There is also provision for an additional supplement for wives (if over age 60) and for children. Disabled persons with special needs can receive additional grants of up to 60 percent of the base amount.[4] Still other special grants, all nontaxable, are available for vehicle adaptation, tools, workplace adaptation, work assistants, and resettlement.

Except for the work and some of the special programs (e.g., vehicle adaptation), the disability system—including pensions and training—is financed by a payroll tax. The payroll tax for the national pension (including the retirement pension) amounted to 8.6 percent in 1978, and the supplementary pensions entailed an 11.75 percent payroll levy (up to an income maximum). The training programs are partly financed by a payroll tax (.4 percent in 1978). The remaining programs are financed by the general government budget.

The Netherlands

In terms of adequacy, coverage, simplicity, and integration, the Dutch system appears even more advanced than the Swedish system. The full range of costs associated with disablement—earnings loss, medical care, special needs—are compensated for through universal (nontargeted) programs based on insurance principles. Most benefits are not means-tested, though both a minimum (equal to the country's net minimum wage) and a maximum benefit exist. And both partial and temporary disabilities are covered. Only in its organization is the system not a fully coordinated one: numerous groups (associations), organized by trade, administer the programs, which in total provide coverage to the entire working population.

The first link in the system's chain is the *Sickness Benefit* program, replacing 80 percent of earnings lost for up to a 12-month period by workers who become sick or disabled. This program is administered by industry-based associations. Employers and unions have, in most cases, negotiated an additional payment up to 100 percent of the pre-sickness, after-tax wage. Interestingly, in the majority of sickness or disablement cases, the employer continues paying the wage and is reimbursed the insured portion covered by the association's sickness fund. The funds are supported by a payroll tax of 1 percent on employees and a varying percentage due to widely disparate sickness records among sectors; hence an element of "experience rating" is a part of the program. In 1982, the average employer tax levy was over 5 percent.

The second link in the system is the *Disability Security* program, the benefits from which begin after the one year of sickness benefit coverage and continue until the normal retirement age of 65 years. This program covers private sector employees with a disabling condition equal to at least 15 percent of their fully functioning capacity. Again, the program is administered by several industry-based associations. Seven classes of disablement are distinguished, and benefit payments depend on both the class to which a worker is assigned and the earnings of the worker before he was disabled. Eighty percent of earnings are replaced for the most severely disabled (requiring at least 80 percent disablement). A substantial majority of benefit recipients are in this class. Gaining access to benefits requires a medical evaluation by doctors employed by the program. The key criterion is the percentage reduction in earning capacity caused by the disability.

Since 1973, labor market considerations have become important in determining eligibility for Disability Security. Lack of suitable employment is generally considered to be caused by someone's handicap, unless the contrary can be proven. The result is that the largest degree of disability is often assigned even if, in medical terms, some capacity to work remains. Application of this criterion, however, requires that the earning capacity of the community be considered as the norm by which the degree of disability is evaluated. Consequently, labor market conditions in the community as well as the worker's age and skills have become relevant factors. Benefits paid in the program are indexed to the general wage level; minimum benefits are equal to the national minimum wage after taxes, and are financed by a payroll tax imposed up to an earnings ceiling.

This simple structure is essentially still in place, although a change in 1976 introduced some complexity into the system. Up to that time, self-employed individuals (e.g., shopkeepers) were not covered by the system. The *General Disability* program, inaugurated in 1976, provided base coverage to the self-employed (if more than 25 percent disabled) and extended the same base coverage to all other disabled individuals of working age (18-65), including those employed in the public sector and those handicapped early in life. At the beginning of 1980, married working women were also included in the program. The basic benefit for those classified as having a disablement of 80 percent or more (the substantial majority of recipients) is equal to 70 percent of the national minimum wage after taxes. For those who are married (or unmarried with a dependent child under the age of 18), the basic benefit is supplemented up to 100 percent of the minimum wage, if the earnings when added with those of the spouse contribute 15 percent or less to the basic benefit. As a result, the Disability Security program has become a supplemental program, paying benefits above this basic minimum to privately employed workers for whom entitlement is higher than the minimum (because of their previous income and degree of disablement).

Receipt of benefits from the General Disability program opens the door to a wide range of other benefits, including special needs, training, transportation, and workplace adaptation.

All of the programs except General Disability apply to private sector workers only. A separate program, the *General Public Pension* program, covers public employees who are found to be permanently disabled. While this criterion is, in principle, more strict than that of the programs for private employees, in practice it is not. Earnings lost by public employees because of sickness or disablement are fully reimbursed for a variable period (which averages nearly two years); i.e., the worker's salary continues to be paid. If, after that period, work cannot be resumed, the worker is automatically covered by the program. The structure of its benefits is similar to that of Disability Security. Nearly all recipients are placed in the most severely disabled class, entitling them to replacement of 80 percent of lost (and indexed) earnings.

Although rehabilitation and training programs are available in the Netherlands, there is no clearly organized structure for such activities except through the large-scale *Social Employment* program, which provides sheltered employment. The program has about about 150 workshops and factories, some employing more than 1,000 handicapped or low-skilled workers. Responsibility for organizing the workshops is assigned to the municipality, but their organization is governed by national government regulations. The national government also provides large subsidies for their operation. Nearly all of the workshops have testing, training, and rehabilitation centers for potential employees, most of whom are referred from the disability pension programs. The wages paid in the shops are at or above the national minimum wage.

The Netherlands also has a quota system which requires private sector employers with more than 20 workers to have disabled employees equivalent to 2 percent of its workforce and to pay them the standard wage for the type of work performed. Noncompliance is, however, substantial, and enforcement minimal.

The Dutch disability system is thus both comprehensive and generous; and, relative to the systems in the other countries studied, it is an integrated system. However, as we will discuss in more detail below, its provisions for replacement of at least 80 percent of lost earnings, and the relatively low level of "real" disablement for which coverage is provided, have caused serious problems for the labor market, as well as the related problem of extremely rapid program growth.

Federal Republic of Germany

In 1974, the German system of income support and rehabilitation services for disabled workers was reorganized and consolidated through passage of the Rehabilitation Equalization Act. This legislation put in place and coordinated a series of programs for disabled workers, producing a well-integrated system.

The first link in this system is, like that of the Netherlands, a sickness benefits program, *Public Health Insurance*. For workers becoming ill or disabled (but, note, *not* disabled due to the job), the program provides interim sick pay equal to 80 percent of lost earnings up to a ceiling. Viewed as transitional, benefits cease when work begins or when the worker is awarded an alternative benefit or pension. Payments can continue, however, for up to 78 weeks. The program pays for medical care as well, and will also pay support rehabilitation and training costs if no other institution does so. The program is supported by a payroll tax of over 11 percent on average, shared equally by employers and employees.

While receiving health insurance benefits, workers may apply for support from the *Public Pension Insurance* program if they are insured under it. This program provides retirement as well as disability pensions. To be eligible for income support, the worker must have been insured for 60 months or more and meet either of the two following conditions: have a handicap that reduces earning capacity by at least 50 percent (called *specific* disability), or be totally disabled (called *general* disability). The amount of support provided is based on the number of periods insured, the income earned during those periods, and the severity of the disability. As an incentive to resume work, income support for a specific disability can be continued for some period after a recipient returns to work.

This pension program provides longer-term income support to those with specific disabilities, but only if the extensive efforts that it devotes to medical and occupational rehabilitation do not succeed. It also provides subsidies to employers who hire disabled workers, work-adaptation subsidies, subsidies for travel to work, and a wide range of other work-related measures.

The Public Pension program is financed primarily by a payroll tax. Because the program covers areas other than disability (e.g., retirement) the tax is high: 18 percent, shared equally by employer and employee, up to an income limit.

An alternative entry into the system is provided through the *Continuation of Wage Payments* provision associated with the *Workman's Accident Insurance* program. For workers who are injured on, or while traveling to or from, their job, wage payments automatically continue for six weeks. At this point interim Workman's Accident benefits equal to 80 percent of lost wages (up to a very high ceiling) can be awarded after eligibility is certified through medical examination. This payment is regarded as a wage replacement. Then, after thirteen weeks, a further determination is made to establish the appropriate level of compensation. A rating is made of the reduction in capacity which has occurred relative to pre-injury capacity. A 20 percent reduction is the minimum for which compensation is paid; total disability is awarded a compensation annuity equal to 67 percent of the predisability gross wage (implying a *net* replacement rate of about 90 percent). Financing is also through a payroll tax, in this case an experience-rated tax on employers.

In addition to these two primary channels of support, the Federal Republic has a number of other disability income support programs. *Aid to Aged Farmers* and *Veterans' Benefits* provide support to two groups who may not be insured under the Public Pension program. Both programs in effect extend the Public Health and Public Pension programs to these groups. Farmers may receive assistance in operating the farm as well as income support equivalent to benefits awarded by the Public Pension program to blue collar workers. Veterans may receive income support benefits commensurate with those in the public health program. The veterans' program provides benefits to persons who are covered by Public Pension Insurance, making cumulation of benefits possible. Benefits in both the farmers' and veterans' programs depend on the extent of disability, and both provide considerable rehabilitation services.

Finally, income support is provided to those with civil service status (which does not include all government employees) through the *Program for Civil Servants*. Its key concept is "inability to perform duties," and de facto nonperformance, along with a medical examination, determines eligibility. Benefits are determined as if the disability were retirement: their amount depends on the number of years counted toward retirement and past contributions to the retirement fund. These three special group programs are largely financed by the General Fund of the national government.

Finally, there is a *Public Aid* program to assist those who fall through the cracks in the workers' accident insurance systems, primarily nonworkers or those who have not been employed long enough to be insured. Income-tested benefits are provided, as is assistance for medical care, housing, and mobility.

To an extent at least equal to that of Sweden, and surpassing that of the Netherlands, the Federal Republic of Germany emphasizes training, rehabilitation, and job placement. In addition to the activities of the programs described, the *Federal Office of Employment* provides major services for employment of those with low skills or handicaps. The office is an umbrella for programs providing similar services, and seeks to place each worker in the labor force to the extent residual work capacity permits.

Disability Policy within Less Integrated Income Transfer Systems

Centralization, integration, and relative adequacy characterize the disability systems affecting working-age persons in Sweden, the Netherlands, and the Federal Republic of Germany. France, Italy, and Israel—and, as we will see, the United Kingdom—have more disjointed and less well structured systems. By and large, their levels of program benefits are lower as well.

France

Social Security programs for disabled working-age persons have been in effect in France since the end of World War II. Salaried workers have been covered since 1947, nonsalaried workers have had a voluntary program since 1948, and disabled farmers have been covered since 1961. Because some programs were noncompulsory insurance systems, large numbers of workers in certain trades were not covered; if disabled they were supported by their families or welfare allowances. Family responsibility for the disabled was in fact the primary means of support. Moreover, until 1957, serious horizontal inequities existed among the programs due to the wide variety of definitions of disability among them. Legislation in 1957 consequently sought to establish a single definition of disability.

A major breakthrough in disability policy toward those of working age came with the *Law of Orientation* in 1975. It established three basic disability programs: Social Security (including work injuries), Social Assistance, and a Work Code that includes quotas, rehabilitation, and special workshops. These programs cover all working-age disabled individuals, including those disabled from birth. The law specified three main objectives: (1) establishment of work rather than income assistance as a primary goal, (2) replacement of family responsibility with collective responsibility for disabled people, and (3) a guarantee of income support up to an established social minimum. All three represented major departures in French disability policy.

The Social Security system contains several disability programs. The first is the *Disability Insurance* program. To be eligible for benefits, one must have contributed for 12 months and worked a minimum number of hours. A medical examination determines whether the applicant meets the criterion of loss of two-thirds of earnings capacity. In this determination, labor market conditions in the area are considered. There are three disability classifications: disabled with residual work capacity, totally disabled, and disabled and needing special help.

Also administered by the Social Security system is the *Work Injury* program. It provides coverage to all salaried workers injured at, or traveling to or from, work. The benefits depend on the ability of the worker to return to the previous job.

A state *Accident Compensation* program is designed to compensate those who are injured in accidents (primarily auto) caused by others. Benefits are determined either through the courts or by individual insurance values, and generally depend on the effect of the accident on work capacity and lost work time, as well as the victim's age.

A rather large *Military Pensions* program provides income support to veterans with disabilities caused or aggravated by military activity. Again, benefits depend on the extent of disability.

The Law of 1975 made major changes in French social welfare programs, which had previously left assistance for disabled nonworkers, workers not eligible for social insurance benefits, and the congenitally disabled up to the family, although some support was provided through a system of family allowances.

The Law of 1975 established a single *Social Assistance* program which provides monthly benefits to working-age individuals who are severely disabled (having disabilities reducing normal capacity by 20 percent or more, or unable to find work). On average, the program provides income support equal to about 50 percent of the legal minimum wage for salaried workers. Attached to the Social Assistance program is a set of compensatory allowances for the disabled who need third-party help or have additional work expenses. These allowances can raise income support well above 50 percent of the minimum income.

The third category of disability programs includes those that are work-oriented. Before 1975, a series of departmental (state) commissions existed for the guidance and work placement of the disabled. Because they were viewed as generally ineffective, the 1975 Law established a new set of departmental commissions under the direction of a national authority (COTOREP). The mandate was to enable those with disabilities to return to work, and the commissions were given a wide range of responsibilities, including classifying the handicapped in terms of type of assistance needed (e.g., work or income support), guiding them into channels consistent with the classification, determining eligibility for special work-related allowances or loans, and granting wage reductions of up to 20 percent to employers hiring the handicapped.

In addition, a set of *sheltered workshops* that had existed since 1960 was to be coordinated with COTOREP's activities. For the most severely handicapped, clinical types of work centers have been developed, paying wages equal to at least 70 percent of the minimum. Those less seriously handicapped are employed in normal business workshops and are paid at least 90 percent of the minimum wage. In each case, the government can supplement the wage in an amount up to 110 percent of the minimum in the clinical centers and 130 percent of the minimum in the normal workshops.

The 1975 Act also established *employment quotas*, stipulating that businesses with 10 or more workers must hire disabled workers as 10 percent of their work force. The quota can be relaxed by 50 percent if the firm awards contracts to the normal sheltered workshops. As with most such quotas in Western European countries, enforcement is uneven and not strict.

The 1975 Act contained other work provisions. *Employment subsidies* of up to 80 percent of the cost of work adaptation and 50 percent of additional management costs were provided; an *Early Retirement* provision was enacted for handicapped workers, and a *Variance from the Minimum Wage* was permitted, under which the government supplements the wage costs of private employers up to (and, in some cases, beyond) the minimum wage.

These changes put France on the road toward an integrated and adequate disability system, containing a full set of insurance, welfare, and work-provision components with organized links between them. Because of the recent nature of these changes and the lag in their implementation, however, the French disability system has not achieved the level of organization and adequacy of the countries surveyed above.

Italy

Disability policy in Italy serves several objectives besides income support and employment opportunities for disabled individuals of working age. It includes the provision of long-run unemployment benefits in depressed regions and early retirement options for low-productivity workers. By and large, the components of the system are not well integrated.

One route of entry into the system is through the *Sickness Benefits* program, a state program for private sector workers in agriculture, industry, and trade. While a sickness benefit can be viewed as a temporary disability benefit, it alone does not guarantee entry into the system of disability benefits. Sickness benefits equal 50 percent of lost income beginning with the fourth day of absence from work and continuing for 20 days. If illness beyond that point continues to cause absence from work, the benefits rise to 66 percent of lost income. After the 20-day period, a disabled worker may be considered eligible for benefits in disability programs, if covered by them.

The *Disability Pension* program, a part of the Social Security system, is the core of disability policy toward working-age people. This income support program provides coverage to workers who are not civil servants and who have made the equivalent of five years of contributions to the system through payment of a payroll tax (in some cases, however, entitlement can be gained by a single year of work). Eligibility for benefits requires a permanent loss, after the beginning of work life, of at least two-thirds of earning capacity. Determination of eligibility requires, first, a medical examination to ascertain the degree of impairment and of likely permanency. Vocational considerations also enter; the worker's residual skills are related to those required for handling his or her previous job or some other job of at least equal status. In addition, since 1969, the "social and economic characteristics" of the area in which the worker lives can be considered. The program can and does mandate treatment as a condition for rewarding benefits, even though the program does not itself operate rehabilitation and training centers.

The amount of benefits awarded depends on the amount contributed to the system (and hence on the number of years of work) and on predisability income. Provision is made for dependents' allowances for the disabled worker's spouse and children. The average per capita benefit level is about 45 percent of per capita income. During the 1970s, benefit levels increased more rapidly than the salary of industrialized workers, and among disabled workers, benefit levels for the self-employed increased more rapidly than for "dependent" workers (in part because they started at a lower level). The minimum benefit level is indexed to the contracted wage in the industrial sector, while the benefit award above the minimum is indexed to the price level. As a result, the ratio of minimum to average benefits is rising.

Interestingly, unlike the other countries studied, disability pensions in Italy are not converted to retirement or old age pensions at a particular age (say, 65); the elderly can be awarded disability pensions. Because two-thirds of pension recipients in Italy are above retirement age, comparisons with other countries are difficult.

The second major program is the *Industrial Injuries* program, a state insurance program covering manual workers (about 66 percent of all workers). Benefits are provided for industrial accidents and about 40 forms of occupational illnesses, whether temporary or permanent, total or partial. Three categories of benefits are available—temporary total, in which 60 percent of earnings are replaced for the first three months of disablement and 75 percent thereafter; permanent partial, in which the benefit is based on an assessment of lost capacity; and permanent total, in which 100 percent of previous earnings (within a floor and ceiling) are replaced. Because industrial injury benefits are nontaxable, *net* replacement rates can lie substantially above these levels. In addition, support for personal assistance, health care, and other social services are provided. The benefits paid in this program are financed through an experience-rated payroll tax in which employers pay the entire premium. Disabled individuals can receive *both* work injury and disability pension benefits; the benefit payments in the programs are not integrated. Indeed, the two programs have quite different bases—one is insurance based and the other takes the form of social assistance. As a result, there are two different payroll taxes and administrative mechanisms.

The *War Pensions* program is the third major income support element in the system. Because these benefits are indemnities for war and war-related handicaps, they can be added to disability pensions, in much the same way as industrial injury benefits. The benefits in this program are quite generous, with the maximum benefit in excess of twice the nation's per capita income; provision also exists for dependent and "survivors" benefits. Further, these benefits are nontaxable, are indexed to general wage increases, and are accompanied by substantial health care and rehabilitation benefits.

A final income support program is *Welfare to the Disabled*, designed to place a floor under those not covered elsewhere. It is income-conditioned, providing a minimum benefit slightly below that of the disability pension program.

In addition to a number of rehabilitation programs, Italy's major effort in the employment area is a rather sophisticated *quota employment* program. The program is designed for partially disabled workers aged 55 or under, each of whom is assigned one of 10 classifications, depending on the severity of the disablement.[5] Employers are given a quota of 15 percent of their work force (in jobs not considered dangerous) which must be filled with partially disabled workers. The quota can be filled by hiring far fewer than 15 percent, if a greater number are from the more-disabled classification. There have been difficulties administering the quota, and many firms apparently do not comply, taking advantage of loopholes in the law.

While Italy's program does have some of the characteristics of a mature system, it also contains a number of serious problems. Beneficiary incidence and benefit awards vary substantially by region, and the program's disability assistance goals are intertwined with its long-term unemployment relief and early retirement aspects. The lack of integration of programs and rather loose administration of some of them results in horizontal inequities.

Israel

Israel has one of the most comprehensive and generous disability systems among the countries we have studied. While the basic framework of the system is straightforward, there are a large number of separate programs providing categorical benefits. The various plans are largely skill- or industry-based; then, as an overlay, the national insurance system has a more or less residual benefit program. The overall system has four basic components: (a) a two-tier system composed of the General Disability program operated by the National Insurance system and a nearly universal wage-related program mandated by collective bargaining agreements (Histadrut), (b) a work-injury program for those experiencing work-related injuries, (c) a welfare-based program assisting those not covered by the general and work-injury programs, and (d) a veterans' program for those injured in military service. In addition, there are numerous programs providing mobility and attendance services for the disabled.

The *General Disability* program of the National Insurance system is relatively recent (1970). It brought under a single aegis a set of already existing programs, and also provided coverage to persons with 50 percent or more disability (including those disabled from birth and housewives of the insured), who were previously uncovered. For those covered before 1970, benefits are financed out of general revenues and compulsory contributions from all workers; benefits for those disabled after 1970 are financed by compulsory contributions alone. Eligibility is established by a disability board which determines if the individual's earning capacity has been decreased by 50 percent by the disabling condition. The board can also direct the individual into a rehabilitation or training program.

Poverty-line benefits (equal to about 25 percent of the average wage) are provided those with high disability ratings. Benefits to those with lower ratings are provided in proportion to the reduction in work capacity. The program also grants dependents' allowances and attendance allowances which can equal the value of the basic benefit. Earnings or benefits from other programs reduce general disability benefits at a 100 percent rate beyond a certain earnings level. General Disability is the most extensive program in terms of recipients.

Complementing this general program is the *Comprehensive Disability Pension* program (administered by the trade union organization Histadrut) which provides age-related disability benefit coverage to a very high proportion of industrial and service workers. Coverage is mandated by collective bargaining arrangements and provides for both partial and total disability, regardless of cause. The program is financed by an employer payroll tax (which covers survivors' insurance as well); it is not experience-rated. Benefits depend on previous wages and the severity of the disability, as well as on the length of time covered. For example, the maximum benefit—70 percent of the predisability wage—is available to workers who joined the system prior to age 30. There is also a minimum benefit of 40 percent of the predisability wage for those covered by the system only after age 55.

The determination of eligibility in this program is unique. If a worker is impaired for three months and is unable to work more than three-fourths time in his or her existing job or other suitable work, benefits are granted for three months. After this period has expired, reapplication must be made. If eligible, a partial benefit payment is awarded if the person can work more than 30 percent of work time, but less than full time. Full pension is granted if no more than 30 percent work time can be achieved. In a sense the benefits are income-conditioned, in that their support plus current earnings cannot exceed 100 percent of prior earnings. The program also provides rehabilitation services and makes loans and grants. Benefits are indexed to the price level, and 75 percent of benefits are treated as taxable income.

While the Comprehensive Disability Pension program is indeed comprehensive insofar as it covers all industrial and clerical workers, it does not cover public servants or the self-employed. Special programs, similar to the Comprehensive Disability program, are available for the first group. These programs are generous, and also serve as an early retirement program. They are noncontributory—i.e., a pure fringe benefit.

Complementing these general disability programs is the *Work Injury* program, operated by the National Insurance system. It covers those injured on the job or while traveling to and from work. Occupational diseases are also covered. Benefits received from this program preclude the receipt of benefits from others. The program has two components: (1) interim benefits for the first six months of work injuries, and (2) the main program, which provides long-term support for those injured while working. It is a compulsory (for employers), contributory, experience-rated program in which employer payroll taxes vary. The program provides benefits which are related to both the severity of an injury and to prior income. For example, a worker with 100 percent disability receives a benefit of 75 percent of his or her prior wage up to twice the national average wage. In addition to the ceiling, there is also a minimum benefit equal to 80 percent of the average wage. Workers whose disability is relatively small—say, less than 20 percent—can receive a one-time grant rather than an annuity.

Eligibility for program benefits is determined by a medical board which is guided by published criteria. In recent years, vocational considerations have also become relevant, and are increasingly used. If vocational considerations are taken into account, a benefit supplement is possible. The program also provides medical care and rehabilitation services, and attendance and mobility allowances as well in the case of severe disability. Note that the benefits are not income-conditioned, although the level of earnings at time of application is likely to affect the probability of acceptance into the program. Benefits are not taxed, but indexing provisions are like those in the Histadrut pension program.

Finally, there is a *Welfare* program for poor individuals, including the disabled and those with chronic diseases or mental illness. It is financed by general revenues, and guarantees the national minimum income (40 percent of the average wage for a family of four, plus health insurance and a rent supplement). The program is income-tested with a 70 percent benefit reduction rate, and, for those with less severe disabilities, participation in a rehabilitation program is a condition for receiving benefits. Eligibility requires that application first have been made for the General Disability program.

The final income support program is the *Military and Hostile Action* program. If impairment was caused by military service, compensation plus rehabilitation services, and also a cash supplement if the person is unemployable, in addition to a long list of special benefits, are available. All benefits are financed by the general fund. They are more generous than those in the General Disability program, providing 60 percent of the average wage to the disabled individual plus supplemental benefits to dependents. Only the cash supplement when the individual is unemployable is income-tested, and even then there is a set-aside. The sum of all cash benefits can equal 90 percent of the average wage for a severely disabled person. Benefits are proportionately smaller when disabilities are less severe. The criteria for eligibility and benefit awards are basically the same as in the work-injury program. Receipt of the military benefits automatically makes one ineligible for other income support.

In addition to these basic support programs, there is a series of special programs. In 1975, an *Automobile Accident Compensation* program was established, in which private insurance pays one-time capitalized benefits based on the degree of disability caused, as determined by the rules and ratings of the work-injury program. The liability is imposed on the responsible driver's carrier; the courts rule on responsibility, not the amount of settlement. While no income test is imposed for the settlement, the amount is likely to affect eligibility and the benefits received from other programs.

For individuals impaired in their motor capacity, a variety of *Mobility Allowance* programs exist. Rather complex, they include cash benefits to support both automobile and other transportation, and allow loans for automobile purchase. The benefits can be very generous (especially those provided to military veterans) relative to the basic disability benefit, in part because of the high cost of transportation and the very high taxes on cars in Israel. And for the disabled who work, the basic mobility allowance can be doubled. Generosity also results from the standard provision of subsidies for automobile purchase and for maintenance as fringe benefits to both private and public sector workers in Israel. The programs are indexed (in some cases tied to the price of gasoline and insurance) and are supported out of the general fund.

Finally, the *Housing Assistance* program grants a special allowance to disabled people. Subsidized loans are available depending on the individual's status, and disablement gives an applicant high priority in this program.

As is true of the income support programs, employment programs are numerous and complex. By and large, *rehabilitation services*—counseling, placement, training, job adaptation, and some wage subsidies—are provided as part of the income support programs. In addition, a *quota system* for handicapped veterans is required in the private sector, though not effectively enforced. A series of *sheltered workshops* is operated by Meshakem, a public corporation. The objectives of this program are not clearly spelled out—e.g., whether the work is permanent or transitional—and the training afforded is limited. Workers are paid the minimum wage, and the output is sold on the open market. Government subsidies cover 35 percent of the costs of the program.

United Kingdom

In general the United Kingdom has a relatively generous and mature social insurance system. In the area of disability policy, however, the system is characterized by unintegrated programs which, taken together, generate a wide variance in the benefits available to equally disabled workers with the same predisability incomes. An effort at modernization was undertaken in 1970, but for a number of reasons, including budget constraints, the effort has fallen short of its goal. To better understand the nature of the current system, a brief description of the pre-1970 structure is helpful.

The system before 1970 includes some elements of the Beveridge Plan of 1942, which called for a *National Insurance and Industrial Injuries* program and a *National Health Service* (both enacted in 1948). These were both insurance programs, financed by contributions from participants. Beneath them, the *National Assistance* program acted as a "safety net," providing coverage to those not in the insurance programs. Although originally the size of the net was expected to shrink in the future, it instead expanded. In 1966, the National Assistance program was replaced by Supplementary Benefits, in part because of the growth and inadequacies of the former. "Discretion" was to be the key in the new act, so as to allow public agencies to respond flexibly to the needs of low-income and disabled people. Instead, in a period of budget limitations, discretion appears to have become the instrument for rationing benefits. In response, a variety of voluntary organizations have been developed to aid low-income and disabled people—in effect assuming a role many expected the state to fill.

Beginning in 1970, a series of new acts were passed: the Chronically Sick and Disabled Persons Act (1970), the Invalidity Pensions Act (1971), the Non-Contributory Invalidity Pension Act (1975), the Non-Contributory Invalidity Pension for Married Women or Housewives Act (1976), the Attendance Allowance Act (1971), and the Invalid Care Allowance Act (1976).

Because of this proliferation of quasi-independent programs, operation of the system can best be understood by tracing the course of one worker who becomes disabled on the job and then one disabled not on the job.

For the one disabled on the job, the key program is the *Industrial Injury Benefit* program, which is part of the national insurance system. If he or she has met the insurability criterion and is incapable of work, 26 weeks of benefits are available. This program pays benefits which largely replace lost income, though a ceiling does exist. Eligibility is determined by an insurance officer or a medical board.

If the disability condition continues for more than 26 weeks, support for the worker is provided by the *Industrial Disablement Benefit*, also a part of the national insurance system. A new eligibility determination must be made and is again contingent on having met insurability standards. In this case, the loss of earning capacity is estimated, and benefits depend on the extent of disability and the previous income of the worker. A worker may also be eligible for benefits under the *Unemployment Supplement* program. The requirement for eligiblity is permanent loss of all, or a substantial amount of, earning capacity. Benefits can be added to benefits in the other programs.

For totally disabled workers who were injured on the job, a *Constant Attendance Allowance* is also available. A *Special Hardship Allowance* is available for those who, while not totally disabled, are unable to work at their predisability job or its equivalent. These benefits can be cumulated with the Industrial Injury Benefit, Industrial Disablement Benefit, and Unemployment Supplement.

For a worker not injured on the job, a different set of benefits applies. If medical criteria are satisfied and if sufficient contributions to the insurance system have been made, the worker can receive benefits under the *Sickness Benefits* program, a part of the national insurance system. Benefits under this program largely replace lost income, though there is a ceiling, which causes the benefit replacement ratio to be lower for high-income than for low-income workers.

After 28 weeks, sickness benefits expire. If the worker is still unable to work, a pension is received under the *Invalidity Benefit* program, inaugurated in 1971. It is also a part of the national insurance system. As a percentage of predisability income, the pension provided in this program is relatively low: however, if the worker is under 60 years of age, an additional allowance is granted. A very low earnings limit is imposed in the plan, reflecting its objective of assisting only the severely disabled.

In addition, a rather low *attendance allowance* program is available for totally disabled workers needing special care. A disability pension is now available for working-age married women (since 1975) and housewives (since 1977) if they are incapable of work for a period exceeding 28 weeks. The benefits paid by these Non-Contributory Invalidity Pension programs are not as high as in the programs in which insured status is essential.

There is also a *War Disablement* program that provides income support to civilians disabled or injured in World War I or II and to military personnel injured in actions after 1946. There is a basic pension awarded for total disability, and proportionately smaller pensions for less severe disabilities. Below the level of 20 percent disability, a single lump-sum payment is awarded. As with the Industrial Injury program, eligibility for the basic benefit gives access to a wide range of supplements: an unemployability supplement, constant attendance allowance, allowance for lowered occupation, treatment allowance, severe displacement occupational allowances, and so on, including an age allowance and a comforts allowance. These military pensions and related benefits are not income-conditioned, and can be added to other pensions or benefits with no offset.

Finally, the *Supplementary Benefits* program (described above) provides support for disabled people who have little or no claim to national insurance benefits. The supplements are typically used to bring benefits from other programs up to a minimum level. The program has an assets test; availability of capital is taken into account in determining eligibility. As with the other cash support benefits, eligibility also carries access to supplementation—in this case for special needs and circumstances.

All of these benefits, with the exception of the Industrial Injury Benefit program, are paid out of the basic national insurance program, which is financed by payroll tax contributions.

In addition to these social insurance benefits, a wide range of other programs also provide services to the disabled. We will briefly describe them.

The *Chronically Sick and Disabled Persons Act* of 1970 was designed to ensure that adequate care and services were provided to the disabled population. The main burden was placed on local authorities, which were required both to ascertain the number of people needing services in their jurisdiction and to provide educational, recreational, and transport services to these people. Increased housing assistance was also mandated, as was improved access to public and educational buildings. Serious delays have been encountered in implementing this act, and wide variance among localities exists.

A large number of programs exist to provide *mobility services*. They provide subsidies for travel to work, automobile purchases and repair, taxi fares for work-related travel, and exemption from road taxes. Many of these allowances are taxable.

Finally, there are a number of smaller programs providing still other ind benefits—housing grants and allowances, telephone adaptations, so on. Many are local in nature.

As with income support programs and in-kind services, employment policies for the disabled are numerous and varied. A *quota system* requires every employer of 20 or more workers to fill at least 3 percent of all jobs with a registered disabled person. Not only is this law not enforced, but there appear to be too few unemployed registered disabled workers to meet the quota. However, only about one-half of the eligible disabled people are actually registered. Related to the quota system is a *designated employment* program, in which certain jobs (e.g., elevator operators) are reserved for disabled people.

Since 1945, a sizable nonprofit company, Remploy Ltd., has provided *sheltered employment* for the disabled. In addition, voluntary organizations and local governments often operate sheltered workshops for the sighted disabled. National government subsidies are awarded all of these types of organizations. Remploy, it should be noted, seeks to compete in the sale of its products with commercial enterprises.

A program of *special employment aids* also exists. In it, national government officers work with disabled people to provide adapted workplaces and special tools and environments within private enterprises. This service is very personalized and, as a result, the program is expensive and limited.

A number of *vocational training and rehabilitation centers* are operated or subsidized by the government to provide these types of services and placement assistance for disabled workers.

In sum, diversity and discretion characterize the disability system of the United Kingdom. The diversity is confusing and contributes to horizontal inequities among disabled people. The widespread exercise of discretion in the award of benefits by program officials appears to exacerbate this problem. In addition to their sheer number, the programs are not well coordinated or integrated. Some are local, some national; some are voluntary, and some are nonprofit subsidized businesses. Many, if not most, are income-tested. And, in spite of the large number of programs, a substantial "safety net" welfare program is required for those who fall through the cracks. For these reasons, then, the U.K. system, in spite of its national insurance base, is classified for our comparative purposes as a nonmature system.

Summary

This chapter has been largely descriptive. We first reviewed the structure of disability programs targeted at disabled working-age people in the United States, where we observed two main types of activity: ameliorative and corrective policies. The ameliorative policies involve primarily income support transfers, some provided as social insurance benefits, others as compensation for work or military-related impairments, and still others as welfare. The corrective measures are composed of subsidies for training and rehabilitation and employment programs such as employer subsidies or assistance to sheltered workshops. In addition, a policy strategy involving both ameliorative and corrective objectives—namely, affirmative action regulations supporting equality of access and mobility—was discussed. Relative to most other industrialized countries, United States policy emphasizes the ameliorative objective. With the exception of the military programs and a large number of special categorical programs, the system is relatively integrated and comprehensive in its coverage. As a result, the United States was characterized as having a mature and developed system.

The ameliorative and corrective characteristics of the United States system are observed in varying degrees in the seven other countries. While some can be roughly characterized as having mature and integrated systems, others cannot. In the former category are Sweden and the Federal Republic of Germany, both of which place emphasis on the work components of the system. The Netherlands has also a mature and integrated system but, like the United States, places substantial reliance on income support programs. All three of these countries, unlike the United States, have a strong commitment to regulatory policy in support of the "right to work" of the disabled. Israel also has an integrated and relatively adequate system, but is characterized by a large number of separate programs with a wide range of special emphases reflecting special circumstances.

The disability systems of France, Italy, and the United Kingdom are less developed than those of the other five. France, for example, has only recently shifted to an emphasis on collective responsibility, rather than family responsibility, for disabled working-age people. In Italy, income support transfers are emphasized, but the welfare—as opposed to insurance—programs for disabled working-age people provide relatively low benefits. Moreover, because there is no automatic shift from disability to retirement pensions when beneficiaries reach retirement age, the relative contribution of the program to income support for the disabled, as opposed to those who have retired early, is blurred. Finally, the programs in the United Kingdom for the working-age disabled are numerous and relatively unintegrated. Some of the disabled receive adequate income support, while others in like circumstances do not fare as well.

Notes

1. For several reasons, these calculations must be interpreted with caution. First, as noted above, some of the benefits may go to disabled persons who are above or below working age, and our adjustments to account for this are crude. Second,

some of the benefits are paid to support the dependents of working-age disabled people. We have treated these as expenditures on behalf of the disabled. Finally, while we call these public expenditures, it is clear that a number of states and local programs on behalf of the disabled are not included in the total.

2. In addition to public expenditures on the disabled, it is estimated that there are another $50 billion of private expenditures (private insurance disability payments) on disabled people. The figures are adjusted from 1975 data in Berkowitz and Rubin (1977).

3. Indeed, in recent years, the proportion of new persons entering the disability pension rolls who receive the supplementary pension is well above two-thirds.

4. The base amount is an indexed accounting unit, equal in 1978 to 12,600 Swedish crowns.

5. The classifications also include some working-age individuals who are not disabled—for example, widows, war orphans, and political refugees.

Chapter 5

The Ameliorative Response: Effects on Program Growth and Labor Supply

Two noticeable phenomena of the past decade in the eight industrialized countries in this study are the sizable growth in public expenditures on (and numbers of recipients of) disability programs aimed at working-age people, and the fall in the labor supply of this age group. Most of this growth has been concentrated in the ameliorative income support programs, centering in most countries on public disability pensions. There has been much speculation regarding the relationship between the liberalization and extension of benefits and their link to benefit acceptance and labor force participation decisions. In this chapter, we will explore the nature of this program growth, develop a model which relates it to work and benefit acceptance decisions, and investigate the evidence regarding this linkage.

The first section presents the record of growth in beneficiaries and expenditures from 1968 to 1978 in the eight countries studied. In the second section, the nature of the economic choice facing potential applicants for disability benefits is discussed, and the various aspects of policy which affect this choice—and its impact on program growth—are spelled out. Only in the United States have models of this linkage been tested empirically, so we use the United States experience in our discussion. This analysis of the impact of policy choices on work effort is presented in the third section. Then, after the patterns of disability income support growth and work effort patterns on a cross-national basis are analyzed, we describe the evidence on programs and their economic consequences for the other seven countries. The last section summarizes the discussion and offers some conclusions.

The Record of Growth in Disability Programs for Working-Age People across Eight Countries

Table 5.1 presents estimates of the growth from approximately 1968 to 1978 in the primary disability income support programs in the eight countries studied. It is this decade which witnessed a highly remarkable growth pattern in most of the countries, and that growth pattern has continued since then in some of them.

In terms of growth in the number of income transfer recipients, the rates of increase for a few of the countries are truly impressive. The Netherlands, for example, experienced an average growth rate of over 11 percent per year. This implies an almost threefold increase in the number of recipients over the ten-year period. Even though the population growth rate in the Netherlands has been very low, the number of recipients increased from 194,000 to 567,000 over the decade. Israel, Italy, and the United States have somewhat lower, though still substantial, rates of growth in the number of beneficiaries. The rates for these countries lie in the 7 to 8 percent range. Even these rates are very large, however, for countries in which the rate of growth of population is in the 1 to 3 percent range. The four remaining countries—France, Sweden, United Kingdom, and the Federal Republic of Germany—have lower growth rates, in the 2 to 5 percent range.

This rapid increase in recipients implies a substantially enlarged income support burden on the working population. Columns 3 and 4 of Table 5.1 show the number of disabled income support recipients in each country as a percentage of the employed population. Looking at this ratio for 1978, substantial variance among the countries is seen. Italy is truly an outlier, with disability recipients of working age totaling 18 percent of the employed work force. The Netherlands, the United States and the Federal Republic of Germany, however, are not far behind; their disability transfer recipients equal from 13 to 15 percent of their employed work force.[1] The lowest percentages are for France, Israel, Sweden, and the United Kingdom, where disability recipients represent 7 to 9 percent of the employed work force.

The growth in the ratio of recipients to the employed population from 1968 to 1978 gives some indication of the growth in the disability burden over this period. For the Netherlands, this percentage tripled during the period, and for Italy it doubled. Growth was not as pronounced in the other countries, although an increase was recorded in all of the countries.

While changes in the ratio of disability recipients to the employed population gives some indication of the increase in the burden of growth in this dependent population on the working population, it is incomplete. Indeed, the ratio of disabled to employed could increase and the burden represented by the disabled group could simultaneously decline if the income of workers increased more rapidly than the taxes required of them for income support payments to the disabled. One indicator of this financial burden would be the ratio of expenditures or income support to the disabled as a percentage of wage and salary earnings or national income. Another measure, though more crude, would be the percentage of total public expenditures which are accounted for by income support payments to the disabled. This measure also suggests how the priority given disability income support policy has changed over time. Columns 6 and 7 of Table 5.1 show this change for the 1968-78 decade. Change in this ratio, it should be noted, reflects the growth in the number of disability recipients, growth in the level of average support payments made to them, and growth in total public expenditures.

A doubling of the ratio is not rare among the countries studied. Italy and the Netherlands both experienced more than a doubling in the share of public expenditures accounted for by income transfers to the disabled, and the percentages for Israel and Sweden have nearly doubled. For the United States, the 1978 percentage is about 1.5 times that of 1968. The lowest relative increase was experienced by the Federal Republic of Germany,[2] while the percentage decreased for France and the United Kingdom.

The absolute level of this ratio of disability expenditures to total public expenditures is enormous in Italy and strikingly high in the Federal Republic of Germany and the Netherlands. In 1978, over one-fourth of total public expenditures were devoted to income support for the disabled in Italy,[3] and nearly 16 percent in the Federal Republic of Germany. The magnitude of this budget share, one could conjecture, is not fully recognized in the countries studied.

The rates of growth of income support expenditures are no less impressive than their level. In none of the countries studied did the increase fall below 10 percent in current prices. For half of the countries—Israel, Italy, Netherlands, and Sweden—the annual rate of growth exceeded 20 percent in current prices. The rate in Israel was about 50 percent per year in current prices.[4] Even when expenditures are expressed in constant dollars (adjusted for inflation), the growth rates are substantial. Again, Israel is in a class by itself with an annual growth rate of nearly 24 percent in real terms. The real growth rate for the Netherlands stood at about 19 percent, while that for Italy and Sweden was about 12 percent.

Rates of growth (in real terms) of the magnitude shown in column 9 are remarkable. Very few real public expenditure series grow consistently over a decade at a rate of 10 percent, yet growth in disability transfer expenditures exceeded this figure in one-half of the countries studied. Disability income support programs were truly a "growth industry" in the period 1968-78, and have remained such in several of the countries under review here.

Table 5.1. Growth of Disability Income Support in Terms of Recipients and Expenditures, Eight Countries, 1968-1978

	Recipients in Primary Programs					Expenditures in Primary Programs			
	Total (000)		Percentage of Employed		Annual Rate of Growth (%)	Percentage of National Government Expenditure		Annual Rate of Growth (%) ca. 1968-78	
	1968 (1)	1978 (2)	1968 (3)	1978 (4)	ca. 1968-78 (5)	1968 (6)	1978 (7)	Current (8)	Real (9)
Federal Republic of Germany[a]	2,955	3,789	11.3	15.1	2.5	12.9	15.7	10.5	5.3
France[b]	1,695	1,833	8.4	8.8	2.6	12.3	6.6	14.1	6.7
Israel[c]	46	93	5.4	8.6	7.3	1.6	2.9	50.0	23.7
Italy[d]	1,727	3,758	9.0	18.0	8.1	10.4	25.6	25.0	12.7
Netherlands[e]	194	567	4.4	13.0	11.3	5.8	13.6	25.9	18.6
Sweden[f]	212	353	5.3	8.7	5.2	2.6	4.3	20.8	11.7
United Kingdom[g]	1,464	1,754	6.3	7.8	1.8	3.8	2.9	11.3	.5
United States[h]	7,079	13,954	9.3	14.7	7.0	5.8	8.0	13.7	6.3

Note: Data were collected by the authors from various country studies, program reports, and official statistics.

[a]Programs included in the data are Public Pension Insurance, Workman's Accident Insurance, Health Insurance (benefits to disabled only), Aid for Farmers, Civil Servants Security, Employers' Benefits, Veterans' Compensation, Public Assistance, Tax Savings, and a variety of in-kind transfers. Because of the possibility of benefit cumulation in some of the programs, the total number of recipients is likely to be overstated to some unknown extent; the rate of growth of recipients is considered to be accurate, however. Data on recipients are for 1967 rather than 1968, and for 1977 rather than 1978. Data for expenditures are for 1969 rather than 1968.

[b]Programs included in the data are Disability Insurance, Military Disability Pensions, Pensions for War Victims, Assistance for Handicapped Adults, Work Accident

and Professional Illness, and Compensatory Allowance. Because disabled people may receive benefits from more than one of the programs, there is some amount of doublecounting in the recipient data. The data are for 1974 rather than 1968, and for 1977 rather than 1978 (i.e., a four-year period only).

[c]Programs included in the data for expenditures are Ministry of Defense Programs for War-Related Disabilities, General Disability Benefits, Mobility Allowance, Standing Loans for Cars, Work Injuries, Prisoners of Zion, Border and Hostile Actions, Welfare Cash Allowance, Histadrut Pension Funds, Disabled through Nazis, and Civil Service Disability Pension. To the extent that some of these expenditures are for purposes of rehabilitiation, the levels are somewhat exaggerated. Because disabled people may receive benefits from more than one of the programs, the recipients of Histadrut Pension Funds, Civil Service Disability Pensions, Mobility Allowances, and Standing Loans for Cars were excluded in recipient data to avoid doublecounting. Data are for 1977 rather than 1978. No exact data for 1968 are available; the earliest years for which reliable estimates are available (1972 to 1977) indicate higher rates of growth for both recipients (10.5%) and expenditures (62.7% in current monetary units) than indicated in the table.

[d]Programs included in the data are Industrial Injury Pension (INAIL), Disability Pensions (INPS), and Benefits to Disabled in Need.

[e]Programs included in the data are Disability Security Act, General Disability Act, General Pension for Public Workers, and Social Employment. The inclusion of the Sickness Benefit Program would exaggerate the total number of recipients and expenditures to some extent. However, because the sickness benefits program provides support for up to 12 months of nonwork due to sickness or injury, it provides benefits to numerous disabled individuals. Similarly, inclusion of the expenditures on and clients of the Social Employment program assumes that the primary purpose of this program is income support to disabled workers.

[f]Programs included in the data are Disability Pensions, Bonus Pension Supplement, Municipal Housing Supplement, National Housing Supplement, Child Supplement, Disability Supplement, Handicap Allowance, and Supplemental Injury. The data for recipients has been adjusted for doublecounting.

[g]Programs included in the data are Sickness and Invalidity Pensions, Industrial Injury Benefits, Industrial Disablement Pension, Non-Contributory Invalidity Pension (NCIP), Housewives' Non-Contributory Invalidity Pension (HNCIP), and Supplementary Benefits to Disabled. The expenditure data exclude the NCIP and HNCIP programs; the recipient data exclude only invalidity recipients in the Sickness and Invalidity Pension programs. A wide range of in-kind benefits are not included in the data. As a result, growth rates are biased downward. The terminal year for the rate of growth calculations is 1975 rather than 1978. The expenditure data include administrative expenses of the pension programs and the entire supplementary benefit programs as well as benefit payments. They also include Supplementary Benefits to the Disabled.

[h]Programs included in the data are Social Security Disability Insurance, Supplemental Security Income, Workers' Compensation, Veterans Compensation and Benefits, and Black Lung. There is some amount of doublecounting in the recipient data.

Program Liberalization and Its Effect on Benefit Acceptance, Work, and Program Growth

As we saw in Chapter 2, the disabled population in the eight countries appears to be remarkably similar. Clearly the differences in the size and growth of disability transfer income reported in Table 5.1 cannot be explained simply by differences in the incidence of impairment. In this section, we use a simple economic framework to describe the nature of the economic choices faced by potential disability benefit recipients and the way in which changes in the benefit scheme will lead to increases or decreases in the size of disability transfer programs. While our illustration of these effects is in the context of the United States disability insurance system, the analysis is directly relevant across all of the countries studied. Then, in the next section, we use this framework to describe and critique research studies which have sought to relate the liberalization of program benefits to changes in the number of applications for benefits and in work effort.

A Simple Work versus Disability Transfer Choice Framework

Workers who are potentially eligible for disability benefits face the choice of either continuing in the labor market (working or searching for a job) or applying for benefits and adjusting labor supply behavior to conform to the eligibility rules of the program. Such potential applicants can be thought of as performing a maximization calculation based on two alternative future life paths. The first path involves continuing in the labor market. The benefits of this path involve the earned income from continued work, less the costs of working, which include the cost of leisure foregone. For the person who becomes impaired, continued work may be at a wage below that which he or she earned when healthy, and future wage and employment prospects are likely to be uncertain. The second path involves application for disabililty-related benefits. Uncertainty also exists on this path, as such benefits are not guaranteed. Moreover, wages are lost during any initial waiting period, and future earnings are constrained by program rules, which may change over time. However, the worker whose application is accepted receives a lifetime and, in most cases (so far, at least) inflation-adjusted disability benefit. Moreover, benefits often depend upon the number of dependents, and full medical care benefits are typically awarded with disability benefits. A rational decisionmaker will, then, choose to work or to be a disability benefit recipient, depending on which option yields maximum well-being.

This framework of choice suggests that, for those people with handicaps, the smaller their potential wage rate, and the lower their probability of finding employment, the more likely they will be to apply for benefits.

Similarly, the more generous the program benefits—including benefits from all sources for which the person is eligible—relative to potential wages, the more likely they are to seek disability benefits. It also suggests that the greater the potential loss in wages owing to program-imposed constraints on the amount that can be earned if benefits are awarded, the smaller the probability of application. Conversely, the greater the uncertainty in future wages and the less the uncertainty of program acceptance, the more likely is application.

Clearly, this statement of maximization behavior is too simple, even though it does give some insight into why different people with the same medical impairment will behave differently in the labor market. Part of this difference in behavior not explained by the framework is due to differences in social outlook, work orientation, and concepts of self-worth among people. Other reasons involve differences in family or community attitudes toward work or toward benefit recipiency (stigma). While these differences are relevant to individual work decision, it is true that the benefit level and work constraint characteristics of disability programs are also important determinants of the work-benefit choices of the impaired. In what follows, we focus on these program characteristics.

Figure 5.1 shows the effect of a disability benefit program on the work effort and benefit acceptance decision. Consider an impaired man who, over the next thirty working days, can earn a daily wage of (*w*) and who has no other source of income. In the 30 working days, he can earn $30*w* if he works every day, and takes no days of leisure. Such a person would be at the $30*w* point on his budget constraint (line *ab*), working the maximum number of days and consuming no leisure. If he does not work at all, he would be at the opposite end of budget constraint *ab*, earning no income and taking 30 days of leisure. Most people, given such a choice, would be somewhere in between *a* and *b*, for example at point *A*, consuming, say, 8 days of leisure and earning $22*w*.

One method of achieving the ameliorative goal of spreading the costs of this person's impairment across society would be to provide him a cash transfer of, say, *B*. This is the amount which society would guarantee all people who had this person's health condition, regardless of the amount worked or of the person's work potential. Such a disability scheme would clearly increase the well-being of this impaired worker—for any given level of work or leisure he would have more total income, because his budget constraint would increase from *ab* to *cd*. Note, however, that the person's new income level will probably not be $22*w* + *B*, if the program simply awards him an income grant. The impaired worker is likely to choose a point on his new budget constraint (line *cd*) to the right of *A'*—a point, for example, such as *A''*, which has more leisure days and less work. In effect, with the income grant he can now "afford" more leisure. This change in work effort is the income effect of an unrestricted cash grant from a disability scheme.

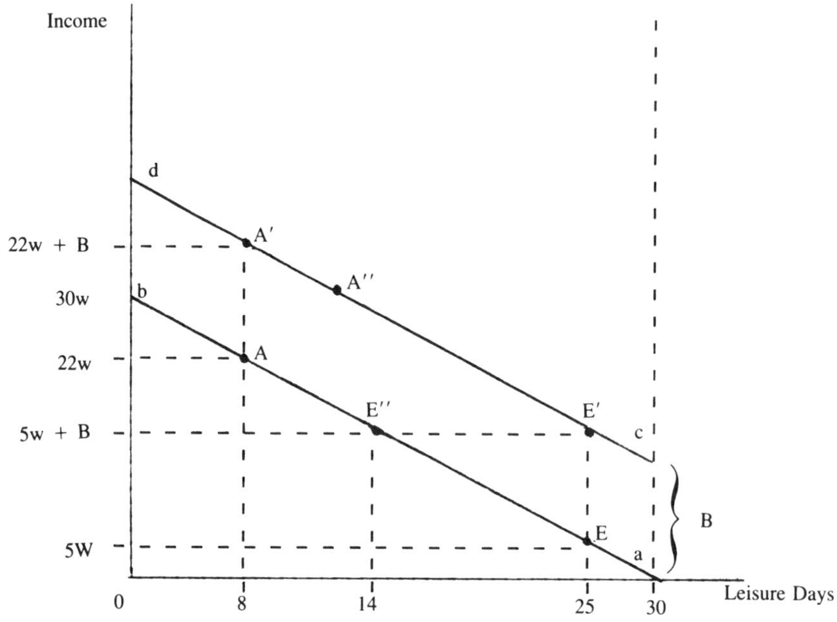

Figure 5.1. The Labor Supply and Benefit Acceptance Decision of the Impaired Worker. Definitions: w = daily wage, in dollars; line ab = budget constraint of worker without transfers; B = cash transfer, in dollars; line cd = budget constraint of worker with transfers; A and E are points of worker's choice between working and leisure.

In this analysis, we assumed the cost of applying for benefits (for example, lost wages, costs of gaining information, out-of-pocket expenses, time, social stigma) is zero, so that every impaired person who is eligible or even potentially eligible will apply. For a given *B* of available benefits, applications will fall as the cost of applying increases. Holding costs constant, applications will rise with increases in benefits or increases in the probability of being accepted into the program, given a specific impairment.

This framework indicates clearly that a reduction in work effort is a natural response to an unrestricted income transfer from the nonimpaired population to the impaired population. No such fall in work effort occurs, of course, if the impaired worker was originally out of the work force.

However, some disability income transfer programs (for example, DI and SSI in the United States) look not only at a potential beneficiary's impairment, but also at his or her work *potential*. Those people capable of "substantial gainful activity" may not be eligible for benefits, regardless of their impairment level. Since the government official determining a worker's work potential does not have the advantage of seeing Figure 5.1, he or she bases the decision on the seriousness of the impairment and on *actual* work experience.

Assume now that anyone who earns more than \$5*w*—that is, anyone who can work more than 5 of the 30 days or, alternatively, who takes fewer than 25 days of leisure—is considered not eligible for benefits regardless of the level of impairment. In this case, the choice facing the worker is more complicated. If he works more than 5 days, he will not be eligible for benefits. However, if he works fewer than 5 days, he has some probability of receiving benefits. For the worker who was at point *A*, this will mean a reduction in wage earnings greater than the gain in benefits. If he chooses to indicate that he needs 25 days of leisure, his total income would be \$5*w* + *B*, which is less than \$22*w*. Whether or not he will for apply for benefits is uncertain. The decision will depend on whether the *additional* leisure time gained if he were to receive benefits would offset the fall in total income. Note, however, that the potential-work-ability rule results in a significant gap in the worker's relevant budget constraint.

Any worker who was working 16 days or less (taking 14 days or more of leisure) will always reduce his work effort to 5 days (ignoring the issue of uncertainty about the ultimate awarding of benefits) and apply for benefits, since he can still receive the equivalent of 16 days of earnings (\$5*w* + *B*) in income while working only 5 days. The budget constraint with such a work-potential conditional benefit structure becomes *cE'Eb*.

As this analysis shows, a system which provides benefits to all impaired workers, regardless of their work potential, will tend to cause the work effort *of each* worker to fall, and will be "target inefficient" in that it provides benefits regardless of actual work effort. By assigning an additional constraint to the system—a rule concerning work potential—those who work *beyond* the level indicated by the rule will not receive benefits and will not change their work behavior. However, some impaired workers with the ability to work beyond the level of the work-potential rule may be induced to reduce their work effort in order to qualify for program benefits.

In our example, such a substitution away from market work is in the interest of those who would have earned between \$5*w* and \$5*w* + *B* initially (that is, who worked from five to sixteen days), since the program rules implicitly tax away all wages earned from days worked between five and sixteen. But even a worker at *A* who is working 22 days might be induced to substantially reduce work effort, if the added leisure is valued more than the lost income.

Moreover, applications for benefits will increase the more liberal is the work-potential rule. Conversely, the further is the work-potential level from the worker's actual position (say, 22 days of work), the less likely is a worker to reduce work effort and apply for benefits. In the extreme case, where any work results in ineligibility for program benefits, a worker would have to choose between completely leaving the labor force and receiving \$*B* in benefits or continuing to work but receiving no benefits. Hence, one measure of the likelihood of benefit application is the ratio of benefits to the potential wage earnings (for example, $B/\$22w$)—the higher this ratio, the greater will be the application rate.

A similar, and perhaps more vivid, way of looking at the potential labor supply reductions attributable to disability cash transfers, and the interaction of the benefit level with work-potential rules, is the following numerical example. Consider a disabled worker who could receive $400 per month of disability benefits as a recipient, but who could earn $600 per month if he worked full time. The structure of the program allows him to earn up to $300 per month and still receive the $400 in benefits, but any dollar earned beyond $300 per month is taken as evidence that the person has work potential too great to be eligible for benefits. This person, then, could voluntarily reduce his earnings to $300 per month, thereby receiving the $400 in disability benefits. His total income would be $700, which would be $100 more than if he worked full time. There is a substantial incentive for this worker to reduce his labor supply.

But this is only part of the story. Often, medical care, housing, and other social benefits are granted along with disability benefits. These serve to make the choice of disability recipiency even more attractive. Moreover, in some countries, disability (and other income transfers) are not taxed, while labor earnings are subject to payroll and income taxes.

Table 5.2 illustrates these incentives. For the worker who could earn $500 per month, being a recipient would yield him an increase of $300 per month in net income. Instead of working to his potential he would limit his earnings to the allowed amount. The same result would occur for the individual who had potential earnings of $750 per month. By cutting back his earnings by $450, he would end up with a total income which was $100 more than he would have if he worked full time. The final case, that of a worker who could earn $1000 of monthly income, yields a situation in

Table 5.2. Benefit-Cost Calculation Regarding the Beneficiary Status Choice of a Worker with Various Potential Monthly Earnings and $400 of Guarantee Level Benefits

	Monthly Earnings Potential					
	$1-$500		$750		$1000	
	Beneficiary Status	Worker Status	Beneficiary Status	Worker Status	Beneficiary Status	Worker Status
Disability benefits	$400	$ 0	$400	$ 0	$400	$ 0
Allowed earnings if a beneficiary	300	300	300	300	300	300
Value of medical and other disability-related benefits	50	0	50	0	50	0
Earnings above the allowed amount	0	200	0	450	0	700
Assumed taxes	0	50	0	100	0	200
Net income	$750	$450	$750	$650	$750	$800

which the individual finds it advantageous to work. But even then, he is only $50 better off, and has far less leisure than if he were a recipient.

Significantly, this simple single-period example in Table 5.2 assumes perfect certainty. In reality, a worker who gambles on working past the allowed earnings amount gives up a lifetime benefit for an uncertain stream of labor earnings. For instance, in the United States, once a worker gives up disability benefits, the worker loses all rights to future benefits. If his earnings fall below the maximum allowed, he must reapply as any other worker. Finally, the example implicitly overstates the amount of free time an impaired worker has for work. As Oi (1978) has emphasized, an impaired worker typically requires more time to perform nonmarket activities as well as market activities. In addition to direct medical care, he might need more rest, have less access to conventional means of transportation, and so on. Because of this, some recipients with high potential earnings who can work only part time are likely to voluntarily constrain earnings to the allowed earnings limit, even though twice or three times that amount could be earned.

Program Liberalization and Work Incentives: An Illustration

This discussion indicates clearly the ultimate dilemma faced by policymakers. A combination of benefit level and allowed earnings must be found sufficient to satisfy the income needs of recipients, but not cause a large reduction in work effort and program costs. In the remainder of this chapter we look at the ways in which policies that liberalize benefits may affect labor supply and benefit acceptance. In Chapter 6, we look at the extent to which liberalized benefits have alleviated poverty and achieved adequacy. The following discussion rests on the United States as an illustration, and shows how changes in the disability benefit law, changes in interpretation of the law, changes in benefits, and changes in the costs of applying can all affect the work-effort choice.

Changes in the Law

As initially enacted in 1954, the Social Security Disability Insurance (DI) program provided benefits only to disabled workers who had reached retirement age. Soon after establishment of the program this restriction was relaxed, and by 1956 workers aged 50 or more became eligible for disability insurance benefits. It was not until 1958 that dependents of disabled workers were eligible for benefits. By 1965, all workers, regardless of age, and their dependents were eligible for disability benefits. Each of these changes increased the population potentially eligible for benefits, and each is likely to have accounted for some of the program growth.

The determination of eligibility for DI involves demonstration of a permanent and total impairment and a waiting period in which no "substantial gainful activity" (SGA)—work earning more than $300 per month—is engaged in. Over time both of these eligibility requirements have been relaxed. For example, in 1965, the test of permanent and total disability was changed to mean that the disability was expected to last at least 12 months or result in death. This increased the probability of application and benefit acceptance for a given impairment.

Changes in the Interpretation of the Law

Both DI and Supplemental Security Income (SSI) have strict medical-impairment criteria for eligibility, but a vocational standard also exists. It considers such personal attributes as age, education, and work experience, and is applied to workers whose impairments are not sufficiently severe to meet the strict medical standards. Although these vocational criteria have only been standardized in published form since 1978, the role of these factors has been expanded over the life of the program. In 1960, fewer than 10 percent of all DI allowances were based on vocational factors. By 1975 these factors accounted for more than 26 percent of all allowances. Because these criteria are more subject to administrative discretion than the medical criteria, their expansion is likely to have contributed to program growth. This is especially true in the case of fringe workers (older, less educated, unskilled workers), whose probability of acceptance into the program with a given level of impairment is significantly affected by the use of such factors. This relaxation has also increased the relative attractiveness of the disability recipiency option.

Changes in Benefit Adequacy

Individual DI benefits have significantly increased in both real and nominal terms since 1956. This increase is caused by the general rise in average lifetime wages on which the benefit is based. But more important, the increases are due to legislated increases in the insurance-based formula, on which DI benefits directly depend. Congress raised the formula seven times between 1954 and 1974. After 1974, the formula was automatically increased with increases in the consumer price index.

The increase in potential disability benefits from the start of the program in 1957 to 1978 has been large. In constant 1978 dollars these benefits increased nearly 80 percent, from $2,937 to $5,265 for the median manufacturing worker with no dependents. Over this same period annual wages increased from $9,781 to $12,941 (in 1978 dollars), an increase of 32 percent. Hence, potential DI benefits for manufacturing workers have grown at more than twice the rate of real wages over those twenty years. This is reflected in the replacement rate (the ratio of disability transfer amounts to the earlier wage rate), which has risen from 30 percent to over 40 percent since 1957. Since DI benefits are exempt from income taxation, the increase in federal and state income taxes during this period for most workers makes the net increase in DI benefits even greater. For the worker with median income, the net replacement rate rose from 35 to 49 percent from 1968 to 1978.

Changes in the law concerning provision of benefits to a disabled worker's dependents have also increased the generosity of the program. Those benefits were first established in 1958. Although the schedules are complex, total benefits for a family with children can range up to 280 percent of the benefit amount if no dependents are present. The total family replacement rate also increased rapidly from 1957 to 1978—from 57 percent to 70 percent.

However, replacement rates vary substantially over the population of DI recipients. The availability of dependents' benefits, together with changes in the law designed to increase relative benefits for low-wage workers, has made the program especially attractive for certain types of families—in particular, large families headed by a low-wage worker. As a result, some workers in this category are potentially eligible for DI benefits close to or even in excess of current wages. Indeed, in 1972, one-third of DI recipients were found to have benefit levels in excess of 80 percent of their wage earnings in the year prior to the onset of disability, and one-quarter of newly entitled beneficiaries in 1973 received *more* in benefits than they earned in 1972.[5] Moreover, those receiving DI benefits for at least two years are automatically eligible for Medicare benefits. As we saw in Figure 5.1 and Table 5.2, an impaired worker considering the decision to stop work and accept DI benefits versus continuing work will compare potential wage earnings and benefits. Increasing benefit adequacy is likely to have contributed to the growth in the DI program.

Changes in the Costs of Application

It takes time and effort for potentially eligible workers to learn about the disability program, to apply for benefits, and to monitor their case through the Social Security system. These direct costs, however, are likely to be but a small proportion of the total costs of establishing eligibility. In addition to direct time and effort costs, the worker must meet the five-month waiting period, implying little or no work during this period and forgoing earnings. Moreover, having once established eligibility, the worker must continue to meet the work-potential rule. Meeting both of these constraints entails present and future reductions in work and earnings, which are likely to be a serious cost to potential DI applicants.[6] In recent years, both of these costs of application have been reduced. The allowed earnings (potential work) figure has been increased to $300 and the waiting period has been shortened from six to five months. These reductions in the cost of application (in the form of lost wages) are also likely to have contributed to the observed program growth.

The Impact of Disability Transfers on Work Effort: Empirical Evidence

The discussion in the previous section provided a framework for predicting the effect of disability program benefits, program eligibility rules, and the interpretation of rules on the choice between continuing work or seeking disability transfers. Using this framework, it is clear that many disability program changes in the countries studied over the past 25 years were such as to increase the attractiveness of the transfer recipiency option relative to the work option for impaired individuals. Replacement rates have risen and eligibility requirements have been relaxed. It would be surprising if empirical studies failed to find that these changes in the terms for granting disability transfers contributed to program growth and reductions in labor supply.

Consider first the decision of an individual to apply for benefits. In the United States, the working-age population with some type of self-reported impairment serious enough to restrict work is over four times the size of the DI beneficiary group. Hence, the opportunities for expansion of the system—and for working individuals to alter their choices regarding continued labor force participation—are substantial.

Using some variant of the economic choice framework discussed in the previous section, researchers have attempted to test a number of hypotheses concerning the effects of disability transfers on people's behavior. The primary hypothesis involves the effect of health status and disability benefit levels on the choice of work or recipiency. Clearly, disentangling the effects of potential labor market earnings, potential disability benefits, and disability status on that choice is very difficult. And studies have experienced varying degrees of success in this effort.[7] All of the available studies of this choice have employed United States data.

Three early studies (Scheffler and Iden, 1974; Berkowitz, Johnson, and Murphy, 1976; and Luft, 1978) attempted to sort out these determinants of disability transfer recipiency and labor force participation. While these studies were plagued with less than adequate data and, in some cases, employed questionable techniques, several interesting results were reported. Luft found that disability status had a substantial negative impact on labor market activity, and that this impact was much greater for women than for men. He estimated that over 6 percent of potential national output is lost because of health status problems, and for individuals with physical limitations, the earnings decline ranges from 33 to 45 percent of expected annual earnings if limitations were not present.

These results are important in that they suggest that the presence of an impairment does lead to a major reduction in expected or potential income. These expected income losses make the work option less attractive for a disabled person, and conversely increase the relative attractiveness of being a recipient of disability transfers.

The Berkowitz, Johnson, and Murphy study was among the first to recognize the complex interaction among health status, availability of disability transfers, personal characteristics, and labor market conditions in the work-effort decision. The authors concluded that, even for those not receiving disability transfers, the presence of impairments significantly reduced work effort. The authors also concluded that the receipt of income transfers that do not constrain work effort—e.g., veterans' pensions—do have an income effect leading to reductions in labor supply, but that these effects are not large. Unfortunately, the authors could not statistically sort out the effect of the major disability income transfer programs, as opposed to health status itself, on the work effort choice.

Two recent empirical studies of the work-effort effects of disability transfers focus on older male workers. These studies are by Parsons and by Leonard and are summarized in Table 5.3. Both are based on a model in which the individual rationally compares the expected income stream associated with being in the labor force with that associated with being a disability transfer recipient, and chooses that which maximizes his economic welfare. The expected income associated with being a labor force participant is proxied by the individual's expected earnings (wage rate), and that associated with reliance on disability transfers is measured by imputed values of disability benefits which would be received were this option chosen. Because "true" health status determines the probability of receiving disability benefits, it is also a determinant of the labor force participation decision in these studies.

Parsons finds that the probability of labor force participation falls significantly as the replacement rate (disability benefits divided by the wage rate) rises. In both of his studies, the estimated response is very large. For each 10 percent increase in real disability benefits (at the mean), Parsons estimates that the labor force participation rate of older men will fall by from .3 percent to .9 percent. Parsons attributes the bulk of the observed decline of about 7 percentage points in the labor force participation rates of older workers in the United States since 1960 to the growth in DI transfer generosity.

Like Parsons, Leonard also addresses the question of the role of disability transfer benefits on the individual decision to work or to seek disability transfer recipiency. And, like Parsons' study, Leonard's also rests on a regression framework in which variables standing for expected earnings, expected transfers, and health status are employed to explain the choice between the work or transfer recipiency. Leonard's −.052 estimate of the elasticity of labor force participation with respect to expected DI benefits is also very large—about 40 percent of the decline in older worker

Table 5.3. Labor Supply Analyses of Disability Transfers

Study	Parsons (1980a, 1980b)	Leonard (1979)	Slade (1982)	Haveman and Wolfe (1983)
Population analyzed	Men, 48-62(a) or 45-59(b)	Men, 45-54	Men, 58-63	Men, 45-62
Data used[a]	National Longitudinal Survey, 1969(a) or 1966(b)	1972 Social Security Survey of Health and Work Characteristics merged with benefit and earnings records	1969 Retirement History Survey	1978 Michigan Panel Study of Income Dynamics, plus information from prior years
Dependent variable	Participation in work force	DI recipiency	Participation in work force	Participation in work force
Program variables	Potential DI/Wage	Expected DI benefits	Potential monthly DI benefits	Expected total income, if a disability transfer recipient
Results	Elasticity of participation with respect to replacement rate = −.09 (1966) or −.03 (1969)	Elasticity of participation with respect to expected benefits = −.052	Elasticity of participation with respect to expected benefits = −.023	Elasticity of participation with respect to expected income as a disability transfer recipient = −.0003 to −.0005

[a]All are cross-section studies.

labor force participation in the United States since the 1950s is attributed to increased benefit levels.

The results of these studies suggest that decisions on "early retirement" and/or the receipt of disability transfers do have a strong economic dimension to them. They also indicate that expected labor market earnings, expected disability transfers, and disability status all play a role in these decisions. Nevertheless, methodological and empirical weaknesses pervade these studies. The disability status variables used to measure "true" health status are often very weak. Further, expected disability transfers and nondisability transfers have been proxied by actual transfers, or other procedures have been used which introduce statistical problems. Finally, little attention has been given to the role of labor demand conditions in explaining the labor supply decisions of workers.

Two more recent studies of this issue have reached quite different results than those of Parsons and Leonard. These studies, one by Slade and the other by Haveman and Wolfe, are also summarized in Table 5.3. Slade finds a distinctly smaller response to disability transfers. His estimated elasticity is about -.023, and is not statistically significant. The most recent estimate is presented by Haveman and Wolfe from a work-status choice model estimated over a sample of men aged 45 to 62. The income flow expected from the labor market and from disability transfer options depends on each individual's observable characteristics. It is assumed that the individual rationally compares these expected income flows and selects the option which maximizes his expected income. The income flows are defined as the *total income flows* associated with each option rather than transfers from only one program, such as Social Security Disability Insurance.

Their results suggest a small but significant response to expected income in the disability transfer option. The elasticity of labor force participation with respect to disability transfer income is –.0003 to –.0005, a response much smaller than those of the other studies. Haveman and Wolfe conclude that no more than 20 to 25 percent of the 1968-78 reduction in the labor force participation rate of older men is attributable to the growth in generosity of the entire portfolio of income transfers available to disabled workers, and not just DI benefits.

From these studies, what have we learned about the work disincentive effect on older workers of disability transfers? There is consistent evidence of a statistically significant effect of disability benefits on the work-status choice—but the estimated effects range from small (Slade, Haveman and Wolfe) to rather large (Parsons, Leonard). The range of estimated elasticities of the response in terms of labor force participation is from -.0003 to -.0005 (Haveman and Wolfe); to –.023 (Slade); to –.052 (Leonard); to –.09 to –.03 (Parsons).[8] The evidence from these studies, after taking account of their methodological strengths and weaknesses, suggests that the leniency in disability benefits accounts for a small, but nevertheless significant, part of the 1968-78 decrease in the labor force participation of older men—perhaps 20 percent, but at the most no more than one-third.

Cross-National Comparisons of Income Support and Work Effort Patterns: A First Approximation

In the first two sections we analyzed the incentives for disability program growth and concluded that the labor supply disincentives—earnings limits, higher replacement rates, high benefit reduction rates—implicit in the major disability programs have contributed to the growth in expenditures and in numbers of recipients. And, in the United States, we have seen that these program characteristics have led to an identifiable and statistically significant reduction in work effort. We speculated that about one-fourth of the U.S. decline in older workers' labor supply from 1968 to 1978 is attributable to the increased generosity of disability transfers. Given these results, one would expect that patterns of work effort reduction among the population of the eight countries studied over time would correspond to the rates of growth of disability program recipients and expenditures across the countries.

In Table 5.4, patterns of male labor force participation for prime-aged and older workers are shown for the 1960s and 1970s. In addition, the table shows average annual percentage rates of change. Because of data incongruities, there are some differences among the countries in the dates to which the rates correspond, and in the age groups being compared.

Looking at the labor force participation rates for the older age group of male workers, one is struck by the substantial differences across countries. For the late 1970s, the rates range from 91 percent for those aged 55-64 in the United Kingdom to 39 percent for those aged 60-64 in Italy.[9] By way of contrast, there is very little difference in the labor force participation for prime-aged men among the countries.

The focus in this table is on the change from the late 1960s to the late 1970s (although the actual years vary) in labor force participation rates for the older group of workers. It is this group which would be primarily affected by early retirement policies, including changes in Social Security retirement pension programs and extensions of coverage or increases in net replacement rates in disability programs over time. And, if the poor economic performance in these countries in the 1970s resulted in unemployment among older workers being disguised by the awarding of disability (or other early retirement) benefits to them, labor force participation rates for this group should also reflect this pattern.

Table 5.4. Male Labor Force Participation Rates by Country for Older and Prime-Aged Groups, 1960s and 1970s[a]

	Older Group (ages)	Participation Rate(%)		Average Annual Rate of Change (%)	Prime-Aged Group (ages)	Participation Rate(%)		Average Annual Rate of Change (%)
		Late 1960s	Late 1970s			Late 1960s	Late 1970s	
Federal Republic								
of German	55-59	86.8	85.8	−0.2	25-49	96.6	96.1	−0.1
(1970-77)	60-64	68.8	47.9	−5.0				
France								
(1962-75)	55-64	78.7	72.1	−0.7	25-54	96.1	95.4	−0.1
Israel								
(1961-75)	55-64	84.0	81.0	−0.3	45-54	93.4	92.9	.0
Italy	55-59	82.0	75.9	−0.8	30-49	97.3	97.8	0.1
(1968-78)	60-64	51.2	39.4	−2.6				
Netherlands	55-59	86.9	79.9	−1.4	25-44	96.4	96.7	0.1
(1971-77)	60-64	73.9	58.0	−4.0				
Sweden	55-59	97.8	89.7	−0.9	25-49	94.5	91.9	−0.3
(1965-75)	60-64	93.0	74.0	−1.1				
United Kingdom								
(1971-75)	55-64	91.0	90.8	.0	25-44	97.9	97.9	0
United States	55-59	90.0	82.9	−0.8	25-54	97.2	95.7	−0.2
(1968-78)	60-64	77.3	62.0	−2.2				

Source: For non-U.S. countries: International Labour Office (relevant years). For the U.S.: U.S. Department of Labor, Bureau of Labor Statistics (1969, 1979).

[a] Actual years covered are cited with each country name.

For all eight of the countries studied, labor force participation rates for older workers fell from the 1960s to the 1970s, in some cases rather radically. While already low in the 1960s in Italy (51 percent), the rate there fell to a very low 39 percent by the late 1970s for workers aged 60-64. This represents an average annual decrease in the labor force participation rate of 2.6 percent. Even for the 55-59 age group in Italy—a group below the male retirement age—the rate fell from 82 to 76 percent—an average annual decrease of nearly 1 percent per year. In the Federal Republic of Germany, the rate for workers age 60-64 fell even more substantially—from 69 percent to 48 percent—a decrease of 21 points or an average annual reduction of 5 percent. Only in Israel and the United Kingdom did this rate for older workers remain high, showing but a slight decrease. These changes over time stand in contrast to the rates for prime-aged workers. On balance, these rates showed some tendency to sag from the 1960s to the 1970s, yet the decreases recorded are small and not unexpected, given the adverse economic conditions of the 1970s.

In general, then, this labor force pattern for older workers suggests that the increasing generosity and coverage of disability programs has led to a decrease in labor force participation—and labor supply—for older workers. On the other hand, a word of caution is in order: to some extent, contributions to this reduction in the labor supply—early retirement—of older workers are also likely to be attributed to the extension of coverage of Social Security retirement programs into age categories below 65. This is the case for the United States, where a Social Security early retirement option is made available to workers at age 62. In Sweden, the Netherlands, and the Federal Republic of Germany as well, the terms under which retirement at less than age 65 could be chosen were liberalized during the 1970s. Failure to recognize such enlarged opportunities for early retirement would result in an exaggerated view of the effect of increased disability program generosity and more lenient eligibility requirements on the labor supply of these workers.

Given the large variance among the countries in the decrease in labor force participation rates from the 1960s to the 1970s, it would be of interest to determine the correspondence of this pattern to patterns in the growth of disability programs across the countries. Table 5.5 permits this comparison. The first column of that table presents an indicator of the extent of the decrease in the male, older worker labor force participation relative to that of prime-aged male workers. It shows that the Federal Republic of Germany, Italy, and the Netherlands experienced large relative decreases in older worker labor supply; the United States, Sweden, and France somewhat smaller relative decreases; and Israel and the United Kingdom quite small relative reductions.

The second two columns are taken from Table 5.1, and report the growth rates from 1968 to 1978 of the number of disability program recipients and

Table 5.5. Patterns of Decrease in Older Male Labor Force Participation Rates and Disability Program Growth, 1960s to 1970s, by Country (in percentages)[a]

	Percentage Change in Ratio of Older to Prime-Aged Worker Participation Rates, 1960s to 1970s			Annual Rate of Growth of Disability Program Recipients, ca. 1968-1978[b]			Annual Rate of Growth of Real Disability Program Expenditures, ca. 1968-1978[b]		
Federal Republic of Germany	−15.4[c]	(2)	(2)	2.5	(7)	(6)	5.3	(7)	(6)
France	−7.4	(6)	(6)	2.6	(6)	(5)	6.7	(5)	(4)
Israel	−3.1	(7)		7.3	(3)		23.7	(1)	
Italy	−15.5	(1)	(1)	8.1	(2)	(2)	12.7	(3)	(2)
Netherlands	−14.8[c]	(3)	(3)	11.3	(1)	(1)	18.6	(2)	(1)
Sweden	−9.5	(5)	(5)	5.2	(5)	(4)	11.7	(4)	(3)
United Kingdom	−.2	(8)	(7)	1.8	(8)	(7)	.5	(8)	(7)
United States	−12.5[c]	(4)	(4)	7.0	(4)	(3)	6.3	(6)	(5)

[a]Rank of country is shown in first set of parentheses; rank of country with Israel excluded is shown in second set.

[b]From Table 5.1.

[c]Mean of percentage change of age group 55-59 and age group 60-64.

real program expenditures, respectively. In both of these indicators of program growth and generosity, Israel, the Netherlands, and Italy rank above the other countries, and substantially above the United Kingdom. With the exception of Israel, then, the pattern is clear: the United Kingdom, the country with the lowest indicator of disability program growth, also has the smallest labor supply reduction among older workers. Countries with greater program growth (the United States, Sweden, the Federal Repubic of Germany, and France) have greater relative labor supply reductions, and the Netherlands and Italy, which have the greatest indicators of program recipiency and expenditure growth, have the greatest labor supply reduction in the older working group.

With Israel excluded,[10] then, the data suggest that those countries which, either deliberately or inadvertently, experienced rapid growth in disability income transfers or recipients also experienced the most rapid decrease in the labor supply of older workers. While this relationship does not establish causality between the growth in disability benefit generosity or reduced eligibility stringency and the reduction in labor force participation rates, it does indicate that a substantial fraction of those older workers who left the labor force during the 1970s replaced some of their forgone earnings by gaining access to disability benefits. The implications of this pattern for economic performance are clear. As has been stressed, both disguising unemployment through induced retirement via disability program recipiency and increasing the generosity of these programs relative to potential earnings leads to labor supply reductions which are concentrated among older workers. Some of these workers have substantial job experience and work skills. While such workers may appear to have relatively low ratios of productivity to wages (especially in economies with strong labor unions and employment security systems), the economic costs associated with their permanent (or long-term) retirement from productive activity would appear substantial. The question of whether or not this cost is too great a price for a nation to pay for hiding inadequate economic performance, providing "generous" pension benefits, or relaxing eligibility standards should appear high on the agenda for public discussion in these economies.

The Sources of Program Growth in Other Countries: Some Speculations

The findings on the sources of program growth in the United States can only suggest the determinants of growth in the other countries studied. In part because of the high unemployment and poor economic situation in these countries in the 1970s, as well as the greater propensity to employ the social welfare system to ease financial hardships, disability benefits appear to have been used to replace and supplement unemployment benefits in many of the countries. This is reflected in alterations of program regulations that gave increased weight to vocational and labor market considerations. In some of the countries studied, disability benefits were viewed as a mechanism for supporting, indeed encouraging, the early retirement of older, less skilled workers for whom employer wage costs exceeded productivity and who, in the absence of constraints implicit in collective bargaining arrangements, would have been released. The effect of this policy was simultaneously to increase the growth of the disability income support system and to camouflage the true level of unemployment.

In this section, we discuss the nature and causes of program growth in the seven other countries. Because of the absence of quantitative research on the subject, this discussion must, of necessity, be more speculative than that for the United States.

Federal Republic of Germany

Relative to the other countries studied, the growth in disability recipients and expenditures in the Federal Republic of Germany was low. As Table 5.1 shows, the rate of real growth in expenditures was about 5 percent. As the figures on disability expenditures as a percent of total government expenditures indicate, the percentage of government spending accounted for by disability programs was relatively high, and rose during the 1968-78 decade from 13 to about 16 percent.

This growth in expenditures appears to be related largely to increased policy awareness of the economic circumstances of the disabled, and the resulting increase in benefits provided them. As the description of the program in the Federal Republic in Chapter 4 showed, benefits provided in the Public Act and Social Insurance programs increased during the 1968-78 decade.

The criteria for eligibility were substantially relaxed during this period as well, largely because of a 1969 decision of the Grand Senate of the Federal Social Court. This decision made the absence of an appropriate job (even part-time) equal to the presence of a health impairment in deciding whether a pension applicant met program criteria. The decision was elaborated on in 1976, when the Grand Senate decided that no appropriate job was available if the Pension or Supplement programs were unable to find suitable work for the applicant within one year.

The effect of these changes in eligibility criteria was to increase the proportion of pensions awarded for "general" conditions of impairment, as opposed to "specific" reductions in earnings capacity in excess of 50 percent. While new general disability pensions accounted for about 70 percent of the total in 1969, by 1975 they had increased to nearly 90 percent. If all of this proportional increase is attributed to the decision of the Grand Senate, the implied increase in annual costs of the new disability recipients in 1975 is estimated to be about 5 percent of total costs.[11] A later study for 1977 attributed a 15 percent increase in expenditures in the pension program to the 1969 ruling.

This evidence, then, suggests that a substantial proportion of the growth in numbers of German recipients and in expenditures is due to extensions of coverage and, especially, to the judicially imposed relaxation in eligibility criteria for the pension program. This relaxation, it should be noted, came at approximately the same time as the economic recession of the early 1970s. These factors, rather than increases in real benefit levels, appear to account for the bulk of post-1969 expenditure growth in the program.

One additional factor should be mentioned. During the 1970s, a flexible age-limit arrangement was introduced into the old age retirement programs. The age limit for receipt of retirement benefits was lowered to age 62 and, perhaps most important, 60-year-old persons who had been unemployed for 1.5 years also became eligible for retirement benefits. Without these changes, the cost increases for general and specific disability pensions would have been much larger.

France

Changes in both the number and pattern of disability recipients and expenditures in France are attributable to the major reorganization of disability policy that has been underway during the last decade. As described in Chapter 4, this legislation culminated in the 1975 act, which established collective (rather than family) responsibility for the economic support of the disabled, integrated pension benefits for the disabled with social assistance, and revised the work code dealing with the labor market classification of disabled workers.

The main impact of this law was to increase the guaranteed support to severely disabled adults not covered by one of the pension plans, replacing family by state support. The extension of coverage and increased adequacy under this system led to major increases in benefits. For example, prior to passage of the 1975 law (e.g., in 1974) the severely disabled were guaranteed benefits equal to about 13 percent of the minimum wage; by 1977, three years later, the guarantee had risen to over 50 percent of the minimum wage. This increase brought the assistance provided this group to a level equivalent to that for aged salaried workers.[12] Largely because of benefit expansion, but also because of other administrative changes associated with the 1975 act, the number of beneficiaries in the severely disabled group rose rapidly—from 80,000 in 1974 to nearly 200,000 in 1977. Because the two largest programs—the disability pension and the war invalid pension—showed almost no growth from 1974 to 1977, the increase under the 1975 act accounts for 90 percent of the growth in total beneficiaries in the system during this period.[13]

In terms of beneficiary growth, then, this single program extension explains much of the increase. However, from 1974 to 1978 expenditure growth for the severely disabled far exceeded the rise in number of beneficiaries—nearly 25 percent per year in current values. This increase reflects expanded levels of benefits in nearly all programs during the period. Much of the increase also resulted from changes brought about by the 1975 law. As Chapter 6 will indicate, from 1974 to 1978 the relative position of those receiving regular disability pensions did not change—the net replacement rate hovered in the 30-40 percent range, with a slight tilt in favor of the poor. The benefit levels for workers experiencing occupationally related disability or illness[14] increased substantially in these years, especially for those with less than median income. By 1978, replacement rates at all predisability income levels were at least 100 percent, and those with low predisability incomes received over 180 percent of their predisability income if they became totally disabled because of employment-related maladies.

The growth in both number of beneficiaries and disability expenditures in France is largely attributed to program extensions and increased benefit levels (especially to lower-income workers) brought about by the 1975 law. Increasing benefits to those disabled by job-related difficulties does not seem to have generated a sudden increase in the demand for benefits. As noted in Chapter 4, however, the changes in the 1975 law largely served to move coverage and benefit levels toward the levels attained in the other countries studied.

Israel

Table 5.1 shows that growth in disability program expenditures was larger in Israel than in any of the other countries studied. As in the case of France, legislation from 1968 to 1978 both extended coverage and liberalized entitlements. In Israel, however, two other forces appeared to support this growth. First, there was a series of court rulings which asserted beneficiary rights, in some cases opening coverage to groups not previously covered. And, perhaps related to developments in the judicial and appeals system, individuals tended to press their claims for benefits more rigorously. As in France, the most rapid growth occurred in the work-related pension programs, where the number of recipients grew by about 12 percent per year during the 1968-78 decade. While the absolute number of recipients was not large in 1978, it was expected to increase because of the extension of coverage offered by recent labor agreements.

The major legislative change during the 1968 to 1978 decade was the 1974 Disability Law, which became a major source of income support for the disabled. Although the passage of this law was expected to result in a major reduction in the number of disabled receiving welfare assistance, that did not occur during the first three years of the law's implementation—the number of disabled on welfare declined only slightly. As a result, the 1974 law led to an increase of 20,000 disability-program beneficiaries in the 1974-78 period—about 2 percent of the labor force. In addition to growth directly related to the General Disability program, beneficiary status in that program carried entitlement to both mobility and attendance benefits (although the disabled person could only take advantage of one of these programs). The number of recipients and expenditures in these programs also increased rapidly.

In addition to developments related to new programs, there has also been program liberalization in other dimensions. Categories of health problems recognized as occupational diseases have been expanded—e.g., to include heart attacks and strokes—and benefit levels have been increased—e.g., by as much as 50 percent in the work injury programs (if the impairment affects ability to work). In the defense-related programs, the wage on which benefits was based increased three times in the 1968-78 decade, and the percentage of this wage covered by benefits grew from 68 to 86 percent. And, as noted, provision for mobility benefits expanded rapidly over the past decade.

Demographic factors appear to have played little role in the rapid expansion of working-age beneficiaries and expenditures. Among that population, the proportion of workers aged 54-65 decreased somewhat over the decade. Moreover, educational levels and occupational status—both related to impairments—improved, and the level of unemployment was rather constant over the period.

Finally, for largely unexplained reasons, the incidence of disability within the Israeli population appears to have increased over the decade. In a 1966 survey, only 2.6 percent of the working-age population reported a health-related work limitation (3.9 percent for men; 1.4 percent for women). In a comparable survey in 1974, the percentage had increased to 4.5 (5.7 percent for men and 3.4 percent for women). Although we have little insight into the causes of this increase, effects of military conflicts and possibly an increasing social awareness of the significance of health problems are factors that should not be neglected.

These program extensions and liberalizations are reflected in the replacement rate changes described in Chapter 6 and, in themselves, account for some of the expenditure growth. In addition, as we have noted, they are likely to increase the demand for beneficiary status. The replacement rate increases registered from 1968 to 1978 were substantial. Except for the Work Injury program, replacement rates increased from 12 to 40 percent. Increases for the low-income population were even more substantial, ranging from 3 to 73 percent. The Welfare, General Disability, and Defense program benefits, it should be noted, strongly favor the poor—for both low-income and average-income groups, replacement rates in excess of 100 percent are not rare.

Such replacement rates, however, tell only part of the story. The 1968-78 decade in Israel saw more rapid relative growth in special benefits (e.g., mobility, housing, and attendance) programs than in cash transfer programs. When these benefits are added to cash benefits, replacement rates become very high indeed. Numbers reported in Chapter 6 for the General Disability program with work-related pensions show that these replacement rates for 1978 were in excess of 130 percent.

The increasing generosity of the Israeli disability system is reflected in the various replacement rates. While high and increasing rates account directly for some of the rapid growth in program expenditures from 1968 to 1978, their indirect effect on the demand for program beneficiary status should not be understated. The incentive for labor supply reductions and early retirement via disability benefits are substantial.

Italy

Table 5.1 shows that, next to Israel and the Netherlands, expenditure growth in programs for the disabled was most rapid in Italy.[15] Unlike Israel, however, that growth is not attributable to any new major legislation or to any substantial increase in benefit levels. A more liberal interpretation of the eligibility criteria appears to be a major cause of increased growth. This is reflected in Table 5.1, where the average rate of growth of beneficiaries (8.1 percent) is relatively close to the rate of growth of real expenditures (12.7 percent).[16]

Largely owing to explicit government policy, the disability pension program has been used as a supplement to unemployment benefits, especially for older workers. When unemployment rose to high levels in the early 1970s, the eligibility criterion concerned with the worker's social and economic environment became a primary one; established in 1969, it was immediately seized upon by program administrators. Because of the high rate of program growth from 1970 to 1975, program instructions emphasized a more restricted use of this criterion, and by 1976 program growth had slowed considerably.

Use of the economic environment criterion is reflected in the regional distribution of disability pensions. By 1978, the number of disability pensions in the poor, high-unemployment southern part of Italy (the Mezzogiorno) had doubled from its 1968 level. In the North, the number of disability pensions increased by about 60 percent over the same period.

The dependence of program growth on high unemployment, combined with the liberalization of eligibility requirements (especially in the Disability Pension program), is reflected in the pattern of replacement rates over the 1968-78 decade, described in Chapter 6. While replacement rates increased somewhat in the Disability Pension program (from 16 to 21 percent of predisability income at the median income level), they were virtually constant in the Work Injury program. Replacement rates favor the poor in both programs, but the gap between the two programs is enormous. In the regular Disability Pension program, the highest replacement rate recorded is 43 percent, which is the lowest recorded in the Work Injury program. For workers of median income and below covered by both Work Injury and Disability Pension programs, replacement rates are well in excess of 100 percent. And, it should be noted, these programs cover the regular industrialized workers; the poorest of working age are covered only by the regular disability pension.

The Netherlands

The Netherlands ranks first in the growth rate of number of disability program recipients and is second only to Israel in the growth rate of program expenditures. The growth in both the population of disability recipients and expenditures on them is rather remarkable in a country with a mature and relatively generous social insurance system. The net increase in disability recipients per year was almost 40,000 in the 1968-78 period. In 1968, the population of disability recipients was about 4 percent of the employed population; by 1978, this had tripled. The factors determining this pattern are complex, and include important changes in coverage, benefit levels, eligibility criteria, and economic conditions.

In 1976, coverage under the Dutch disability system increased substantially through passage of the General Disability Act, which extended coverage to the self-employed and those handicapped early in life. Before 1976, only employees in the public and private sector were automatically covered. This single change in coverage added 71,000 persons to the disability rolls. About 14 percent of the increase in number of disability recipients can, therefore, be attributed to this fundamental change in the scope of coverage by the system.

A second important change—in the regulations regarding program eligibility—was made in 1973, coincident with the downturn in economic conditions in the Netherlands. The eligibility criteria for the primary disability pension program had long admitted an individual's vocational and employment circumstances as a consideration of eligibility. The 1973 regulation went one large step further. It stated that any inability on the part of a person with some handicap to find employment was to be attributed to the handicap. Because the downturn in economic conditions and the rising unemployment fell most heavily on older, less educated workers, the new regulation applied most directly to them. And because the chances of finding a job for people in this category were judged to be quite low, most of the accepted applicants were awarded the highest benefit—80 percent of their prior wages. This change in regulation, then, moved the disability pension program in the direction of a long-term unemployment-early retirement program. It, together with the poor employment conditions in the Dutch economy in the mid-1970s,[17] was another determinant of the rapid growth in beneficiaries during this period.

A third determinant concerned incentive effects, which, as we have seen, were at work in other countries as well. Because the demand for disability recipient status is related to the benefits which that status affords, high and increasing levels of disability benefits must also be a factor accounting for the growth in the number of recipients. Under the General Disability Act, the base benefit awarded for full disability is equal to the *net* minimum wage (which is a high percentage of the median wage in the Netherlands). For private sector employees, this is supplemented by up to 80 percent of the previous wage.[18] This percentage is greater than that for unemployment benefits granted after the first six months of unemployment, leading to a desire on the part of the unemployed to substitute disability for unemployment benefits.

In addition to the generally high level of disability benefits, their average benefit level has also been increasing in the Netherlands, owing largely to the system of indexing, which is employed for all social benefits. Rather than being tied to the price level, the benefits are adjusted in line with increases in collectively bargained wage contracts. The rise in level is also due to the increase over time in the average degree of disability for which awards are made.[19] As a result, from 1969 to 1977 the average annual real benefit awarded increased by one-third—an average annual increase of 3.6

percent in real benefits in the Disability Pension program. High and increasing benefit levels would appear to be the third important factor accounting for the rapid growth in Dutch disability rolls.

Two other determinants of the rapid growth in expenditures should be mentioned. During the high-unemployment period of the 1970s, the rate of termination of benefits due to physical recovery sagged, and the average duration of recipiency increased. Also, during this same period in-kind subsidies in the form of mobility and home care allowances increased rapidly—in percentage terms more rapidly than cash benefits.

In many ways, then, the determinants of program growth in the Netherlands parallel those in the other countries—the use of disability pensions to assist long-term unemployed workers, increases in coverage and benefit levels, and a relaxation in eligibility requirements. What is surprising is the enormity of the growth given the extensiveness of the pre-1968 system. About two-thirds of the total growth in expenditures is accounted for by growth in the total number of beneficiaries. This experience suggests the absence of any "natural" limit to the potential population of disability beneficiaries.

In 1981, the first results of a large and important micro-analysis on the determinants of access to the Disability Security program became available.[20] They showed that the access probability for employees is strongly influenced by the physical demands of the job and by age. Moreover, the employer can exert substantial influence on the access probability by means of counseling: jobs and workload can be adapted to functional limitations of workers. The financial strength of the firm also appears to be an important factor, reflecting the influence of the decisions of employers, based on the profitability of the job. The replacement rate has a statistically significant though quantitatively quite moderate influence. In the study, the variable pertaining to career prospects as perceived by the employee showed significant results, which is indicative of the influence of a decisionmaking process on the part of the employees.

Using the data gathered for this analysis, estimates were made of the working capacity of disability beneficiaries.[21] Working capacity was defined as the ability to perform a job that is commensurate with one's physical and mental capacities and in accordance with one's training and former profession. When entering the Disability Security program after one year of sick leave, 29 to 48 percent of those awarded a benefit appeared to be able to perform their former, or at least other kind of, work, commensurate with their training and experience. It was estimated that within a few years after program entry, as many as 51 to 71 percent of those who became entitled to disability benefits would be able to do such work. By contrast, comparatively few people actually do leave the disability rolls to secure work. This leads to the conclusion that indeed a substantial quantity of working capacity is sheltered in the Dutch disability program.

Sweden

Table 5.1 indicates that growth in the number of beneficiaries in the Swedish disability system was relatively low in the 1968-78 period. The growth in expenditures, however—11.7 percent per year—places Sweden well up in the ranking of the countries studied.

A major factor in the growth of Swedish disability programs in the 1968-78 decade was the depressed state of the economy beginning in the mid-1970s. Moreover, during the 1960s and 1970s the Swedish economy underwent substantial structural changes: forestry was mechanized, the textile industry suffered serious losses, and shipbuilding was being phased down. The number of firms going out of business rapidly increased. In addition, Sweden during this same period adopted policies designed to achieve substantial equalization of wage differentials within industries. This change was likely to have increased the wages of older workers (or those with some physical impairment) above their perceived productivity to a larger extent than for prime-aged workers. As a result, low-productivity workers became prime targets for layoff or release by employers confronted with excess capacity and low demand.[22] Note, however, that while this change would contribute to growth in the number of recipients, it does not explain the rapid growth of expenditures relative to recipients.

During the 1960s, trade unions had urged that older workers not be included in Sweden's active labor market policies, one aspect of which involves worker relocation in response to employment opportunities. This pressure on the part of the labor unions was supported by employer groups. In Sweden, as well as some of the other North European countries, job security is a basic principle, especially for older workers. Hence, employers experience difficulty in releasing older workers, even when business conditions are bad. To the extent that access to disability pensions is available, and the level of the pension is attractive, employers can use encouragement and subtle pressure to induce older workers to leave their jobs in favor of disability pension status. Employer and union interests in Sweden therefore coincided in seeking a liberalization of eligibility requirements in disability pension programs and a more generous level of benefits.

This combined pressure received a legislative response in 1970. Disability pension eligibility requirements for older workers were eased, and a partial retirement pension for workers aged 60 to 65 was introduced. In addition, a special bonus pension supplement was created for those with no (or low) national supplementary disability pension, and the special supplement was periodically increased during the 1970s. While this change extended coverage of the pension system to more citizens, its greatest relative effect was on expenditure growth, since the effect of this change was largely to supplement benefits of those who were already recipients.

A further policy change consisted of the elevation of the disability classifications employed in the program. For example, those classified as one-third disabled prior to 1970 were classified as 50 percent disabled after 1970, and benefit payments increased commensurately. Like the first change, this had a major impact on expenditures, since it elevated the benefits already being paid.

Finally, in 1970 and 1974 pension regulations for older workers (those over 63 years; changed to 60 years in 1974) were liberalized. Labor market considerations were to be weighed along with medical considerations. After 1972, workers over 60 no longer had to pass a medical test to receive disability benefits; eligibility was fulfilled if the person had exhausted his or her unemployment benefits and if the person or the employment office could not find available work in the same area and occupation.

Perhaps an even more fundamental determinant of program growth than these changes in the early 1970s was the structure of the National Supplementary Pension System. The rules of this system were set in the 1950s, but the way in which they were structured made it increasingly attractive over time for an older worker to become a disability pensioner. During the 1960s and 1970s, program benefits rose as a proportion of average earned income.

Since the structure of the basic supplementary pension and the legislative and administrative changes of the early 1970s were put into place when unemployment was low and many vacancies existed, the stage was set for the economic downturn of the mid-1970s. With these changes, rapid growth in the number of recipients and in expenditures on disability income support programs was both facilitated and encouraged.

In the last half of the decade, other changes occurred that worked in the same direction, and growth was further stimulated. In 1977, for example, the law was changed so that only the existence of a disabling condition, and not its cause, was the criterion on which benefits were granted. This change allowed chronic alcoholism to be the basis for a pension. Given the magnitude of the problem of alcoholism in Sweden, this was not a trivial change.

The effects of a policy change in a nondisability area should also be noted. In 1976, the age for retirement pensions was reduced from 67 to 65 years. The result was that for the years 1975-77, about 50,000 recipients were transferred from the rolls of disability pension programs to the old age program, artificially reducing the number of recorded disability program recipients.[23]

In the case of Sweden, then, both trade unions and employers came to favor a policy of disguised early retirement for older workers. The political pressures thus generated led to changes in both disability and retirement pension laws in the early 1970s, which encouraged this outcome. Laws were passed which extended coverage and increased benefits. These same pressures encouraged a liberal interpretation of the eligibility requirements which did exist. When adverse economic conditions set in during the 1970s, these program provisions created the sponge which absorbed the excess labor supply. As a result, the labor force participation rates of older workers fell substantially during the 1968-78 period, and expenditures for a growing number of disability recipients rose rapidly.

United Kingdom

As our description in the previous chapter of the disability policy systems made clear, before 1970 no universal pension system for the disabled existed in the United Kingdom. Only the Supplementary Benefits—a basic welfare program—provided general benefits to the disabled, and then only if they had sufficiently low income. In addition, those who had made sufficient contributions to the Social Security system were eligible for medical and unemployment benefits. While there was provision for a long-term medical benefit, it was designed for the sick who were expected to return to the work force, not for the disabled. In 1971, the Invalidity Pension program was introduced as a contributory extension of long-term medical benefits. In 1975, this was supplemented by Non-Contributory Invalidity pension legislation to cover those, including housewives, with insufficient contributions. Moreover, although benefits are not indexed, successive governments have kept them in line with the rate of inflation. No legislation, however, passed during this period was designed to increase these benefit levels for those who were already recipients.

The limited nature of the legislative program for the disabled is reflected in the slow increase in both disability recipients and expenditures. In real terms, expenditures grew at a rate of only .5 percent per year. This was the slowest growth of any of the countries studied. And this pattern is what one would expect, given the small increase in the incentive to draw benefits, as reflected in the replacement rates shown in Chapter 6. The only noticeable increase in replacement rates is that for the Contributory Invalidity program (plus supplements). While these rates did not increase rapidly over the period, their level is rather high. By 1978, the only median-income workers who would not fully replace lost income through transfers were those without contributions (a rather small group). Replacement rates for lower-income workers are substantially above unity.

This story of low growth, however, does not reflect the rather noticeable shift in the United Kingdom toward providing assistance via in-kind rather than cash benefits. If changes in housing allowances for the disabled, mobility allowances, and health care and attendance allowances were reflected in the recipient and expenditure data, growth in the disability system would be recorded at a higher level than that reflected in Table 5.1.

Summary and Conclusions

The decade of 1968-78 witnessed rapid growth in income support programs for the disabled working-age population in the developed world. In the eight countries included in our study, the 1968-78 average annual percentage change in number of recipients ranged from 1.8 percent in the United Kingdom to over 11 percent in the Netherlands, and the median percentage increase among the countries was equal to 6 percent per year. Expenditures grew at an even faster rate, from an average annual percentage rate of 10.5 percent in the the Federal Republic of Germany to 50 percent in Israel, in current prices. The median rate of increase was 21 percent. In real terms, expenditures changed from .5 percent in the United Kingdom to nearly 24 percent in Israel, with a median rate of growth of 11 percent per year.

The more rapid growth of real expenditures as compared with recipients indicates that real benefits per recipient have increased during the 1968-78 decade. Table 5.6 summarizes this growth in real expenditures per recipient. For one-half of the countries (Israel, Sweden, the Netherlands, Italy), this per recipient growth rate over the years 1968-78 is well in excess of rates of real economic growth, suggesting that the average disability recipient experienced increases in *transfer benefits* at a faster rate than the average citizen experienced an increase in income.[24] The only countries which are clear exceptions to this pattern are the United States and the United Kingdom.

The determinants of program growth are complex, and vary from country to country. In nearly all of the countries, however, there has been a tendency toward relaxation of the criteria for program eligibility, typically involving the introduction of vocational and labor market considerations into the decision. Moreover, legislated increases in average payments occurred in most of the countries—as indicated in the net replacement rate

Table 5.6. The Growth in Number of Disability Recipients Relative to Disability Expenditures, 1968-1978

	Rate of Growth of Real Expenditures per Recipient
Federal Republic of Germany	2.7%
France	4.0
Israel	15.3
Italy	4.3
The Netherlands	6.6
Sweden	6.2
United Kingdom	−1.3
United States	−.7

Source: Calculated from Table 5.1.

estimates analyzed in Chapter 6—improving the attraction of the benefit recipiency option. When these changes are combined with the high unemployment and slow economic growth experienced during the 1968-78 decade, a perfect recipe exists for an increased flow of low-skill older workers from the labor market to disability pension status. The supply of such benefits, as well as the demand for them, has increased.

A plausible scenario for the 1968-78 decade, though varying over the countries, might run as follows:

> As economic growth faltered in the mid-1970s, older workers with more or less serious impairments became targets for layoffs and, if out of work, found obtaining a job increasingly difficult. Public officials responded by introducing relaxed eligibility criteria into disability programs, making access to them less difficult. They became a form of extended unemployment benefits. This option was attractive to older workers, as benefit payments became increasingly more adequate, and little stigma was attached to receipt of disability income support. Employers, likewise, found this development attractive, as it made release of long-term older, low-skilled, or impaired workers less difficult. With large cohorts of better educated youths and women entering the labor market, replacement of older workers was not difficult. Disability income support programs became an instrument to encourage early retirement.

The program growth described in this chapter has important implications for the dependency burden placed on the working population, the growth of government expenditures, and labor supply. Some indication of these effects is found in Table 5.1. For example, in all of the countries studied, the ratio of disability program recipients to the employed population increased substantially—in about one-half of the countries it at least doubled. Whereas in 1968 the median ratio of disabled transfer recipients to the employed population was .07, by 1978 the median ratio had increased to .12. In the Federal Republic of Germany, Italy, the Netherlands, and the United States, there were 7.5 or even fewer workers for every disability recipient by 1979. Similarly, disability programs accounted for a rapidly growing share of tax revenues and public expenditures in all of the countries studied. In Italy, about one-fourth of a heavy tax burden went to support these programs; in the Netherlands and the Federal Republic of Germany, about 15 percent of the tax burden is attributable to disability income transfers. Among the eight countries studied, the median percentage of national government expenditures accounted for by disability income transfer programs had risen from 7 percent to 10 percent from 1968 to 1978.

Notes

1. As mentioned in the note to Table 5.1, the figure for the Federal Republic of Germany may be overstated because of some undetermined amount of doublecounting.

2. The figure for the Federal Republic of Germany is biased downward to some extent because of the introduction during the decade of a flexible age limit provision in the retirement pension program, which encouraged some who would have received disability pensions to accept early retirement pensions at age 60 or 62 instead.

3. It should be noted that disability pensions are paid to those over 65 years of age in Italy, making this figure somewhat difficult to interpret.

4. As the discussion in Chapter 4 implied, this rapid growth is accounted for by the institution of the General Disability Law in 1974 and the Yom Kippur War in 1973.

5. See Lando and Hopkins (1977).

6. Clearly, a handicapped worker from whom any type of work is impossible will have no opportunity to earn wages. For such a person, the costs of gaining eligibility are only the time and effort costs. But the worker with a severe impairment, yet able to continue working, is in quite a different situation. This worker must consider whether the expected gain from DI benefits is sufficiently high to warrant refraining from substantial work over the five-month waiting period, in addition to confining work to below the work-potential rule level thereafter.

7. The following paragraphs draw from Wolfe (1982), who presents a detailed review and critique of the major efforts to estimate the work effort impacts of disability policy.

8. Haveman and Wolfe (1982) attempt to reconcile the two polar estimates—their own and those of Parsons—by replicating Parsons' model using more recent data. By correcting Parsons' procedures in defining expected disability benefits, neglecting eligibility considerations, and confounding the wage and benefit variables, they obtain results which closely approximate their own.

9. It should be noted that for the substantial majority of workers in Italy, retirement age is 60 years for men and 55 years for women.

10. The outlier status of Israel, and the basis for its exclusion, would apparently stem from several factors: the relative immaturity of its Social Security system, the rapid growth of population resulting from immigration, the growth in the number of disabled due to military action, and the emphasis given to full employment and economic growth. The first three factors would account for the rapid growth of disability program recipients and expenditures. The last explains the small decrease in labor force participation of older workers.

11. This analysis is concerned only with the general versus specific split of new recipients, and does not impute any of the increase in the total number of recipients to the ruling. From 1969 to 1975, the total number of pension recipients increased from 129,000 to 278,000.

12. It should be noted that a special compensation benefit is associated with the disability allowance, providing assistance to those requiring third-party care.

13. The total number of beneficiaries grew by more than 2.5 percent per year from 1974 to 1977.

14. Expenditures in this category account for over 40 percent of total expenditures in the disability system.

15. Italy ranked second, behind the Netherlands, in growth of number of beneficiaries.

16. In Israel, for example, the comparable percentages were 7.3 and 23.7.

17. From 1971 to 1978, the number of unemployed in the Netherlands rose from 70,000 to 205,000.

18. For public sector employees, the replacement rate is 100 percent for the first 1.5 to 2.5 years, falling to 80 percent thereafter.

19. This happened in the face of a decreasing average age of the disability award, and evidence of an increase in the average state of health of new disability recipients.

20. P. de Jong, H. Bruinsma, L. Aarts, and J. P. Hop, "Determinant-enonderzoek WAO; fase 1, determinanten van WAO-toetreding; een eerste totaalbeeld" (Analysis of the determinants of disability), Social Security Council/Center for Research in Public Economics, Zoetermeer/Leyden, October 1981.

21. Leo Aarts, "Working Capacity of the Disabled," paper presented at the Expert Group Meeting on the Determinants of Access to Disability Benefits, Zoetermeer, The Netherlands, 16-17 November, 1982.

22. This pattern is reflected in the data on the number of older men, relative to those in other age groups, who are disability pensioners. From 1967 to 1976, the percentage of men 60-64 who were disability pensioners rose from 11.2 to 22.6, while the percentage of those 30-39 stayed virtually constant.

23. Offsetting this to some extent was the takeover from private insurance companies of 25,000 pensioners by the Employment Injury program. This takeover occurred in the last half of the 1970s.

24. This rate of growth of benefits per recipient should be interpreted with care. If the composition of programs was constant over the period, the rate would unambiguously indicate increasing generosity in average program benefit. However, with changing program composition, increasing true program benefit generosity could occur even though the rate was negative. This could happen, for example, if a new program was instituted that provided coverage to a previously uncovered group of disabled persons, but granted a relatively low level of per recipient benefits.

Chapter 6

Ameliorative Responses: Has Adequacy Been Guaranteed?

In discussing the growth and labor supply effects of the primary disability income support programs, we emphasized the influence of the benefit structure and of other program characteristics on labor supply and participation rates. A key element in our discussion was the incentives which such programs exert on work effort. Labor supply effects are of concern to policymakers, yet it must be recognized that reductions in labor supply are an inevitable side effect of any program which attempts to provide income assistance to the handicapped population.

In this chapter, we again consider various replacement rate levels. Here, however, we focus on the degree to which disability income support programs provide an adequate replacement for earnings losses and a level of support which minimizes the probability that disabled people will fall into poverty. This issue of "program adequacy" is considered by many to be the central issue in disability support policy. We concentrate on the adequacy of the United States disability system, in particular the adequacy of the three major ameliorative public programs. The degree to which these programs provide income replacement and keep disabled workers from falling into income poverty is measured. To the extent available, evidence from the other countries studied is also provided.

Income Adequacy in the United States Disability System

For the United States, Table 6.1 gives detailed estimates of benefit and replacement rates across programs in relation to preimpairment income levels of recipients. In analyzing the effect of disability benefits on the labor supply choices of individuals, the relevant comparison is between *potential* program benefits and *potential* labor market earnings. However,

Table 6.1. Potential Disability Benefits and Income Replacement Rates for Three Hypothetical Workers in Two-Member Families under Major U.S. Disability Programs, 1968 and 1978[a]

	Benefit Provided and Income Replacement Rate					
	Worker Earning One-Half Average Annual U.S. Income during Lifetime of Employment		Worker Earning Average Annual U.S. Income during Lifetime of Employment		Worker Earning Twice Average Annual U.S. Income during Lifetime of Employment	
Disability Program	Disabled in 1968	Disabled in 1978	Disabled in 1968	Disabled in 1978	Disabled in 1968	Disabled in 1978
Disability Insurance[b]						
Annual benefit rate	$1,102	$2,904	$1,606	$4,470	$ 1,876	$ 5,937
Gross income replacement	43%	59%	31%	45%	18%	30%
Net income replacement	45%	59%	35%	49%	21%	35%
Disability Welfare[c]						
California						
Annual benefit rate	$1,866	$3,864	$1,866	$3,864	$ 1,866	$ 3,864
Gross income replacement	72%	78%	36%	39%	18%	20%
Net income replacement	77%	78%	41%	42%	21%	23%
Texas						
Annual benefit rate	$1,164	$2,273	$1,164	$2,273	$ 1,164	$ 2,273
Gross income replacement	45%	46%	23%	23%	11%	11%
Net income replacement	48%	46%	25%	25%	13%	13%
Workers' Compensation[d]						
District of Columbia						
Annual benefit rate	$1,617	$4,586	$3,235	$6,115	$ 3,640	$12,229
Gross income replacement	63%	93%	63%	62%	35%	62%
Net income replacement	67%	93%	70%	67%	41%	72%
Oklahoma						
Annual benefit rate	$1,617	$3,051	$2,080	$3,900	$ 2,080	$ 3,900
Gross income replacement	63%	62%	40%	39%	20%	20%
Net income replacement	67%	62%	45%	43%	24%	23%
Worker's expected annual income, 1968						
Before tax	$2,574		$5,147		$10,294	
After tax	$2,439		$4,589		$ 8,789	

Worker's expected annual income, 1978			
Before tax	$4,943	$9,887	$19,774
After tax	$4,943	$9,147	$16,925

Sources: Data from the Social Security Administration and, for Workers' Compensation, from the U.S. Chamber of Commerce.

[a]At time of disability, each worker is assumed to be age 45, male, head of a two-person family with a non-working wife, totally disabled as of January 1968 (or January 1978), receiving no outside income in any form, and taking the standard deduction on federal income taxes. All replacement rates assume the worker is covered *only* under the program in consideration. No adjustment for state tax liability is included. U.S. average annual income used here is for workers with taxable earnings under OASDHI, i.e., covered employment, plus contributing self-employed persons. Farm and nonfarm workers are included.

[b]In addition to assumptions in footnote a, each worker receiving benefits under the Social Security Disability Insurance program (DI) is assumed to have been working since age 21 in a job covered by Social Security payroll deductions and to meet all necessary qualifications for DI benefits. These income replacement calculations are substantially increased with the presence of dependents in the household.

[c]Until 1972 the program was Aid to the Permanently and Totally Disabled (APTD), administered entirely at the state level (through district or local offices) with matching federal funds. Since 1974, Supplemental Security Income (SSI) has been administered at the federal level through the Social Security Administration; states have the option of supplementing the federal payment. Benefits varied widely across states; Texas and California are representative of the range of potential benefits provided.

Each worker is assumed to be *not* receiving DI benefits because of not having worked 20 of the past 40 months as of January 1968 (or January 1978), to be living in his own home with cooking facilities, to have wealth (as defined by SSA) below $2,250, and to meet all other necessary qualifications. It should be noted that for those living in the home of others the benefit would be significantly less. APTD payments were made according to developed state cost standards and were divided by basic needs (rent and other than rent) and a variety of recurrent needs varying by state such as laundry, home nursing care, telephone, transportation, drugs and hearing aid upkeep. The benefit figure used in the calculation is for basic needs only using April 1968 cost standards. The basic federal SSI disability payment was $189.40 for an individual with an ineligible spouse (effective mid-year 1978); the California supplemental payment was $132.60 for an individual. The mid-year payment is assumed to be applicable throughout the year. The California SSI payment does *not* include cashed-out food stamps. Texas provided no supplement to the federal SSI payment in 1978.

[d]Workers' Compensation benefits vary dramatically across states. The District of Columbia and Oklahoma are representative of the range of potential benefits provided.

The skewness of the distribution of potential benefits across states should be noted. In 1978, 40 states would have provided a gross replacement rate equivalent to Oklahoma's (63%) for the worker earning one-half average U.S. income, and all but eight states would have replaced income at the same rate as D.C. (63%) for the worker earning average U.S. income. For the worker earning twice annual U.S. income, 40 states would have replaced between 30-61% of income. In 1968, 38 states would have provided an income replacement rate of between 55-63% for the worker earning one half average U.S. income and 10 states would have replaced more than 63%. For the worker earning average U.S. income, 33 states would have replaced between 40 and 62% of income with 9 states greater than 62%. All but four states would have replacement rates below 39% for the worker earning twice average U.S. income.

in order to assess program adequacy, it is the level of potential program benefits relative to the *preimpairment* wage which is relevant. The issue is the degree to which government programs cushion the income loss associated with the onset of unexpected impairments. Thus, the measure used in this chapter is the proportion of the after-tax, preimpairment wage which is replaced by program benefits. This measure understates the relative attractiveness of disability benefits for this same group of workers if their potential postimpairment level wage income is less than their preimpairment level. Estimates are shown for three prototypical workers, each in a family of two persons, who experience impairments indicating total permanent disability. They differ only in their wage earnings histories. The first worker is assumed to earn one-half the average annual wage of the median worker over his or her lifetime, the second exactly the median, and the third earns twice the median. Wage replacement rates are shown for both in 1968 and 1978. We further assume that each worker is eligible for benefits in only one of the three programs—DI, SSI, and Workers' Compensation—at a time.

The table indicates a major increase in replacement rates over the past decade in all of the programs. For the largest program, the Disability Insurance program, the net replacement rate for the average income worker rose from 35 percent to 49 percent from 1968 to 1978. For the average income worker, replacement rates in the Workers' Compensation and SSI programs changed relatively little. The variance in benefit levels among the states is still substantial in both of these programs, however. For example, for the average income worker in 1978, the replacement rates in the SSI program vary from about 25 percent in the low benefit states to about 42 percent in the highest benefit states. The table also indicates that all of the programs provide a higher replacement rate for the low wage worker than for the worker with twice the average income. As would be expected, the SSI program, as a welfare program, has a higher replacement rate for low relative to high wage workers than the other programs.

Handicapped workers are often eligible for benefits for more than one of the three programs. In addition, there are still other programs providing income support to handicapped workers, primarily the veterans' programs and Medicare. Where benefits from more than one program are cumulated, the replacement rates for some workers may approach or exceed unity.

Moreover, programs such as DI and SSI provide additional benefits for dependents of disabled recipients. Replacement rates for DI increase significantly with the number of dependents. For the other programs, the replacement rate remains relatively constant. The effect of dependents' benefits on replacement rates is seen by comparing the estimates in Table 6.1 (two-member families) with those in Table 6.2 (four-member families).

The primary benchmark for measuring the effectiveness of public policy in the United States is the degree to which social programs have removed

Table 6.2. Potential Disability Benefits and Income Replacement Rates for Three Hypothetical Workers in Four-Member Families under Major U.S. Disability Programs, 1968 and 1978[a]

	Benefit Provided and Income Replacement Rate					
	Worker Earning One-Half Average Annual U.S. Income during Lifetime of Employment		Worker Earning Average Annual U.S. Income during Lifetime of Employment		Worker Earning Twice Average Annual U.S. Income during Lifetime of Employment	
Disability Program	Disabled in 1968	Disabled in 1978	Disabled in 1968	Disabled in 1978	Disabled in 1968	Disabled in 1978
Disability Insurance						
Annual benefit rate[b]	$1,558	$4,033	$3,117	$7,764	$ 3,960	$ 9,095
Gross income replacement	61%	82%	61%	79%	38%	45%
Net income replacement	64%	82%	68%	85%	45%	54%
Disability Welfare						
California						
Annual benefit rate	$1,866	$3,864	$1,866	$3,864	$ 1,866	$ 3,864
Gross income replacement	72%	78%	36%	39%	18%	20%
Net income replacement	77%	78%	41%	42%	21%	23%
Texas						
Annual benefit rate	$1,164	$2,273	$1,164	$2,273	$ 1,164	$ 2,273
Gross income replacement	45%	46%	23%	23%	11%	11%
Net income replacement	48%	46%	25%	25%	13%	13%
Workers' Compensation						
District of Columbia						
Annual benefit rate	$1,617	$4,586	$3,235	$6,115	$ 3,640	$12,229
Gross income replacement	63%	93%	63%	62%	35%	62%
Net income replacement	67%	93%	70%	67%	41%	72%

Table 6.2. (cont.)

Disability Program	Benefit Provided and Income Replacement Rate: Worker Earning One-Half Average Annual U.S. Income during Lifetime of Employment		Worker Earning Average Annual U.S. Income during Lifetime of Employment		Worker Earning Twice Average Annual U.S. Income during Lifetime of Employment	
	Disabled in 1968	Disabled in 1978	Disabled in 1968	Disabled in 1978	Disabled in 1968	Disabled in 1978
Oklahoma						
Annual benefit rate	$1,617	$3,051	$2,080	$3,900	$ 2,080	$ 3,900
Gross income replacement	63%	62%	40%	39%	20%	20%
Net income replacement	67%	62%	45%	43%	24%	23%
Worker's expected annual income, 1968						
Before tax	$2,574		$5,147		$10,294	
After tax	$2,574		$4,814		$ 9,036	
Worker's expected annual income, 1978						
Before tax		$4,943		$9,887		$19,774
After tax		$4,943		$9,462		$17,300

Sources: See Table 6.1.

[a]See notes to Table 6.1 for assumptions concerning workers and benefit calculations under the various disability programs. This table assumes the worker is head of a four-member family with three eligible dependents.

[b]Maximum family benefit rate.

people from poverty. The poverty line, adjusted for family size and farm or nonfarm residence, is defined as the minimum level of income necessary to provide an adequate living.

While the poverty line measure is an important benchmark for judging program adequacy, it must be cautiously interpreted when it is applied to those with special needs, such as the disabled. Underlying the measured poverty line for a family of any given size, structure, and location is some assumed average level of "needs." As a result, the poverty line for those with special problems—for example, mobility, the need for special appliances, or the need for special living arrangements—will be too low. The evaluation of any support program based on such standard poverty lines will yield an exaggerated estimate of the extent to which the real needs of beneficiaries with special problems are actually being met. With this note of caution in mind, the extent to which disability income support programs remove beneficiaries from income poverty can be used as a measure of "adequacy."

Table 6.3 provides evidence on the extent to which existing disability programs keep beneficiaries from falling into income poverty in the United States. The situations of three prototypical workers, each in a family of two persons (say, husband and wife) and who experience impairments indicating total permanent disability, are analyzed. Once again the workers are assumed to differ only in their wage earning histories; the first worker earns one-half the average annual wage of the median worker over his or her lifetime, the second earns exactly the median, and the third earns twice the median. The degree to which potential benefits from each program match a poverty income level is found for both 1968 and 1978. We further assume that each worker is eligible for benefits in only one of these programs at a time.

A major finding of Table 6.3 is that, while it was still possible in 1978 for workers to fall into poverty because of total disability, it was far less likely than in 1968. The major variation appears to be across the states rather than across programs. For example, in a state such as Texas, which provides no state supplement to the SSI program, only 52 percent of poverty-line income is guaranteed. In California, on the other hand, the guarantee is 89 percent. With respect to DI, the median worker is guaranteed benefits above the poverty line in 1978. It is those who have near poverty-level earnings, even when healthy, that are most likely to fall below the poverty line if they become totally disabled. But it is exactly this type of worker who is most likely to be eligible for income support from SSI. In addition, there are still other programs not presented here which are likely sources of income support to such a worker, primarily Food Stamps and Medicare. When benefits from these programs are cumulated, it is likely that few workers receiving disability benefits—DI, SSI, or Workers Compensation—fall into poverty.

Table 6.3. Potential Disability Benefits Relative to the Poverty Level for Three Hypothetical Workers in Two-Member Families under Major U.S. Disability Programs, 1968 and 1978[a]

Expected Income and Poverty Level[b]	Benefit Provided and Benefit as a Percentage of Poverty Level					
	Worker Earning One-Half Average Annual U.S. Income during Lifetime of Employment		Worker Earning Average Annual U.S. Income during Lifetime of Employment		Worker Earning Twice Average Annual U.S. Income during Lifetime of Employment	
	Disabled in 1968	Disabled in 1978	Disabled in 1968	Disabled in 1978	Disabled in 1968	Disabled in 1978
Worker's expected annual gross income in year of disability	$2,574	$4,943	$5,147	$9,887	$10,294	$19,774
Poverty level in year of disability	2,242	4,360	2,242	4,360	2,242	4,360
Disability Insurance						
Annual benefit rate	$1,102	$2,904	$1,606	$4,470	$ 1,876	$ 5,937
Percent of poverty level	49%	67%	72%	103%	84%	136%
Disability Welfare						
California						
Annual benefit rate	$1,866	$3,864	$1,866	$3,864	$ 1,866	$ 3,864
Percent of poverty level	83%	89%	83%	89%	83%	89%
Texas						
Annual benefit rate	$1,164	$2,273	$1,164	$2,273	$ 1,164	$ 2,273
Percent of poverty level	52%	52%	52%	52%	52%	52%
Workers' Compensation						
District of Columbia						
Annual benefit rate	$1,617	$4,586	$3,235	$6,115	$ 3,640	$12,229
Percent of poverty level	72%	105%	144%	140%	162%	280%
Oklahoma						
Annual benefit rate	$1,617	$3,051	$2,080	$3,900	$ 2,080	$ 3,900
Percent of poverty level	72%	70%	93%	89%	93%	89%

[a]See notes to Table 6.1. for assumptions concerning workers and benefit calculations under the various disability programs.

[b]The poverty level is that reported by the U.S. Bureau of Census for a two-member family. The figures used here are weighted averages of farm and nonfarm workers' poverty-level incomes.

Table 6.4 retains our previous assumptions about work histories but looks at a family of four (say, husband, wife, and two children). The results do not change substantially for the DI program since additional benefits are provided to a disabled worker with dependents. But for both SSI and Workers' Compensation, benefits do not typically increase because of family size. However, Aid to Families with Dependent Children (AFDC) does provide an additional source of income for some low income families with children. Nevertheless, poverty status is much more likely for larger families with a disabled head receiving either SSI or Workers' Compensation benefits than for smaller families.

The results of Tables 6.3 and 6.4 show that for the great majority of workers who become sufficiently disabled to be eligible for DI, SSI, or Workers' Compensation, benefits are large enough for them to remain above the poverty line. However, for those with impairments or poor health not sufficient for eligibility for these programs, no strong "safety net" exists. Much of the current debate with respect to the "welfare" role which the disability income support system should play centers around the provision of aid to this sizable portion of the impaired population. And, it should be noted, removal from income poverty as it is defined in the United States is not synonymous with program generosity or even "adequacy." Nor does it imply a major redistribution of income. The poverty line in the United States lies at about 40 percent of median income.

Income Adequacy of Disability Programs in Other Countries

As suggested earlier, no final judgment on the adequacy of public program benefits can be made without an estimate of the special needs of the group of individuals on which benefits are targeted. Ideally, then, one would like to have estimates of both the income level required to meet the basic needs of the target group and the income attained by the target group from program benefits, earnings, and other sources. In none of the countries studied is evidence available on either the basic income needs of the disabled or the total income levels achieved by the disabled. What is available are bits and pieces of data, and some general impressions. In the following sections, we provide a rough evaluation of program adequacy based on this evidence. In evaluating adequacy, a relative norm is used—program benefits are assessed in relationship to median or average income in the particular country, rather than to any absolute standard. In addition, Table 6.5 displays the pattern of replacement rates for high, median and low-wage workers in each of the countries studied. It summarizes a number of the features which are discussed in the following paragraphs. The data for the United States are taken from Table 6.1, and are included for purposes of comparison.

Table 6.4. Potential Disability Benefits Relative to the Poverty Level for Three Hypothetical Workers in Four-Member Families under Major U.S. Disability Programs, 1968 and 1978[a]

	Benefit Provided and Benefit as a Percentage of Poverty Level					
	Worker Earning One-Half Average Annual U.S. Income during Lifetime of Employment		Worker Earning Average Annual U.S. Income during Lifetime of Employment		Worker Earning Twice Average Annual U.S. Income during Lifetime of Employment	
Expected Income and Poverty Level[b]	Disabled in 1968	Disabled in 1978	Disabled in 1968	Disabled in 1978	Disabled in 1968	Disabled in 1978
Worker's expected annual gross income in year of disability	$2,574	$4,943	$5,147	$9,887	$10,294	$19,774
Poverty level in year of disability	3,531	6,630	3,531	6,630	3,531	6,630
Disability Insurance						
Annual benefit rate[c]	$1,558	$4,033	$3,117	$7,764	$ 3,960	$ 9,095
Percent of poverty level	44%	61%	88%	117%	112%	137%
Disability Welfare						
California						
Annual benefit rate	$1,866	$3,864	$1,866	$3,864	$ 1,866	$ 3,864
Percent of poverty level	53%	58%	53%	58%	53%	58%
Texas						
Annual benefit rate	$1,164	$2,273	$1,164	$2,273	$ 1,164	$ 2,273
Percent of poverty level	33%	34%	33%	34%	33%	34%
Workers' Compensation						
District of Columbia						
Annual benefit rate	$1,617	$4,586	$3,235	$6,115	$ 3,640	$12,229
Percent of poverty level	46%	69%	92%	92%	103%	184%
Oklahoma						
Annual benefit rate	$1,617	$3,051	$2,080	$3,900	$ 2,080	$ 3,900
Percent of poverty level	46%	46%	59%	59%	59%	59%

[a]The hypothetical workers have the same characteristics as those in Table 6.3 except that they are household heads of a four-member family. A spouse and two dependent children make the family eligible for additional benefits subject to a family maximum. See notes to Table 6.1. for assumptions concerning worker and benefit calculations under the various disability programs.

[b]The poverty level is that reported by the U.S. Bureau of Census for a four-member family. The figures used here are weighted averages of farm and nonfarm workers' poverty-level incomes.

[c]Maximum family benefit rate.

Federal Republic of Germany

While the disability income support system in the Federal Republic is relatively comprehensive and well integrated, it is not among the more generous of the systems studied. As the replacement rate data in Table 6.5 indicate, income lost through disablement is replaced at more than 80 percent only in the Accident Insurance program. For beneficiaries in other disability income support programs, expected income attainment in 1978 would appear to be in the range of 40 to 70 percent of median income. Perhaps most surprising is the relative lack of progressivity in the German system. For example, the replacement rates of the Public Pension Insurance system are lower for individuals with one-half the median income than for those at the median level—or at two times the median, for that matter.

France

In France, the measure closest to the poverty line of the United States is the government-stipulated minimum wage. Some sense of adequacy can be obtained by comparing average annual benefits in various programs to the income level which would be achieved by a full-time, full-year worker employed at this minimum wage. On average, the standard disability pension, supplemented by the compensatory allowance, provided about 50 percent of the minimum-wage-based annual income in 1977, the latest year for which full data were made available. The guarantee of resources for those employed in sheltered workshops provided a somewhat higher level of support—about three-fourths of the minimum annual income. It should be noted that these data reflect average benefits, with a substantial variance around this level; some recipients therefore receive income support less adequate than that reported. On the other hand, the minimum wage was raised substantially in 1981-82, reducing inadequacies.

As Table 6.5 indicates, from 1968 to 1978 the relative position of those receiving regular disability pensions did not alter; net replacement rates stayed in the 30-40 percent range, with a slight tilt in favor of the poor. The benefit levels for workers with occupationally related disability or illness increased substantially during this period, especially for those with less than median income. The 1978 replacement rates at all predisability income levels were at least 100 percent, and those with low predisability incomes received over 180 percent of that predisability income through Workers' Compensation.

For several reasons, these estimates should be considered as lower bounds on the average level of income obtained by the disabled population. First, some recipients are able to add benefits from a second program to those of a primary program, sometimes with no offset to benefits in the

Table 6.5. Net Replacement Rates in Income Support Programs for Disabled Workers, by Country and Income Level, 1968 and 1978

	1968			1978		
	One-half Median Income	Median Income	Twice Median Income	One-half Median Income	Median Income	Twice Median Income
Federal Republic of Germany						
Public Assistance	70%	39%	21%	68%	38%	21%
Public Pension Insurance	58	65	60	60	67	65
Accident Insurance	77	86	91	82	91	90
France						
Disability Pension	39	35	28	24	33	36
Workers' Compensation	133	100	80	182	100	97
Guaranteed Support	—	—	—	63	33	18
Israel[a]						
Work Injury	76	84	58	75	86	86
General Disability						
Alone	—	—	—	80	46	26
With work-related pensions[b]	71	78	91	123	110	110
				(185)	(145)	(130)
Welfare	44	24	14	57	32	19
Defense	181	100	58	195	112	65
Italy						
Work Injury	122	87	43	121	88	44
Work Injury with Disability Pension	159	106	53	167	111	56
Disability Pension	32	16	13	43	21	20
The Netherlands[c]						
Disability Security Act	92	80	55	92	80	76
				(100)	(92)	(85)
General Disability Act	NA	NA	NA	100	77	41
General Public Disability Pension	NA	NA	NA	100	85	85

Sweden[d]						
Disability Pension and Supplement	105	73	55	117	88	66
Employment Injury Insurance	110	83	49	93	95	78
Social Assistance	114	64	38	109	69	50
United Kingdom						
Industrial Disability and Supplement	176	102	56	178	107	60
Contributory Invalidity Pension and Supplement	118	69	38	160	96	54
Non-Contributory Invalidity Pension and Supplement	118	69	38	119	72	40
United States						
Disability Insurance	45	35	21	59	49	35
Disability Welfare						
High state	77	41	21	78	42	23
Low state	48	25	13	46	25	13
Workers' Compensation						
High state	67	70	41	93	67	72
Low state	67	45	24	62	43	23

[a]The mean income level, rather than the median, is used as the basis for comparison.

[b]Prior to 1974, only the work-related pension program existed. Numbers in parentheses include special benefits.

[c]The data for one-half the median are for the "minimum income" level as defined in the Netherlands. The entries are gross replacement rates; net rates where available are in parentheses.

[d]Median income for married men aged 45-49 in 1967 and 1977 are used as the base for the calculation. If the median income of all males was used, the replacement rates for the Social Assistance Program would be higher. Those for the Disability Pension and Employment Injury Programs are likely to be higher, but in some benefit calculations could be reduced. Most recipients of the Disability Pension also receive Supplemental Benefits from negotiated pension plans, agreements between the trade unions and employers' organizations, the national government or local governments.

primary program, and sometimes with only a partial offset. Moreover, a wide range of in-kind benefits accompany and supplement these cash transfers. Disabled recipients are also able to supplement their incomes through work, again with little offset to benefits in some of the programs. Even after making some implicit allowance for these considerations, the level of adequacy of disability income support programs in France would appear to be among the lowest of the countries studied. And it should be noted that these estimates implicitly assume that the relationship of the minimum wage to the basic needs of the disabled is the same as for the remainder of the population. As noted above, this assumption leads to an overstatement of the adequacy of program benefits.

Israel

The replacement rates shown in Table 6.5 illustrate the rapid growth of the disability income support system in Israel during the decade of the 1970s. The replacement rate increases are considerable—with the exception of the Work Injury program, they rose from 12 to 40 percent, and increases for the low-income population range from 3 to 73 percent. The Welfare, General Disability, and Defense program benefits favor the poor—for both the low-income and the average-income groups, there are some replacement rates in excess of 100 percent.

The replacement rates in Table 6.5 describe mainly cash transfers, but the 1968-78 decade in Israel was one of more rapid relative growth in the special benefits (e.g., mobility, housing, and attendance) programs than in the cash transfer programs. When these benefits are added to cash benefits, replacement rates are considerably increased. The numbers in parentheses for the General Disability program with work-related pensions show these replacement rates for 1978—all are in excess of 130 percent. Somewhat lower levels of adequacy are provided for those who are not insured, and who must rely on the welfare-based disability scheme. With special benefits included, however, it appears that three-fourths of median income is attained by most of this group of disabled. Finally, the very special position of those covered by military-related programs should be emphasized. Even with no consideration of special benefits, attainment of median income status is the norm for this group. Among the countries studied, Israel would appear to rank in the top two or three in terms of benefit adequacy.

Italy

Evaluation of adequacy in the Italian system must be separated into two parts. First, the disabled of median income with Work Injury program coverage are able to achieve about 85 to 90 percent of median income without cumulating the benefit with the disability pension. When the benefits are cumulated, total benefit payments can rise to well over the median income level, even for those with low earnings histories. This pattern of recipiency, it should be noted, covers the regular industrialized workers, the higher-paid segment of the Italian working class. For the second group—low-paid workers eligible only for the Disability Pension—the situation is quite different. For this group with median incomes prior to disablement, less than one-fourth of median income is provided by benefits. Even for this group, the evaluation needs to be tempered, however. First, the disability pensioner can earn up to one-third of his or her previous earnings with no loss of pension, and many of these benefit recipients do work. Moreover, given the generally assumed importance of the unreported economy in Italy, it is likely that many, if not most, disability pension recipients earn well over the one-third limit permitted by the program. Because of tax benefits accruing from unreported earnings to both employers and employees, this practice is widely viewed as providing a major supplement to the relatively low disability pension benefit. Finally, a number of disability pension recipients are also entitled to war-related benefits, which can be added to the disability pension with no offset.

Because of the operation of the underground economy and the possible cumulation of benefits, the adequacy of disability benefits in Italy is difficult to evaluate. Given the relatively high proportion of total recipients in the work-related injury program, and the opportunities for unreported work, it is likely that the adequacy of the Italian system is, relative to the median income in that country, in the upper half of the countries studied. However, as we noted in Chapter 4, the sickness benefit program and the welfare programs provide relatively meager benefits.

The Netherlands

With little question, the provision of income support to disabled workers in the Netherlands is among the most adequate—indeed, generous—among the countries studied. During the 1960s, the Netherlands adopted a minimum income figure (which has since the early 1970s been automatically adjusted to accord with wage changes and which has been additionally increased several times) designed to represent a reasonable standard of living. All disabled individuals in the Netherlands are guaranteed this level of basic support.

As Table 6.5 indicates, those receiving the General Public Disability Pension in 1978 had a guaranteed income support of 85 percent of median income. The net replacement rates are even somewhat higher, since minimum benefits are equal to the national minimum wage after taxes. These levels of support are only the base guarantee; a wide range of supplemental benefits (e.g., rent supplements) are also available to basic program recipients. Moreover, up to 12.5 percent of previous earnings can be received from work with no benefit reductions, and income from sources other than earnings (e.g., spouse earnings or capital income) do not lead to reductions in disability benefits. Even when the special needs of the disabled are taken into consideration, the income support system in the Netherlands assures them a position well up in the distribution of economic well-being.

Sweden

In spite of the emphasis on work in the Swedish disability system, it, like the Netherlands, ranks high among the countries studied in terms of adequacy. A 1978 general survey of the income status of the disabled provided a picture of the adequacy of income support programs. It indicated that the severely disabled had an average household income amounting to about 80 percent of average income of the nondisabled, because the average pension income is less than average nonpension income, and a far higher percentage of the disabled are pensioned. When adjustment for the smaller average size of disabled households is taken into account, however, the per person income level of the two household types is comparable.

The adequacy of the Swedish system can also be sketched through a brief review of the major disability transfer programs. The largest income support program is that of disability pensions. As Table 6.5 shows, those receiving the supplementary as well as the basic national pension were afforded rather generous income levels in 1978—almost 90 percent of median income. Those without supplementary pensions, but receiving the bonus pension supplements (not on table), have income levels well above the poverty line. This group of pensioners have lower incomes than those receiving the supplementary pensions, however. Municipal housing supplements are also available to all disability pensioners, though their amounts vary widely across municipalities. The residual group—those not eligible for the basic national pension with supplementary or bonus pensions—fare rather poorly. If not institutionalized, they fall into the poverty class in Sweden. Moreover, some of them are not eligible for subsidized or sheltered employment; their economic status depends on how they fare in the open labor market, aided by any sickness benefits for which they qualify. The failure of coverage for this group (of unknown but probably small size) marks a gap in the system. However, data from the national survey of 1978 suggest that the average income of this group is not substantially below that of the nondisabled population. On balance, the disability income support system would appear to be fairly adequate for those who qualify for full pensioning. Among recipients of the basic national pension, however, the level of support varies substantially, depending on eligibility for pension supplements. And some disabled workers are not eligible for any pension support.

Evaluation of the adequacy of the system must also take into account the large sheltered and subsidized private sector employment programs in Sweden. For those so employed, wages are comparable to those in equivalent regular labor market employment, though some special supplements are not available. Variability also results from the fact that some of those in sheltered employment are paid on a lower wage scale than in the regular workshops.

Overall, Sweden appears to rank above average in program adequacy among the countries in this study. Those fully covered do rather well, but the variability in support provided and gaps in coverage detract from the high level of average support given the fully covered.

United Kingdom

As Table 6.5 indicates, the replacement rates for individuals covered by the disability system of the United Kingdom are substantial, especially for those with low predisability incomes. In 1978, no individual in the system was likely to fall below 70 percent of median income for his or her family size. These high replacement rates are in part due to the ability to cumulate benefits from more than one program in the system. Rarely does an individual receive benefits from only one program.

The problems concerning adequacy in this system stem from the diverse criteria for program eligibility and the variance in the levels of income support. This diversity leaves gaps in coverage, creates inequities among equally disabled individuals, and induces rather wide variance in benefit levels. The data available also indicate that impaired workers who remain in the work force—largely because of inadequate program coverage—do not fare well. A higher proportion are unskilled workers, two-thirds find their choice of job limited, nearly one-half state that their hours of work are constrained, and they experience an unemployment rate nearly triple that of nonimpaired workers.

While the average benefit is quite adequate, the variance around that mean appears to leave many of the disabled inadequately protected. The problem, then, is largely one of horizontal equity. The large variance in income support provided equally disabled individuals detracts from the system's adequacy. Largely for this reason, program adequacy in the United Kingdom would not place it in the upper half of the eight countries.

Summary

The top tier of countries, judged in terms of adequacy, would include the Netherlands, Israel, Sweden, and perhaps Italy. The United Kingdom ranks below this set of countries because, as we have just seen, high average benefit levels are offset by substantial variance around the average. This problem of horizontal equity and variance in income support also lessens the adequacy of the Swedish system. France, the United States, and the Federal Republic of Germany fall in the lower half in terms of benefit levels.

Our assessment, it should be noted, is based largely on the evidence assembled for this cross-national study, and a good deal of judgment is required in interpreting that evidence. The judgments of other observers may vary from our own. It should also be emphasized that our assessment of adequacy in each country is based on the relationship of the average benefit level (and variance around that average) at various income levels, and that the assessment depends on each country's median income rather than an absolute standard of program adequacy.

Chapter 7

Corrective Responses: Approaches and Outcomes

The emphasis in the last three chapters centered on public programs that are ameliorative in nature, providing income support to disabled workers. We described the nature of these programs in the United States and the seven other countries studied, and analyzed the causes and consequences—primarily regarding labor supply and the adequacy of income support—of their structure and growth. In this chapter, our focus changes. Here, we emphasize policies designed to fulfill the corrective goal of disability policy. In this discussion, both programs that seek to increase the capacity of workers to earn income (e.g., vocational rehabilitation programs) and those designed to modify the structure of labor markets for disabled workers (e.g., employment subsidy, quota, or sheltered work programs) will be included.

We first discuss some of the major policy issues which underlie the alternative strategies which constitute corrective policy. The major programs in the United States which seek to achieve this corrective goal and their growth over the last two decades are described in the next section. The following section provides a brief survey of these approaches in the other countries studied. Finally, we develop a framework for measuring the effectiveness of these programs, review past studies using this methodology, and reach an overall assessment of the success of these programs.

The Corrective Goal: Policy Issues

Programs designed to increase the earning capacity and work effort of the disabled have a different underlying philosophy from that which governs ameliorative programs. Programs with a corrective goal are best viewed as investments designed to reduce the aggregate costs of disability, rather than to distribute its burden more evenly across society, and hence are subject to the benefit-cost type of appraisal. For this strategy, the presumption is either that the person with an impairment is not in that state permanently and that the condition can be improved by appropriate treatment, or that the workplace and the labor market—in particular, labor demands—can be altered so as to provide work opportunities for all but those with the most serious handicaps. In either case, work is the ultimate goal and income receipt tied to work effort is viewed as preferable to cash transfers. Underlying this view is the belief that the self-esteem of handicapped workers depends on their being active and participating members of a productive society. Income support alone will not provide this.

As with the income support strategy, this view leads to a set of important policy questions: Should the primary focus be on the disabled individual, or on the labor market in which he or she is expected to operate? Should the disabled person's condition be treated so as to correct it, or should the individual be trained for a new set of tasks consistent with the condition? If the latter, should the government provide the requisite employment directly, or should it either subsidize private sector employers to provide work opportunities or mandate such employment via quotas? Or should a system of sheltered workshops providing adapted working conditions be established and supported?

Several concrete programs rest on this work-oriented philosophy. Some or all of them are present in each of the countries which we have studied. Typically, they stand independent of the income support, social-security-based programs, and they are often administered or supported by agencies quite different from those administering the income support programs. While integration of the two strategies would seem essential, such integration is rare. Although several variants of these programs exist, the most prominent forms are vocational rehabilitation and training, operation and/or subsidization of sheltered workshops, subsidies for employment and training, and implicit or explicit employment quotas.

The first, and most common, of these corrective approaches is the vocational rehabilitation and training strategy. In most countries studied, central government sponsorship or subsidization of a rehabilitation program for workers, especially those injured on the job, is a central component of disability policy. In most cases, skill training along with medical treatment is emphasized. In some programs, placement services are provided with rehabilitation and training. Referral into the program is often from workers' compensation or social security pension programs. Because provision of rehabilitation and training is a costly strategy, offering such services to all disabled workers would not be efficient. Determination of those workers for whom provision of such services would lead to a resumption of work or increased earnings is one of the important issues which must be addressed in designing rehabilitation programs.

A second work-oriented strategy is the provision of sheltered work. In most of the countries studied, national governments either provide financial support to workshops offering work to disabled workers in a protected (or adapted) environment or directly sponsor and administer such enterprises. In some cases, these activities are viewed as transitional, and their success is judged by the placement of workshop employees in regular jobs. In other cases, the workshops are viewed as providing permanent jobs for those hired. A large number of issues must be addressed in the design of such programs: the choice of products to be produced or services provided, selection of participants from among the pool of disabled workers and determination of the wages to be paid them, the extent of the public subsidy to be provided, and the design of subsidy arrangements to encourage sensitivity to costs on the part of workshop managers.

A third corrective strategy involves public provision of subsidies to private employers who agree to provide employment, training, and often job adaptation for disabled workers, or direct public employment of these workers. While not widely used heretofore, this strategy is increasingly being studied and experimented with—for all disadvantaged workers, not just the disabled. The primary issues confronted in designing such programs include the setting of a subsidy rate sufficient to induce hiring and training (but not so high as to provide a windfall to firms), ensuring that the workers subsidized would not have been hired in the absence of the program, and establishing and enforcing eligibility criteria to ensure that the subsidy is not awarded for the hiring of nondisabled or marginally disabled workers.

A fourth strategy is regulatory in nature. In the United States it falls under the generic term "equal access." It combines "affirmative action" with mandated changes in the work environment in an attempt to increase jobs for handicapped workers. Several of the countries studied, including the Federal Republic of Germany, Italy, the Netherlands, and the United Kingdom, have legislation which is even more explicit with regard to reserving jobs for the handicapped. Under the generic term "right to work," hiring quotas in these countries are mandated for both public and private employers. As will be seen, the level of the quota varies substantially among countries, although all of the countries share the characteristic of poor enforcement of the quotas.

The following sections describe the use of these work-oriented programs to achieve corrective goals in the countries studied and present evidence on their effectiveness in creating employment and generating earnings on the part of disabled workers.

Work-Oriented Programs in the United States

Expenditures on the direct provision of services to disabled workers form a small fraction of total disability expenditures in the United States—in the

1970s less than 5 percent of total federal disability expenditures were devoted to the provision of rehabilitation and other services.[1] But, as discussed in Chapter 4, this measure greatly understates the public sector commitment to the corrective goal in that period. In this section we will discuss the growth of the more traditional programs—vocational rehabilitation and sheltered workshops—as well as of the major new programs—job subsidies, public employment, and equal access—which played a major role in disability policy in the 1970s.

The Vocational Rehabilitation Program

From its inception in 1920, the program established by the Vocational Rehabilitation Act has undergone numerous changes, gradually expanding over the years from a provider of strictly vocationally related services for clients likely to find employment in the labor force to a program offering multiple vocational and psychological counseling services to handicapped individuals regardless of their employment potential. Initially, federal responsibility was small, involving a minimum of interference with individual state plans. Today the federal government administers federal funds to all approved state Vocational Rehabilitation programs and is the primary regulator of rehabilitation policy in the United States.

The basic philosophy of vocational rehabilitation has evolved from a purely market orientation (the reintegration of physically disabled individuals into the work force when such investment yields an economic return) to a broader viewpoint seeking to help all disabled—whether they be physically, mentally or economically handicapped, and regardless of the severity of the handicap or the return on that investment. In short, the program broadened its focus from those with traditional physical and mental handicaps to those who are the "employment handicapped." In response to this shift in philosophy, the rehabilitation program has increasingly provided services to handicapped persons when these services are of help in achieving a way of life which is economically and psychologically rewarding.

The 1965 amendments to the Vocational Rehabilitation Act marked the first time that the basic medical eligibility criteria for services were altered. The amendments extended services to people believed to be in "socially" handicapping situations, such as those who were in poverty. This group, when added to those with traditional physical or mental impairments, forms what we call the "employment handicapped." The abandonment of the medical model of rehabilitation and the use of rehabilitation funds for economically disadvantaged groups—the employment handicapped—was consistent with the government philosophy in the 1960s that retraining and education were keys to eliminating poverty in America.

Expenditures on rehabilitation increased from $39 million at the start of the 1960s to $579 million at their close, with the great bulk of the increase occurring after 1965. An alternative measure of program growth is captured in Table 7.1. It reports both the number of clients served and the number of clients reported rehabilitated each year. After a leveling off of clients in the 1950s, the number served quadrupled over the next fifteen years, the greatest gain occurring between 1965 and 1975. The ratio of clients rehabilitated to clients served rose to around 30 percent in the 1960s, but during the 1970s fell back into the 25 percent range of the years before. The cost of rehabilitation, however, doubled in real terms between 1960 and 1975, the great part of the increase coming between 1965 and 1970. By 1980, clients served, clients rehabilitated, and real expenditures per client rehabilitated had all fallen below 1975 levels.

Program changes made in the 1970s represented a greater shift in program goals than those of the 1960s. The first change was the requirement that those receiving SSI (initiated in 1974) were required to take vocational rehabilitation when it was offered or forfeit their SSI benefits. This may in part explain the fall in the ratio of rehabilitated clients to total clients in the 1970s, since the work disincentives in the SSI program may well have discouraged program participants from obtaining employment and becoming classified as rehabilitated.

An alternative explanation of this decrease in the successful rehabilitation ratio may be related to the other major development in the law in the 1970s, when the Vocational Rehabilitation Act of 1920 was replaced by the Rehabilitation Act of 1973. This change marked a turning point in the goals and the priority system under which rehabilitation services were provided in the United States. The 1973 Act required that priority for rehabilitation services be given to the *most* severely handicapped. Since 1974, the percentage of clients with severe handicaps has steadily increased, and in

Table 7.1. Vocational Rehabilitation Clients and Cost per Client Rehabilitated in the United States, 1940-1980

Year	Clients Served (thousands)	Clients Rehabilitated (thousands)	Ratio of Rehabilitated to Served	Program Expenditures per Client Rehabilitated (current dollars)	(1967 dollars)
1940	65.6	12.0	.18	$ 343	$ 817
1945	161.0	41.9	.26	235	436
1950	225.7	59.6	.26	492	682
1955	209.0	58.0	.28	666	830
1960	298.0	88.3	.30	892	1,006
1965	441.3	134.9	.31	1,140	1,206
1970	875.9	267.0	.30	2,167	1,863
1975	1,244.3	324.0	.26	3,152	1,955
1980	1,168.0	277.0	.24	4,343	1,758

Source: U.S. Department of Health, Education, and Welfare (1970, 1980).

1980, 55 percent of clients served were severely disabled. Over this period the success rate for this group has been below the success rate of less severely disabled clients. This in part explains the fall in the percentage of clients rehabilitated from its high point in the 1960s. Surprisingly, the real cost per rehabilitated person was relatively constant between 1970 and 1980, in spite of the change in severity levels.

The final change of the 1970s occurred in 1978, when the Rehabilitation Act of 1973 was amended. The principal alteration was the authorization for states to use rehabilitation resources for the severely disabled even if they had no chance of returning to market work; a sufficient goal was the return to "independent" living. Blunting the force of this directive, however, was the fact that no provision for federal matching funding for formal independent living rehabilitation programs was established.

During these sixty years of rehabilitation efforts, then, program goals and priorities have greatly changed. At the start, the Vocational Rehabilitation program was limited to those unemployed handicapped individuals who showed the greatest promise of returning to the work force. The philosophy was simple—returning these individuals to gainful employment meant more productivity to the nation as a whole. In the 1960s and 1970s, services were progressively extended, first to reach the entire group of employment handicapped, and ultimately to focus on those with the most serious handicaps. These changes dramatically enlarged the client population by changing the definition of disability from a purely medical model to one that considered economic and social characteristics. The result has been a larger and more expensive program, but one that serves different and certainly wider goals.

Sheltered Workshops

The goal of regular sheltered workshops is the provision of *transitional* employment designed to enable impaired workers to pass successfully into the work force of the able-bodied. Skill training is not emphasized. As we saw in Chapter 4, these workshops are heavily subsidized by federal and state government, even though they are private activities. In addition, they can be exempt from paying the federal minimum wage. "Certificated programs," however, still must pay wages "commensurate" with those in the competitive labor market, and in no case may a client in a certificated program be paid less than 50 percent of the federal minimum wage. Moreover, at its discretion the Department of Labor may set minimum wages of between 50 and 100 percent of the federal minimum for individual programs and workers.

In the 1970s a major policy change established separate programs for the severely disabled who were judged to have low productivity in the job market. "Work activity centers" were established to provide longer-term or even *permanent* employment to these handicapped workers. This program was part of the more general move to target rehabilitative services on the more severely handicapped.

The average hourly wage for all workshop clients was $.70 in 1973, less than half the federal minimum wage.[2] This low average wage is partly attributable to the tremendous growth of centers serving the mentally retarded. Public policy measures on behalf of the retarded and the movement for "deinstitutionalization" of mentally disabled persons have been the main factors behind this growth. Programs for retarded workers now account for half of all the workshop operations in the United States.

Direct Job Creation

The ameliorative and corrective programs we have so far discussed rely on traditional market failure arguments to justify the role of the government. Direct job creation programs, the major corrective strategy in the 1970s, rely upon a quite different rationale for public sector intervention. As we described in Chapter 3, these programs attempt to offset the adverse side effects of market intervention policies and constraints which form a wedge between employer-borne gross wages and the perceived marginal product of low-wage workers, as well as between net wage received by labor and the supply price of work. These policies and constraints include minimum wage policy, government workplace regulation, and the policies of labor unions. For employers, the direct job creation programs reduce the wage costs of hiring disabled and other employment-handicapped workers; for workers, the programs increase the possibility and reward of finding a job and holding it.

Direct Employment

Governmental policy began to focus on stimulating the demand for employment-handicapped workers in the early 1970s. Disabled workers, youths, minorities, and those with low education were the primary target groups. In the United States, the Comprehensive Employment and Training Act of 1973 (CETA; phased out since 1981) was the focal point of efforts to generate jobs for such workers in the public sector. By 1978, the CETA program reached its peak employment of about 750,000 workers, a number representing about 10 percent of the unemployed population. Federal exenditures on CETA in that year totaled $5.7 billion. By 1980, the target group objectives of the program were being met. Nearly all of the participants were either poor or were living in a family that was receiving welfare benefits. Somewhat fewer, though still an overwhelming majority, were either unemployed or structurally underemployed, and about one-half were themselves receiving welfare benefits. About 60 percent were nonwhite.

While no estimates are available regarding the number of physically or mentally disabled who were employed in the program, the "employment handicapped" and the disabled working-age populations overlap.

Employment Subsidies

During the 1970s, the United States experimented with a variety of subsidy programs designed to reduce the costs to employers of hiring certain classes of workers or additional workers regardless of their characteristics. The first sizable effort of this sort was the Work Incentive (WIN) program, designed to subsidize a major share of the wage bill of welfare recipients who were given jobs. This program, initiated in the 1960s, was never very effective—the target group typically had few job skills, the program was not well publicized, and it entailed substantial recordkeeping and administrative reporting on the part of employers. While the target group—welfare recipients—has a high rate of disability incidence, hiring a disabled person per se did not qualify an employer for the subsidy.

The second sizable program was the New Jobs Tax Credit of 1977-79, described in Chapter 4. In this program, no target group was indicated; the purpose was to increase employment per se, not the employment of any particular group. Again, because low-wage workers were favored in the subsidy structure, disabled workers were likely to have been favorably affected by this program, even though it was not directly targeted on them.

The most recent employment subsidy was the Targeted Jobs Tax Credit of 1979-81, also described in Chapter 4. Among the target groups were individuals referred from Vocational Rehabilitation agencies, youths from low-income families, Vietnam war veterans, certain welfare recipients, and students in vocational education programs. Gaining certification of eligibility for the subsidy could be at the initiative of either the worker or the potential employer, and both employers and target groups were informed of the program and encouraged to make use of it. Few results are available regarding the extent to which disabled workers secured jobs through it.

Regulation

Changes in U.S. public policy toward the disabled in the 1970s were affected by the argument that the handicapped represent a distinct minority group subject to economic discrimination, in the same way that blacks and women are considered minority groups. As in the earlier Civil Rights movement, it was argued that government's responsibility should be to reduce or eliminate this discrimination. Public intervention to achieve this corrective goal was based on the radical "equal access" rationale we outlined in Chapter 3. According to this rationale, society should be compelled to change the network of private relationships which prevent the disabled minority from being fully integrated into all aspects of society.

The Vocational Rehabilitation Act of 1973 was the most significant of the laws relying on this radical justification. Section 501 of Title V of this act mandates affirmative action in the hiring practices of the federal government. Section 502 addresses the problems of architectural barriers, and establishes a board to ensure compliance with the architectural accommodations standards determined by the government.

Section 503 requires those who provide contracted services to the federal government to take affirmative action in the employment and advancement of qualified handicapped individuals. This part of the act requires detailed outreach procedures in the recruitment of handicapped workers and in the design of specific internal procedures to ensure that all handicapped applicants and employees receive the same benefits and opportunities as other workers.

Section 504 states that no otherwise qualified handicapped individual may be excluded from any program receiving federal financial assistance. In the United States this includes hospitals and health facilities, universities and colleges, public school districts, and states and municipalities. It also includes private employers if they participate in federally funded programs.

A major difficulty in implementing the law has been the lack of a precise definition of (or at least a consensus on) what Congress meant both with regard to who the handicapped are and what society's commitment to them was under the act. The percentages in Table 2.3 (Chapter 2) showed that in 1978 about 20 million people between the ages of 18 and 64 considered themselves to have at least some work limitation. However, in developing their response to the Rehabilitation Act of 1973, directives from the U.S. Department of Health, Education, and Welfare (HEW) contended that as many as 35 million people might be considered handicapped under the law. This lack of consensus on definitions has been a major factor in delaying regulations for implementation of the 1973 law. Not until 1978 did HEW, the first federal agency to do so, issue such regulations.

Policy Approaches across Countries

As with corrective policies toward disabled workers in the United States, a diversity of approaches to increasing the earnings capacity and work effort of disabled working-age people exists across the countries studied. Some rely on the full range of instruments designed to integrate the disabled into the work force—rehabilitation and training, sheltered workshops, employment subsidies, and mandates imposed on private employers regarding the employment or retention of disabled workers. The Netherlands is an example. Others give only passing attention to labor market policies for the disabled, relying on one or two instruments. An example is

Italy. This section presents a brief description of the labor market policy approaches among the countries studied.

Federal Republic of Germany

Labor market policies toward disabled working-age people in the Federal Republic have undergone a major change since the beginning of the 1970s. The "Action Program of the Federal Republic of Germany for the Promotion of the Rehabilitation of Handicapped Persons" (1970) is still in effect; its principle is that rehabilitation takes precedence over a retirement pension. The Rehabilitation Equalization Act of 1974 stipulated that, by 1980, 80 percent of all disabled working-age people should be integrated into employment and social life.

Supplementary legislation assigned the Federal Labor Office (FLO) primary responsibility for the occupational training of disabled workers and their placement in the work force. Because of this responsibility as well as its knowledge of the situation in different segments of the labor market, other agencies providing such services were required to consult with the FLO.

The FLO, with nine subdivisions at the state level and 142 local labor offices, is a semipublic, self-governed institution. Its tripartite governing body is composed of trade unions, employers, and state representatives. It is responsible for the administration of unemployment insurance and for the implementation of all labor market policies (training measures, living subsidies, short-term work compensation, public work creation, placement and counseling services). Most of the costs of "active labor market policy" are paid out of the unemployment insurance fund (1.5 percent of the payroll paid by employers, 1.5 percent paid by employees). All of these services except vocational rehabilitation apply to both disabled and nondisabled workers. The share of expenditures by the FLO on vocational rehabilitation increased from 0.4 percent in 1968 to about 3.5 percent in 1978. In terms of gross domestic product, the increase was from 0.01 percent (1970) to 0.08 percent (1978). Whereas the FLO financed only 29.6 percent of all vocational rehabilitation in 1968, its share of costs increased to 71.2 percent in 1979. These figures show that the goal of integrating the disability programs designed to increase earning capacity appears to have been at least partly reached.

There are four main policies in the Federal Republic that are intended to increase the earning capacity or work effort of the disabled: vocational rehabilitation and training, sheltered workshops, wage subsidies to employers for hiring disabled workers, and the "right to work" quota rule.

Vocational rehabilitation programs focus on both individuals and institutions. Those programs targeted on individual disabled workers involve a sequence of activities designed to integrate them into the work force. Comprehensive work tests are provided in order to ascertain working capacity. These are followed by the provision of medical aid and/or training to increase physical, mental, or social capacities. Finally, assistance in job placement is provided. Institutional programs support the establishment of vocational rehabilitation centers and of sheltered workshops. In 1978 there were 24 "vocational training workshops" for 7,000 handicapped youths who could not find a training opportunity in a private or public enterprise owing to their handicap. In addition, "vocational supporting workshops" for handicapped adults offer facilities for the retraining of 12,000 individuals, a number double the 1970 level. Both types of facility seek to train the disabled and to reintegrate them into work and society. Expenditures by the FLO in 1978 for vocational rehabilitation were about DM 550 million, of which 79 million were provided for institutional programs.[3]

The second type of program aimed at the integration of disabled persons into the work force is that supporting sheltered workshops. This policy is a more recent one. In 1962 there were 500 workers in 17 workshops; in 1968, there were 140 workshops with about 5,000 clients; by 1978 there were about 40,000 placements in 268 workshops. The government's explicit objective is to create 60,000 sheltered work positions.

A relatively new policy measure involves wage-cost subsidies to employers who hire severely disabled persons in addition to the mandatory quota (see below). The subsidy, a lump-sum grant, ranged between DM 8,000 and 18,000 in 1980, depending on the circumstances: the maximum amount is paid for hiring disabled workers who need personal assistance, or for severely disabled young persons whose primary activity is vocational training. Employers who do not fulfill their quota obligation receive one-half of the subsidy amount under specific circumstances.

This program was initiated in 1976 and has since been renewed twice. It appears to be a permanent institution, at least as long as the adverse labor market conditions for disabled workers persist. From 1976 to 1981, the FLO spent about DM 300 million on the program; a total of 32,000 disabled workers were supported from 1976 to 1981. The program is financed out of the compensation fund raised from the quota rule.

Under legislation for the protection of severely disabled persons passed in 1974, a quota system was instituted which requires all public and private employers who have at least 16 employment positions to reserve a minimum of 6 percent of those positions for severely disabled persons.[4] If found to be in noncompliance, employers must pay DM 100 a month into a fund which is used to support wage-cost subsidies for hiring and training disabled workers. In 1978, 4.8 percent of all work positions were so filled, compared to 3.8 percent in 1975.

Two causes could account for the failure of the quota to be met. Either the fine is set too low or, as employers claim, the number of disabled people meeting the requirement is insufficient to permit the quota to be reached.[5] The latter factor is likely to be eliminated as a cause of noncompliance, since the definition of eligible handicapped people has been widened. Prior to 1974, the cause of disablement was a relevant factor; since 1974, only the health status of the disabled person is considered relevant.

Despite the increase in employment of disabled workers brought about by the quota, the number of unemployed disabled workers increased from 24,000 in 1975 to 54,000 in 1978. The implied unemployment rates for disabled workers increased from 3.8 percent to 6.2 percent over those years, as compared to the average unemployment rate in the Federal Republic of Germany of 3.5 percent in 1978.

The magnitude and growth of the first three programs, both in terms of clients and expenditures, is shown in Table 7.2. From 1970 to 1978, the number of clients served by these programs grew from 85,000 to 201,000, a growth rate of over 11 percent per year. Actual expenditures increased from DM 192 million to 1,008 million over those years, a rate—on average—of nearly 23 percent per year. The rate of increase in the more recent years was even greater.

In addition to these public spending programs and the quota rule, two other components of German labor market policy toward the disabled should be mentioned. The jobs of severely disabled workers are under special protection: dismissal requires the approval of public welfare centers, which are charged with improving the working conditions of disabled employees. In addition, a spokesperson for the disabled must be elected in every firm in which more than five disabled people are employed. The rights of this spokesperson, however, are restricted to information and advice on matters which concern the disabled. That person is allowed to attend workers' council meetings, but is not a member in his or her own right.

France

French labor market policy toward the disabled, like income support policy, was substantially modified during the 1970s. As in most of the countries studied, rehabilitation and sheltered employment form the mainstays of French policy. In addition, a quota system exists, and there is a fledgling employment subsidy arrangement. A serious incentive problem resulting from a guaranteed income regardless of workplace or productivity affects French labor market policies, impeding the success of programs in returning workers to normal employment. We will consider each of these in turn.

Prior to 1975, commissions existed in the departments (states) of France to classify disabled workers and to guide them into productive employment. While 40,000 cases per year were handled by the commissions, two-thirds of

Table 7.2. Persons Served by and Public Expenditures on Major Labor Market Programs for the Disabled, Federal Republic of Germany, 1970-1978 (expenditures in DM million)

	1970			1978		
	Persons	Current Expenditures	Expenditures in 1970 Prices	Persons	Current Expenditures	Expenditures in 1970 Prices
Vocational rehabilitation	80,000[a]	192[b]	—	157,400[c]	928[d]	—
Sheltered work positions	5,000[e]	2[f]	—	40,000	23[f]	—
Employers' wage subsidies	—	—	—	6,000	80[e]	—
Total	85,090	192	192	201,400	1,008	660

Source: Official goverment statistics.

[a]Number of cases finally processed in administrative terms; about 45 percent were subsequently integrated into the labor force.

[b]Share of the Federal Labor Office (FLO) is DM 67 million (34.9 percent); the sum includes the institutional support, and the estimate assumes an equal share spent by the FLO on institutions and on individuals.

[c]47,300 received financially supported vocational training, job service or special training assistance; 30.4 percent of the 157,400 were subsequently integrated into the labor force.

[d]Share of FLO is DM 555 million (59.8 percent); see also note a. In 1979, the FLO's share increased to 71.2 percent.

[e]Estimated.

[f]A grant by the FLO for sheltered work is included in vocational rehabilitation; this number is, therefore, an underestimate.

the disabled were not in contact with the commissions and therefore did not receive classification. Depending on the classification given (A, B, C, or incapable of work), clients were provided appropriate services (averaging 2 months) and either placed in sheltered workshops (20 percent), or received occupational retraining (30 percent), or were employed in the normal environment (50 percent).

Owing to concern with the administrative functioning of this system, it was reorganized in 1975. Each department was assigned a single commission; three rather than four classifications were used, each with a more specific definition; more careful placement and treatment procedures were implemented; wage reductions were allowed for employers of the handicapped in work environments; and provisions for forcing private sector hiring of the disabled were pursued. This new arrangement appears to have achieved a better record in terms of determining appropriate treatment and fulfilling the recommendations made.

One of the placement options for the commissions is in sheltered workshops. In France, they take two forms—Centers of Helping by Working (operated by the Ministry of Health) and Protected Workshops (operated by the Ministry of Labor). The former category is reserved for the most severely disabled—wage payments are at a very low level, and sales are made at below-market prices. Revenues in this component barely cover the very low salaries provided the 16,000 workers employed in these programs. The second component, protected workshops, are more like normal businesses. These factories employ about 2,500 workers and operate in the competitive market; revenue from sales is the primary means of financing. The effort in these shops is to seek the successful transition of workers to the normal labor market. Subsidies are provided by both the local and national governments to cover expenses peculiar to employing disabled workers.

Two problems affect the operation of the workshop system. First, the competition between the two forms of workshops has created an abrasive relationship between them: charges of unfair competition have been levied by the Protected Workshops against the Centers of Helping because they sell goods at below-market prices. Second, the 1975 Act guaranteed income to handicapped workers up to the minimum wage regardless of the place of work or productivity. As a result, salary differentials within the protected work sector and between protected work and normal private employment have been effectively eliminated. As a consequence, there is little incentive provided sheltered work employees to either increase their productivity (work classification) or to attempt the transition from sheltered work to the open labor market.[6]

Two other programs should be mentioned. The quota system in France requires all private businesses employing more than ten workers to have a proportion of disabled employees amounting to 10 percent of their work force (3 percent in the case of public sector workers). Enforcement of the quota has been difficult, and firms have resorted to two primary ways to fill the quota—retaining their workers injured on the job, and subcontracting work to either of the types of sheltered workshop.[7] From 1962 to 1974, the percentage of workers who were handicapped and covered by the quota fell from about 8.5 percent to 6 percent.

Finally, subsidies are available to private employees to support 80 percent of the incremental costs of job adaptation and 50 percent of the incremental management costs of employing the handicapped. These subsidies have seldom been used.

Israel

Understanding the structure of labor market programs for the disabled in Israel is difficult, owing to the variety of programs, limited data, and inconsistent quality of the data available.

There are two main programs for returning the disabled to productive work—vocational rehabilitation and sheltered workshops. Vocational rehabilitation services are provided under several auspices. Each major income support program—for example, those under National Insurance and the Defense Ministry—operate their own rehabilitation programs. In the late 1970s, about 20 percent of Defense Ministry and 10 percent of National Insurance beneficiaries participated in rehabilitation programs—a total of about 70,000 people. In addition, the Ministry of Labor and Social Affairs operated rehabilitation and vocational training centers serving nearly 40,000 disabled workers.

In all of the rehabilitation programs, efforts are extensive, averaging about two years. Eligibility for them is based on the degree of medical disability—for example, two years of training is provided to workers with a disability rating of 35 percent, three years to workers with a 65 percent rating. In addition to vocational training, a variety of other services are provided, including formal education, counseling and placement services, and assistance in gaining self-employment.

Related to these training programs—in particular, to the placement efforts—are provisions for government financing of the salaries of trained workers placed in private industry. Government support for special job-related assistance and job adaptation is also available.

The second major component of the Israeli system, sheltered employment, is large and plagued with controversy. In 1958 a public corporation called Meshakem was formed, with government support, to provide sheltered employment to disabled workers. In 1980, about 6,000 workers were employed in Meshakem centers, representing .5 percent of the total

Israeli labor force. Much of the controversy over the program concerns the nature of the employment provided—long-term menial jobs with little training or provision for advancement—and the lack of concern with income support. The typical worker in Meshakem centers works five-hour days at the minimum wage, gaining total earnings of less than 40 percent of the average wage. Because of the absence of training, the rate at which workers make the transition to regular employment is negligible. While 65 percent of the Meshakem budget is covered by sales—mainly contracts for services at below-market prices—the remainder is covered by public subsidy. In recent years, efforts have been made to move Meshakem activities toward light manufacturing; nevertheless, participation in the program has been declining by about 6 percent per year[8] and the public subsidy per worker has been increasing at 7.5 percent per year.

In contrast to several of the other countries studied, Israel has not adopted designated employment or quota regulations, except in the case of those disabled while in the military.

Italy

The case of Italy is unique among the countries studied. Low priority is assigned to rehabilitation by the national government. Indeed, legislation in 1978 assigned responsibility for rehabilitation to the regional governments. The limited amount of training available to handicapped workers is provided in integrated facilities serving both handicapped and nonhandicapped workers. Only when the handicap is so severe that it impedes normal work procedures in a firm are special courses provided.

The main focus of labor market policy toward the disabled in Italy is a complex employment quota system which, since 1968, has covered nearly all categories of disabled workers except those over 55 years of age or those with zero work capacity. Under the system, a uniform quota is imposed on employers, requiring that 15 percent of their work force be disabled employees. Different categories of disabled workers carry different weights, with the most severely disabled contributing substantially to filling the quota. Enforcement of quota regulations has been difficult. The percentage of disabled employees in private firms has hovered around 3 percent, edging up slightly in the last few years. This proportion lies far below the 15 percent quota. In the public sector, the quota system appears to perform better—at the end of the 1970s, nearly 13 percent of the work force in that sector was disabled. However, the unemployment rate among disabled workers registered for quota employment is high—35 percent in 1977. The low percentage in the private sector is in part due to the conditions required of private firms: disabled workers must not only be paid regular wages, but also the employer must pay all of the social security contributions.

The Netherlands

While no single policy for rehabilitating or improving the labor market position of handicapped workers prevails in the Netherlands, a number of individual programs serve this goal. The primary programs are Social Employment, the General Disability Act provisions for assisted employment, and a number of wage subsidy programs. There is also a quota system imposed on private employers for hiring disabled workers.

The Social Employment program consists of approximately 150 workshops or factories providing employment to disabled workers. In 1980, 75,000 workers were so employed—a figure equal to about 1.5 percent of the country's total labor force. Motivated by the "right-to-work" principle prominent in Dutch social policy, this program provides workers with full employment status (including social security coverage) and pays wages equal to 105 to 140 percent of minimum disability pension benefits. Most of the employees work in industrial centers, producing items under contract which are sold at a competitive price; other workers are employed in administrative centers and in "open-air" projects. While individual municipalities run the programs, substantial subsidies are provided by the national government. In recent years, the total public subsidy has equaled about 80 percent of total program costs, which amounted to Dfl. 3,200 million. While the program provides some testing and training services, few employees—1.3 percent—make a successful transition to regular private employment. The program is unique among the countries studied, but has been subject to several criticisms. One concerns the incentives implicit in the subsidy arrangements, which provide little inducement for cost control or efficient operation since, at the margin, additional costs are passed on by managers and municipalities to the national government. A second criticism concerns the interaction of disability pensions and Social Employment wages: when the two income sources are combined, many Social Employment workers have no financial incentive at all to make the transition to regular employment.[9]

The General Disability Act supports a large number of activities designed to maintain or improve the opportunities for gainful employment of disabled workers. These include expenses for adaptation of workplaces, special transportation needs, and medical support, including appliances. In 1978, over 100,000 awards for special provisions were made at a total cost of Dfl. 124 million. Only about one-fourth of these, however, were directly work related.

Another program under the General Disability Act attempts to find suitably adapted employment for the disabled. In 1980, almost 34,000 disabled were covered by this program, 39 percent of them new beneficiaries in that year. Of the total number of people served, about 40 percent were employed both before and after receiving the service; presumably their jobs were made more suitable because of the intervention. Only about 28 percent of previously unemployed clients were employed after the reintegration effort. The more successful efforts were those involving the least disabled and younger workers.

A wage subsidy program for hiring the disabled was initiated in 1977. A maximum wage subsidy of 60 percent (up to Dfl. 21,000) for the first twelve months, with a 30 percent subsidy for an additional three months, is provided to an employer who hires a registered unemployed handicapped worker. At least 20 hours a week of work is required, and the maximum annual wage payment permitted is Dfl. 36,000 (1979 value). The program was very small during its first full year—fewer than 1,000 unemployed handicapped workers were hired, at a government cost of Dfl. 13 million (1979).

The final policy involves quota legislation. Employers with more than 20 workers are required to employ 2 percent of their work force as registered disabled persons, and those employees must be paid the standard wage for their occupation. Noncompliance entails a fine of Dfl. 1,000 plus adverse publicity. As in most of the quota systems in the countries studied, enforcement is lax and noncompliance widespread, even though a quota increase to 5 percent is being considered.

Sweden

Among the countries studied, Sweden has not only made the strongest commitment to employment of the disabled but has also devoted the largest share of resources to attainment of that goal. It is official government policy that impaired people of working age should be rehabilitated both medically and vocationally.

The primary administrative instrument for achieving this objective is the Labor Market Administration (LMA), a multilevel government agency. The basic responsibility of the LMA is to evaluate job opportunities for the disabled in the labor market and, if it is determined that the handicapped person can work, to implement special programs matching employment with available skills. These responsibilities are undertaken through LMA operations at the national, county, and local levels. At the highest level, the National Labor Market Board formulates rules, interprets legislation, and oversees program implementation. At the lowest level, local employment offices deal directly with clients and play the key role in allocating individuals to programs. The local office is also responsible for classifying workers as disabled, relying on medical reports and classifications from other public authorities. The concept of disability used by the LMA is broad: any person judged to have difficulty in keeping a job in the open labor market because of some physical or mental condition can be classified as disabled.

The LMA and the programs for which it is responsible have grown rapidly since the 1960s. From 1965 to 1980, the LMA budget rose from 1 percent to 2.5 percent of GDP. Policies targeted on disabled people represented 3 percent of the LMA budget in 1960, but 17 percent in 1980. In terms of the total government budget, disability policies administered through the LMA rose from less than .1 percent in 1960 to nearly 1 percent in 1980. In the latter year, over 70,000 clients were served by LMA employment offices.

The LMA and its employment offices are responsible for five primary programs affecting the employment of disabled workers. The largest programs—or set of programs—concern labor market training. While these training programs serve all workers having employment difficulties, over one-third of the clients are classified as disabled workers. The standard procedure in the programs is, first, to administer comprehensive work tests in order to ascertain working capacity, then to provide training to increase physical, mental, or social capacities, and finally to assist in job placement.

The second program involves sheltered workshops. In Sweden the workshops are supported, and in most cases sponsored, by the national government. In 1982, they employed 23,450 disabled workers in 370 workshops. In 1981, total expenditures for the shops were SK 3.1 billion, of which SK 2.1 billion were covered by government subsidies. These subsidies included rent, machinery, and operating (including wage) costs. Wage levels in the workshops are determined by negotiation between the board responsible for state enterprises and the trade unions. Wages are relatively high—though at the low end of the private sector wage distribution for unskilled workers—and as a result, government subsidies to the workshops were 170 percent of the total wage bill.

The third, and most innovative, aspect of Swedish policy toward the disabled is what is now called "work with wage subsidy," previously known as "semisheltered" employment. It has two basic components: public sector employment and wage subsidies for private (mainly industrial) enterprises. For the former, the Labor Market Board pays 100 percent of the wage costs of disabled workers in national government agencies and supports one-third of the wage costs of workers hired by municipal agencies. Both full- and part-time work are offered. For the private sector component, long-term support for disabled workers is provided, and at a rate that is high relative to similar programs elsewhere. In the first year of employment, 75 percent of the wage paid is subsidized; to reflect the fact that worker productivity varies with training and experience, the subsidy rate drops to 50 percent in the second year, 25 percent in the third and fourth years. In 1981, 32,500 persons were employed in this program.

Another program is termed Special Relief, provided to disabled and other disadvantaged workers with labor market difficulties. These work relief projects take a variety of forms, including open-air and administrative jobs, and are operated by local governments. Because they cover both disabled and nondisabled workers, statistics on the program related to the disabled are difficult to obtain.

The final type of labor market activity undertaken by the LMA on behalf of disabled workers consists of grants for motor vehicles and their adaptation, tools and equipment, workplace adaptation, work assistants, and resettlement for self-employment.

All of these programs except those for labor market training are supported by general revenues; the training programs receive financing from an .8 percent payroll tax.

The magnitude and growth of these programs, both in terms of clients and expenditures, is shown in Table 7.3. From 1968 to 1978, the number of clients grew from 23,000 to 61,000, a growth rate of over 10 percent per year. Actual expenditures increased from SK 486 million to SK 2.5 billion (or .58 percent of GDP) from 1968 to 1978, a rate of 18 percent per year; in constant values, the growth rate was nearly 9 percent per year. The labor market component of public policy toward disabled workers in Sweden has thus grown rapidly, reflecting the government's commitment to returning disabled workers to productive employment and paralleling the rapid growth in public transfers to the disabled.

Beyond this public spending program, two other aspects of Swedish policy should be mentioned. For several years the Job Security Law has stipulated that age, health, or reduced working capacity are not sufficient conditions for laying off workers, unless the employees are eligible for full disability pensions. This "antiredundancy" provision is complemented by the Promotion of Employment Law, which authorizes county labor market boards to apply moral suasion and other pressures to induce employers to hire disabled workers.

These programs illustrate Sweden's strong commitment to placing disabled workers in jobs. There has been little discussion concerning the potential conflict between this goal and the generous disability and early retirement transfer benefits for which the disabled are eligible.

United Kingdom

Like its income support policies for the disabled, labor market policies for disabled workers in the United Kingdom are also disparate and relatively unintegrated. There seems to be no overriding philosophy regarding work and the disabled. The following outline of the primary labor market programs describes the most important ones and gives some indication of the number of clients served by each, although the data needed to assess the programs' growth and impact are notoriously weak.

The Industrial Employment Rehabilitation Services program is the

Table 7.3. Persons Served by and Public Expenditures on Major Labor Market Programs in Sweden, 1968-1978 (expenditures in SK millions)

	1968			1978		
	Persons	Current Expenditures	Expenditures in 1970 Prices	Persons	Current Expenditures	Expenditures in 1970 Prices
Archive work	4,922			15,362		
Sheltered work	7,801			17,175		
Work with wage subsidy	286			11,687		
Vocational rehabilitation	1,789[a]			2,794		
Special relief work[b]	8,300			14,100		
Total	23,098	486	480	61,118	2,534	1,097

Source: Swedish National Labor Market Board, *Labor Market Statistics* (for the years cited).
[a]1969.
[b]Data are for 1967 and 1977 and include some older nondisabled workers.

primary training and rehabilitation program undertaken by the government. In 27 centers scattered around the country, services are supplied to disabled or long-term unemployed workers. In 1979, net expenditures on the programs were about £12 million. Together, these centers can provide services to about 3,000 people at a time. However, because the training courses offered are typically from four weeks to six months, the total number of people served over the course of a year is substantially greater—in 1980, about 14,000 people attended the centers. Only about half of those taking courses obtained employment within six months after completing them.

The second major labor market program is a sheltered workshop system in the form of a government-operated program known as REMPLOY. It began in 1945 and now consists of a series of about 90 factories employing 8,200 workers in 1981. These enterprises primarily produce basic manufactured items (e.g., furniture) and market them through a variety of channels. Entry to the shops is restricted to the disabled who are registered with the employment service. The workshops vary substantially in the extent to which they are oriented toward work or training—some provide mainly vocational training and occupational therapy, others provide a work environment similar to the private market.

In addition to REMPLOY there exist nearly 120 workshops for the blind and partially sighted (the "sighted disabled"). About 5,000 individuals are employed in these enterprises, two-thirds in workshops for the blind. The shops are operated by municipalities or voluntary organizations, and are eligible for government subsidies.

In 1981, over £60 million were provided by the national government in support of sheltered employment. Neither the REMPLOY workshops nor those operated for the sighted disabled have been particularly successful in moving clients into the private sector labor market. Only 2 to 3 percent of REMPLOY clients succeed in making that transition; and the proportion in the remainder of the shops is virtually zero.

A third program concerns provision of placement and resettlement services by the Department of Employment. Nearly 600 disablement resettlement officers are employed by this program to assist disabled (including blind) people in finding employment. The focus is on the person and not on the work environment; special tools and equipment can be provided, and assistance is granted to facilitate adjustment to the workplace. The placement task is difficult, as the program lacks the means to provide incentives to private firms to hire disabled workers. Approximately 60,000 disabled people per year receive services from the program; this compares with a total of about 70,000 disabled people who are registered as unemployed.

These are the major service programs targeted on the disabled. Perhaps a more effective employment program is found in government regulations on private businesses regarding the hiring of disabled workers. Two schemes in particular should be noted. Under the disability quota system, every employer of 20 or more workers is required to fill 3 percent of the job slots with handicapped workers. In practice, this regulation is only sporadically enforced, and the fine is an insignificant £100. In 1980, 68 percent of all firms failed to meet their quota, an increase from 1960, when 38 percent of covered firms were below the quota. Part of the difficulty lies in the magnitude of the quota—indeed, if all of the registered disabled were hired, the average percentage achieved throughout the economy would be just slightly over 2 percent. Despite this, it seems likely that the real effect of the quota on employment of disabled people may exceed that of the vocational training, sheltered workshops, or placement and resettlement programs. Many large corporations, for example, not wishing to attract the bad publicity which accompanies noncompliance, are likely to increase employment of the disabled because of the quota. In 1979, a publicity scheme in the form of a "Fit for Work Award" was introduced to support the quota legislation. The awards are given annually to the 100 firms which best carry out constructive policies for hiring the disabled.

Related to and supplementing the quota system is a "designated employment" provision, under which certain occupations (e.g., elevator operators and parking lot attendants) are reserved for disabled people. Able-bodied individuals can be hired for these positions only if no disabled workers are available. In recent years, about 5,000 such reserved positions were filled by disabled workers.

Finally, there are several more general labor market programs which provide services to the disabled. These include the Training Opportunities Scheme (TOPS), in which 4,500 out of 75,000 participants are disabled; the Youth Opportunity program; the Special Temporary Employment program; and the Community Industry program, which provides work experience and placement services for disadvantaged youths. Another general program is the Job Introduction Scheme, an employment subsidy program begun in 1977. It grants a subsidy of £30 per worker per week to firms for four months if target groups, including disabled workers, are hired. As with the other programs in this category, little information is available on the number of disabled persons affected by the programs or expenditures on disabled workers in the programs.

Have Public Programs Been Effective?

Vocational Rehabilitation

Economic analyses of the effectiveness of rehabilitation programs have been of two types. The first concerns studies undertaken to determine if government expenditures on rehabilitation yield government budget savings in excess of the expenditures. These are, in essence, financial studies focusing on the impacts of publicly financed rehabilitation on net public revenues. They were mostly initiated by those who saw rehabilitation as a cost-effective way of reducing federal expenditures. The second type of study involves standard benefit-cost analysis techniques to evaluate the full social efficiency impacts of rehabilitation programs.

The difference between the two approaches is shown in the following benefit and cost accounts. In the financial analysis account, all of the benefits and costs accrue to the government budget; the entries in the economic analysis account refer to the social efficiency gains and losses of the program. Note that in the financial analysis, no consideration is given to social and psychological benefits to the rehabilitated worker or to society as a whole.

Financial Analysis

Benefits	*Costs*
Increased taxes due to earnings increases	Program expenditures
Reduced income support payments due to earnings increases	

Efficiency Analysis

Benefits	*Costs*
Present value of earnings increases due to rehabilitation	Labor costs of the rehabilitation activity
Sociopsychological benefits of rehabilitated worker and society as a whole	Capital costs of the rehabilitation activity
	Forgone income of the client during rehabilitation
	Forgone productivity from displacement of other workers due to employment of the client

Beginning in the early 1960s, numerous studies of the economic effects of vocational rehabilitation programs in the United States were undertaken. Almost uniformly, these studies yielded estimates of benefits relative to costs which were very high—benefits of twenty times the costs were not unusual.[10] The analyses used standard procedures: the earnings of program clients after receiving training were compared with their earnings in the period (week, month, year) before training, this difference was projected into the future (sometimes with adjustments for normal productivity growth or expected job loss), and the discounted present value of this gain was compared to the discounted present value of program costs (sometimes with adjustments for forgone income during training and other components of cost not directly stated in program accounts). The studies employed crude benefit-cost techniques—there were no control groups; before-after earnings comparisons were suspect; guesses were made regarding the durability of the earnings increases into the future; and they failed to consider some components of real costs. As a result, they were generally viewed with suspicion, though the sizable benefit-cost ratios produced did not lead to serious doubts regarding the overall economic worth of the program. Elsewhere we have detailed the results of these studies (Burkhauser and Haveman, 1982). Here we report their principal findings as they relate to the issues of priorities and goals of the rehabilitation system.

A major element in the studies concerns the impact of the program on specific groups of clients—age groups, racial groups, gender groups, and types of disability. Conley (1965, 1969), for example, suggested on the basis of his results that the benefits of providing services to low-productivity groups—older workers, those with low education, blacks, and those with severe disabilities—might be more efficient than supplying services to groups who have been more successful in the labor market. Such evidence suggested that rehabilitation services should be targeted to low-productivity clients, both because of "social need" and because of a higher return on investment in a narrow economic sense. It supported the arguments for reordering priorities in the rehabilitation program. Worrall's (1978) results, however, were significantly different. He found that it is more efficient to provide services to young, married, nonwhite, and less severely disabled people. These results must be used with caution, since they are based on estimates of the average benefit-cost ratios of rehabilitation services supplied to various groups of disabled workers. Decisions on program allocation among various groups requires information on the effects of expenditures at the margin—marginal benefit-cost ratios.

Since 1965, the Social Security Administration has been permitted to spend an amount equivalent to 1.5 percent of total Disability Insurance benefits to rehabilitate program recipients. In fiscal year 1980, $113 million was spent on the Beneficiary Rehabilitation Program (BRP), and 96,000 beneficiaries received services. This program was to continue only if the savings to the DI trust fund created by the discontinuance of benefits due to rehabilitation exceeded the expenditures from the trust fund. The appraisal of effectiveness implied by this criterion is a variant of the financial account analysis described above—instead of analyzing the effects of the program on the entire government budget, only effects on the DI budget were recognized.

The selection of DI beneficiaries as BRP cases is made by the state vocational rehabilitation agencies. Counselors are instructed to choose clients who are likely to be able to return to sustained, competitive employment. Those with impairments so severe that they cannot be expected to perform in competitive employment and those who can medically recover on their own are excluded.

Analysis of the results of the program are controversial. Treitel (1975) concluded that over the period from 1966 to 1973 the program succeeded in meeting the goals set by Congress. While the ratio of reductions in DI benefits to program expenditures fell in 1972 and 1973, it remained above 2.

The methods used in estimating this ratio are open to criticism. Most important, the study assumed that recovery would not have occurred if the disabled persons had not been on the BRP program, even though contradictory evidence exists. In addition, the analysis assumed that Social Security retirement (OASDI) benefits are taken by workers at age 65, and that rehabilitated workers continue in the labor force until that age. In fact, workers with low earnings histories tend to take OASDI benefits at age 62 rather than age 65, which pattern significantly reduces the measured return to rehabilitation efforts. Finally, the study failed to take account of the fact that some of the participants in the BRP program who are classified as rehabilitated return to the DI program at a later date. All of these assumptions cause the estimated success ratio to be biased upward.

The U.S. General Accounting Office (1976) reevaluated BRP, using the same methodology but looking more closely at the selection process. The results of this study throw serious doubt on Treitel's initial conclusions, even though the study failed to consider the early retirement and return-to-the-rolls effects mentioned above.

As we have noted, the Rehabilitation Act of 1973 signaled a change in emphasis for rehabilitation services. In response, Congress required the BRP programs to attempt rehabilitation of the hardest cases first.[11] It is unclear what effect this has had on rehabilitation effectiveness or the ability of the BRP program to meet the financial test imposed by Congress. However, it is clear that increased emphasis on the severely disabled is likely to reduce the successful rehabilitation rate and raise the costs per client.

What, then, can be concluded from these studies? First, in terms of a social benefit-cost criterion, the vocational rehabilitation program does appear to yield substantial net benefits. Although the available studies are methodologically flawed, it seems unlikely that improved procedures and data would overturn the results. However, because the benefit-cost calculations yield average rather than marginal benefit-cost estimates, little evidence exists on the efficiency of expanding the program beyond its present size. Second, although the evidence is not strong, it appears that concentrating rehabilitation activities on younger, less disabled, and more productive workers is likely to be more efficient than focusing on those in the disabled group with the most severe handicap.[12] This conclusion calls into question the current policy of both the Vocational Rehabilitation and BRP programs. Finally, because of the small number of DI beneficiaries who leave the rolls (even after rehabilitation treatment), the high average age and the severity of disability of DI recipients, and the favorable income transfer options available to them relative to work options, the continuation of the BRP program, which diverts DI funds to rehabilitation activities, would seem to be questionable.

Sheltered Workshops

The framework for evaluating the efficiency of sheltered workshops is somewhat different from that of rehabilitation and training efforts. In this case, the focus is on the enterprise rather than the worker and the effort is designed to determine if the value of the resources entering the enterprise (the labor of the disabled workers and administrative and supervisory staff, materials and other inputs, the services of capital equipment) is greater or less than the value of the output of the enterprise, the increased productivity of the disabled workers, and their social and psychological well-being. This framework has been applied to sheltered employment programs in the United Kingdom, the Netherlands, and the United States.

In one study undertaken in the United Kingdom (Morgan and Markeham, 1978), analysis was performed on each of the three types of sheltered workshops—REMPLOY employing 8,000 sighted disabled in 87 factories, and a set of 52 workshops employing 3,000 blind workers. The analysis was done from both an economic perspective and from the perspective of the government budget.

On the benefit side, the value of the output produced by the shops is assumed to be equal to the sales of the workshops net of stock adjustment. Payments received by the shops, such as the Value Added Tax and the Regional Employment Premium, are properly ignored since they involve transfers of income rather than compensation for real output produced. The rehabilitative services of workshops and the psychological benefits which the disabled derive from sheltered employment are acknowledged on the benefit side, but no attempt is made to quantify these benefits. There are two categories of benefits completely ignored in the study: reduction in medical or psychological care costs owing to the workshops, and third-party benefits.

On the cost side, the analysis considers the real opportunity costs of all inputs used by the workshops. The rather strong assumption is made that the opportunity cost of employing clients is zero. While not an unreasonable assumption for most, there are at least a few clients who would produce some output of value in the absence of the workshops. Shadow prices are assigned to land and capital resources employed in order to estimate the resource costs associated with their wage. The major category of costs ignored is that associated with other workers and resources in the economy left unemployed because of displacements caused by the existence of the workshops.

The results of this study varied widely by the type of workshop. Sizable net economic costs were recorded for the workshops employing only blind individuals. And even though the other two types of program indicated net economic benefits, the results for the entire set of shops were dominated by those of the blind workshops. Overall, net resource costs of about £100 per worker were recorded for the entire program. The financial results were also negative on balance. The net costs to the government budget of providing sheltered employment (as opposed to providing income support and other benefits) to disabled workers totaled £215 per worker in 1974-75.

A similar type of benefit-cost comparison has been done for the large industrial centers component of the Social Employment program in the Netherlands (Haveman, 1977). That program, as noted above, employs about 75,000 workers, or 1.5 percent of the total Dutch work force. The evaluation study of that program documented its growth in clients, expenditures, sales, and subsidies over the past decade, analyzed the incentives for efficiency in the subsidy arrangements employed in financing program deficits, and performed a benefit-cost analysis of the program. The study reached several conclusions concerning the causes of the rapid growth of the program, including the adverse effects on performance of both the financial incentive arrangements and the interaction of disability pension program benefits and the employment program.

In the benefit-cost analysis, the net social costs of the program per worker were estimated. These were treated as the social costs required to yield whatever nonmeasurable benefits (such as social and psychological well-being of the workers) the program was producing. Estimates of these net social costs were large and rising rapidly. In 1970, the cost to society of providing each industrial center worker with whatever sociopsychological benefit the program yielded was about Dfl. 1,500-2,000. By 1973, this social cost had risen to Dfl. 5,500-7,500, and was estimated at Dfl. 7,500-10,000 per worker in 1976. If this same social cost estimate applies to Social Employment workers in the open-air and administrative component of the program, the total social cost of the program in 1976 was estimated to be at least Dfl. 500 million. These large costs were attributed in part to the perverse incentives implicit in the program, and the inability of the national government to impose fiscal and efficiency controls on the operation of the program. The direct or indirect benefits stemming from increased client sociopsychological well-being would have to exceed the net social cost of the measured categories if the program were to yield positive net social benefits. The study thus was quite sober in its assessment of the contribution the program was making to social welfare.

The most recent study of the social efficiency of sheltered workshops was done for a large sample of workshops in the United States (Christainsen, 1981). This study was more comprehensive than either the British or Dutch studies in that an effort was made to measure the third-party benefits of the workshops; namely, the value to citizens generally of work provision to disabled workers. On the benefit side of the account, the study estimated the value of workshop output, the value of the increased productivity of clients attributable to the workshop, and the value of third-party benefits. Benefits in the form of increased sociopsychological well-being of clients and the workshop-induced reduction in medical care costs were considered as unmeasurable. The elements of the social cost of the system which were measured included the client productivity if he or she had not been employed in a workshop, operating costs of the facilities, the resource cost of the volunteer time provided to the facilities, and the value of other resources displaced by the workshops.

As in the Dutch study, partial benefit-cost calculations were made—net benefits were estimated excluding the two categories of unmeasurable benefits. Because of the uncertainty in the estimates of some of the values, upper and lower bounds were presented.

Substantial differences in net benefits were observed among the different types of shops. Regular program shops appeared to generate substantial net benefits. Work activities centers for the severely disabled, on the other hand, appeared to generate significant net resource costs. This suggests that channeling resources toward severely disabled clients—for example, via work activity centers—yields substantially smaller economic welfare gains than efforts targeted on the moderately disabled. The output of severely disabled clients is depressingly low; resources devoted to rehabilitation and training do not appear significantly to enhance their productivity.

With an average daily attendance at workshop establishments of 55 clients in 1973, an upper-bound estimate of partial net benefits per shop is $74,269 (in 1973 dollars). A lower-bound estimate is -$101,768. If there were 3,000 shops in existence at that time, this implies aggregate (partial) net benefits between -$305 million and $223 million.

Despite the attempt to estimate third-party benefits of sheltered workshops, the difference between the upper- and lower-bound estimates of partial net benefits per client for the overall workshop system is approximately the same as in the Dutch study—about $3,000. As in the Dutch study, however, no attempt was made to measure the extent of the psychological benefits clients receive, or the value of reduced medical costs which may result from sheltered workshops. These omissions create additional uncertainty in interpreting the results.

The results of all these sheltered workshop studies, then, give some cause for concern regarding the effectiveness of this corrective strategy. Except for the regular sheltered workshops in the United States, the unmeasured benefits to society (for example, the social and psychological well-being of the workers or the freeing of care time of other family members) must be substantial in order to compensate for the measured net social costs attributed to the enterprise activities.[13]

Demand-Side Programs

In determining the effectiveness of rehabilitation efforts or regular sheltered workshops, it must be noted that disability is defined with respect to the performance of the economy. If a handicapped person's functional limitation restricts his or her ability to compete in the labor market, society has several options. On the one hand, it may seek to rehabilitate the person so that the impediment can be overcome. Alternatively, society may seek to adjust prevailing economic conditions so that the impairment becomes less relevant. Or, society may choose to compensate the handicapped person directly through an income support program. Finally, a strategy incorporating aspects of all these approaches may be chosen. A cost-benefit analysis of rehabilitation programs, holding constant the income support system and the performance of the economy, is likely to yield different results from one in which these other aspects of the system are also allowed to vary.

The concept of a labor market queue is appropriate in considering this issue. If such a queue exists, less severely disabled workers stand ahead of those with more severe handicaps. In a fully employed, high-demand economy, both workers at the front and those far back in the labor queue are likely to find employment. Rehabilitation and training in such a regime is likely to enhance the earnings of all workers in the queue. However, with low demand, workers back in the queue are unlikely to be employed. And the implications for rehabilitation programs in this low-demand situation are important. Training provided the most severely disabled is less likely to generate employment and earnings gains in such an environment than in a high-demand situation, and less likely to improve earnings and employment of these workers than it is those with less severe disabilities. In a low-demand, high-unemployment situation, then, the advisability of concentrating resources on rehabilitation services or regular sheltered workshops without considering the demand side of the labor market seems open to question, as does the strategy of focusing training resources on more rather than less severely disabled persons. It is to the effectiveness of strategies designed to more directly increase the demand for low-skill, employment-handicapped workers, that we now turn.

Comprehensive Employment and Training Act of 1973 (CETA)

From 1973 to 1981, over $50 billion was spent on the CETA program. Evaluation of the benefits of a direct job creation program, such as CETA, encounters several difficulties. The first problem associated with direct job creation programs involves "displacement effects"—the reduction of employment somewhere as an offset to the job creation impacts of the program. Because the primary objective for this strategy is employment creation, its evaluation must be in terms of its net job creation impact, defined as the differences between the employment level in the economy with the policy and that without it. One consistent finding appears to be that in the early days of CETA, when few constraints were imposed on the governmental units which administered the program, the net-to-gross jobs ratio approached zero in the long run because local authorities were able to divert CETA funds to expenditures which would have been financed anyway. In the mid-1970s, however, CETA shifted to a much more targeted program. As local authorities were forced to hire people with more serious employment handicaps, it is likely that the net job creation effect rose since the skill mix of the target group workers hired tended to be not in conformance with that of regular public employees.

A second problem involves the resource and budget costs of the net jobs created by this approach. The budget costs per *net* job created are quite high. A recent, though rough, estimate of budget costs is based on the assumption that displacement is 20 percent in public employment programs, and suggests a cost per job for public employment programs of over $9,000 (Sawhill, 1979). Although these estimates do not consider the increased tax revenues generated by the extra employment, or the reduced transfer payments, they do suggest that the taxpayer cost per job created is close to, if not in excess of, the net earnings of the new employees.

It is apparently difficult for public sector direct job creation efforts targeted on low-productivity workers to meet the benefit-cost efficiency test. While diverting such workers into a direct job creation program is likely to entail relatively small losses from alternative activities (especially if the alternative to participation is voluntary employment), these workers do require associated inputs in the form of materials, equipment, and supervisory personnel, all of which comes at full cost. The key issue, then, is the value of the output produced. Because the output of public job creation programs is not marketed, its value is hard to measure. This is especially true if the basic motivation for the program is to "keep occupied" members of the target groups or to provide them work experience or training, rather than to use the public sector to achieve some defined objective or to produce some identifiable good or service.

The most comprehensive benefit-cost evaluation of the CETA program (Bassi, 1982), covering the mid-1970s, found that the average annual *net* taxpayer cost of the program was about $5,000, while the average annual post-program wage gains were less than $700. When discounted, with an assumed length of wage gains equal to five years, the effectiveness-cost ratio (calculated from the taxpayers' viewpoint) was from about .5 to .6. Activities under CETA which emphasized training had a substantially more favorable evaluation. It should be emphasized that these results do not represent full social benefit-cost evaluations. Rather, the costs are calculated from the perspective of the taxpayer, while benefits are from the client's point of view. The benefits would appear to be the more narrowly defined of the two, excluding the value of goods produced while the clients were publicly employed, as well as all third-party benefits. Indeed, the program was initially set up to provide financial assistance to local governments which wanted to provide additional public services. The benefits of these public services should be included in any evaluation. Nevertheless, it was results such as these that led the Reagan administration, with the consent of the Congress, to eliminate the CETA program and its 300,000 government-provided jobs.

The Supported Work Demonstration

A variant of the public employment and training strategy was the large Supported Work research and demonstration program instituted in the United States in 1975.[14] The basic objective of the program was to provide individuals having severe employment problems with work experience of about one year. The work experience was offered under conditions of gradually increasing demands, close supervision, and work in association with a crew of peers.

Four groups of employment-handicapped workers were eligible for the program: female long-term recipients of welfare (AFDC); ex-offenders recently released from prison; former drug addicts recently in treatment; and young school dropouts, often with a delinquency record. The characteristics of the participants, all of whom were volunteers, suggests the severity of the handicaps which they faced in the United States labor market. Fewer than one-third had graduated from high school, most were black or Hispanic, fewer than one-quarter were married, the number of weeks worked in the twelve months prior to participation averaged six to seven (except for the female welfare group), and the arrest rates ranged from 54 to 100 percent.

The Supported Work program was unique in that it included a full-scale benefit-cost evaluation to assess its impacts. The benefit and cost results were presented from three perspectives—that of society as a whole, that of the workers themselves, and that of the rest of society (taxpayers).

Overall, the results indicated far more favorable program effects for some of the groups than for others. The cost-benefit calculation for the AFDC group revealed that, primarily because of the employment and earnings gains of participants after they left the program and because of the value of the goods and services produced by them while they were in Supported Work, the net benefit to society was considerable. The program for ex-addicts was economically effective, especially when the gains from a reduction in destructive behavior, drug-related and other criminal offenses in particular, are added to those resulting from increased employment and earnings. However, Supported Work had no significant long-term impact on the earnings, employment, criminal activity or drug abuse of the youth group, and the program's benefits for youth fell short of its costs. No clear-cut evaluation result was possible for the exoffender group.

Employment Subsidies

The New Jobs Tax Credit (NJTC) of 1977-79 and its successor, the Targeted Jobs Tax Credit (TJTC), have not been fully evaluated. The evaluation studies of the NJTC tried to measure the employment increases in the construction and retailing industries attributable to the subsidy, net of displacement within these industries (e.g., Bishop and Haveman, 1979). By and large, however, these studies failed to consider the possible displacements in other sectors of the economy. The preferred models attribute at least 20 to 30 percent of the observed employment increase (1.3 million jobs between mid-1977 and mid-1978) in these industries to NJTC. Other studies, based on different data and techniques, also suggest a substantial effect on the NJTC. Although they focus on the net intrasector employment effects, and hence fail to consider some possible channels of displacement, the employment effects attributed to the job creation measure appear to be significant.

Such findings have important implications for overall macroeconomic policy. Both NJTC and TJTC had as their goal employment generation for low-skill, employment-handicapped workers. Such job creation measures will have important impacts on macroeconomic relationships in the economy, especially if the programs are successful. If such programs are effective, employment will increase at a substantially greater rate than output, as the NJTC results suggested. A direct result of this is a fall in productivity—output per unit of labor input, as it is measured in the United States—when inputs grow faster than output. Similarly, if employment of target-group workers results in an increase in labor force participation from those in the group who are discouraged workers, employment may increase but measured unemployment may remain relatively unchanged, or even increase.

Surely it is an open question as to whether or not such changes in macroeconomic relationships are desirable. Declining productivity, for example, does have implications for economic growth and the maintenance of international competitiveness. On the other hand, the reduction in productivity may be evidence that low-skill workers are being removed from unemployment and idleness and transferred into the productive sector. In this case, these adverse side effects on macroeconomic relationships are evidence that direct job creation efforts are, indeed, producing the intended effects.

Second, both of these programs were put into place under economic circumstances which were, at best, inhospitable to job creation. Unemployment in the United States throughout the 1977-82 period was over 7 percent and ranged up to 10 percent, and a quasi-recession was in evidence throughout the period. More important, expectations for expansion and rapid growth were weak, and in many sectors nonexistent.

Equal Access Regulations

The relatively recent passage (1977) of "equal access" regulations in the United States, and the delay in their implementation, makes any evaluation of them difficult. As mentioned in Chapter 4, only a few studies have been undertaken, and their results are controversial. Smith (1980) summarized the findings of two private consultant studies commissioned by the U.S. Department of Health, Education, and Welfare. Both studies estimated the cost of the initial architectural modifications necessary to adhere to the regulations established under Section 504 of the Rehabilitation Act of 1973. The costs estimated by the HEW consultants were compared with the cost estimates provided by the affected institutions. The results varied greatly. The HEW studies estimated costs to be between $1.3 billion and $1.5 billion, while the institutions put their costs at between $3.8 billion and $5.7 billion.

A second group of institutions especially affected by both Section 502 and Section 504 are the nation's heavily subsidized public transportation systems. Although the regulations regarding transportation services for the handicapped were issued in 1979, they have been embroiled in controversy ever since. At the heart of this controversy are the twin concerns of cost of implementation and effectiveness in reaching and serving the handicapped population.

Currently, the regulations require transit systems to equip buses with lifts for wheelchairs, to install elevators in underground and above-ground rail stations, and to modify rail cars and buses to accommodate wheelchairs. It was estimated that $6.8 billion (in 1979 dollars) would be needed to implement the Department of Transportation regulations over the next 30 years (U.S. Congressional Budget Office, 1979). Two-thirds of this amount would be required for adaptation of transit buses and corresponding maintenance and operating costs, and much of this would be required for modification and expansion of the country's bus fleet. The main objection to the plan was that after these expenditures were undertaken, it was estimated that no more than 7 percent of all severely disabled handicapped persons were expected to be served. When these expenditures were averaged over this limited number of wheelchair and other severely disabled passengers, the regulations were estimated to cost approximately $38 per trip. In contrast, transit trips by the general public cost, on the average, $0.85 per trip. This comparison highlights the issue of the cost of implementing the regulation relative to the benefits provided to the disabled.

The efforts to implement the requirements of the 1973 Rehabilitation Act and later amendments to it have become enmeshed in bureaucratic and legal problems. This result is not unexpected, given the complex nature of the issues, the lack of a clear-cut understanding of the term "handicapped," the resistance of the private sector to what is viewed as yet another constraint on the choices open to it, and the problems inherent in multi-agency jurisdiction. As a result, confusion, delays, and uncertainty have plagued the entire "equal access" area. And hanging over the entire area is the potential for huge social cost, relative to the expected benefits, to achieve the objectives of the legislation.

Conclusions

In this chapter we have reviewed the variety of programs and policies to deal with disabled workers in the labor market, again emphasizing the programs and approach taken in the United States. There, the main efforts are represented by the Vocational Rehabilitation program and, related to it, a large system of sheltered workshops. During the decade of the 1970s, a number of programs to create jobs for the disabled via employment subsidies and public employment have been undertaken. The same period saw the passage of regulations designed to ensure "equal access" to employment and mobility for the disabled. Until the last few years, supply-side efforts were limited to training, counseling, placement, and medical services; demand-side efforts to low-paying sheltered employment.

Other countries studied have undertaken a wide variety of corrective measures, including those listed above. For example, France, Germany, Italy, the Netherlands, and the United Kingdom have quota systems which require private (and in some cases public) employers to reserve job slots for the disabled. While the nature of the quota arrangements vary widely, most are characterized by poor enforcement. The only exception is the Federal Republic of Germany, and its enforcement has been controversial in the weak labor market of the 1980s. Sweden has the most extensive system of work-oriented programs among the countries studied. The efforts extend from subsidized private employment arrangements to sheltered work to training and rehabilitation. Italy, on the other hand, relies almost exclusively on the private employment quota system, while the Netherlands is notable for its large Social Employment and sheltered work effort. In none of the countres studied do these efforts appear to work at cross-purposes with the disability transfer programs. Moreover, those countries emphasizing supply-side strategies—the United States, Sweden, and the United Kingdom—appear not be have recognized fully the difficulties of this approach in an economy characterized by high unemployment.

The evaluations of this corrective strategy yield mixed results. The benefit-cost analyses of vocational rehabilitation programs—while flawed in data, methodology, and projections—suggest substantial earnings and employment gains of recipients attributable to the services provided. They also indicate that younger workers, married workers, and those with less severe disabilities respond more favorably to training and rehabilitation than do older and more severely disabled workers. Evaluations of sheltered workshop efforts are more difficult to interpret. Analyses have focused on those cost and benefit components which are measurable and on which data exist. While net social costs are typically registered, the unmeasured benefits—for example, the sociopsychological well-being of the workers-against which these costs are to be set may themselves be substantial.

Evaluations of employment subsidy and public employment programs also yield mixed results. Studies of employment subsidies indicate a high employment impact, but gives little indication of the employment effect on disabled workers. Public employment efforts also show some net payoff when training is provided and target groups are carefully distinguished.

The evaluations, then, have yielded results which are mixed and uncertain. On the basis of them, it is difficult to make a strong case for the reorientation of policy from ameliorative toward corrective policy.

Notes

1. In 1973, it was estimated that only 3 percent of total federal disability expenditures were devoted to direct services to the disabled. See Berkowitz, Johnson, and Murphy (1976).
2. See U.S. Department of Labor (1977).
3. Although exchange rates have fluctuated widely over the past few years, to provide some idea of dollar equivalence we list the exchange rates of the foreign currencies mentioned here, as of October 1983: German mark = \$.38; French franc = \$.125; Israeli shekel = \$.016; Italian lira = \$.006; Dutch guilder (Dfl.) = \$.34; Swedish krona = \$.128; British pound = \$1.50.
4. A severely disabled person is defined as one whose working capability has been reduced by at least 30 percent of standard capability.
5. According to a recent survey (1980), the number of disabled people with an officially acknowledged reduction in working ability of at least 30 percent was 3.4 million at the end of 1979—5.6 percent of the population. Of this number, 1.4 million, or 41 percent, were employed. The remainder, of which 4.1 percent were children and students, were not employed.
6. For example, the lowest-paid worker in a sheltered workshop would, with the wage guarantee, earn 90 percent of what would be earned in private employment. The highest-paid sheltered workshop employee would earn an equal amount in either sheltered work or private employment—about 130 percent of the minimum wage.
7. Up to 50 percent of the quota can be met in this way.

8. While the reasons for this decline are not well understood, the lack of attractive jobs in combination with the increased adequacy of disability benefits are often cited as the primary reasons.

9. In 1979, 62 percent of Social Employment workers were entitled to a disability income support benefit. This benefit is paid only when it is higher than the sheltered workshop wage, which is the normal market wage with a minimum equal to the legal minimum wage. Not all of those employed by the centers are eligible for a disability pension—those admitted not because of a handicap but because they were socially maladjusted, and those entering with a handicap *before* they were entitled to a disability security benefit, do not receive disability income support.

10. Many of these studies are reviewed in Kisner (1973).

11. Since 1980, expenditures on this program have been substantially reduced. In addition, a major change in financing criteria has occurred. Now benefits are reimbursed to the states only if they result in a successful rehabilitation. The implications of this new guideline is that when states take on the rehabilitation responsibility, it is likely that they will target funds on those with the highest probability of successful outcome.

12. On the other hand, it is not unreasonable to hypothesize that the sociopsychological effects of disablement and earnings loss are greater for older than for younger workers, suggesting that efforts targeted at this group may be more efficient.

13. This conclusion must be tempered by the results of a small survey of British sheltered workshop employees. The governmental costs of providing sheltered workshop employment to these workers was set against the tax payments received from their earnings. This option was then compared to that of transfer benefit recipiency. The study concluded that neither the recipients nor the government were gainers from the sheltered workshop option relative to the transfer recipiency option. See Gennard and Wright (1978).

14. This discussion draws heavily from Kemper, Long, and Thornton (1981).

Chapter 8

Fundamental Issues in the Evolution of Disability Policy

Numerous economic and ethical issues are confronted in framing efficient and equitable public policy toward disabled workers. When these issues are viewed from the particular historical or institutional perspective and objectives of a single nation, another dimension of complexity is added. In this chapter, we identify five important policy issues which cut across all of the countries included in this study, and discuss pros and cons of the relevant policy approaches in three of the areas. The discussion relates equally to the mature disability systems of all of the industrialized countries studied.

Were resources abundant, the economic issues which we have emphasized in this volume would be less serious than they in fact are. Rapid program growth would probably continue to be welcomed by many as a sign that the social commitment to share broadly the total costs of disability—or to invest in corrective measures to reduce those costs—could be fully implemented. There would be less concern with the distinction between the insurance and redistributive purposes of income transfers, as no real purpose would be served in separating these two goals—the protection against income loss due to impairment could converge with the usually lower guarantee of minimal economic security to all, including disabled people. And, finally, the right to work could be granted to more individuals, including some of the disabled—as could the right to equal access to mobility, health care, education, and housing—without continuous concern for the cost of assuring such equality.

Resources are not abundant, however, and cost—real social cost—is the issue. Rapid transfer program growth, the equalization of economic status through income and service grants, and the assurance of equal access to work, mobility, and education all entail costs. The loss of work effort, the administrative burdens, the high marginal tax rates on both beneficiaries and taxpayers, and the use of resources to achieve and maintain equal access are all costly side effects of sharing and reducing the costs of disability.

Because of this undeniable presence of social costs associated with measures to ameliorate and correct disability problems, beyond some point it is not desirable to move in either of these dimensions. The benefits must be set against the costs, and the trade-offs recognized and confronted. Indeed, within any country, trade-offs exist in establishing both the optimal level of national commitment to the disabled population, and in providing an efficient mix of programs. As the previous chapters and Part Two of this book show, considerable variation exists among the countries studied, both in the policy approaches taken toward the disabled population and in the social costs borne to ameliorate or correct disability. Some of these intercountry differences can be explained by differences in the costs and benefits of similar programs across countries, or by differences in the ability of different governments (or by quasi-public union-industry partnership agencies) to administer complex income maintenance or work-related programs. Another part can be explained by differences among the countries in general economic conditions: level of GNP, structure of production, unemployment, and economic growth vary substantially among the countries studied. Moreover, different levels of real wealth and the distribution of that wealth among individuals may also explain some of these differences. However, in addition to these factors, much of the difference appears to be cultural. The salient distinction between United States policy and that of the mature social welfare systems of most other industrialized democracies is in the attention paid to the costs of sharing or reducing the burden of disability. This difference is clearly seen in the readiness to grant the "right to work" to the disabled population, or to accept "equal access" as an inviolable principle, irrespective of cost. In general, concern with the cost of attaining these goals has been a continuing issue in policy debates in the United States; the same explicit concern about costs is scarcely found in most of the other countries included in the study.

As we have emphasized, the cornerstone of U.S. disability policy has been the ameliorative response of income maintenance. For many of the other countries, however, relatively more emphasis has been placed on job provisions. Only since the 1970s has something of a convergence in the policy mix among countries occurred as the United States began a substantial and highly controversial shift toward the more corrective approach of direct job creation and equal access programs.

In part because of this convergence, the 1980s promise to be a turbulent period for disability policy in both the United States and most other industrialized democracies. Economic growth has been low in all of the countries studied; and the rapid expansion of policies toward the disabled population has had both distributional and economic growth implications. All of the countries are in the process of reevaluating their approaches to disability policy in the context of these rising costs and limited resources. This chapter provides a framework for such a reevaluation. We distinguish five broad areas of likely policy conflict, and discuss three of them in some detail.

The *first* issue concerns the appropriate ameliorative response to the disabled population, and its place in a more general income support policy. That is, what is the appropriate level of disability cost which should be borne by society at large, and by what criteria should assistance to the disabled be allocated among potential claimants for it? In formulating this response, choices must be made which affect the system's eligibility criteria, the breadth of protection it provides, its tax and benefit structure, and the administration of the programs.

The *second* issue, while not independent of the first, concerns the appropriate corrective response for disability policy, and its role in a more general employment policy. Policy choices made in this regard concern the extent to which the public sector (or quasi-public "partnership" agencies in some countries) should seek to reduce unemployment by emphasizing job provision for the disabled, as opposed to more general employment efforts. Decisions concerning the willingness to emphasize rehabilitation and training, as well as more direct intervention in the market—targeted job subsidies, job creation, or job quotas—as opposed to broader employment and growth policies, are central to this issue.

The *third* issue, while also corrective in nature, concerns the extent to which a society should attempt to alter its socioeconomic structure so as to accommodate impaired citizens. To what degree should society be transformed so that impairments are made more or less irrelevant to normal interactions? The major questions involve determining what "equal access" implies, assessing the costs and benefits of providing equal access, and defining the role government regulations should play in achieving equal access.

A *fourth* issue, while relevant to the debate on the evaluation of disability policy, involves the interrelationship between disability programs—both ameliorative and corrective—and programs targeted on other distressed groups, such as the long-term unemployed. Should the portfolio of benefits available to individuals declared to be disabled—income support, health care, housing, employment quotas, training—be more generous than that available to other groups of disadvantaged workers? While little evidence exists on the extent of these disparities across countries, either in this volume or elsewhere, claims of inequity exist in many of the countries included in this study. There seems little doubt that this issue will be an important one in the evolution of disability policy over the next decade. Little more than this can be said within the scope of this study.

The *final* issue is also one about which few data and little information are available. It concerns the effect on migration decisions of differentials in benefit levels and eligibility criteria among political jurisdictions. This may concern not only migration within and/or toward the United States but also within the European Communities and/or toward them. The countries of the European Communities have very generous social security regulations for intra-Communities migration. Those eligible for social benefits, including the disabled, place both social and fiscal burdens upon the jurisdiction in which they reside. In a period when the costs of social policy are viewed as excessive, the possibilities of exporting these burdens through reduced benefits may influence the formation of disability and other social welfare policy. While little of concrete nature can be said about this issue, the potential for destructive defensive actions among countries should not be ignored (see Veldkamp, 1970).

In the following sections, we will discuss the first three of these issues in some detail, as this study has focused on these particular issues.

The Ameliorative Response: Income Support Policy

In most of the countries included in this study, economic policy operates under the presumption that free markets generally provide an efficient mechanism for allocating and distributing many scarce resources. Thus, to a large degree, but with some government guidance, prices in these markets are permitted to be determined by the actions of individual consumers, producers, and providers of productive services.

In Chapter 3, we presented arguments within this framework for government intervention in the disability insurance market. We argued that the existence of externalities in this market causes prices to be inefficient, and a less than optimal amount of insurance to be purchased. In addition, we argued that efficient allocation of resources is only one goal of society and that it may be reasonable to sacrifice some efficiency if it leads to a better distribution of income. It is important to distinguish these two justifications for government intervention in the disability insurance markets, because they have quite different, and in some cases opposite, effects on prices and economic behavior.

One public sector intervention attempts to reduce inefficiencies by adjusting the relative price arrived at in a free, but inefficient, market. It is expected that at the new price, total productivity will increase. A second form of intervention creates inefficiencies in a free and efficient market by the alteration of prices. It is expected that the new price will decrease total productivity, but will increase the income of some group deemed worthy. We define the first form of intervention as the *insurance goal* of government policy and the second intervention as the *welfare goal*. The weight given to these two goals within and across programs is at the heart of income transfer policy discussion in the United States, and increasingly in other industrialized countries with a well-developed system of disability programs.

Some government income transfer programs are welfare-based, while others take the form of social insurance. Government programs based solely on welfare principles redistribute income to assure that all citizens—disabled or not, unemployed or not—are able to achieve some minimum level of social adequacy. On the other hand, government programs based solely on private insurance principles directly relate the benefits which any individual expects to receive to the contributions expected of the individual. These programs also provide a guaranteed level of social adequacy, but only to those who fall victim to the insured risk. Coverage in such insurance-based programs is based on the individual's previous earnings or contributions. Hence, any income distribution or labor supply changes which occur should be similar to those caused by private insurance.

A public disability program based solely on private insurance principles would provide protection to the entire population based on quid pro quo individual payments set equal to the market value of the protection which is provided. Such a program would be motivated by a market failure—the lack of a private insurance market—which causes an underprovision of insurance. In achieving its goal it does *nothing* directly to enable those unable to afford such protection to purchase it. On the other hand, a public disability program based solely on welfare principles is a social mechanism which allows part of the cost of a disability to be shared by the healthier portion of society, with no quid pro quo expected from the disabled themselves. Provision of such protection, however, tends to cause market inefficiencies—for example, labor supply reductions—which reduce total productivity.

Disability insurance programs provide an excellent example of the conflicts between these two policy goals. Revenue usually comes from a wage tax; benefits are based on covered earnings with varying health (and, in some cases) earnings tests on beneficiaries. Each of these characteristics is fundamental to a narrow, health-related insurance system, targeted to workers, which links benefits to past and current contributions and not to current income needs. In such a system, severity of impairment would affect the size of the benefit, but no means test would be imposed. Such a system would meet insurance goals.[1] In addition, if eligibility criteria were firm, such a system would guard against outside market forces—for example, a slack labor market with high unemployment—affecting the likelihood of getting benefits. Hence, by design it would do little to aid a wider potential constituency. The system would not offer benefits to those who are homemakers, to the long-term unemployed, or to those who are simply poor.

Consider, by way of illustration, the case of the United States. As we have seen, a large Disability Insurance (DI) program has existed since 1958. However, prior to the 1970s, welfare benefits had been provided to a relatively small segment of the impaired population, through federal grants to states for the Aid to the Blind (AB) and the Aid to the Permanently and Totally Disabled (APTD) programs. Because the United States had no general income support policy to aid low-income people, pressures to accommodate a wider welfare goal were put on all parts of the disability system, both the insurance-based DI program and the welfare programs.

One result of this pressure was the introduction in 1974 of the Supplemental Security Income (SSI) program. SSI protected all those previously eligible for AB and APTD by standardizing the minimum benefit requirements across states. SSI also increased the level of benefits and the potentially eligible population in most states. This expansion was a major step in providing a welfare-based program to severely disabled people who were either ineligible for DI or for whom prior welfare benefits were considered inadequate—it placed a "safety net" under the severely disabled. Because SSI bases benefits on need, those eligible for DI on health grounds, but lacking a sufficient record of contributions to the Social Security system, are protected. This program, unlike the other major income support programs in the United States, breaks the link between market work and program eligibility.

The passage of the SSI program was a major expansion of the federal government's commitment to redistributing income to those with low income within a disability context. It is significant that in establishing this program, society accepted a commitment to assure some minimum income to individuals based solely on their health condition. SSI, however, is a universal moral commitment neither to the poor nor to those in ill health. Like DI, it still attempts to separate the "qualified" impaired population—the severely disabled—from all other poor people. Hence, it is of little help to those who are poor but not severely disabled, or those who are severely disabled but not poor.

The ameliorative response in the other countries studied has also been through a combination of insurance and welfare-oriented programs. As we discussed in Chapter 4, in each of the mature systems (Federal Republic of Germany, Netherlands, Sweden), the principal disability-related income support program is not income-tested and is wage-related. In each of these countries, a payroll tax is used to finance the program and benefits are related to previous wage earnings. However, in each country, this primary pension program is also sensitive to welfare goals. In Sweden, the insurance aspects of the Supplementary Benefit Pension are coupled with a flat Regular Disability Pension. As a result, major welfare benefits are provided within the basic disability social insurance program; this tendency is also found in other parts of the income security system. In the

Netherlands, this is also the case. The insurance aspect of the Disability Security program (which replaces some percentage of earnings) is tempered by a generous minimum benefit for low earners. The Federal Republic of Germany, in contrast, has as its major income maintenance program the Public Pension Insurance program, which is much closer to a true insurance program than its counterparts in any of the other countries, including the United States. However, the Federal Republic also has a separate income-tested welfare program—Public Aid—which operates much like SSI in the United States.

In the United States, the debate over the degree to which government should redistribute income through the disability system has been a continuous one. The same has not been true in most of the other countries until recently. Those who favor an increase in the commitment to income redistribution support a broadening of the definition of a "qualified" impairment as a means of establishing a universal "safety net" for all poor people. The political commitment to such reform clearly varies with general economic conditions.

The pressure for increasing the commitment to redistribution tends to be exercised on two levels. The first is direct pressure on the government to explicitly increase the commitment of public programs to aid those with some health problem who are either disadvantaged or long-term unemployed—to increase the tilt in favor of the poor in the distribution of disability benefits. Proposals in this vein suggest relaxing the eligibility criteria of ongoing programs, increasing benefit levels of those at low relative to high levels of economic status, or creating new programs or new bases for benefit entitlement. The second type of pressure involves the administration of programs and the interpretation by both beneficiaries and administrators of the rules by which they are operated. It is this type of pressure—reflected in data on program applications or acceptances—on which we focused in Chapter 5.

This second type of pressure is subtle to analyze and is related to the first. The dynamic is perhaps something like the following: Through a conscious policy choice, disability program benefit levels are increased or the stringency of eligibility determinations is reduced. These changes are interpreted by those who view themselves potentially eligible as a willingness of society to bear a greater share of the cost of disability. Seeing an increased probability of being eligible or of receiving larger benefits if eligible, these people increase their efforts to gain access to the now more attractive programs—numbers of recipients and levels of expenditures rise. To the extent that some of these individuals change their behavior in response to program characteristics, a problem of "moral hazard" arises. Clearly, the more generous these programs, the greater the moral hazard problem.

In Chapter 5, we observed that both the mix of welfare and insurance goals and the size of disability programs based on an ameliorative commitment vary across the mature economies included in this study. The extremely generous welfare aspects contained in the social insurance programs in Sweden and the Netherlands provided replacement rates near or exceeding 100 percent at low income levels. In the 1960s, replacement rates in these countries exceeded one-half, even for high-income beneficiaries. The social insurance programs in both the Federal Republic of Germany and in the United States were much less generous across all income levels in the 1960s. However, welfare programs were available in both of these countries, and for those eligible low-income workers, replacement rates of 70 percent were not unusual. Ten years later, while all four countries showed some increases in replacement rates, the United States showed the greatest increase in the replacement rate of its social insurance system across all income groups.

One inevitable consequence of this increase in program generosity in the United States has been that, as unemployment increases, DI and SSI have become important potential sources of aid to those most vulnerable to economic downturns—older workers, the impaired, the unskilled. It is such marginal workers who have applied for DI benefits. In reponse to this pressure, eligibility criteria have been relaxed through the use of vocational considerations. Much the same pattern is observed in several of the other countries included in this study. In effect, then, decisions in disability insurance programs have been intimately related to government policy toward low-income or unemployed people in general. In the absence of alternative antipoverty or income-replacement programs, or in the absence of a strategy to achieve full employment through more general fiscal and monetary measures, the pressure to shift disability insurance programs toward more general welfare programs seems inevitable.

The recognition that disability pensions have an effect on work incentives—and that this effect is likely to be exacerbated by the income distribution features of the program—will be important in future discussions over the benefit levels and eligibility criteria of such programs. This is especially so in light of the strong commitment to income redistribution in all of the countries studied. Thus, the thrust of the disability policy debate in the next decade is likely to center on the asserted need to continue to include specific welfare-related goals in insurance-based disability programs, and to relax the conditions for access to and the benefits provided by these programs. The continued policy of liberalization will confront increasing costs in a low-growth, high-unemployment situation.

The Corrective Response: Employment Policy

In addition to issues regarding the generosity of disability benefits, and the means of providing income support, policymakers must also consider the relationship of disability policy to employment policy. This relationship arises in several guises. We have seen that disability income support expenditures increase during economic downturns. Similarly, there is evidence that liberal eligibility requirements and generous benefit levels in disability income support programs tend to discourage work effort and encourage early retirement. On the other hand, government support for vocational rehabilitation, job training, sheltered workshops, or employment subsidies is designed to increase the employment of disabled workers. Clearly, policies designed to induce increases in the labor supply of disabled workers interact with those that provide income support. And aggregate employment or selective employment policies interact with all of these. In this section, we will deal with some of these relationships of disability and employment policy, raising a number of issues which must, in some way, be resolved as policy evolves. Again, the discussion will be illustrated with United States policies, although the basic questions cut across countries.

Disability Pensions and Work Effort

Since disability income support programs offer income protection to those workers most susceptible to unemployment during economic downturns —older health-impaired workers or the unskilled—the demands for program benefits increase during recessions because of the inclusion of work-related characteristics of individuals and labor market considerations. Moreover, as the standards for disability eligibility have been lowered to include work-related characteristics, the sensitivity of these programs to market conditions has increased. And, as the share of an individual's costs of disability borne by these programs increases, they become more attractive alternatives to continued work or job search.

The degree to which disability income support programs should be used by government to explicitly encourage the early retirement of older, impaired workers is an important public policy question. Currently, most workers in industrialized countries are covered by unemployment insurance benefits which provide income support for some limited period of time. Often, benefit duration is expanded in periods of high unemployment. Rather than rely on continually expanding general unemployment insurance, one policy alternative is to use disability income support or early retirement programs as a means of dealing with long-term unemployment. In fact, in most of the mature industrialized countries studied, long-term unemployment is an important and, in the case of the Netherlands, is de facto a sufficient condition for eligibility to disability programs. Especially for workers who are difficult to reemploy (i.e., older and impaired workers, or those with low skills), disability programs have been viewed as a means of extending unemployment benefits—or, more accurately, providing early retirement benefits—to those not "expected" to work by society. A less charitable interpretation would describe this policy as "hiding unemployment."

The evidence of the role of disability programs in reducing measured unemployment and the labor supply of older workers was reviewed in Chapter 5. Coincident with the increase in such benefit programs, the labor force participation rate of older workers has fallen dramatically over the last decade for most of the countries in our study. For men aged 60 to 64, the average annual percentage reduction in participation rates in the Western European countries with mature disability systems—the Federal Republic of Germany, the Netherlands, and Sweden—was -5 percent, -4 percent, and -1 percent, respectively, during the 1970s. In the United States it was -2.2 percent. These patterns compare with only very minor changes in the participation rate of prime-age groups in these countries during that period. A nontrivial cause of this change is probably the explicit increase in replacement rates and the reduction of eligibility criteria in both disability and retirement programs in these countries.

In an environment with high unemployment and slow economic growth, the political value of using the disability system to hide unemployment or induce early retirement is recognized, but the costs of such a policy must also be considered. Workers with employment handicaps who once find themselves on the disability rolls are likely to remain permanently out of the labor force. Thus, short-run political gains may be achieved at the expense of a larger and more permanent class of inactive workers, or of workers permanently subsidized in public sector jobs.

Rehabilitation and Sheltered Workshops

In most of the countries studied, disability policy has long incorporated a commitment to increasing the ability of disabled workers to overcome their impairments through rehabilitation and job training. However, the resources committed to this effort relative to income support vary substantially across countries. In calculating the benefits and costs of these efforts, little weight has been given to the social and psychological benefits of work. Nevertheless, evaluations of these programs appear to show that they did succeed, even with a narrowly framed benefit-cost framework.

The reluctance to employ rehabilitation efforts as more than a cost-reducing mechanism in the United States is in sharp contrast to many of the other countries studied—especially Sweden and the Federal Republic of Germany—where the social and psychological benefits of work are given great weight, and where rehabilitation and job placement form a central element in disability policy. In these countries, protection for the disabled has typically been provided within the context of a protected job (or at least preparation for such a job) which the government would supply either directly or through the use of subsidies or the enforcement of quotas.

In the United States, a major change in this regard appeared during the 1970s. The creation of "work activities centers" within sheltered workshops and the change in priorities which targeted training services to those most severely handicapped shows that work for its own sake is being given more weight in United States disability policy. Earlier studies which purported to show that investments in the severely handicapped were likely to yield high returns in market productivity, however, have subsequently been shown to be overly optimistic. It remains to be seen whether such priorities will continue in the present era of shrinking budgets.

Another movement toward a "European approach" to disability was the requirement in the United States that persons collecting SSI benefits due to a disability be required to take vocational rehabilitation training when it was judged to be beneficial. This is a first step toward compulsory work as part of a disability strategy in which work is valued for its own sake.

Whether this work-oriented trend in the United States will continue, or whether its relative emphasis in other countries will be maintained, will be an important subject for debate in future years. Indeed, where labor demands for able-bodied workers are low and long-term general unemployment widespread, the case for a work-oriented approach seems less compelling. If disabled workers, even with training and rehabilitation, are unable to secure work, the benefits of such activities may fall substantially and the net benefits of these programs may become net costs.

Direct Job Creation

Direct intervention in the labor market has always been a far more controversial policy in the United States than in the other countries studied. Hence, the relative emphasis on income support rather than jobs for the disabled in the United States, where even those who favor a jobs strategy for the working-age disabled have emphasized the less interventionist approach of providing rehabilitation and job training. This is in sharp contrast to most of the other countries in our study, where direct job creation measures are common. Employment quotas have long been on the books (although country statistics suggest that such quotas appear to be weakly enforced) and specific government jobs are available exclusively to the disabled in most of the other countries.

In the mid-1970s, however, several policy initiatives were enacted in the United States which, implicitly at least, argue that government has a role in directly stimulating the demand for less productive, employment-handicapped workers in order to increase their work effort. These employment subsidy, public employment, and "equal access" programs were discussed in Chapter 7. While these measures from the 1970s can be considered as first steps toward government intervention designed to encourage the employment of disabled workers, they are largely untested.

However, the evidence suggests that major increases in the employment of those currently receiving disability benefits are not likely to occur without major intervention to stimulate private sector employment demands. While increased rehabilitation efforts could be effective for younger disabled workers, no easy solutions exist for older, unskilled disabled workers. Even in Sweden and the Federal Republic of Germany, where commitment to reintegrating the disabled into the work force through workplace adaptation, counseling, and occupational resettlement is a strong one, there has been a substantial reduction in the labor force activity of these groups. In these countries, and in the Netherlands, very generous income maintenance systems offer an "early retirement" option to such fringe workers. And increased labor market activity is not likely to occur without major employment creation programs or a significant improvement in overall economic conditions. And, as evidence in Chapter 7 indicated, the costs of the former of these approaches are large absolutely, and in relationship to their benefits as well. On the other hand, efforts to encourage such fringe workers to stay in the labor force by simply tightening eligibility requirements or reducing benefit levels in income support programs are not likely to achieve this goal without substantial hardship, unless the overall growth in employment in the 1980s is substantially greater than during the 1970s.

An Ameliorative and Corrective Response: "Equal Access"

Direct intervention in the labor market during the 1970s moved United States disability policy into a new role in trying to integrate the disabled into the economy of work. While new in the United States, this commitment was longstanding in the mature social welfare systems of other industrialized countries. However, another commitment made by the United States in the 1970s—equal access—reflects a new dimension of disability policy virtually unknown in the other countries. Beginning in the 1970s, the United States took steps to guarantee the disabled "equal access" to education, employment, and mobility. By declaring that a barrier-free environment is a fundamental "right" of disabled people, the government, for the first time, stated its intent to adjust social norms to accommodate the handicapped, rather than to provide assistance to the handicapped in their efforts to adjust to social norms.

This commitment to such a major structural change signaled a radical new element in disability policy, an element first supported by political action groups among the handicapped population. While these groups defined the equal access issue, by the end of the 1970s the government itself accepted the proposition that handicapped people should be assured full integration into the productive processes of society. Using the civil rights legislation of the 1960s as a model, the government—through legislation in the 1970s—guaranteed handicapped people "equal opportunity" in employment and education, and "equal access" to all public facilities.

As a means of sharing or reducing the costs of disability, this new approach goes well beyond income support or rehabilitation, or even direct job creation. Indeed the commitment to the "equal access" principle goes well beyond even the most elaborate corrective response efforts of some of the countries studied to develop networks of sheltered workshops and to subsidize selected industries which make their workplaces accessible to handicapped employees. All of these programs—or programs like those in Israel which make in-kind transfers available to the "transportably" handicapped—are based on the more traditional concept of integrating the handicapped into society. They do not reflect a commitment to a legal concept of "equal access." Only in Sweden, which recently required new mass transit and multiple-dwelling units to provide minimum access to the handicapped, has this new and fundamentally different approach to handicapped rights become an issue.

The equal access provision, in effect, states that society at large will bear the costs required to make major social institutions and facilities adapt so that the characteristics of the disabled no longer impose as large a set of costs on them. In one sense, this approach is an ameliorative response—the burden of disability costs borne by the disabled is reduced, with additional costs being shifted to the nondisabled. It can also be viewed as a corrective response if it is believed that, by the provision of equal access, the total costs of disability are reduced by an amount greater than the costs required for adaptation. To the extent that implementation of "equal access" objectives entails large costs, such a benefit-cost framework is appropriate for evaluating the effectiveness of this strategy.

The principle of "equal access" and subsequent legal attempts to define it are modeled on civil rights legislation. Few criticize the goals espoused in the rhetoric of this legislation. But there are major differences between preventing discrimination against racial and sexual groups and providing equal access to the handicapped. The primary difference concerns the social and taxpayer costs of this provision, in comparison to its benefits. Clearly, if the provision of equal access to, say, public transportation facilities would lead to a substantial increase in ridership by the handicapped, and in turn increased employment, income, and social activities of this group, diversion of nontrivial amounts of society's resources to this purpose could be justified. However, if these gains did not occur, attainment of the "equal access" goal would have to serve as an inviolable principle. The question then is: What is the cost required to attain "equal access," and are these costs less than the value of achieving this goal?

As suggested, the costs of assuring equal access to the handicapped are likely to be of a different order of magnitude than assuring equal opportunity to racial minorities and women. Equality of treatment by sex and race does not require adapted workplaces, specialized machines, specialized training, altered cafeteria and toilet facilities, alternative means for building entry and movement between floors, and wide aisles and doors. While discrimination plays a role in employment, education, and mobility decisions regarding both the handicapped and racial and gender groups, the relative contribution of such attitudes toward the unequal status of the handicapped would seem to be substantially smaller than in the case of the other groups. Conversely, the real costs of securing true equal opportunity for the handicapped are likely to be substantially higher. At the present time the magnitude of these costs is unknown and, in essence, will depend critically on the regulatory decisions which are made in this area, and on how they are enforced. Efficient decisions regarding the enforcement of this regulatory legislation requires knowledge of the aggregate costs associated with various levels of regulatory stringency.

The need for some process to ensure that both the costs and the benefits of various regulatory and enforcement options become reflected in such decisions is essential if serious resource misallocations are to be avoided. While the need for such a decisionmaking mechanism would appear to be required primarily by efficiency concerns, it should be noted that important equity impacts are also at stake. While some social benefits targeted on a group tend to benefit all members of the group equally, others may disproportionately benefit certain subgroups of the larger group. For example, while the benefits of general retirement programs are distributed relatively equally among the aged population, welfare-based programs benefit the poor among the aged population. Similarly, policy choices among various "equal access" options are likely to convey substantially different benefits to subgroups among the disabled. The degree and type of impairment are likely to be important variables. Analyses of benefits and costs of "equal" options must distinguish those among the handicapped who will be helped or hurt in moving to higher or lower levels of guaranteed access.

Summary

In this chapter, we have distinguished those areas of potential conflict on which public debate on disability policy will focus during the next decade. In discussing the future evolution of disability policy, a number of basic propositions should be clearly recognized. First, the share of disability costs to be borne by taxpayers depends primarily on an overall view of the optimal level of government intervention in society, and the role disability programs should play in this intervention. Hence, it must be recognized that disability income support—or employment or equal access—policy is really only a subset of larger economy-wide income support or employment policy. Similarly, the regulatory nature of equal access legislation is a subset of a broader use of regulation to alter market processes. A second proposition is that each of the major disability policy issues is related to the others. A strong equal access program, for example, could no doubt reduce the costs of both income support and job subsidy programs. Similarly, a strong disability income support system would render superfluous many job support and equal access goals. And, of course, several economic conditions and especially the strength of labor market demand will greatly affect the optimal mix of these programs.

The final mix of programs should rest on the share of costs society is willing to remove from handicapped people, as well as notions regarding the most efficient and equitable means of sharing this burden. These judgments are ultimately based on values, and no single correct and socially optimal solution can be found by data and analyses. In ongoing discussions on the level and type of disability assistance, for example, it should be recognized that those who emphasize jobs for the disabled cannot claim that they clearly are more efficient than income transfers. Rather, their position simply reflects a stronger commitment to a "right-to-work" goal—defined as the availability of a job to any citizen who wants one—and a greater willingness to assign the associated costs of this commitment to society as a whole. Nevertheless, in the discussion over such a strategy, any decision to place major emphasis on the right to work for the disabled should explicitly confront the costs of that choice. Such a choice may well be made, however, if the commitment to the right-to-work objective is sufficiently strong. Hence, the ultimate resolution of this issue should not be decided only on cost-effectiveness grounds, but on some social judgment regarding the size and configuration of public intervention evolved through the political process. However, recognition of the full costs of such a commitment is important if the political process is to promote the general welfare. The same is true regarding the "equal access" issue.

As government disability programs have expanded in all dimensions—transfers, training, employment creation, and equal access—the costs have been substantial, both in budgetary and in resource-allocation terms. The primary disability policy issues in the 1980s concern just these costs. Is there a willingness to accommodate new commitments in a climate of public sector austerity? If retrenchment—or reorientation—is required, should corrective or ameliorative responses be emphasized? And within each strategy, what are the benefits of various options relative to their costs? The issues addressed in this chapter were presented within this benefit and cost context. The public choices which must be made will be difficult ones. And all along the line the benefits of various options to both the disabled and society as a whole, both in terms of measured and unmeasured effects, must be appraised and compared with the costs. This comparison, in turn, must be tempered by both value judgments and commitments already made.

Note

1. If this were a pure insurance system, taxes paid would be exactly offset by the insurance value received and the "tax" would not alter the payments received for working. It would only change the mix of income payments.

References to Part One

Aarts, Leo. 1982. "Working Capacity of the Disabled." Paper presented at the Expert Group Meeting on Disability Research, Zoetermeer, The Netherlands, November 16-17.

Allan, Kathryn H. 1976. "First Findings of the 1972 Survey of the Disabled: General Characteristics." *Social Security Bulletin, 39* (October), 18-37.

Bassi, Laurie J. 1982. "CETA—Is It a Cost Effective Method for Increasing the Earnings of Disadvantaged Workers?" Research Paper, The Urban Institute, Washington, D.C.

Berkowitz, Monroe, Johnson, William, and Murphy, Edward. 1976. *Public Policy toward Disability.* New York: Praeger.

Berkowitz, Monroe, and Rubin, Jeffrey. 1977. "The Costs of Disability: Estimates of Program Expenditures for Disability, 1969-1975." Mimeographed. Bureau of Economic Research, Rutgers University, August.

Bishop, John, and Haveman, Robert. 1979. "Selective Employment Subsidies: Can Okun's Law be Repealed?" *American Economic Review, 69,* 524-530.

Burkhauser, Richard, and Haveman, Robert. 1982. *Disability and Work: The Economics of American Policy.* Baltimore: The Johns Hopkins University Press.

Christainsen, Gregory B. 1981. "Sheltered Workshops as a Means of Benefiting the Disabled." Ph.D. Dissertation, University of Wisconsin-Madison.

Conley, Ronald W. 1965. *The Economics of Vocational Rehabilitation.* Baltimore: The Johns Hopkins University Press.

Conley, Ronald W. 1969. "A Benefit-Cost Analysis of the Vocational Rehabilitation Program." *Journal of Human Resources, 4,* 226-252.

Culyer, Anthony. 1974. "Economics, Social Policy, and Disability." In D.S. Lees and B. Shaw, eds., *Impairment, Disability, and Handicap.* London: Heinemann.

Gennard, John, and Wright, M. 1978. "A Sheltered Workshop." *Department of Employment Gazette,* Vol. 86. London: HMSO.

Gliedman, John, and Roth, William. 1980. *The Unexpected Minority.* New York: Harcourt, Brace, Jovanovich.

Haveman, Robert H. 1977. "A Benefit-Cost and Policy Analysis of the Netherlands' Social Employment Program." Special Report no. 15, Institute for Research on Poverty, University of Wisconsin-Madison.

Haveman, Robert H., and Wolfe, Barbara. 1982. "Disability Transfers and the Work Effort Response of Older Males: A Reconciliation." Paper presented at

NBER Conference on the Incentive Effects of Government Spending, November.

Haveman, Robert H., and Wolfe, Barbara. 1983. "Disability Transfers and Early Retirement: A Causal Relationship?" Discussion Paper no. 723-83, Institute for Research on Poverty, University of Wisconsin-Madison.

International Labour Office. Various Years. *Yearbook of Labour Statistics.* Geneva: ILO.

Kemper, Peter, Long, David A., and Thornton, Craig. 1981. *The Supported Work Evaluation: Final Benefit-Cost Analysis.* New York: Manpower Demonstration Research Corporation.

Kisner, L. 1973. *A Review of Benefit-Cost Analysis in Vocational Rehabilitation.* Supplemental Studies for the National Commission of State Workmen's Compensation Laws. Washington, D.C.: GPO.

Lando, Mordechai E., Cutler, Richard R., and Gamber, Edward. 1982. *1978 Survey of Disability and Work: Data Book.* U.S. Department of Health and Human Services, Social Security Administration. Washington, D.C.: GPO.

Lando, Mordechai E., and Hopkins, Timothy R. 1977. "Modeling Applications for Disability Insurance." Conference Paper for the American Economic Association Meetings, December.

Leonard, Jonathan. 1979. "The Social Security Disability Program and Labor Force Participation." Working Paper no. 392, National Bureau of Economic Research, Cambridge, Mass.

Luft, Harold. 1978. *Poverty and Health.* Cambridge, Mass.: Ballinger.

McMillan, Alma W., and Bixby, Ann Kallman. 1980. "Social Welfare Expenditures, Fiscal Year 1978." *Social Security Bulletin, 43* (May), 3-17.

Morgan, P. L., and Markeham, P. 1978. *Economic and Financial Analysis of Sheltered Employment.* Research Paper no. 5, Department of Employment, London, United Kingdom.

Nagi, Saad. 1979. "The Concept and Measurement of Disability." In Edward Berkowitz, ed., *Disability Policies and Government Policies.* New York: Praeger.

Oi, Walter. 1978. "The Impact of Disability on Full Income." Conference Paper for the American Economic Association Meetings, August.

Parsons, Donald O. 1980a. "The Decline in Male Labor Force Participation." *Journal of Political Economy, 88,* 117-134.

Parsons, Donald O. 1980b. "Racial Trends in Male Labor Force Participation." *American Economic Review, 70,* 911-920.

Riley, Lawrence E., and Nagi, Saad Z., eds. 1970. *Disability in the United States: A Compendium of Data on Prevalence and Programs.* Columbus, Ohio: Division of Disability Research, Department of Physical Medicine, The Ohio State University.

Sawhill, Isabel V. 1979. Testimony before the Joint Economic Committee, U.S. Congress, *Hearings,* February 21, pp. 74-84.

Scheffler, Richard M., and Iden, George. 1974. "The Effect of Disability on Labor Supply." *Industrial and Labor Relations Review, 28,* 122-132.

Scott, Robert A. 1969. *The Making of Blind Men.* New York: Russell Sage Foundation.

Slade, Frederic P. 1982. "Labor Supply under Disability Insurance." Working Paper no. 860, National Bureau of Economic Research, Cambridge, Mass.

Smith, Mary F. 1980. "Prohibiting Discrimination against Handicapped Individuals by Recipients of Federal Financial Assistance: Section 504 of the Rehabilitation Act of 1973." Report no. 80-191 EPW, Congressional Research Service, Education and Public Welfare Division, Washington, D.C.

Treitel, Ralph. 1975. "Effect of Financing Disabled Beneficiary Rehabilitation." *Social Security Bulletin, 38* (November), 16-28.

U.S. Congressional Budget Office. 1979. *Urban Transportation for Handicapped Persons: Alternative Federal Approaches.* Budget Issue Paper for Fiscal Year 1981, Washington, D.C.

U.S. Department of Health, Education, and Welfare. 1970. *Statistical History of the Federal-State Vocational Rehabilitation Program, 1920-1964.* Washington, D.C.: GPO.

U.S. Department of Health, Education, and Welfare. 1980. *Fifty Years of Vocational Rehabilitation in the United States.* Social and Rehabilitation Services Administration. Washington, D.C.: GPO.

U.S. Department of Labor, Bureau of Labor Statistics. 1969. *Employment and Earnings.* January. Washington, D.C.: GPO.

U.S. Department of Labor, Bureau of Labor Statistics. 1979. *Employment and Earnings.* January. Washington, D.C.: GPO.

U.S. Department of Labor, Employment Standards Administration. 1977. *Sheltered Workshop Survey,* Vol. 1, June.

U.S. General Accounting Office. 1976. *Report to the Congress: The Social Security Administration Should Provide More Management and Leadership in Determining Who Is Eligible for Disability Benefits.* HRD-76-105.

U.S. Office of Management and Budget. 1979. *The Budget of the U.S. Government: Fiscal Year 1980.* Washington, D.C.: GPO.

Veldkamp, G.M.J. 1970. "Towards Harmonization of Social Security in the EEC." In Alfred Kamin, ed., *Western European Labor and the American Corporation.* Washington, D.C.: Bureau of National Affairs.

Waldron, I., Herald, J., and Dunn, D. 1982. "How Valid Are Self-Report Measures for Evaluating Relationship between Women's Health and Labor Force Participation?" *Women and Health, 7,* 53-66.

Wolfe, Barbara. 1979. "Impacts of Disability and Some Policy Implications." Discussion Paper no. 539-79, Institute for Research on Poverty, University of Wisconsin-Madison.

Wolfe, Barbara. 1980. "How the Disabled Fare in the Labor Market." *Monthly Labor Review, 103* (September), 48-52.

Wolfe, Barbara. 1982. "The Demand for Disability Transfers: Recent Research and Research Needs." Paper presented at Expert Group Meeting on Disability Research, Zoetermeer, The Netherlands, November 16-17.

Worrall, John D. 1978. "A Benefit-Cost Analysis of the Vocational Rehabilitation Program." *Journal of Human Resources, 13,* 285-298.

Part Two

Disability Policy in Seven Countries

Chapter 9

Disability Policy in the Federal Republic of Germany

Martin Pfaff and Walter Huber

Public policy toward disabled workers has a long tradition in Germany. It has always constituted an important part of the overall social security system, and has evolved both in terms of the quality of the provisions made and of the quantity of economic resources devoted to its pursuit. Indeed, a central part of Bismarck's social reforms may be found in the Disability and Old Age Insurance Act of June 22, 1889 (passed into law in January 1891), which instituted a system of workers' pensions. This earlier law was extended and amended by the Disability Insurance Act of July 19, 1899, and included in the National Insurance Act in 1911. Since then, a series of legal provisions has expanded public disability programs considerably, and in addition to public programs, private disability insurance is now offered, largely as a complement to life insurance.

As a part of the overall social security system, public programs aiding disabled workers are financed on a pay-as-you-go basis through contributions make by employees and employers and through public transfers allocated out of the federal budget to social security funds. Financing problems arise in the context of the overall developments affecting the system of social security—for example, large-scale unemployment tends to exert twin pressures on social insurance institutions, on the one hand via reduced employees' and employers' contributions, and on the other hand through the increasing number of individuals classified by doctors or judges as disabled.

The issues which this chapter addresses may be summarized by the

Martin Pfaff is Professor of Economics, University of Augsburg and International Institute for Empirical Social Economics; Walter Huber is Health Economist, Dr. Karl Thomas GmbH Chemisch-pharmazeutische Fabrik, Biberach an der Riss.

following questions: (1) How large is the disabled population of the Federal Republic of Germany? (2) What are its demographic and socioeconomic characteristics? (3) What form does public policy toward the disabled take? Specifically, what kinds of transfers (monetary, real, implicit) are provided by the various institutions? (4) How are these public programs financed? (5) Do benefits conveyed by various programs cumulate in favor of particular groups of disabled? (6) Is the system of rehabilitation efficient and effective? (7) What factors are responsible for the rising costs of such rehabilitation programs? (8) What are the effects of rehabilitation and the monetary programs on the supply of labor? (9) What policy measures would improve the situation of the disabled in the future?

The Disabled Population of the Federal Republic of Germany

Definitions of Disability

An exact medical definition of disability appears impossible to find. Even the terms "health" and "ill health" cannot be defined exactly because they represent overlapping categories. Moreover, "ill health" and disability can be distinguished mainly in terms of their time sequences. Hence we conclude that degrees of disability cannot be measured exactly in medical terms: Medical experts can only observe individual symptoms, interconnections, and the determinants that affect the normal functioning of organs or systems of organs, but there is a subjective element that must be considered, too.

Neither the National Insurance Act, the Employees' (White Collar Workers') Insurance Act, nor the Social Code contains a definition of disability; in fact, the term is not even used in these laws. The Social Report of the federal government (Bundesminister für Arbeit and Sozialordnung, 1978, p. 185) defines three types of health status:

1. "General disability" is defined as physical impairment which leads to a permanent loss of health and to a handicap (which, however, is not caused by a work accident, an occupational disease, or by political events).
2. "Illness" is defined as a temporary loss of health which is expressed in a temporary inability to work.
3. "Work accidents and occupational diseases," fall in between the extremes defined by disability and illness; they cause a permanent reduction or loss of the ability to earn income while generally leading to a temporary inability to work.

There is similarly no satisfactory definition of the concept of handicap:

> Existing legal definitions of handicap are either based on a principle which attributes a handicap to a certain cause or involves a mere enumeration; or

> else, a certain handicap is automatically associated with the responsibility of a particular public institution which undertakes the rehabilitation of handicapped persons. (The Lord Mayor of Berlin, 1978, p. 2)

Other legislative definitions which distinguish the degree of disability by the detriment to health are utterly misleading. For example, there exist three definitions—in the Federal Security Act, the National Insurance Act, and the Equalization of Burdens Act—whose only common feature is an attempt to define "a general disability to work" (see Goetz, 1975, p. 162). Although the terms for a reduction in a general ability to work found in the accident insurance system and the Veterans' Welfare Program are linguistically dissimilar, they are identical in meaning. In practice, however, these terms barely correspond to the actual decrease in the general ability to work (ibid.).

Accordingly, we define disability solely in terms of its effects: We call those workers disabled whose ability to pursue gainful employment has either been reduced or lost temporarily (but for an unforeseeable span of time) or permanently. Among the determinants of disability are congenital diseases, work accidents, occupational diseases, aftereffects of political events, diseases caused by environmental damages, and the aftereffects of diseases.

Disability represents a dynamic concept. It refers to a specific individual: Only in conjunction with a particular type of work will a specific disability arise. For instance, the loss of a finger would cause a greater degree of disability to a pianist than to a judge. From this example the dynamic nature of disability becomes evident: Through reeducation an individual's specific occupation may change, and hence reduce the degree of his disability.

Size of the Population

The size of the disabled population can be estimated from statistics of rehabilitation programs, by summing up of persons who receive a disability pension, and from census and microcensus data. Section 51 of the Handicapped Persons Act requires the collection of statistics pertaining to rehabilitation programs. But as Christian (1976, p. 85) has pointed out, one cannot derive from these statistics the total number of the disabled within the Federal Republic. Such a procedure would neglect two essential problems: (1) not all individuals being rehabilitated can be considered disabled since many of them do not show generally recognizable characteristics of a disability—some are only threatened by disability; (2) the number of individuals rehabilitated is likely to be considerably smaller than the number of disabled, as the statistics comprise only those rehabilitation measures which have been completed.

Furthermore, only those institutions responsible for rehabilitation measures have been included in the statistics (Statistisches Bundesamt, 1978a, p. 56, n. 2)—Public Pension Insurance including Aid for Aged Farmers, Workmen's Accident Insurance, the Veterans' Welfare Program, and the Federal Office for Employment. Many disabled persons do not participate in rehabilitation programs, and thus are not included in the rehabilitation data. For these reasons, an estimate obtained in this fashion is bound to underestimate the size of the disabled population.

Estimating on the basis of recipients also entails several problems that result in an underestimation of the size of the disabled population: Only those persons can be included who receive pensions from Public Pension Insurance, Workmen's Accident Insurance, or from the Veterans' Welfare Program. Thus disabled persons who have not been employed and hence have not accumulated any claims against security institutions and are supported by Public Assistance or by members of their families are not being counted. Furthermore, the cumulation of more than one transfer to the same person cannot be identified from these data, which may result in either an over- or an underestimation of the size of the disabled population.

The supplementary survey to the microcensus of 1976 provides us with perhaps the best data source for estimating the size of the disabled population (Statistisches Bundesamt, 1978b). Estimations were determined by identifying those individuals who declared themselves to be disabled (subjective element), and those who may be considered disabled on the basis of objective criteria such as the receipt of a disability pension from Public Pension Insurance, Workmen's Accident Insurance or the Veterans' Welfare Program, quite independently of whether or not such individuals declare themselves to be disabled.

Table 9.1 provides an overview of the size of the disabled population on the basis of this latter alternative: We may consider either the 3.3 million persons who declared themselves disabled, or the 4.25 million persons who

Table 9.1. Size of Disabled Population (in thousands and percentages)

Group	Total		Male		Female	
	No.	%	No.	%	No.	%
Disabled (Self-reported)	3,299	77.6	1,700	51.5	1,599	48.5
Recipients of a disability pension who did not report themselves disabled	953	22.4	655	68.7	298	31.3
Total	4,252	100.0	2,355	55.4	1,897	44.6
Those officialy recognized for pensions	2,542	59.8	1,708	67.2	834	32.8

Source: Statistisches Bundesamt (1978b, p. 493).
Note: Male and female columns include share of percentage totals in column 1.

additionally include those who receive disability pensions. There is yet a third alternative, which entails counting only those disabled who have been officially recognized as such. But this would underestimate the size of the population, since individuals who were disabled just prior to the survey and whose applications for official recognition were not yet processed are not included.

If we accept that the disabled population consists of 4.25 million persons, this amounts to 7 percent of the total population. These figures, however, could underestimate the extent of the problem simply because the interviewer asked individuals only how they would judge themselves. Their judgments could not be verified, since the interviewers themselves had no medical training (ibid., p. 492). Moreover, most individuals are not likely to admit to a mental handicap within their families (Klee, 1974, p. 27). Add to these inhibitions another possible cause of underreporting: the economic situation (the high rate of unemployment, the pressures for rationalization, and the drive for increased performance and competition) prevailing at the time of the interview (Runde, 1979, p. 10).

The decennial census of the population could have provided us with the most reliable estimate of the size of the disabled population. However, during the preparatory phase of the last census, in 1970, political interest pertaining to this segment of the population was less pronounced. Hence, no questions pertaining to disability status were included, even though the inclusion of such a question had been demanded (Klee, 1974, p. 27). Since then the government has focused on this problem: Section 51 of the Handicapped Persons Act of April 29, 1974, calls for a survey of the disabled to be undertaken every 5 years. This survey was undertaken for the first time in the latter part of 1979 (Deutscher Bundestag, 1978b, p. 5). On the basis of this instrument the size and situation of the disabled population in the Federal Republic of Germany can be assessed for the first time in a more objective fashion.

The following analysis is based on microcensus data of May 1976 relating to physically, mentally, and emotionally disabled individuals. A limitation should be recalled: Some 953,000 individuals are excluded—even though they were the recipients of disability pensions and thus could be classified as being disabled by objective standards—because they did not declare themselves disabled. Thus we focus our discussion on the 3.3 million persons who did so report themselves.

Demographic Characteristics

A change in the structure of the disabled population in terms of sex composition can be observed in comparing the results of the microcensuses of 1962, 1966, and 1976 in Table 9.2.[1] The declining share of men can be explained by the gradual demise of those, predominantly men, disabled as a

Table 9.2. Disabled Persons by Sex, 1976 (in thousands and percentages)

Year	Total	Male		Female	
		No.	%	No.	%
1962	3,722	2,849	76.6	872	23.4
1966	4,054	2,791	68.8	1,263	31.2
1976	3,299	1,700	51.5	1,599	48.5

Source: Statistisches Bundesamt (1978b, p. 502).

consequence of World War II. This change in composition becomes even more evident from the comparison by age and sex, shown in Table 9.3. The increasing share of females aged 65 and above among the disabled population is also attributable to the increasing share of older women in the population as a whole. Possibly, older women show a greater tendency to be disabled than men; alternatively, they may tend to admit the presence of disability more readily than men do. On the whole, however, the share of women among the disabled is clearly lower than that of men.

Up to the age of 65 the share of disabled women is considerably less than that of men. Since, at the same time, the share of women in the labor force is substantially smaller than that of men, one can conclude that the probability of disablement is relatively greater for the working population than for the nonworking population, or that women are less susceptible to health problems (see Table 9.4).

Table 9.3. Disabled Persons by Age and Sex, 1976 (in thousands and percentages)

Age	Total		Male		Female	
	No.	%	No.	%	No.	%
below 15	138	4.2	74	4.4	63	3.9
15-25	176	5.3	99	5.8	79	4.9
25-40	314	9.5	174	10.2	140	8.8
40-50	357	10.85	217	12.8	141	8.8
50-65	1,070	32.4	625	36.8	443	27.7
over 65	1,244	37.7	511	30.0	733	45.8
Total	3,299	100.0	1,700	100.0	1,599	100.0

Source: Statistisches Bundesamt (1978b, p. 493, and 1979, p. 225).

Table 9.4. Disabled Persons of Working Age (in thousands and percentages)

Age	Total	Total[a]	Male	Male[a]	Female	Female[a]
15-25	176	2.00	99	2.21	79	1.83
25-40	314	2.36	174	2.52	140	2.19
40-50	357	4.55	217	5.45	141	3.65
50-65	1,070	11.11	625	15.72	443	7.83
Total	1,917	4.85	1,115	5.77	803	3.97

Source: Statistisches Bundesamt (1978b, 1979), and own computations.
[a]As a percentage of the resident population.

In each age group the total number of disabled individuals consists (1) of those persons who became disabled within this age span, and (2) of surviving persons who were already disabled at a younger age. The number of disabled persons will increase to the extent that improvements in curative medicine have lowered the mortality rate of the disabled by a greater extent than preventive care has tended to reduce the risk of disability.

Undoubtedly, the official recognition of a handicap is of import with regard to the eligibility for the receipt of monetary and real transfers. In May 1976 barely half of the 3.3 million disabled had been officially recognized, as is evident from Table 9.5. The share of individuals not officially recognized is particularly high in the case of those under 25 years and above 65 years of age. Furthermore, more women are in this group.

Table 9.5. Disabled Persons by Age Group and Official Recognition (in thousands and percentages)

Age	Official Recognition				
	Total	Without		With	
		No.	%	No.	%
below 25	314	187	59.6[a]	127	40.4[a]
25-40	314	159	50.6	155	49.4
40-65	1,427	550	38.6	876	61.4
65 and over	1,244	813	65.3	431	34.7
Total	3,299	1,709	51.8	1,589	48.2
			Male		
below 25	173	102	59.0	71	41.0
25-40	174	80	45.8	95	54.2
40-65	842	212	25.2	630	74.8
65 and over	511	254	49.6	258	50.4
Total	1,700	647	38.1	1,053	61.9
			Female		
below 25	141	85	60.3	56	39.7
25-40	140	79	56.7	61	43.3
40-65	584	338	57.9	246	42.1
65 and over	733	560	76.3	174	23.7
Total	1,599	1,062	66.4	536	33.6

Source: Statistisches Bundesamt (1978b, p. 495).
[a]Share of column 1.

The determinants of these patterns are by no means obvious. The following suppositions may, however, be indicated: (1) individuals below age 25 have not yet been able to accumulate adequate claims against the pension system; (2) individuals aged 65 and above are already receiving old age pensions and hence do not have any claims toward a disability pension; (3) due to their lower labor force participation, women have fewer opportunities to press claims for disability payments.

Even though the reports of disability were based on the subjective response of the individuals surveyed, the degree of disability which is based on the degree of reduction in ability to earn (expressed as a percentage of

Table 9.6. Disabled Persons by Sex and the Degree of Reduction of Ability to Earn, 1976 (in thousands and percentages)

Sex	Total(A)	Without Reduction of Ability to Earn		Total(B)		With Reduction of Ability to Earn[a]							Application for Pension Submitted, Not Yet Decided
						below 50%	50-59%	60-69%	70-79%	80-89%	90-99%	100%	
Total	3,299	1,709	51.8[b]	1,589	48.2	31.4	14.3	8.9	10.7	8.6	3.5	18.6	4.1
Male	1,700	647	38.1	1,053	61.9	30.7	16.1	9.5	10.4	9.1	3.9	16.9	3.4
Female	1,599	1,062	66.4	536	33.6	32.9	10.7	7.7	11.2	7.5	—	21.8	5.4

Source: Statistisches Bundesamt (1978b, p. 496).
[a]Percentage of Total (B).
[b]Percentage of Total (A).

that of a healthy individual) has to be officially recognized. Table 9.5 indicates that of the 3.3 million considered here, 3 out of 6 have not received any official recognition of the reduction in their ability to earn; 1 out of 6 has been recognized as having his ability to earn reduced by less than 50 percent, and 2 out of 6 have been recognized as being seriously disabled (see Table 9.6)—the latter amounting to more than 1 million persons.

The microcensus provides rather limited information with regard to the cause of a disability. Only three categories are presented: "accidents," "war injuries," and "other causes." Because of these undifferentiated categories, 61 percent of disabled males and 92 percent of females associated their disability with "other causes." The limited validity of these answers can be deduced from the fact that only 471,000 mentioned "war injuries" as cause, whereas the statistics of the Veterans' Welfare Program recognize over 1 million persons qualifying for veterans' benefits.

Economic Status

The disabled participate in the labor force far less than the able-bodied. While 41.8 percent of the total population were employed in 1976, only 28.2 percent of the disabled worked (see Table 9.7), males representing a larger

Table 9.7. Disabled Labor Force by Type of Impairment and Labor Force Participation, 1976 (in thousands and percentages)

Type of Impairment	Total		Male		Female	
	No.	%	No.	%	No.	%
Impaired function of upper limbs and shoulder	103	42.2[a]	88	51.1[a]	—	—
Impaired function of lower limbs and hips	242	31.0	192	43.5	50	14.6
Impaired function of spine	124	38.5	88	56.7	36	21.4
Other types of physical impairments (incl. hairlip)	236	27.1	152	39.9	84	17.1
Chronic disease and deformations of internal organs	86	26.3	68	32.4	—	—
Impaired sight (incl. blindness)	54	27.3	41	42.8	—	—
Impaired hearing, including deafness and inability to speak	33	26.0	24	38.0	—	—
Mental and behavioral impairments, including seizures	47	12.4	28	18.7	—	—
Total	931	28.2	687	40.4	245	15.3

Source: Statistisches Bundesamt (1978b, p. 497)
[a]Share of disabled labor force among total disabled population (correspondingly grouped).

share of the disabled labor force than females (40.4 percent and 15.3 percent, respectively). Type of disablement is a factor in the different rates of labor force participation: The physically handicapped obviously have better chances of being integrated into work and society than those with damaged sensory nerves or with abnormal behavior patterns.

One would assume that the granting of official recognition would imply the seriousness of a disability; thus one would expect smaller rates of employment among those with official recognition. When comparing Table 9.7 with Table 9.8, however, the opposite pattern emerges: Persons with a recognized disability exhibit a higher rate of employment than the total number of disabled persons (34.3 percent vs. 28.2 percent, respectively). This could be the result of an overrepresentation of working-age persons within the group of persons with a recognized disability (see Table 9.5). Furthermore, these persons are more likely to be required to seek employment. We may presume (without being able to prove it) that this group is also overrepresented among the applicants for official recognition, as they are more likely to fulfill the requirements for the award of benefits (for example, in the public pension system). An above average employment rate may be noted also for those with a decrease in ability to work of 50 to 79 percent: This involves mainly men with war injuries who have, however, become fully integrated into the normal labor force (Statistisches Bundesamt, 1979, p. 225).

The distribution over professions of persons in the labor force corresponds to that of able-bodied workers (see Table 9.9). However, if the survey data of the Bureau of the Census could be broken down further, it would probably reveal that the disabled are more likely to occupy lower-level positions.

Corresponding to the low level of labor force participation, only a small

Table 9.8. Disabled Persons with Official Recognition, by Degree of Decreased Capability and Participation in the Labor Force (in thousands and percentages)

Degree of Decreased Ability to Work (%)	Total		Male		Female	
	Total (No.)	Employed (%)	Total (No.)	Employed (%)	Total (No.)	Employed (%)
below 50	500	38.4	323	52.6	177	13.0
50-59	227	52.4	170	57.1	58	37.9
60-69	142	44.4	100	51.0	42	—
70-79	169	42.0	109	51.4	60	—
80-89	136	25.0	96	30.2	40	—
90-99	56	—	41	—	—	—
100	295	10.8	178	12.9	117	—
Total	1,525	34.3	1,018	42.8	507	17.4

Source: Statistisches Bundesamt (1979, p. 226).

Table 9.9. Disabled and Ablebodied Labor Force by Professional Status, 1976 (in thousands; percentages in parentheses)

Professional Status	Labor Force			
	Disabled		Ablebodied	
	All			
Self-employed and unpaid family workers	164	(17.6)	3,354	(13.5)
Civil servants, white collar workers[a]	378	(40.6)	10,891	(43.9)
Blue collar workers[b]	389	(41.8)	10,567	(42.6)
Total	932	(100)	24,821	(100)
	Male			
Self-employed and unpaid family workers	117	(17.0)	1,895	(12.2)
Civil servants, white collar workers[a]	267	(38.9)	6,011	(38.8)
Blue collar workers[b]	303	(44.1)	7,579	(48.9)
Total	687	(100)	15,485	(100)
	Female			
Self-employed and unpaid family workers	47	(19.3)	1,459	(15.6)
Civil servants, white collar workers[a]	111	(45.3)	4,880	(52.3)
Blue collar workers[b]	87	(35.4)	2,997	(32.1)
Total	245	(100)	9,336	(100)

Source: Statistisches Bundesamt (1976b, p. 497).
[a]Including trainees in recognized commercial and technical apprenticeships.
[b]Including trainees in recognized industrial apprenticeships.

share of the disabled derive their main source of income from work (see Table 9.10). The microcensus reports only the main sources of income. Thus we may assume that the total net income reported reflects the joint effects of several sources of income. Not surprisingly, the highest monthly net incomes are found for persons for whom wages and salaries are the main source of income. The majority of disabled persons however, lives on pensions (47 percent); among these, 36 percent showed a net income of more than DM 1000 per month. (However, this figure may also reflect past employment).

Disability gives rise to various problems, including a decrease in income and difficulty in coping with everyday situations. One would assume that this segment of the population would be more likely to live with healthy members of an extended family than would be the case for the able-bodied. The empirical evidence indicates the opposite, however: While 57.1 percent of the total population live in one- or two-person households, almost three-quarters of the disabled (72.8 percent) belong to the category of small households. While almost 7 percent of the total population are disabled, households with disabled persons account for 8.6 percent. Thus, these households are smaller on the average than those of the able-bodied, frequently consisting only of disabled persons.

Table 9.10. Disabled Persons[a] by Main Source and Level of Income (in thousands; percentages in parentheses)

Main Source of Income	Total	Monthly Net Income (DM)								Self-Employed Farmers and Family Members Who Help in the Work		No Income or Income Not Reported	
		under 600		600-1000		1000-1400		1400 and over					
Employment	859	49	(5.7)	117	(13.6)	254	(29.6)	367	(42.7)	46	(5.4)	27	(3.1)
Pension	1,549	360	(23.2)	547	(35.3)	320	(20.7)	243	(15.7)	25	(1.6)	54	(3.5)
Family support	585	87	(14.9)	—	—	—	—	—	—	—	—	475	(81.2)
Other income[b]	306	119	(38.9)	51	(16.7)	—	—	—	—	—	—	106	(34.6)
Total	3,299	616	(18.7)	731	(22.2)	591	(17.9)	623	(18.9)	75	(2.3)	662	(20.1)

Source: Statistisches Bundesamt (1979, p. 227)
[a]With and without official recognition.
[b]Including unemployment insurance and other types of public aid.

Public Policy Toward the Disabled

Public programs aiding the disabled are administered by a large variety of institutions. Apart from the four branches of social insurance—public pension, public health, workmen's accident, and unemployment—we also note other institutions, such as those administering welfare programs. Further complexity results from the principles which give rise to benefits: Some institutions grant benefits on the basis of what kind of damage and aftereffects occurred, such as benefits granted on the basis of the so-called finality principle; other institutions structure their pattern of benefits primarily on the basis of what caused the damage, that is, in line with the principle of causality. This implies, for example, that the same kind of damage would lead to different benefits depending on whether it was caused by a work accident, a disease, or by an ordinary accident. Nonetheless, we attempt to systematize these institutions and identify the programs undertaken by them in aid of the disabled population.

First, we turn to those parts of the social security system which have been structured in line with Section 2 of the Rehabilitation Equalization Act of August 7, 1974, namely, Public Pension Insurance, Workmen's Accident Insurance, Public Health Insurance, Public Aid to Aged Farmers, Veterans' Benefit and Veterans' Welfare Programs,[2] and Public Employment Programs (under the Employment Promotion Act). After discussing these programs we turn to those for civil servants, and to the programs for the disabled within the framework of Public Assistance.

Public Pension Insurance

The purpose of Public Pension Insurance is the maintenance, improvement, and restoration of the ability to work and earn if or when this ability is endangered or reduced by illness, other infirmities, or by a general weakening of physical and mental capabilities (Dembowski and Schröder-Printzen, 1976): "If this goal cannot be attained either via medical or occupational rehabilitation, monetary transfers should compensate for the lost ability to earn income" (p. 38; authors' translation). The idea behind this policy should be evident: In the interest of both the individual as well as society it appears more meaningful and preferable to aim primarily at safeguarding and restoring physical and mental health and the ability to engage in gainful employment. This guiding principle has been set forth in Section 7 of the Rehabilitation Equalization Act.

These medical rehabilitation measures are regularly granted under the public pension programs: (1) medical treatment; (2) medication and medical dressing; (3) medical treatment including therapeutic gymnastics and physical mobility therapy, speech therapy, and occupational therapy; (4) orthopedic and other aids; (5) tests of the ability to bear stress and work therapy. They are mainly provided in health spas and other special institutions, which also provide board and lodging of the individuals to be rehabilitated.

Among the occupational rehabilitation benefits offered to enhance the individual's ability to seek and find gainful employment are the following: (1) assistance to keep or obtain a job, including services and benefits which help persons to take up work as well as incentive payments to employers for employing additional workers; (2) assistance in finding and trying out a job; (3) assistance designed to enable an individual to either adjust to the labor market opportunities, or to seek further education, training, and retraining, including the completion of formal schooling; (4) other types of assistance designed to enhance disabled individuals' chances for seeking gainful employment in the general labor market or within special workshops. Furthermore, the costs for board and lodging are included whenever participation in rehabilitation programs requires a stay away from home. These various types of assistance are aimed at integrating the individual into the labor market permanently, if possible. In selecting one or more of the types of assistance available, an individual, his aptitude, preferences, and his past experiences are considered.

Supplementary benefits include interim payments, the coverage of certain costs which are immediately connected with an occupational rehabilitation program, and the coverage of travel expenses; under certain circumstances payments for household help and other benefits necessary to ensure the success of rehabilitation measures are made.

A disablity pension is paid in case of specific (limited) or general disability (under the Miners' Pension Insurance—in case of the reduced ability to work as a miner). An individual is entitled to receive pensions for specific disability if and when he has been insured for a least 60 months. According to the National Insurance Act (Section 1246), the White Collar Workers Insurance Act (Section 23), and the National Miners' Insurance Act (Section 46), the term "specific disability" can be defined as follows: "An insured individual is considered to be specifically disabled if, due to illness or other infirmities or due to physical or mental deficiencies, his ability to work has been reduced to less than half of that of a physically and mentally healthy person with similar education, training, knowledge and skills."

A higher degree of invalidity is associated with the concept of general disability, defined in the Imperial Insurance Act (Section 1247), the White Collar Workers Insurance Act (Section 24), and the National Miners' Insurance Act (Section 47) as follows: "An insured individual is generally disabled if, due to illness, other infirmities or physical or mental deficiencies, he is not able to carry out regular work in the foreseeable future or if he is at most able to earn a negligible income through work."

Despite or because of these legal definitions, the terms remain controversial. Bley (1975, p. 113), for example, considers the concept of specific disability to be one of the most questionable in the entire social insurance law. Aye and his colleagues (no date, n. 3, sec. 1246), speak of a legal fiction which presupposes that a person whose ability to earn has been reduced by more than half is unable to carry out his occupation.

The computation of the pension accruing in the case of specific or general disability follows the general pension formula, with the exception that per year of insurance different incremental rates are applied, in contrast to old age pensions.

Workmen's Accident Insurance

Workmen's Accident Insurance covers work accidents, including accidents en route to work, and occupational diseases. Under Section 537 of the National Insurance Act, accident insurance provides several types of benefits. Specifically, it compensates for the damages caused by work accidents (1) through measures to restore the ability to work and enhance employment and job opportunities, and through easing the aftereffects of the accidents; and (2) through workmen's compensation payments to injured individuals.

The aim of medical treatment is to remove or reduce the injury or health impairment as well as the reduction in the ability to work caused by the accident, to avoid its becoming worse, to ameliorate the consequences wrought by the accident, and also to integrate the injured into a job commensurate with ability to perform according to one's skills, aptitudes, preferences, and prior activities, if possible, on a permanent basis. In addition, occupational aid can be granted to further the professional advancement of the injured. Various administrative agencies of Workmen's Accident Insurance can also provide medical treatment for those who are insured under Public Health Insurance. Even if medical treatment is not directly provided, reimbursement to health insurance funds from accident insurance funds is still required for expenses incurred in connection with the work accident.

If an injured individual is unable to work he is entitled to receive an interim payment from the first day that his disability has been attested to by a medical examination. In practice the interim payment begins usually 6 weeks after the accident, since within this period an employee is entitled to receive his (gross) income from his employer even while sick.[3] Because the main purpose of the interim payment is to provide a substitute for wages earned, it is immediately discontinued when an injured individual again receives income from work. Furthermore, an interim payment is not made when the injured person is entitled to receive an equal amount of sick pay from public health insurance.

The interim payment amounts to 80 percent of the regular wages or salaries of the injured party. However, as far as the law goes, wages and salaries are only considered up to a maximum amount of DM 36,000 annually, unless the accident insurance agency expressly provides for higher ceiling amounts.[4]

Compensation payments are made to injured individuals whenever their reduced ability to work continues beyond the 13th week after the work accident. Pension payments are granted when an insured individual's ability to work is reduced by at least 20 percent (in which case he receives a partial pension). An individual's ability to work prior to the accident is defined as 100 percent, whether the individual was healthy prior to the accident or partially disabled. The pension payment is computed by comparing the earnings before the accident with the reduced earnings after the accident. If an individual becomes generally disabled as the result of an accident he receives the full pension, which amounts to two-thirds of his annual wage income (subject to a ceiling).

Public Health Insurance

Both Workmen's Accident Insurance and Public Health Insurance may be liable for benefits in the same case, even though one covers work accidents and the other general illness. There are remarkable parallels in the provisions of both institutions. The Rehabilitation Equalization Act extended the types of benefits to be granted by Public Health Insurance to equal those awarded by the other medical rehabilitation institutions within the social insurance system. The same law also provides (similar to the provisions of Workmen's Accident Insurance) for treatment in hospitals, health spas, and in special institutions as part of the Public Health Insurance benefits. However, health insurance provides these benefits only in a subsidiary fashion—that is, only if no other institution within the social security system is responsible for providing them.

Like accident insurance, health insurance provides for monetary transfers in the case of sickness, with the aim of compensating the sick for the loss of work income. The sick pay has a transitional character, however; there is no provision for a permanent monetary transfer to be paid in the case of reduced ability to work (as would be the case with public pensions or Workmen's Accident Insurance). A sick individual is entitled to pay only if his illness causes him to be unable to work. Accordingly, the sick pay is discontinued (similar to the interim payment in the Workmen's Accident Insurance) when an individual receives work income even during his sickness.

The Federal Office of Employment

The Employment Promotion Act provides the legal foundation for the activities of the Federal Office of Employment. Among its goals is the occupational integration of physically, mentally, or emotionally handicapped individuals. Any institution wishing to initiate an occupational rehabilitation program must consult the Office first. Furthermore, whenever a question of competence between occupational rehabilitation institutions arises, the Federal Office becomes responsible for the occupational rehabilitation until the question can be resolved.

The Federal Office provides job placement and counseling, support for vocational training and education, and assistance for entering new jobs. To assure complete and permanent integration into a job following rehabilitation, a specially designated employment agent of the Federal Office develops a comprehensive design for integration, in cooperation with a medical doctor and a psychologist, who note the professional opportunities open to the disabled person.

The Office also gives financial support for the individual who participates in training or education designed to further his or her occupational opportunities.

Aid for Aged Farmers

Recently, disability benefits under the auspices of Aid to Aged Farmers have been changed to provide benefits in line with those offered by other programs. The Farmer Health Insurance Act of August 10, 1972, includes self-employed farmers under Public Health Insurance. In addition to general coverage, farmers are provided with help to continue running their farm or household during an illness or treatment in a health spa, or they are reimbursed for costs incurred for such a purpose.

The Rehabilitation Equalization Act provides farmers with rehabilitation opportunities in line with those granted by Public Pension Insurance for Blue Collar Workers. In case of disability, Aid for Aged Farmers provides cash benefits prior to the farmer's reaching the age at which he becomes eligible for receiving an old age pension.

Veterans' Benefit and Veterans' Welfare Programs

The public program designed to help veterans and other persons who suffer as a result of military action attempts to reduce the ill effects of health impairments by means of medical treatment, rehabilitation, and monetary transfers. For this group as well, the Rehabilitation Equalization Act provides for an equalization of benefits with those granted under Public Health Insurance. Benefits granted to veterans are geared to the specific situation of the individual; their aim is to enable the individual to maintain an adequate life style. Veterans' pensions are based on the severity of the damage and on the typical needs of the disabled. Accordingly, the benefit scales are rather complex in structure.

Programs for Civil Servants

In marked contrast to the provisions of Public Health Insurance, the benefit programs for civil servants are not based on the concept of specific or general disability, but rather on "inability to perform duty." The civil servant can be considered unable to perform his duty when he has been ill for 6 months, or if he has not performed his duties for more than 3 months and there is no chance that he will become fully restored within a further period of 6 months (Bundesminister für Arbeit und Sozialordnung, 1977, p. 152).

In contrast to Public Pension Insurance, the pay level of the civil service pension depends on only two factors: (1) that part of the last income earned which is considered for retirement income; and (2) the number of years of service which may be applied toward retirement income. In case of disability prior to normal retirement age, it is assumed that the civil servant has reached a retirement income level which he would have reached at his normal retirement age and that he worked until his normal retirement age. Undoubtedly, these provisions result in more favorable treatment of civil servants as ompared to other employees. Civil servants also enjoy other privileges which we shall not elaborate on here.

Public Aid

The main task of public aid is to provide cash and real transfers in cases where no other institution within the system of social security is responsible. It provides for persons or groups not adequately covered by the other social security institutions (for example, individuals who have never been employed, or individuals who have not yet accumulated sufficient claims against other social security institutions because they have not worked a sufficient time).

Public Assistance (cash benefits granted toward the general sustenance of an individual) is based on formulas depending only on the income and wealth of the individual; other forms of public aid depend on individual needs. Medical care is granted to individuals who, due to illness or disability, are unable to live without help from others. The type of service granted depends on the degree of the impairment. Public aid aims not only at restoring ability to work, but also at integrating the handicapped into the social life of the community. In addition to the benefits granted by other institutions toward occupational and medical rehabilitation, public aid covers other types of assistance, such as help in finding and keeping an apartment which is suitable to the specific needs of a handicapped or disabled person.

Monetary and Real Transfers under Various Programs

The Social Budget provides an overview of the types of benefits available to disabled individuals:

1. Explicit transfers or grants are made directly to an individual by particular social security institutions.

2. Implicit transfers or grants result whenever the financial obligation imposed on an individual is reduced in view of a particular consideration (for example, a tax reduction or a reduction in the social insurance contributions available to some individuals but not to others); implicit transfers are also termed indirect benefits within the Social Budget.

3. Monetary transfers are cash benefits paid to individuals.

4. Real transfers include transfers in kind as well as services which are granted by the social security institutions to citizens, either free of charge or else for a fee (which may or may not cover full costs).

5. Indirect benefits are not identified as such in the Social Budget; a breakdown is made by granting institutions into monetary or real transfers only, and not into explicit versus implicit transfers.

Table 9.11 provides an overview of the magnitude of the various types of benefits granted in the case of work accidents and disability. Monetary transfers designed to compensate for an income loss amounted to 73 percent of all transfers in 1969; their relative share was reduced to 63 percent by 1977 and they were expected to amount to only 61 percent of all transfers in 1982. In absolute amounts monetary transfers increased by 72 percent within the time period 1969-75, while real transfers increased by 155 percent. This discrepancy in the increment of monetary versus real transfers is likely to persist into the future: In the period 1975-1982

Table 9.11. Transfers in Connection with Work Accidents and Disability, by Type of Transfer, 1969-1982 (in DM millions)

Type of Transfer	1969	1973	1975	1977	1982
Monetary transfers	7,666	11,416	13,178	15,541	21,263
Regular income maintenance payments	7,568	11,279	13,013	15,350	21,005
Single payments	98	137	165	191	258
Real transfers	2,775	4,873	7,075	8,978	13,481
Cash refunds	240	371	569	719	1,052
Goods and services	1,840	3,302	4,958	6,158	9,498
General services and benefits	695	1,200	1,548	2,101	2,931
Total	10,441	16,289	20,253	24,519	34,743

Sources: Bundesminister für Arbeit und Sozialordnung (1976, p. 249, for 1969 and 1973; 1978, p. 213, for 1975, 1977, and 1982)

[a]Preliminary estimates: for assumptions on which projections are based, see Bundesminister für Arbeit und Sozialordnung (1978, pp. 66, 166).

monetary transfers are expected to rise by 61 percent while real transfers should increase by 91 percent. In 13 years (1969-82) monetary transfers should thus grow by 177 percent while real transfers should increase more strikingly by 385 percent.

The benefits granted by various institutions covering work accidents and disability are shown in Table 9.12. In 1969 the share of indirect benefits among the total benefits granted for work accidents and disability amounted to 2.9 percent; it was expected to decline to only 1.3 percent by 1982. During the same time period, indirect transfers were expected to

Table 9.12. Transfers Related to Work Accidents and Disability, by Type of Institution (in DM millions)

			1969	1975	1977	1982
0	Total Social Budget	(a)	DM 4,352	DM 8,435	DM 9,706	DM 12,944
		(b)	6,089	11,819	14,815	21,799
1	Social Security	(a)	3,393	5,932	6,895	9,131
		(b)	4,416	7,539	6,307	12,954
10	General Systems	(a)	3,282	5,730	6,664	8,818
		(b)	3,058	4,614	6,040	8,413
101	Pension Insurance	(a)	195	322	441	618
		(b)	3,058	4,614	6,040	8,413
1011	for Blue Collar Workers	(a)	131	222	292	412
		(b)	1,881	2,808	3,623	5,114
1012	for White Collar Workers	(a)	36	62	99	144
		(b)	640	1,035	1,425	2,079
1013	for Miners	(a)	28	38	50	62
		(b)	537	771	992	1,220
103	Health Insurance	(a)	826	1,804	2,100	2,754
		(b)	—	—	—	—
104	Workmen's Insurance	(a)	2,261	3,604	4,123	5,445
		(b)	—	—	—	—
12	Special Systems	(a)	1	4	5	7
		(b)	29	87	108	140
122	Aid for Farmers	(a)	1	3	4	6
		(b)	22	67	83	108
123	Specific Pension Programs	(a)	—	1	1	1
		(b)	7	20	25	32
13	for Civil Servants	(a)	100	169	190	256
		(b)	1,189	2,352	2,612	3,615
14	Supplementary Systems	(a)	9	28	35	50
		(b)	140	486	546	786
2	Employer Benefits	(a)	920	2,404	2,703	3,667
		(b)	240	392	464	640
3	Compensation (Veterans'	(a)	—	—	—	—
	Compensation)	(b)	38	78	81	110
4	Public Aid	(a)	39	99	108	147
	(Public Assistance)	(b)	1,093	3,435	4,582	7,651
001	Direct Benefits	(a)	4,352	8,435	9,706	12,944
		(b)	5,787	11,444	14,434	21,354
5	Indirect Benefits	(a)	—	—	—	—
	(Tax Savings)	(b)	302	375	381	444

Source: Bundesminister für Arbeit und Sozialordnung (1978).
Note: (a) = work accident; (b) = disability.

increase by 47 percent, while direct transfers were expected to grow by 238 percent. The following patterns of growth are expected to hold for the same period: Direct benefits within the social security system should increase by 182 percent, employers' benefits by 271 percent, benefits to veterans by 190 percent, public aid by 589 percent, health insurance by 233 percent, and accident insurance by 141 percent. Within the public pension insurance system, expenditures for white collar workers were expected to experience a particularly large increase (by 229 percent) compared to those for blue collar workers and miners.

These forecasts indicate that there will be a somewhat unequal growth of benefits within the various social security institutions. But how are these expansions to be financed in the future? We turn to this question in the next section.

The Financing of Disability Programs

Public programs aiding disabled workers are financed partly through social security contributions by employers and employees, and partly through public transfers from the general exchequer. Based on the principle of the solidarity of the insured, social security contributions are made by employers and employees on the basis of statutory provisions. The principle of solidarity is limited, however, insofar as those incomes which are beyond a certain ceiling are not subject to social security contributions (and benefits). Thus the effect of the financing of public programs aiding the disabled shows a regressive pattern. Rehabilitation benefits, however, are granted without regard to the social security contributions made in the past. Given the two distributional patterns of financing on the one hand, and of benefits on the other, it is not surprising that one arrives at a pattern of redistribution which may be considered to be socially undesirable (see Brück, 1976, p. 70).

There are several reasons and justifications for public subsidies out of the general budget to programs aiding disabled individuals (ibid., p. 69).

1. The aftereffects of wars have resulted in a reduced number of contributors and in a higher rate of disability. Since these effects are not the sole responsibility of the insured persons, the government and the population as a whole are responsible for such grants in aid to the ocial security institutions.

2. The government guarantees the benefits to individuals. Hence it has to come to the assistance of the parafiscal institutions responsible for dispensing social security benefits, especially where the general economic policy of the government can be held responsible for added expenditures of the social security institutions. As an example we may cite the increase in disability pension payments to the disabled which results in the case of high unemployment.

The various types of revenues accruing to social security institutions are not tied to particular expenditure categories. We therefore cannot examine the financing of individual programs, but must look at the entire revenue structure of the various social security institutions. The public pension insurance system is financed primarily by contributions, amounting to 18 percent of gross wages or salaries (up to an income ceiling). One-half is paid by the employer, the other half by the employee. Ever since the last century the federal government has provided subsidies to public pension insurance institutions. However, they have decreased strikingly within the last decades: Since 1955 the share of federal government subsidies in the revenue of the blue collar and the white collar public pension insurance programs has decreased by two-thirds (Bundesminister für Arbeit und Sozialordnung, 1977, p. 110).

Workmen's Accident Insurance is financed mainly by contributions which are paid solely by the employer. The contributions are raised at a rate which is adequate to cover the expenditures of the previous business year. The amount of the contributions depends on the wages of the insured in a particular enterprise, and on the degree of risk of accidents in the enterprise. This implies that the principle of causality is applied to the benefits or expenditure side, as well as to the revenue side of accident insurance, since there appears roughly an equivalency between contributions made and the number and the severity of the accidents that actually occurred in an enterprise.

The institutions of the public health insurance system are financed via contributions by their members. In rare cases public grants in aid are made. The average contribution rate amounted to about 11.3 percent as of July 1, 1976 (ibid., p. 204). These contributions are paid half by the employers and half by employees. Public Pension Insurance pays contributions to Public Health Insurance for its retirees; similarly, the recipients of interim payments are covered in return for health insurance contributions paid by the institution responsible for their rehabilitation; contributions for the unemployed are borne by the Federal Office of Employment.

The benefits awarded by Public Aid, veterans' programs, and civil service programs are financed out of the budget of the federal government of state and local governments.

Efficiency and Effectiveness of Rehabilitation Measures

The rehabilitation of disabled workers provides a more meaningful and fulfilling life to the disabled individual in terms of work and general integration in society. In addition, rehabilitation may contribute toward reducing the financial burdens imposed on the public pension insurance institutions. Even though rehabilitating individuals involves expenditures, it can lead to a reduction of total costs in a case where an individual is able to resume work, due to the reduction in pension payments and the increase in social security contributions that individuals make from their work income after the successful completion of their rehabilitation.

The economic efficiency of rehabilitation measures can be assessed with the aid of benefit-cost analysis. However, it would appear that such an analysis is of limited usefulness insofar as the social benefits of rehabilitation are generally stressed over and beyond the economic aspects. Thus an economic analysis can only assess part of the benefits accruing to society from rehabilitation. On the other hand, in periods of budgetary pressures and high tax burdens, an economic justification appears called for in cases involving investments in human capital. Since expenditures for rehabilitation do involve such investments they can also be judged by the criteria applicable to public investment projects.

Earlier Work: A Critique

Two types of efficiency analysis have generally been performed in the Federal Republic of Germany regarding rehabilitation measures.

1. From the point of view of an institution responsible for such expenditures, a rehabilitation measure is considered to be efficient if the inflow of funds into the institutional budgets resulting from a successful rehabilitation measure exceeds the outflow in the form of expenditures necessary for said measure.

2. A more satisfactory type of analysis of rehabilitation measures, which looks at the economic productivity of such measures, is one where a rehabilitation measure is considered to be efficient if, after rehabilitation, an individual makes a contribution to gross national product (less the contribution which he would have made had he not been rehabilitated) which exceeds the economic costs necessary for his rehabilitation.

Undoubtedly, these two approaches to the assessment of the economic efficiency of rehabilitation measures can be faulted when compared with the requirements of an encompassing benefit-cost analysis (a question we return to later). Several studies of the efficiency of rehabilitation measures are based on relatively small samples. Pflueger (1960) took gross income as a measure of the benefits of rehabilitation measures and arrived at a relationship of benefits to costs of 36:1; he also computed the relationship of the inflows of the institutions responsible for these costs to the costs of rehabilitation (3:1). Undoubtedly, these conclusions are not statistically representative as they were based on 136 individual cases only. Furthermore, Pflueger analyzed only cases which had been successfully completed, and assumed that the successful rehabilitation measure would continue up to age 65.

Similarly, Jochheim (1958) analyzed 105 cases of occupational rehabilitation of war victims. Here, again, unsuccessful cases were left out of consideration. He concluded that, from the point of view of the institution responsible for meeting the costs of rehabilitation, the costs of retraining would be amortized within a period of 5 years.

One must conclude, however, that both of these investigations lend little support to the thesis postulating the high productivity and efficiency of rehabilitation measures (Rahner, 1965, p. 85). In further analysis, Wolfslast (1968) analyzed the medical rehabilitation measures carried out by the public pension insurance institutions on the basis of cross-sectional data. In contrast to the two authors cited above, he did consider, however, additional investments which become necessary if rehabilitation measures have to be repeated: On this basis the costs of rehabilitation will increase by roughly 25 percent (p. 192). However, he only analyzed measures which involve an improvement or restoration of the general ability to work, and not such measures which merely aim at maintaining the ability to work. As a measure of benefits, he took the income losses which were avoided through rehabilitation measures and found that 6 years after completion of the rehabilitation measure these were three times as high as the costs required for said rehabilitation measures.

A more satisfactory benefit-cost analysis was carried out by Heier and Winterstein (1973) for blind persons and victims of tuberculosis. They were able to take as a basis of the benefit computation the actual incomes accruing to individuals (compared to the incomes generally accruing to all employees, as was the case for other investigations). Heier and Winterstein concluded that, depending on the specific profession, economic investments in rehabilitation of the blind and of tuberculosis victims would be amortized within a period of 2 to 5 years. Furthermore, for individuals living outside the cities, this amortization period would be roughly 2 months longer than would be the case for individuals living within big cities (p. 260). From the point of view of the institutions carrying out these rehabilitation measures, such a measure was fiscally efficient after 4-7 years.

A third type of efficiency analysis of occupational rehabilitation measures was carried out by Ehrenberg (1974) on two simulation models. This approach goes beyond the point of view of the individual institution incurring costs, insofar as he analyzed the cash inflows and outflows of all public households, including parafiscal institutions (this approach clearly neglects, however, the benefits accruing at the level of the overall economy). On the basis of the cash receipts and costs accruing to all public institutions, he arrived at a benefit-cost ratio of 9.1:1 and 10.8:1 for the two model types analyzed. However, Ehrenberg disregards the possibility that an individual will not be able to secure employment after completion of his rehabilitation measure. Furthermore, by assuming that the disability occurs at age 20 or 35, and that the individual once rehabilitated will continue to work until age 63, he arrives at overstated estimates of benefits accruing from rehabilitation.

In a second analysis he attempts to take account of the uncertainties associated with these hypothetical computations, particuarly regarding the assumption that individuals will continue to work up to age 63. He obviates these problems by looking only at periods of amortization. Thus he concludes that the costs incurred for rehabilitation measures will be covered by return flows into public budgets within 4 years in the case of an employee who is entitled to receive general disability pensions, in 4.5 years if he is entitled to receive specific disability benefits, and, finally, in about 8 years of professional activity in the case of an employee who has not earned any claims against Old Age Insurance.

The studies reported thus far lead to the following conclusion. Even with a very conservative interpretation of the figures reported, rehabilitation must be considered to be one of the most efficient investments in human capital. However, we must qualify this conclusion, since productivity and fiscal efficiency of measures will differ: The more differentiated and decentralized the social security system is, the greater will be the discrepancy between the results obtained from these two types of analysis. Even though the benefits to be granted to disabled individuals toward their rehabilitation are specified by law, individual institutions can exercise some discretion. Accordingly, these institutions will be motivated to consider their fiscal efficiency in terms of the expenditures and inflows into their own budgets, rather than overall economic efficiency (or even the fiscal efficiency of the total public system). The more universalized a system of social security is, the more efficient a rehabilitation measure will appear, in terms of the inflow of payments to be expected from an individual after his rehabilitation. Given rather selfish interests of particular institutions, one could thus conclude that the chances for the economic efficiency of a measure appear greater the more unified the institutions which are responsible for carrying out rehabilitation. Thus we must conclude that the pronounced differentiation existing among the social security institutions of the Federal Republic of Germany has an adverse effect of the pursuit of rehabilitation measures (Pflueger, 1960, p. 75).

All of the empirical analysis reported on must be faulted on well-known theoretical grounds (see Huber, 1979, pp. 84-86): (1) All of these analyses focus on fiscal considerations rather than on the overall economic productivity of a measure; (2) all studies ignore the problem of discounting benefits and costs; (3) in estimating the opportunity costs of alternative measures only nominal costs were considered, and it was thus assumed that the costs involved in financing rehabilitation measures involve only a curtailment of consumption and not of investment; (4) these analyses ignore the fact that the costs of rehabilitation measures are financed to varying degrees from general taxes and social security contributions (however, depending upon the predominance of one as compared to the other mode of financing, the results of benefit-cost analyses would differ depending upon whether the share of consumption or savings has been reduced, and thus different opportunity costs would have to be applied); (5) the benefits of rehabilitation measures are generally assessed in terms of increased work incomes, but investigators do not inquire as to whether sufficient demand exists for the skills of the person to be rehabilitated; (6) an employer may provide employment to a person who has been rehabilitated simply because he wants to avoid the legally required payments to public institutions if he does not fulfill his quota of disabled employees, or else, in order to obtain public subsidies—in both cases productive labor is not being increased; they simply entail a redistribution of labor market opportunities if and when another potential employee is excluded from participation in the production process (the individual who has been employed after rehabilitation does obtain the work income; furthermore, from the point of view of the institution carrying out rehabilitation measures, such a project is fiscally efficient, although an overall economic productivity of this measure may not be assured as long as another individual who may have been more productive cannot obtain work) (see also Pflueger, 1960, p. 78); (7) by assuming that the work income achieved actually corresponds to the marginal productivity of labor, the analysis assumes the relevance of marginal productivity theory in determining wages; (8) if and when a successful rehabilitation measure leads to a nonmarginal change in the supply of labor, the average work incomes prevailing before the pursuit of such measures may not be adequate indices of benefits resulting from rehabilitation.

Despite these shortcomings, there is little doubt that further analyses of the economic efficiency of rehabilitation would tend to substatiate the conclusions reported thus far. Futhermore, even if economic analyses should suggest lower (or even negative) productivity, rehabilitation may still be recommended on other grounds.

Effectiveness of Medical Rehabilitation Measures

Three types of indicators of the degree of effectiveness of medical rehabilitation measures may be envisaged:

1. Objective success: This measure is of interest to the public pension insurance system only indirectly; since the aim of rehabilitation is defined not in terms of health (which very often cannot be measured with the aid of a technical apparatus) but rather in terms of the ability to earn income (see Wannenwetsch, 1970, p. 302).

2. Subjective success: Insofar as individuals are motivated to obtain

disability pensions, any subjective statement indicating success or failure of particular rehabilitation measures has to be treated with caution (ibid.).

3. Legal (economic) success: A measure is said to be successful if it serves to maintain, improve, or restore a person's ability to earn; only this type of measure is considered to be legally relevant (Gercke, 1965, p. 226).

The effectiveness of rehabilitation measures could also be judged by the following questions: (1) Is the individual, after the completion of a measure, able to resume or continue an economically gainful activity? (2) Is the individual unable to pursue an economically gainful activity, only due to health reasons? On the basis of these criteria we would conclude that, in the year 1975, 93.4 percent of medical rehabilitation measures showed a positive result. There are no significant differences by sex; however, above average success rates may be noted for the group aged 30-60. There is a relatively low success rate to be found in the case of those who are over 60. This would imply that the determinants of disability, although not the deficiencies which are due to age, had been removed (see Table 9.13).

This evidence constitutes, however, only a limited indicator of the success of rehabilitation measures: At least 30 percent (Huber, 1979, p. 90) of the persons rehabilitated received training for the maintenance of a general work ability, which implies that they were not disabled in the first place. Thus, the success rates may have been overstated simply because this group of individuals naturally would show a very high probability of success.

Thus the results of a survey undertaken by Schwarze (1977) concerning the effectiveness of medical rehabilitation measures for retired persons and individuals about to retire are of interest. Schwarze subdivides the sample, consisting of 12,842 individual cases, into three groups. Group A consists of individuals applying for pensions who may be characterized by fictitious

Table 9.13. Results of Medical Rehabilitation by Age and Sex of Rehabilitated Persons, 1975

Age and Sex	Total	Continued Working (%)	Continued Working after Occup. Rehabilitation (%)	Work Impossible for Health Reasons (%)	Work Impossible for Personal Reasons (%)
Under 20	11,617	85.0	1.0	4.0	10.0
20-30	39,172	85.8	2.7	5.6	5.9
30-40	113,518	90.1	2.4	4.3	5.2
40-50	208,018	90.6	2.3	5.1	2.1
50-60	254,908	90.0	2.1	6.5	1.5
60-65	91,947	87.6	1.5	8.4	2.5
65 and over	22,437	53.9	0.4	28.4	17.3
Total	741,617	88.5	2.1	6.6	2.9
Male	478,656	87.8	2.6	6.5	3.2
Female	262,961	89.7	1.2	6.8	2.4

Source: Statistisches Bundesamt (1977, p. 46).

specific or general disabilities. Group B consists of applicants for pensions whose applications had been denied. Group C consists of specifically or generally disabled and retired individuals. The success of rehabilitation measures is lower for all three groups in the case of men compared to women. This difference can be explained as follows: After rehabilitation some men could have been employed at least part time (but not full time), but they could not obtain part-time jobs. A general disability pension therefore had to be awarded to them. In contrast, such part-time jobs were considered at least at that time available for women to a sufficient extent.[5] As a result no specific or general disability pensions had to be awarded to women; and they were classified as having been fully rehabilitated. In the case of group C the success of rehabilitation is considerably greater. However, only the total discontinuation of pension payments was treated as a successful rehabilitation, whereas those cases in which a general disability pension could be converted into a specific disability pension would also have to be viewed as a successful form of rehabilitation.

On the whole one could therefore conclude that rehabilitation measures were fairly successful in the case of pensioners and those who were in the process of applying for pensions. This conclusion would be substantiated when one considers that by a solely medical definition of general disability even better results could have been reported. A comprehensive way of assessing the success of medical rehabilitation is possible when the duration of success is taken into account. In view of the variability in the subjective judgment pertaining to the success or failure of rehabilitation, one has to accord greater credence to the objective indices. They generally tend to be more stable than the former (Gercke, 1965, p. 232). For this purpose Wannenwetsch (1975, p. 230) developed the method of comparing the periods of specific work disability prior to and after the conduct of the rehabilitation measure. Some empirical evidence can be obtained from a set of surveys undertaken by the Association of Public Pension Insurance Institutions. A 1 percent sample was drawn from a population of 80 percent of all persons who completed medical treatment within institutions during the year 1966 (Kaufmann, 1976)—5,352 persons. The success of a rehabilitation measure was determined by comparing the periods of specific work disability (1) within the last 12 months prior to medical treatment, and (2) prior to the examination of the success of a rehabilitation measure (undertaken 1.5 years after the medical rehabilitation had been completed).

Based on the degree of severity of the illness, the sample was subdivided into five groups: group I—work performance endangered; group II—work performance reduced; group III—specific disability; group IV—specific disability with the danger of a general disability; group V—general disability. Thus we can reach some conclusions about the success of medical rehabilitation measures (differentiating among individuals who are actually disabled and those persons whose work performance was only endangered):

1. The more a person's work performance was reduced prior to medical rehabilitation, the smaller the success rate of rehabilitation measures.

2. The success rate with regard to pensioners (groups III-IV) corresponds roughly to the results reported by Schwarze (as stated above).

3. For the disabled in groups II-V there was a positive result for two-thirds of all cases. Thus we conclude that the data reported in Table 9.13 overstate the success of rehabilitation measures. This is due on one hand to the confusion caused by the law which provides for a lumping together of prevention and rehabilitation measures, making it impossible to isolate the success rates of actual rehabilitation measures. On the other hand, on the basis of medical results we may draw only indirect conclusions about the future, that is about a persons' ability to perform on a job (Gercke, 1965, p. 231). A successful rehabilitation measure, however, would involve this very long-term effect.

Effectiveness of Occupational Rehabilitation Measures

Similar to the situation reported for medical rehabilitation, occupational rehabilitation measures are characterized by a high success rate immediately following the conclusion of the measure. Interestingly enough, the inability of individuals to resume economic activity owing to personal reasons correlated highly with age. Since the evidence pertaining to those over 65 years is not at all representative we may conclude that the success of occupational rehabilitation (training, retraining, further education, etc.) will decrease with increasing age of the person to be rehabilitated (see Table 9.14).

However, because not all institutions carrying out rehabilitation measures are included in reported statistics, the true overall structure of results of rehabilitation measures may deviate from those reported. This seems to be so, since the persons covered by Public Health Insurance and Public Aid, which were not included, exhibit other distributions of relevant socioeconomic characteristics (a higher share of children and retired persons). Therefore, we may expect a larger number of persons going through rehabilitation who cannot be reintegrated into economically gainful activities due to health reasons (Statistisches Bundesamt, 1978a, p. 58).

As in the case of medical rehabilitation, we may also doubt whether these results are an exact representation of the true situation. All investigations which are concerned with the long-term success of professional rehabilitation measures deal with only some aspects of the problem. Thus, analyses

Table 9.14. Results of Occupational Rehabilitation by Age and Sex of Rehabilitated Persons, 1975

Age and Sex	Total	Continued Working (%)	Work Impossible for Health Reasons (%)	Work Impossible for Personal Reasons (%)
Under 20	20,891	95.8	0.2	4.0
20-30	7,181	81.8	4.1	14.4
30-40	6,506	76.9	6.9	16.2
40-50	3,901	73.8	9.4	16.8
50-60	860	74.7	7.2	18.1
60-65	38	65.8	—	34.2
65 and over	10	70.0	10.0	20.0
Total	39,387	87.4	3.1	9.5
Male	28,688	86.3	3.7	10.1
Female	10,699	90.4	1.6	8.0

Source: Statistisches Bundesamt (1977, p. 46).

of their success exist either for certain types of disability (see Heier and Winterstein, 1973; Seibert and Winterstein, 1973), or else they pertain only to some of the institutions carrying out rehabilitation measures (see Meier, 1976), or to some types of benefits granted by these institutions (Hofbauer, 1977).

The analysis undertaken by Hofbauer (1977) may be considered statistically representative; it focuses on the rehabilitation and retraining measures which both in quantitative and qualitative terms are most important. In the course of his investigation over 10,000 persons who had started retraining and rehabilitation measures in 1971 were questioned as to the process of rehabilitation and as to the occupational activities undertaken after its completion.[6] The study comes to the following conclusions: 3 months after completion of the occupational rehabilitation measure 79 percent were employed. At the time of the investigation, 4 years later, this share had surprisingly increased to 85 percent. Within the same time period, however, the share of individuals who were still pursuing the particular occupations for which they had been trained during occupational rehabilitation declined from 73 to 70 percent. Considering that this time period was characterized by severe cyclical and structural labor market problems, we may conclude that these occupational rehabilitation measures were highly successful.

If one accepts as an additional indicator of the success of these measures the subjective evaluation of the persons who had been rehabilitated toward the professional status change made possible through rehabilitation, then a success rate of 75 percent was reached. Fifty percent stated that they had experienced an improvement in their work status, while 25 percent reported that they were able to maintain their status when compared to the time prior to the disability. Two further subjective indicators pertaining to satisfaction with income and work satisfaction were assessed to reflect the overall situation. Only 28 percent of the persons surveyed reported that the total professional situation had worsened. The greatest variance was observed in the subjective measure pertaining to the characteristics "severity of the disability" and "gross work income earned at the inception of the disability" (see Table 9.15).

Table 9.15. Share of Persons Rehabilitated Whose Occupational Situation Was Worse than before Disability, by Income before Rehabilitation and Severity of Health Impairment (percentages)

	Health Impairment				
Gross Income before Disability (DM)	Severe	Medium	Light	Not Ascertained	Total
under 600	27	(12)	(8)	(25)	19
600-800	27	(20)	(11)	(39)	18
800-1000	26	19	11	(27)	(19)
1000-1250	34	27	15	(23)	25
1250-1500	39	28	21	(30)	29
1500-2000	52	43	32	(40)	41
2000-3000	55	(61)	48	(62)	54
3000 and over	(63)	(71)	(100)	(67)	(71)
Not employed; not specified	(35)	(30)	(14)	(27)	25
Total	36	29	20	28	28

Source: Hofbauer (1977, Table 15, p. 73).
Note: Numbers in parentheses are not significant.

We find a negative correlation between the degree of severity of the health impairment and the objective indicator of success ("job opening which corresponds to the occupational rehabilitation measure"). Apart from this, the type of rehabilitation measure undertaken (retraining on the job or outside an enterprise) shows the strongest influence on the success of the retraining measure; this holds both in the short run (immediately after conclusion of the measure) and also in the intermediate run (when the survey was made). The results are shown in Table 9.16. (One must qualify these results, however: In order to eliminate the impact of the recession only those cases which were completed by June 30, 1974, were included).

The success of retraining measures carried out within enterprises is evident: More than 50 percent of those rehabilitated persons remained in the firms where they had been retrained (see Hofbauer, 1977, Table 9, p. 71). Evidently a retraining measure undertaken within the enterprise reduces the prejudice of employers pertaining to the supposedly lower productivity of disabled persons, particularly as regards their impact on increasing the costs of production.

Within the Federal Republic of Germany only 12 percent of all occupational rehabilitation measures are undertaken within the enterprise.

Table 9.16. Share of Persons Rehabilitated before July 1, 1974, Employed in Occupational Retraining at Time of Interview (1975), by Type of Retraining and Severity of Health Impairment (percentages)

Type of Measure	Health Impairment				
	Severe	Medium	Light	Not Ascertained	Total
Retraining in enterprise with official certification	73	83	81	(54)	78
Retraining in enterprise without official certification	(55)	(67)	(86)	(64)	69
Retraining outside enterprise with official certification	68	73	78	60	72
Retraining outside enterprise without official certification	58	68	70	(47)	64
Total	66	73	77	57	71

Source: Hofbauer (1977, Table 12, p. 72).
Note: Numbers in parentheses are not significant.

However, in the labor market district of Augsburg, as an example, this was increased to 53 percent of all cases simply by intensive efforts of the public employment agency in contracting, counseling, and educating enterprises within the field of rehabilitation. These results suggest that there is a considerable potential for the improvement of occupational rehabilitation measures.

The Realization of the Objectives of Rehabilitation Policy

As we have pointed out, on the whole rehabilitation measures have succeeded in integrating the disabled. This, however, is only one objective for the evaluation of the overall effectiveness of rehabilitation policy.

Consideration of program goals contained in social legislation as well as those enumerated by the Stiftung Rehabilitation (Rehabilitation Foundation) provides a less striking picture of success. Section 7 of the Rehabilitation Equalization Act states "Disability Pensions should be awarded only upon the conclusion of rehabilitation measures, or if the success of such rehabilitation measures cannot be expected." The goals postulated by the Stiftung Rehabilitation (1974) are even more explicit: "By the late seventies every year 80 percent of all disabled of working age should be integrated completely into employment and social life" (p. 9). A review of statistics pertaining to new disability pensions, however, shows how little practical substance there is to the principle "rehabilitation prior to pension." In 1979, in 79 percent of all cases of specific or general disability pensions awarded under Public Pension Insurance for Blue Collar and White Collar Workers, no rehabilitation measures had been undertaken within five years prior to the awarding of the disability pension (Verband Deutscher Rentenversicherungsträger, 1978, p. 86).

Thus we must conclude that the objective of total reintegration of disabled and handicapped persons is not being pursued with the intensity called for by social legislation.

Economic Issues Regarding Pubic Policy toward the Disabled

Determinants of the Growth of Disability Programs and Costs

The striking increase of public benefits for the disabled can be seen by looking at expenditures under various programs. Their relative import can also be assessed when these increases in expenditures are related to other types of economic indicators. As Table 9.17 shows, the growth in compensation for work accidents and disability cannot be accounted for by factors such as increases in price levels, economic growth, and changes in the population structure alone. Even if these changes are taken into account, a significant share of the increase in program expenditures can be related to these economic and demographic factors only in an indirect fashion. For this reason we shall investigate alternative explanations for the disproportionate increase in expenditures by these programs.

The risks inherent in work may be a major determinant of the increase in the number of disabled individuals and thus of program costs. We can measure the risks by means of an indicator which expresses the number of reported fatal accidents in industrial enterprises per 1,000 insured individuals. This indicator suggests, however, that the number of reportable accidents (those which lead to an interrution of work for more than 3 days) has decreased steadily since the 1960s (with the sole exception of the year 1969). A reduction in fatal accidents has occurred since 1948 (Hagenkötter,

Table 9.17. Expenditures in Relation to Work Accidents and Disability

	1969	1972	1975	1978[a]
Total expenditures	DM 10,441	DM 15,776	DM 20,254	DM 25,723
DM per capita	171.59	255.80	327.58	420.12
Percentage of social budget	6.80	7.04	6.13	6.39
In DM 1970[b]	10,775	14,251	15,115	18,146
Percentage of GNP	1.75	1.91	1.97	2.03

Source: Huber (1979, p. 110)
[a]Preliminary estimates.
[b]Deflated by consumer price index for middle-income worker households.

1974, p. 208). This increase in the safety of the workplace can be attributed, among other factors, to the increased activities and competence of public offices supervising industrial employment, the institutions in charge of Workmens' Accident Insurance, and to trade unions.

The increase in the number of disabled workers could also reflect heightened awareness of the problem on the part of the legislators. In the declaration of government policy of 1969, the goal of "humanization of work life" was proclaimed. Increased awareness has also resulted from the federal government's action program for improvement in the rehabilitation of the physically handicapped, presented in April 1970. A major determinant of the increase in costs may thus be the improved benefits awarded to the disabled through Public Aid, the provision of social insurance by the Handicapped Act, the inclusion of farmers and their dependents in Public Health Insurance, and, last but not least, the Rehabilitation Equalization Act.

An increase in expenditures is also the result of broader eligibility criteria: When the new Seriously Disabled Act went into force on May 1, 1974, the number of persons eligible for benefits increased because benefits are awarded on the basis of the presence of a handicap or disability, irrespective of cause. Between May 1974 and July 1978 the number of employed persons recognized officially as seriously disabled increased from 430,000 to over 800,000 (Deutscher Bundestag, 1978b, p. 19). It is evident from the continuing large number of new applications for recognition as seriously disabled (320,000 applications were received during the fourth quarter of 1978) that this is an established trend.

Effects of Court Decisions

Since the legislative definition of disability is rather vague, the judiciary has played an important role in giving concrete meaning to this term. The judiciary therefore also exerts a significant impact on the growth of expenditures of various institutions responsible for rehabilitation. We attempt here to estimate the economic consequences of judicial decisions on the basis of decisions by the Federal Social Court with regard to the interpretation of the terms "specific" and "general disability."

The Grand Senate of the Federal Social Court passed a verdict on December 11, 1969, that persons who can only work part time are eligible for disability pensions when only full-time jobs are available. Following this verdict, there was a marked increase in the share of disability pensions under Public Pension Insurance. If one assumes that the change in the structure of specific and general disability pensions noted for 1969 is solely due to the verdict of the Federal Social Court, then one can simulate the economic consequences of this verdict, which has turned out to be rather expensive from the point of view of the public pension insurance institutions; solely the costs for the new entrants into the group of disability pension recipients increased per month by almost DM 10 million.

Public Health Insurance conducted a special survey of individuals entering its program during the period July 1, 1977, through September 30, 1977 (Deutscher Bundestag, 1978a, p. 69):

> The special survey led to the conclusion that out of the expenditures of the Public Health Insurance system made for specific and general disability, roughly 15 percent were due to the decision of the Federal Social Court in the matter of specific and general disability of part-time workers; according to the situation prevailing in 1977 this amounts to roughly 1.4 billion DM per year.

One must add, however, that due to the time periods selected the actual impact on expenditures might have been understated: In the third quarter of every year the labor market generally improves. In the period under investigation the level of unemployment was below average (by about 80,000 persons). This certainly affected the granting of disability pensions as well. Furthermore, this estimate of expenditures does not include the costs of the succeeding years. Insofar as the average duration of specific and general disability pensions is about 6 years (see Verband Deutscher Rentenversicherungsträger, 1977, p. 141), we actually have to assume that this verdict accounts for a much larger share of the increase in expenditures. As a result, greater integration of public pension and unemployment insurances has been achieved, but this has clearly imposed burdens on the public pension insurance program.

The Effect of Disability Benefits on the Supply of Labor

In the preceeding section we analyzed economic consequences resulting from the verdict of the Federal Social Court of December 11, 1969, and December 10, 1976,[7] focusing on the price component of the overall increase in expenditures. We now turn to the second dimension affected by these verdicts—that of quantity. In focusing on the concrete definition of disability, the court verdict caused a considerable share of persons who previously would have been eligible for specific disability pensions to now be entitled to general disability pensions. Thus, a group of persons who would have been taken off the labor market for a limited period of time only or who would have been available only for certain tasks was completely removed from the labor market. Now general disability, as defined by law, may apply to persons who in fact are not generally disabled.

If there had been no changes, the share of these two types of disability pensions would not have changed between 1969 and 1970. Undoubtedly, however, a change in the age composition of the population will increase the share of all disability pensions among all the pensions granted to the total population. Nevertheless, this should have no impact on the relationship between specific and general disability pensions. We would expect that only medical causes would lead to a change in the relationship of these two types of disability pensions. Since we have no reason to assume that these causes have changed, we must assume that the verdicts of the Federal Social Court are the sole or major determinants of the change in the pattern of specific versus general disability pensions.

With the help of a simple simulation model we can conclude that in the year 1977 more than one quarter of a million persons were kept out of the labor market due to the verdict of the Grand Senate of the Federal Social Court of December 11, 1969. If one assumes that in the case of an abstract definition of disability the whole group would have become unemployed, we must conclude that in 1977 the unemployment rate would have increased from 4.5 to 5.6 percent but for these verdicts (see Huber, 1979, p. 116-120). However, it is only reasonable to assume that some persons would have continued to work even after they had become specifically disabled. Furthermore, employers will often release workers only when they can assume that they will be taken care of by the social security system. Thus we may conclude that the legislation, in fact, indirectly caused the unemployment of those aged 58 and 59 years. By introducing an early retirement with old age pensions for persons 60 years of age after a period of unemployment of at least one year, the employers and the unions were able to develop what has been euphemistically termed "social plans," which in effect amount to the unemployment of older workers. Generally, older persons who are specifically disabled have great difficulty securing employment even if the overall labor market is improving. After the verdict of 1969 they now are entitled to general disability pensions which are higher by 50 percent than the specific disability pension and as high as the old age pension. The verdict of 1969, by defining the residual ability to earn in concrete terms, has exerted a similar impact on unemployment. Even if it had been possible previously to find a part-time job or another type of employment for an individual whose ability to earn had been reduced, the employers and the unions are no longer motivated to do so simply because they know that a person who becomes unemployed is not thrown into a dire economic situation.

Thus the judiciary anticipated in the year 1969 what became law in 1972: (1) eligibility for old age pensions, already at age 60 for persons unemployed for 1 year within the last 1 1/2 years; (2) eligibility for early retirement pensions for persons aged 62, which applies to specifically disabled, among others. The verdict focusing on a concrete definition of disabilty led to a reduction of the retirement age for unemployed persons with a specific disability.

What may come as a surprise in Table 9.18 is the fact that the labor supply of women has decreased more than that of men, also in absolute terms, even though one would expect that it would correspond to the share of women in the labor force. This can be explained partly by the fact that among women the share of recipients of a specific disability pension among all pensioners has decreased more strikingly than in the case of men. This implies then that for labor market reasons, more specifically disabled women were classified as generally disabled than was the case with men. Or, in other words, even if the medical situation and the situation recognized by the social insurance system are equal regarding a recognized specific disability, men are more likely to obtain a suitable job than are women. This suggests evidence of the discrimination against women in the labor market from a different angle.

Thus far we have analyzed the effects exerted by various measures on the

Table 9.18. Reduction in Labor Supply (Workers Leaving Labor Force) due to 1969 Verdict of the Federal Social Court, 1970-1977

	Male Workers			Female Workers			
	Blue Collar	White Collar	Total	Blue Collar	White Collar	Total	Total
1970	2,602	1,094	3,696	1,434	629	2,063	5,759
1971	13,633	4,470	18,103	6,674	2,872	9,546	27,649
1972	31,681	9,227	40,908	15,921	6,524	22,445	63,353
1973	48,994	13,454	62,448	27,752	10,582	38,334	100,782
1974	64,679	16,172	80,851	42,321	15,943	58,264	139,115
1975	79,839	17,700	97,539	59,930	24,583	84,513	182,052
1976	91,842	18,967	110,809	77,765	34,877	112,642	223,451
1977	104,268	18,142	122,410	95,251	43,112	1,138,363	260,773

Source: Huber (1979, p. 120).

total supply of labor. Now we turn to the impact that public programs aiding disabled workers have on individuals' specific financial situations and thus on their decision to work. In order to obtain these facts a simple simulation model was applied to the case of three married persons without children who belong to different income classes. It was assumed that person B's income corresponds to the average gross wages of all persons insured by Public Pension Insurance for Blue Collar and White Collar Workers, while person A obtains half, and person C double, person B's income. It is further assumed that married women do not work and that they do not begin to work after their husbands become disabled. On the basis of these assumptions we estimated the income that each one of these three persons could expect from one of the three institutions called upon in such situations, viz., Public Pension Insurance, Workmen's Accident Insurance, and Public Aid.

In order to compute the amount of compensation under Public Pension Insurance the following additional assumptions were made:

1. The insured had 40 insurance years.

2. Within this period his income did not change in relation to the income of all the other insured persons.

3. C's income exceeded the ceiling of wages subject to social security contributions. Therefore, his disability pension could not simply be based on double the claims of B (since they exceeded the ceiling). We thus base his pension claims on the ceiling income of the year in which he became disabled.

We can compute the ratio of the gross income an individual receives after becoming disabled to the one that he obtained prior to his disablement. This ratio we term his gross wage replacement rate. In order to derive the net wage replacement rate, taxes and social security contributions have to be considered as well. Furthermore, the ceiling of wages subject to social security contributions was taken into account in calculating contributions to the public pension and unemployment insurance systems. However, health insurance contributions were computed on a basis of total income, using the rates applicable to the public health insurance system. Furthermore, in order to enable us to make a comparison over time, these wage replacement rates were computed for the years 1968 and 1978. Table 9.19 notes the different benefits granted by the various programs.

Generally, the wage rates under Public Aid are lower than those under the Public Pension and Workmen's Accident programs. An exception is found only for person A (a person with one-half of the average income). This results from a pattern of rates which are independent of the level of

Table 9.19. Gross and Net Income Replacement Rates Applicable to Benefits Granted under Various Programs, 1968 and 1978

Person	Public Assistance 1968	Public Assistance 1978	Public Pension Insurance 1968	Public Pension Insurance 1978	Accident Insurance 1968	Accident Insurance 1978
Half the Average Income						
Gross wage replacement rate	60.5	55.7	50.9	49.3	66.7	66.7
Net wage replacement rate	69.8	68.3	57.6	60.4	77.0	81.7
Average Income						
Gross wage replacement rate	30.2	27.9	50.9	49.3	66.7	66.7
Net wage replacement rate	39.1	37.9	64.5	67.1	86.2	90.7
Twice the Average Income						
Gross wage replacement rate	15.1	13.9	45.0	41.6	66.7	60.8
Net wage replacement rate	20.5	20.7	59.9	65.4	90.5	90.1

Source: Huber (1979, p. 125).
Note: See text for explanation of assumptions used in the simulation.

income earned prior to the disability. Furthermore, we note that in the case under investigation Public Aid benefits increased less than the overall level of income. Thus we may conclude that, in view of the low level of benefits awarded, a disincentive to work may not exist; or, in any case, may not be very pronounced.

In the case of Public Pension Insurance, benefits awarded are dependent on income, or rather on the level of contributions made. This leads to equal gross wage replacement rates in the situation of persons A and B. However, the lower gross replacement rate noted for person C results from the fact that contributions have to be paid only up to a certain wage ceiling. That the gross replacement rate decreased from 1968 to 1978 is due to the change in the method of computation applied in arriving at the general wage basis for determining benefits. The higher the increase in annual wages, the greater the discrepancy between benefits and current income due to the time lag existing between changes in wages and changes in benefits awarded. The net wage replacement rates exceeded gross wage replacement rates in 1978 because of, on the one hand, increased taxes and social security contributions on wages, and on the other the reduction in the burdens imposed on pensions (since in 1978 pensioners no longer had to pay the 2 percent contribution to Public Health Insurance which was required in 1968).

Disincentives to return to the labor market seem to be somewhat higher than in the case of Public Aid. In addition, in many cases individuals were classified as generally disabled precisely because no job was available to them. The incentive to work provided by the reduction of income by about 40 percent which follows becoming disabled, however, is reduced further by the regulations that provide for a complete discontinuation of general disability pensions if and when the individual earns additional wages of over DM 500 (in 1979). In contrast, specific disability pensions are granted quite irrespective of the amount of additional income a person is able to earn. Thus it is conceivable that a person's postdisability income would be higher than the income earned prior to disablement.

The maximum accident pension, granted in cases of 100 percent disability, amounts to two-thirds of the last wages earned, subject to an upper ceiling of DM 36,000 annually. In 1968 none of our three workers, A, B, or C, drew incomes in excess of that amount, and in 1978 only person C exceeded this limit. This would imply that after becoming disabled person C would obtain only 46 percent of his last gross income or 68 percent of his last net income. However, all but one of the branches of accident insurance laid down higher annual wage ceilings, ranging drom DM 48,000 to DM 84,000. In estimating wage replacement rates we assumed that we were dealing with a branch of accident insurance applying an annual wage ceiling of DM 48,000. On the basis of this limitation the net wage replacement rate for 1978 amounts to "only" .901. If we were to assume, however, that the disabled person had been insured with an institution whose upper limit amounts to DM 60,000, then he would obtain 99 percent of his predisability income after disablement.

Thus we may assume that in view of the high wage replacement rates the financial incentive to seek work is rather slim. Furthermore, we must also consider the fact that accident insurance does not take account of the labor market situation, i.e., a maximal pension is granted to completely disabled persons. For such persons, however, the chance to obtain work which corresponds to their physical and mental abilities is rather limited.

The number of disabled is not solely determined by the actual health status of the labor force. It is also influenced, as Schewe and Zöllner (1957) and Jahn (1961) have indicated, by overall economic development. The import of economic development becomes evident when one considers that in periods of high unemployment an insured person desires to retire and obtain a pension when the danger of losing his job is increased. As has been pointed out, the general disability pension acruing to an average wage recipient in 1978 (see Table 9.19) corresponds roughly to the level of unemployment benefits (which amounts to 68 percent of the net wage income). Thus it is understandable that an insured person whose ability to work has been reduced would tend to attempt to qualify for a disability pension rather than become unemployed and draw benefits, since the latter are granted for a limited time only and may even be associated with a decline in social status.

This line of reasoning would imply that the attempt to receive a disability pension stems predominantly from causes which are within the perview of the applicant. However, that notion ignores the fact that the concept of disabilty (at least since the 1969 verdict of the Federal Social Court) involves, besides health status, a second component, i.e., the potential for obtaining a job. It is precisely the latter which is influenced and limited by the tendency of employers to fire workers (see Jahn, 1961, p. 92). Thus, the labor market situation becomes the overriding factor in determining an individual's decision to apply for a disability pension.

However, no perfect correlation between the number of new disability pensions sought and granted and the extent of unemployment can be observed. Rather, the relationship roughly follows a pattern corresponding to the one shown in Figure 9.1. In phase I the rate of unemployment increases. This affects first of all, and to a disproportionate extent, those whose performance is impaired; it leads to a significant increase in newly granted disability pensions. If and when the economic situation deteriorates further, this increase in new disability pensions will continue, however, only up to an upper limit (ZI_{max}). In this situation some individuals will retire who, in spite of their reduced ability to work, had been employed in situations of high employment (ibid.). Thus we disagree with Schewe and Zöllner (1957), who assume that this upper limit is

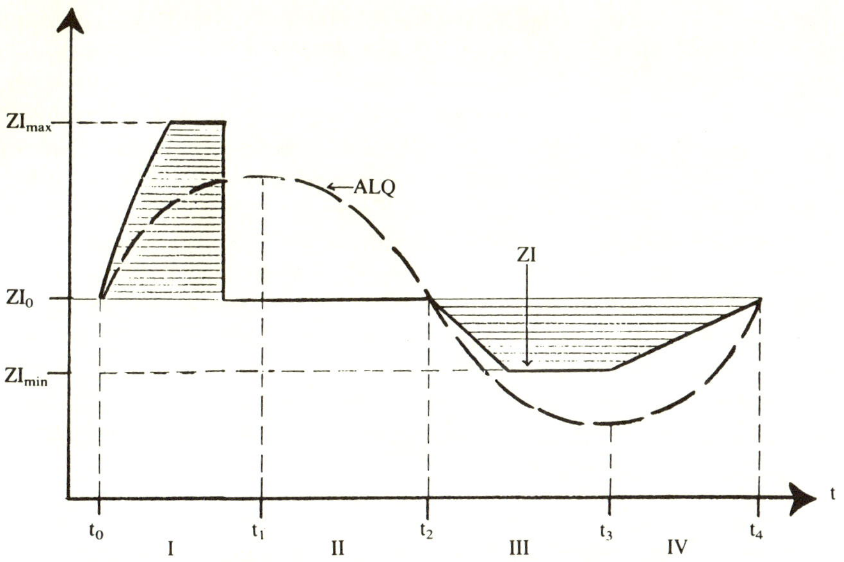

Figure 9.1. Theoretical Relationship between the Unemployment Rate (ALQ) and the New Disability Pensions (ZI).

determined by "prerequisites of the physical capability to perform" (p. 40). Rather we conclude that it is determined by the properties of the preceding business cycle upswing: The longer it lasts and the stronger and more pronounced it is, the more likely it will be that disabled individuals will be drawn into the productive processes in spite of their limited ability to perform. Thus, the more pronounced and the longer the cyclical upswing the more new disability pensioners follow the upswing. A prolonged and pronounced business cycle upswing results in a delay of applications for disability pensions which is caught up during the following recessionary phase; this will also influence the level of ZI_{max}. Once this delayed effect has worked itself out the number of new disability pensions decreases to the level ZI_0.[8]

As the level of unemployment decreases and as the economy approaches full employment (phase III) the newly disabled are being kept in their jobs to an increasing extent. However, we cannot assume that there will be no new additions to the disabled at all. Rather, their number will correspond to a lower limit (ZI_{min}) determined by "a physiological morbidity or biological invalidity which exists irrespective of the labor market situation" (Schewe and Zöllner, 1957, p. 40). The more suddenly the business cycle downturn occurs, the faster the number of disability pensioners will again increase.

Opinions differ as to how far the economic situation can explain the variance in the number of new disability pensions (Schewe, 1959, p. 375;

Zöllner, 1959, p. 728). Schewe and Zöllner maintain that the health status of the insured person does not exert any demonstrable influence on the extent of disability found in the economy. Jahn, however, maintains: "Thus we must conclude that the occurrence of disability noted within a particular year must, after all, be considered an expression of the given health situation, even though it is strongly influenced by the respective potential of the economy to offer or maintain employment for persons whose ability to perform has been impaired" (Jahn, 1961, p. 101). Schewe's conclusion (1959, p. 735), that the best therapy against disability is full employment, would imply the prerogative of economic policy over social policy, with the consequence that social policy is merely meant to cure symptoms, not to get at the causes.

Distributive Effects of Public Programs in Favor of Disabled Workers

The pattern of financing benefits is a major determinant of the distributive patterns resulting from public programs in favor of disabled workers. Insofar as social security contributions represent a fixed proportional share of income up to an upper wage limit and do not increase beyond this upper limit, the overall pattern of the incidence of social security contributions is regressive for higher incomes. However, if we assume that the incidence of grants in aid made out of the Public Exchequer in favor of the institutions responsible for social security programs corresponds roughly to the overall incidence of public tax receipts, this conclusion becomes modified, as the progressive effects of the direct taxes are more significant than the regressive effects of indirect taxes (see Pfaff and Schneider, 1979, p. 25). (This conclusion abstracts from a shifting of taxes and thus it assumes that the concept of impact incidence applies.)

The combined distributive effect of financing and benefits under Public Pension Insurance has to distinguish between cash benefits on a more permanent basis (pensions) and in-kind or real benefits (rehabilitation programs). Since benefits are computed roughly according to a proportionate formula, one might argue that there is little redistribution between higher and lower incomes as such, even though we must take into account the fact that persons who retire with disability pensions at an early age "get more out of the system than they pay in."

With regard to rehabilitation measures, which are more or less independent of the amounts contributed by a person prior to the beginning of the measure, one may argue that lower income groups, though they pay less in absolute terms (the same relative share), get as much out of the system as middle income groups do. Higher-income groups (with incomes above the wage levels subject to social security contributions), on the other hand, have to pay a smaller share of their income than do middle and lower income groups, while getting the same benefits. This distributive effect would be even worse if we assumed that rehabilitation measures for higher income individuals tend to be more expensive.

For those programs which are being financed solely out of taxes (for example, Veterans' Benefits and Public Aid) we can assume that the burden is being imposed in a progressive fashion. Since the recipients of disability pensions from Public Aid are generally found in the lower-income groups, we can only assume in this case that the redistribution of income results from a shift from individuals with higher incomes to those with lower incomes.

The Reform of Public Programs Aiding Disabled Workers

Public discussion in the Federal Republic of Germany with regard to reform of the social security system stems largely from the problems of financing Public Pension Insurance. Pensions are increased annually in line with increases in gross wages. Proposals currently being discussed would change these increases in pensions in line with the development of net wages only. Due to inflation, more and more wages have reached income brackets with progressive tax rates. This in effect leads to a larger increase of pensions compared to net wage increases. Such an effect is considered to be undesirable on social policy grounds.

Another proposal would aim at the taxation of pension incomes in line with the taxes being levied on wages. This, of course, does not immediately ameliorate the financial position of the public pension program, as long as those tax revenues are not passed from the Federal Exchequer to Public Pension Insurance by way of increased grants in aid, for example. A further possible way to reduce the pressure on the public pension insurance system is the requirement that pensioners pay contributions to Public Health Insurance. Thus far, health benefits awarded to the retired are being financed simply through a transfer between the parafiscal budgets of the public health and public pension insurance systems. Under the new proposal certain percentages of the pension income should be deducted as contributions to Public Health Insurance.

Apart from these changes, which focus on the expenditure side of the fiscal and parafiscal budgets, several changes on the income side can also be considered. Owing to technological developments and the increase in capital intensity of production, the number of job openings has decreased; thus, the share of contributions to Public Pension Insurance made by employers has also decreased. In order to compensate for such changes several proposals are being discussed: The employers' contribution to the old age insurance system should no longer be based on the wage bill but on the overall turnover or on the capital intensity of the enterprise. The latter is of particular interest. As compared to a contribution based on value added or to the current practice of tying employers' contributions to the number of wage earners and their wage income, such a system would be less sensitive to cyclical fluctuations in employment; furthermore, it would exert no disincentives to the creation of jobs.

Additionally, it is very likely that during the next decade the benefit scheme used by Public Pension Insurance will be reformed. Among the possible reforms is a change in the current system whereby recipients of specific disability pensions would only be allowed to earn wages up to a certain level without loss to their pension. One proposal envisages the determination of the extent of the disability pension commensurate with actual income loss.[9] Similar proposals have been advanced by representatives of public pension insurance institutions (see, for example, Ruland, 1979). Furthermore, in determining the specific disability pension, the examination rules on whether to reconsider the expectation that the insured person can carry out another type of activity. (This point was touched upon above.)

Whether a person can be expected to take up a different job should no longer be tied to the ambiguous concept of "decrease in social status" associated with the new type of job potentially open to the disabled. One should instead maintain that a person cannot be expected to take a new job if it involved an income reduction of, say, more than 10 or 20 percent.

The number of unemployed disabled persons is increasing. Enterprises beyond a certain number of employees are required to make available 6 percent of all jobs to disabled persons, but more and more employers do not comply with this quota. Proposals have been discussed which would lead to a change in the existing quota system favoring the disabled. Insofar as employers can circumvent providing jobs to the disabled within this quota simply by making a monetary tax contribution, some have asked for an increase in these contributions in order to motivate the enterprises to provide job openings also to the seriously disabled. Others argue in favor of a reduction in the obligatory quota: In their view the financing of rehabilitation should not fall primarily on the enterprise. We need not speculate here as to what extent contributions levied on enterprises as part of production costs are ultimately passed on into prices and borne by consumers. One should point out, however, that employers receive a large share of the contributions they make in the form of subsidies for providing jobs for the seriously disabled. A better integration of the disabled into employment and social life could also be achieved by passing regulations regarding the provision of part-time jobs. Such a law could easily be fashioned in line with the current law favoring the seriously disabled.

Notes

1. The decrease in the proportion of the disabled among the total population (or the constancy of this proportion resulting when the 735,000 are included) is unlikely

to be observed in the real world; it represents an artifact resulting from the use of different concepts of disability.

2. These programs are aimed at veterans and their dependents as well as at other persons subjected to damages on account of war or military action.

3. As the Continuation of Wage Payments Act does not apply to workers who have been employed either for a short period or a negligible extent, these individuals receive interim payment immediately.

4. In the case of most agencies, a wage ceiling of DM 48,000 or more holds.

5. This assessment prevailed until the verdict of the Grand Senate of the Federal Social Court, December 11, 1976.

6. In all, 7,584 cases were included (see Hofbauer, 1977, p. 49).

7. The verdict of 1976 gave a new and clearer definition of what is meant by the "availability" of a full-time job.

8. This is due to the assumption that those with reduced abilities to perform will be dismissed first, and leads to a situation whereby such an effect will always be noted before the maximum level of unemployment (t_1) has been reached.

9. Among the proposals made by the German Federation of Trade Unions, see Leingärtner (1977, p. 153).

References

Aye, H. A., W. Göbelsmann, P. Müller, H. Schieckel, and U. Schroeter. No date. RVO Gesamtkommentar. Mimeo volume. Wiesbaden: Chmielorz.

Blaha, H. 1978. Ist die Arbeits- und Erwerbstätigkeit medizinisch meßbar? Oral report presented at a seminar in Wildbad Kreuth, Bavaria, November 25.

Bley, H. 1975. *Sozialrecht*. Frankfurt: Metzner.

Brück, G. W. 1976. *Allgemeine Sozialpolitik*. Cologne: Bund-Verlag.

Bundesminister für Arbeit und Sozialordnung, ed. 1976. *Sozialbericht 1976*. Bonn: Kohlhammer.

Bundesminister für Arbeit und Sozialordnung. 1977. *Ubersicht über die Soziale Sicherung*. Bonn: Referat Presse- und Öffentlichkeitsarbeit.

Christian, W. 1976. Statistik der Rehabilitationsmaßnahmen. *Die Rehabilitation, 15*(2), 84-90.

Dembowski, H., and G. Schröder-Printzen, eds. 1976. *Schriftenreihe zum Sozialgesetzbuch*. Sozialgesetzbuch Band 1. Cologne: Bund-Verlag.

Deutscher Bundestag. 1978a. *Rentenanpassungsbericht 1978*. Drucksache 8/1615, March 10. Bonn: Heger.

Deutscher Bundestag. 1978b. *Lage der Behinderten und Weiterentwicklung der Rehabilitation*. Drucksache 8/2190, October 16. Bonn: Heger.

Ehrenberg, H. 1974. Von der Notwendigkeit und den Möglichkeiten einer unfassenden, auf die gleichen Ziele ausgerichteten Wirtschafts- und Sozialpolitik. In A. Christmann, W. Hesselbach, M. Jahn, and E. Mommsen, eds. *Sozialpolitik-Ziele und Wege*. Cologne: Bund-Verlag.

Gercke, W. 1965. Methodische Gesichtspunkte für eine Erfolsbeurteilung der Heilmaßnahmen der Rentenversicherungsträger. *Deutsche Rentenversicherung*, no. 4, 226-237.

Goetz, E. 1975. Die Bedeutung der Minderung der Erwerbsfähigkeit. *Das öffentliche Gesundheitswesen, 37*, 161-169.

Hagenkötter, M. 1974. Sicherheit am Arbeitsplatz. In A. Christmann, W. Hesselback, M. Jahn, and E. W. Mommsen, eds., *Sozialpolitik*. Cologne: Bund-Verlag.

Heier, D., and H. Winterstein. 1973. *Rehabilitation von Schwerbeschädigten in Bayern*. Nürnberg: Kohlhammer.

Hofbauer, H. 1977. Verlauf und Erfolg beruflicher Umschulung bei Rehabilitanden. *Mitteilungen aus der Arbeitsmarkt und Berufsforschung*, *10*(1), 47-73.

Huber, W. 1979. Effizienz und Effektivität öffentlicher Unterstützungsprogramme für invalide Arbeitnehmer—Theoretische Grundlagen und empirische Befunde. Ph.D. thesis, Faculty of Economics and Social Science, University of Augsburg.

Jahn, E. 1961. *Frühe Erwerbsunfähigkeit im internationalen Vergleich*. Cologne: Bund-Verlag.

Jochheim, K. A. 1958. Grundlagen der Rehabilitation in der Bundesrepublik Deutschland. *Arbeit und Gesundheit, 64*, 114-139.

Kaufman, F. W. 1976. Ergebnisse katamnesischer Erhebungen nach medizinischen Rehabilitationsmaßnahmen der Rentenversicherung. *Deutsche Rentenversicherung*, no. 1, 28-49; no. 2, 99-124.

Klee, E. 1974. *Behindertenreport*. Frankfurt: Fischer.

Leingärtner, K. 1977. Neugestaltung der Leistungen für erwerbsgeminderte und erwerbsunfähige Versicherte in der Gesetzlichen Rentenversicherung. In *Grundlagen der Sozialversicherung, Festschrift für Kurt Brackmann*. St. Augustin: Asgard-Verlag.

Lord Mayor of Berlin, ed. 1978. *Die Situation der Behinderten in Berlin (West)*. Berlin: Senatskanzlei.

Meier, H. H. 1976. Berufliche Rehabilitation—Eine Betrachtung des gesamten Komplexes Rehabilitation und des Erfolges von Rehabilitationsmaßnahmen am Beispiel von Berufsförderungswerken des norddeutschen Raumes, Ph.D. thesis, University of Göttingen.

Pfaff, M., and M. Schneider. 1979. Unterscheiden sich beitragsgedeckte Systeme sozialer Sicherung hinsichtlich ihrer ökonomischen Voraussetzungen und Wirkungen—insbesondere auch im Hinblick auf die Umverteilung? Paper presented at the colloquium: Die Rolle des Beitrags in der Sozialen Sicherung. Tutzing, Starnbergersee, July 3-6.

Pflueger, W. 1960. Aufwand und Erfolg von Maßnahmen der Arbeits- und Berufsförderung für behinderte Personen—Ein wirtschaftwissen-schaftlicher Beitrag zu Grundsatzfragen der Rehabilitation. Ph.D. thesis, University of Nürnberg.

Rahner, E. 1965. Kosten- und Ertragsanalysen im Gesundheitswesen Versuch einer ökonomischen Beurteilung von gesundheitspolitischen Maßnahmen in der Bundersrepublik Deutschland, Ph.D. thesis, University of Saarbrücken.

Ruland, F. 1979. Moglichkeiten zur Reform der Versicherungsfälle Berufs- und Erwerbsungfähigkeit. Paper presented at Sozialrechtliches Kontaktseminar, University of Bamberg, October 29-30.

Runde, P. 1979. Soziologie der Behinderten—Forschungsstand und Perspektiven. In R. Runde and R. G. Heinze, eds., Chancengleicheit für Behinderte. Neuwied und Darmstadt: Luchterhand.

Schewe, D. 1959. Die Bedeutung der vorzeitigen Invalidität. *Bundesarbeitsblatt, 11*, 728-734.

Schewe, D., and Zöllner, D. 1957. *Die vorzeitige Invalidität in der Sozialen Rentenversicherung: Umfang, Entwicklung und Bestimmungsgründe.* Berlin: Duncker und Humblot.

Schwarze, F. 1977. Medizinische Rehabilitation in der Angestellen-versicherung bei Rentenantragstellern und Rentnern, ihre Effektivität and ihre Effizienz. *Deutsche Rentenversicherung, 5,* 313-325.

Seiberth, P., and H. Winterstein. 1973. *Rehabilitation von Querschnittgelähmten in Bayern.* Stuttgart: Georg Thieme.

Statistisches Bundesamt. 1977. Rehabilitationsmaßnahmen 1975. *Wirtschaft und Statistik,* 42-46.

Statistisches Bundesamt. 1978a. Rehabilitationsmaßnahmen 1976. *Wirtschaft und Statistik,* 56-58.

Statistisches Bundesamt. 1978b. Körperlich, geistig und seelisch behinderte Personen. *Wirtschaft und Statistik, 8,* 491-497.

Statistisches Bundesamt. 1979. Strukturdaten über Behinderte. *Wirtschaft und Statistik, 3,* 224-228.

Stiftung Rehabilitation. 1974. *Auf dem Weg zur umfassenden Rehabilitation.* Heidelberg: Selbstverlag.

Verband Deutscher Rentenversicherungsträger. 1977. *Der Rentenzugang und der Rentenwegfall im Jahr 1976.* Frankfurt: Verband Deutscher Rentenversicherungsträger.

Verband Deutscher Rentenversicherungsträger. 1978. *Der Rentenzugang und der Rentenwegfall im Jahr 1977.* Frankfurt: Verband Deutscher Rentenversicherungsträger.

Wannenwetsch, E. 1975. Die Messung der Effektivität und Effizienz in der Rehabilitation. *Die Angestelltenversicherung, 6,* 229-230.

Wolfslast, J. 1968. *Cost-benefit Analyse im Gesundheitswesen.* Hamburg: Weltwirtschaftsarchiv.

Zöllner, D. 1959. Neuere Untersuchungsergebnisse über Entwicklung und Ursachen der vorzeitigen Invalidität. *Bundersarbeitsblatt,* 723-727.

Chapter 10

Disability Policy in France

Beatrice Majnoni d'Intignano and Jacqueline Repellin

Characteristics and Principles of Public Policy toward the Disabled in France before 1975

Public policy toward the disabled in France since 1945 can be conveniently divided into three main periods.

First, the years from 1945 to 1957 saw the progressive development of measures designed to deal with the financial consequences of a handicap (setting aside, for the moment, consideration of the set of conditions implied by that term). These measures were inspired by a concern to *compensate* the handicapped according to the circumstances of the disability and also by the notion of *assistance*.

Second, during the years 1957-75 we can detect the development of a consensus concerning certain fundamental rights of the disabled: (1) the right to a minimum amount of resources; (2) the right to education, training, and physical rehabilitation; (3) the right to work; (4) the right to the aid of a personal attendant; (5) the right to housing.

Finally, since 1975, policy toward the disabled has seen both consolidation and attempted rationalization of laws affecting the status of the disabled, and a considerable evolution in the philosophical bases of that policy—first, in replacing the notion of *family responsibility* for the disabled with that of *collective responsibility* (for instance, the resources of the handicapped person's family are no longer taken into account in

Beatrice Majnoni d'Intignano is a member of the Department of Economics, University of Paris, and Economic Advisor to the Public Hospitals of Paris; Jacqueline Repellin is a member of the Institut d'Etudes Politiques, Paris.

allocating benefits); and second, in the movement away from the notion of "assistance" toward that of "self-reliance."

We shall briefly consider the main legislative and administrative measures of these years.

A general scheme of social insurance for disabled salaried employees throughout France was first established by the Plan de Sécurité Sociale, which became effective in January 1947. The plan was implemented after earlier efforts, such as in 1946, to cover the whole French population within the framework of a single social security scheme were defeated by the hostility of independent workers, who refused to be enrolled in the general scheme. After the 1947 plan was implemented, the only workers not covered under this system were salaried employees who before that date had benefited under various special schemes that gave them analogous advantages. There followed several pieces of legislation that extended forms of social insurance to the self-employed.

Self-employed agricultural producers, whether owning or renting their land ("exploitants agricoles") were first brought under the Act of 25 January 1961 by a scheme of social insurance which covered them in particular against the risk of disablement from a nonoccupational illness. A second Act, of 22 December 1966, made it obligatory for self-employed persons in agriculture to be insured through a special program against accidents and illnesses of an occupational nature or those incurred at work.

Self-employed persons outside of agriculture were covered by the Act of 17 January 1948, which established a compulsory scheme of old age allowances and provided each of the groups involved (craftsmen, industrial and commercial professions, medicine, law, accountancy, or those in activities closely allied to one of these groups) with the opportunity to establish disability programs, participation in which would be compulsory for members of the trade or profession.

There was some delay in implementing these schemes: craftsmen were covered in 1963, those in industrial and commercial activities in 1975. Among those in professional and technical occupations, disability insurance schemes have been gradually introduced for doctors, dental surgeons, pharmacists, veterinary surgeons, accountants, engineers, technicians, and others.

Finally, over the fifteen years after 1948, special allowance schemes were introduced. Some are (or were, before 1975) paid by the Caisse d'Allocations Familiales (Family Allowance Department)—for instance, the allowance for handicapped adults who were not receiving old age or disability benefits equal to the amounts paid under the social security scheme, the retirement scheme, or other schemes established by special legislation. Others were paid by Aide Sociale (public welfare) to those disabled persons unable to receive a pension or allowance under the various social security schemes because their handicap was congenital, and therefore they had never worked, or because they were in some other way ineligible.

Running parallel to this complex tangle of social insurance schemes entitling disabled persons to protection in the form of pensions, annuities, or allowances, there has developed a body of legislation aimed at the occupational and social rehabilitation of disabled persons.

The first legal steps to aid occupational retraining were taken for the benefit of victims of the First World War. The Act of 1924 obliged employers to include among their employees a certain percentage of servicemen disabled during the war. At the same time, the Office National des Anciens Combattants (Veterans Office) was created; it progressively introduced forms of reeducation and professional training. These measures gradually extended to those disabled by accidents at the work site or by occupational illnesses. Thus the only persons left without coverage were those whose infirmities were congenital or had been acquired before their entry into an occupation.

The first legislation in favor of civilian invalids dates from the Liberation. An administrative order of 3 July 1945 allocated compensatory awards and established occupational retraining programs for the blind. The Act of 2 August 1949 extended these rights to all "severely disabled" persons. A decree of 29 November 1953 set up the Commissions Départementales d'Orientation des Infirmes (CDOI; local organizations for the guidance of disabled persons). Their task was to assess the ability of disabled persons to undertake employment or to receive occupational training. A further decree, 20 May 1955, extended to all physically handicapped persons the legislation establishing the employer's obligation to hire servicemen and those disabled by accidents at work.

The period since 1954 has seen the creation by the Ministry of Health of "Centres d'Aide par le Travail" (Work Assistance Centers; CAT), a form of sheltered workshop where the most severely disabled can receive medical and educational care as well as being provided with employment. The first attempt at consolidating all those measures came with the Act of 23 November 1957 (implemented in the decree of 26 July 1962), which introduced a coherent system aimed at the rehabilitation or retraining of disabled workers. The Act established a legal definition of disability: "Every person shall be considered to be a disabled worker if the chances of his acquiring or retaining employment are effectively reduced by virtue of a lack of, or diminution in, physical or mental capabilities." The 1957 Act provided in particular for setting up protected workshops and centers for arranging work in private homes, to enable people to work when their handicap would otherwise prevent them working in an ordinary environment. It established specific rights at work: priority of employment, special hiring conditions, trial periods which might not be interrupted except following consultation with the work supervisor, pay control, and eventual abatement of salary because of the handicap. It also established rights to reeducation and occupational training with the expenses to be paid by the state or the social security system. Finally, it created an advisory body attached to the Ministry of Labor: the Conseil Supérieur pour le Réclassement Professionel et Social des Travailleurs Handicapés, which acts as a liaison agency among the administrations concerned, the employers' professional organizations, the unions, and the principal associations for the handicapped. However, this act has been only partly implemented: in 1972, only 12,981 persons benefited from professional retraining, and only 49 of them were in public employment.

Over the years it became increasingly clear that coordination and a simplification of the entire system were greatly needed. This was the object of the Loi d'Orientation of 30 June 1975, which marks a new and important departure in the treatment of the handicapped by adopting what might be called a global and unified approach.

The first concern of the act was to consolidate legislation benefiting the disabled. Essentially this was contained in three texts. The first was the Social Security Code: its principal acts regarding insurance protection against the risk of disability and accidents at work have already been noted. Second is the Code de l'Aide Sociale et de la Famille (Code of Social and Family Aid) aimed at the most unfortunate. Finally are the provisions governing employment, notably the Act of 23 November 1957 on the rehabilitation and retraining of handicapped workers.

The 1975 Act dealt with all those persons with a physical, sensory, or mental handicap. It covers every stage of the handicapped person's life—i.e., from birth for someone whose affliction is congenital, or from the diagnosis of lasting aftereffects where an illness or accident is concerned. Further, it embraces several aspects: prevention, orientation, retraining, employment. Finally, this policy is aggregative, in that for its realization it calls on all the organizations concerned: public services, social security organizations, families, associations, groups, public and private enterprises, professional organizations and employers' unions.

Of all these objectives, occupational rehabilitation or training constitutes an essential priority. We will examine it in detail in this study.

The scope of the Act is implied by its length—no fewer than 62 articles. Many decrees have been needed to apply it—some not taking effect until January 1978, the date at which, by Parliamentary order, the dispositions contained in the Act were to come into force. In the sections that follow, we assess its provisions in detail. First, however, we turn to a crucial preliminary: clarification of the term "disabled" as it is understood in the French legal and administrative system.

The Demand for Disability Policy

The Definition and Classification of Disability

The flexibility and all-encompassing character of the concept of "handicap" in the new law meant that it was preferred, in 1975, to the concept of "disability" or "infirmity," until then used by law. The last two terms describe the state of an individual that prevents him from enjoying one of his faculties and is thus self-explanatory. "Handicap," however, has to be understood in relation to an activity, especially work. It is a result, whereas "infirmity" is primarily a cause. It is possible to imagine handicaps not related to infirmities and infirmities not resulting in a handicap.

"Infirmity" implies a permanent and fixed condition; "handicap" no longer does. It is considered today as an evolving condition, and one that encompasses certain illnesses which, without complying exactly with the definition of infirmity, nevertheless still entail a handicap for the afflicted person. "Handicap" must also be distinguished from "disfunction," which relates more to social functions than to physical or physiological ones. The Loi d'Orientation of 1975 tries to deal only with physical, sensory, or mental handicaps, excluding from its ambit the social handicap.

An important exception to the all-encompassing concept of handicap has, however, been made in the field of employment. "Unable to work" has been replaced by the simple "impossible to find work," but it is still necessary for this impossibility to be linked to a physical or mental handicap. The ordinary unemployed person does not come within this legislation, any more than the socially maladapted or the "dropout." The replacement of one formula by another is, however, an indication of an important change. The two notions in effect do not overlap at all, for "unable to work" must be considered a complementary condition of infirmity, and "impossible to work" an autonomous condition. (In reality, of course, one can accept the presumption that it will be impossible for someone more than 80 percent disabled to find work, whereas below this figure there must be proof.) "Unable to work" was assessed in connection with work actually done by the claimant before his infirmity; "impossible to find work" takes account not only of the ability of the disabled person but also of the state of the labor market without reference to a specific job.

"Handicapped" is not an easy concept to define, encompassing as it does a multiplicity of causes whose relative significance may change as social or medical circumstances change or individuals grow older. It is clear, though, that the definition involved more than medical issues: social norms play a role in defining particular individuals as "handicapped."

The relative nature of the concept explains the difficulty of restricting it to a precise definition. Indeed, the Loi d'Orientation does not try to provide one.[1] Under such conditions, drawing up an inventory of handicaps and their causes promises to be an especially complex task. The Economic and Social Council in its report of March 1979 (Viot, 1979) on the occupational rehabilitation and training of handicapped persons adopted the following classification.

1. The handicap can in the first place be assessed according to how it affects the handicapped individual. In general, there are several types. *Motor handicaps*: Motor disability (cerebral or functional), or mutilations, are the more immediately noticeable ones, posing problems of mobility, access to work, and adaptation of the place of employment or more generally of living quarters. *Sensory handicaps*: If blindness and deafness are obvious obstacles to the accomplishment of normal professional activity, the diminution of other perceptive faculties can also make it impossible to accomplish certain tasks. *Mental handicaps*: Alteration or diminution of mental faculties. *Relational handicaps*: These often border on mental handicaps but can equally reveal difficulties of social adaptation. *Physical handicaps*: Malformation or alteration of certain organs. *Multiple handicaps*: Handicaps are frequently interrelated; thus their adverse effects are cumulative.

2. The *degree* of incapacity must be considered, in order to measure the decrease in capacity for work; this comparison is by no means automatic, for the nature and organization of the work play an important role.

3. The handicap can be defined according to its *"natural"*(congenital malformation, accident at birth) or *"accidental"*origin (trauma arising from car accidents or work accidents for the most part, or other causes).

4. The handicap may develop or occur before or after entering professional life.

In sum, the Council report emphasizes that handicaps become manifest in relation to a particular environment. From this point of view, the work environment, or usual patterns of behavior and work habits, impose criteria of "normality," the merits of which are dubious: one can suffer from a handicap without its affecting one's abilities at work and, conversely, conditions at work may be responsible for revealing certain handicaps.

Another interesting approach is to base the different categories of handicap upon people's perceptions of them. A study carried out in 1978 (*Revue Française des Affaires Sociales*, 1978) shows that these perceptions are built around two principal issues: the degree to which communication is possible; and the degree of autonomy or dependence (capacity to take care of oneself).

These categories can be further classified into four types: (1) Handicaps arising from accidents, polio, and motor defects. Persons suffering from these handicaps are the least distressing by virtue of being the more autonomous and the least different; communication is possible. (2) The handicaps of extreme old age and chronic illness. Even if persons so handicapped have become completely dependent, they have at least belonged to the normal world. (3) Sensory handicaps. People who are blind or deaf and dumb are capable of looking after themselves but do arouse some distress in others, as life is perceived to be difficult without these senses. (4) The mentally handicapped, properly so-called, constitute the truly distressing cases; they are living beings, but also those with whom most people can least identify. The extreme example of noncommunication is represented by mental illness.

Measuring the Size of the Disabled Population

The Quality of the Statistical Sources

Because so few statistics are available, it would be illusory, even misleading, to try to do more than give a general idea of the characteristics of the disabled population in France. The shortcomings both of official statistical organizations and of specialized institutions in this domain are well known; currently there seem to be no signs of change. The Ministry of Health, the Direction de l'Action Sanitaire et Sociale (Agency for Health and Social Action), the Institut National de la Statistique et des Etudes Economiques (INSEE; National Institute for Statistics and Economic Studies), and the Institut d'Etudes Demographiques (Institute of Demographic Studies) answer every question on the subject by supplying a rough estimate of the aggregate number of handicapped people, with no breakdowns of the population by age, sex, economic status, or the precise origin of the disability. More seriously, the census of population on which these statistics are based was carried out in 1974; even then it drew upon old statistics, and has not been brought up to date since.

This lack of detailed and accurate information is the major obstacle to any economic approach to the problem of occupational training and employment of the handicapped. Every scientific approach will be condemned to failure as long as the shortcomings of the French administration in this area continue—even though the government of France is centralized and in theory has the means to carry out investigations into the demography and the economic status of the handicapped, and the costs of public policy toward them.

The only data that could be collected are restricted in scope, incomplete, and of varied origins. They are based on different definitions of "handicap," relate to different years, and use conflicting criteria or variables. It is difficult to compare their findings. The following presentation can thus be considered as merely an approximate picture of the disabled population.

Only three credible sources are available:

1. *The 1962 Census*, in which questions about the disabled were introduced; unfortunately, this approach was not repeated in the later

censuses of 1968 and 1975, so that it is impossible to make comparisons across time. The 1962 results made it possible to measure the prevalence of different handicaps in various age groups among the population as a percentage estimate of the number of handicapped belonging to an age group compared with the effective total number of persons in that age group. It is the only exhaustive estimate we can make, and provides the basic document on which later work relies. The Census used a *self-definition* of handicap.

2. *The preparatory work* for the Seventh Social and Economic Five-Year Plan and the Planning, Programming, and Budget Study of the disabled concerning occupational training and employment of handicapped adults. Unfortunately, these estimates date back to 1974 and were not brought up to date. Since they rely on the 1962 census, they also rely on a *self-definition* of handicap.

3. *Disablement statistics* provided by all the programs paying allowances of any kind to the handicapped, and statistics from the institutions receiving the handicapped: psychiatric hospitals, asylums, special institutions, accommodation centers, and work centers. To use these figures is to take an *institutional* approach, relying on the data of programs providing assistance.

The data presented in this report have been coaxed from these three sources. Traditional techniques of demographic analysis have been used, as follows. The total number of the handicapped is derived from applying to the population at large the rates of prevalence for different kinds of handicaps and mortality rates among different age groups in the population. The institutional approach has also been used.

Under these conditions, it is useless to offer annual statistics. According to the available data, we will select an estimation of the number of handicapped before the Act of 1975 and one taken from after it, so as to judge the impact and implementation of the Act.

The prevalence of handicap within the population. The demographic enumeration of handicap starts from its origin, as measured by its prevalence, which may differ according to age. Among the young,*physical deficiency* of a *congenital*origin, afflicting the severely defective with an I.Q. between 30 and 50, who work slowly and can do only simple, repetitive tasks, and the severely retarded—less than 30—is not affected by age (see Figure 10.1a). Deficiencies that are acquired through an accident that is pathological in origin, or that reflect relational problems arising from lack of affection or sociocultural deficiencies, become more prevalent with age (Figure 10.1b). Here, the shape of the curve can be explained by the tolerance or intolerance of the environment for the handicapped person; a slight defect generally becomes more manifest at about school age or occupational training age, when the family and then the employer can fairly easily accept it or compensate for it.

By contrast, the rate of prevalence is in the shape of an inverted Gauss curve for those who suffer from a slight mental handicap—those with an I.Q. of 70 to 85, who can lead independent lives with special teaching, or those who are mentally defective, with an I.Q. between 50 and 70, who will always need psychological or intellectual help (Figure 10.1c). For several years these handicapped have received training in the Centres Médio-Psycho-Pédagogiques (CMPP), in the Instituts Médico-Pédagogiques, or Instituts Médico-Professionels (IMP) according to need. This public or private training assists the handicapped to become reintegrated into the mainstream at an older age than the vast majority of normal

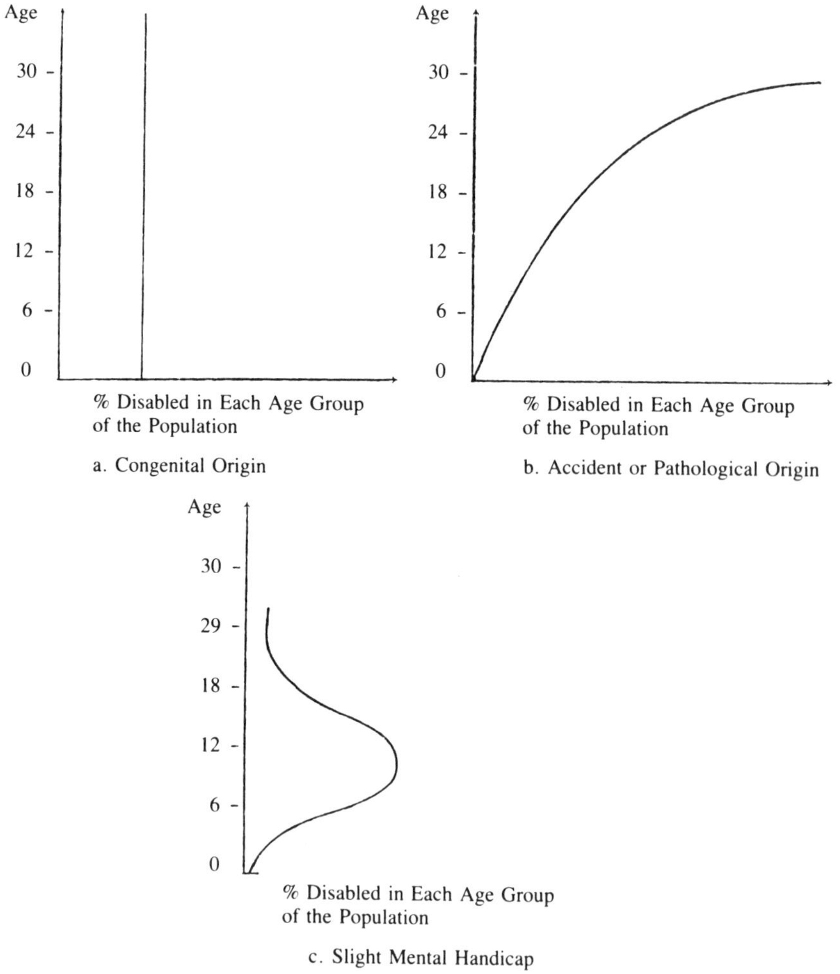

Figure 10.1. Prevalence of Handicaps of Various Origin in the Younger Population.
Source: Planning, Programming, and Budgeting Study (RCB, 1977).

individuals. The organizations are reimbursed by the social security schemes.
normal individuals. The organizations are reimbursed by the social security schemes.

Figure 10.2 shows the interaction of age and origin of the handicap in influencing prevalence in the adult population. It seems that handicaps that are rooted in an illness form a larger part of the overall rate of prevalence as age increases, whereas death diminishes the prevalence of congenital handicaps with increasing age, war (even among elderly people) remains an insignificant cause, and accidents only a modest cause, even though the size of the population affected increases with age.

The application of these rates of prevalence to the French population aged 15-60[2] reveals the size and the composition of the disabled population by age and origin of the handicap. Looking at the numbers in Table 10.1, we can clearly see that the disabled under 30 are few in number and that the congenitally disabled are mainly between 30 and 40. The general total slowly increases and the number of those handicapped as a result of illness slowly overtakes the total number of congenitally handicapped. Around 45 or 50, illness becomes a major cause, generating a rapidly growing number

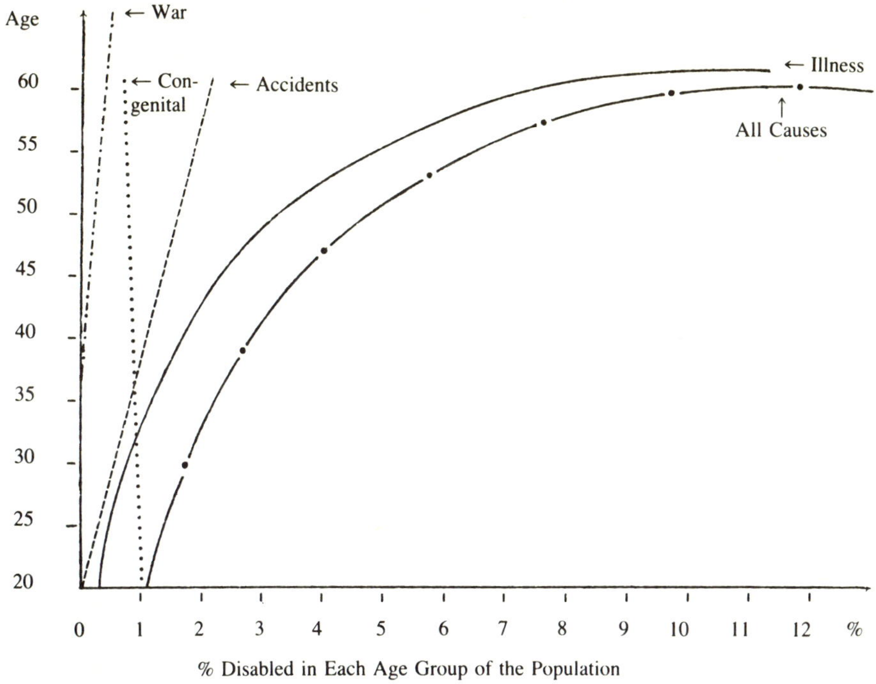

Figure 10.2. Prevalence of Handicaps in the Adult Population.
Source: Planning, Programming, and Budgeting Study (RCB, 1977).

Table 10.1. Changes in the Handicapped Population in France Aged 15 to 59, 1974-1980 (Demographic approach)[a]

	Estimate		Change			Distribution	
Handicap, by Origin	1974	1980	Absolute	Relative 1974/80 (%)	Annual (%)	Per 1,000, 1974	Per 1,000, 1980
Congenital or juvenile							
Sensory	35,400	37,000	1,600	+ 4.5	+ 0.7	35	33
Motor	52.200	54,000	1,800	+ 3.4	+ 0.5	52	49
Severely defective	104,900	109,000	4,100	+ 3.9	+ 0.6	105	99
Comatose	59,500	62,000	2,500	+ 4.2	+ 0.7	59	56
	252,000	262,000	10,000	+ 4.0	+ 0.6	251	237
Accidental							
At work	88,000	95,000	7,000	+ 8.0	+ 1.3	87	86
Traffic	47,000	60,000	13,000	+ 27.7	+ 4.2	47	54
Other	16,000	17,000	1,000	+ 6.2	+ 1.0	16	15
War	23,000	15,000	− 8,000	− 34.8	− 6.8	23	14
	174,000	187,000	13,000	+ 7.5	+ 1.2	173	169
Illness							
Psychological	130,000	141,000	11,000	+ 8.5	+ 1.4	129	128
Other	450,000	514,000	64,000	+ 14.2	+ 2.3	447	466
	580,000	655,000	75,000	+ 12.9	+ 2.0	576	594
Total	1,006,000	1,104,000	98,000	+ 9.7	+ 1.6	1,000	1,000
Total per 1000 inhabitants	34	35	b	b	b	b	b

[a]Application of prevalence rates of handicapped to total population.
[b]Number is negligible.

of disabled people. Thus we estimate that there are about 1,000,000 disabled people between 15 and 60 in France; half of them are over 45, a quarter are congenitally handicapped and 60 percent handicapped through illness. In all, the handicapped constitute 3.5 percent of the total active population, but those over 55 constitute more than 13 percent of their age group. We can imagine the difficulties that their integration into the world of work poses, given the competition to which young people of today are subjected when they leave school and the difficulty that people over 40 encounter trying to get back into employment, especially since the recession of 1975.

Factors Affecting the Size of the Disabled Population

The prevalence of handicap within different groups is currently changing. Two kinds of factors are operative.

Factors causing apparent increase. As aids for the handicapped are perfected, diagnosis improved, and the activities of specialized organizations become more widely known, people with existing handicaps "rise to the surface." Currently this factor is increasing the apparent prevalence of handicap, as it does for unemployment.

Factors causing real increase. Progress in preventive medicine and medical technology have reduced pathological and mortality factors and increased the numbers of persons who survive although handicapped. Down's Syndrome victims live longer, for instance; auto accident victims survive, but suffer from impairments; the rapid shrinking in the rate of perinatal and neonatal mortality following the introduction of the perinatal program of the sixth Social and Economic Five-Year Plan has unfortunately caused an increase in number of congenitally handicapped; some environmental factors such as urban crowding, or work conditions such as noise pollution, are increasing the number of people with relational and social handicaps.

Factors causing real diminutions. These are numerous. They include advances in the field of vaccination—poliomyelitis has vanished, as to all intents and purposes has tuberculosis; therapeutic progress, for instance in the treatment of congenital malformation; better prenatal care and the use of preventive abortions should there be an abnormality of the fetus; increasingly early diagnosis and intervention in relational problems at an early age.

Growth of the disabled population between 1974 and 1980. We do not believe it is possible to estimate the aggregate influence of these factors on the rates of prevalence of handicap. The projection in Table 10.2 is purely demographic; the INSEE statistics have been used as a basis, and the

Table 10.2. Annual Fluctuations in Numbers of Newly Handicapped Aged 15 to 59, 1974-1980

Handicap by Origin	Entries	Departure	Balance	Annual Variation in Composition
Congenital or juvenile				
Sensory	960	700	260	+ 0.7
Motor	1,520	1,220	300	+ 0.5
Severely defective	4,680	4,000	680	+ 0.6
Comitial	1,660	1,240	420	+ 0.7
	8,820	7,160	1,660	+ 0.6
Accidental				
At work	3,500	2,330	1,170	+ 1.3
Traffic	3,800	1,630	2,170	+ 4.2
Other	800	630	170	− 1.0
War	0	1,340	−1,340	− 6.8
	8,100	5,930	2,170	+ 1.2
Illness				
Psychological	8,700	6,870	1,830	+ 1.4
Other	61,300	50,630	10,670	+ 2.3
	70,000	57,500	12,500	+ 2.0
Total	86,920	70,590	16,330	+ 1.6

Source: Notes et études documentaires.

variations in the demographic composition of the handicapped comes from changes in the "age pyramid."

The aggregate growth rate is about 10 percent for the period—1.6 percent per annum, representing 16,000 newly handicapped people annually. Three-quarters of them were handicapped by illness, the older war victims (decreasing at a rate of 6.8 percent p.a.) giving way to young people disabled in road accidents (increasing 4.2 percent p.a.) or at work (increasing 1.2 percent p.a.).

Severity of Handicap

Since the definition of "handicap" is relative, and the degree of social tolerance and the level or type of protection markedly influence the number of handicapped people, it is appropriate to estimate the number of "severely" handicapped—those who need special living or working arrangements, whether special equipment or a personal aide. By making this distinction we diminish the number of persons handicapped by somatic complaints, mental illness, and behavioral difficulties. This choice is partly arbitrary, but the statistics are more credible and give us the minimum number of handicapped people. Our statistical approach is no longer demographic but institutional, since the health and social organizations also devote research to the help given to the disabled. The available information is presented in Table 10.3. These estimates are very rough and the comparison can be considered only an approximate indicator. Note that about half the disabled are considered "severely handicapped."

Table 10.3. Estimated Numbers of the Severely Disabled in Relation to the Total Disabled Population

	Severely Handicapped[a]	Total Handicapped[b]
Mentally defective	150,000	150,000
Comatose condition	45,000	120,000
Physically handicapped		
Motor	200,000	200,000
Sensory	85,000	111,000
Visual	38,000	66,000
Auditory	47,000	47,000
	285,000	313,000
Other	—	482,000
Total	480,000	1,065,000

[a]Ministère de la Santé (1976).
[b]Notes et études documentaires.

Employment Status of the Disabled

The disabled of working age constitute about 3.35 percent of the total working-age population (Table 10.4). A higher percentage, 4.9 percent, of those employed in agriculture is disabled, and a lower one in the private or public sector—2.6 and 2.9 percent. It is normal to find that very few among the declared unemployed are disabled; since 1975 the probability of the disabled person getting a job has been very low because of the increasing number of unemployed, in general; thus they simply stop looking for work. Employment does not seem very different in the disabled and the nondisabled populations; the percentage of disabled "not working" is about the same as the percentage of disabled in the total working-age population.

We can provide only very partial information on working handicapped people. Table 10.5 combines public and private business information; the data come from the health and social security statistics or answers to written questions to the government by Parliament, or are Ministry of Health estimates, some from 1974, some from 1975.

Table 10.4. Employment Status of the Disabled, 1974-1975

	Disabled	Total Population	Percentage of Population Disabled
Working age	987,000	29,441,000	3.35
At work or declared unemployed	736,670	22,042,000	3.34
Working in agriculture	100,000	2,026,000	4.9
Working in public sector	44,770	1,715,900	2.6
Working in private sector	544,900	18,305,100	2.9
Declared unemployed	12,000	1,000,000	1.2
Not working	250,000	7,399,000	3.37

Source: Estimates from the Ministry of Health.

Table 10.5. Sectors of Employment of the Disabled, 1974-1975 (Round numbers)

	Number	Percentage
Sheltered institutions		
AP	12,000	1.3
CAT	23,000	3.2
	35,000	4.5
Self-employed	100,000	13.8
Private sector		
Accident at work	344,800	47.4
Other origins of disability	200,100	27.6
Public sector		
Education, reeducation	1,700	0.2
Second-stage training	70	
Postal and telecommunications	3,000	0.4
Other administrations and local organizations	40,000	5.5
Total working	725,000	100.0
Registered as unemployed	12,000	
Without work	250,000	
	987,000	

Source: Estimates from the Ministry of Health.

Around 70 percent of disabled people work. Half this number (47 percent) includes those injured at work. Only a small percentage of the total number of positions occupied by handicapped people (6 percent) are in the public sector, and sheltered-work institutions play an equally marginal role (4.5 percent). Unfortunately, there are no recent figures on the employment by economic sectors.

The Economic Characteristics of Disability Policy

Programs for the Compensation of the Handicapped

Currently, there is a multitude of programs designed to assist the handicapped and to make essential resources available to them. This legislative diversity can be explained both on historical grounds and by the nature of the handicap.

Along with the general program for salaried workers there thus exist many special programs. Although the Social Security Plan adopted in 1945 proposed the progressive unification of the various programs for social protection and the extension of this protection to everyone, the social climate has not allowed integration of the preexisting special programs (public servants, miners, local organizations and the like). The latter programs offer better protection, which the salaried workers have refused to finance. The programs receive varying proportions of their funds (ranging from 20 percent to 70 percent) from the state budget.

The nonsalaried (i.e., those self-employed, such as craftsmen or farmers), excluded originally from the general program, preferred (according to them) to create so-called "autonomous" schemes to avoid having to reveal the size of their incomes and inheritances, as they would have been obliged to do had they been integrated into the salaried workers' scheme. Moreover, the creation at different times of the various social security organizations over many years has meant that the separate parts of the current system are built on foundations so different that the financial aids given to the handicapped show important disparities.

Depending on the handicap's origin, the compensation program and the organization charged with responsibility for the individual will differ. The net result is that the compensation to which the handicapped person may lay claim relates neither to his needs nor the gravity of his affliction, but rather to the category into which he falls according to his disability. Even more disturbing is that certain persons may suffer from different handicaps of such kinds that they are dependent on distinctly separate legislative measures. Thus a veteran injured in the war and benefiting under a military pension may subsequently, as an employee, suffer a disabling accident at work. Thus *dispersion* and *heterogeneity* characterize the French system of compensating the handicapped. Recognition of this situation, deplored by all and criticized by the associations for the handicapped, has for many years led to the creation of study groups whose object it was to conceive ways to consolidate the system and propose concrete solutions. Yet the first real reform undertaken, the Act of 1975, unfortunately is still only partly implemented.

Eligibility requirements. Disparities prevail in the current system of indemnity—from one scheme to another and through all aspects of regulation, whether regarding the nature of the handicap, the threshold of incapacity qualifying the applicant for benefits, other eligibility conditions, or the way in which indemnity is calculated (Inspection Générale des Affaires Sociales, 1976).

Nature of the handicap. The different programs offering pensions, annuities, or allowances have no uniform conception of the handicap that entitles the handicapped person to a benefit. Some adopt the criterion of *physical incapacity*, evaluated upon a scale of the amount of physical incapacity caused by the infirmity, the so-called IPP (incapacité physique partielle). In this category are military pensions, the Aide Sociale program, and the program covered by the Caisses d'Allocations Familiales. Others are related to *total or partial incapacity to work or earn* an income, whatever the occupation. Under this definition, a worker is considered to be an invalid if, regardless of occupation, his physical condition prevents him from earning a salary higher than one-third of the remuneration that normal workers in the same category can expect to receive. This is the definition established by the general program for salaried employees, as well as by the program for salaried agricultural workers.

A third group of programs defines the handicap in terms of incapacity to *exercise one's original occupation*. This is the case for many special social security programs, principally the program for civil servants and state employees, the program for employees of local government, and that for staff of national transport enterprises, such as the National Railways. Also included are certain of the professions and the program for agricultural producers.

Finally, a handicap can also be regarded as a certain *degree of inability to work* in one's chosen occupation. A small number of programs adopt this approach—essentially some of the professions, such as accountants, engineers, and veterinary surgeons.

Benefit thresholds. These are not an issue for those programs using as their criterion of handicap the complete incapacity to exercise an occupation or undertake any other remunerative activity. For the other schemes, benefit thresholds vary within very wide limits. For military disability pensions and war victims, and the special social security program for sailors, the incapacity level is 10 percent. For disability pensions under the general program for salaried workers, the program for wage-earning agricultural workers, and certain of the professions, it is 66.66 percent. For allowances to handicapped adults paid by the Caisses d'Allocations Familiales, and the compensation awards paid by Aide Sociale, the incapacity level is 80 percent.

Eligibility conditions are generally expressed in the form of a minimum period of prior contributions which varies according to the social security program. (Over the age of 60, old age insurance replaces disability pensions.) This strictness varies greatly. For instance, for the general program, it is 12 months and 800 hours work p.a.; for the special mines program, it is 2 years; and for the National Railways program, it is 15 years. Conversely, no particular condition is required for allocating benefits in the category of accidents at work and occupational illness, or for military pensions, which are supposed to be financed by those responsible for the disability and not by the contributions of the handicapped themselves.

The method of calculating benefits calls for considerations which, because of their technical complexity, are beyond the scope of this study. Here we merely point out the hierarchical structure payments. Table 10.6 shows the disparities in the benefits paid to handicapped persons according to their previous occupations, as a ratio of the minimum allowance given by the general program. Miners, seamen, and civil servants, in particular, are in a relatively favorable position.

Table 10.7 presents similar indices for annual benefits to wage earners injured in an *accident at work* or afflicted by *occupational illness*. This category of disabled people clearly embraces those getting better treatment; in addition, no minimum incapacity is required for eligibility, and if individuals have a low level of incapacity, they may well add a near-normal salary to the benefits they receive.

Table 10.6. Disparities in Benefit Levels (Minimum allowance under general program = 100)

Benefit Program	Annual Income Index
General program for salaried workers and agricultural program: Minimum	100
Maximum: Invalids in Group 1	275
Group 2	464
Group 3	954
Average sum	234
Miners' program, single basic rate	324
Solicitors, clerks, and employees: Minimum	100
Clerks: Invalids in Group 1	259
Group 2	324
Group 3	788
Seamen	
Minimum	338
Maximum	1,211
Gas and electricity industries (average)	483
Civil servants:	
Minimum	230
Average for middle-level servants	1,485

Source: Inspection Générale des Affaires Sociales (1976).

Table 10.7. Benefits According to the Level of Incapacity: Accidents at Work and Occupational Illness (Unit base 100 = minimum allowance under the general program)

Level of Incapacity		Annual Benefit Rate
10%	Minimum	33
	Maximum	135
30%	Minimum	101
	Maximum	406
50%	Minimum	169
	Maximum	676
66%	Minimum	331
	Maximum	1,325
100%	Minimum	2,700
	Maximum	3,780

Source: Inspection Générale des Affaires Sociales (1976).

Finally, Table 10.8 shows the relative level of *military disability pensions*; currently this category of the handicapped is also in a favorable situation.

Reforms Introduced by the 1975 Law

The Loi d'Orientation of 30 June 1975 constituted an important step toward rationalization, but left six large programs for the handicapped. To these can be added the special programs, which we have decided to omit from the discussion because of their specific nature and the small numbers involved. Of the six programs, only two have been remodeled by the Act.

Table 10.8. Military Disability Pensions (Unit base 100 = minimum allowance under the general program)

Level of Incapacity	Annual Benefit Rate
65%	165
85%	261
85%; severe handicap status	334
100%	336
100%; severe handicap status	535
Requires help of third person	984
Severely handicapped, requires help of third person	1,172

Source: Inspection Générale des Affaires Sociales (1976).

The structure of the four programs left intact reveals the primitive foundations of the system of social protection for the disabled. Even today, it is still chance and not social need which determines which shall apply to a particular person. For each program, Table 10.9 shows the funding organization, beneficiaries, origin and nature of the handicap, and the benefit threshold.

The two programs restructured by the 1975 law are essentially concerned with the *congenitally disabled* who have never worked and thus do not come within any social security program, but they also cover handicapped persons to whom the preceding programs fail to provide adequate resources according to current social conceptions of action to help the poor. Careful study of the list of those entitled reveals that this Act is not only concerned with a marginal or rejected part of the population (which appears at first glance to be the case, and which would greatly reduce the scope of the Act), but that the text could in theory apply to the entire disabled population.

Unlike the four systems examined above, the allocation of benefits is now based *not on the origin of the handicap* but on *the need of the handicapped person*, who is no longer given assistance because of the handicap but because he or she is an individual with need for a certain amount of resources that has been brought about by a handicap. Consequently, we no longer base our classification on the cause of the handicap, but on the *nature of the organization* charged with meeting the need.

Before the 1975 Act, these programs were characterized by two essential traits—complexity and the supremacy of family over collective (state) responsibility. For adults there existed no fewer than five allowances. The allowances were paid only if the family's resources did not enable it to assume care of the handicapped person. Three "basic" allowances in effect guaranteed the disabled a minimum income equal to the old age minimum: (1) the "allocations aux handicapés adultes" (AAH), funded from the Caisses d'Allocations Familiales; (2) the "supplementary" allowance to the Fonds National de Solidarité, which was the responsibility of the general health insurance scheme; (3) the "monthly allowance" for social assistance, funded by Aide Sociale. Two allowances, the so-called "expenses compensation," provided (4) the increased allowance for continuous help by a personal attendant; (5) the allowance to severely disabled workers to whom allocations were very uncertain.

The 1975 Act had a real effect upon the complexity of the system—the five existing allowances were replaced by two.

The *"allocation aux adultes handicapés" (AAH)* replaced the first three allowances (Article 35 of the Act). This benefit is granted to handicapped persons with a permanent incapacity of 80 percent or, if incapacity is less, to those who find it impossible to obtain work. The monthly amount is equal to one-twelfth of the aggregate amount of the annual allowance given to retired salaried workers—"allocation aux vieux travailleurs salariés" (AVTS)—and the supplementary allowance of the Fonds National de Solidarité. In August 1976, it was 708.33 Frs per month. This allowance cannot be cumulated with an old age or infirmity benefit of an equal amount; if the latter is less, the allowance is reduced accordingly. However, it can be cumulated with the assets of the disabled person and, if applicable, of his or her spouse, up to the AVTS ceiling in force. That ceiling is doubled if the interested person is married, and it is increased by half for each dependent child. In August 1976, the ceiling was 8,200 Frs per annum for a single person.

Conditions for recipiency of the AAH are set out in Table 10.10. Table 10.11 presents the relative income level of those qualifying for this allowance as a percentage of the legal minimum wage. After the introduction of the 1975 reform, the amount of the AAH represented 45.6 percent of the minimum wage. This percentage has noticeably increased since then, to 47.3 percent, 50.50 percent, and finally 53.4 percent in 1979. But despite the relative improvement in the situation of handicapped people receiving the AAH, this allowance currently hardly exceeds half the minimum income of a wage earner.

The AAH is disbursed and financed like a family benefit and is thus administered by the Caisses d'Allocations Familiales. In addition, Aide Sociale pays sickness and maternity insurance contributions for persons receiving the AAH.

The *"allocation compensatrice"* compensatory allowance; Article 29 of the Act), dispensed by Aide Sociale, is granted to every disabled adult who does not benefit from a comparable social security program and who is afflicted with a permanent incapacity of at least 80 percent that makes the help of a personal attendant necessary for acts essential to existence or adds additional expenses to the cost of pursuing occupational activities.

Benefit amounts of the allowance are fixed with reference to increases in sickness benefits for those falling into the third group of the general social insurance program. They vary according to the nature and permanence of the assistance needed or according to the importance of the supplementary

Table 10.9. The Four Programs Left Intact after the 1975 Law

Program	Funding Organization	Beneficiary	Origin of Disability	Threshold	Nature
1. Military disability pensions; pensions for war victims	Departmental offices of the Anciens Combattants	Veterans	Wound, accident, or illness attributable to military service	Disability of 10% or more	Permanent physical incapacity
		Civilian war victims	Wound, accident, or illness suffered because of war		
			Plus the aggravation of preexisting disability because of war	Only the degree of aggravation will be taken into account unless the aggregate disability is 60% or more; this level is then taken	
2. Accident compensation (not mutually exclusive)	(a) common law compensation (b) indemnity from insurance	All victims of bodily harm caused by others	Essentially traffic accidents (excluding travel to work)	(a) Common law compensation: considers the total prejudice suffered by reason of the tort (aggregate compensation in the judge's discretion) (b) Individual insurance: compensation limited	Relevant consideration: % incapacity; % age of victim; % effect on work

				initially to the true amount in the contract-fixed sum	
3. Work accidents; occupational illness	Social security work, accident department (Caisse primaire d'assurance maladie)	All salaried workers, victims of accident at work, or occupational illness	Accident at work AND travel to work Illness of an occupational origin	No minimum	Inability to work in a particular occupation
4. Disability insurance (extension of sickness insurance)	Social security invalid department (Caisse primaire d'assurance maladie)	Each insured person who has complied with contribution requirements for at least 12 months, and who has completed the minimum number of hours of work Over age 60: old age pension Beneficiary groups: Those able to continue to work; unable to work, but no need for a third person's help; help of third person necessary	Disabling illness Accident incurred in the normal course of daily life	Work capacity reduced by 2/3	General inability to work evaluated with reference to the labor market in a given area

Table 10.10. Eligibility Conditions for AAH (adult handicapped), 1976 (in francs)

Handicap of 80% incapacity or more	Annual amount (%SMIC)	Annual ceiling of resources: Rights existing before June 30	Annual ceiling of resources: Rights existing + continued after July 1	For hospitalized people (% of SMIC)	Qualifying conditions
Single person	7,680 (45.6%)	7,200	8,200	Reductions of 3/5, giving 3,216 (19%)	Resident in France or D.O.M.
Married or cohabiting without dependent child	7,680 (45.6%)	14,400	16,400	If no dependent, reduction of 2/5, giving 4,824 (28.6%)	Aged > 20 Incapacity no less than 80%
Married or cohabiting with dependent child	7,680 (45.6%)	14,400 + 3,600 per dependent child	16,400 + 4,100 per dependent child	If no parents reduction of 1/5, giving 6,432 (38.2%)	Not in receipt of old age pension Corresponding invalidity
Two or more dependent children				No reduction; 8,040 (47.8%)	No recuperation
Need for third party help					Indemnity given by CAF or Mutualité Sociale Agricole

Table 10.11. Income of the Disabled under AAH as a Percentage of the Minimum Wage in France

	*Income as a % of SMIC**		
	1977	*1978*	*1979*
Handicapped under age 20:			
Educational allowance	14	19	13.5
1st category complement	21	21.6	20.3
Handicapped over age 20, with incapacity ≥ 80%	47.3	50.5	53.4
Compensatory allowance for a third person	from 43.2 to 91.7	from 46.4 to 93	from 46.5 to 93
Handicapped over age 20, with incapacity ≤ 80%; incapable of work	47.3	50.5	53.4
SMIC = Minimum legal wage (francs)	19,020	21,756	24,151

expenses, respectively. For 1977-79 this allowance fluctuated between 43 percent and 93 percent of the minimum wage, according to the gravity of the handicap; thus it is probable that the allowance is often insufficient to allow the handicapped person who receives no help from his family to obtain satisfactory care.

The asset ceiling is equal to that of the AAH, increased by the amount of the compensatory allowance granted; income from work done by the disabled person is only partially taken into account. Further, the Act of 1975 instituted a guarantee of resources for the benefit of those handicapped persons pursuing an occupation. Legally, such resources cannot be considered an "allowance," but rather an "added extra to income from work." We will later describe the technicalities of the asset guarantee, when we consider government action in the field of occupational rehabilitation.

Table 10.12 summarizes the disability benefit programs. How many people are assisted by this varied menu of programs? Any figures that we come up with can only be estimates, since published data are lacking. The figures in Table 10.13 are verbal estimates by program officials. Note the rapid increase in the number of those benefiting from the AAH, which can be explained by gradual disappearance of the monthy allowance paid by Aide Sociale. Note also that the number of beneficiaries under the assets guarantee is still modest (35,000) if compared with the number of war disabled (690,000).

Considered financially, this attempt at simplification by the Loi d'Orientation reinforced the supremacy of collective over family responsibility. In effect, it did away both with the necessity to take into account the resources of the handicapped person's family in assessing benefits and with repayment of benefits from inheritances, except when the next of kin are neither spouse, children, nor any other party permanently responsible for the handicapped person.

Together the measures we have just outlined show definite progress

Table 10.12. The Two Disability Benefit Programs Restructured by the Act of 1975

	Pre-1975	Post-1975
Allocations Familiales Awards paid to handicapped adults whose resources are below a certain figure and who are not in receipt of old age disablement benefits of an equivalent sum to that under a social security scheme, or special legislation	AHA	AAH *Conditions:* Handicapped persons over 16 with a disability of at least 80%, or for whom it is recognized as impossible to find work *Amount:* Equal to the minimum old age pension, be it AVTS + supplementary FNS allowance
Aide Sociale Awards paid to persons handicapped before coming within the scope of social security (e.g., the congenitally handicapped)	Monthly allowance from Aide Sociale Two compensatory awards to cover expenses: (1) increased amount for the constant help of a third person; (2) allowance to severely handicapped workers	*Compensatory allowance:* Paid to every handicapped person who is not under a social security scheme, and who has a disability of at least 80%, when his condition necessitates help of a third person, or supplementary expenses in order to exercise a professional activity
Fonds National de Solidarité	Supplementary FNS allowance; since 1958 the responsibility of the general sickness insurance program	

Table 10.13. Number of Program Beneficiaries Aged 25-60, 1974 and 1977

Type of Allowance	*1974*[a]	*1977*[a]
Housing	46,756	47,637
CAT	22,781	31,230
Domestic help	4,700	7,000
Disablement	718,300	701,306
War invalids	699,000	691,800
AHA, subsequently AAH	80,000	195,000
Increase for personal attendant	105,000	104,000
Compensatory allowance	18,000	20,000
Guarantee of resources	nonexisting	35,000

Source: Estimates from program officials.
[a]Numbers do not represent total number of disabled, since individuals may receive benefits from more than one source.

toward consolidation of programs for the handicapped. However, this progress is only a first step. In particular, it would be preferable to entrust the administration of compensatory allowances to the Caisses d'Allocations Familiales, already responsible for the AAH; this arrangement would end once and for all intervention by Aide Sociale in a system the complexity of which discourages its intended beneficiaries.

Next, it seems more rational to eliminate the Caisses d'Allocations Familiales loop altogether, and confine the whole structure of benefits to the Caisses Primaires d'Assurances Maladie, part of the general social security program which already manages many pensions and annuities (disability insurance, occupational illness, work accidents).

Proposals for Unifying Disability Programs

There have been many proposals to reduce the multiplicity of handicap compensation programs. We have singled out those of Michel Lévy, director of the Centre Technique National d'Etudes et de Recherches sur les Handicapés et les Inadaptés (CTNERHI). These proposals revolve around two major themes (Levy, 1978; 1979): First, administration of all programs would be confined to a single common organization called the Fonds National des Handicapés (National Fund for the Handicapped). The fund would be managed locally, in each department or major commune, by officials of existing programs—for example, Caisses Primaires d'Assurance Maladie. Consequently, it would act as a pivot for a gradual unification of the awards paid under the various programs currently in existence. Lévy further proposes that the fund be once again integrated into the general social insurance program, more particularly the Caisse Nationale d'Assurance Maladie, of which, henceforth, it would constitute the invalid branch. This system would have the substantial advantage of facilitating coordination between the different programs for which some individuals, by the nature of their handicaps, are eligible.

Second, the different kinds of benefits would be combined into three allowances: (1) *subsistence allowance*, designed for handicapped persons who cannot follow any occupation, would constitute a substitute for earned income and provide for the material needs of the disabled; (2) *compensation* for *earnings lost* where illness or accident prevents the individual from pursuing the kind of employment he held before he became handicapped; (3) *compensation* for the *extra expenses* that the handicap makes necessary.

Obviously, this unification could only be effected gradually and must consider the rights of each person within each program. Transitional measures would thus be provided. The proposed scheme would do away with special occupational considerations; but it would possess the advantages of relative simplicity, equality, and encouragement of occupational and social rehabilitation. "Balancing the interests of a certain objective against the financial constraints or political difficulties of its application highlights not so much the technical content as the political choices which only the legislator can make" (Lévy, 1979).

Occupational Rehabilitation and Employment of the Handicapped

The Loi d'Orientation for the handicapped has affirmed that priority be given to research into the integration of handicapped people into a social and occupational environment that is as near normal as possible. A lag is evident between the good intentions of the drafters of the Act and the current reality, but this legislation is still the best means of halting the slide toward permanent welfare status.

The necessary components of occupational integration are, first and foremost, identification of the handicap and counseling for the handicapped person, and second, sheltered work or living environments (centers specifically set up for handicapped, of which the sheltered workshop discussed below is one example), which, it may be hoped, will constitute the first step toward the ultimate return to *an ordinary work environment*. We will examine each of these aspects in turn.

Identification of the Handicap and Counseling for the Handicapped

Before the Act of 1975, occupational counseling for the handicapped was provided by the Commissions Départementales d'Orientation des Infirmes (CDOI)—departmental commissions for the guidance of the disabled. These organizations would identify the handicap and evaluate its severity according to four categories (A, B, C, or incapable of work). There are no statistics to enable us to characterize the cross-section of handicapped people that came before these commissions—we do not know their age, their social and occupational status, their handicap, or the benefits they are receiving.

The commissions dealt with 40,000 dossiers a year, and each person received an average two months' counseling or rehabilitation. Over several years the general pattern of dispositions hardly varied at all. Some 50 percent of those seen were directly placed in a "normal work environment," about 30 percent received occupational retraining, and about 20 percent were placed in sheltered workshops (RCB, 1977).

What conclusions can one draw about the effectiveness of these commissions? First, two-thirds of the newly handicapped did not appear before a commission, either because they did not know of it or because they mistrusted it. Further, few of the placements recommended by the CDOI were actually put into effect. Figure 10.3 shows the relationship between actual entry into reeducation centers, placement in protected work establishments, direct placement, and the dispositions recommended between 1971 and 1974. The picture is not an encouraging one; these committees appear to have largely failed, and no incentives to hire the handicapped were ever offered to employers. Against this background of relative failure, the Act of 1975 set up the COTOREP—the "Commissions Techniques d'Orientation et de Réclassement Professional"—in ways designed to counteract the inadequacies of the previous system.

These commissions, one for each department of France, are the mechanisms for implementing the 1975 law. Their tasks are manifold:

1. To identify the characteristics of handicapped workers (that is, those persons coming within the legal definition of "handicapped") and to classify cases referred to them under three categories: sound; disabled with more than one-third the productive capacity of a sound worker; handicapped with less than one-third such capacity, assessed according to the demands of a particular workplace.

2. To provide assessments and guidance to the worker and to establish a set of norms by which a worker's placement in the appropriate establishment may be effectively determined.

3. To determine whether the condition of the disabled person justifies *allocation of benefits*, such as the compensatory allowances.

4. To assess the feasibility of financial assistance—such as loans—to the handicapped person wishing, for example, to set up a business.

5. To allow employers to decrease the wages of a handicapped worker in relation to those of a sound worker.

The commissions play a demanding and fundamental role. The Code du Travail fixes maximum authorized wage decreases at 20 percent for workers whose output is less than normal. In fact, larger cutbacks have in practice developed, for the current state of the labor market gives employers the upper hand. The rapid and widespread growth of unemployment means COTOREP will be forced to accept diminutions of the income offered to disabled workers to maintain the level of offers of employment.

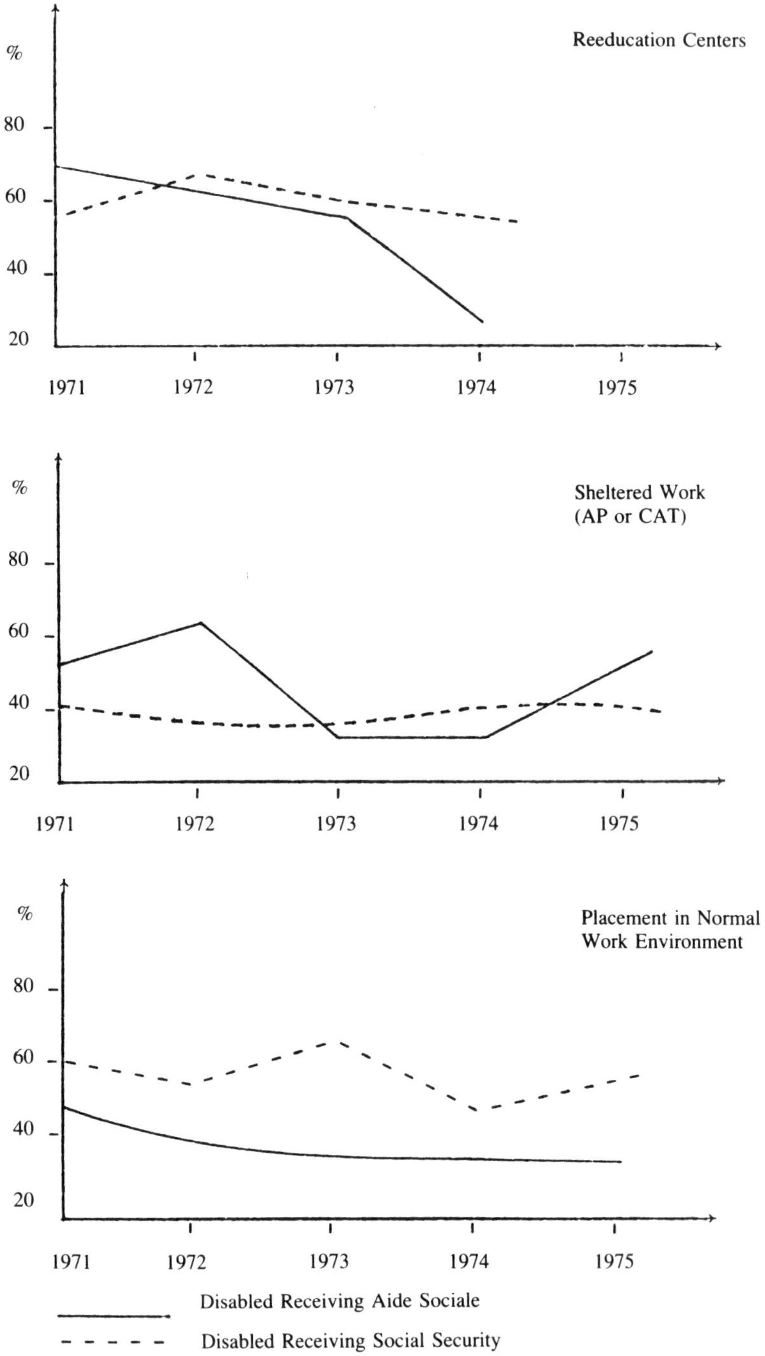

Figure 10.3. Actual Placements in Rehabilitation or Employment as a Percentage of Total Recommendations by the Counseling Agencies (CDOI and COTOREP)

Each commission hears representatives of the administration and of the various interested organizations to ensure an exhaustive representation of the different points of view. COTOREP has no power to force an employer to take on a handicapped worker, but its decision brings into play the system of the obligation to employ. The guidance that COTOREP offers may lead to either an immediate possibility of employment or the first stages of reeducation. In this study, we will not be examining the latter—strictly speaking, they fall within the medical domain. By way of example, Table 10.14 underlines the difficulty of translating opinion into action, despite the very obvious advances over the situation before the Act of 1975, especially where sheltered workshops and, to a lesser extent, direct placements are concerned.

The Economic Effectiveness of Employment in a Protected Environment

Sheltered workshops began to appear only around 1960. Two types are officially recognized: the Centre d'Aide par le Travail (CAT; Center of Helping by Wórking), and the Atelier Protégé (AP; Protected Workshop). The AP provides the handicapped worker with the conditions necessary to pursue an occupation in surroundings resembling those of a normal business. The CAT tries to provide employment in an environment which in addition assures almost complete social protection.

Administratively, the AP is under the Ministry of Labor; its position approaches that of a business committed to making a profit. The CAT is under the Ministry of Health and retains an essentially clinical orientation. In 1976, the CATs opened their doors to 16,000 handicapped people, often with a relatively poor capacity for work; the AP served some 2,500 persons whose work capacity was high.

These differences lend themselves to an interesting economic analysis. The APs are part of industry, sometimes as manufacturing units, more often as subcontractors within the businesses or organizations creating them, and thus have to be competitive. Sales returns are the principal

Table 10.14. Outcome of COTOREP Guidance

Opinion Given	Total (1)	%	Realization (2)	Percentage Realization (2)/(1)
Readaptation	1,198	3.9%	—	—
Professional reeducation	10,266	33.7	5,689	55.4%
Direct placement	13,991	45.9	4,869	34.8
Protected work center	4,983	16.4	2,408	48.3
	30,438	100	12,966	average 46.34%

means of financing salaries and social and legal charges and paying for raw materials, although at the end of the year the organization may receive a public subsidy. Only those supplementary costs attributable to the difficulties peculiar to the handicapped—access, work rhythms, etc.—can be funded, subject to agreement, by subsidies from local or social security organizations. Thus in practice, the APs are acquainted with the problems faced by management in general. In the first place, before they can even employ the handicapped workers they must establish a footing in an industrial sector and determine a demand they can supply. Here they may have a very restricted range of possibilities. Some sectors currently offer the prospect of well-paid employment (electronics, telephones, electrical equipment, light engineering). Other, more numerous, sectors make it hard for the APs to compete.

In the second place, management is made more hazardous by the departure of workers who, having acquired a particular technical skill and overcome their handicap, are generally required to leave the AP. Some workers may be made available to other employers under three-month contracts (renewable only once) which establish for the employer and the handicapped worker precise conditions of employment, subject to the worker's availability. These contracts are intended to facilitate the worker's movement from a protected to a normal environment.

The CATs offer industrial work at a much lower technical level, coupled with medical and psychological care. Almost always this means subcontract work. Funding, which is based on a standard "daily rate" paid per worker per day, places them firmly outside the private sector. Sales returns do not cover the salaries of management and supervisory personnel. The only costs met by the CATs are the salaries paid to the handicapped workers and their various special benefits ("pécules"). The products of the CAT are thus marketed at an abnormally low price in relation to conditions prevailing in the industry thanks to hidden subsidies. Given that the cost per hour of work done in a CAT establishment is about 2.5 times the minimum wage (the SMIC[3]) for workers paid according to that wage, and that the average output of the handicapped persons in these centers is about 0.5 the norm (RCB, 1977), the hourly subsidy for work done by a handicapped person in a CAT is as follows: H.S. $= 0.5\ (2.5 \times \text{SMIC} - \text{SMIC})$. In 1979 figures, H.S. $= 0.5\ (2.5 \times 11 - 11) = 8.25$ Frs. On average the handicapped person employed in a CAT works 1500 hours, and, as we noted, about 16,000 persons are employed in these centers. Thus the total subsidy per year is about 198 million Frs, or about one quarter of the total public expenditure on CATs. The different treatment of the AP and CATs seems to be at the same time economically prejudicial and socially a source of injustice.

Effectively the CATs are providing the APs with unfair competition, by reason of this hidden subsidy. The CATs are in a position to sell cheaper than the APs, sometimes forcing the APs out of the market. The APs cost about one-third of what the CATs cost to run. This ratio can only increase as personnel costs are heavier in the CATs, and their costs are growing more rapidly. Finally, the AP is encouraged to improve production because all its members are financially interested in doing so, whereas the CATs feel less need.

This analysis suggests that in future it would be advisable to prefer the AP to the CAT system, as one more step toward abandoning the notion of assistance (the help of an outside party for a handicapped person) in favor of a kind of financial aid that would not differ fundamentally from the aid given to large sectors of industry in difficulties. For instance, the extra overheads linked to the worker's handicap might be assumed, just as the expenses of a shrinking industry in difficulties might be assumed or the development of a new technology subsidized. Aid to the AP is in the nature of an *investment subsidy*—a fixed sum without interest—as opposed to aid to the CAT, which is a subsidy to running costs proportional to amount of time worked; the AP structure thus doubly favors the disabled: it encourages them to pursue industrial projects reflecting the state of the market and the product in question, and giving the AP an equipment subsidy allows increased productivity, adding value and improving revenues. Conversely, running-cost subsidies allow the CAT to be content with mediocre productivity and do not reward the efforts of disabled workers.

Numerous administrative and staffing constraints that are beyond the scope of this study stand in the way of change. But assuming for the moment that these were overcome, let us consider the cost of such a solution to the organizational problems of employing the handicapped. A Planning, Programming, and Budgeting Study (the French acronym is RCB, Rationalisation des Choix Budgétaires) was carried out in 1976 to calculate the approximate cost of two alternative policies (RCB, 1977).

Policy 1. Prolongation of Current Trends: Preserving the AP/CAT Duality

The full complement of positions for employment of the handicapped can be estimated from general demographic statistics, which have established that the existence of more than 70 such positions per 100,000 inhabitants in a geographical area tends to attract the disabled from other regions. This threshold can thus be taken as a norm. If the administration were to gradually introduce, between 1980 and 1986, the number of jobs indicated by the norm, growth in the number of employment positions would proceed along these lines:

Years	Total Need	AP	CAT
1976	18,500	2,500	16,000
1980	24,400	2,900	21,500
1986	30,500	3,500	27,000

Policy 2. Progressive Elimination of CATs by Converting Them into APs

Though this policy would be expensive to begin with because of its investment demands, it holds out the prospect of ending third party assistance, and of firmly establishing the status of salaried employees for handicapped workers. In conjunction with the guarantee of assets it shows itself as financially very advantageous, after a few years, for the social organizations and the public authorities concerned. This difference arises from the increased productivity which, it is estimated, will accompany these changes in financial and administrative structures. Such progress would make possible a revolving investment fund, under the AP current administrative structure. Figure 10.4 compares the costs of both policies and sketches the reduction over time in the collective cost that would result from a Type 2 policy.

Curiously, the public authorities have so far refused to commit themselves to a choice and, despite advantages of Policy 2 which are both human and financial, have contented themselves with recommending to the Directions Régionales de l'Action Sanitaire et Sociale (DRASS), the local executives of the relevant ministry, that they encourage the creation of APs when the characteristics of the population accepted by the CATs so allow (circular of Dec. 8, 1978).

Employment in the Ordinary Environment

The obligation to employ the handicapped goes back to an old provision: the Act of 1924, which obliged businesses to employ war victims. The 1957 Act extended the principle to those injured at work and to other handicapped, and the 1975 Loi d'Orientation more precisely specified the circumstances of the obligation, which is still today the focal point of public directives aimed at procuring employment for the disabled.

Every private business employing more than 10 salaried workers is obliged to employ handicapped persons, to constitute up to 10 percent of its total staff; in the public sector the percentage is reduced to 3 percent. Experience has shown that the obligation in this form does not, however, match recruiting needs as businesses perceive them. Juridically, the obligation has come to be seen as a simple examination of the priority of each handicapped candidate; thus certain businesses can quite easily not employ any handicapped workers at all and still be within the letter of the law. Although the law has worked well for the slightly handicapped, it remains inoperative as far as the placement of severely handicapped persons is concerned. More often than not, positions reserved for handicapped persons go to employees of the business who suffer accidental work injuries, frequently mild. Thus, the general consensus seems to be that the obligation to employ handicapped persons has contributed more to the

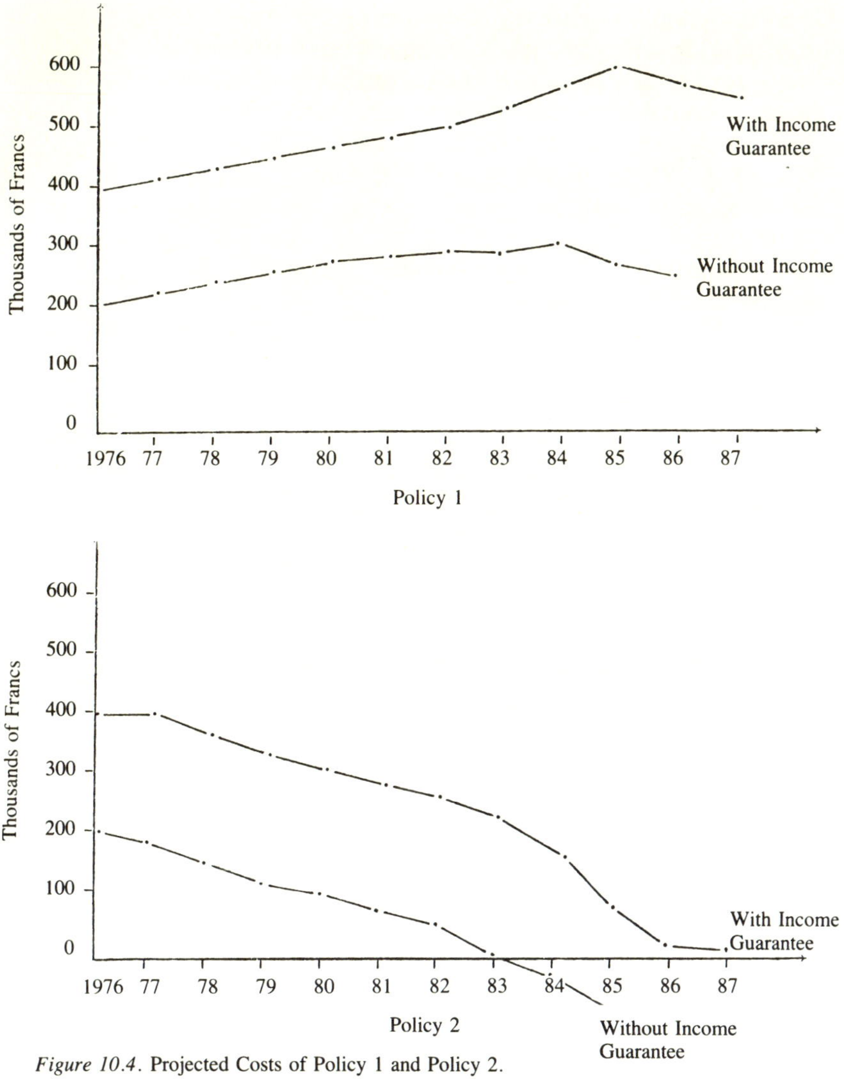

Figure 10.4. Projected Costs of Policy 1 and Policy 2.

reclassification of those injured in accidents—certainly laudable in itself—than to the hiring of workers already handicapped, its true object. Since 1975, businesses have been allowed to fulfill 50 percent or more of this obligation by offering subcontracts to "établissements de travail protégé," for example, APs.

These circumstances make apparent the delicate link between encouragement to employ handicapped people in a normal environment and supplying subcontract work in a protected environment. Today, legislation gives public authorities the means to provide, with the flexibility required by differing degrees of handicap, either employment or a sufficient volume of manufacturing contracts. It is to be hoped that the law will be applied with more vigor in the future, for the percentage of handicapped who were benefiting from this law did not seem to grow appreciably over the last years before the Act of 1975 (Inspection Générale des Affaires Sociales, 1976). The amount of employment available to handicapped people will, in the years to come, be under the control of the public authorities, who currently have the power to force the hand of business. Thus, the problem is more one of political will than economic policy. It is a disturbing possibility that the increasing number of unemployed will make it difficult for disabled people seeking employment to compete with those already unemployed.

Year	No. of Businesses	Total No. of Salaried Employees	Handicapped Empoyees	% of Handicapped Beneficiaries Under Obligation to Employ
1962	80,623	5,939,279	485,004	8.47%
1971	108,613	8,773,745	666,637	7.66%
1974	104,295	10,427,102	619,629	5.97%

The Incentive to Employ: Economic Measures

Any hope of appreciably increasing the number of offers of employment to the handicapped probably rests with such incentives. Since 1978, the financial help granted to encourage employment of handicapped workers in business, local organizations, and public establishments has included setting up a position (adapting the machinery or tools, the environment, or access to work; aid is limited to 80 percent of the extra cost incurred), and supplementary costs of management (aid is limited to 50 percent of the extra expenses incurred in employing handicapped workers).

These conditions are, objectively considered, very favorable to business, but surprisingly little use has been made of them. Three years after their adoption, the funds made available to cover the adaptation of workplaces have only been fractionally consumed by business—in 1978, hardly three-quarters (Inspection Générale des Affaires Sociales, 1978)—and proposed projects seem few and are not increasing. Perhaps it is too early to judge, as information is insufficient and procedures still too centralized. It may be those businesses already wary of employing any additional person, because of the financial and legal obstacles to letting such a worker go, that fear the inflexibility accompanying the establishment of a job for a disabled person. They wish to conserve maximum flexibility of organization, allocation of work within the business, and above all the freedom to lay off or fire workers.

The Role of the National Agency for Employment

The ANPE (Agence Nationale pour l'Emploi) has established a network of "prospecteurs-placiers" (employment agencies) for handicapped workers (PPTH). Their task remains imprecise; they have not taken over the role of interviewing and advising the handicapped. In fact the special organization required to perform such a function is not assured by the agency, and the prospecteurs-placiers are geographically unevenly distributed. This particular action has not yet produced the results anticipated because priority has been given to generating incentives to employ handicapped persons. Most offers of work to the handicapped continue to be prompted by personal motives, but it is to be hoped that gradually increasing awareness of these financial incentives will change this state of affairs.

Improving Employment Opportunities for the Handicapped

Several proposals for improving the supply of jobs available to handicapped persons have been offered. One would base the employment obligation not on the number of workers employed in a business, but on turnover of workers; this measure, although favorable when employment is growing, would be futile in the current business climate of decreasing employment. A second measure would set a different value on hiring a newly handicapped worker as compared to those already working for the firm, by crediting him with a different weight when working out the balance of obligatory employment.

A third measure, following similar lines but harder to put into practice, would give more weight in calculating the obligation to employ those workers whose handicap is greater than a certain level of incapacity. That level would, however, be difficult to establish if it were to have significant effect. Finally, it seems advisable to establish penalties to ensure more rigorous adherence to the thresholds.

It is especially the small and medium-sized businesses that will create most positions for handicapped workers in years to come; any tampering with the obligation to employ should first consider their attitudes toward the offer of employment. For example, such firms would welcome a simplification of the procedure and better information on incentives for employment. At the moment these are poorly understood by the relatively small and undeveloped personnel departments of small businesses.

A final comment concerns access of the handicapped to public employment. Whereas one would expect the state, as an employer, to lead the way, one finds a similar or even greater reluctance by government. Two principal issues may be mentioned here, although we will not discuss them in detail.

First is the exclusion of "category A" (highly paid) jobs from the field of "reserved positions" for public employment. Second is the existence of "special" or "supplementary" criteria of aptitude, which may be applied at the discretion of the different employing administrations.

The Guarantee of Resources:
A Secondary Income for Disabled Workers

Article 32 of the Act of 1975 guarantees a minimum of resources to every handicapped worker whether employed for wages or not. When the unpaid disabled person takes up regular work constituting the normal exercise of an occupation, the guarantee of resources is determined according to conditions fixed by ministerial directive. If he or she earns wages, the guarantee of resources varies, according to whether such activity is earned or in the ordinary production sector, or in an AP or a CAT. The guarantee is fixed according to the minimum wage (SMIC), and a system of bonuses to disabled workers in APs or CATs allows more of this revenue to be guaranteed when production exceeds fixed minima.

In the normal working environment, the minimum guarantee of resources is fixed at 100 percent SMIC. The state reimburses any cutback in a handicapped worker's wages authorized by a COTOREP decision. This compensation cannot in any case exceed 20 percent SMIC, but it can push the guaranteed resources up to one salary equal to 130 percent SMIC, as the following example illustrates:

Salary Paid	% SMIC (as of 1 Jan. 1978)	Complementary Remuneration	% SMIC	Total	% SMIC
1395.20	80	348.80	20	1744	100
1918.40	110	348.80	20	2267.20	130

When the disabled worker occupies a protected work position, although within the normal work, the minimum guarantee of resources is fixed at 80 percent SMIC.

In sheltered workshops (AP), the guarantee of resources is fixed at 90 percent SMIC. For those earning the estimated minimum salary, which is 33 percent of SMIC, the complementary remuneration is 56.67 percent SMIC (it can be more, e.g., when the salary paid during a trial period is less than one-third of the SMIC, so as to push the salary up to the guaranteed minimum 90 percent SMIC). With the bonus system, total salary can reach 130 percent SMIC.

In CATs the guarantee of resources is fixed at 70 percent SMIC, starting from wages equal to 15 percent SMIC. When work remuneration is less than 15 percent, the complementary amount cannot exceed 55 percent SMIC. With the bonus system, the salary can reach 110 percent SMIC.

This guarantee is the financial expression of collective responsibility, imposing on the state that part of the cost of paying salaries of which the business is relieved. What are its macroeconomic effects?

Figure 10.5 shows the future cost to the public authorities, depending on which policy is adopted—maintaining the dual system, or phasing out the CAT (RCB, 1977). The analysis of this result implies that progressive abandonment of the CAT formula will be markedly less costly and at the same time more efficient.

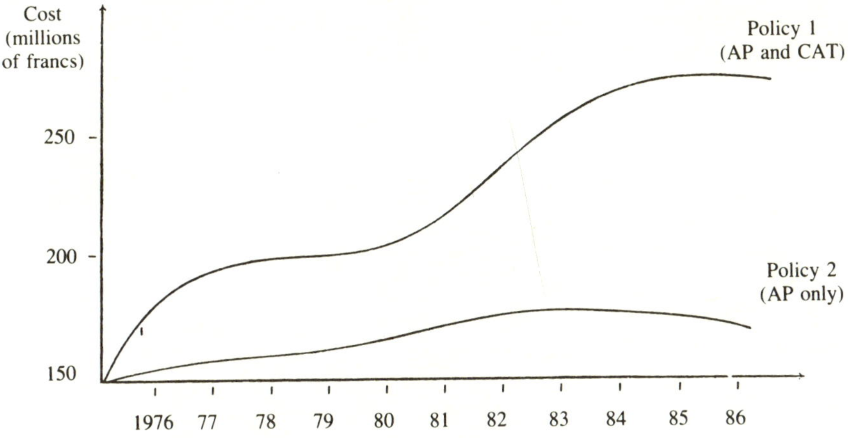

Figure 10.5. Aggregate Cost of Guarantee of Resources.
Source: RCB (1977).

What are the microeconomic effects of the guarantee of resources? What is its influence on the behavior of the handicapped person who is seeking work?

The guarantee modifies the relative attractiveness of the different formulae for finding work that are offered to the disabled in the normal or sheltered work environment while at the same time correcting the variations in benefits between the schemes. Within the sheltered workshops, application of the guarantee destroys differentials in ultimate resources (salary plus complement); those in charge of these establishments complain that this is a disincentive to work—that it discourages effort, and that the bonus system is insufficient to offset this effect. The following example illustrates this state of affairs in a CAT (Unit = Francs).

Category	Salary paid by CAT	Complementary Resources	Total Resources
1	130	1055	1185
2	220	1055	1275
3	340	1029	1369
4	430	984	1414
5	650	874	1524

Between the first and the fifth categories the initial difference in salary was 520 Frs; after the complementary benefits are received it was no more than 339 Frs.

The revenue disparity between the *protected and normal* environment is equally reduced. The guarantee of resources has a redistributive effect which considerably lessens the handicapped person's financial incentive to progress toward a normal environment, or into a job which is pursued under circumstances closer to normal. The difference between the minimum and the maximum amount of the guarantee of resources in these two environments is very slight.

	Min.	Max.
Ordinary sector	SMIC	130%
AP	90% SMIC	130%
CAT	70% SMIC	110%

Just as for employers, this system leaves a great deal up to the personal motivations of those participating. These observations show how difficult it is to strike a balance between, on the one hand, productive justice: the goal of occupational rehabilitation demands that all accomplishments be recognized, which means remuneration in proportion to work done; and, on the other hand, distributive justice: the desire not to penalize those whose handicap makes it impossible for them to work, which means that all are remunerated at approximately the same rate.

In this context the economic argument is compelling. The occupational rehabilitation of a disabled person costs ten times less than providing such a person with care; thus the unit cost speaks in favor of the first solution. Furthermore, the law accords priority to rehabilitation, as a necessary preliminary to financial autonomy and social integration. More philosophically considered, this policy reflects the preeminence traditionally given to work in our system of values. However, this moral precept has of late years come into question; new views have stressed the role that activities linked to leisure and education will play, in years to come. This trend will no doubt suit many disabled people currently condemned by the gravity of their affliction to tasks which are extremely simplified, fragmented, and little valued.

Attached to this already complex problem of the guarantee of sufficient resources to allow a decent life style is that of housing and the disabled person's financial contribution thereto.

The Right to Collective Housing and Its Financing

As far as *individual* housing is concerned, the 1975 Act widened eligibility requirements for a rent allowance. For collective housing, the problem is more complex: To encourage the autonomy of disabled persons, the 1975 Act provided that the costs of accommodation and maintenance in occupational rehabilitation and CAT establishments as well as in hotels were to be apportioned as follows. (1) The disabled person pays the full amount for his accommodation as long as this does not take his resources below the minimum. (2) Aide Sociale pays any excess.

Two criteria come into play to determine the minimum disposable resources left to the accommodated disabled persons: the nature of the accommodation and the condition and responsibilities of the disabled person.

Where the establishment assures full board and lodging, the disabled person must each month have at his own disposal at least 10 percent of his total monthly resources if he does not work. This amount must represent at least 1 percent of the annual level of the Allocation aux Adults Handicapés (AAH). If he does work, one-third of his earned income or of the guaranteed resources and 10 percent of his other resources must be at his own disposal. This minimum cannot be less than 30 percent of the monthly AAH. Where the tenant regularly takes at least five main meals per week outside the establishment, 20 percent of the monthly AAH allowance is added. Where the establishment only offers accommodation without board, the disabled person must each month dispose of resources at least equal to the level of the AAH, if he does not work. If he works, one-third of his earned income and 10 percent of his other resources, plus an additional amount of 75 percent of the monthly AAH, must be at his own disposal.

Where the tenant is responsible for the upkeep of a family, he has larger amounts at his disposal. If he is married without children, and his spouse does not work for a reason recognized as valid by the committee for admission, he must have 35 percent of the monthly AAH at his disposal, and another 30 percent of the monthly amount for each child or dependent.

The compensatory allowance varies with the circumstances of the disabled person. If he does not work and receives a compensation allowance for the help of a third party, its payment is suspended by an amount fixed in proportion to the help which he receives by the staff of the establishment in which he lives. The maximum suspension is 90 percent. If he does work and receives a compensatory allowance for supplementary expenses linked to his occupational needs, he keeps it for his own use, unless it is reduced by expenses for services provided—notably, provision of specially modified transportation.

These methods of calculating resources distort the economics of work by the handicapped just as the guarantee of resources does; they are a true disincentive to work, by limiting to 5 percent the growth of minimum resources left to the disabled in some form of collective accommodation. This is particularly true for psychiatric institutions.

Replacement Rates of Income for the Disabled: 1968 and 1978

In calculating these rates for the three main programs, we assumed a person of prime working age, head of a two-person family, who has become disabled. We set income levels at half the average, average, and twice the average. The 3 × 3 matrices in Table 10.15 show strong disparities among the situations of the disabled, depending on whether they receive a disability pension, a replacement income because of occupational illness, or a disability welfare pension.

The first situation—disability pension—does not change the predisability income schedule; it simply changes the level of income, which is about 33 percent of predisability income. This situation did not change between 1968 and 1978.

The second situation—occupational illness—is very different. First, benefits are much higher (between 78 percent and 190 percent of predisability income); second, the pension is redistributive. Lower-income beneficiaries receive the higher pension; average-income beneficiaries maintain the same level of resources; those who use to receive high incomes now receive a lower percentage in this postdisability pension. Compared to 1968, this population of disabled is doing better and better because their disability is linked to their employment.

The third situation—welfare program—is quite redistributive; all disabled get the same pension, that of the elderly. But this income is very low (32% of the average income). The situation is much better than in 1968, but for these people life is very difficult. However, the number of persons concerned is also low.

Financial Aid to Handicapped Workers from Public Funds: Macroeconomic Aspects

There is currently in France no complete economic study of the source and amount of revenue allocated to the disabled. Lacking full, appropriate, and significant data, our survey has therefore confined itself to noting the great increase of expenditure in order to show, on the one hand, the principal organizations and their roles, and on the other hand, distribution of the aggregate amount among the beneficiaries.

This approach led us to select four main areas to investigate: (1) What are the systems of financing help for the disabled, and what are their idiosyncracies? (2) What is the respective contribution of each organization? (3) How has the number of beneficiaries grown? (4) What is the role of this aid in the total social effort of the nation, and how has it developed over the years?

Table 10.15. Replacement Rates among the Three Main Programs, 1968 and 1978 (in francs)

1968	Half Average Income	Average Income	Twice Average Income
Predisability gross income (pre-DGI)	7,950	15,900	31,800
Taxes	358	1,339	4,053
Predisability net income (pre-DNI)	7,592	14,561	27,747
Program I: Disability Pension			
Disabled gross income (DGI)	2,570	6,140	8,160
Taxes	0	92	381
Disabled net income (DNI)	2,570	5,048	7,779
DGI/pre-DGI	32%	32%	26%
DNI/pre-DNI	39%	35%	28%
Program II: Occupational Illness and Accidents at Work			
Disabled gross income (DGI)	10,734	15,900	24,912
Taxes	659	1,339	2,774
Disabled net income (DNI)	10,075	14,561	22,738
DGI/pre-DGI	135%	100%	78%
DNI/pre-DNI	133%	100%	80%
Program III: Social Aid		Nothing (unless entering old-age program)	
1978			
Predisability gross income (pre-DGI)	20,400	40,800	81,600
Taxes	0	1,791	8,785
Predisability net income (pre-DNI)	20,400	39,009	72,815
Program I: Disability Pension (by "Caisse primaire d'Assurance maladie")			
Disabled gross income (DGI)	6,957	14,707	26,820
Taxes	0	0	308
Disabled net income (DNI)	6,957	14,707	26,512
DGI/pre-DGI	34%	36%	33%
DNI/pre-DNI	34%	38%	36%
Program II: Occupational Illness and Accidents at Work			
Disabled gross income (DGI)	38,763	40,800	78,884
Taxes	1,571	1,791	8,198
Disabled net income (DNI)	37,192	39,009	70,686
DGI/pre-DGI	190%	100%	97%
DNI/pre-DNI	182%	100%	97%
Program III: Disability Welfare (AAH)			
Disabled gross income (DGI)	12,900	12,900	12,900
Taxes	0	0	0
Disabled net income (DNI)	12,900	12,900	12,900
DGI/pre-DGI	63%	32%	16%
DNI/pre-DNI	63%	33%	18%

Our tentative evaluation has, however, run into several important difficulties. First, certain categories of expenditure have not been investigated by any organization, public or private; this is notably the case with the efforts of businesses using their own resources, funds paid by private associations and local organizations, for which all that is known is expenditure relevant to social aid. Further, time constraints have made an exhaustive presentation of the data impossible (even the administration refuses to attempt it). Thus the figures presented below concern only public aid and aid given by social security organizations. However, this limitation does not noticeably affect our conclusions, as aid from associations and business is only a tiny part of the whole. Second, the government's figures are delayed; thus the latest figure available to us are for 1977.

Finally, the benefit structure is currently being changed; the persisting overlap between the benefits that fall under the pre-1975 scheme and the benefits gradually being phased in since the Act of 1975 adds to the difficulty of describing the flow of financial aid.

The Financing System in France

Certain developed countries have clearly opted for a system of publicly financed social expenditure. Others, on the contrary, prefer to let private organizations intervene by means of insurance. In France, no such choice has been explicitly made, for historical reasons; funding remains a hybrid, relying on both public and private funds. Thus three large sources of funding coexist:

1. Social Security contributions by employers and insured people. Juridically this means funds managed by private organizations; economically, this means obligatory deductions over and above taxes paid. In France, contributions form the major part of the nation's social effort; but the social allowances paid each year, when taken as a whole, exceed the annual state budget (115 percent) and the allowances paid by the social security programs represent about 75 percent of the nation's total social effort (Ministère du Budget, various years).

For the disabled these funds are distributed by the Caisse d'Assurance Maladie—disablement, work accident, and occupational illnesses departments—and by the Caisse d'Allocations Familiales.

2. Local taxes, paid to local organizations that fund part of Aide Sociale. This represent a small part of all benefits paid to the disabled.

3. General revenues derived from various taxes on groups and private individuals and from indirect taxation. These funds are distributed to the working-age disabled people by three large ministries—Health, Labor, and Veterans.

The nature of the allowances has already been described earlier. Figure 10.6 shows the three routes by which the funds may pass from the taxes or contributions to the disabled people.

Evaluating the Financial Flow

Benefits in cash, paid directly to the disabled person, must be distinguished from those in kind—services placed at the disposal of the disabled: accommodation, subsidies to AP, and CAT, or domestic help.

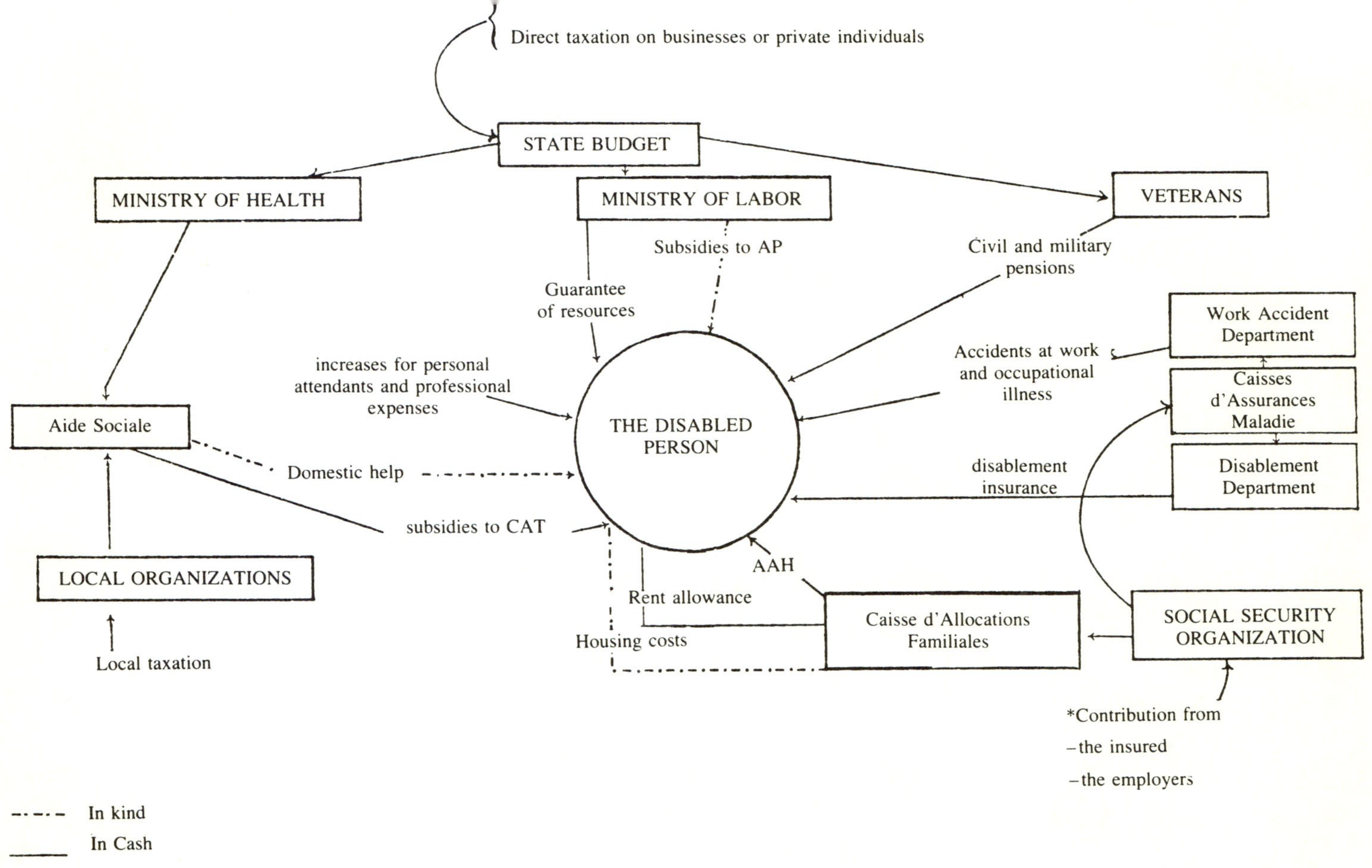

Figure 10.6. Funding of Disability Benefits.

Table 10.16. Cash Benefits Disbursed (in millions of francs)

Type of Allowance (before 1975)	1974	1975	1978 (or 1977)	Type of Allowance (post-1975)
Invalidity	2,187	2,559	3,965	
War disabled	4,244	4,539	5,893	
Work accident/occupational illness	8,774	10,436	10,951	
Rent allowance	49	95	173	
AHA	118	56[a]	1,877	
Monthly allowance	331	405[a]	212[a]	AAH
Supplementary FNS allowance	581	874[a]	570[a]	
Increase for personal attendant	663	750	1,921	
Compensatory allowance	100	423	193	Compensatory allowance
			485	Guarantee of resources
Total	17,047	20,137	25,340	

Sources: Annual reports of Inspection Générale des Affaires Sociales, of the Mission charged with following application of the Act of 1975, Caisse Nationale d'Assurance Maladie des Travailleurs Salaries; and information from the Veterans Ministry.

[a]Allowances being phased out since 1975.

Table 10.16 shows, for each category, the total level of benefits paid (in millions of francs) during 1974, 1975, and 1978—dates chosen to show the effect of the 1975 reform.

It appears that allowances in kind (Table 10.17) represent a very small part of the total, although they are slowly increasing. In 1974 they constituted only 4 percent of the total, in 1977, 7 percent. This expenditure comprises direct aid to the APs and CATs, a fact which makes it clear that, financially considered, the attempt at occupational rehabilitation remains a timid one. In particular, although the RCB study showed the strong social and economic profit to be had from the APs, the efforts focused upon them remain negligible, and the unchanged amount of money being spent on their equipment points to a reduction in efforts to launch new sheltered workshops.

Cash still constitutes the principal means of aid to the disabled (Table 10.18). Three-fifths of such aid goes to those injured at work or suffering occupational illnesses, or to war invalids.

Table 10.17. In-Kind Benefits Disbursed (in millions of francs)

Type of Allowance	1974	1975	1978 (or 1977)
Housing	507	641	918
CAT	204	338	807
AP	—	6	12
Domestic help	17	24	36
Total	728	1,009	1,773

Source: See previous table.

Table 10.18. Disability Benefits, Total Social Welfare Benefits, and GNP (in millions of francs)

	1975	*1976*	*1977-78*
In-kind benefits for the disabled	728	1,009	1,772
Cash benefits for the disabled	17,047	20,137	25,343
Total	17,775	21,146	27,115
Total social welfare payments	343,050	404,880	469,250
1. Benefits to disabled as % of total social welfare payments	5.2%	5.23%	5.8%
2. Total social welfare payments as % of GNP	23.6%	24.26%	26.09%
Benefits for the disabled (1 × 2) as % of GNP	1.23%	1.27%	1.45%

Sources: Tables 10.16 and 10.17, plus Ministère du Budget, *L'effort social de la nation;* annually.

The total amount of benefits paid to disabled adults represents just over 5 percent of the nation's social effort—that is, of all aid from which the members of the society benefit to improve their social condition and provide security against the risks of daily existence (Ministère du Budget, various years); it represents only 1.25 to 1.50 percent of GNP. We are obviously talking about very modest expenditure, and remember that this is for the entire working-age handicapped population—about 20 percent of the French population aged between 15 and 60.

Financial Contributions by Government Agencies

Comparing the contributions of Social Security, Aide Sociale, and the state budget in general—setting aside the share for Aide Sociale—to the financing of benefits for the handicapped population (Table 10.19), Social Security plays a preponderant role, supplying about 70 percent of all funds budgeted. Passage of the 1975 Act did not affect the aggregate amount contributed by Social Security, but merely added to it the contributions of the Caisse d'Allocations Familiales (which have increased from 3.7 percent to 11 percent).

The contribution by Aide Sociale is stable at around 7-9 percent. Since the compensatory allowance is now granted with more reluctance, this percentage should not vary greatly in the future.

Finally, the share paid out of the state budget which disburses benefits to the war-injured (23 percent of the total), will undergo rapid growth in expenses associated with the guarantee of resources (currently 2 percent) which is still being established and is not as yet benefiting the large numbers of eligible disabled.

Contrary to expectations, costs of benefits to the war-injured will hold steady as a result of the numbers of injured generated by the Algerian war and the rapidly rising level of benefits.

Table 10.19. Budget Share of Government Agencies

	1974		1975		1978		Direction of Change
	Amount	%	Amount	%	Amount	%	
1. *Covered by Social Security*							
CNAM (illness)							
Invalidism	2,187		2,559		3,968		
Occupational illness or accident at work	8,774		10,436		10,951		
	10,961	(61.6)	12,995	(61.5)	14,919	(55.9)	
CAF (family)							
Rent allowance	49		95		173		Growing
AAH	118		56		1,877		Growing
Housing costs	507		641		918		Growing
	674	(3.7)	792	(3.7)	2,968	(10.9)	
FNS supplementary allowance	581	(3.3)	874	(4.1)	570	(2.1)	Dwindling
Total Social Security	12,216	(68.7)	14,661	(69.33)	18,457	(68.8)	
2. *Covered by Aide Sociale*							
Monthly allowance	331		405		212		Dwindling
Increase for personal attendant	663		750		1,021		Dwindling
Professional cost allowance	100		423		196		
Domestic help	17		24		36		
Cost of CAT placement	204		338		807		Stable or Decreasing
	1,315	(7.4)	1,940	(9.2)	2,272	(8.4)	
3. *Covered by State Budget (less Social Aid)*							
Guarantee of resources					485	(1.8)	Very strong growth
AP subsidy			6		12		
War injured	4,244		4,539		5,893		
Total from State Budget	4,244	(23.9)	4,545	(21.5)	6,390	(23.6)	
Grand Total	17,775	(100)	21,146	(100)	27,115	(100)	

Disability Benefit Levels

Income levels of handicapped French workers are not known. Partly to try to offset the lack of accurate and complete statistics, we have calculated the average value, in current francs, of the individual benefit for each category of disabled, and the relationship between this average allowance and the minimum legal wage (hourly SMIC). This we have called the *SMIC coefficient of multiplication* (Table 10.20). The resulting figure cannot be considered as any kind of estimate of the average income of the disabled. First, some handicapped people—we do not know how many—receive several allowances. Second, income levels among the disabled vary greatly. Third, the disabled worker receives income from work as well as from disability benefits. However, this calculation does show the value of each kind of disability benefit relative to the minimum salary of the ablebodied worker. It is an indication of the relative economic status of the disabled which at the same time takes into account increasing prices and the rising wages of the most disadvantaged groups.

From Table 10.20, a relative decline in the circumstances of the war-injured is obvious. Their annual average represents 933 "SMIC hours" in 1977 as against 1084 "SMIC hours" in 1974. To a lesser degree, the benefit paid to disabled people who need the help of an assistant has diminished in value also: in 1974 it represented 1,127 "SMIC hours," but in 1977 it represented no more than 1,074. The situation of these disabled people has clearly become more difficult.

In contrast, the position of the average beneficiary of a disability pension or a compensatory allowance has slightly improved, represented by increases in "SMIC hours" from 543 to 619, and from 960 to 1,051, respectively. The principal rise, however, has been in the AAH, which has grown from 263 "hours" to 1,053—a figure that demonstrates improvement in the relative situation of those handicapped whose status was marginal before the Act of 1975 (essentially the congenitally disabled and those not otherwise covered by an existing program).

Finally, the guarantee of resources represented in 1977 an average of 1,516 "hours." This figure seems high in comparison with the coefficients of multiplication found for the other benefits, especially when one considers that it is generally given as a complementary benefit rather than as primary income source. Thus the most rapid growth has been in newly introduced benefits: AAH and the guarantee of resources. The development of the legal structure of aid to the handicapped appears as an important factor in the growth of their purchasing power.

Conclusion

The Act of 1975 makes aid to the disabled a collective obligation. By deemphasizing family responsibility, it abandons the notion of

Table 10.20. Disability Benefit Levels in Terms of Annual Average per Individual and Equivalent at Hours of Minimum Wage

	1974			1977		
	Number of Beneficiaries	Average Individual Benefit	SMIC Coefficient of Multiplication[a] (hours)	Number of Beneficiaries	Average Individual Benefit	SMIC Coefficient of Multiplication[a] (hours)
In-kind benefits						
Housing	46,756			47,637		
CAT	22,781			31,230		
Domestic help	4,700			7,000		
Cash benefits						
Disablement	718,300	3,045	543	701,336	5,656	619
War invalids	699,600	6,071	1,084	691,800	8,528	933
AHA (AAH)	80,000	1,475	263	195,000	9,625	1,053
Increase for personal attendant	105,000	6,314	1,127	104,000	9,817	1,074
Compensatory allowance	18,000	5,374	960	20,000	9,607	1,051
Guarantee of resources				35,000	13,857	1,516

Source: Preceding tables.

[a]Represents value of average benefit in terms of hours worked at SMIC (the minimum legal wage). SMIC as of March 1974 = 5.60 Frs per hour; as of April 1977 = 9.14 Frs per hour.

"assistance" in favor of the principle of social responsibility. It endeavors, furthermore, to encompass all aspects of the life of a disabled person so as to unify administrative procedures and rationalize the disparate and heterogeneous set of programs through which aid to the disabled was previously disbursed. However, the legislature has stopped short of a complete reshaping of the diverse pieces of legislation that determine benefits to the disabled. Disparities in payments, even flagrant inequalities, continue to exist. The Act itself is a source of costly inconsistencies among programs as a whole. In particular the lack of liaison between the programs leads to a reliance largely on good faith to avoid unnecessary duplication of benefits.

Detailed analysis of financing mechanisms before and after 1975 shows little change or improvement in the roles of the agencies involved. The principal modification has been to transfer from Aide Sociale to the general Social Security program (family allowance branch) almost all responsibility for paying benefits to disabled people who do not otherwise qualify for a pension or allowance.

Nor have some desirable administrative changes been implemented. For instance, all intervention by Aide Sociale has now been eliminated where minors are concerned, but not for adults.

On the other hand, one could question the appropriateness of assigning to the Caisses d'Allocations Familiales new managerial responsibilities for the handicapped, when the Caisses Primaires d'Assurance Maladie, already accustomed to administering disability pensions under the general program, are well equipped to cope with this task and have at their disposal already suitable medical service.

As for benefits—in kind or in cash—no noticeable change has yet occurred. Benefits in kind, intended to adapt the occupational and social environments to fit the needs of the disabled, remain insignificant, despite some slight growth, in relation to benefits in cash, based upon the nature of the handicap.

One group of the handicapped is seen to have particular advantages. Those disabled by accidents at work and by occupational illness are in a very favorable position compared to other disabled people, notably the congenitally disabled, for whom integration into society demands a cumbersome and too often insufficient infrastructure.

In establishing employment opportunities for the disabled, the public authorities have favored the Centres d'Aide par le Travail (CAT) over Ateliers Protégés (AP). The former, of course, offer the more seriously handicapped occupational help combined with indispensable medical and social care, whereas the APs provide merely a work site adapted to the needs of the disabled and thus are chiefly directed at the only slightly disabled. Economically speaking, this situation has driven the APs and CATs, because of their respective pricing systems, into competition, which is as destructive to their financial goals as to their social ones.

Finally, the Act poses, under the same rubric as the guarantee of resources, a difficult choice between two contradictory though equally legitimate philosophies:

1. The desire financially to compensate the handicapped, which assures all disabled people of almost identical resources, regardless of productivity, so as not to penalize those whose handicap makes it impossible for them to work.

2. The desire to integrate the handicapped into the mainstream of society by the indirect path of occupational rehabilitation, which involves recognition of effort made and thus remuneration in proportion to work done.

The relative importance of the allowances in kind and in cash seems to prove that despite the law's affirmation of occupational rehabilitation as a primary means of social reintegration, the first philosophy continues to inspire current policy.

Thus it would appear that the 1975 Act, even if it does reestablish the rights of a disabled person to a decent life, to work, and to equality with others, is not the instrument of an economic change that will enable the disabled to become at least partly self-sufficient individuals instead of burdens on the state. The principle is certainly reaffirmed, but the means are not provided. Implementation of the Act has been inexcusably delayed in ways that cast doubt upon the genuineness of the public authorities' desire to implement real and profound reform. More serious is the fact that the promulgation of specific decrees and administrative circulars which do not conform to the principles set forth in the Act are distorting the intentions of the legislators, making essential provisions of the Act completely ineffective.

Aid to the disabled must, in the years to come, become one of the priorities of social and economic policy. Currently, it is clearly not seen as such.

Notes

1. For the World Health Organization, whose definition is currently in favor, "handicap" is characterized as the presence, lasting or transitory, of a psychological, physiological, or somatic disorder, which can result in a functional diminution—i.e., partial or total inability to carry out certain motor, sensory, or mental activities within the capacity of a normal individual. The net result is an incapacity "to exercise one or several functions which generally are considered essential elements of daily life" (World Health Organization, 1980).

2. We have chosen age 15 as the age at which young people begin to enter the work force, and 60 as the age at which handicapped people can generally benefit by early retirement.

3. "Salaire minimum interprofessionnal de croissance." The figure is linked to the rate of growth of the economy and to the rate of inflation.

References

INSEE (Institut National de la Statistique et des Etudes Economiques). Annually. *Comptes de la Nation: Documentation française.*

Inspection Générale des Affaires Sociales. 1976, 1978. *Rapport annuel.*

Lévy, Michel. 1978. Où en est l'action en faveur des handicapés? *Regards sur l'actualité*, no. 37 (*Documentation française*).

Lévy, Michel. 1979. L'harmonisation des régimes de compensation des handicaps. *Cahiers du Centre Technique Nationale d'Etudes et de Recherches sur les Handicapés et les Inadaptés* (CTNERHI).

Ministère de la Santé. 1976. Estimation du nombre de personnes atteintes d'un handicap sévère. Service des études et du financement.

Ministère du Budget. Annually. L'effort social de la Nation: Notes bleues du Ministère du Budget. *Documentation Française* (INSEE).

RCB(Rationalisation des Choix Budgétaires). 1977. Etude de Rationalisation des Choix Budgétaires: L'insertion professionnelle des handicapés adultes. *Statistiques du Travail.* Supplement to monthly bulletin no. 51.

Revue Française des Affaires Sociales. 1978. Les personnes handicapés et l'opinion. January/March.

Viot, M. 1979. L'insertion professionnelle des handicapés. Report to the Economic and Social Council. *Documentation Française* (INSEE).

WHO(World Health Organization). 1980. International classification of impairments, disabilities, and handicaps. Geneva: WHO.

Chapter 11

Disability Policy In Israel

Jack Habib, Haim Factor, and Vincent Mor

Policies toward the disabled have not commanded major attention in Israel. The prevailing public image was and is that the disabled are a small and deserving group; this sympathy has been translated over the years into an ever growing body of entitlements. The pace of growth has accelerated in recent years, and has been paralleled by a rapid growth in the number of recipients. The result is that the public image has become obsolete: the number of nonaged beneficiaries of some form of disability benefit now approaches 100,000, or 8.6 percent of the labor force, and many of the disabled are economically better off than they were before impairment.

The Israeli system is comprehensive in its coverage: each of the main groups for the disabled is covered by a separate categorical program (or programs), and coverage extends even to compensation to housewives for the loss of homemaking capacity. It is, on the whole, highly coordinated in that the receipt of benefits in one program excludes that in others to avoid duplication of benefits.

A noteworthy characteristic of the system is that medical services and a range of vocational rehabilitation services are fully integrated with the income support programs, and access for these services is available at a single point. A second aspect is the broad view taken toward the needs of the disabled: personal care and mobility needs are fully recognized and provided for on an entitlement basis. These are also accessible at the single entry point for basic income replacement and rehabilitation aid.

In the first two sections of this chapter we summarize the main income support and employment programs; the next section focuses on special

Jack Habib and Haim Factor are affiliated with the Brookdale Institute of Gerontology and Adult Human Development in Israel; Vincent Mor is in the Division of Biology and Medicine, Brown University.

benefits for the disabled. We then calculate the levels of benefits for various types of impairments, document the growth in disability programs, and analyze the various contributory factors, including changes in entitlements and replacement rate.

We conclude with a review of key policy issues and suggest the need for a comprehensive revision of existing policies.

Income Maintenance and Earnings Replacement Programs for the Disabled

Public policies in Israel follow a categorical approach to the disabled, making distinctions among groups of the disabled on the basis of both value orientations and historical factors. There is less categorical differentiation in rehabilitation services, although here too there are groups that have preferential access.

Income support programs distinguish among injury sources—work-related, military, automobile accidents; all other sources are lumped together in the category of "generally disabled." The type of benefits to which the last group is entitled varies with the extent to which its members are insured in the workplace and the particular sector of the labor force in which they are employed. The welfare system deals with those not eligible for any other programs.

Disablement and Work Injury (Covered through National Insurance)

The National Insurance work-injury program covers those injured as a result of employment, defined to include accidents on the way to work and occupational diseases. Two subprograms divide the clientele into short-term and long-term disability. The latter, our sole concern here, insures against both partial and full disability, with benefits geared to the level of disability and predisability wages. It is a compulsory program, financed by employer contributions based on a regularly adjusted industrial-branch experience rating.

Eligibility for benefits is determined by a rating based on a medical scale and work-capacity-impairment evaluation. The law provides for a supplement to the rating of up to 50 percent "in consideration of the profession, age and sex of the disabled." Rarely applied in the past, this clause has come into use recently as a result of several court rulings. The program has been transformed into one in which work-capacity considerations play a more important role.

Although the program has a reputation for not penalizing income or employment, employment status at the time of application may influence the medical board decision.

An important feature of the benefit structure is the possibility of benefits capitalization when the disability rating is 20 percent or more. The number who have chosen to capitalize is significant. This right is frequently denied, and attempts by applicants to contest the use of such discretion have consistently failed in court. The reason for denial is to ensure that the capitalized benefit is used for a legitimate rehabilitative purpose and that alternative income is or will be available. In the rating range of 5-20 percent, only a one-time grant is provided. Additional benefits include extensive medical and rehabilitative services. Special monthly benefits for attendance and one-time grants for housing and automobile purchase are available on a discretionary basis to those with at least a 75 percent disability. These benefits have recently been expanded and substantially revised.

Eligibility for a work-injury benefit precludes eligibility for most other programs. Moreover, many programs require prior application to the work-injury program before consideration for benefits.

General Disability
(Covered through National Insurance)

General disability funding began in 1970, and the program was enacted by law in 1974. It brings under the National Insurance roof almost all persons who have a disability that reduces work capacity by at least 50 percent and who are not covered by other programs. It includes those disabled prior to 1970, those disabled from birth, and, more recently, disabled housewives whose husbands are insured. A program providing benefits to families with disabled children is the latest to be enacted.

For those disabled prior to 1970 or before age 19 (termed the "previously disabled"), the program is a pure transfer, without contributory requirements. Seventy-five percent of the benefits for these groups are financed out of general revenues, the remainder from contributions of the entire working poulation. For those disabled after 1970 (termed "newly disabled"), benefits are financed entirely from compulsory contributions.

The eligibility and rating process is complex. An individual must first establish that predisability earnings are reduced by at least half. If he receives a 35 percent disability rating from the required medical examination, the client is usually sent for a rehabilitation assessment. Finally, he is sent before a disability board composed of a doctor, an employment counselor, and a social/rehabilitation worker for a determination of his work capacity. This committee has broad discretion. Work history is a factor influencing the decision. Rehabilitation program participants are entitled to the maximum benefit regardless of their disability rank.

The benefits provide a poverty-line income. Special dependents' allowances in addition to the universal child allowance are available to maintain this standard. For the newly disabled, dependents' benefits are earnings-related; the previously disabled receive the entire benefit. National Insurance makes occasional random checks on earnings status, but no regular reporting is required. Just as earnings above the disregard are penalized at a 100 percent rate, so are benefits from any other programs.

In addition to the basic cash benefit there is an attendance allowance set at a maximum of 100 percent of the basic benefit (if the disabled lives alone, 150 percent) for a person with a 75 percent disability rating and the maximum score on an "activities of daily living" (ADL) functioning test. Recipients have the option of receiving either the attendance allowance or an allowance under the mobility benefits program, described next.

Mobility Benefits

This assistance, designed to compensate for the loss of independent movement, is provided any disabled person except those entitled to similar benefits under the military and hostile action program (see below). The mobility benefits previously offered to those injured at work were recently consolidated with this program. Disability is based on a fixed numerical scale reflecting motor capacity impairment. Determination is made by a special medical board of the Ministry of Health. Benefits take the form of monthly payments and a loan to cover automobile import customs, the latter being equivalent to 150-200 percent of a car's value. The amount of benefit depends on whether the disabled person is employed, whether he purchases a car, whether he drives it himself, and on his disability rating.

A premium is placed on work and earnings. Anyone earning above the basic disability pension is entitled to a 100 percent increase in the monthly benefit; that benefit is available only to those employed, if they do not have a car. Those receiving general disability benefits must choose between attendance and mobility benefits.

Work-Related Disability Programs

A significant percentage of the labor force is insured against disability through collective bargaining arrangements.

The *Civil Service (Treasury) program* serves tenured public servants within the central government. This is a noncontributory system financed by general revenues and can be viewed as a pure fringe benefit. In practice it also serves as an early retirement plan for undesirable workers.

Disability is defined as reduction in work capacity resulting in inability to perform work that a person of the same age and sex can perform. The disability board may determine that a worker needs to be moved to another position rather than receive a benefit. That is, in fact, the frequent request of applicants, particularly those with physically demanding tasks.

Partial benefits are geared either to years of service or to disability degree, whichever yields the greater amount. Thus, a person with a 25 percent disability rating and 35 years of service can receive the full benefit of 70 percent of his predisability wage. This reflects the system's additional function as an early retirement plan. There are no penalties on subsequent income, but the individual may not continue work within the Civil Service.

A benefit based on years of service may be received in addition to any rights under the work-injury program, but a benefit based on degree of disability precludes the right to a work-injury benefit.

The Histadrut Comprehensive Disability pension is an employer-financed compulsory plan for industrial and service workers. It is part of a comprehensive survivors' and disability retirement plan requiring contributions from employer and employee.

Disability is determined by a medical board. Its standards require that the applicant's work capacity must have been affected by injury or illness for at least three months and he is unable to work at least 3/4-time in his previous job, or another suitable job, without doing injury to health. A full pension equal to 70 percent of predisability wages is granted those unable to work more than two hours a day.

A worker is not entitled to receive these benefits if also entitled to work-injury or veterans' benefits. He may, however, receive general disability benefits.

Welfare

The system of welfare and social services, jointly financed by the Ministry of Labor and Social Affairs and the local municipal authorities, is designed to provide for those with low incomes who are deemed deserving but who are not eligible for a National Insurance benefit. As part of the application process a person must be classifed in one of the following categories: aged, having a disability or chronic disease, mentally ill, women heading families with children, unemployable, and low income due to family size. In 1982 it was legislatively mandated that this program be transferred to the National Insurance Institute in a somewhat revised format.

Welfare provides a minimum cash income coordinated with the child allowances provided by National Insurance. Welfare recipients receive free health insurance, have their National Insurance contributions paid, and are given a rent supplement. Special benefits, such as basic household goods and home care, which will continue to be administered by welfare, depend on municipal budgetary conditions and a discretionary assessment of need.

A person who claims he cannot work and is not eligible for any other disability program may receive a benefit if it is deemed that he is not employable or that the labor exchange is unable to find him a job.

The benefits income test includes a disregard and imposes a penalty of less than 100 percent in order to moderate the effect on incentives. Once a year, all recipients must report their earnings status and reapply.

Automobile Accident Compensation Act of 1975

This act eliminated negligence from the classification of auto accidents by instituting the no-fault principle. Benefits provided under the laws are not different from those formerly provided under civil law, but strict limits are placed on compensation for pain and suffering. Specific regulations were adopted gearing benefits to age, number of hospital days, and degree of permanent disability. For loss of earnings, a maximum of three times the worker's past average wage was established. In contrast to civil law, where no compensation could be obtained until the final court ruling, the act provides for payment of immediate medical expenses and a basic living allowance, and the courts may rule that compensation be made on an annual rather than a one-time basis if the claimant has no other means of livelihood.

The law adopted the disability rating scale used in the National Insurance work program: loss in earnings is defined as the difference between what a claimant would have earned if uninjured and what he will earn after the injury over his entire lifetime. The difference is summed and capitalized for a one-time payment. While attempts are made to adjust estimates of income loss for future expectations, there is no provision for additional claims should disability status change.

Because the benefit level is tied to current earnings, there is a strong disincentive against returning to work until the final ruling is made. The disabled person is entitled to claim benefits under other programs, although generally the damages received will be deducted in determining eligibility for benefits.

Disablement through Military and Hostile Action

Persons injured as a result of military or hostile action are eligible for support under one of two programs—soldiers are entitled to benefits from the Defense Ministry, civilians to benefits from the National Insurance "Border and Hostile Action Program." Because the two programs are very similar, we will describe only the first.

The Defense Ministry covers all impairments due to accident or illness in military service, whether incurred during duty or travel. The program provides both compensation and rehabilitation. The scale used to measure disability is essentially that of the work-injury program, except that a 130 percent disability rating is assigned to special categories such as paraplegics and the brain-damaged.

Benefits are diverse and complex. The basic cash transfer is linked to the salary of a lower-echelon civil servant, which is about 60 percent of the average wage. A cash supplement is provided if the disabled person does not work or is unemployable. Besides generous home care and mobility allowances, there are many additional benefits in the form of extensive housing assistance, sales tax exemption on consumer durables, and free telephone calls.

Special supplementary benefits are reserved for those who have limited work capacity. Eligibility is considered when rehabilitation efforts have failed and the disabled cannot earn an adequate living (defined as 60 percent of the average wage). A committee composed of a doctor, social workers, and vocational advisor must submit its recommendation to an administrative commission having final authority. There is a regular follow-up of supplementary benefit recipients.

Those eligible for Defense Ministry benefits are denied eligibility under most other programs.

Disablement through World War II or the Holocaust

These laws complement German laws compensating those disabled from Nazi actions in World War II. They provide benefits to the disabled who are ineligible for any foreign benefits or whose foreign benefits are below the Israeli level of benefits. Germany provides benefits to those whom it recognizes as "members of the circle of German language and culture." Israel undertook to indemnify former residents of countries now Communist. This classification of "Germans" and "non-Germans" has no rigid rules. The German interpretation of "German circle" has been increasingly liberal, enabling new claimants to apply for benefits.

Despite the lapse of the final claims date and the old age of most of the people who suffered from Nazi persecutions, the number of recipients has continued to grow significantly in recent years, due to liberality of the laws, especially one article that sets aside the time limit on new claims if there is a "special reason."

In determining eligibility, those disabled by war action are examined by a medical board of the Indemnity Authority, using Defense Ministry regulations, and those disabled through Nazi persecutions are examined by a National Insurance medical board where work-injury regulations apply. The structure of benefits and their levels are then linked to these two programs.

Housing Assistance

The Ministry of Housing, with the participation of the Ministry of Health, provides housing assistance to the disabled in the form of special consideration within an extensive network of programs for the general population.

Assistance is granted young couples on the basis of a point system that assigns additional points to a disabled person who is unemployed, or partially employed, and who has proper medical certification. An 80 percent disability rating or blindness grants many more points. The program makes loans available to cover part of the purchase price of a home, and disability status may increase the maximum loan by as much as a third.

Another program, which provides loans to moderate- or low-income families for the purchase or renovation of their homes, recognizes inadequate living arrangements compounding disability as a special source of need. The disabled who live alone are also recognized as a special group because of the scarcity of small units.

A joint committee of the Ministries of Health and Housing exists to assess the needs of the disabled.

Tax Treatment of the Disabled

There have been many changes in tax treatment of the disabled over the years. There has always been full exemption of earned income and pensions for those who have a 100 percent rating or are disabled or blind. There is a large exemption for property income, but the disabled may not receive the exemption on both sources of income simultaneously. A variety of additional exemptions for various groups with less severe disabilities were abolished as part of a general tax reform in 1975. In return, the level of general benefits was raised from 20 percent to 25 percent of the average wage.

Income from disability pensions has special tax status. Benefits from the programs of the Defense Ministry, Hostile Action (civilian), and Disabled by the Nazis are fully tax exempt. Seventy-five percent of National Insurance benefits were included in taxable income up to 1978, but now are totally exempted. Work-related benefits are the only form of disability benefits that are subject to tax. Here too, however, there has been a liberalizing trend; recently the percentage of benefits subject to tax was reduced to 60 percent.

Links among Programs

We now turn to an analysis of links among programs as they bear on the several groups of disabled. The extent of overlap is governed by a priori limitations on the sources of disability or by the way in which the receipt of benefits in one program affects the right to and the level of benefits in a second. Because the links between the various programs and the welfare system are particularly intricate, we shall deal with them at the outset.

We must distinguish between monthly cash benefits and various forms of special assistance. A disabled person who applies for a monthly welfare benefit is required to apply first to other disability programs, in particular to general disability. If eligible for support under these other programs, he is ineligible for welfare regardless of benefit level. If he is deemed not sufficiently disabled to receive benefits under National Insurance, he cannot receive welfare on the basis of being disabled. If, aside from his impairment, he has additional problems that affect his employability, he may receive welfare under the more general category of being unemployable, but his probability of getting welfare on this basis is much lower. These links illustrate the residual role played by the welfare system since adoption of the general disability law.

Eligibility for special benefits under welfare is not, however, so restricted, being potentially available to any disabled person who meets the income requirements and has a demonstrable need. The relationships between eligibility for special benefits under welfare and under National Insurance are unclear. Under National Insurance, the generally disabled may receive either a mobility or an attendance allowance. The question of how receipt of either affects eligibility for special benefits under welfare has not been resolved. While cash benefits from National Insurance enter into the welfare means test for special benefits, it is not clear whether attendance and mobility allowances are included. Moreover, no clear rule governs the link between a cash attendance benefit from National Insurance and the assessment of need for in-kind home care services under welfare.

Summary of Support for the Disabled

Those injured as a result of military service are provided for almost exclusively by the Defense Ministry. If partially injured they may be eligible for occasional additional support, as from the Housing Ministry. If they receive benefits, they may not claim damages under civil law.

In a parallel way, those disabled as a result of work receive almost all of their support from the work-injury program under National Insurance. With the exception of those in the civil service, they may not simultaneously receive a work-related disability *pension*. A public employee may receive, at the individual's option, benefits either from National Insurance or from a pension. If he chooses to receive severance pay, he gives up the right to a disability pension (and retirement as well) and he will receive benefits from National Insurance. If he chooses to forego severance pay, he is entitled to a disability benefit from the civil service that will supplement his National

Insurance benefit up to a maximum of 90 percent of previous wages. In this case he will be also entitled to retirement benefits.

The disability benefits provided public employees over and above their National Insurance benefits are, in a sense, in lieu of severance pay. As the government system is noncontributory, there is an apparent preference for annuities as opposed to one-time benefits. This is also reflected in the fact that public employees cannot capitalize their pension rights when leaving the government, whereas other employees can.

The worker who sues his employer under civil law is entitled only the amount of damages in excess of that which he receives from National Insurance. This includes that part of his wages not replaced by National Insurance or additional compensation for pain and suffering. Employers generally participate in a special insurance program to cover themselves against such claims. This insurance covers only the claims in excess of National Insurance benefits, as employers cannot be held liable for any more (although previously they could). If the accident involves an automobile (automobile accidents that occur on the way to work are recognized as work accidents), then it is covered under the automobile insurance law. In this case National Insurance is entitled to deduct 75 percent of the damages paid to the worker.[1]

All other groups of disabled may receive general disability and mobility benefits from National Insurance and additional support from several other programs. They may simultaneously receive a work-related disability pension, but the pension is taxed at 100 percent in the means test applied to National Insurance benefits. The newly disabled may therefore lose their dependents' benefit; the previously disabled may lose their full National Insurance pension.

Damages received in civil cases are fully deducted from the previously disabled persons rights to benefits, and are deducted at a rate of 75 percent from those in the category of the newly disabled. If, for example, a person was injured in an auto accident, he may retain only a small portion of any damages that he is awarded. Housing assistance may be obtained from the Ministry of Housing, and assistance in purchasing medical aids from the Ministry of Health.

Employment Policies for the Disabled

For the most part, Israeli programs designed for employment of the disabled fall within the context of income maintenance and income replacement programs, and consequently they reflect the same categorical distinctions made by the income transfer programs. It is instructive to begin by examining the available evidence on the extent of employment of those who have had some form of impairment. Data are available for two groups, those receiving a benefit from the work-injury program and those receiving a benefit from the Defense Ministry.

In April 1974 a study was conducted of a representative sample of 532 recipients of disability benefits from the Defense Ministry who applied for benefits in the years 1967-70—i.e., the study came four to seven years after application. They were compared to a group of the same age serving in the reserves. The study found that at the time of the survey 64 percent were employed full-time on a regular basis, 10 percent were employed part-time, and 13 percent were students (primarily for advanced degrees). Only 13 percent were neither studying nor employed. When asked to evaluate their work capacity a smaller number (6 percent) claimed they could not work at all and about one-third of those not working had made efforts to find work in the past year. Only 8 percent of the impaired were receiving the supplementary assistance provided to the disabled, defined as unable to work. This is only slightly higher than the percentage who claim they cannot work. The participation rates are particularly meaningful in light of the very high benefit levels provided in the Defense Ministry's program and the considerable bonus provided those defined as unable to work or temporarily unemployed.

In interpreting these findings it is useful to keep in mind some basic characteristics of this group of disabled. Only 11 percent have a disability rating of 75 percent, 20 percent are rated between 50-75 percent, and at the other extreme, 25 percent have a rating between 19 and 24 percent. Unfortunately, we do not have a breakdown of labor force activity by disability rating. While there is a wide spread of disability ratings, a very large group has medically oriented problems of work adjustments. Sixty-seven percent worked before their impairment; of these about half were employed in jobs that required continuous physical effort—skilled or semi-skilled industrial jobs. When asked if they could return to the same type of work, 75 percent replied that they could not.

The high rates of labor force participation may in no small measure be due to the extensive rehabilitation opportunities available to this group and the special access privileges granted this group in the labor market. All recipients in the Defense Ministry's program receive at least some assistance from the rehabilitation department. The vast majority reported that they found their jobs through the special labor exchange operated by the Ministry; in addition, 14 percent received training, 12 percent were given financial assistance to establish self-employment, and 24 percent were assisted in pursuing higher education.

In 1973 the National Insurance Institute conducted a survey of a sample of 1,140 recipients of disability benefits in the work-injury program (the great majority) and a small group in the hostile action program (Reiss, 1973). As in the Defense Ministry's sample, the full range of disability levels is covered: 6 percent had a rating above 75 percent, 11 percent between

50-75 percent, and 47 percent were rated between 20-34 percent. At the time of the survey, 75 percent were employed and 59 percent were employed full-time on a regular basis. Of the 24 percent not working, 18 percent had never worked since their injury. When asked to evaluate their work capacity, 50 percent defined themselves as capable of working full-time (14 percent without any limitations as to type of work) and only 9 percent as unable to work at all. Thus about 15 percent of the disabled reported that they were not working but were able to work at least part time. Of particular interest is the relationship between degree of disability and the extent of employment, presented in Table 11.1. The variation in the rate of employment is moderate in the 20-74 percent disability range, and somewhat greater if the distinction between full and part-time employment is made. There is, however, a precipitous drop in labor force participation for those with a disability rating above 75 percent. The subjective evaluation of work capacity (not shown on table) also varies with the medical disability rating. Five percent of those with a 20-34 percent disability rating claimed they could not work at all, as opposed to 10 percent with a rating of 51-74 percent, and 21 percent of those over 75 percent.

There is evidence that the extent of adjustment problems was quite widespread. Those claiming inability to do the same type of work as before impairment constituted 72 percent of the disability and 81 percent of those who returned to work. Of the impaired, 69 percent worked in jobs requiring continuous physical effort prior to impairment, but only 20 percent did so after impairment. Almost all of those working part-time stated that the reason was medical.

Rehabilitation

Rehabilitation services are provided within the context of each of the major income support programs. Voluntary organizations provide services to select subgroups of the disabled. In addition, the Ministry of Labor and Social Affairs, through the Labor Exchange and various training centers, provides additional services that are not limited to any specific group.

Table 11.1. Employment and Degree of Disability, 1973 (percentage distribution of participants in work-injury and hostile action programs)

	Medical Disability Rating (%)				Total
Employment Status	20-34	35-50	51-74	75+	Disabled
Working	79	77	70	43	75
Full-time	64	59	44	24	59
Part-time	15	18	26	19	16
Not working	19	22	29	57	24
Worked during the year	3	3	3	1	3
Did not work	16	19	26	56	21
Unknown	2	1	1	0	1

Source: Reiss (1973).

The total number of recipients of rehabilitation services cannot be determined because the same person may be simultaneously listed by more than one program—if, for example, National Insurance sends someone to a course sponsored by the Ministry of Labor, he will be listed by both. Confining ourselves to those receiving services through the National Insurance and Defense Ministry programs, we arrive at an estimate of about 6,800 persons in 1977-78. They represent about 16 percent of those receiving benefits in the Defense Ministry program, and 9.3 percent of recipients of National Insurance benefits.

The number of those receiving rehabilitation services has been growing over time, as shown in Table 11.2. The growth rate of rehabilitation in the Defense Ministry has matched the rate of growth in number of recipients. Rehabilitation through self-employment has grown almost twice as fast. The overall rehabilitation program of National Insurance has grown tremendously since the introduction of the general disability law in 1974. Only a small proportion of these rehabilitants were previously receiving such services from the Ministry of Labor and Social Affairs. Over the same time there has been a decline in rehabilitants among the work-injured, due perhaps to increased pressure on the staff of the rehabilitation department.

Access to and take-up of rehabilitation services in all programs tend to be concentrated around the time of application for the benefits. Rehabilitation efforts in most cases last up to two years. An outstanding feature is the availability of a wide range of services under common auspices. This simplifies the process of applying for the various benefits. It enables the rehabilitation department to have a comprehensive view of the needs and motivation of the disabled.

Lack of reliable data prevents us from describing rehabilitation efforts. We can only indicate the nature of the opportunities provided and the extent of financial benefits and incentives. In general, eligibility is based on degree of medical disability. A lower rating is usually required than that needed for benefits. There are four major forms of rehabilitation: counseling and placement services; formal education; vocational training; and self-employment. Counseling and placement are available to all the disabled, either through the various categorical benefit programs or through the Labor Exchange, which maintains a registry of the disabled who request its help in seeking employment. Counseling and placement services vary from program to program. The most comprehensive form includes personal counseling and regular contact with a professional social worker, intensive vocational testing and observation (generally at the vocational testing stations of the Ministry of Labor and Social Affairs), and supervised attempts at job placement. This level of service is in theory available to recipients of benefits from the Defense Ministry or through National Insurance or welfare; in practice, there may be budgetary or bureaucratic constraints on actual availability. For example, the generally

Table 11.2. The Growth of Rehabilitation and Employment Programs for the Disabled of Working Age over Various Periods

	Total in 1977-8		Average Rate of Real Growth (%) over Period of Years		
	Expenditures (mill. 1978 IL)	Recipients	Expenditures	Recipients	
Rehabilitation and Placement					
Ministry of Defense (excl. placement)[a]	39.0	1,770	10.5	9.3	1969-77
National Insurance[b]					
General Disability	10.5	1,955	97.2	7.7	1975-77
Work Injured	6.0	805	−0.8	−4.4	1971-77
Border and Hostile Actions	0.9	287	20.1	15.0	1971-77
Ministry of Labor and Social Affairs[a]					
Welfare Division[c]	16.3	1,800	17.0	13.3	1970-77
Labor Division[d]	12.0	1,760	—	—	
Labor Exchange	—	2,833	—	2.5	1971-77
Sheltered Employment[a]					
Meshakem	131.4	5,057[e]	−0.7	−6.3	1968-77
Others	12.3	600	—	—	
Sheltered	(11.9)	(370)	—	—	
In-home Employment	(2.7)	(230)	—	—	
Self-Employment[a]					
Ministry of Defense	109.6	1,976	20.6	17.7	1969-77
Ministry of Labor and Social Affairs	4.9	100	—	—	
Rehabilitation and Employment for the Retarded and the Blind	13.9	2,344	6.6	5.4	1968-77

Note: Numbers in the table cannot be totaled because National Insurance sends its rehabilitants to programs operated by the Ministry of Labor and Social Affairs and pays a large portion of the program cost.

[a]Number of recipients is the total number during the year.

[b]Number of recipients in April 1978.

[c]Includes numbers of places in rehabilitation centers, participation in public rehabilitation centers, and training in various settings.

[d]Number of places in vocational diagnosis centers. In 1978, 3,000 individuals received this service.

[e]Not including some special programs for the retarded and blind.

disabled with medical disability ratings of 20 percent who are ineligible for cash benefits are formally eligible for rehabilitation services but in practice do not receive them. The level of placement services provided by the Labor Exchange is generally thought to be inadequate. Thus, independent placement services have been set up by the Defense Ministry and the various rehabilitation frameworks to undertake placement efforts on a more informal basis.

Training specifically targeted at the disabled is provided in rehabilitation centers or in vocational training courses under the sponsorship of the Ministry of Labor and Social Affairs (ca. 3,500 in 1977), not including the blind and retarded). Yet referral and financial support are generally provided by the program through which income support is received. Each program has its own financing criteria. Eligibility for training support is available for up to 24 months to recipients of National Insurance benefits with a disability rating of 35 percent, and for 36 months if their disability rating is 65 percent. The support criteria for expensive formal education are more severe. The general disabled are eligible only if it is viewed as essential to their rehabilitation and if they have a disability rating of 65 percent; for the work injured, 50 percent is required.

Access to higher education is much more extensive in the Defense Ministry, and the percentage of beneficiaries is much higher. Aside from receiving full financial support for training, the rehabilitant is provided with additional benefits, including a regular monthly living allowance and allowances for transportation costs, school supplies, rent, and a supplementary food allowance if the course requires the disabled to live away from home. In most programs the monthly living allowance is set at the level of benefits for someone with a 100 percent disability ratings. As a result there is considerable incentive for the partially disabled to participate in disability programs. This factor is particularly significant in the work-injury and the Defense Ministry programs, where the vast majority of recipients have partial disability ratings but a significant number receive full benefits. For the generally disabled the advantages are much less significant.

Various groups of disabled are provided assistance for self-employment. This option is available on a relatively minor scale in the welfare system, but on a much larger one in the Defense Ministry's program. The option was until recently very common in the work-injury program as well. However, assistance in that program is granted on the basis of capitalization of benefits and represents an alternative not only to other forms of rehabilitation assistance but to the receipt of an ongoing benefit as well.

On-the-Job Training, Aid to Employment, and Job Adaptation

Additional forms of assistance linked with a specific employer or position are also available. The rehabilitation departments of National Insurance and the Ministries of Defense and Labor and Social Affairs are all willing to finance the salary, under certain circumstances and for a limited period, of a disabled person who is placed in private industry.

Funds are available to purchase special aids required to enable the disabled to maintain a specific job or to make adaptations in the workplace itself. Little documentation of the extent of these activities or of the criteria for assistance are available. National Insurance has established certain guidelines which provide a maximum equivalent to about $1,000 for those with at least a 50 percent medical disability rating. This may be used to purchase special equipment or to make adaptations in the job surroundings.

Designated Employment Quotas

Social policy in Israel has tended to reject imposition of quotas as a means of promoting equality of opportunity for various groups. The one notable exception concerns those disabled in military service. According to the laws governing the Labor Exchange, an employer may be compelled to hire disabled veterans up to a certain limit. In addition, disabled veterans by law have priority for some positions: tellers in theaters, ticket takers in public transportation, those on guard duty, those running refreshment stands in factories, etc.

There have not been any direct studies of the implementation and effects of these programs. The law is apparently rarely used to compel employment but is more often used to prevent arbitrary dismissal.

Providing Physical Access to Employment

A set of Ministry of Interior regulations was adopted in 1971 to establish compulsory standards for access to all buildings serving the general public—public services such as government ministries, clinics, post offices, museums, or schools; and commercial services such as banks, department stores, restaurants, hotels, sports facilities and banquet halls. The motive was not so much to give access to employment as to provide access to a citizen or consumer. The provisions specify access ramps, width of entrance and hallways, door types, elevators in multistory buildings, bathroom facilities adapted to the disabled, public phones at an accessible height, a 5 percent allocation of all parking space to the disabled, reserved places in self-service restaurants serving more than 25 people, and special seating in movie theaters.

Responsibility for implementation lies with the municipal planning authorities. In new construction, the regulations do not appear to be strictly enforced. The reasons are unclear, and organizations representing the disabled have expressed their dissatisfaction.

Sheltered Employment: The Meshakem

Sheltered employment for the disabled is provided by a number of organizations ranging from nonprofit organizations to government ministries. A minimum of 6,000 disabled persons representing a little over 0.5 percent of the labor force are so employed.

Sheltered employment in Israel is primarily confined to low-paying menial jobs geared toward the least skilled sections of the labor force. We do not know whether this emphasis reflects the needs of the disabled or an explicit view of the cost/benefit ratio associated with providing sheltered employment.

The dominant organization is the Meshakem, a public corporation founded in 1958, designed for those who cannot easily be absorbed into the regular labor market. Initially, the Meshakem was established to provide employment for disabled and aged workers during the period of mass immigration when there was severe unemployment. As the economy developed and full employment was achieved, the basic question arose as to whether the goal was to provide permanent employment or to prepare the disabled for eventual employment in the regular labor force. While this equivocation is still not fully resolved, it appears that the Meshakem will confine itself to providing long-term employment.

Similarly, there is some equivocation between viewing employment as an end in itself and viewing employment as a means of reducing dependency on the rest of society. There seems to be little if any concern with increasing the overall income of the disabled.

Ten categories of employment are offered by the Meshakem. A large percentage are menial service jobs; there are as well several light industries such as dressmaking or bookbinding.[2]

The Meshakem generally works on a commission or contract basis with the organizations using its services—for the most part large organizations such as municipalities, government offices, and the army. It is frequently granted exclusive rights in providing certain services, and the prices provided are often below the market price. In other cases it wins its contract in open bids.

A 1974 report on the Meshakem argued that the types of employment provided to the disabled were in many cases inappropriate and based on primitive methods, lacking any attempt to raise productivity or to provide opportunities for advancement (Shapira, 1973). This was attributed to a reluctance to undertake riskier projects involving capital investment and to an inability to shake loose from the role of providing menial employment to the least capable, which had developed in the early years of the service. The report recommended that the Meshakem initiate an industrialization program emphasizing light and service industries employing modern technology to enhance both productivity and job opportunities. It also recommended that a range of services be designed to provide the supervision and support required by the disabled. A basic issue raised by these recommendations concerns the kinds of workers requiring sheltered employment in a full-employment economy. The author of the report felt that prime-age disabled workers would be able to get jobs in the open market unless they were unskilled. As a result, the only way to meet the more diverse skill requirements of light industry would be through more effort to attract aged workers having the requisite skills to work alongside the disabled. This was also justified on the basis of the genuine need to develop employment opportunities for the aged.

The rough guideline for eligibility is that a worker have a level of productivity between 40 percent and 99 percent of the average. Employment conditions in a particular area also enter in. In development towns, established in peripheral areas or for new immigrants, the medical requirements are known to be applied less severely. Efforts to accept all referrals are constrained by a shortage of available work slots. Whereas in the past the number of work days was rationed, reflecting the overall scarcity of employment opportunities in the economy, such limitations have been dropped. In most cases the work day is limited to five hours. Workers are provided with the official minimum wage rate (about 40 percent of the average wage for full-time employment) and are granted fringe benefits common throughout the Israeli economy. The most significant fringe benefit is a pension providing for 35 percent of the last monthly wage after 10 years of employment. Sick pay is provided, and absenteeism due to sickness is a serious problem. There is no wage differentiation on the basis of type of work nor any system of incentives and advancement.

Of the 1977-78 operating budget of IL 182.5 million (IL 131.4 million for the nonaged recipients), 65 percent was covered by sales and the rest by government support. The Meshaken must have its annual budget approved, and fiscal control is exercised by the ministries that finance the annual deficit. The Meshakem does not have a formal development budget. Investment funds are financed by soliciting grants from a range of government ministries. We have not been able to document the magnitude of the development budget.

Efforts at industrialization are modestly reflected in the data on the growth of the Meshakem: light industry grew from 2.5 percent in 1968-69 to 10 percent in 1977-78, while most other sectors declined in absolute terms. The pattern of subsidies by sector also changed significantly: in the early years the subsidy per worker was highest in the industrial sector, where it is now among the lowest.

Growth of the Meshakem

Tables 11.3 and 11.4 describe the Meshakem's growth. To evaluate the pattern one must distinguish between two groups of participants, regular and special. Since the period of mass unemployment in the early years of the state, Israel has had a public employment program concentrated on the unskilled. This program has declined in importance and is being gradually

Table 11.3. Growth of Meshakem Sheltered Employment for Nonaged Recipients, 1969-1978

	1969-70	1970-71	1971-72	1972-73	1973-74	1974-75	1975-76	1976-77	1977-78	Average Annual Growth 1969-77	1977 as % of 1969
Number of recipients up to 65	8,540	8,414	8,274	7,974	7,618	6,811	6,145	5,438	5,057		59
Annual growth (%)	—	−1.5	−1.7	−3.6	−4.5	−10.6	−9.8	−11.5	−7.0	−6.3	
Of these: regular recipients[a]	—	4,844	—	6,002	5,354	5,016	4,611	4,316	3,975		
Annual growth (%)			23.9		−10.7	−6.3	−8.0	−6.4	−7.9	−2.9	
Total expenditures (mill. 1978 IL)[b]	139.2	137.1	182.8	169.0	201.1	171.6	141.3	137.0	131.4		94
Annual growth (%)	—	−1.5	33.7	−7.6	18.9	−14.7	−17.7	−3.1	−4.1	−0.7	
Total subsidy (mill. 1978 IL)[c]	42.7	43.7	77.8	63.8	91.4	69.5	52.8	52.2	45.0		05
Annual growth (%)	—	2.3	78.0	−18.0	43.2	−24.0	−24.1	−1.2	−13.8	0.7	
Average expenditure per recipient (ths. 1978 IL)	16.3	16.3	22.1	21.2	26.4	25.2	23.0	25.2	26.0		59
Annual growth (%)	−30.6	0	35.6	−4.0	24.5	−4.5	−8.7	9.5	3.1	6.0	
Average subsidy per recipients (ths. 1978 IL)	5.0	5.2	9.4	8.0	12.0	10.2	8.6	9.6	8.9		78
Annual growth (%)	−27.5	4.0	80.8	−14.9	50.0	15.0	15.7	11.6	−7.3	7.5	

Source: Hameshakem, budgets and financial reports for the various years.
Note: Values for IL are for 1978.
[a]Regular = disabled, as opposed to only unskilled.
[b]Average annual growth 1970-77.
[c]Calculated on the basis of the proportion of aged to nonaged recipients.

Table 11.4. The Composition of the Meshakem and Rate of Subsidies by Type of Work, 1969-1978 (1978 values of IL)

Type of Work	1968-69 No. Workers	1968-69 No. Work Days	1968-69 Exp. (mil. IL)	1968-69 Subsidy per Worker per Year (ths. IL)	1968-69 Sub. per Work Day	1973-74 No. Workers	1973-74 No. Work Days	1973-74 Exp. (mil. IL)	1973-74 Subsidy per Worker per Year (ths. IL)	1973-74 Sub. per Work Day	1977-78 No. Workers	1977-78 No. Work Days	1977-78 Exp. (mil. IL)	1977-78 Subsidy per Worker per Year (ths. IL)	1977-78 Sub. per Work Day	1977 Sub. per Worker as % 1968 Sub.
Absolute total	6,849	1,581,864	148.7	4.9[a]	21.2	6,151	1,462,958	212.5	10.4[a]	43.7	4,353	1,038,466	134.3	5.9[a]	24.5	120
Percentage distributions and amounts																
Gardening	42	39	42	IL 5.9	IL 27.2	42	39	37	IL 11.1	IL 58.4	36	32	32	IL 6.1	IL 28.7	103
Building maintenance	29	30	26	2.7	11.1	23	25	20	10.4	41.0	16	13	11	5.0	24.1	185
Janitorial services	4	5	4	0.8	4.4	7	7	7	7.2	29.4	7	7	6	3.1	12.0	388
Watchmen	6	7	6	3.3	12.6	2	2	2	9.6	40.3	—	0	0	—	5.3	161
Manufacturing clothing	4	4	5	10.4	43.7	4	4	4	14.6	58.3	5	5	6	8.7	35.9	84
Plant nurseries	2	2	2	2.4	4.0	1	1	7	8.2	33.7	2	2	2	7.4	33.1	308
Simple clerical work	1	1	1	1.0	4.7	1	0	0	5.2	40.2	0	0	0	4.7	24.8	470
Light industry (e.g., bookbinding)	2	2	6	8.1	37.5	6	5	10	10.1	44.4	10	8	17	3.3	16.6	41
Rehabilitation	—	—	—	—		—	—	—	—	—	3	5	6	4.2	9.3	—
Miscellaneous	10	9	9	7.6	33.8	14	16	13	9.4	34.6	21	26	20	7.6	25.8	100

Source: Hameshakem, budgets and financial reports for the various years.
[a]The difference between subsidy per worker here and in Table 11.3 is due to administrative costs which are not related to specific type of work.

phased out, remaining quantitatively significant only in a few scattered development towns. In 1969 all participants in the program were shifted to the auspices of the Meshakem, almost doubling its size. These participants were disproportionately concentrated in menial jobs, such as gardening and maintenance. We refer to them as special recipients and whenever possible have separated them out.

The overall number of participants in 1977-78 was only 60 percent of the number in 1969-70; the annual rate of decline has been 6.3 percent (Table 11.3). The number of regular participants, which grew in the early seventies, subsequently declined rapidly and is now only two-thirds of the 1972-73 peak. The level of real expenditures and of subsidy is similar to that at the start of the decade, having peaked in the mid-1970s. An obvious consequence has been a rise in the average real subsidy per recipient, using 1969 as a base, of 7.5 percent per year.[3] The current subsidy level is, however, below the mid-1970s peak. When aged participants are included in the growth figures, the number of participants is stable over the whole decade and the level of expenditure and subsidy reveals a modest increase.

How can the program's overall decline be explained? There was considerable turnover in the Meshakem program during the 1970s. The average number of years on the program has actually declined. In 1967-68, 28 percent had more than 10 years experience, whereas in 1977-78 the percentage had declined to 15 percent. New participants joined at a rate of about 1,000 per year, while 1,800 left on average in the years 1972 to 1978. Part of the explanation lies in the accelerated rate of withdrawal of aged recipients in response to the extension of pension rights and expanded National Insurance old age benefits. The aged have indeed declined as a percentage of all participants. Still another factor may have been the expanded adequacy of disability benefits for those of working age. In 1974, with the adoption of the National Insurance disability program, there was a reported decline in the hours worked of many participants so as to meet the income test of that program. Others may have been induced to withdraw from the program, although this has not been documented. This effect has been somewhat offset by the referral of the National Insurance rehabilitation department of a significant number of disabled in the younger age groups.

A new factor is the changing attitude toward unskilled physical labor that plays a large role in the Meshakem. It has been necessary to phase out these jobs because of an absence of takers. This, together with the difficulties inherent in developing industrial jobs, raises the possibility that supply factors have also been a constraint. In other words, the supply of attractive jobs may not have increased sufficiently to meet the actual and/or potential demand. In various discussions with the program administrators, this claim has been made. Thus it may be that the increased availability of transfers has accelerated a decline in the readiness to assume unattractive menial jobs. Similarly, insufficient jobs of an attractive nature has inhibited the participation of younger persons. Finally, there has been some development of other sheltered employment opportunities. We do know the full extent of these developments, but they may have lured potential applicants from the Meshakem.

We conclude by listing a number of basic questions that underlie our discussion:

1. What is the nature of sheltered employment in a full employment economy and on what groups should it be targeted? Should it be confined to those with minimal skill levels, or should it include persons with a range of skills?

2. To what extent should the Meshakem alter its basic orientation from that of providing a minimum wage to that of realizing the full earnings potential of the disabled?

3. Considering its present policies, will there be a demand for employment in the Meshakem as the coverage and adequacy of income support expands? On the other hand, if wage levels and jobs are made more attractive, how can a shift of workers out of open employment be avoided?

4. The major constraint facing the Meshakem is the scarcity of development funds. As a result it must balance the desire to provide additional employment opportunities with that of offering more attractive ones. What is the optimal balance between expanding employment opportunities and creating more attractive capital-intensive jobs?

Special Benefits for the Disabled

A frequent subject of discussion concerns the special needs of the disabled and the range of special benefit programs related to those needs. In this section we evaluate two major forms of special programs in Israel: attendance allowances and mobility allowances.

Attendance Allowances

The term "attendance allowances" covers a range of cash benefits as well as in-kind services geared to those who, for reasons of health, require assistance in order to prevent bodily injury and/or to provide for personal care. While those eligible for attendance allowance may also be eligible for a variety of other "additional" benefits, we will not discuss these additional assistance items. Major consumer durables, such as washing machines or medical equipment, although they constitute important aids in the provision of personal care, are not included in attendance allowances.

Personal services include a range of activities. A distinction is frequently made between personal care, homemaking activities (shopping, heavy housecleaning), and medically oriented services provided by nurses. A particular program will generally emphasize one of these areas, although in practice parts of these areas may be simultaneously provided.

The attendance allowance programs are operated under various auspices and with considerable variability in their provisions. The most recent is for those receiving general disability benefits from National Insurance. This program will soon be serving the largest group of disabled and is of particular interest both because of its quantitative significance and because it may well serve as a model for the expansion of benefits of this kind to other groups. A demonstration project preceding national implementation provided information for the final development of eligibility criteria and procedures.

Attendance benefits are generally targeted on the severely disabled in recognition of the nonlinear relationship between the level of disability and the incumbent costs and difficulties of daily living. That is, the most severely disabled are entitled to a measure of assistance more than twice that afforded an individual who is half as disabled. Several means are used to focus on those potentially in need of such services. One approach limits eligibility to those with a certain minimum disability rating; a second applies a formal direct test of functional capacities; a third allows for exercise of discretion in assessing the level of need. These are often used in combination.

The major disability programs (work injury, veterans', and general disability) require a minimum medical disability rating as a prerequisite for eligibility and only then apply more direct measures of need. The general disability and, until recently, the veterans' program, applied functional capacity scales to rate the degree of assistance needed, if at all, in such areas as getting about, dressing, bathing, eating, toilet, living alone.

Recently, as the result of pressure from the organization of disabled veterans, a major adjustment has been made in the eligibility procedures for an attendance benefit from the Defense Ministry. The benefit is now granted automatically to all those with a disability rating above 50 percent. The amount provided rises with the disability rating and is geared toward the average benefit that these groups received in the past on the basis of the functional scale. A person who feels that he deserves a larger benefit may request that a calculation be made on the basis of the scale. This is used to raise, but not to reduce, benefits so that this new procedure in effect serves to increase the overall level of benefits and extend them to a much wider population.

The National Insurance and the Defense Ministry programs have several common elements. In both programs benefits are provided in the form of a grant in cash rather than in kind and at remarkably similar levels. The maximum benefit for National Insurance is about 1.5 times the basic disability pension, and for veterans it is 25 percent higher. In both cases the existence of potential family support could, in certain instances, reduce these benefits by a third. The main distinction in the pattern is that benefits in the veterans program bear a continuous relationship to the scale, while there are only three benefit levels in the National Insurance program. There is no particular rationale presented in either program for the level of benefits. Nor is there any specification of the assumed number of hours of personal care required, the expected share of the burden to be borne by the family, or the cost of purchasing the remaining hours of care needed. On the basis of current rates for home and personal care services we estimate that the maximum National Insurance benefit is the equivalent of 11 hours of care per week, and 14 hours is the equivalent of the Defense Ministry benefit.

The major substantive difference between the Defense Ministry and National Insurance general disability attendance benefits is in the areas of need covered by the scale. The Defense Ministry scale includes homemaking activities in addition to personal care needs. Difficulties in homemaking generally arise at lower levels of medical impairment and should lead to a much broader distribution of eligibility for benefits. Thus, persons with problems in meeting their homemaking needs would not be eligible for any assistance in the general disability program.

The initial intent of National Insurance was a two-tiered program of benefits, one directed toward the compensation of personal care needs and the second to home care needs. Somewhat different criteria were anticipated for both programs, and conceivably persons might receive one benefit but not the other. Personal care criteria were to be largely based upon the client's ability independently to perform critical tasks of daily living in personal care. Home care benefits, on the other hand, were to take into consideration not only the individual's functional capacity, but also the availability of family members and other unpaid persons to perform homemaking activities, like cooking and cleaning. The obvious value assumption inherent in this twofold approach is that home care tasks can be performed by family members. Thus, full provision of homemaking duties could lead to overcompensation. In order to understand why a separate program for homemaking needs did not take shape, we need to describe the process by which the final program was developed.

Given the rapid growth in the population of general disability recipients when the attendance allowance program was being planned, management control issues were seriously considered. It was felt that greater management control could be exercised through the development of highly explicit criteria which would allow for only limited delegation of decision-making authority. Program growth could be then controlled by adjustments in the eligibility criteria if it was found that too many persons were meeting the initial criteria.

Demonstration Project Findings

The desire to use explicit eligibility criteria was further reinforced by National Insurance findings from a demonstration project conducted in a middle-sized city for over a year.[4] The participants were persons already receiving general disability benefits with at least a 75 percent medical disability rating, plus a sample of recently eligible recipients. Both samples were fairly small (70 incumbent recipients and 57 new recipients). A principal aim of the project was to determine the extent of eligibility for attendance allowance benefits so as to determine what level of funding the program would require. Of additional interest was the refinement of eligibility determination procedures. In view of the potentially massive task of evaluating need for special services, it was hoped that the demonstration project would suggest ways to streamline assessment procedures.

Some 23 percent of those evaluated were found to be in need of home care assistance and 29 percent were found to meet the criteria for personal care need. Perhaps the most important finding of the study was that despite the relatively independent criteria used to determine the need for home care and personal care, there was considerable overlap in eligibility for the two benefits. The substantial relationship between eligibility for home care and for personal care prompted the program planners to abandon the separate determination of home care eligibility.

The home visits by investigating nurses and social workers revealed that on the whole the level of personal care received by the needy disabled was quite good. The major source of this care was the family. Less than 20 percent of those found eligible (for attendance benefits) for either home or personal care were receiving any services from the Ministries of Health or Labor and Social Affairs, and only 8 percent were receiving personal or home care services. Despite the assessment that providing care for the disabled was a burden for the families, there was little or no indication of inadequate personal care or other unmet needs. This finding is consistent with those reported for populations of disabled or chronically ill in England and the United States (Sainsbury, 1975; Simkins and Tickner, 1978; Sherwood, 1975). The finding that most needs were already being met by the family also helped to resolve the question of whether the benefits should be provided in cash or kind—the cash benefit and the wider range or options it provides was deemed preferable.

Other Attendance Programs

Most other programs are quite different from the National Insurance for the generally disabled and the Defense Ministry's programs. They do not make use of any clearly defined functional criteria and are based almost exclusively on professional discretion. They tend to take into account the availability of family support and thus directly penalize families making greater efforts. The benefits are generally provided in kind, and their variation with the degree of functional capacity is much less clearly defined. In the program of the Ministry of Labor and Social Affairs, the upper level is 90 percent of three times the basic benefit (54 percent of the average wage). This is higher than that provided by other programs, but the sum is generally limited by municipal budget constraints. Moreover, a means test penalizes income at a rate of half of every IL 1 of income above a disregard. The breakeven income for eligibility is, however, quite high (about 50 percent above the average wage).

The pattern of attendance care benefits in the work-injury program is unique. The amount of benefit is linked to the level of need on a discretionary basis, but the maximum for any given individual is a function (1/3) of his wage-related basic benefit. As a result the benefit varies both with the degree of disability (in the range of 75-100 percent) and with the level of predisability wages. Is there any possible justification for this pattern? One would have to argue that the level of needs for personal care is a function of one's overall living standard. In point of fact, the inverse is typically the case, with the better-off purchasing more home and personal services (cooks, maids) prior to disability. Unless the discretionary element in the eligibility decision is used to equalize actual benefits, the pattern of attendance benefits will prove unjustifiably regressive.

Mobility Benefits

Benefits for the physically disabled specifically designated to compensate for loss of independent movement are termed mobility benefits. In Israel such benefits generally take two forms—a monthly cash benefit which can be used by the recipient for whatever purpose he chooses, or a grant or long-term, low-interest loan to enable the beneficiary to purchase an automobile. The benefits are not mutually exclusive; frequently the regular allowance is granted to cover the operating costs of an automobile which the beneficiary has purchsed with the help of grants or subsidized loans.

There are two major programs of mobility benefits for the disabled in Israel: one for disabled veterans, and a second, administered by National Insurance, for beneficiaries of both the work-injury and the general disability programs. The latter also serves those who are not entitled to benefits from either source but meet the separate eligibility criteria of the mobility program. Other, minor programs exist—the Ministry of Labor and Social Affairs provides transportation to disabled persons in need of medical care and meets the transportation costs (buses, taxis) of a small number of persons who have been rehabilitated and placed in jobs.

The mobility benefits available under National Insurance are administratively distinct from either the work-injury or the general disability program. Need is established directly from medical factors. Included are impairments such as neurological disorders resulting in the complete or partial paralysis of lower limbs; amputations of the lower limbs; and back problems. A minimal 40 percent disability is associated with any of the qualifying impediments. The classes of impediments and the disability percentage associated with them in the mobility regulations are identical to those in the general medical listing.

There are three types of benefits in the National Insurance program. One is a monthly cash allowance which is designed to meet current transportation expenses. The other two provide loans and limited grant assistance in meeting the purchase price of an automobile.

Unlike those in the National Insurance program, mobility benefits from the Defense Ministry are not a separately administered program. Benefits include a government-owned automobile for the disabled person's full personal use in case of 100 percent disability of both legs, low-interest loans and partial grants for the purchase of an automobile if disability is at a designated level (a lower level permits eligibility if a car is necessary for work), monthly allowances covering operating costs, and bimonthly transportation allowances for those without cars. The mobility benefits cover practically all recipients of basic benefits in the disabled veterans' program.

In comparison with the range of benefits provided by the National Insurance program, the disabled veterans' program is more comprehensive both in terms of the range of potential recipients and in the scope of the benefits. Even a moderately disabled veteran can purchase a car without investing any of his own capital. The most severely disabled may purchase the more expensive and larger American model cars. The level of monthly maintenance benefits is much higher. The emphases of the Defense Ministry's program are quite different from those of National Insurance; its benefits are viewed as contributing to the overall standard of living of the disabled rather than as direct compensation for special needs and expenses, and there is less emphasis on giving an advantage to those who are employed.

The Levels of Benefits in Disability Programs

In this section we compare the total levels of benefits provided for the major categories of disabled: military disablement, work-injury disablement, and the generally disabled. To a lesser extent we also analyze how benefits vary within programs according to the severity of disability and the level of earnings or earnings capacity. In some programs the particular type of impairment affects the level of benefits. Sometimes these impairments are explicitly singled out (as in the military program), and sometimes their functional implications lead to benefits conditioned on special needs, such as attendance allowances. We have therefore constructed hypothetical cases in which the nature of the injury is specified along with the associated medical disability rating. In order to assess eligibility for various benefits, the family and earnings status of the individual have been specified as well. The analysis is based on the four cases, described as follows:

Case 1. Paraplegic: disability rating of 100 percent; married, no children; earned the average wage before disability; now unable to work.

Case 2. Hemiplegic (left side disabled from a stroke): disability rating of 60 percent; married, two children over 18; earned the average wage before disability; now unable to work.

Case 3. Cannot use right arm: disability rating of 60 percent; married, two children; earned the average wage before disability; now earns half the average wage.

Case 4. Sight lost in one eye: disability rating of 35 percent; married, two children; earned the average wage before disability; now earns average wage.

These cases reflect a range of impairment. At the lower end of the scale we presumed that the disabled person would be able to earn an average wage; at the other end we presumed that he could not work at all. In the middle range of severity (60 percent) we contrast a disabled person who cannot work with one who earns a modest income. Income is set at a level allowing eligibility for general disability benefits. As a base we assumed a wife and two children; our stroke victim was presumed to be at least middle-aged and therefore his children were presumed to be over 18. We assume the paraplegic has no children so that he is eligible for benefits from the Housing Ministry, which has special programs for newly married couples. This does not distort the overall comparison as the number of children does not seriously affect the level of benefits.

We must first decide what kinds of benefits are to be included in the calculation. Certain benefits, such as access to police protection or public parks, are not directed at any particular social group. Other benefits, such as housing assistance or children's allowances, may be directed to those with certain social characteristics; many disabled have these characteristics and accordingly receive these benefits. Finally, there are programs that offer benefits specifically to the disabled. We have tried to confine ourselves to benefits that are over and above what a nondisabled person of working age would receive; thus child allowances received by the general population are not included. The level of housing benefits is calculated as the supplement received by the disabled person relative to the housing benefits available to the general population. Taxes on benefits are subtracted, so that we estimate net income. Welfare benefits not readily available to the nondisabled have been included.

Realistically, not all benefits are received by those eligible. In comparing programs we have calculated the maximum possible available benefit level.

In the case of two mutually exclusive benefits for which the disabled is eligible, only one is counted, generally the higher. Where receipt of benefits depends upon a test of functional ability, the benefit is counted only if there is a reasonable probability of eligibility on the basis of the functional implications of the particular impairment. These are a rather strong set of assumptions. To the extent that there are differences across programs in the extent of actual utilization, our comparison will not necessarily reflect typical program differences.

In addition to benefits available on an ongoing basis, there are many irregular and one-time benefits. There is a serious problem in trying to reduce them to a common denominator. One approach would be to calculate the imputed annuity value of each irregular or one-time benefit. Because of the complexity of such calculations and the various assumptions that must be made, we calculate the annuities values only for Case 1, the 100 percent disabled case, using the Hansen-Weisbrod (1968) formula.[5] To implement this approach we must assume a discount rate, the age of beneficiary, and life expectancy of the beneficiary. As a simpler alternative we have evaluated the level of benefits a given type of disabled person could receive during the first year of program eligibility. This procedure biases the comparison in favor of programs with a high ratio of nonannual to annual benefits. From conversations with various program personnel and review of budget figures, it appears that recipients tend to make use of most one-time benefits early in their career as beneficiaries.

The relative level of benefits by program is summarized in Table 11.5. The benefits provided by the Defense Ministry are distinctly greater than those provided to all other disabled groups. Regular benefits are between two to three times the benefits in other programs, except for those with low disability ratings. The advantage of the Defense Ministry is even more dramatic in terms of total benefits. Here differences increase with a decrease in the severity of impairment. This pattern reflects the exceptional role that irregular benefits play in the military program.

The unique position of those injured in military service reflects an explicit judgment by policy makers and public opinion in Israel. There is clearly little chance of integrating military benefits with those of other groups in the interest of a more uniform system. The level of benefits in this program, and the unusual weight of one-time benefits, is generally conceived of as sound social policy.

Several problems arise with respect to irregular benefits. The receipt of those benefits is much less uniform and thus increases variance in economic status when the severity of disability is held constant. This variance is not necessarily related to variation in needs but rather is positively correlated with the economic and social status of the disabled. The receipt of such benefits is for the most part linked to the purchase of various consumer durables and therefore requires some contribution on the part of the

Table 11.5. Percentage Comparisons of Levels of Benefit across Programs Using Defense Ministry Benefit as the Standard

Degree of Disability	Defense Ministry		National Insurance Work Injury		National Insurance General Disability: Welfare; No Work History		National Insurance General Disability: Histadrut Pension Fund		National Insurance General Disability: Civil Service Pension Fund	
Regular benefits (monthly or annual)										
Case 1: 100%; unable to work	100	(100)	63	(63)	39	(39)	54	(54)	45	(45)
Case 2: 60%; unable to work	100	(99)	52	(52)[a]	31	(31)	46	(46)	38	(38)
Case 3: 60%; earns half average wage	100	(68)	28	(19)	12	(8)	26	(18)	28	(19)
Case 4: 35%; earns average wage	100	(12)	94	(11)	—		—		82	(10)
Grand total first-year maximum benefit[b]										
Case 1: 100%; unable to work	100	(100)	38	(38)	4	(4)	21	(21)	21	(21)
Case 2: 60%; unable to work	100	(38)	42	(16)[a]	8	(3)	33	(13)	42	(16)
Case 3: 60%; earns half average wage	100	(28)	7	(2)	3	(1)	6	(2)	10	(7)
Case 4: 35%; earns average wage	100	(10)	11	(1)	—		—		18	(2)

Note: Figures in parentheses indicate percentage comparison to 100% Defense Ministry benefit level.

[a]Assuming he receives 50 percent supplement to his disability rating; without supplement the percentages would be 52 for regular benefits and 28 and (11) for first-year maximum benefit.

[b]Benefits awarded by the courts in civil damages suits have not been included.

disabled to the purchase price or imposes operation and maintenance costs. This fact has the additional disadvantage of encouraging consumption and of imposing the welfare losses typically associated with benefits in kind. We should note that some of the regular benefits, such as mobility allowances, share some of these features. The regular mobility allowances are a major source of advantage enjoyed by Defense Ministry beneficiaries. The unusual emphasis on these special benefits within the military program has been a major factor in creating demands for them in other programs as well.

In interpreting these results it is useful to keep in mind that the comparison has been made for someone with average earnings prior to impairment. As this wage rises the relative advantage of the Defense Ministry declines in relation to other groups. We must remind the reader that the pattern of actual utilization of irregular benefits will also affect the comparison.

The differences in the level of benefits for the work injured and generally disabled are by contrast not very great. The magnitude of these differences varies with the severity and type of impairment and between regular and total benefits. However, no meaningful pattern of variation is apparent. The work injured are advantaged at some disability levels and disadvantaged at others. The largest difference is in total benefits for those who are totally disabled, so that irregular benefits are a major factor in creating disparities across programs in the level of benefits. This comparison suggests that benefit integration among programs is feasible and, in any case, that there is considerable room for rationalizing the differences in benefit levels.

In comparing the variation in benefits within programs, we found that benefits decline with the severity of impairment in all programs. The decline in total benefits is particularly large, reflecting the fact that irregular benefits are often targeted on the severely disabled. Regular benefits do not vary proportionally with medical disability rating in the upper range of the scale. Benefits for those with 60 percent disability are more than 60 percent of the benefits of someone with a 100 percent rating, if we assume that in either case the recipient is unable to work. In the Defense Ministry this is true whether the recipient with a 60 percent rating can work or not. Yet in the lower end they are always highly progressive. Those with 35 percent disability rating do not receive any benefits in several programs. In others they receive between 10 percent and 20 percent of the benefits of those with a 100 percent rating.

Comparing the two examples of 60 percent disability, we were able to obtain insight into the role of work capacity in determining benefit levels. Someone unable to work at all receives a substantial bonus in all programs. In the Defense Ministry this takes the form of a special supplement to the basic benefit. In the other programs the individual receives a disability rating that exceeds the rating he would receive on medical grounds. We have assumed in calculating benefits that the hemiplegic receives a 100 percent disability rating in the National Insurance disability and work-related programs. In the work-injury program the rating based on work capacity is limited to 150 percent of the medical rating, i.e., 90 percent in this case.

There are two important sources of variation in benefits that are not observed in these tables. One is variation in the level of predisability earnings and the second is variation in current earned income. These patterns will be examined in the part of the next section where we deal with work incentives.

Sources of Growth

While this study is concerned with the full range of disability programs, we have particular interest in the general disability program, one of recent vintage in Israel. Its growth reflects the phased implementation of benefits for various groups of disabled. The adoption of the general disability program exerted, in and of itself, a major quantitative influence and has been a large factor in the growth of the entire disability system. In analyzing this program we focus on its absolute magnitude, the potential for future growth, and the need for review of the concomitant development of entitlements for work-related pensions.

Taking a broader view, one finds a clear pattern of rapid growth in all disability programs that have been in existence over the ten-year period on which we focus. There is a clear trend, throughout the system, towards expanding and liberalizing entitlements. Both changes in legislation and changes in procedures, often resulting from court rulings, have contributed to this trend. Further, there is evidence, admittedly more tentative, of an increased tendency for an individual to assert a claim to benefits.

Table 11.6 summarizes the dimensions of disability program growth from 1968 to 1977. Expenditures for the disabled, defined to include the main cash benefit programs, in 1977 constituted 1.7 percent of the gross national product (GNP) and 2.9 percent of government expenditures (excluding defense expenditures). Five years before, expenditures were only 0.7 percent of GNP and 1.8 percent of the civil budget. Real expenditures grew by 177 percent over this period.

The total number of disability benefit recipients grew from a minimum estimate of 56,745 in 1972, or 5.8 percent of the working-age population, to 93,415 in 1977, or 8.4 percent—an increase of 65 percent. This is shown in Table 11.7.

The major benefit programs all grew at a rapid rate, as shown in Table 11.8. In the 1970s the number of recipients in the work-injury program increased at an average annual rate of almost 3.7 percent and in the Defense Ministry program at a rate of 9.5 percent. The annual rate of increase for

Table 11.6. Rates of Disability Expenditures to GNP and Nonmilitary Government Budget, 1968-1977 (expenditures in mill. IL, current prices)

	Expenditures				Percentage of GNP (Percentage of Civil Government Budget)							
	1968	1972	1974	1977	1968		1972		1974		1977	
GNP[a]	14,037	29,484	54,235	138,921								
Civil government budget[b]	4,382	12,019	24,729	83,840								
Total disability benefit expenditure[c]		*210.9*	*701.4*	*2,354.6*			*0.7*	*(1.8)*	*1.3*	*(2.8)*	*1.7*	*(2.8)*
Ministry of Defense	23.8	65.7	307.0	785.7	0.2	(0.5)	0.2	(0.5)	0.6	(1.2)	0.6	(0.9)
Natl. Ins. General Disability	—	—	9.6	495.5	—		—		0.0	(0.0)	0.4	(0.6)
Natl. Ins. Mobility Allowances[d]	—	—	8.5	267.4	—		—		0.0	(0.0)	0.2	(0.3)
Natl. Ins. Work Injury	15.9	39.9	81.4	228.9	0.1	(0.4)	0.1	(0.3)	0.2	(0.3)	0.2	(0.3)
Natl. Ins. Other (Pris. of Zion & Border Action)	0.8	2.2	10.2	46.1	0.0	(0.0)	0.0	(0.0)	0.0	(0.0)	0.0	(0.1)
Welfare	—	29.7	84.9	110.5	—		0.1	(0.2)	0.2	(0.3)	0.1	(0.1)
Histadrut Pension Funds	—	9.6	17.6	62.5	—		0.0	(0.1)	0.0	(0.1)	0.0	(0.1)
Disabled by Nazis (total)	23.0	63.8	182.2	358.0	0.2	(0.5)	0.2	(0.5)	0.3	(0.7)	0.3	(0.4)

[a]Source is Bank of Israel annual reports, 1968-77.
[b]Source is proposed government budget, 1978.
[c]Not including medical care in all programs; also excludes civil service pension expenditures because data not available. Does not include rehabilitation activities of the Ministry of Labor and Welfare, which were 40 mill. IL in 1977; a part of these is included in National Insurance figures.
[d]Including standing loans for cars.
[e]Not including survivors' benefits.

Table 11.7. Rates of Disability Recipients to Population and Civilian Labor force by Main Disability Program Recipients, 1968-1977

	Absolute Numbers				Percentage of Civilian Labor Force (Percentage of All Aged 18-64)							
	1968	1972	1974	1977	1968		1972		1974		1977	
All population (000, aged 18-64)	1,529.2	1,734.6	1,840.5	1,940.7								
Civilian labor force (000, aged 18-64)	866.7	982.9	1,042.2	1,117.7								
Recipients of Disability benefits												
Ministry of Defense	10,621	14,384	18,676	24,081	1.2	(0.7)	1.5	(0.8)	1.8	(1.0)	2.2	(1.2)
Work Injury[a]	4,172	4,797	6,298	8,012	0.5	(0.3)	0.5	(0.3)	0.6	(0.3)	0.7	(0.4)
General Disability	—	—	1,537	22,327	—	—	—	—	0.1	(0.1)	2.0	(1.2)
By Nazi action (total)	15,850[b]	19,940	22,400	23,750	1.8	(1.0)	2.0	(1.1)	2.1	(1.2)	2.1	(1.2)
Welfare	—	17,624	20,700	15,245	—	—	1.8	(1.0)	2.0	(1.1)	1.4	(0.8)
Total[c]		56,745	69,611	93,415			5.8	(3.3)	6.7	(3.8)	8.4	(4.8)
Histadrut Pension Funds	932	1,465	1,792	2,632	0.3	(0.2)	0.4	(0.2)	0.4	(0.2)	0.6	(0.3)
Civil Service Pension	1,550	2,127	2,582	3,691								

[a]Excludes recipients of capitalization and grants.

[b]Estimate.

[c]Excludes recipients of Histadrut pension funds, civil service pension, and mobility allowance owning to overlap with other programs; excludes recipients of military action programs because data not available (1,466 recipients in 1978).

Table 11.8. Growth of the Major Disability Programs over Various Years (excluding medical care expenditures)

Disability Program	Years	Average Rate of Real Growth (%) Expenditures	Recipients	Average Benefit	Absolute Total 1977-78 Expenditures (mill. 1978 IL)	Recipients
Ministry of Defense[a]	1968-77	21.6	9.5	11.0	1,183.3	24,081
National Insurance						
General Disability (basic benefit)	1974-78	124.1	109.3	7.1	742.2	22,327
Newly disabled		(103.0)	(89.2)	—	(477.2)	(14,078)
Previous disabled		(94.7)	(104.7)	—	(269.0)	(8,249)
Mobility Allowance[b]	1976-78	16.6	12.6	3.6	118.9	6,200
Standing Loans for Cars[b]	1976-78	10.2	4.9	5.1	283.8	2,280
Work Injury	1968-77	10.9	3.7	7.0	344.7	8,830
Others (military action)	—	—	—	—	69.4	1,446
Welfare Cash Allowance	1972-77	−2.0	−2.9	0.8	166.4	15,245
Histadrut Pension Funds[b]	1971-77	11.3	11.6	−0.3	94.1	2,632
Treasury						
Disabled by Nazi action	1968-77	12.3	4.6	7.3	630.4	23,750
Civil Servant Pension	1968-77	—	10.1	—	—	3,691

[a]Includes aged recipients.

[a]A large portion are recipients of general disability benefits.

recipients of work-related pensions was around 11 percent, for mobility benefit recipients, 13 percent. Expenditures have grown at an even faster rate, with a resulting significant increase in average expenditures per recipient in most programs.

Changes in Entitlements

The most significant development in the last ten years has been the extension of entitlements to the generally disabled. This resulted from the adoption of several new programs and alterations in existing ones. These developments have been particularly concentrated in the last five years.

The general disability law, adopted in 1974, has become the major source of basic income support for the disabled. Previously, the disabled could turn to welfare for support. The consequent shift in eligibility and benefit levels is quite intricate. Whereas the welfare benefit is fully income-tested, the basic benefit for a newly disabled beneficiary in the general disability program is not. Because the level of predisability wages plays a major role in the general disability program, newly disabled persons with relatively high current earnings can receive benefits. For example, someone who earned twice the average wage before his disability may earn up to the current average wage and be eligible for half the basic benefit.

For the previously disabled, the differences in the entitlement of benefits will in principle be much smaller, as in both programs the benefits are income-tested. However, in judging the effective differences it is necessary to consider the different ways in which the means test is implemented. In welfare the disabled must reapply and report on income annually. No regular reporting is required by National Insurance; random irregular checks are carried out instead.

The programs also differ in the way they treat the newly disabled who have some other source of transfer income (e.g., work-related pension). These persons are not eligible for welfare, while they may receive a full benefit in the general disability program. As there is a significant group that has a work-related disability pension this difference could be significant.

What was the quantitative impact of the introduction of general disability? Did the numbers of disabled receiving welfare decline proportionately?

The total number of general disability recipients grew from 1,537 in 1974, the year the program was introduced, to 29,502 in 1978. From 1977 to 1978 the rolls grew by almost 8,000. In 1974-75 there were 20,700 disabled recipients of welfare or, perhaps more relevant, 14,017 who received support for a full year. The number of generally disabled does not seem large in comparison with this figure. Welfare expenditures represented one-eighth of the total spent on the disabled in 1974, while general disability represented one-fifth in 1977. What is surprising is that the number of disabled welfare recipients declined only moderately. Thus the introduction of general disability increased the overall number of recipients by over 20,000, or about 2 percent of the civilian labor force.

The rate of receipt of general disability benefits rises sharply with age, as shown in Table 11.9. Among men aged 55-65 the proportion of recipients is 7.1 percent. Moreover, the contribution of the general disability program to the overall rate of recipients of disability benefits is much higher in the higher age groups. This program also accounts for most recipients with several medical impairments.

Aside from these basic programs, there are a number of supplementary programs. These include the mobility programs and loans for automobile purchases. Moreover, subgroups among the generally disabled may be eligible for substantial wage-related benefits, either through participation in a pension fund or through the courts in the case of automobile injuries. Entitlements in both areas have undergone major developments. The number of work-related disability pensions (civil service and Histadrut), while still relatively small in magnitude, has been growing at a rate of 10 percent per year over the decade. Aside from the growth in recipients there has been a much more significant extension of coverage for employed workers. Most workers are already insured (at a rate of 70 percent) in labor contracts that were signed over the years for the public sector and for clerical workers in all sectors. In 1979 all industrial workers were included in such arrangements.

In both the Defense Ministry and the work-injury programs, there has been increasing liberalization of the eligibility criteria. Both programs cover injuries arising from a specific source, and the courts have given impetus to liberalizing rules that link the injury to the specified source.

Another factor in the growth of disability programs has been changes in benefit levels. The recent introduction of work-capacity criteria into determination of disability rating in the work-injury program, for example, has led to systematic increases in the level of the disability rating, often as much as 50 percent. Eligibility for special benefits has significantly expanded, particularly in the case of mobility benefits. The Defense Ministry program has also increased benefit levels.

Demographic Factors

The rate of disability has been shown to be related to such socioeconomic factors as age, education, and occupation. The state of the economy as reflected in the rate of unemployment also has an effect on the relative tendency to apply for benefits.

In the period under study there have been major changes in these variables, to which we may attribute part of the growth in recipients and

Table 11.9. Age and Sex of General Disability Beneficiaries and Rate in Relation to the Civilian Labor Force, 1977

		Men					Women				
	Total	Total	18-34	35-44	45-54	55-65	Total	18-34	35-44	45-54	55-65
Disabled after 1970	20,382	13,725	3,606	1,307	2,978	5,834	6,657	2,718	668	1,839	1,432
Disabled before 1970	9,968	6,547	1,700	1,265	1,564	2,018	3,421	1,205	802	829	585
Total	30,350	20,272	5,306	2,572	4,542	7,852	10,078	3,923	1,470	2,668	2,017
Civilian labor force (000, aged 18-64)[a]	1,150.3	742.2	334.0	158.4	144.2	110.6	405.1	226.7	77.3	68.1	33.0
Rate of disabled to civilian labor force (%)	2.6	2.7	1.6	1.6	3.1	7.1	2.5	1.7	1.9	4.0	6.1

[a]Estimates of age-sex breakdown based on 1977 unpublished National Insurance Institute data.

benefits. The Israeli population is aging rapidly: the population over 65 increased from 6.4 percent in 1968 to 8.3 percent in 1977. However, the age structure of those 18-64 years old has not significantly changed; if anything, it is younger. There have been shifts of a more significant nature in the educational, occupational, and industrial distribution. These should have contributed to a decline in disability rates, as the percentage of educated workers in white collar occupations rises and the percentage employed in industry and agriculture declines.

Unemployment rates were low throughout the period we are studying. They varied from 4.5 percent in 1969 to 2.6 percent in 1973 for the population over 14. For the working-age population, unemployment rates were lower (3.7 percent in 1969, 3.3 percent in 1977-78), with an upward trend since 1978.

Thus the demographic trends and trends in employment patterns should have contributed to a decline in disability. They cannot serve to explain the rapid rates of increase that we have observed.

The Incidence of Disability

There have not been any national surveys designed to estimate the extent of disability in the population. In a 1966 national labor force survey, all those who generally worked less than 35 hours in the last year, or worked less than 26 weeks in the last year, and who were not studying or engaged in housework at the time of the survey, were asked the question: "Do you have a physical defect, disability or disease which prevents or interferes with your working?"

In 1974, all those who regularly worked less than 35 hours per week in 1973 or who worked less than 40 weeks that year, were asked to indicate the principal reason for not working or only working part time. The possible options available to respondents were (1) sickness or disability; (2) age over 65 for a man, over 60 for a woman; (3) sought employment but could not find it; (4) housewife; (5) student; (6) other.

This set of data has obvious limitations. It relates only to limitations in the *amount* of work, and provides no estimates of those limited in the *kinds* of work they can do. It does not clearly differentiate between impairment and temporary illness. The 1966 estimates exclude impaired persons who are students or who define themselves as homemakers. The 1974 data exclude the impaired who may have another reason for not working—being a student or housewife—that they consider primary.

Despite these limitations, the data provide a benchmark, probably more reliable for men than women. Table 11.10 provides estimates of persons with health-related work limitations by age and sex as well as the incidence of disability in the general working population in 1974. According to the survey, there were 1,459,513 Israelis of working age (18-64) in 1974. Those

Table 11.10. Estimated Prevalence of Health-Related Work Limitations by Age and Sex, 1974 (percentages in parentheses)

Age	Total	Disabled Men			Disabled Women		
		Total	Household Head	Not Household Head	Total	Household Head	Not Household Head
Total, 18-64	65,946 (100)	40,919 (100)	26,998 (100)	13,921 (100)	25,027 (100)	8,325 (100)	16,702 (100)
18-34	15,334 (23)	10,545 (26)	3,805 (14)	6,740 (48)	4,989 (20)	829 (10)	4,160 (25)
35-54	27,972 (42)	15,198 (37)	11,011 (41)	4,187 (30)	12,774 (51)	3,981 (48)	8,793 (53)
55-64	22,440 (34)	15,176 (37)	12,182 (45)	2,994 (22)	7,624 (30)	3,515 (42)	3,749 (22)
% Disabled among Total Population of Each Group							
Total, 18-64	4.5	5.7	5.0	8.1	3.4	11.0	2.5
18-34	2.3	3.1	2.1	4.2	1.5	3.3	1.3
35-54	5.0	5.6	4.2	63.6	4.4	14.7	3.4
55-64	10.3	14.4	12.1	69.9	6.4	15.0	4.2

Source: Israel Central Bureau of Statistics, *Income Survey*, 1974; includes those not working full time on a regular basis for medical reasons.

reporting health-related conditions or impairments as the reason for not working full time accounted for 4.5 percent of the total population, or 65,946 persons.

Some 60 percent of the disabled are men. They constitute 5.7 percent of the national male population (Table 11.11). Disabled women constitute only 3.4 percent of the female population. Given the manner in which the disability definition was derived, it is probable that the incidence of disabled women is an underestimate. Women with health-related limitations whose primary role is housewife may not have labeled themselves as sick or disabled when reporting why they were not employed. About 85 percent of the disabled do not work at all; among men alone that percentage is high, at 81 percent. Some 13 percent of the population of nonemployed males have a health-related work limitation. Among men employed part time, only 1.9 percent attributed partial work to health. The incidence of disability increases sharply with age (Table 11.10), more dramatically so for men (from 3.1 percent to 14.4 percent), and particularly men who are not household heads (4.2 percent to 70 percent). These patterns are what we would expect.

The number of years of education is strongly related to disability status, particularly among men—23.4 percent of those without any education, as opposed to 1.6 percent of those with 13 or more years of schooling, are disabled. Presumably the correlation of age, education, and type of work the uneducated generally perform produces this differential likelihood of being disabled. Continent of origin is also related to disability status: men born in an Asian or African country have an above-average rate, 8.1 percent.

The incidence of disability is higher in the 1974 survey than in that for 1966. In general, however, the relationships described in the 1974 survey data between disability status and various demographic factors remain fairly constant from 1966 to 1974. If we accept the evidence of a trend increase in the extent of reported health-related work limitations, it must be remembered that these are not necessarily synonymous with an increase in the incidence of medical impairments or even in their consequences for employment. A shift in the social awareness of the legitimacy of disability as a reason for not working, or even a voluntary decrease in the labor force participation of the disabled, could lead to increased reporting of health-related work impairments.

The estimates presented here do provide a useful reference point for comparison with program data on the extent of disability. We have totaled up the number of recipients in programs which require at least a partial reduction in employment (general disability and welfare) and an estimated percentage of recipients in other disability programs who work less than full time (using various special surveys). We arrive at a figure of 3 percent of the total working-age population who report work limitations. Given the

Table 11.11. Estimated Prevalence of Health-Related Work Limitations by Work Status, Marital Status, Education, and Sex, 1974 (population aged 18-64; percentages in parentheses)

	Number and Percentage Distribution of Disabled			Prevalence of Disabled in Total Population (%)		
	Total	Men	Women	Total	Men	Women
Total	65,946 (100)	40,919 (100)	25,027 (100)	4.5	5.7	3.4
Work status						
Work	9,924 (15)	7,978 (19)	1,945 (8)	1.7	1.9	1.2
Not work	56,022 (85)	32,941 (81)	23,082 (92)	6.9	13.3	4.1
Marital status						
Married	41,334 (63)	29,288 (71)	12,046 (48)	3.8	5.5	2.1
Divorced	3,642 (6)	1,046 (3)	2,596 (10)	19.3	19.0	19.4
Widowed	6,970 (11)	1,039 (3)	5,931 (24)	14.8	28.7	13.7
Single	14,000 (21)	9,546 (23)	4,454 (18)	4.8	5.5	3.7
Years of education						
0	14,299 (22)	6,947 (17)	7,352 (30)	12.9	23.5	9.0
1-8	32,642 (49)	22,802 (56)	9,840 (39)	6.7	9.5	4.0
9-12	15,215 (23)	8,895 (22)	6,320 (25)	2.6	2.9	2.2
13+	3,631 (6)	2,275 (5)	1,356 (5)	1.4	1.6	1.1
Unknown	159 (0)	—	159 (1)	3.2	—	6.4
Origin						
Asia or Africa	33,077 (50)	22,045 (54)	11,032 (44)	6.0	8.1	4.0
Europe or America	23,500 (36)	13,261 (32)	10,239 (41)	4.6	5.4	3.8
Israel	9,369 (14)	5,613 (14)	3,756 (14)	2.4	2.9	1.9

Source: See Table 11.10.

fact that almost all of these recipients are men, they represent a little less than 6 percent of the total male working-age population. This estimate is strikingly similar to the percentage of men reporting limitations in 1974, shown in Table 11.10. This figure suggests that the coverage of disability programs is very nearly universal.

Incentives

The typical economic analysis emphasizes the effect of program structure on incentives to apply for benefits and on the decision to work. The level of benefits and the penalties imposed on earnings are generally featured in this analysis.

If one takes a more realistic view, there is need to consider other elements. For example, the formal and the actual penalty on employment may be very different, because it may be fairly easy to underreport earnings. In this context, the penalty rate is an expected rather than a single definite value. While such considerations arise in all income maintenance programs, they may be particularly relevant to disability programs, where review procedures tend to be more lax.

Programs that have no earnings penalty do not force the individual to choose between work and receiving a transfer. Even in these programs, however, one would not expect the number of recipients to be determined only by the size of the population potentially eligible. The level of benefits and the nature of procedures for establishing eligibility could still influence the rate of application. Moreover, the extent of benefits is influenced by very subjective decisions about the degree of medical disability (or perhaps potential work capacity). Individual assertiveness, efforts at medical rehabilitation, the degree to which falsification and exaggeration are accepted norms of behavior, and the tendency to pursue opportunities for appeal will all affect the final rate of recipients. Thus, the preference for work versus leisure and the level of benefits are factors determining the overall rate of recipients even when there is no direct penalty on earnings.

Replacement Rates

Gross and after-tax replacement rates in programs for the work injured and the generally disabled are presented in Tables 11.12 and 11.13. Rates have been calculated for a disabled person who has a 100 percent disability rating and a dependent spouse.

In the work-injury program the basic replacement rate is 75 percent of previous wages. Since work-injury benefits are exempt from tax, the net rate is higher and reaches approximately 85 percent for those who earned the average wage before impairment. The effect of tax exemption begins to be felt at earnings levels above 50 percent of the average wage, the tax threshold, and is regressive.

For the generally disabled person, we have three separate calculations. One is based on the assumption that he receives a general disability benefit; the second, that he is also entitled to a work-related pension; and the third, that he receives welfare as opposed to a general disability benefit.

As the general disability and welfare programs basically provide a minimum income, the replacement rates are substantial at low wage levels, and then decline sharply as wages rise. The differences in minimum benefit level between the general disability and welfare programs are reflected in Table 11.12. For the general disability program, the replacement rate is substantial even at the average wage (40 percent). After taxes these rates are a bit higher (46 percent), reflecting once again the exemption of benefits from tax. Unusually high rates of replacement occur when both general disability and work-related pensions are received. The gross rate exceeds 100 percent over a broad range, and is 97 percent for those with average earnings. The net rates exceed 100 percent over the entire range. The difference between gross and net rates for this group is particularly large for those with a 100 percent disability rating, as they are fully exempt from tax. Those with less than a 100 percent rating must pay taxes on 75 percent of the work-related pension.[6]

From 1968 to 1978 there was an expansion of replacement rates. In the work-injury program this resulted from a change in the level of maximum

Table 11.12. Gross and After-Tax Replacement Rate in Selected Disability Programs, 1968 and 1978 (percentages)

Predisability Gross Earnings	Gross Replacement Rate					After-Tax Replacement Rate				
		General Disability					General Disability			
	Work Injury	Alone[a]	Work-Rel. Pension[b]	Welfare	Ministry of Defense[c]	Work Injury	Alone[a]	Work-Rel. Pension[b]	Welfare	Ministry of Defense[c]
1978										
Twice average wage	65[d] (75[e])	20	83	14	49	86[d] (99)[e]	26	110	19	65
Average wage	75	40	97	28	98	86	46	110	32	112
Half average wage	75	80	123	57	195	75	80	123	57	195
1968										
Twice average wage	44[d]	—	70	11	45	58[d]	—	91	14	58
Average wage	75	—	70	22	89	84	—	78	24	100
Half average age	75	—	70	43	179	76	—	71	44	181

Notes: Rates calculated for a person 100 percent disabled, with a dependent spouse. Gross rate = basic benefit divided by previous gross earnings; after-tax rate = basic benefit divided by previous after-tax earnings. The 100 percent disabled are exempt from income tax. We assume no post-disability earnings. The 1968 average wage was 593 IL per month; for 1978, 7,000 IL per month.

[a]The National Insurance general disability program started in 1974.

[b]For 1968 this includes only the Histadrut work-related pension.

[c]Benefits resulting from limited work capacity.

[d]Maximum insured wage in 1968: 700 IL (1.2 of average wage); in 1978, 12,100 IL (1.7 of average wage); in 1980, 63,000 IL (3 times the average wage).

[e]Parenthetical figures are replacement rates in 1980; changes due to increase in maximum insured wage.

Table 11.13. Gross and After-Tax Replacement Rate in Selected Disability Programs, 1978 (percentages)

	Gross Replacement Rate (%)					After-Tax Replacement Rate (%)				
		General Disability					General Disability			
Predisability Gross Earnings	Work Injury	Alone	Work-Rel. Pension	Welfare	Ministry of Defense	Work Injury	Alone	Work-Rel. Pension	Welfare	Ministry of Defense
Basic and current special benefits										
Twice average wage	102	36	99	41	123	135	47	131	54	163
Average wage	150	72	128	81	247	171	81	147	93	282
Half average wage	225	144	187	162	494	225	144	187	162	494
Basic and current special benefits, and annuity value of one-time benefits										
Twice average wage	199	106	168	41	328	263	140	223	55	433
Average wage	344	211	267	83	656	392	241	305	95	
Half average wage	612	422	464	165	1,311	612	422	464	165	1,311

Note: See general note to Table 11.12.

insurable wage in relation to average wages. An additional change is the tax exemption of National Insurance benefits for the partially disabled that went into effect in 1978; those with a 100 percent disability rating were exempt in both years. The generally disabled who were previously eligible only for welfare now enjoy the more generous terms of the general disability program. Welfare benefits themselves have risen. Those who previously had only a work-related pension can now enjoy a general disability benefit as well, although the numbers receiving the two pension are as yet small.

The treatment of family size in both disability programs, together with the amounts of taxation, may lead to signficant variation in replacement rates according to family size. In many countries generous dependents' benefits in disability programs lead to a sharply rising pattern of gross replacement rates with family size, whereas exemption for dependents in the tax structure have an opposite effect on after-tax replacement rates. In Israel, work-injury and work-related programs do not provide for dependents' benefits. It is true that dependents' allowances are provided in the general disability program, but they are subject to a severe means test with the result that a person eligible for a work-related benefit in effect does not receive it. Moreover, consideration of children in the tax structure is provided in the form of allowances. As a result there is little variation in replacement rates with family size, whether before or after tax. For those receiving only a general disability benefit, this is not the case. If the recipient is eligible for a full benefit, the replacement rate, in percentage, for someone with predisability earnings equal to the average rate has the following pattern:

	Single Person	Couple	Couple + 2
Gross replacement rate	25	38	48
After-tax replacement rate	32	43	58

In calculating replacement rates we have not allowed for various forms of supplementary benefits, which add up to a sizable proportion of total benefits. The treatment of these benefits raises several questions. If they are viewed as compensation for increased needs arising from impairment, they do not reflect an increase in real income. As such they should not have an income effect on the decision to work. In the absence of such compensation, the calculated nominal replacement rates are an overestimate of the relative real income of the impaired. If they exceed the extent of actual increase in needs, then they contribute to the real replacement rates and should be included.

Consider the role of special benefits (mainly mobility allowances) in determining the nominal ratio of benefits to predisability earnings (Table 11.13). It is clear that with special benefits, replacement rates are well over 100 percent for the vast majority of insured persons. At the average wage, gross replacement rates tend to be about 50 percent above predisability earnings for the work-injured and 30 percent above the generally disabled. After tax they range from 47 to 71 percent. Even the general disability and welfare programs provide between 72-81 percent of previous wages, and 81-93 percent after tax. The Defense Ministry program offers more than double the level of previous earnings. At least in nominal terms we can see how considerable the special benefits are. Moreover, we have not included various benefits received on a one-time basis. To combine them with ongoing benefits we have converted them to annuities using the Hansen-Weisbrod (1968) formula. The major component of one-time benefits is the exemption of taxes on automobiles (taxes exceed 100 percent in Israel). If this component is not included, one-time benefits have a relatively small effect, except for the Defense Ministry program. With the value of these tax exemptions, imputed replacement rates are more than doubled for all groups of disabled.

The Extent of Penalties on Earnings

We confine our evaluation of penalties on earnings and employment to the generally disabled, which is the major group explicitly subject to these penalties.

We consider the penalties imposed by the general disability program and those imposed by this program in conjunction with the work-related pensions of the Histadrut. The calculations are for a disabled family head with two children, and they take the tax system into account as well.

The general disability program enables workers with predisability wages that were particularly low to receive a full benefit even if the reduction in work capacity is less than 75 percent. This is because if income is below the level of the basic benefit, he is eligible for a full benefit regardless of previous income. Because of this clause, there is a very large penalty on earnings in the range immediately above. The marginal rate then follows an oscillating pattern up to 50 percent of the predisability wage, where it is again very high as the disabled person is no longer entitled to benefits. The oscillating pattern is the consequence of rounding the disability rating into four groups (100 percent = 75 to 100; 74 percent = 66 to 74; 65 percent = 56 to 65; 60 percent = 50 to 55).

When the Histadrut pension is also accounted for, the basic pattern remains unchanged. The magnitude of the marginal rate is higher at some levels because of the tax system and lower at others because the dependents' benefit is no longer applicable. The level of the penalties at 25 percent and 50 percent of previous wages are, however, much higher. This is shown in Table 11.14.

Because of the extensive ranges over which the marginal rates are 100 percent, these calculations are not fully revealing. In order to see the

Table 11.14. Marginal Tax Rates in General Disability Program with a Work-Related Pension (family of two or more persons)[a]

Predisability Wage (w_o)	Postdisability Wage as % of w_o							
	0-24	25	26-34	35	36-44	45	46-49	50
Half average wage								
Before-tax marginal rate	0	1,250	0	433	0	241	0	2,884
After-tax marginal rate[b]	0	1,250	0	433	0	241	0	2,884
Average wage								
Before-tax marginal rate	0	1,759	0	609	0	339	0	4,060
After-tax marginal rate[b]	25	1,545	25	551	25	318	25	3,533
Twice average wage								
Before-tax marginal rate	0	3,033	0	1,095	0	538	0	7,000
After-tax marginal rate[b]	35	2,399	35	852	35	445	35	5,491

Note: Marginal tax rates here are changes in benefits due to increase in 100 IL current wages.

[a]Family is newly disabled, in general disability program. Recipients of the work-related pension are not eligible for dependents' benefits in the general disability program.

[b]Refers to inclusion of the general income tax system.

broader picture, Figure 11.1 traces the relationship between disposable income and earnings for the general disability program of National Insurance, with eligibility for a work-related pension. Regardless of predisability wage, for the generally disabled there is little if any gain from working. There is, however, one important qualification. We have assumed that the programs monitor the earnings of the disabled over time and that they adjust the disability rating in response to fluctuations in earnings. In practice, there is actually little monitoring.

Policy Issues

There has been a persistent and remarkable increase in benefits for the disabled, in particular for the generally disabled. The increase has resulted from many isolated decisions made on a number of fronts—from the development of social insurance, from tax policy, from the collective bargaining process, from the judiciary's resolution of indemnity claims, and from the judicial interpretations of laws and regulations. There has been no overall guiding principle governing these decisions; there has been very little awareness of their cumulative consequences.

Accordingly, there has been no discussion of the interrelatedness of these developments. Specific events received attention and were the subjects of controversy, but were almost never perceived in the broader context.

This state of affairs reflects the divided authority for decision-making with respect to disability policy. It also attests to the absence of a process of monitoring and reporting on the development of social policy. It is not, however, within the limits of this study to evaluate the sources of these developments. Our concern is evaluation of the consequences.

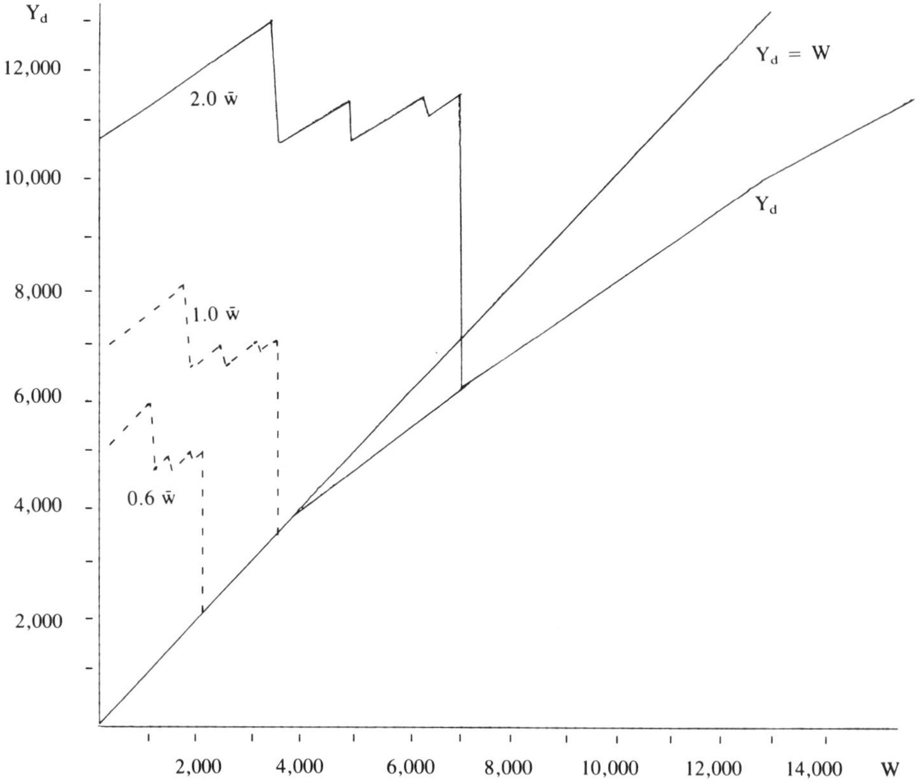

Figure 11.1. Disposable Annual Income (in 1978 IL) Related to Earnings for the Generally Disabled with Work-Related Pensions

Y_d = disposable income; W = postdisability earnings.

One consequence has been that benefits are now substantial for almost all groups of disabled. Today most who are in the labor force and who are injured, under any circumstances, will receive substantial wage-related benefits. After-tax wage replacement rates for non-work-related injuries easily exceed 100 percent. If various special benefits are considered, postdisability benefits are well above predisability earnings. There is little awareness of this state of affairs, among either public officials or in the academic community. These levels, at least for the generally disabled, seem to have evolved almost inadvertently. Despite the attention to developing programs of special benefits, there is little attention to their effects on overall replacement rates.

The development of benefits for the generally disabled and the expansion of special benefits for all groups of disabled have had important consequences for another basic issue of disability policy: differential treatment of various groups among the disabled. In our analyses of replacement rates in the previous section and of the level of benefits in the section before that, we have estimated the magnitude of these differences and their sources.

One striking consequence of recent developments has been that the generally disabled, traditionally viewed as a disadvantaged group, have achieved preferred status in many instances. Most of those injured in an accident at home or in an auto accident will, if fully disabled and unable to work, receive higher benefits than if injured on the job, as they may receive both a national insurance and work-related pension. Someone who is medically rated at 50 percent disabled and whose work capacity is equally reduced will also receive higher benefits in the general disability program.

This state of affairs gives rise to two questions. Traditionally, the work-injured have been viewed as a group with preferred claims to compensation. Has the status reversal been intentional? If the work-injured no longer have a recognized right to preferential status, why shouldn't programs for these two groups—work injured versus disabled from other causes—be integrated? The response to the first question is clearly that the developments were unplanned. The response to the second question raises many questions that we cannot address here.

It is a commonplace that those covered within the Defense Ministry's program have a privileged position. Every now and then the magnitude of benefits in this program or the size of the advantage over other groups of disabled is subject to criticism. The rationale for "special treatment" has been questioned in light of the fact that more than half are injured in daily activities (e.g., auto accidents, illness), not in battle or training. The extent to which these sources of impairment are recognized is linked to how the rules for defining "due to military service" are interpreted, and criticism is directed to the liberality of these interpretations. Even those whose injuries result from misconduct are frequently eligible for benefits.

This kind of program integration is complex and sensitive. One problem is that the program deals for the most part with very young persons who have not as yet established an earnings record or completed their education. Thus it would make little sense to adopt a benefit structure related to previous wages or to impute an expected predisability wage. The second problem relates to the magnitude of present benefit differentials. If we consider only basic benefits, the differentials are not very great and may go in either direction depending on the level of predisability wages at which the comparison is made. Those who would have had earnings above the average had they not been injured will generally do better in the work-injury or general disability program. The differentials become large, and favor Defense Ministry recipients, when various special and one-time benefits are considered.

The ideological arguments for and against integration have been reviewed elsewhere (see Miller, Kretzmer, and Procaccia, 1979), and we shall not repeat them. The particular importance of maintaining morale and incentives within the context of the Israeli national security situation weighs heavily toward maintaining at least some differential. Differentials reflect popular sympathies as well. Moreover, given the size of the differences, full integration of benefits would seem impossible. There is a case for arguing that the benefits in the Defense Ministry program are too high and should be reduced on some gradual basis over time. This would reduce the differentials as well.

Strategy of Support

We now turn to the question of support strategy for the generally disabled. The development of social insurance for the generally disabled in Israel was accompanied by a divergence of views with respect to the appropriate goals and strategy for implementing them. These divergences are reflected in the ongoing debate between those who favor a universal social insurance approach to income maintenance and those who would rely on income-tested benefits to guarantee a minimum income. A policy recommendations committee delivered a report in 1972 advocating a two-tier system: the top tier would provide a benefit tied to predisability wages; the bottom tier would grant a minimum benefit to those without an earnings history or would supplement the income of those with low wages. The committee's recommendations were opposed, and only the bottom tier was enacted, in a form that incorporates both selective and universal elements and that distinguishes the eligibility criteria between the "newly" and "previously" disabled (after and before April 1970). Adoption of a top tier to provide wage-related benefits was rejected.[7]

Developments within the social insurance system were accompanied by gradual extension of coverage of work-related disability pensions. These pensions are a component of the work-related retirement pension system. This system, the only source of wage-related retirement pensions in Israel, has been characterized by a high rate of wage replacement. The extension of coverage has, almost inadvertently, led to the development of a universal wage-replacement orientation for the generally disabled. In contrast to the 1972 recommendations, the top tier is provided in the context of various work-related schemes (three or four major ones). Moreover, it provides a 70 percent wage replacement rate as opposed to the 50 percent recommended by the commission. We predict that this relatively unobtrusive program will become the major source of disability benefits and their growth in the future.

Several issues arise in reviewing these developments. Does the particular combination of selective and universal elements characterizing the program for the newly disabled within National Insurance make sense as a coherent policy? Does this policy make sense in relation to the development of the work-related system? Does the system for the previously disabled make sense in relation to the alternative of dealing with them in a purely welfare framework? Can the distinction between the previously and newly disabled be justified? Do the level and pattern of benefits that have emerged from developments in the work-related and social insurance systems represent a justifiable set of policies?

One major consequence of the decision not to develop a two-tier system of disability insurance within National Insurance has been the uncoordinated growth of its systemic components. The unusually high replacement rates for the the generally disabled have been one consequence of this failure to link the National Insurance and work-related systems. In the context of national pension system proposals, suggestions were made to reduce the combined replacement rates. However, it is unclear whether measures to reduce benefits will be included in the final proposals. If adopted, the basic replacement rate would be reduced from 105 percent to 90 percent for a two-person family earning the average wage.

Another consequence of the system's organizational duality has been the creation of two entirely distinct procedures for defining disability in the bottom and top tiers. The basic concept of disability underlying the two systems is the same—both condition eligibility for benefits on reduction in work capacity. Yet one cannot rationalize these procedural differences on any substantive basis. Indeed, there is something of a paradox. The value of the work-related benefits is potentially much greater, but the procedures for defining disability and the rules governing the determination process are more elaborate and explicit within National Insurance. Moreover, the disability determination process within National Insurance is uniquely integrated with rehabilitation efforts. Thus the greater administrative effort is made where the payoff to being exact is lowest. One can find additional differences in administrative procedures that would appear to have no rationale, such as the provisions for monitoring disability status over time.

A more fundamental issue is why general disability programs should rely on direct assessment of work capacity as opposed to the more purely medical concepts applied to the other major disability programs. In evaluating these options one must distinguish between a system in which work capacity is the sole criterion, as in the work-related programs, and one that combines an explicit medical prerequisite with a final decision based on work capacity, as in the National Insurance disability program.

A Summing Up

Many of the issues summarized here are currently under debate in Israel. As part of this debate, the authors offer their own proposal.

We propose a two-tier benefit structure. The bottom tier would be a flat-rate benefit geared to a medical rating. In addition to serving basic income maintenance goals, it may also be viewed as more generally compensating the disabled and as replacing special advantages often provided within the income tax structure. It would make basic support available without labeling the disabled as having functional work limitations or conditioning support on the highly precarious assessment of work capacity.

The top tier would provide wage-related benefits for those deemed to have clear and permanent reductions in full work capacity and which are viewed as largely independent of current labor market conditions. The receipt of such benefits would not be earnings-tested; those entering the work force would be viewed as having made exceptional efforts that should not be penalized. This two-tier structure represents a synthesis of the principles inherent in programs for the work-injured with those of the generally disabled; a full integration of the benefit structures for these two groups would be possible on this basis.

To avoid the pressure of including persons whose difficulties are related to temporary labor market conditions, we recommend the creation of a special category of temporary but renewable benefits for those with medical impairments who are deemed unemployed due to temporary labor market conditions. There would be rigorous provisions for monitoring changes in their status. This would avoid the present practice of denying the productive capacity of many impaired persons who are still able to make a productive contribution.

Notes

1. The burden for reclaiming benefits that have been paid to the worker in the past is on the insurance company. National insurance sues the insurance company to collect its full share of the claim. In many cases the insurance company fails to collect from the individual.

2. Almost 5 percent of workers at the Meshakem have completed high school. In many cases arrangements are made for them to work in the open market, generally with some partial subsidy by the Meshakem. This represents a departure from the role of providing sheltered employment.

3. The subsidy is calculated as the difference between current expenditures and revenues. It does not include the investments in buildings and equipment or their real amortization.

4. This description of the demonstration project is based on a series of internal National Insurance reports. A final report has not as yet been issued.

5. The imputed annuity per pound is

$$\text{An} = \frac{r}{1-(1+r)}\,n$$

where r is real market interest rate (or discount rate) and n is the number of periods for which benefits are imputed.

6. This percentage was recently reduced to 65 percent; our calculations are based on 75 percent.

7. For those disabled before the law was enacted, a purely selective approach was recommended by the committee and was, in fact, adopted.

References

Hansen, W. L., and Weisbrod, B. 1968. An income net-worth approach to measuring economic welfare. *American Economic Review, 58*, 1315-1329.

Miller, A., Kretzmer, D., and Procaccia, U. 1979. *The rights of the handicapped in Israel: Proposals for reform.* Faculty of Law, Hebrew University, Jersualem. [In Hebrew.]

Reiss, Esther. 1973. Survey of those injured at work and in hostile action. Preliminary draft. Department of Research and Planning, National Insurance Institute, Jerusalem. [In Hebrew.]

Sainsbury, Sally. 1975. Registered as disabled. Occasional Papers on Social Administration, No. 35. London: C. Bell.

Shapira, Monica. 1973. *The future of the Meshakem.* Jerusalem: School of Social Work, Hebrew University.

Sherwood, S., ed. 1975. *Long-term care: A handbook for researchers, planners, providers.* New York: Spectrum Publications.

Simkins, J., and Tickner, V. 1978. *Whose benefit?* London: Economist Intelligence Unit, Ltd.

Chapter 12

Disability Policy in Italy

Lucia Vitali

In Italy, as in most European countries, one cause of the growth in public expenditures in the last decade is the increasing share absorbed by social programs, both in current values and in real terms. The percentage of national resources spent on all transfer payments is reaching high levels; social security alone is absorbing more than 20 percent of gross national product (GNP). While the economic intervention of the state in the field of social policy is increasing, budget deficits are growing along with public expenditures. The state is in fact faced with keeping economic growth from falling to unacceptable levels, after the boom years of the late 1950s and early 1960s.

On the other hand, productivity is growing, and as a consequence an increasing part of the working-age population, especially the younger and the older age groups, is kept out of the labor market, where activity rates are low for the young as well as for the population 60 years and older, and even those under 60. Early retirement and the increasing number of disability pensions are relevant components of this phenomenon. The state is therefore urged to give assistance to a growing number of nonactive people: their identification, and among them those who are disabled, is one part of this chapter.

In the Italian context, increased transfer payments to families and firms are also aimed at counterbalancing and mitigating old and new distributive problems, such as between industrialized and rural areas, and between the active and nonactive labor force populations (Forte et al., 1978). This chapter will analyze some of these aspects; it is, however, important to emphasize at this point how closely related and mutually influenced they are, and how their interdependence contributes to further aggravation of "the fiscal crisis of the state."

Lucia Vitali is Associate Professor in the Faculty of Statistical Science, University of Rome.

The expenditure for disability programs is one of the many facets of the welfare role of the state. Here we will describe the various social programs for the disabled and try to relate them to the economic and social conditions of the country.

Information on the Italian disabled population and their income levels is scanty. In the following pages we attempt to put together information gathered from all available sources about a subject that has received very little or no attention by economists up to now. From available estimates, the Italian disabled population seems to constitute about the same percentage as in most European countries—i.e., about 10 percent of the total population seems to suffer from some kind of serious impairment. The same incidence is often quoted in international reports on this phenomenon.

In the decade under examination, the 1970s, the incidence of disabilities recognized for entitlement to benefits grew at a very fast rate. From 1968 to 1978 our estimate is that the amount of cash benefits increased from nearly 4 million to 7.6 million lire. Unfortunately, no census or survey is available to measure the incidence of disability per se. The 1978 survey of those not in the labor force indicates that nearly 600,000 people between 14 and 70 years of age—i.e., 4 percent of those outside the labor force—are not working because they are physically unable to engage in work activity (53 percent are men, 47 percent are women; Istat, 1979). Apart from this information, no other source was available to estimate, or even guess, the size of the universe which can be defined, objectively or subjectively, as disabled. This chapter therefore relies mainly on data relating to recipients of the various programs, and the analysis on the whole employs statistics so collected.

Principal Features of the Main Disability Programs

The most important benefits are directed to the following groups of recipients: (1) workers injured while performing their job, insured through Istituto Nazionale delle Assicurazioni contro gli Infortuni sul Lavoro (INAIL); (2) workers affected by impairment not caused by job performance, insured through Istitutio Nazionale della Previdenza Sociale (INPS); (3) both partly and seriously disabled people with earnings below a certain limit and with no earnings record; the state pays these benefits.

Another instrument of social policy which is of great importance for disabled people of working age (but below 55) is the "quota" employment program—the obligation of employers with more than a certain number of employees to employ a quota of disabled persons. Those eligible are disabled people belonging to groups 1 and 2, above, and having a residual working capacity of at least one third.

The essential social policies for the disabled consist of those described above. A few other programs of relatively minor importance will be described at the end of this section; they are mostly discretionary and their number and cost, compared to the INPS and INAIL programs, are definitely less relevant.

INAIL

The first disability to be considered for compulsory insurance (before the end of the nineteenth century) was *industrial injury*. The risk to be covered related to the frequency of accidents causing impairment or permanent disease to employees while performing their work. Today the INAIL program is still based on insurance principles, as if it were performed by a large, nationwide insurance company. In fact it is founded on an agreement between INAIL and the employer, which favors the worker and entitles him to a benefit if industrial injury takes place.

The financial burden of the INAIL program is carried entirely by the employer. This program—the first form of social insurance to be put into law—was motivated by the need to protect employers from having to pay on their own for the death, or permanent disability, of their employees. Today it covers nearly 10 million workers, half the number of employed people: the obligation excludes all white collar and service workers, and covers only those workers whose job involves a risk situation (the specific definition is discussed in the next section). INAIL cash benefits are received by over one million disabled workers; 70 percent of them are industrial workers and 30 percent are agricultural employed and self-employed workers. The share of agriculture is increasing continuously. Total expenditure of INAIL benefits for 1978 was over 1,007 billion lire.

Within the one million beneficiaries, a further distinction needs to be made. Those who have completely lost working capacity (i.e., with a degree of disability over 80 percent) number nearly 21,000 people, 2 percent of all beneficiaries; among them 20 percent are in agriculture and 80 percent are in industry. Industrial injury benefit is equal to previous earnings for this group of totally disabled (100 percent of earnings at the time of the accident, within a ceiling and a floor); and it carries entitlement to other benefits, such as for attendants, unemployment compensation, and other discretionary benefits in cash and in kind, apart from health care and, when needed, artificial limbs and other health equipment.

Benefits are calculated as a specific replacement of previous earnings. Nearly 80 percent of recipients have a work-capacity reduction of 40 percent or less, and receive a maximum benefit equal to 25 percent of earnings (if below a fixed ceiling). The minimum benefit is equal to 10 percent of earnings for a 20 percent disability. Later, we will discuss the organization and working of each program and give more detail on the relation between degree of disability and level of benefits.

INPS

The disability program of the Istituto Nazionale della Previdenza Sociale (INPS) does not relate degree of disability to level of benefit. Instead, the benefit is granted to workers who qualify by degree of *reduced earning capacity* (above 66 percent). The INPS disability program also has an insurance origin—social insurance against disability, old age, and death (survivors). Social insurance contribution toward these three risks is equal to 24 percent of all gross earnings (excluding family allowances), and has no ceiling.

The employer pays two thirds and employees pay one third. In practice, payroll taxes do not affect the worker's level of earnings, as it is the employer that carries the burden of the whole social security contribution. The INPS social insurance program covers 87 percent of all those employed; 12.2 million are employees in the private sector and 5.1 million are self-employed (10 percent of all employees and self-employed are in agriculture). While employees' social security contributions are rather high (24 percent of gross earnings for the pension system alone), the self-employed, since their initial entry into social insurance, have been asked for a very low contribution. Today the self-employed pay a contribution for old age, disability, and survivors' pensions that is equal to less than one tenth of that paid by the average industrial workers. Benefits for the self-employed are, on the whole, slightly lower; the redistributive effects are mostly in favor of agricultural workers. The outstanding feature is that, out of 5.3 million disability pensions, about 30 percent are granted to those self-employed in agriculture (mostly women over 60).

Of all INPS disability pensions, 84 percent are at the minimum level—i.e., around 20 percent of the salary of the average industrial worker—and a minimum disability pension is cumulable along with other social security benefits *and* a salary.

In 1978, total expenditures for INPS disability pensions were 7,580 billion lire. It should be emphasized that this pension can be granted at any age, and that among all recipients only one third are below retirement age. It is not uncommon for an older worker who lacks a sufficient number of contributing years for an old age pension (the minimum is 15 years) to get a disability pension (for which the minimum is 5 years of contribution). Furthermore, while the INAIL benefit is based on partial or total loss of *working* capacity, the INPS pension is based on the loss of *earning* capacity. This means that it is the economic conditions (i.e., the labor market situation) of the area in which the worker lives that are to be considered, while his health conditions, in practice, are sometimes of minor importance.

State Aid to the Severely Disabled in Need

In contrast, the third program is based on the health of the applicant. The program for severely disabled people in need does not require any individual work history. The work incapacity must be over 66 percent and must be due to physical or mental disability. It is a relatively recent program, initiated by a law of 1971, which extended to disabled people with income below a certain level the benefits previously granted only to the blind, the mute and deaf, and the mutilated. Detailed statistical information on this program is not yet available.

This benefit, and the "social pension" to people over 65 with earnings below a minimum, are the two programs in the social security system which do not require any social security contribution on the part of the recipient (or on account of the recipient). The benefit paid to the disabled in need is very low, equal to 15 percent of the salary of an average industrial worker. It is paid to people between 18 and 65 years of age. A disabled person over 65 receives a social pension (of the same amount). The disabled under 18, if entitled, receive an attendants' benefit (an amount 10 percent less than the total benefit). We estimate that nearly one million disabled with no work history receive benefits from this program, with an expenditure of 850 billion lire in 1978.

Other Benefits

All recipients in these three programs are also free beneficiaries of medical care, since entitlement to the cash benefit also involves full health care. Total expenditures for health services, including hospital care, were, in 1978, over 10,000 billion lire: how much of it went to the disabled was not always recorded. In this chapter we will try to indicate the share of health expenditure involved in each program, even though in Italy health care is free and no distinction is made between disabled and nondisabled patients.

Regarding employment training and placement for the disabled, a large educational program has been underway since 1975 at the regional level. It is directed mainly to people under 18. Fragmentary information from a few of the nineteen regions which can offer training courses for disabled and handicapped people was available only at the qualitative level.

More quantitative information was available from the program of "quota employment," which in its present form started in 1968. It reaches nearly 600,000 people each year (roughly 1.5 percent of the working age population) whose disability varies between one third and two thirds. Under the program, disabled people with at least a 33 percent residual working capacity have the right to be employed by private firms with more than 35 employees and by public institutions and in state jobs in even higher proportions within each new group of entrants.

This obligation imposed on the employer is based on the belief that the productivity of the disabled worker does not differ from that of the nondisabled, and therefore no kind of subsidy or payroll tax relief is granted to the employer. As indicated later in this chapter, the law is felt to be an unfair burden, especially by firms which must be labor-intensive.

Figure 12.1 outlines the main characteristics of programs for the disabled in Italy.

The programs described above cover virtually all of Italian social policy toward the disabled. Training and education for disabled people under age 18 is another important program at the regional level. Apart from the almost permanent benefits just described, a number of subsidiary, temporary benefits are paid by various social security institutions. In addition to the 1,007 billion lire spent on pensions, INAIL spent 7.8 billion in 1978 in subsidiary benefits for the totally disabled and 78.2 billion for health rehabilitation. INAIL temporary benefits to its injured, insured workers absorbed 262.7 billion lire. Among other relevant social security expenditures, sickness cash benefits—including births and tuberculosis—were 1,311.47 billion; 1,154.14 billion were spent on unemployment benefits; and 1,802 billion on family allowances. In 1978, the various social insurance institutions paid subsidies and "assistance" sums up to a total of 25 billion lire. This amount does not specify the share given to disabled people; yet some payments were made to injured workers (4.2 billion) and for deaths at work (1.6 billion). No other amounts can be listed as payment to the disabled, since these payments are recorded under general titles (i.e., need, sickness, or "other").

In our search for disaggregated data, we can point to the nearly 70 billion lire spent for thermal treatments (excluding INAIL expenditure). It is reasonable to suppose that the majority of recipients were disabled workers or pensioners, but none of the two had separate registration. As to "social assistance" to disabled people in institutions, or to children of the disabled (for scholarships, vacations, etc.), in 1978 INAIL spent 8.5 billion lire and other bodies spent 66.4 billion lire (see Ministero del Bilancio, 1979, pp. 623, 633, 647, 649). The basic information available demonstrates the increasing expansion of disability programs, both in the number of recipients and in the level of benefits.

The following sections analyze each of the most important programs, underlining those aspects that are contributing to greater expansion.

INPS Disability Pensions

Istituto Nazionale della Previdenza Sociale provides social security cash benefits for 87 percent of all workers. Only public administration employees and a few minor categories are excluded. In 1978, expenditure

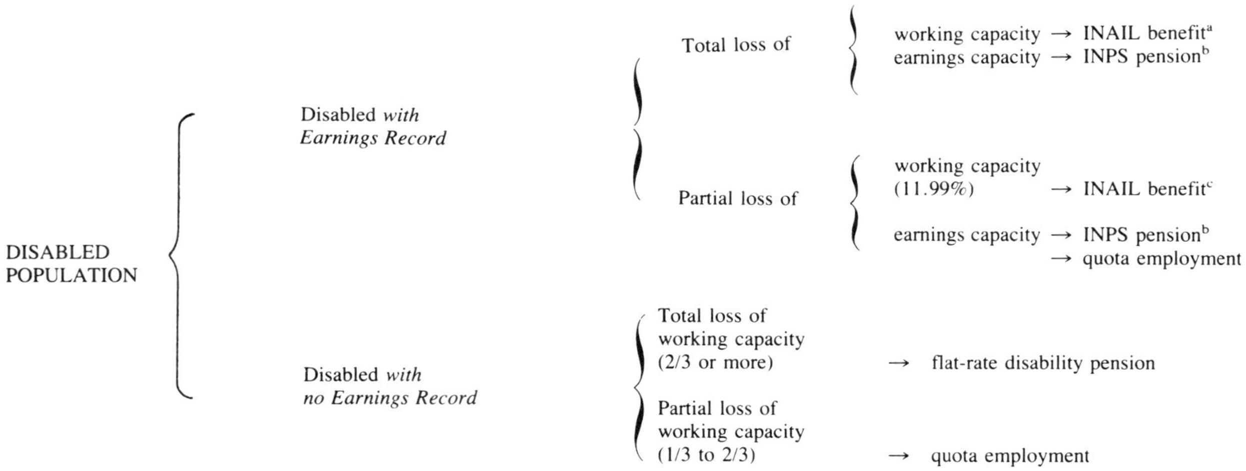

Figure 12.1. Recipients and Benefits in the Italian Disability Programs

Note: INAIL industrial injury benefit and INPS disability pension are legally cumulative, as long as the injured worker has a contribution record of at least 5 years.

[a]Replacement rate: 100% (within a ceiling and a floor).

[b]Replacement rate: according to length of working period and amount of contribution.

[c]Replacement rate: according to degree of disability.

for all INPS pensions was 18,792 billion lire (8.5 percent of GNP), of which over 40 percent went to disability pensions—7,579 billion lire for 5,277 pensions, equal on average to 25 percent of the average wage of the industrial worker.

Disability Definition

The present concept of disability was first defined in Article 10 of Royal Decree Law No. 636 of 1939: "The insured worker, whose earning capacity in occupations *suited to his ability* is permanently reduced because of illness or physical or mental impairment by at least *two thirds*, is considered disabled" (emphasis added). At the time, this definition applied only to manual workers; for nonmanual workers earning capacity could be reduced by only one half. In 1971 the Constitutional Court extended the 50 percent criterion to all workers. The concept was subsequently redefined by a law of June 1975, which restricted benefits to manual *and* nonmanual workers whose earnings capacity was reduced by at least two thirds. Since 1975, therefore, white collar workers have experienced a restricted definition of disability, while blue collar workers (the great majority of beneficiaries) have experienced more generous terms—in the period 1971-75 old age pensions increased at a yearly rate of less than 3 percent and disability pensions at a rate of over 6 percent (INPS, Notizie Statistiche, 1979, pp. 27-28).

Earning Capacity

The INPS definition of disability refers to earning capacity, i.e.: (a) the worker's capacity for work, meaning the capacity to use his ability profitably; and (b) the "general adequacy" of the worker to provide himself with an income through his work; this capacity refers to his ability to use his remaining health and his education, and his ability to adjust to new environments and acquire new working techniques.

"Occupations suited to his ability" refers to a condition which will allow the worker to perform an activity equitably related to his strength and his capability, and involves a fair evaluation of his training and preparation. This concept was originally formulated only for employees, but it has recently been extended, by direct or indirect reference to the law, to self-employed workers—to farmers in 1957, to artisans in 1959, and to retailers in 1966. The law does not really give a precise definition of disability, but establishes a relationship between "medical" invalidism and invalidism which gives entitlement to a pension.

Permanent Character of Impairment

The law states that disability deriving from illness or physical or mental impairment is the most important factor in determining entitlement to a pension. Illness is a long-term disease and impairment is a chronic condition or injury. The medical test of disability (the assessment of disability from a medical point of view) is merely technical and is one of the elements used for the subsequent assessment of invalidism as part of INPS administrative procedures. The medical assessment concerns the degree of impairment and the extent to which it is *permanent*. It also considers the worker's residual working capacity with reference to technical and professional ability, and establishes whether a working activity would further undermine the worker's health.

Suitability of Occupation

According to the current interpretation of the law, "occupations suited to his ability" includes activities that are different from the worker's original job, provided that they are of a similar nature. An occupation is considered suitable when the worker, because of his capacity and adaptability, can actually do a job of equivalent status by using his remaining physical capacity and his knowledge and technical ability without undergoing retraining. It is widely recognized, however, that because of increasing specialization the "range of occupations suited to his ability" is limited, so that earning capacity generally refers to the *worker's original occupation*. Thus residual earning capacity has a very restricted meaning.

Reviews and Terminations

As to the permanence of the disability, the interpretation of the law is quite clear: permanent reduction of earnings capacity entitles a worker to a pension, but can be reviewed and revoked, if, e.g., a worker's residual earnings capacity improves and rises above one third; then, according to the law, the pension is terminated. The permanent character of reduced earnings capacity remains, even if there is a possibility of an improvement in the worker's condition as a result of medical treatment (or surgical operation) after the pension has been granted.

In theory, it is also accepted that INPS can temporarily withhold the pension if the worker refuses to undergo treatment (Law No. 1827, 1935).[1]

"Normal" Earnings

Disability must be currently existing, permanent, and medically ascertained. It must also entail a minimum degree of reduced earnings capacity, a threshold which must be passed in order to qualify for a pension. The law refers to "normal" earnings (guadagno normale).

The earnings standard intended to determine whether an impaired worker, using his remaining physical or mental capacity in an occupation suited to his ability, is able to earn more, or less, than one third of the salary earned by a healthy worker in the same labor market conditions. The problem of defining normal earnings has given rise to a great many legal disputes, and the task is even more difficult when the assessment concerns self-employed workers. The criteria adopted are usually subjective and leave room for considerable discretion. A disability benefit is not (or should not be) granted as a form of indemnity or compensation, as is a war pension or industrial injury benefit. The impairment in this case is not due to the performance of a work-related activity. It is the reduction in earning capacity, not in work capacity, that is the test, and this requires that labor market conditions should be taken into consideration.

The social and economic conditions of the area in which the applicant lives have to be taken into consideration when evaluating his invalidism. In poor areas, evaluation of the social and economic situation prevailed in practice, especially during the early 1970s, over every other consideration, and the disability pension actually became a sort of indemnity for those who lived in jobless areas. In fact, the law itself gives considerable discretionary power to the committee which makes the decision concerning eligibility.

The criterion of referring to the worker's economic situation was established in 1969 (the law states "an evaluation of social and economic aspects") and has been applied on a very broad scale. When it was introduced, it was expected that it would decrease the number of disability pensions in richer areas. Experience has proved this wrong. The 1978 figures indicate a tendency toward a more restricted use of this criterion. Since 1975 the need for a more restricted policy has been underlined in INPS official documents (INPS, 1977, p. 184), and the rate of increase of new disability pensions fell sharply from 1976 (down 40 percent for 1976 in the category of employees; previously it was about 10 percent per year; INPS, 1979, p. 97).

Assessment of Invalidism

Requirements include the following:

1. A "strictly objective" medical test, to ascertain the presence of illness or physical or mental impairment permanently injuring the health of the worker.
2. Investigation of the ability and labor skills of the worker. This is largely subjective and concerns the "personality" of the applicant, with reference to his technical and professional aptitudes and his capability of applying them to the appropriate working opportunities.
3. A sociological evaluation of the social and economic environment and its positive or negative influence on the profitable and continuous use of the worker's capability on the labor market.
4. A quantitative definition of the reduction in earnings capacity, which must reach a certain level (at least two thirds) for the applicant worker to be eligible for a pension.

The social, economic, and environmental aspects are part of the concept of invalidism. The "working personality" of the applicant is therefore evaluated in terms of environmental conditions permitting its expression, and factors other than medical disability are considered. Age is one of the most important, although it has already been taken into consideration at the medical stage. Others are mental capacity and cultural background, propensity to acquire new technical or professional ideas, the ability to use residual capacity in learning an activity similar to the previous one, and any other element the INPS Committee considers relevant.

Aptitudes

Article 10 of the 1939 law, cited above, refers to occupations suited to the worker's ability. Suitability concerns fitness to do the job with average efficiency and productivity, according to ability and talent, with normal use of strength, and with no danger of further impairments or damage to health. This refers to vocational aptitude.

Problems in Evaluating Disability

The evaluations are made by INPS doctors, who are specialists in forensic medicine. It is the doctor's task to assess all possible factors contributing to the "personality" of the applicant as a worker, keeping in mind that in no circumstances can he accept an occupation of lower status than his previous one.

It often happened, in the past, that no evidence of a medical test was provided with an application. However, the diagnostic tests necessary to prove that an application is unfounded are costly. All applicants are tested carefully by the INPS doctor, who can often be compelled to conduct yet another test by both the worker and by the doctor whom he has permission to bring with him. This second doctor often comes from a "patronato," an agency (usually a union agency) which assists workers in various bureaucratic procedures. There are about thirty of these institutions covering the whole country and they are financed by the Ministry of Labor out of social security contributions (66.2 billion lire in 1977). Their assistance usually constitutes a useful form of prescreening. Yet they play a relevant role in legal disputes, giving assistance to workers who want to appeal. It is important to point out that expenses for legal disputes are always paid by INPS, even when the appeal is rejected. The medical administrative staff and doctors of INPS do not always receive copies of previous hospital treatment or industrial injury invalidism tests, and the cost of medical tests needed to check previous tests is very high. The amount of this expenditure was over 12 billion lire in 1977, mostly concentrated in southern areas.

For the evaluation of disablement of self-employed workers, it has been suggested that reference should be to the precise job the farmer, artisan or retailer performs, not to similar ones, for obvious reasons. The excessive number of disability pensioners among self-employed workers (see Table 12.4, below, and discussion in the next paragraph) is due to the fact that these categories of workers are more numerous in rural and depressed areas.

Obviously, the "social and economic aspects" are strictly related to economic growth and labor market conditions, to technological developments and applications, and to labor mobility. In the South, labor supply notoriously exceeds demand, and geographical consideration is therefore important, since in determining disability there must be reference to the province where the worker lives. In the North, labor supply is more equal to demand and the geographical principle is extended to the whole region considered. Where the demand for labor is limited, applications for disability benefits are more numerous and have often been accepted with more generosity. At the beginning of 1978, within the system for employed workers there were 103 disability pensions for every 100 old age pensions. In Lombardy the ratio was 44 to 100, and the North as a whole fell below the national ratio. In the South, on average, the ratio was 250 to 100; the highest ratio was 669 to 100, in Enna, Sicily. For the self-employed in agriculture, Enna had a ratio of 1,552 to 100, whereas the national average for the same category was 282 to 100.

Given this situation, it is understandable that there are more petitions and appeals in depressed areas. Although no statistical geographical distribution of appeals is available, the concentration of expenditures for medical tests in certain areas, recorded in unpublished provincial INPS medical reports, is indirect evidence.

Rejected Applications: Appeals and Petitions

Once the necessary evaluations and medical tests have been performed, an application can be rejected for one of the following reasons:

1. No impairment has been found that would result in a reduction of earnings capacity within the prescribed limits.
2. No impairment has been found that would result in a reduction of earnings capacity within the prescribed limits, as demonstrated by the fact that the worker has a suitable occupation, the performance of which does not exhaust his capability, nor is the occupation of lower level than he should expect, or badly paid, or offered as charity.
3. The impairment was present before the applicant began his working life.

Appeals lodged by a worker, or by a labor union agency (patronato) on his behalf, are examined by the provincial INPS offices. When the appeal is lodged by a worker without assistance from an agency, a new medical examination is made by a doctor different from the one who rejected the case; if the worker is assisted by an agency, the medical examination is carried out by the two doctors, one from INPS and the other one from the agency. Very often the opinions expressed by the two doctors differ; this leads to a new appeal. After the medical examination, a committee composed of doctors, representatives of workers, employers, and INPS administrative staff express a final opinion. Final responsibility for granting the pension lies with the committee and the director of the local INPS office, who acts as chairman. Employees and self-employed workers are referred to different committees.

The same procedure can be repeated at the regional level. A new medical examination takes place, conducted by different doctors. In practice, the procedure is similar to the previous one. Very seldom do opinions differ when the impairment itself is examined, although this involves high costs for tests and specialized medical examinations. Dissension can however be very strong concerning nonmedical factors.

Controversial cases can be brought to court, and trials have often given the judge considerable discretionary power. Judges of the Constitutional Court, called upon in a few cases, have recently stated that "the social and economic conditions of the area should be considered a marginal complementary element in the inquiry toward the ascertainment of earnings capacity" and such conditions cannot reverse the result of the medically ascertained working capacity. Probably because of this sentence, the number of court appeals has recently decreased. Although this suggestion may be of help in restraining the generosity of certain provincial and regional INPS committees, the law itself has not been changed, even though a restrictive proposal was submitted to Parliament in July 1978. It was not discussed before the elections, and was reintroduced for the approval of the new Parliament in October 1979. In June 1982 it was still up for approval.

Review of Disability Benefit Entitlement

The review and revocation of disability pensions are regulated by the laws of August 28, 1924, and April 14, 1939. Periodical reviews are not compulsory; the law simply indicates the possibility of reviewing the benefit for pensioners under 65 years of age (whose incidence is shown in Table 12.4). There are no statistical data for geographical distribution by age. It is, however, reasonable to suppose that new disability pensioners above pension age are to be found mostly in underprivileged areas.

In practice, reviews are conducted only for recent cases that were dubious at the time the pension was granted. Pensions granted because of blindness are never reviewed. In theory, pensions can be revoked not only when physical conditions improve, but also when other elements of the decision context have changed. This second criterion has rarely been applied.

Preventive Medicine and Health Rehabilitation

All workers who are insured for disability through INPS and are suffering from certain illnesses, i.e., respiratory (asthma and bronchial asthma) and rheumatic diseases, can be treated at the expense of INPS at thermal baths and spas. Such cures are prescribed to, and paid for, active workers only when they do not have another social security institution which can provide them. These provisions, sometimes largely discretionary, are found in other disability programs. They are directed toward the use of effective, although ancient, natural therapeutic resources.

INPS does not organize any work rehabilitation or retraining programs for disability pensioners, the main reason being that it is only the worker's original occupation that can be considered for his earnings capacity assessment.

Statistical Information

Tables 12.1-12.3 offer data on INPS disability pensions. Statistics for Table 12.2 are taken from the old age, disability, and survivors' system for employees and refer to the last occupation of new disability pensioners for the year 1976. Compared to the 1976 percentage distribution of employment in the same industries, it is evident that some groups are overrepresented. Agricultural employees are evidently favored in the granting of disability pensions, as their share in the universe of beneficiaries is 32.7 percent (38.1 percent of all women disabled pensioners were agricultural employees) as compared with 8.1 percent of all employees. To a lesser degree, male construction workers get disability benefits more easily, and the same happens in the large category of "other services." Agriculture and "services and other" are also the groups in which new pensions are granted to people well over pension age (Table 12.1).

Size of the INPS Disability Program

The INPS disability pension schemes are a mixture of social insurance and welfare, as found in other parts of our social security system.[2] This hybrid marriage is exemplified in disability pension benefits.

Entitlement to a disability pension is gained after 5 years of contributions, compared to 15 years required for an old age pension.[3] The welfare element in disability pensions became more important between 1970 and 1975, when greater attention was given to the social and economic situation of the particular area (often the province) in which the applicant lived, in accordance with the 1969 law. Furthermore, between 1971 and 1975 the number of disability pensions increased because the reduction in earnings capacity was fixed at 50 percent instead of the previous (and present) 66.6

Table 12.1. Percentage Distribution of New INPS Disability Pensions by Age, Sex, and Economic Sector, 1976 (not including self-employed workers)

Age	Agriculture			Industry			Services and Other			Total		
	Men	Women	Both	Men	Women	Both	Men	Women	Both	Men	Women	Both
under 24	.1	.1	.1	.2	.4	.3	.2	.2	.2	.2	.2	.2
25-29	.5	.6	.6	1.2	1.7	1.3	1.2	.9	1.0	1.0	.9	.9
30-34	1.2	1.7	1.4	2.5	2.9	2.6	2.5	1.7	2.1	2.1	1.9	2.0
35-39	3.2	4.6	3.9	5.4	4.8	5.2	4.8	3.7	4.2	4.6	4.2	4.4
40-44	8.6	10.2	9.4	10.7	9.6	10.5	9.2	7.0	8.1	9.6	8.7	9.2
45-49	18.4	20.6	19.5	18.5	18.6	18.5	16.4	15.3	15.8	17.6	17.8	17.7
50-54	28.5	34.7	31.6	26.2	32.3	27.5	24.8	23.3	24.0	26.4	28.9	27.5
55-59	25.2	18.2	21.6	23.0	17.6	21.8	22.9	23.4	23.1	23.6	20.6	22.3
60-64	11.5	7.2	9.3	10.4	8.6	10.0	11.8	13.0	12.5	11.2	10.0	10.7
65-69	2.2	1.7	2.0	1.6	2.8	1.9	3.4	5.5	4.5	2.4	3.7	2.9
70-74	.6	.3	.5	.3	.7	.4	1.6	3.0	2.3	.8	1.6	1.2
75-79	—	.1	.1	—	—	—	.8	1.7	1.3	.3	.9	.5
80+	—	—	—	—	—	—	.4	1.3	.9	.2	.6	.5
	100.0	100.0	100.0	100.0	100.0	100.0	100.0	100.0	100.0	100.0	100.0	100.0
Number	47,142	48,514	95,656	63,210	17,735	80,945	54,783	61,075	115,858	165,135	127,324	292,459

Source: INPS, *Notizie statistiche* (1979).

Table 12.2. New INPS Disability Pensioners among Employees (Non-Self-Employed Workers) and Distribution of All and Disabled Employees, by Sector, 1976

Sector	New INPS Disability Pensions per 100 Employees			General Distribution of Employees (%)	Distribution of New INPS Disability Pensioners among Employees (%)
	Men	Women	Both		
Agriculture	28.5	38.1	32.7	15.1	8.1
Manufacturing	13.5	11.9	12.8	28.2	34.4
Construction	22.4	1.9	13.7	8.6	10.2
Power, gas, and mining	.9	.1	.5	1.0	1.3
Transport	1.4	.1	.8	5.8	6.1
Distribution	1.4	2.0	1.6	17.5	10.0
Banking and insurance	.2	.1	.1	1.4	2.0
Other services	29.4	37.9	33.1	10.7	11.5
Public administration	1.8	1.7	1.7	11.7	16.4
No indication	0.5	6.2	3.0		
	100.0	100.0	100.0	100.0	100.0

Source: INPS, *Notizie statistiche* (1979).

Table 12.3. Percentage Distribution of New INPS Disability Pensions, by Cause and Sex, 1976

Disability	Men	Women	Both
Epidemic and infectious diseases	1.3	1.7	.9
Gland and metabolic diseases	3.2	2.7	3.9
Tumors	3.9	3.8	4.1
Diseases of the nervous system	10.4	10.1	10.8
Diseases of the circulatory system	31.3	28.1	35.4
Respiratory system diseases	11.5	15.8	6.1
Digestive system diseases	3.4	4.3	2.2
Genito-urinary system diseases	1.1	.9	1.4
Arthritis and rheumatism	28.1	26.7	29.2
Senility and ill-defined diseases	4.6	4.2	5.4
External causes (accidents, poisoning, etc.)	1.2	1.7	.6
	100.0	100.0	100.0

Source: INPS, *Notizie statistiche* (1979).

percent. A shorter contributory period than for old age pensions and a recent period of easier entitlement are two of the main reasons for growth in the number of beneficiaries over time.

The percentage distribution of the different INPS pensions in the period 1960-78 is shown in Table 12.4. The ratio of disability to old age pensions has been declining considerably. Mention needs to be made again of the two fundamental elements in this growth: there is no upper age limit on obtaining a disability pension (in 1977, nearly 500 new pensions went to people over 80), nor is the benefit converted to an old age pension when retirement age is reached.

At the end of 1978, over 67 percent of all disability pensioners were above retirement age. If disability pensions were granted only to people below that age, Table 12.4 would show a rather different distribution. It is reasonable to suppose, in the absence of quantitative evidence, that the majority of disability pensions are paid to workers who, because of precarious employment, have not paid the longer contributory period needed to be entitled to an old age pension, but who have reached the five-year period of social security contributions, and usually qualify for a disability pension because of their old age (old age is, as the saying goes, an illness in itself). Another explanation of the large share of INPS disability pensions is that this benefit is cumulative with earnings, as it is a "reduced" earnings capacity that entitles one to the benefit, not a total loss of such capacity.

Table 12.4. Number and Percentage Distribution of INPS Old Age, Disability and Survivors' Pensions, 1960-1978

	Number of Pensions	Percentage Distribution		
		Old Age	Disability	Survivors'
1960	5,323	61.0	23.0	16.0
1961	5,598	59.4	24.3	16.3
1962	5,815	57.8	25.6	16.7
1963	6,073	55.7	27.3	17.0
1964	6,404	53.6	29.2	17.2
1965	6,863	51.5	31.2	17.3
1966	7,248	49.5	33.2	17.3
1967	7,793	48.3	34.6	17.1
1968	8,112	46.7	36.4	16.9
1969	8,863	48.5	35.5	16.0
1970	9,599	48.3	35.6	16.1
1971	10,278	47.1	36.6	16.3
1972	10,963	45.5	37.8	16.7
1973	11,316	44.3	38.8	16.9
1974	11,642	43.3	39.8	16.9
1975	12,031	41.7	41.2	17.1
1976	12,126	40.6	42.7	16.7
1977	12,377	39.9	43.1	17.0
1978	12,110	38.9	43.1	18.0

Source: INPS, *Notizie statistiche* and *Allegati statistici,* various years.

Note: Categories of workers covered include private sector employees; self-employed farmers, artisans, and retailers; and a few small groups of those with higher average earnings (telephone and power workers, etc., for a total of 500,000 active workers), excluding public administration employees.

Incidence of Self-Employed Workers

Table 12.5 shows the percentage distribution of old age pensions and disability pensions for the four largest categories of pensioners: employees, farmers, artisans, and retailers. In the 22 years examined (self-employed farmers were the first to be covered by social security, in 1957), disability pensions have increased much more than old age pensions in all categories, but farmers and artisans recorded the fastest growth of disability pensions and the ratio is now almost equal to 3 to 1 for both schemes. In the case of retailers, the figures refer to the last 11 years only, but the trend of the ratio is practically the same as for the two other categories of self-employed workers.

The excessive growth in the number of disability pensions, especially in the 1970s, cannot be explained simply by focusing on self-employed workers. It is also due to the changes in legislation described previously, since growth in disability pensions has in fact been recorded in all categories of INPS insured workers. New beneficiaries are usually well over 50 years old. All beneficiaries above pension age are evidently old people recognized as disabled because of senility; of all invalidism pensions in the employees category, nearly 5 percent were granted because of senility in 1978 to workers up to 80 and more years of age.

Table 12.5. INPS Disability versus Old Age Pensions among Employees and Self-Employed, 1958-1968 (percentage distribution)

	Employees		Self-Employed Workers					
			Farmers		Artisans		Retailers	
	Old Age	Disability	Old Age	Disability	Old Age	Disability	Old Age	Disability
1958	70.9	29.1	—	—	—	—	—	—
1959	69.6	30.4	100.0	—	—	—	—	—
1960	67.6	32.4	99.9	.1	—	—	—	—
1961	65.9	34.1	98.0	2.0	97.0	3.0	—	—
1962	64.3	35.7	95.0	5.0	94.1	5.9	—	—
1963	63.1	36.9	91.3	8.7	91.3	8.7	—	—
1964	61.9	38.1	84.2	15.8	90.2	9.8	—	—
1965	60.8	39.2	76.3	23.7	80.2	19.8	—	—
1966	59.5	40.5	69.6	30.4	72.3	27.7	—	—
1967	58.7	41.3	62.1	37.9	65.6	34.4	—	—
1968	57.8	42.2	55.4	44.6	59.8	40.2	100.0	—
1969	56.8	43.2	49.5	50.5	55.0	45.0	98.6	1.4
1970	56.6	43.4	45.3	54.7	50.7	49.3	97.0	3.0
1971	55.6	44.4	41.6	58.4	46.7	53.3	87.9	12.2
1972	53.9	46.1	36.9	63.1	40.4	59.6	74.1	25.9
1973	52.9	47.1	33.7	66.3	36.8	63.2	68.4	31.6
1974	41.7	58.3	31.3	68.7	33.9	66.1	64.2	35.8
1975	51.1	48.9	29.6	70.4	31.6	68.4	60.3	39.7
1976	50.4	49.6	28.2	71.8	29.1	70.9	56.0	44.0
1977	49.9	50.1	26.4	73.6	27.8	72.2	52.5	47.5
1978	50.2	49.9	26.2	73.8	27.5	72.5	51.0	49.0

Source: INPS, *Notizie statistiche,* various years.

The question may be raised of whether the number of disability pensions going to older beneficiaries should be subtracted from the total. Subtraction did not seem adequate, since under present legislation the reduction in earnings capacity can depend, among other causes, on old age itself.

The year 1978 reflected a reduction in the number of new beneficiaries, mainly because the excessively permissive policy of the previous decade was coming to a halt. There was also a tendency toward a lower number of agricultural self-employed pensioners, due to the higher incidence of mortality because of a higher percentage of old people among these beneficiaries; the number of terminations because of death was higher than the number of new pensions.

Incidence of Disability Pensioners above Retirement Age

Table 12.6 indicates the distribution of INPS disability pensioners in the four major employment categories, according to the old age pension threshold. The old age pension threshold is 60 for men and 55 for women in the employees category, and 65 for men and 60 for women in the three categories of self-employed workers. The difference in threshold probably accounts for the lower percentage of new pensions above retirement age in

Table 12.6. Percentage Distribution of All New INPS Disability Pensions by Sex, Relation to Retirement Age, and Type of Employment, 1977

	All Disability Pensioners			New Disability Pensioners		
	Men	Women	Total	Men	Women	Total
Employees						
Below retirement age	39.4	22.4	31.3	86.1	62.4	75.7
At or above retirement age	60.6	77.6	68.7	13.9	37.6	24.3
Farmers						
Below retirement age	43.1	24.1	31.3	96.6	86.6	90.9
At or above retirement age	56.9	75.9	68.7	3.4	13.4	9.1
Artisans						
Below retirement age	55.1	31.7	44.7	95.2	74.9	86.6
At or above retirement age	44.9	68.3	55.3	4.8	25.1	13.4
Retailers						
Below retirement age	62.4	44.6	53.0	91.2	72.9	81.4
At or above retirement age	37.6	55.4	47.0	8.8	27.1	18.6

Source: INPS, *Notizie statistiche* (1970).

the self-employed scheme. Before reaching the specified age for old age pension, the self-employed person applies for a disability pension, as at least one impairment is commonly found in a person over 60, especially if living in a depressed area. Many self-employed workers, however, apply and receive a disability pension as soon as they reach the minimum contributory period, as there is no obligation to leave their occupation. (Mean age, shown in Table 12.7 below, is usually higher among the self-employed.)

Contributions to self-employed systems are very low and entry (especial-

Table 12.7. Mean Age of All and New INPS Disability Pensioners in Relation to Retirement Age, 1977

	All Pensioners			New Pensioners		
	Men	Women	Total	Men	Women	Total
Employees						
Total	61.7	63.3	62.4	51.5	52.3	51.9
Below retirement age	51.3	48.5	50.3	49.6	47.5	48.4
At or above retirement	68.5	67.5	68.0	63.5	60.2	61.3
Farmers						
Total	65.2	65.4	65.3	54.4	52.4	53.2
Below retirement age	57.5	53.0	55.3	53.9	50.8	52.2
At or above retirement	71.1	69.4	69.9	67.5	62.5	63.3
Artisans						
Total	62.5	62.6	62.5	54.1	54.3	54.2
Below retirement age	56.1	52.9	55.1	53.4	51.5	52.7
At or above retirement	70.3	67.1	68.5	67.3	62.7	63.6
Retailers						
Total	61.3	59.7	60.4	55.8	54.7	55.2
Below retirement age	56.7	53.2	55.2	54.7	51.6	53.2
At or above retirement	68.8	64.9	66.4	67.4	62.9	63.9

Source: INPS, *Notizie statistiche* (1979).

ly for farmers) is rather easy, as requirements are not strict. In fact, more farmers are insured under the old age, disability, and survivors' pension systems than there are farmers in the labor force. Those who enter the scheme may have a low-income occupation; they contribute the minimum period to be entitled to a disability pension, which will augment their earnings.

Geographical Analysis

The growth of disability pensions has been greatest among self-employed workers, especially farmers. It is in the Mezzogiorno, where agriculture and pre-industrial manual occupations still play an important role in the distribution of employment, that disability pensions are most numerous. The following tabulations show the percentage distribution of disability pensions between the North and the rest of the nation. The population distribution was 46 percent in the North and 54 percent in the rest of the nation.[4]

	Disability Pensioners (%), 1978	Old Age Pensioners (%), 1978
North	37.3	64.4
Center and South	62.7	35.6

	Disability Pensioners, 1978		Old Age Pensioners, 1978	
	North	Center/South	North	Center/South
Employees	39.5	60.5	66.0	34.0
Farmers	35.0	65.0	61.8	38.2
Artisans	27.6	72.4	50.4	49.6
Retailers	36.1	63.9	53.7	46.3

The geographical distribution of female disability pensioners indicates a higher percentage in the most industrialized part of the country, gradually decreasing toward the areas where female participation in the labor force is very low:

	All	Employees	Farmers	Artisans	Traders
Northeast	57.6	55.9	63.1	35.5	48.1
Northwest	55.0	53.4	45.7	35.7	49.5
Center	50.4	44.7	60.5	38.2	53.0
South	48.7	43.1	68.9	49.8	51.3

Geographical distribution of disability pensioners evidently indicates that they are more numerous where unemployment is higher, while their incidence is smaller in the industrialized areas of the North.

Age and Sex of INPS Disability Pensioners

The majority of disability pensioners are women and, on average, they are older than men. Table 12.7 shows that new pensions for women are granted to relatively younger beneficiaries as compared to men. Among farmers, older women are so numerous that there are more women than men among disability beneficiaries in this category (not shown on table). There are more men than women in the other categories, with the exception of retailers, where women are again the majority.

The mean age among INPS disability pensioners is now stable, at around 52 years for employees and 54 for self-employed workers. Generally, new pensions are granted to men who are a few months younger, and women a few months older, than the mean age. Table 12.8 shows that the highest

Table 12.8. Percentage Distribution of INPS Disability Pensioners by Age and Category, 1978

Age	Employees	Self-Employed			Minor Categories	Total
		Farmers	Artisans	Retailers		
20-24	—	—	—	—	—	—
25-29	.3	.1	.1	.2	—	.2
30-34	.6	.3	.5	.4	.1	.5
35-39	1.6	.7	1.4	1.2	.5	1.3
40-44	3.3	1.5	2.8	2.6	1.2	2.7
45-49	7.0	3.4	5.1	6.3	3.1	5.7
50-54	12.7	7.5	9.7	13.2	6.6	10.9
55-59	13.6	10.4	13.2	18.3	8.5	12.7
60-64	20.8	23.6	28.9	34.2	19.7	22.5
65-69	18.3	24.5	24.0	18.9	21.4	20.5
70-74	12.2	18.1	11.0	3.4	19.5	13.7
75-79	6.1	8.6	2.5	.9	12.1	6.6
80-84	2.5	1.1	.6	.3	4.6	1.9
85-89	.8	.2	.2	.1	1.8	.6
90-94	.2	—	—	—	.8	.2
95+	—	—	—	—	.1	—
Total	100.0	100.0	100.0	100.0	100.0	100.0

Source: INPS, *Notizie statistiche* (1979).

proportion of INPS disability pensioners is to be found in the 60-64 age group (the totals by sex are 23.2 percent of all men and 21.8 percent of all women), but it is important to stress that over 23 percent of all disability pensioners are in the 50-59 age group. Note the cumulative frequency of INPS disability pensioners by age in 1978:

	Up to 64 years	Up to 69 years
Employees	59.6	78.4
Farmers	47.4	71.0
Artisans	61.8	85.7
Retailers	76.0	93.5

Family Composition and Child Allowances

Social insurance disability pensioners in the farmers' group are usually older than those in the other categories. These workers are in general older, on average, than workers in other economic sectors, and they tend—notwithstanding their disability pensions—to remain active longer. This is partly due to migration from agriculture to other economic sectors, a phenomenon of great importance in Italian economic development, especially in the 1950s and 1960s. As a consequence, there are fewer family members in farmers' families, where fewer than three disabled pensioners out of ten have children and/or wife allowances.[5] The same applies to retailers, while employee and artisan pensioners receive larger family allowances (more than 40 percent of total INPS disabled pensioners). On average, more than 90 percent of disability pensioners have at least a wife (or husband) allowance; the differences relate to the number of children, with particular reference to farmers' families: The distribution of disabled pensioners receiving family allowances, 1978 INPS data, is as follows:

	Disability as % Total Pensioners	% Dis. Pensioners with Family Allowance		
		Wife/Husband	Children	Total
Employees	42.5	89	70	159
Farmers	26.8	98	34	132
Artisans	40.5	91	53	144
Retailers	29.6	90	78	168

Amount of INPS Disability Pension Benefit

In the period 1968-78, the employee disability pension has, on average, increased by 16 percent in real terms, while self-employed disability pensions have increased by over 30 percent; nearly the same increase in real terms was registered for old age pensions in the respective categories. Employees have thus seen their pensions increase less than the self-employed, whose benefits were, at the start, at a very low level and have therefore increased at greater speed. The benefit level for employees is related to the number of contributions paid and to the last 10 years of salary level. In the employee category, 40 percent of old age pensions and 15 percent of disability pensions are above the minimum level. The programs for self-employed workers, on the other hand, started during the last two decades and required very low contributions to their insured workers: the benefits therefore are all at minimum level (amounts are given in Table 12.12). In spite of the payment of massive state contributions (over 80 percent of this expenditure) and of deficits of programs, benefits are counterbalanced by a workers' contribution equal to 6 percent of benefit.

Nevertheless, there have been increases in the average amount of benefits, due to legislative changes granting very favorable adjustments and

Table 12.9. Average Amount of INPS Pensions for Non-Self-Employed Workers, 1960-1978 (thousands of lire)

	General Program		Minor Programs	
	Old Age	Disability	Old Age	Disability
1960	145	144	502	385
1961	150	145	582	365
1962	218	196	617	474
1963	227	199	689	637
1964	233	200	774	549
1965	319	264	886	610
1966	322	267	833	665
1967	336	274	1,009	701
1968	374	307	1,186	721
1969	427	360	1,243	947
1970	449	380	1,328	1,037
1971	499	403	1,477	1,205
1972	625	492	1,848	1,323
1973	677	519	2,406	1,532
1974	824	668	2,773	1,773
1975	1,007	836	3,375	2.332
1976	1,229	1,013	3,961	2,648
1977	1,519	1,215	4,475	2,820
1978	1,821	1,546	5,413	3,544

to changes in the amounts, particularly at the minimum level (Tables 12.9 and 12.10). A most marked increase is evident for the minimum benefit in the group of self-employed pensioners, especially in the last ten years (Table 12.11).

In the past, the amount of all INPS pensions was related to the amount of social security contributions paid by each worker. Since 1968, earnings-related pensions (when above the minimum level) are computed with reference to the last best salary (precisely, to the average earnings in the three best years among the last ten) and to the length of the period of contribution. Retirement pensions in the general program for employees have the lowest percentage of "minimum" pensions (still the majority—i.e., 54 percent in 1977), while a much higher percentage of minimum pensions (84 percent) is to be found among disablement benefits granted to employees of the general scheme. Minimum-level disability benefits have a stronger "welfare" connotation, especially in the program for self-employed workers, where 99 percent of all pensions are at the minimum level (more than 99 percent among farmers, who receive the large majority of disability pensions).

Table 12.12 shows the acceptance rate of applications, and Table 12.13 shows the growth in expenditures for INPS disability pensions, for all pensions including old age, disability, and survivors' pensions, social security expenditures for the period 1968-78, and the pensions' share of gross domestic product (GDP). Deflated indexes for GDP and expenditures are also indicated. In real terms, disability pension expenditure increased at

Table 12.10. Average Amount of INPS Pensions for Self-Employed Workers, 1960-1978, (thousands of lire)

	Farmers		Artisans		Retailers	
	Old Age	Disability	Old Age	Disability	Old Age	Disability
1960	65	68	67	98		
1961	65	68	67	68		
1962	65	68	129	120		
1963	129	133	129	127		
1964	129	132	128	132		
1965	156	162	156	170		
1966	158	166	160	179		
1967	160	168	164	183	155	
1968	176	183	180	198	170	196
1969	237	246	242	257	234	256
1970	242	246	245	258	235	251
1971	254	258	260	269	249	262
1972	321	325	325	333	315	328
1973	338	342	344	350	333	344
1974	467	475	470	487	457	479
1975	747	756	743	771	734	765
1976	893	905	891	923	878	913
1977	1,018	1,030	1,018	1,054	1,003	1,030
1978	1,211	1,235	1,211	1,235	1,190	1,210

a yearly rate of 16.7 percent in the period 1968-78, while the GDP growth rate was 3.3 percent and while total pensions and social security expenditures increased by 11.0 percent and 5.6 percent respectively.

INPS disability pensions are year by year absorbing an increasing part of national resources.

Table 12.11. Minimum Monthly Amounts of INPS Pensions, 1962-1978, in Lire (parentheses indicate ratio of pension to per capita income)

	Employees			
Date of New Amount	over 65 years		under 65	Self-Employed
July 1, 1962	15,000 (.40)		12,000 (.32)	10,000 (.26)
January 1, 1965	19,500 (.39)		15,600 (.31)	12,000 (.24)
May 1, 1968	21,900 (.35)		18,000 (.29)	13,200 (.21)
January 1, 1969	25,000 (.36)		23,000 (.33)	18,000 (.26)
January 1, 1971	26,200 (.32)		24,100 (.29)	18,850 (.23)
June 1, 1972	27,450 (.31)		25,250 (.28)	19,750 (.22)
July 1, 1972	32,000 (.36)		30,000 (.34)	24,000 (.27)
June 1, 1973	33,750 (.32)		31,650 (.30)	25,300 (.24)
January 1, 1974		42,950 (.35)		34,800 (.28)
January 1, 1975		55,950 (.40)		47,800 (.34)
July 1, 1975				55,950 (.40)
January 1, 1976		66,950 (.38)		66,950 (.38)
January 1, 1977		79,650 (.38)		76,250 (.36)
January 1, 1978		102,500 (.38)		91,100 (.34)
January 1, 1979		118,700		103,300

Note: There are 13 monthly payments in a year (double monthly payment in December).

Table 12.12. Acceptance of Applications for INPS Disability Pensions (thousands)

	Accepted	Total Cases Examined	Acceptance Rate (%)
1963	230.3	799.5	28.8
1964	293.4	880.3	33.3
1965	311.8	918.6	33.9
1966	345.2	1,022.3	33.8
1967	384.6	1,079.1	35.6
1968	365.1	1,033.5	35.3
1969	322.8	916.2	35.2
1970	363.4	981.9	37.0
1971	433.5	1,017.7	42.6
1972	437.5	945.9	46.3
1973	442.4	1,042.5	42.4
1974	422.4	1,029.8	41.0
1975	446.2	1,061.8	42.0
1976	387.8	1,009.1	38.4
1977	341.6	932.6	36.6

Source: INPS, *Notizie statistiche* (various years).

Financing of INPS Pensions

The state contributes a monthly flat amount of 12,000 lire to the payment of each pension, including the larger pensions. For either old age or disability, at the time of computation of a new pension, if the contribution period and the amount of salary combined do not result in an amount above the minimum level, a minimum pension is granted, largely subsidized (over 70 percent) by active workers paying their social security contributions. All schemes are administered on a pay-as-you-go basis, with no accumulation of reserves.

While minimum pensions are practically at the same amount for all categories, active workers in the self-employed groups pay a per capita contribution that is about one-tenth of the average earnings-related contribution paid by employer and employee in the employee scheme. The 1979 report on manpower by the National Economic and Labor Council (CNEL, 1979) calculated the 1977 average productivity level per employed person, at 1970 prices: 1,715,000 lire for an agricultural worker, as compared to 4,232,000 lire for an industrial worker. Because of the lower level of agricultural earnings, disability programs are in effect used to support the low income of rural areas. The dichotomy of the Italian labor market should also be kept in mind: in the northern areas there are possibilities for steady work, while in the South there is a different growth rate and occupations are usually precarious. Rarely—on average—can a worker in the South achieve a contributions history so continuous as to qualify for an old age pension, yet he will usually reach, by adding together

Table 12.13. Total Expenditures and Index for INPS Disability Pensions, All General Insurance Pensions, and Social Security, 1968-1978

	Current Values, billions of lire				Percentage of GDP		
	INPS Disability Pensions (1)	All Pensions (incl. Veterans) (2)	Total Social Security (3)	Total GDP (4)	(1)	(2)	(3)
1968	805.7	3,403.0	7,533	46,953	1.7	7.2	16.0
1970	1,154.3	4,978.3	9,055	57,937	2.0	8.6	15.6
1971	1,387.7	5,711.0	10,680	63,056	2.2	9.1	19.9
1972	1,863.2	7,265.4	12,321	69,026	2.7	10.5	17.8
1973	2,097.8	8,020.8	14,337	82,503	2.5	9.7	17.4
1974	2,888.9	9,957.8	17,203	101,723	2.8	9.8	16.9
1975	4,091.3	13,252.1	22,618	125,378	3.3	10.6	18.0
1976	5,080.8	16,271.0	27,565	156,657	3.2	10.4	17.6
1977	6,028.6	19,944.0	33,319	189,878	3.2	10.5	17.5
1978	7,579.5	25,216.0	41,590	220,743	3.4	11.4	18.8

	Deflated Indexes				
	(1)	(2)	(3)	(4)	Cost-of-Living Index
1968	100.0	100.0	100.0	100.0	100.0
1970	128.8	131.6	108.1	111.0	111.2
1971	144.5	140.8	118.9	112.7	119.2
1972	182.8	168.8	129.3	116.2	126.5
1973	184.1	166.7	134.6	124.3	141.4
1974	214.6	175.1	136.7	129.7	167.1
1975	257.9	197.8	152.5	135.6	196.9
1976	271.6	205.9	157.6	143.7	232.2
1977	270.9	212.2	160.1	146.4	276.2
1978	266.7	210.1	156.5	133.3	352.7

pieces of contributions spread on a longer period, the five years required for a disability pension based on earnings capacity. Sometimes the five-year period is achieved by enrolling in the farmers' program when one is not a farmer. The majority of benefits, on the other hand, are at the minimum level; the self-employed workers' programs, especially for farmers, have in the last five years accumulated huge deficits, and yet their contributions have not been raised.

The INPS average contribution to the old age, disability, and survivors' pension system for employees was estimated at one million lire in 1978; the rate was 23.7 percent of earnings. No ceiling is fixed—i.e., the contribution rate applies to the entire gross salary. The yearly flat-rate contribution for old age, artisans and retailers was 95,000 lire, but the yearly rate for farmers was only 60,000 lire. The social help given to these categories of workers is justified by their being reputedly economically worse off than the majority of employees, especially in the case of agricultural workers.

Adjustment of INPS Pension Benefits to Price and Wage Increases

The growing expenditure for disability pensions (and for social security pensions in general) is due to the recent extension of coverage to new categories as well as increases in amount and changes in adjustment regulations. These mechanisms will continue to affect future expenditures. In the period 1971-75, INPS pensions were linked to the price index: the yearly increase was 4.8 percent, 4.7 percent, 5.1 percent, 9.8 percent, and 13 percent, but in some years the government decided on increases to match wage raises (see Table 12.14). According to the law of June 3, 1975, every January the adjustment mechanism is applied as follows: (a) pensions above the minimum level are adjusted to the price index and to average increases in real value (i.e., excluding wage price indexing, or sliding scale increases); (b) pensions at minimum level are adjusted to the wage increases of the minimum contractual wage of the industrial sector (including price indexing of these wages).

The 1975 law has not only introduced this more costly (and inflationary) mechanism, but has also raised by over 30 percent the amount of minimum pension. The result was a greater increase in pension expenditure than the GDP. For disability pensions (and all pensions) in the future, it seems reasonable to anticipate a continuous increase in real value, in the face of an inflationary situation that apparently still remains well above 15 percent.

The adjustment mechanism presently in effect is under discussion and, possibly, revision. One of the indexing proposals being discussed among experts indicates growth in GDP as a more adequate yardstick.

Review and Pension Revocation

Controls on INPS disability pensions are rather limited, mostly in deference to the income support function of these benefits. Furthermore, since the law states that reviews must stop when the disabled worker reaches the age of 65, controls can only be exerted on one-third of the total number of disability pensions.

Nevertheless, INPS unpublished data for 1976 and 1977 indicate that recently there has been more control. About 3 percent of all disability pensions granted to people of working age have been reviewed, and 2.86 percent of them have been revoked—in 1976, 51,381 pensions were reviewed, and of them 45,795 (valued at 47 billion lire) were revoked. In 1977, 54,783 were reviewed and 43,758 were revoked, valued at 53.5 billion lire. Control is also exerted when pensions are questioned at the time of initial granting. This is not a random check; it affects primarily those cases that are strongly disputed by the Committee, when entitlement is first decided.

Table 12.14. Rates of Increase in INPS Disability Pensions, 1966-1978 (percentages)

	Number	Total Expenditure	Average Amount
1966	11.2	11.8	—
1967	11.2	13.1	.9
1968	11.0	19.8	9.3
1969	10.6	27.5	19.7
1970	10.9	12.4	3.6
1971	11.5	20.2	4.8
1972	11.0	34.3	22.4
1973	10.7	12.5	5.1
1974	10.5	37.8	31.3
1975	10.4	43.1	37.1
1976	10.3	22.8	19.2
1977	10.1	18.7	17.4
1978	10.1	25.7	25.0

Source: INPS, *Allegati statistici ai rendiconti* 1977 (1979).

INAIL Industrial Injury Pensions

The state covers industrial injury risks for all workers performing any potentially dangerous working activity. Nonmanual workers are usually excluded from the program. In 1978, about 52 percent of the active labor force was insured against industrial injury through the Istituto Nazionale delle Assicurazioni contro gli Infortuni sul Lavoro (INAIL).

Article 2 of the law of 1965 gives this definition of such injury: "Industrial injury insurance covers all cases of injury resulting from violent cause while performing a working activity, from which death or long-term working disability (permanent or temporary), or a temporary absolute incapacity to work for more than three days, is derived." Injury can therefore be considered as entitlement to benefit when (1) it causes an impairment to the *working capacity* of the worker; and (2) it has been caused by violence (i.e., an unusual, extraordinary cause) in a short space of time. The cause of injury must be related to the workplace, and it can sometimes take into account—for purposes of evaluating the amount—pre-existing pathological conditions of the worker, as long as they are relevant to measuring the extent of damage.

Article 3 of the law of 1965 takes into account a series of 40 *occupational diseases* resulting from dangerous working activity. Recently, various mental illnesses have been added to the list, but they are considered only to the extent that they are indirectly the result of the injury and worsen the individual's general health status. The list tends to keep compensation under fairly strict control: each illness is related to a particular aspect of work and to a maximum indemnification period, on the basis of past medical and forensic experience. Therefore, the worker who is affected by one of the specfific diseases on the list does not have to demonstrate that the impairment is due to his work activity, as he does for industrial injury; the fact of being employed in that specific work activity is in itself sufficient evidence.

Disabilities from silicosis and asbestos have special regulations, tending to protect completely the workers affected (Articles 140 to 177 of the 1965 law).

Financing

The industrial injury program is administered in accordance with rigorous insurance criteria, and employers are the only contributors. They are required to pay according to the degree of danger of the activity (premiums paid to INAIL are based on the frequency of injury in the factory and in the sector to which it belongs, according to a very sophisticated distinction) and to the amount of salaries. On average, the yearly contribution is less than 5 percent of salaries. The INAIL contribution can therefore vary each year, according to previous injury record, kinds of working methods and procedures, prevention measures, site of plant, use of materials or equipment, manpower composition. Regulations are very strict in controls and penalties levied on the employer (Art. 16 of the 1965 law), and they can result in a higher contribution for future years or in a bonus credited because of an unanticipated good record.

The agricultural program has a different financing method. Agricultural employees are insured by their employers, who pay 3.5 percent of the daily wage for 156 days a year. Self-employed workers pay a yearly amount of 750 lire. The obviously insufficient amount of these contributions has resulted in growing deficits for the agricultural program of INAIL. Whereas the industrial program is based on partial capitalization of premiums, the agricultural system is based on the pay-as-you-go method, which has lost its meaning in face of constantly growing expenditures and inadequate financing. The deficit of the agricultural program for 1978 was 312 billion lire, and the total deficit of the system was over 1,536.2 billion. In 1968, the total deficit was 9.5 billion lire.

Benefits to Injured Workers

Injured workers are entitled to benefits in all recognized cases, and the employer's violation of the obligation to pay industrial injury contributions does not affect the worker's rights to receive the following: *Cash benefits*, which can be in the form of daily compensations for temporary full disability, a pension for permanent disability, allowances to totally disabled workers in case of continuous need for personal attendants, survivors' pensions, burial allowance, and discretionary lumpsums. *Health care*, covering medical tests, surgical and medical treatment, and appliances needed as a result of the injury. *Assistance benefits* for social services to impaired workers.

Temporary full disability allows up to 60 percent of earnings in the first three months and up to 75 percent after that, to a maximum of 4.5 million lire a year. A permanent disability pension is based on the degree of loss of working capacity (starting from a loss of 11 percent) and on the amount of previous earnings. Levels of indemnities are carefully listed according to the degree of working capacity lost; the law actually states the replacement rates.

Total loss of working capacity entitles the worker to a pension equal to previous earnings, with a floor of 2,448,000 lire a year and a ceiling of 4,547,000 lire, and to a personal allowance of 35,000 lire a month if personal care is needed (this allowance was raised to 250,000 a month in April 1982). For a loss of between 11 and 99 percent, the pension replaces a quota of earnings whose amount depends on the severity of impairment. INAIL benefits are a compensation and therefore are not subject to taxation, even when they are temporary.

Review of a Permanent Disability Pension

Both injured workers and INAIL can decide to review the benefit, in case of changes in the physical condition of the worker. These changes must be directly related to the industrial injury or occupational illness.

In the case of industrial injury, review is possible within ten years of the first assignment of the pension; after that, no change is possible. The law sets the timing of reviews, which can be conducted at specified intervals, for a maximum of six reviews in the ten-year period. In the case of occupational illness, the maximum time within which the benefit can be reviewed is 15 years; first review can be done within six months after the termination of temporary total incapacity, or one year after the impairment; other reviews are at one-year intervals. In practice, reviews take place at least every three years, often at the request of the worker himself, when he feels that his working capacity has further deteriorated.

Pensions resulting from silicosis and asbestos can be reviewed any time the illness intensifies.

When there are serious reasons to believe that the accident was the worker's fault, or when the consequences have been intentionally exaggerated, the case can be reviewed and brought to court on INAIL's initiative; and, with absolute priority over other labor cases, the judge can decide on termination of the benefit. Penalties to the worker can include conviction. All trial expenses are paid by INAIL.

Health Care

INAIL pensioners can undergo treatment at any time, so long as it is considered possible to recover at least part of the lost working capacity. A pensioner who refuses, without valid reason, to undergo the prescribed treatment will have his benefit withdrawn.[6] Health care provided by INAIL has proved to be efficient and to give beneficial results. Although it rarely happens in practice, the worker can be treated by a private doctor or hospital and receive a reimbursement from INAIL.

Because of the 1980 reform of health services, INAIL hospitals have recently become the responsibility of regional administrations. Injured workers continue to be treated there.

Assistance Benefits

In principle, benefits of this kind are granted to workers who receive a severe disability benefit—i.e., workers who have lost from 80 percent to 100 percent of their working capacity. For disability pensioners with greater work capacity, the law allows the payment of discretionary assistance benefits depending on their financial resources. Among various minor provisions, INAIL grants a "training benefit" to those disabled workers who register in a retraining course organized by the Ministry of Labor.

The fact that the regulations cited above are given in the same article seems particularly indicative of the lack of interest in rehabilitation and retraining of injured workers. INAIL used to have a few centers for rehabilitation—training school, a form of protected workshop, with activities such as bookbinding or printing techniques. Five centers were still in operation in the late 1960s. They were closed in 1970 on the grounds that they were too costly and produced few results.

High costs involved facilities, equipment, teaching staff salaries, and training benefits. Few workers attended the courses, and their attendance was usually very short, since most of them tried to return to their previous occupations if they could. Regular clients were too few to justify operating the centers. Unfortunately, no quantitative data on the centers could be collected. A recent law (December 30, 1978) on training and rehabilitation has set the general framework for a new policy of rehabilitation and training courses for workers and for disabled people. The responsibility lies with the regions (administratively active since 1972). Each region is now expected to report to the Ministry of Labor on existing programs for disabled people.

Incidence of Industrial Injuries

The incidence of injuries among the working population has risen noticeably since the 1950s. Growing industrialization, rapid urbanization and training of many industrial workers, and the mechanization of agriculture have brought about a steady increase of injuries. A lower incidence in certain sectors is simply the result of a stronger impact of recession (constructions and wood industries are notable examples, as shown in Table 12.15).

Table 12.15. Incidence of Industrial Injury per 1000 Active Workers, by Economic Sector, 1972 and 1978

Sector	1972	1978
Agriculture	167.8	n.a.
Chemistry	129.6	94.4
Construction	266.2	125.7
Power and gas	70.8	29.7
Wood industry	224.2	34.7
Steel	198.9	250.5
Mining	206.4	44.8
Textiles	79.2	102.3
Transport	118.7	73.8
Others	64.2	203.8
National average	154.6	145.4

Source: INAIL, *Annuario statistico.*

Expenditures for INAIL Benefits

Both the number and amounts of INAIL pensions have been growing since World War II, especially since 1965. In that year, increases in amounts were first decided and at the same time an adjustment mechanism was enacted which ties, every three years, the benefit to the average rate of growth of the industry to which the worker belongs. The percentage of GDP spent on INAIL benefits, however, has increased steadily, but has recently risen to a higher proportion (Table 12.16). On average INAIL

Table 12.16. INAIL Industrial Injury Pensions and Expenditures, 1960-1978

	Number of Pensions (thousands)	Average Amount of Direct Pensions (thousand lire)	Total Expenditure for Direct and Survivors' Pensions (billion lire; percentage of GDP)	
1960	460	58	32.2	15%
1961	490	68	39.9	17
1962	525	93	58.1	21
1963	535	109	69.6	22
1964	562	128	85.3	25
1965	592	163	114.1	31
1966	628	163	135.1	34
1967	662	162	139.2	32
1968	701	196	175.9	37
1969	744	198	187.7	36
1970	775	196	194.0	33
1971	799	271	274.5	44
1972	840	271	287.5	42
1973	881	275	303.4	37
1974	932	391	453.9	45
1975	924	417	476.5	41
1976	998	399	496.5	35
1977	1,032	696	764.9	40
1978	1,058	709	1,007.0	46

benefits did not increase more than national income because, to a certain extent, they did not experience the massive influence of income maintenance distortions as for the INPS disability program.

Because of its "insurance" administration, INAIL expenditure growth has been supported by a reasonably consistent guarantee derived from capitalized reserves. The easier pay-as-you-go administration of contributions and benefits used in the agricultural program shows dangerous signs of insufficient financing, the same problem that has affected INPS programs for that sector. Here again, the agricultural sector has been aided by requiring lower contributions than benefits granted. Its benefits are not much lower than INAIL industrial benefits (on average, 550,000 lire annually, compared to 840,000). Therefore, the INAIL agricultural system has been constantly receiving "loans" from the industrial system to counter the growing deficit. The resources made available for this operation have been partly derived from capitalized reserves, and therefore the returns to the INAIL-funded system are decreasing.

Moreover, the additional portion which is added to the benefit because of the adjustment mechanism must be paid on a pay-as-you-go system. Each pension at the start requires its own capitalization: when an adjustment is decided, the contributions must be increased correspondingly. The remarkable increases in benefits (Table 12.16) have heavily distorted the insurance administration of the scheme, and have reduced its capital formation.

Adjustment Mechanism for Industrial Injury Benefits

The adjustment mechanism enacted in 1965 relates INAIL pensions to changes in earnings: every three years, pensions are adjusted to the average earnings of the group to which the worker belonged when the computation was originally made. Since 1965, pensions have been revised in July of the years 1965-68, 1971-74, and 1977, with increases of 55, 20, 35, 45, and 90 percent. Beginning in July 1983, the INAIL pensions for temporary disabilities are revised annually.

How the adjustment mechanism has affected expenditure for the industrial program in the period 1974-78 is indicated by the following tabulation. The figures refer to direct pensions only and are taken from the unpublished INAIL budget for 1978.

	Current Value, Billion Lire	Index Number
1974	272.2	100
1975	313.3	115.1
1976	358.6	131.8
1977	497.4	182.7
1978	664.1	244.0

War Pensions

A 1978 law (no. 915), regulating and coordinating previous legislation, lists in detail the kinds of disablement and illness which entitle a veteran to a war pension, to a temporary subsidy, or to a lump sum payment. The first article defines the war pension as an indemnity, and Article 28 states that it is integrated with other state pensions and subsidies. A war pension can therefore be added to another pension, with no limitation in amount, but it cannot be added to an industrial injury benefit; it can, however, be renounced in favor of that benefit if its amount is higher than the war pension.

Although a cumulative indemnity, a war pension is adjusted to *wage* increases. The number of direct beneficiaries has obviously decreased; it is below 1 percent of the total population and 1.8 percent of the labor force. With time, generous extensions have been made to widows (even if remarried, if her husband earns less than 2.4 million lire) and orphans (even if married, and regardless of sex). The total number of pensions for 1978 was as follows, arranged by decreasing amount of average benefit received: mutilated and invalids, 365,331; widows and orphans of war victims, 176,304; widows and orphans who are beneficiaries of survivors' pensions, 111,151; parents and dependent relatives (in absence of the above), 107,632; for a total of 760,418.

The amount of pension for a veteran disabled in war action can be as high as 8.3 million lire a year for a man with more than one impairment; survivors' pensions are in a limited amount (from 1.2 million for a wife or for children under 21 up to .5 million a year), but the same family can receive more than one pension.

Children of severely disabled veterans are entitled to the same provisions as orphans (i.e., a survivor's pension, assistance for education, and employment programs). The recent law provided larger pension amounts to all recipients (the 1978 expenditure was nearly 700 billion lire; total expenditure for 1979 was 1,184 billion).

War pensioners usually add a salary to their benefit. Although quota employment for the whole category is strictly applied, some severely disabled war pensioners may not work because the degree of disablement would make their presence harmful to the other employees and/or the equipment. As compensation for their total working incapacity, up to the age of 65 they are entitled to a special benefit of 50 thousand lire monthly in addition to the pension. In Italy the yearly amount of pensions is usually divided into 13 monthly installments, two of which are paid in December (the same applies to salaries). The thirteenth payment is not due to war pensioners if they are employed.

A large part of the program focuses on health care and health rehabilitation. Educational aid and training courses are provided to orphans. No separate record of relative expenditure is available.

War pensions or benefits are not computed in the total amount of yearly earnings for either tax or welfare or social security purposes. They can therefore legally be included with other benefits, and are totally tax exempt.

Total expenditures for war pensions, including survivors' pensions, for the five years 1974-78 were 500.8 billion lire in 1974, 535.8 billion in 1975, 544.9 in 1976, 628.6 in 1977, and 728.1 in 1978 (*Relazione generale ed Economica*, 1978, p. 479).

Employment of Handicapped and Disabled People

Legislation before 1968

The history of employment policy toward disabled people is marked by fragmented legislation, reflecting the piecemeal formation of our system of public assistance and social policy.

It is well known that those who suffer from a disability cannot easily find entry into the labor market, especially when unemployment affects a high percentage of the labor force. Legislation has therefore attempted to give the disabled the opportunity for economic independence. The first law was passed in 1917 (Law 15.6.1917, no. 1032; modifications, consolidations, and extensions followed in Law no. 312, 1921, Law no. 375, 1950, Law no. 367, 1963) and concerned mutilated and disabled soldiers. It provided compulsory employment to people disabled in the war and was motivated by social, moral, and economic concerns. Patriotic considerations and gratitude were mixed with a real need for manpower, reduced by war casualties. Once the principle was established, it was in time extended to persons who had become disabled during military service in time of peace (Law no. 142, 1953), to war orphans and widows (Law no. 365, 1958), to service (military and public administration) orphans and widows (Law no. 1288, 1965). After the promulgation of the republican constitution in 1948, in which the right to work was strongly underlined, the legislature has at different times issued regulations for the protection of the rights of various categories of disabled people.

Quota employment regulations were established for various groups. The regulations differed in coverage and enforcement, degree of applicability, and size of each group covered. They included the following categories: workers mutilated and injured by industrial injury (Law no. 1222 of 1947 and no. 851 of 1966); blind people (Law no. 595 of 1957, no. 778 of 1960, no. 155 of 1965 and 231 of 1967); the deaf and the mute (Law no. 308,

1965); people who had recovered from tuberculosis (Law no. 35, 1953) and people mutilated and disabled for cause other than war or work (the large group of the so called "civil" disabled people, to distinguish them from military disabled people).

The legislation shows that the path to acceptance of the right to work for impaired people has been twisted and difficult. It has been subject to various pressures and motivated by humanitarian and political concerns, or simply by concern for social justice. State intervention was at each occurrence directed in favor of a different category of disability, according to its nature and causes and regardless of regulations concerning other groups. Some of the categories had better protection than others; some of the disabled were not covered at all. In 1968 a new law unified the previous legislation, and compulsory employment was extended to those who had no specific regulations protecting their working rights. This led to enlargement of the category of the civil disabled, while distribution among other categories remained untouched.

Quota Employment: Present Legislation and Application

Law no. 482 of 1968 contains "general regulations concerning compulsory employment in public institutions and private enterprises." Although still based on differentiation of the various categories of disabled people, it aims at equalizing the right to work by avoiding the disparities (especially against certain of the civil disabled) created by previous legislation.

The 1968 law covers various categories of disadvantaged people (i.e., war disabled, war civil disabled, service disabled, industrial injury disabled, civil disabled, orphans and widows, the deaf and mute, blind people, and workers who have had tuberculosis, and refugees of Italian nationality, such as those returning from former colonies). The common elements of this legislation concerned: (a) an overall quota of 15 percent, although its distribution among the various categories respected their different weights (at the time); (b) the introduction of a "sliding principle," according to which the openings reserved for a certain category can be covered by the disabled of another category in case the first is full, as is now the case with the war disabled; (c) a unified administration in the provincial employment office, through committees composed of representatives of the various organizations of disabled and disadvantaged persons.

Eligibility for Quota Employment

The law does not apply to disabled and handicapped people over 55 years of age, nor to those who have lost their working capacity completely, according to results of the provincial doctor's examination (they are granted a state welfare pension instead, if they live in a low-income family). It also does not apply to those whose presence at the workplace, because of the nature or degree of disablement, may cause harm to the health or safety of the other employees or to the safety of the equipment.

The categories of disability and the percentages allotted to each category, within the 15 percent quota, are as follows:

War disability: veterans who suffered impairment during military action that prevents them from work. Their quota is 25 percent of the 15 percent quota (i.e., 3.75 percent).

War civil disability: nonmilitary personnel whose impairment results from injury or illness caused by war action. Their quota is 10 percent (1.5 percent).

Service disability: people whose impairment is due to, or worsened by, military or civil service in a state (including local, provincial, or institutional) authority. Their quota is 15 percent (2.25 percent).

Industrial injury disability: workers who have working capacity reduced by more than one third from industrial injury or illness. Their quota is 15 percent (2.25 percent).

Civil disability: people affected by physical impairment reducing their working capacity by between one and two thirds, including workers who have had tuberculosis and excluding the four above categories and the deaf and mute. Their quota is 15 percent (2.25 percent).

Blindness: people who are completely blind or have one tenth of sight or less when using lenses. They are included in the quota of a particular category according to the cause of their blindness.

Deafness and dumbness: people impaired from birth or before learning to speak. Their quota is 5 percent (.75 percent).

Widows and orphans of war, service, or industrial injury pensioners or victims. Their quota is 15 percent (2.25 percent).

Blind people have special employment slots in the following categories: teachers, telephone operators, massage therapists in hospitals. The group of the deaf and mute has quota employment in firms employing more than 100 employees; they are usually trained to be accountants.

Employment Assignments

Every provincial employment office has a committee composed of the director of the provincial employment office (chairman), a doctor who is a provincial employment officer, a representative from each of the following associations: ONIG, ANVCG, UNMS, ANMIL, ANMIC, ONOG, ANFCDG and ENS,[7] three employee representatives (trade unions), and three employer representatives. The committee writes down the list of applicants, applying the stated priorities. The employer under quota is therefore obliged to hire the first one in the list. The disabled worker's application must contain information on education, training, qualifications, family composition and income, and nature of disability. It must be accompanied by a legal medical certificate proving the right to employment, by all documents relating to work qualifications, and by a declaration from a medical officer stating that the impairment will not cause harm to other employees or the equipment in the premises. Strict medical tests are not always performed.

Salary and Duration of Employment

All disabled and handicapped workers are entitled to the standard economic, normative, and administrative treatment set forth in the Statute of the Rights of the Workers (Law no. 300, 1970), in conformance with national contracts, and must follow all obligations therein.

The most important point in the 1970 law concerns dismissals. In the case of nondisabled workers, dismissal can take place (a) for clearly justified reason; (b) for "just cause" (which can refer to a whole group of employees, in the case for example of an unproductive plant in the process of being closed down, and it gives right to an earnings replacement higher than the unemployment benefit); (c) for health reasons, which only concerns disabled workers. Dismissal for low productivity is not permitted. A recent declaration from the Constitutional Court (April 1979) stated that the outcome of the three-month trial period should not distinguish between disabled and nondisabled workers. As to (c), a medical determination can be requested by the disabled employee or by the employer and is performed by a committee of doctors to verify the adequacy of the worker for the post, or vice versa. Following the decision of the medical committee, the worker can be assigned to a different job or dismissed.

All "civil" disabled workers have the right to a maximum period of 30 days off for treatment, apart from their vacation. The provincial doctor decides the duration of the period required. Usually the treatment is in a thermal institution. The worker receives his normal salary from the social security institution.

More than ten years after the 1968 law on quota employment was enacted, the following conclusions can be drawn:

a. Quota employment is generally applied to a lower number of people than stated in the law, especially in those areas of the country where unemployment is worse; discretionary application of the law is encouraged because the employer has a chance of being exempted; penalties consist of fines decided in 1968, whose amount has never been adjusted to real money value.

b. Employers often resist quote employment of disabled people, which s usually considered an undue imposition with no offset (wages and social security contributions do not differ from the ones paid for a nondisabled worker).

The employment of disabled workers is imposed by provincial employment offices on employers who are under the quota level. This often means that the complying employer considers this duty to be a welfare, charitable obligation toward unproductive people. On the other hand, it is not unusual to find disabled people who have little working qualification or training and are nonetheless entitled to a disability pension; they consider their employment a right rather than special help to compensate for their difficulty in finding a job.

According to data derived from Ministry of Labor bulletins, in 1977 there were 601,229 disabled workers registered for quota employment; of these, 211,053 (35 percent) were not employed. Of those employed, 307,571 were in private firms and 82,614 worked for local authorities. Table 12.17 shows the percentage distribution of these workers by type of disability.

The favored groups in the quota employment law are now almost nonexistent (i.e., the war disabled and people with war-related disadvantages). Their percentage within the 15 percent quota remains, yet their applications are declining, which is one reason why a reexamination of the law is being urged by various groups of disadvantaged people.

No data were available for quota employment in government jobs. They are given different quotas for disabled workers: 15 percent of manual workers, 15 percent of lower-level clerks, and 40 percent of ancillary

Table 12.17. Percentage Distribution of Employed Disabled Workers, by Category

	1975	1976	1977	1978
Percentage of Disabled Workers				
War disabled	21.2	18.8	17.5	16.5
War civil disabled[a]	6.5	6.5	6.3	6.2
Service disabled	8.7	8.6	8.6	8.6
Work disabled	19.1	19.0	18.9	18.8
Civil disabled	41.7	44.1	45.7	46.9
Deaf and mute	2.8	3.0	3.0	3.0
	100.0	100.0	100.0	100.0
Percentage of All Disadvantaged Workers				
War disabled	15.9	14.1	13.0	12.3
War civil disabled[a]	4.9	4.9	4.7	4.6
Service disabled	6.6	6.5	6.4	6.4
Work disabled	14.4	14.2	14.1	14.0
Civil disabled	31.4	33.0	34.0	34.9
Deaf and mute	2.1	2.1	2.2	2.2
Other categories	24.7	25.2	25.6	25.6
	100.0	100.0	100.0	100.0

Source: Ministry of Labor bulletins for the various years.
[a]Refers to civilians disabled in wartime.

workers. Disabled people have 15 percent of all posts in the higher ranks of the civil service, provided they pass the national civil service examination.

According to our estimate, public administration disabled workers numbered nearly 250,000 in 1978, while private employers had given work to nearly 400,000. According to our calculations, the incidence of quota employment on all public administration jobs is 12.6 percent, instead of the 15 percent stated in the law. Since state jobs are assigned by means of a national competition, in all new groups of entrants the percentage of disabled to be hired is filled. Private firms, on the other hand, often try to escape through the exemptions allowed by Article 13, recognizing that certain types of work imply the categorical exclusion of disabled workers.

According to our calculations, the incidence of quota employment in private firms is around 6 percent of those so obliged (i.e., employing more than 35 employees), and 3 percent of all private firms. Another indication from data of the Ministry of Labor is that for 1978 the rate of unemployment of disabled workers who asked to be hired under quota was equal to 35.1 percent. Including the estimated value of disabled workers employed in government jobs, the incidence of unemployment among these disabled workers is close to 26 percent. Of all categories, the "civil disabled" are the ones with a lower employment rate (45.5 percent). All other disabled categories are over 80 percent (97 percent of the war disabled are employed).

Table 12.18 shows that official unemployment of disabled workers has been constantly increasing, especially in recession years, until very recently. The increase in the number of applicants with "civil disability" reveals a growth surpassing expectation; it is, however, probable that this category was certified by provincial doctors exercising less rigor. This generosity may sometimes result in improper use of the legislation—distortion of the law in a context of widespread unemployment and underemployment, intentionally aimed at favoring the "disabled" worker by giving him priority. In fact, the applicants to quota employment in the category of "civil disabled people" are more numerous in the depressed areas of the South, even in those where population density is below national average.

Table 12.18. Unemployed Disabled Workers as a Percentage of All Unemployed Workers, by Region, 1968-1977

	North	Center	South	Islands	All of Italy
1968	2.7	10.6	5.0	5.4	4.8
1969	4.4	17.2	7.8	9.1	7.9
1970	4.8	17.1	8.5	8.0	8.4
1971	5.0	18.7	10.3	9.8	9.7
1972	6.0	22.3	12.5	12.6	11.8
1975	6.7	26.3	16.9	17.3	15.3
1976	7.1	22.4	17.1	15.6	15.0
1977	6.6	19.6	16.9	15.6	14.3

Training Those with Severe Disability

Various proposals have been made to change the regulations of quota employment, especially by the associations of disabled people who are generally dissatisfied with the placement. For some, the need for reform focuses on adjusting quotas according to the actual percentage distribution of each group of disabled in the various categories. More advanced associations tend, however, to take into consideration that, within the reform of public assistance, which is slowly being decentralized to regions, more importance should be given to training and placing the young disabled and handicapped.

A law of 1971 (no. 118) set a new direction in social policy for placement of the disabled. These people are if possible trained in ordinary courses, together with nondisabled unemployed workers (this implies that no separate record is kept). Only when noticeable handicaps are present can regional authorities organize specific courses for the training of handicapped. The application of this law has been very slow and difficult, not only because it coincides with a period of increasing depression, but also because adequate preparation of social workers is still in the formative stage. The same law emphasizes the importance of training the young with severe impairments, in order to avoid the high cost of institutionalization and income maintenance.

In some areas of the North, small factories in Parma and Mantua, where unemployment is practically nonexistent, a few experiments with on-the-job-training have recently been tried in a limited, rather atypical way, administered at the local level. The results are not yet significant. They involve only a few hundred workers, some mentally deficient and some young people with polio. Their employer gets a small per capita subsidy from the local authority. The national associations of handicapped and disabled people have applauded these experiments, which indicate an important change in the employer's attitude toward the severely disabled. The need for better protection of the right to work, even for severely disabled people, is in fact beginning to be accepted in public opinion. However, one of the main points presently under discussion concerns the extension of quota employment to mental disability, which is excluded by Article 5 of the 1968 law on quota employment.

The 1971 law does not refer to employment, even though it emphasizes the importance of training the handicapped. At present, therefore, the recognition of disability in a person who is mentally handicapped cannot grant the right to quota employment (as the recognition of other disability does), although it grants the right to medical assistance, education, protected workshops if made available by regional authorities, pensions, and other cash assistance benefits. Quota employment is restricted to people with physical handicaps. However, in order to take into consideration the experiments in on-the-job-training described above, the Ministry of Labor recently agreed to allow, where possible, such experiments and asked to be informed about the results. The problem is whether such policies can be effective, and whether they can be exported out of a "full employment" area. A certain degree of disappointment is felt among the organizers of the experiment; according to verbal information, actual placement has been very unsatisfactory and fell far short of its goal.

Disabled People with No Earnings Record

Assistance to the poor who are severely disabled or handicapped includes free medical care, training, education, gradual removal of "buildings barriers," and cash benefits.

The whole field of social assistance is changing because it is passing from the central government to regional authorities; consequently responsibilities for implementation of the laws are not yet definite. Furthermore, reform of both health care and public assistance are underway. Appropriate coordination among different powers and jurisdictions should in the end result in central planning of national policy, delegating operations to regions, and passing from the regional level to the provincial level for implementation. Presently there are two kinds of provisions, health assistance and cash benefits, for which a record of expenditure can be reported.

A partial survey by the Ministry of Health shows that, in 1976, out of the 43,500 handicapped people interviewed, 55 percent lived in an institution (Table 12.19 describes the institutionalized). Dividing the type of handicap into physical or mental, or both, among all those surveyed, 21,200 (55 percent men, 45 percent women) had a physical handicap, 9,600 (64.5 percent men, 35.5 percent women) had a mental handicap, and 12,700 (44 percent men, 56.4 percent women) had both. A few handicapped people are taken care of in their homes (2.2 percent) and most have day care or temporary care in the institutions surveyed (42.8 percent). Among those hospitalized, men are the majority; women more frequently are kept in their families, unless they are so severely disabled that they need constant personal care.

It is interesting to note that 74 percent of men and 73 percent of women are under 20 years. The survey does not provide very detailed information on the mortality rate of these groups, but it is probable that its high level is an explanation for this composition; the fact that from 18 years on these people can count on a small pension of their own does not seem an adequate explanation for the limited number of older people in these institutions.

Among the regions that have the highest concentration of institutions for the handicapped in their territory, Lombardy, Tuscany, and Lazio are the

Table 12.19. Percentage Distribution of the Institutionalized Disabled, by Age and Sex, 1976 (partial survey)

Age Group	Men	Women	Total
0-5	7.2	9.1	8.0
6-10	35.2	34.0	34.7
11-15	24.7	20.2	22.8
16-20	7.3	10.2	8.5
21-25	3.1	6.9	4.7
26-30	9.4	5.2	7.7
31-35	4.4	2.0	3.4
36-40	3.0	2.7	2.9
41-45	1.7	.8	1.3
45-50	1.8	2.9	2.2
51-60	1.1	2.6	1.7
61-70	1.1	3.3	2.0
71 +	—	.1	.1
Total	100.0	100.0	100.0
Number	11,589	8,429	20,018

Source: Ministry of Health, partial survey of state-subsidized institutions for the disabled, 1976.

leaders: these three regions have 45 percent of the total population and 37 percent of the institutions surveyed. The same regions, being well provided with hospitals and homes, usually accept patients coming from underequipped or less qualified areas, and the handicapped should be no exception.

The daily cost for a severely disabled person who is hospitalized or confined in a home was estimated at 30,000 lire a day in 1978. Our estimate is that the total was nearly 200 billion lire. Most private and charitable institutions are also subsidized by the state. In many areas, strong resistance has been raised to the legislation ordering that responsibility, and power, be transferred from private institutions to regions. In the meantime, information and data on expenditure and costs are considered, when available at all, strictly confidential. Some of these institutions, however, try to key their activity to better policy for the handicapped, putting aside the "welfare philosophy" and preparing the handicapped person for a role of his own in society. The attitude of old handicapped people is unfortunately passive and unchangeable, but the young, even when severely disabled, can find in more work-oriented institutions a learning background which will enable them to be self-sufficient economically.

Permanent Cash Benefits to the Severely Disabled in Need

People who are mutilated or disabled, over 18 years of age, and with annual earnings below 2,400,000 lire, whose disability—ascertained by government medical staff—is so severe that they have extremely limited (33 percent) or no working capacity, receive from the state the following benefits.

a. *Disability pension*, for those citizens over 18 who have been declared totally disabled by provincial health committees. The pension amount is 71,000 lire a month (13 payments in a year).

b. *Monthly benefit*, for the disabled between 18 and 65 who have a working capacity reduced by over 66.6 percent. In theory, this benefit is terminated if the recipient is working. Its amount is 65,000 lire monthly (13 payments in a year). After 65, the pension is converted to a *social pension*, of the same amount, paid by INPS. If living in public institutions, recipients receive half the amount.

c. *Attendance benefit*, for severely disabled people below 18 years (65,000 lire monthly). These benefits are given to disabled children and terminated when they reach 18. Blind people can have the same benefit only if they are over 18, which is one of the many small inconsistencies presently existing in the social policy toward severely disabled people in the low-income population.

All state benefits are adjusted for changes in cost of living according to the same rule as for the INPS minimum pension—i.e., the amount is adjusted every January 1 to the increases in contractual wages. At the beginning of 1978, the number of disabled receiving these benefits was 312,145. The program started in the late 1960s; being relatively recent, it is undergoing a great expansion. By the end of 1978, 80 percent of the 672,154 applications had been accepted.

With passage of Law no. 33 in 1980, pressure groups of families of the severely disabled obtained total equivalence between benefits for the severely disabled and war disability pensions. Furthermore, the attendance benefit was raised to 120,000 lire a month.

Population Estimates, Replacement Rates, and Economic Aspects

Estimates of the Disabled Covered by Public Programs

On the basis of the information we gathered, we estimate the 1978 disabled population as follows: recipients of INPS disability pensions, 5,276,969; recipients of INAIL work injury benefits, 1,058,002; severely disabled with no earnings record (including 5,065 receiving health care only, because above income limit, and 537,723 presumably accepted applications within the year), 854,933; war pensions to mutilated and disabled soldiers, 365,331. (The quota employed has not been taken into consideration because they can be assumed to be recipients of one or more disability benefits.)

A few corrections can be made to the total figure of 7.6 million disabled people. First, the incidence of INPS disability pensions should be reduced to give a more accurate estimate of the "really disabled" beneficiaries. In order to produce an acceptable value, the incidence of INPS disability pensions in the northwest area of the country has been applied to the rest of the nation. The northwest is known as the "industrial triangle" (including Turin, Milan, and Genoa), where unemployment rates have always been lower than elsewhere and per capita income higher. Local social and economic conditions should not influence the decision to grant an INPS disability pension. Applying the northwest incidence of disability pensions to the resident population of the rest of Italy, we get a theoretical total number of INPS disability pensions of 3,878,000. Therefore, the estimate of INPS disabled pensioners given above should be decreased by 1.4 million.

Another reasonable correction relates to the fact that INAIL pensioners above a certain degree of invalidism and/or living in jobless areas apply to INPS in order to obtain a disability pension in addition to workmen's compensation. Considering the weight of the "socioeconomic conditions" clause, the estimate is that 40 percent of all INAIL disabled workers receive an INPS disability pension (of all those with a working disability of over 21 percent we subtracted 20 percent who may not have filled the five-year contribution period requirement). About 400,000 beneficiaries of INAIL have therefore already been counted in the group of INPS disability pensioners.

It therefore seems reasonable to subtract from the total of 7.6 million an amount of 1.8 million (i.e., 1.4 million INPS disability pensioners who would not be considered disabled from a medical point of view, and .4 million double beneficiaries). The corrected total of 5.8 million disabled seems more realistic. It indicates that about 10.3 percent of the total population is disabled, or 27 percent of the labor force and 29 percent of the employed population.

It is well known that the "underground" economy includes to a considerable extent employed pensioners and those receiving social security. Various efforts have been made to estimate the size of this phenomenon; the most reliable indication of it is in the fact that Istat (Central Statistical Office) has been increasing the GDP data by nearly 10 percent to take into account the resources produced by the underground economy. The question of the actual cumulative effect of benefits and earnings is therefore strictly related to the characteristics of the labor market; where the cost of labor is high because of the high incidence of social security contributions (on average 50 percent of earnings for the industrial worker) the prospective employee who is receiving social security will find an easy placement with tax-evading employers.

An INAIL disability pension is granted to workers injured on the job; it is compensation for an injury (or disease) which has occurred because he is a worker. There is no minimum length of a contributory period for entitlement, but if the employer evades INAIL contributions this penalty is very severe. The INAIL benefit is a social insurance compensation that the worker receives, completely separate from other benefits from other programs. The recipient of this benefit can therefore legally add it to an INPS pension (if he qualifies and has the necessary social security payments) and/or other benefits such as a war pension or survivor's pension. As to cumulation with earnings, it is INAIL itself, through its provincial committees, that takes care of placing its pensioners on a quota job if an injured worker has not found a job by himself. This of course does not apply to the totally disabled.

The welfare program obviously excludes all earnings-related benefits and is strictly means-tested.

Replacement Rates of Disability Benefits

Given the possibility of overlap of INAIL and INPS disability benefits, and the legal overlap of the INAIL pension, the INPS minimum pension, and earnings, the calculation of replacement rates is relevant only if it refers to *totally* disabled workers. The ratio of this group to the rest of the disability recipients is very small (24,000 versus one million in the INAIL program); the ratio presumably should be smaller in the INPS program.

We have considered the case of a worker 30 years old, married, with no children (i.e., with one dependent), who has become totally disabled. Net replacement rate in the INPS program is given in Table 12.20 by average earnings, half the average earnings, and twice the average earnings, for the years 1978 and 1968. The reader should keep in mind that the disabled pensioner can draw both his benefit and a normal salary; this is true of a worker with a five-year or longer contribution period and a severe health impairment, who nevertheless continues to work. Having paid contributions to the insurance system, he is entitled to his disability benefit because the disability risk has become reality. The law allows him to draw no more than the minimum amount, which he can add to his salary up to retirement. After retirement, his disability pension will be recomputed to take into account the whole contribution period. It should be emphasized that old age and disability pensions are based on the same method of calculation.

The INPS definition of disability, on the other hand, defines reduced earnings capacity as earnings less than one-third of normal; the pensioner is therefore entitled to add up to one third by the definition of INPS invalidism.

Suppose now that the same totally disabled worker of 30, married, no children, and ten years of social security contribution, has injured himself at work. He can draw both INAIL and INPS benefits. The 100 percent replacement rate for INAIL lies between a minimum and a maximum

Table 12.20. Monthly Net Replacement Rate for the INPS Disability Benefit, by Salary Amount (thousand lire)

Amount of Salary	Amount of Benefit	Replacement Rate	Family Allowance	Replacement Rate (total)
1978				
Half of average salary (242.6)	102.5	42%	9.0	46%
Average salary (485.1)	102.5	21	9.0	23
Twice average salary (970.3)	190.0	20	9.0	20.5
1968				
Half of average salary (69.3)	21.9	31.6	4.2	37.6
Average salary (138.5)	21.9	15.8	4.2	18.8
Twice average salary (277.0)	49.2	17.8	4.2	19.3

annual earnings amount (2,448,000 and 4,547,000 in 1978, and 680,000 and 1,265,000 in 1968). In this case the totally disabled worker will not only receive his 100 percent replacement rate (as long as his earnings are within the amounts stated), but he will also be entitled to an INPS benefit and family allowances (Table 12.21).

Effects of Financing on the Demand for Labor

An example of the peculiarity of the Italian situation lies in the fact that financing both INAIL and INPS programs through heavy social security

Table 12.21. Monthly Net Replacement Rate for the INAIL Total Disability Benefit and for Additional INPS Benefit by Salary Amount (thousand lire)

Amount of Salary	Amount of Benefit	Unemployment Benefit	Total INAIL Replacement Rate (%)	INPS Benefit[a]	Total Replacement Rate (%)
1978					
Half of average salary (242.6)	242.6 (100%)	50.0	121	111.2	167
Average salary (485.1)	378.9 (78%)	50.0	88	111.2	111
Twice average salary (970.3)	378.9 (39%)	50.0	44	119.0	56
1968					
Half of average salary (69.3)	69.3 (100%)	15.0	122	26.1	159
Average salary (138.5)	105.4 (76%)	15.0	87	26.1	106
Twice average salary (277.0)	105.4 (38%)	15.0	43	43.4	53

[a]Including family allowance.

contributions has no adverse labor supply effect, contrary to what one would suppose. In the context of "guaranteeing" earnings, which is a primary determinant in the Italian labor market, workers' wages have increased in real value in the last decade. Social security contributions paid by the worker have not affected the amount of wages. The INPS payroll tax for pensions has been constantly increasing (18.8 percent in 1968; 23.7 percent in 1978), but the worker's salary has not decreased. In addition, the worker's real purchasing power has been safeguarded, and the employer's social security payments have constantly increased. Italy is the one country of Western Europe with the highest social security contributions for industrial workers in relation to salaries, which are lower than the average European salary. Since the cost of labor is high because of social security contributions, payroll taxes have an adverse effect on the demand for labor, and some employers prefer the less costly forms of employment provided for them by the permissive social security programs.

Activity Rates and Disability Benefits: Some Aspects of the Labor Market

If we compare labor force activity (participation) rates for 1968 with those for 1978 for men only, we find a decrease from 81.5 percent to 79.1 percent. Because, however, of growing female participation, total activity rates have increased from 54.4 to 57.3 percent. To separate activity rates of those age groups where disability pensions are more numerous (from 50-54 to 60-64), Table 12.22 shows specific activity rates by sex for 1968 and 1978.

The Italian labor market is evidently characterized by low activity rates. In the last decade female participation increased from 28.6 to 36.3 percent in the 14-64 age population; without this phenomenon, activity rates would be lower. In contrast with this official labor force description, there is an "unofficial" market which employs at least 10 percent as much again of the total employed population. Our estimate of two million "underground"

Table 12.22. Labor Force Participation Rates by Age and Sex, 1968 and 1978

	Men		Women		Total	
Age Group	1968	1978	1968	1978	1968	1978
14-19	66.3	61.2	35.1	42.0	50.5	51.9
30-49	97.3	97.9	29.7	39.3	62.3	68.1
50-64	76.0	72.7	19.0	22.5	46.6	46.7
45-49	95.2	96.5	29.3	35.1	60.6	65.1
50-54	91.6	91.1	25.9	31.7	57.6	60.7
55-59	82.0	75.9	18.8	21.3	49.9	47.6
60-64	51.2	39.4	12.0	10.4	30.9	24.2

Source: Istat, *Annuario di statistiche del lavoro* (1969, 1979).

Note: The Istat series on which the table is based changed in 1978; the 1968 figure includes an estimate of hidden employment.

workers is rather restrictive, but it is based on recent evaluation of the GDP figure. The mean age of INPS disability pensioners is slightly over 50, and starting with the 50-54 age group, official activity rates fall. Although not available, the number of those recipients who officially continue to work is in fact smaller than the number of those pensioners who are in the unofficial labor market. The lowest activity rates are in the 60-64 age group, where we find the highest incidence of INPS disability pensions (Table 12.9). However, it is in the 50-54 and 55-59 age groups that the increase of beneficiaries is noticeable, and it is reasonable to suppose, in the absence of adequate data, that at least the majority stays in the labor market. This is quite certainly true of the agricultural sector.

Another characteristic of the Italian labor market is the absence of mobility. The 1970 Statute of Workers in effect guaranteed the jobs of employees, by forbidding dismissal, but at the same time it made mobility even more difficult, if not impossible. A disability pensioner of 50 years of age can risk a certain mobility once he has the certainty of a basic minimum on which to rely. He offers himself on the labor market at a lower cost than the official worker, and both he and his employer evade taxation. The labor market presents an appearance of strong, stable employment in large firms, in contrast to precarious, hidden, mobile employment in small enterprises. The fact of being guaranteed a disability pension, or similar social security benefits, permits the precarious employee to wait for a job in the "stable" labor market (private and public large enterprises). This phenomenon results in a segmentation of the labor market and in a growing number of unfilled vacancies in less appealing jobs.

Future Directions of Policy for the Disabled

The whole system of disability assistance has shown a strong increase both in the number of beneficiaries and in the average amount of benefits. The social insurance disability pension is clearly being used as a means to support low-income families. The same tendency is suggested by the deficit in the agricultural segment of the industrial injury program. Disability is evidently one of the instruments by which resources are transferred. The Italian economy is increasingly changing from an economy which produces growing wealth to an economy which simply transfers growing amounts of given wealth.

As stressed in the previous pages, the INPS minimum pension is almost entirely paid out of financial "integrations"—the amount contributed by the state to make up the difference between what a worker has actually paid in and what his minimum pension level actually is. This is true especially for the agricultural segment, which has developed growing annual deficits, up to 8,000 billion lire, in the last decade. Reform of the INPS program is especially needed to stop the effects of one cause of expenditure growth: by restricting it to the work-disabled only, the welfare element will be eliminated.

On the other hand, the number of agricultural beneficiaries seems now to be decreasing, partly because of deaths and partly because of the slightly more restrictive criterion recently adopted in this sector. Yet other determinants will remain constant, such as the leveling of the great majority of pensions to the minimum benefit, and the continuous adjustment of these amounts to the rise in contractual wages. Both of these effects will continue to produce expenditure increases in the next years, and in the absence of an increase of contributions by self-employed workers (some of them are, however, presumably well over the poverty line), the budget deficits of the INPS programs for the self-employed will continue to grow. At the same time, because of the adjustment mechanism, the amount of minimum benefits is increasing more than is the cost of living.

The permissive attitude in granting benefits, especially toward the self-employed, was originally aimed at redistributing income in favor of those sectors of the economy that needed support (such as agriculture and manual trades). The 100 percent take-up of these groups seems to entail, as a side effect, a similar percentage take-up for precarious employment of beneficiaries. In order to achieve better results, INPS disability programs should undergo changes. It is still (in 1982) not certain that the reform of INPS disability will be enacted; it would, however, provide consistent benefits to the totally disabled, while partial disability benefits would be temporary, monitored, and of limited duration. Nevertheless, for the next few decades those disability pensions now being paid would continue.

A more selective approach in granting benefits is the crucial change to be made to fight the present inadequate and unfair egalitarianism, which results in small benefits being given to many, and does not protect the really needy. At the same time, the need for less permissive integrations between benefits and earnings is another crucial problem to be solved: with selectivity in granting benefits, many working beneficiaries would have to choose between work and pension.

The share of expenditure devoted to the welfare program will also presumably increase in the coming years. The present expansion in the number of beneficiaries will certainly be followed by increases in the amounts of benefits. The severely disabled in this program are already asking for much higher amounts, and the social pressure of public opinion is very strong.

With reform of the social insurance disability program, which could stop the present disguised minimum-guarantee function of INPS benefits and at the same time provide sufficient benefits to workers whose health conditions justify them, enough resources could be made available for the means-tested program for the needy disabled with no earnings record.

Many of these problems are being debated at the political level, and the press is keeping the problem of disability before the eyes of the public. This situation may create expectations that are acceptable from a social point of view, but which contrast with the extent of resources available. Giving high priority to a strictly selective approach in granting disability benefits is the only answer. The Italian situation promises a high proportion of GDP devoted to disability expenditures, which consist of spreading numerous benefits of limited amount. A stricter standard for entitlement to benefits would certainly permit a more efficient distribution of present expenditures, giving more consistent benefits to a smaller number of people.

Notes

1. This regulation is not applied in practice because of an article of the Constitution which establishes that "The State protects health as a fundamental right of every human being and in the interest of the community and assures medical care to the poor [a national health service was in the process of being implemented in 1979]. No one can be compelled to undergo treatment unless the law requires it. The law cannot, in any case, infringe on the limits imposed by the respect due to every human being."

2. On the assistance component of the Italian social security system, see Vitali (1978).

3. For employees, the five-year contributory period can be reached after one year of actual work and four years of voluntary social security contributions (of a lower amount).

4. Data on geographical distribution have been calculated from INPS official reports. Northwestern regions are Piemonte, Val d'Aosta, Lombardia, and Liguria. Northeastern are Veneto, Friuli-Venezia Giulia, Trentino-Alto Adige and Emilia Romagna. Central are Toscana, Umbria, Marche and Lazio. Southern are Abruzzi and Molise, Campania, Puglia, Basilicata, Calabria, Sicilia, and Sardinia.

5. Family allowances granted to INPS pensioners are minimal amounts—i.e., 9.5 thousand lire a month for each family member. Children receive the allowance until they are 18 (26 if students).

6. See note 1.

7. The acronyms designate associations of the following: war disabled, civilian war victims, (military) service mutilated and disabled people, industrial injury workers, "civil" disabled people, war orphans, families of war victims, and the deaf-and-mute.

References

AREL [Agenzia di Ricerche e Legislazione]. 1978. *Il riordinamento del sistema pensionistico italiano: analisi e proposte.* Doc. (78) 2, Rome.

Banca d'Italia. 1979. *Relazione annuale 1978.* Rome.

Castellino, O. 1976. *Il labirinto delle pensioni.* Bologna: Il Mulino.

Censis [Centro Studi Investimenti Sociali]. Various years. *Rapporto sulla situazione sociale del Paese.* Rome.

CNEL [Consiglio Nazionale dell'Economia e del Lavoro]. 1979. *Rapporto sulla manodopera.* Rome.

Eurostat [Statistical Office of the European Community]. 1978. *Les handicapés et leur emploi.* Brussels.

Fausto, D. 1978. *Il sistema italiano di sicurezza sociale.* Bologna: Universale Paperbacks il Mulino.

Ferrari, Gennaro, and Lagonegro, Guiseppe. 1971. *Le assicurazioni sociale: Manuale.* Giuffré.

FORMEZ. 1979. *Il conto consolidato della spesa pubblica in Campania, per l'anno 1977*, prima stesura, non pubblicato. Rome.

Forte, F., et al. 1978. *La redistribuzione assistenziale: Costi e benefici della spesa pubblica in Italia.* Milan: Etas Libri.

INAIL [Istituto Nazionale delle Assicurazioni contro gli Infortuni sul Lavoro]. 1978. *Notiziario Statistico 1977, Ginnaio/Marzo.* Rome.

INPS [Instituto Nazionale della Previdenza Sociale]. Various years. *Notizie statistiche.* Rome.

INPS. 1978. *Rendiconti dell'anno 1977.* Rome.

INPS. 1979. *Allegati statistici ai rendiconti 1977.* Rome.

Istat [Central Statistical Office]. 1978. *Indagine sulle pensioni 1975* (No. 13). Rome.

Istat. 1979. *Rilevazione delle forze di lavoro, 1978* (Supplement to *Bollettino Mensile di Statistica).* Rome.

IST.I.SS [Istituto per gli Studi sui Servizi Sociali]. 1975. *Formazione e collocamento degli invalidi.* Rome.

IST.I.SS. 1978. Evoluzione dell'assistenza agli handicappati in Italia: prospettive istituzionali e organizzative. Rome. Unpublished.

Ministerio del Bilancio. 1979. *Relazione generale sulla situazione economica del Paese.* Rome.

Ministero della Sanita, Centro Study. 1975. *L'associazionismo tra gli invalidi.* Rome.

Morcaldo, G. 1977. *Analisi della struttura dei trattamenti pensionistici e della sua evoluzione.* Contributi alla ricerca economica, Servizio Studi della Banca d'Italia. Rome.

Relazione Generale sulla Situazioni Economica del Paese (various years). Presented to Parliament by Ministro per Bilancio e la Pro-grammazione Economica e Ministro del Tesoro, ed. Istituto Poligrafico dello Stato. Rome.

Reviglio, F. 1977. *Spesa pubblica e stagnazione dell'economia italiana.* Bologna: Universale Paperbacks il Mulino.

Reviglio, F. and Forte, F. 1975. *La finanza della sicurezza sociale.* Turin: Utet.

Vitali, L. 1978. *The expansion of social security in Italy.* Geneva Papers (Association Internationale pour l'Etude de l'Economie de l'Assurance), No. 10. Geneva.

Chapter 13

Disability Policy in the Netherlands

Han Emanuel, Victor Halberstadt, and Carel Petersen

Social policy toward disabled workers has received a great deal of public attention in The Netherlands due to the increasing number of benefits and beneficiaries. With the number of disability beneficiaries over 700,000 in 1982,[1] or over 15 percent of the labor force, and with one of the most generous benefit systems among the highly industrialized countries, the economic effects of these policies deserve analysis.

This chapter has seven sections. In the first we give a brief sketch of the Dutch social security system. Section 2 presents characteristics of the physically handicapped population in The Netherlands. Section 3 describes the Dutch disability programs, and Section 4 the beneficiaries of those programs. Section 5 focuses on the application of the disability criterion, which is rather loose, and the problems this creates. Section 6 analyzes expenditures on the disability programs, and the final section examines economic issues related to security and employment programs for the disabled.

The Dutch Social Security System

The Macroeconomic Context

As in other Western countries, expenditures on the public sector in The Netherlands have risen tremendously over the last decades. Between 1963

Han Emanuel is Financial and Economic Secretary, Social Security Council, Zoetermeer; Victor Halberstadt is Professor of Public Finance, Leyden University; and Carel Petersen is Assistant Professor of Economics, Erasmus University, Rotterdam. Kees P. Goudswaard of Leyden University provided valuable assistance.

and 1980 the average annual growth rate was approximately 7.2 percent (in constant prices), expenditures rising from Dfl. 44.9 billion to 145.0 billion. As a share of gross domestic product,[2] public expenditures rose from 37.3 percent in 1963 to 57.6 percent in 1980. This implies an average annual growth of 1.2 percent of gross domestic product.

A relatively large part of this growth is caused by the rapidly expanding social insurance sector, defined as the combination of programs that are (mainly) financed by specific payroll taxes and administered by publicly recognized organizations run by representatives of trade unions and employer associations (plus, in some cases, board members appointed by the Crown). Other schemes—e.g., unemployment of longer duration, sheltered workshops, public assistance, rent subsidies, and the old age, widow and orphan, and disability pensions for civil servants financed from the state budget—are counted as part of the government sector. Regrouping these data as *income transfers*, independent of the source of finance but with a distinction between income transfers related to disability and other characteristics on the one hand, and material government outlays and salaries, etc., of civil servants on the other, gives the results shown in Table 13.1.

During the period 1963-1980 the share of material government outlays as a percentage of gross domestic product rose by over 23 percent, disability income transfers by 204 percent, and other income transfers by 80 percent. The average annual growth rate of expenditures (in constant prices) amounted repsectively to 5.8 percent, 11.6 percent, and 8.2 percent. This shows the relative weight of the disability problem. The relative rise in other income transfers is due to the increasing costs of medical care and the effect of demographic factors (aging of the population).

Table 13.2 presents the corresponding development of the rise in number of income recipients, classified by main source of income and measured in man-years. A steady decline in the relative number of employed from 1963 onward is apparent. In 1963 the ratio of the number of employed to the number of beneficiaries was 3:1; in 1976 it was somewhat below 2:1. The number of disability beneficiaries, including those on sick leave for less than a year, increased by 210 percent between 1963 and 1980, reaching 960,000 in 1980, which corresponds to an average annual growth rate of 6.9 percent.

The total population aged 15-64, including nonworking youth (students), housewives, and early retirees, amounted to 9.2 million in 1980. This implies that more than 1 out of 10 working-age individuals received a disability benefit.

The growth of the number of nondisabled beneficiaries as measured in man-years can largely be explained by the worsening employment situation in the market sector, and by the rise in the proportion of old people in the total population.

Table 13.1. Public Sector Expenditures by Type (1976 prices; in billions of Dfl. and percentages)[a]

	1963	1968	1971	1974	1976	1978	1980	Average Annual Growth Rate, 1963–1980
Material								
government	Dfl. 27.3	Dfl. 41.1	Dfl. 51.8	Dfl. 58.4	Dfl. 66.3	Dfl. 70.7	Dfl. 71.2	
outlays[b]	(22.9%)	(24.3%)	(25.6%)	(25.4%)	(27.9%)	(28.1%)	(28.3%)	5.8
Income								
transfers[c]								
Disability	3.2	6.6	9.4	13.3	15.9	19.1	20.6	
benefits[d]	(2.7)	(3.9)	(4.6)	(5.8)	(6.7)	(7.6)	(8.2)	11.6
Other	13.9	24.6	32.5	41.5	48.5	52.9	53.1	
benefits	(11.7)	(14.6)	(16.0)	(18.1)	(20.4)	(21.0)	(21.1)	8.2
Total	44.4	72.3	93.7	113.2	130.7	142.7	145.0	
	(37.3)	(42.8)	(46.2)	(49.3)	(55.0)	(56.7)	(57.6)	7.2

Source: Derived by the authors from data and estimates from the Central Bureau for Statistics, the Ministry of Social Affairs, and the Ministry of Finance 1982 Budget Memorandum.

[a]Numbers in parentheses are percentages of the gross domestic product at market prices.

[b]Includes civil servant salaries and investment.

[c]Includes benefits in kind, etc.

[d]Includes sickness benefits and all disability benefits and provisions in kind, but excludes costs of medical care.

Table 13.2. Number of Income Recipients (in thousands of man-years and percentages)

	1963	1971	1976	1980
Market sector[a]	3560 (64%)	3780 (58%)	3500 (51%)	3360 (47%)
Government and semi-government sector[b]	610 (11)	800 (12)	950 (14)	1000 (14)
Total employment	4170 (75)	4580 (70)	4450 (64)	4360 (61)
Public sector benefits				
Disability[c]	310 (6)	540 (8)	750 (11)	960 (13)
Other[d]	1080 (19)	1430 (22)	1715 (25)	1830 (26)
Total number of beneficiaries	1390 (25)	1970 (30)	2465 (36)	2790 (39)
Total number of income recipients[b]	5560 (100)	6540 (100)	6915 (100)	7150 (100)

Source: Based on statistical material from the Social Economic Council, the Central Bank of The Netherlands, the Social Security Council, and the Central Bureau of Statistics.

[a]Includes self-employed, after downward correction for days of absence due to sickness.

[b]After downward correction for days of absence due to sickness.

[c]Includes SBA (private and semicollective sector), DSA, GDA (only in 1976), and GPPA, TRM and SEA (including those covered by GDA or DSA).

[d]Includes unemployment benefits, old age pensions, widow pensions, and Public Assistance Act beneficiaries.

General Characteristics

In the Dutch social security system, benefits are given across the board—i.e., they are not means-tested, and the whole adult working population is covered, with no further categorization. In the case of benefits to replace loss of earnings above the minimum wage level, a separate legislation covers civil servants; the military and the self-employed are excluded. Nearly all feasible risks of loss of earnings or incurrence of "unbearable costs" (e.g., of medical care and raising children) are covered, each within a separate legal scheme. Most of these programs are fully or mainly financed by a separate payroll or income tax levied on a percentage of wages earned or on total taxable income up to a certain limit. Payroll taxes on earnings are shared between employers and employees in different proportions. Taxes on wages earned are in all cases withheld at the source through a pay-as-you-go system.

There are three main subsystems in the social security scheme:

1. Programs covering demographic "risks" (old age, widow and orphan benefits, child allowances) administered by regional bodies (called Councils of Labor) capped by a central organization (called the Social Security Bank).

2.Programs ensuring cash benefits in case of loss of earning capacity through unemployment (up to 6 months), sickness (first year), or disability (after the first year, from the age of 18 to the age of 65),[3] administered by statutory semipublic bodies organized by branches of industry (misleadingly called Trade Associations).

3.A program ensuring finance of medical care, administered by true associations, usually organized on a regional basis (called Sick-Funds).

The government is represented on the boards of the first group of organizations but not on those of the last two groups. In addition, there are supervisory bodies on which the central trade unions and employer associations are represented and to which the government appoints Crown members: the Social Security Council for the first two groups of programs and the Sick-Fund Council (on which the members of the sick-funds and their "collaborators"—physicians and other professionals—are also represented) for the last one. The first two subsystems are under the administration of the Minister of Social Affairs and Employment, the last one under the Minister of Welfare, Health and Culture.

The demographic programs covering all Dutch residents[4] entitle beneficiaries to flat-rate benefits which vary according to marital status (old age), number of years as resident of The Netherlands (old age and widow and orphan allowances), or the assumed burden imposed by a child, depending on age, whether studying or not, and whether living at home or elsewhere (child allowances). Cash benefit programs cover a percentage of earnings lost for the privately employed only,[5] except for the so-called General Disability Security Act (GDA) which has flat-rate benefits[6] and coverage analogous to the old age benefit insurance scheme. The medical costs program, which finances only the first year of illness, covers the privately employed up to a certain maximum wage, the unemployed, the self-employed (with earnings not exceeding that same maximum) on a voluntary basis, and the aged with incomes up to a lower maximum. Coverage includes not only these groups but also their dependents. Costs of medical care after the first year of illness are covered by another program which is compulsory for all residents.

All cash benefits are wage-indexed twice a year (with a time lag of 6 months) and have a guaranteed minimum equal to the after-tax minimum legal wage. The legal wage minimum (introduced in 1969) is an important element in the structure of wages. It is, in comparison to other countries, substantial (as of January 1, 1981, Dfl. 1880.00 per month for an adult married man), and is indexed twice a year to the rise in average collectively bargained wages in the private sector. Also, it should be noted that wages and benefits are supplemented by a tax-free system of child allowances, which are, again, substantial. Program-specific benefits do not contain family allowances[7] and are taxable by the progressive general income tax and, up to a ceiling, by the specific proportional payroll taxes.

Some schemes have been partly financed from general revenue, but contributions have been withdrawn in recent years. At present they only include (1) a contribution to the costs of disability cash benefits to the privately employed; the full costs of disability benefits in cash or in hand to the early handicapped (this is a permanent legal obligation of the government but has been recently brought up for reconsideration); (2) the payroll tax for the General Disability Act for publicly employed (paid by each public administration for its employees as an employer); and (3) a contribution to financing the costs of medical care for the aged. The first two contributions are financed from the budget of the Minister of Social Affairs and Employment, the last from the budget of the Minister of Welfare, Health and Culture.

Social insurance covers only the risks of the first 6 months of unemployment; it is then succeeded by another unemployment program (2 years; 7 years for those aged 58 or over), fully financed from general revenue through the Ministry of Social Affairs and Employment. In addition, for those unemployed more than 2.5 or 7.5 years and those struck by income losses or excessive costs (e.g., the cost of an old age home) who are not insured, there exists a General Public Assistance Program (GPAP; in Dutch: Algemene Bijstandswet, or ABW). This program is financed from general revenues and administered by the local government under supervision of the Minister of Social Affairs and Employment. The GPAP ensures to all needy residents a benefit at most equal to the minimum wage (after taxes) and/or reimbursement of exceptional costs (e.g., due to illness or commensurate with the previous way of living); it also covers those unemployed who have not previously been privately employed.

Not within the realm of social insurance but relevant to our subject is the social employment program. This scheme is fully financed from general revenues and administered by the local government under the supervision of the Minister of Social Affairs and Employment. In addition, we should mention the existence (since 1946) of a legal quota system which, on paper, forces larger employers to take on a minimum number of handicapped employees equal to a certain percentage (2 percent) of their work force. In 1981, legislation was proposed to increase this quota to 5 percent, with sanctions. Finally, the public regional employment offices should be noted. Under supervision of the Minister of Social Affairs and Employment, these employment offices have the exclusive right to mediate work for the involuntarily unemployed and have special departments for the disabled.

The Disabled Population in the Netherlands

An attempt to identify and describe the disabled workers in The Netherlands requires an estimate of the size and composition of the disabled population as a whole. The only data available are from a survey carried out by the Central Bureau of Statistics (1974-76) in 1971/72. The concept of disability used in this survey, which is an ongoing source of analysis, relates in no way to the different disability programs which will be discussed in the next section. In fact, the survey was aimed at obtaining data only about *physically handicapped* persons of 5 years and older in The Netherlands, and is based on self-reporting. However, within the population of beneficiaries of disability programs, the subset of physically handicapped shows a relative decline over time, as will be discussed. It is likely that the (socio-)psychically handicapped form a substantial and possibly increasing part of the total disabled population. Therefore, the dated estimate of the physically handicapped which is available provides useful but insufficient information about the present size and composition of the disabled population.

The Data Base

In the 1971-72 survey, the physically handicapped are defined as persons who have one or more permanent functional limitations to at least a minimum degree. Functional limitations are defined as disturbances in the functioning of, e.g., limbs, sense organs, and stamina. For each function it was determined to what degree a person must suffer from a disorder for the term physically handicapped to be applicable. The degree of severity may vary from moderate to very serious.

A random sample of about 70,000 persons was drawn from the Dutch population of 5 years and older. The persons included in the sample were first approached by mail. The response rate was 83 percent. All respondents who (or for whom was) reported some handicap (about 31 percent) were visited in order to obtain more detailed information. This method implies that in the first instance the respondents or those responsible for them decided themselves whether they should be considered physically handicapped.

There is a question as to whether the 1971-72 data provide a more or less reliable basis for the generation of corresponding estimates for 1978. There are at least three reasons why, if the same survey were administered in 1981-82, we might see a different picture: (1) the general state of health, irrespective of age, may have deteriorated; (2) the average age of the population has increased, which results, at constant age-specific incidence rates of physically handicapped, in a higher overall percentage of disabled; (3) as a result of malfunctioning of the labor market more people may report themselves handicapped.

There are no reasons to suppose that the first factor is a real one, although there has been a substantial increase of traffic accidents, reported cases of carcinoma and heart failures. This has most probably been overcompensated by a decline in work accidents and diseases with permanent consequences originating in the workplace.

As to the second factor, some increase of the average age can be observed. Over the period 1971-81, this increase was, however, very moderate. This suggests that a straight extrapolation of the 1971-72 data to 1981 will not be substantially incorrect. In a recent estimate by the Central Bureau of Statistics, on the basis of the 1972 age-specific incidence rates the overall incidence in 1981 was estimated at 9 percent, an increase of only 0.3 percentage points as compared with 1971.

With respect to the third possible determinant of change over time, it can be concluded that while the functioning of the labor market has worsened, considerable quantitative insight into its importance as a factor stimulating manifest physical disability is missing. Presumably the worsening of labor market situations results in changed perceptions with respect to the moment one reports oneself handicapped and therefore in somewhat higher incidence rates.

In our opinion, the relative figures of the 1971-72 survey can be considered as reliable, rough approximations for 1981, although they may slightly underestimate the reality of 1981. Because of the population growth between January 1971 (11.9 million persons age 5 years or older) and January 1981 (13.3 million) the absolute figures have to be increased by 11.8 percent. This results in an estimate of approximately 650,000 physically handicapped of working age in 1981. It should be kept in mind, however, that the concept of physically handicapped and the methodology of self-reporting of the survey reflect a vast difference from the concepts and methodologies used in different programs, as will be discussed later.

Size and Demographic Composition of the Physically Handicapped Working-Age Population

In the 1971-72 survey, more than 1 in 11 persons (8.7 percent) in the population of those aged 5 years and older considered themselves or were considered by their elders to be physically handicapped. Among those aged 20-64 (which comprises nearly all of the working population)[8] approximately 580,000, or 8.2 percent, considered themselves physically handicapped. Approximately 32 percent of these appeared to have only one functional limitation in a moderate degree.

Within this part of the population, age is clearly an important variable in explaining the prevalence of physical invalidity as well as its degree. In those aged 60-64 years, nearly 1 in 4 persons considered themselves to be physically handicapped. The great difference between men and women in the share of physically handicapped within the higher age brackets is remarkable. Presumably this is correlated with the greater participation of men in both the labor force and in travel (traffic accidents). Table 13.3

Table 13.3. Physically Handicapped Population, Degree of Handicap, Age, and Sex, 1971-72 (in percentages)

	Degree of Handicap[a]							
Age	1	2	3	4	5	6	7	>7
Men								
20-24	50.0	10.4	27.1	8.3	—	—	—	4.2
25-29	46.9	10.2	18.4	8.2	6.1	4.1	—	6.1
30-34	40.0	12.0	22.0	12.0	10.0	2.0	2.0	2.0
35-39	41.8	12.7	21.5	13.9	1.3	1.3	1.3	6.3
40-44	32.8	14.3	26.9	9.2	4.2	2.5	5.0	4.9
45-49	27.6	11.8	31.8	12.4	8.8	2.4	2.9	2.4
50-54	28.5	10.4	32.1	17.6	5.0	2.7	0.9	2.8
55-59	21.8	10.7	33.6	15.4	9.7	4.7	1.0	2.9
60-64	22.0	9.2	34.5	14.5	8.1	5.6	1.7	4.5
Women								
20-24	58.0	6.0	26.0	2.0	2.0	2.0	2.0	2.0
25-29	50.9	8.8	15.8	7.0	1.8	3.5	5.3	7.1
30-34	57.7	9.0	20.5	2.6	2.6	5.1	—	2.6
35-39	48.5	14.1	19.2	8.1	3.0	2.0	—	5.0
40-44	43.3	15.7	17.9	13.4	3.7	0.7	0.7	4.3
45-49	36.4	16.0	19.8	11.1	5.6	3.7	1.2	6.1
50-54	30.0	12.1	17.4	15.9	9.2	5.3	2.9	7.2
55-59	29.2	13.3	23.7	13.3	7.9	2.5	1.2	8.7
60-64	28.0	12.9	19.4	17.9	8.6	2.9	2.2	8.3

Source: Central Bureau of Statistics (1974-76).
[a]1 = lowest degree of severity; 5 = highest degree; 6 and above = more than one handicap.

shows that the average degree of handicap also rises sharply with age. Illness and old age are by far the most important causes of functional disorders.

With respect to geographical distribution, it appears that the share of the physically handicapped in the population is positively correlated with degree of urbanization. According to the Central Bureau of Statistics 1971-72 survey (1974-76), only 6.8 percent of those residing in rural municipalities, but 9.9 percent of those residing in urban muncipalities, considered themselves physically handicapped.

Economic Status

It is remarkable that the percentage unemployed among the total population of working age is higher than that among the physically handicapped (see Table 13.4). This difference may partly be caused by the definition of handicap used. But the most important explanation is that many potentially unemployed physically handicapped in fact enjoy a disability benefit or, e.g., in the case of married women, withdraw from the labor market. The relatively low percentage of the physically handicapped who attended school or who were studying as compared with the total population may also have been influenced by the definition, although the

Table 13.4. Labor Force Status of the Physically Handicapped Compared to that of the Total Population, Age 20-64 years, by Sex, 1971-72 (in percentages)

Labor Force Status	Physically Handicapped			Total Population		
	Men	Women	Total	Men	Women	Total
School/Study	0.5	0.1	0.3	3.3	0.3	1.8
Employed (incl. self-employed)	49.3	11.5	29.8	86.2	27.7	57.2
Unemployed	1.4	0.4	0.9	3.9	2.7	3.3
Pensioned, living off a social benefit	48.8	6.9	25.9	6.4	1.9	4.2
Housewife	—	81.4	43.0	—	67.3	33.4
Unknown	—	—	—	0.2	—	—

Source: Central Bureau of Statistics (1974-76) and CBS 1975 labor force sample survey.

educational level of the disabled population is definitely lower than that of the total population.

Income distribution by socio-occupational status of physically handicapped wage earners is given in Table 13.5. A fair number of those physically handicapped and working for a wage or salary are to be found in the above-average income brackets. It might be well to note also that for men self-employment rather than social security benefits is the most important source of income, while for women it is support from their partner.

Disability Programs

Sickness Benefits

The oldest (introduced in 1934) and, in terms of money spent, one of the most important programs in the area of cash benefits in case of sickness and disability is the Sickness Benefit Act (SBA; in Dutch: Ziektewet, or ZW). The SBA provides for a cash benefit payment during an individual's first year of inability to work due to illness, accident, or pregnancy, starting from the third working day of absence. The minimum payment guaranteed is 80 percent of earnings. However, administration is by branch of industry (or in some cases even by a small group of enterprises) and the law provides the possibility of increasing this ceiling, on a collective bargaining basis, to 100 percent and/or of waiving the first two "waiting days"; in most cases full use is made of these two possibilities.

The Sickness Benefit program can be considered to be mainly insurance against wage costs to the employers. Usually wages payment is simply continued in case of illness and the employer is reimbursed (for 100 percent, 90 percent, or 80 percent of the costs, depending on the branch of industry) by the Trade Association, of which he is a compulsory member. It is not

Table 13.5. Distribution of Physically Handicapped Wage Earners,[a] by Occupation and Income, 1971-72 (in percentages)

Annual Income[b] (in thousands of Dfl.)	Type of Occupation[c] Higher-Level Employees	Middle-Level Employees	Lower-Level Employees	Service Workers	Factory Workers	Total Employed
0-3	—	1.6	4.6	8.6	0.9	0.6
3-7	—	3.1	16.0	27.0	13.5	4.1
7-12	—	10.9	29.8	36.0	47.2	41.6
12-17	2.4	27.1	28.2	16.9	29.3	36.4
17-22	16.7	24.8	9.9	—	6.1	11.6
22-32	28.6	17.8	2.3	2.2	1.3	2.9
32+	57.2	3.1	0.8	1.1	—	—
Unknown	11.9	11.6	8.4	7.9	1.7	2.9
Total number in population	9,000 +	28,000 +	28,000 +	19,000 +	49,000 +	37,000 = 170,000

Source: Central Bureau of Statistics (1974-76).

[a]Includes only those disabled whose principal source of income is labor.

[b]By way of comparison, the median annual earnings of the total population of wage earners was Dfl. 14,000 in 1971 and Dfl. 15,500 in 1972.

[c]Classification, based on profession and number of people supervised, by the Central Bureau of Statistics.

surprising therefore that the payroll tax for this program is mainly borne by the employer.[9] Under certain conditions (e.g., availability of good medical auditing facilities) large employers are allowed to bear their own risks, in which case no payroll tax is levied. These "own risk bearers" employ roughly 20 percent of the insured. In the case of the unemployed, the Trade Association acts as their employer and pays the payroll tax of 1 percent. The average payroll tax for this program, set separately by each Trade Association or by more homogeneous groups of employers, called "risk-groups", varied between 2.8 percent and 24.8 percent in 1978. The average level of these taxes showed a long term upward trend, from 6.1 percent in 1968 to 7.3 percent in 1980.

Each Trade Association and the Joint Administrative Office (JAO), in which a number of them cooperate, has a medical service which judges the medical grounds for applications for sickness benefits. The JAO employs hundreds of doctors specialized in social insurance medicine, who are supervised by a medical adviser, in the 27 district offices. Trade Associations, which are self-administered, employ only a medical adviser, and in some cases a few other doctors; otherwise they rely for the screening of cases on private physicians who are paid on the basis of the number of cases handled. With some larger employers the Trade Association or JAO only takes over the judgment of cases after 10 weeks of illness; before that the case is handled by the medical staff of the employer. Very large employers, like Phillips or Shell, usually have cases of sick leave judged by their own medical service during the first full year of sickness.

The number of applications for sickness benefits (usually through the employer) has been growing steadily (with fluctuations from year to year owing to epidemics) and reached well over 5.5 million a year by 1980. During the recession that started in that year, the number decreased considerably. Most cases of sick leave are of short duration: 80 percent are terminated within a fortnight. It is clear that with such a large amount of cases, each cannot be expertly investigated, even though all self-administering Trade Associations and the JAO employ large numbers of lay investigators to visit those reported sick from the same or next day to within at the most two weeks after the application form has been received. Investigators report to the medical staff, which concentrates on suspicious and more serious or lengthier cases.

Disability among Privately Employed

The Disability Security Act (DSA; in Dutch: Wet op de Arbeidsongeschiktheidsverzekering, or WAO) took effect on July 1, 1967. It covers all privately employed individuals up to the age of 65, and provides, after the first year of illness (covered by the SBA), a benefit which depends on previous earnings and the degree of disability. The maximum benefit, paid monthly, is 80 percent of the previous wage (calculated as an average per working day, regardless of actual working hours) when a disability of 80-100 percent is established. However, the benefit can never fall lower than the legal minimum wage, both net of taxes. Since the General Disability Act (GDA; in Dutch: Algemene Arbeidsongeschiktheids Wet, or AAW) came into force on October 1, 1976, the DSA benefit has been reduced along with the GDA benefit for those who became disabled or sick after October 1, 1975, while the older cases, which are not eligible for a GDA benefit, continue to get the full DSA benefit.

The DSA has created the most explosive Dutch social security program, mainly because of the growth in the annual number of applicants and the average length of their stay within the program. The payroll tax for the DSA, which is not differentiated by branch of industry, is levied as a uniform percentage of earnings below a ceiling, with an exemption for the low-income brackets.[10] Before the program was started it was thought that its payroll tax would eventually reach a level of 4 percent, to be shared evenly by employers and employees. In fact, over the first three quarters of 1976, just before the introduction of GDA, it reached 10.2 percent, of which employers paid 6.65 percent. Without the reduction in program costs because of GDA benefits to DSA beneficiaries, and without a temporary contribution from general revenue, it would have reached 11.2 percent in 1978 just to cover program costs.

The law defines as disabled a person who as a consequence of illness or infirmity, fully or partly, is unable to gain—with labor which is commensurate to his force and capabilities and which, in view of his training and previous profession, he can reasonably be asked to perform at the place where he works or worked last or at a similar place—what physically and mentally healthy persons of the same kind and similar training at such a place usually gain through labor. The same definition of disability has been used since 1919 in a program which preceded the DSA. A similar definition is applied by the German social security program for the disabled. But what makes the case of the DSA program rather exceptional is that benefits are so high relative to earnings lost and that the minimum degree of disability entitling an individual to a benefit is remarkably low, namely 15 percent.

Until 1963 disability benefits were extremely low, depending on number of years worked, were not adequately indexed, and (except in the case of accidents at work and professional diseases) not given if the degree of disability was less than 65 percent. As of 1963 these benefits were supplemented to a maximum level equal to the average wage of an unskilled worker—regardless of number of years worked—fully indexed to the wage level and dependent on the degree of disability. For the first time a number of classes of degree of disability were identified, each corresponding to a different percentage of the maximum benefit. The minimum degree of disability entitling an individual to a benefit was lowered to 45 percent, later to 33 percent. These developments were taken to extremes by the DSA (1967), which distinguishes the current classes of degree of disability and corresponding relative benefits levels presented in Table 13.6.

It is clear that such a fine distinction by degree of disability is very difficult to make on purely medical grounds. In fact, the last column shows that the large majority of cases are in the 80-100 percent category; the remaining are mainly cases in which individuals continue to work, part time for a while or full time at a lower wage, with their old employer.

Over the years the percentage of cases assigned a degree of disability of

Table 13.6. Degree of Disability and Corresponding Benefit Levels

Degree of Disability	Benefit as Percentage of Previous Wage[a]	Percentage of Beneficiaries as of Dec. 31, 1980
15-25%	10	2.1
25-35%	20	3.1
35-45%	30	2.0
45-55%	40	4.1
55-65%	50	1.6
65-80%	65	2.2
80-100%	80[b]	84.6

[a]Includes GDA benefit; $\frac{100}{107}$ × daily wage rate.

[b]Never lower than 100 percent of the legal minimum wage after taxes.

80-100 percent has gradually increased. This tendency has been enforced by another feature of DSA legislation. The disability criterion of the DSA (and the GDA) is related to the capability to do *other work* of acceptable characteristics. This is markedly different from the criterion applied to establish entitlement to sickness benefits, which relates to one's previous work. As a consequence, when applying the definition the labor market situation is implicitly taken into account because jobs of the given description may not be available to a disabled person. The law, in a special provision, explicitly recognizes this, although it is implicitly contained in the general definition of disability mentioned before. Moreover, from the beginning of 1973 it has been accepted that lack of employment possibilities related to the handicap cannot be distinguished from a general lack of employment possibilities due to economic conditions, and that lack of "suitable" employment possibilities can be taken as sufficient reason to assume a 80-100 percent degree of disability, even if in medical terms a capacity to work remains, unless the contrary can be proven.

The DSA, like the SBA and the GDA, is administered by trade associations, of which there are 26. Eighteen of these cooperate in the Joint Administration Office (JAO, in Dutch: Gemeenschappelijk Administratie Kantoor, or GAK). Both trade unions and employer associations (by trade of industry) are represented on the boards of the trade associations and the JAO. All have to consult an advisory body, the Joint Medical Service (JMS; in Dutch: Gemeenschappelijke Medische Dienst, or GMD), whose administrative activities are also taken care of by the JAO, on individual admissions to the program (both for cash benefits and provisions in kind).

Admission for cash benefits is judged at the end of the first year of sickness. As the administration of SBA and DSA benefits is by the same trade associations, application is automatic. The trade association prepares, without interference by the disabled, the documentation needed by the JMS. This procedure is laid down by law, as the JMS has exclusive responsibility for such judgments. For this purpose it employs large numbers of both physicians and so-called "work experts" and can make use of legal experts of the JAO. But the number of applications for DSA cash benefits (and provisions in kind) has been much bigger from the start than the JMS could cope with. As most cases seemed straightforward and could be assigned an 80-100 percent degree of disability without the need for a later reassessment, in 1969 an agreement was reached between the Federation of Trade Associations and the JMS which allowed Trade Associations to decide which cases belonged to those categories that had to be put before the JMS for assessment and which to categories they could assess themselves, with only summary reporting to JMS. This agreement was adapted in 1976 to provide room for GDA applications. The legality of these agreements, however, is a matter of dispute.

Basic Disability Benefits and Provisions in Kind

The General Disability Act (GDA) entitles all those disabled who were previusly gainfully employed, those disabled before the age of 17,[11] and individuals aged 18-64 who have been sick or disabled for a year to a basic flat rate benefit (differing only for married couples and single persons, and by degree of disability), of which the maximum net of taxes is equal to the minimum wage after taxes.[12] The benefit structure has very recently (January 1, 1980) been changed, together with the acceptance of married working women as beneficiaries. Every disabled person is now entitled to the same basic benefit (which, however, is lowered by 10 percent for each year of age, less for those under 21), the level of which depends only on the degree of disability, the maximum of which net of taxes is equal to 70 percent of the legal minimum wage after taxes. For both married and unmarried persons with a dependent child under the age of 18 this is increased to 85 percent of the net minimum wage if his/her earnings and those of his/her partner together contribute 15-30 percent to the basic benefit, and 100 percent if earnings add to 15 percent or less. If both partners are disabled, their benefits are proportionally reduced until the sum reaches these levels. The law also entitles individuals to provisions in kind to maintain or restore ability to work, or to facilitate adaptation to life as a handicapped person, regardless of their possibilities of gainful employment.[13]

Actually, the GDA meant an improvement only for the self-employed. Benefits and provisions to the early handicapped and the publicly employed were already financed by the government from general revenues. The disability criterion and the different classes of degree of disability distinguished are the same for the DSA as for the GDA program, except that entitlement to a GDA benefit only applies if the disability is at least 25 percent.

The total number of DSA and GDA beneficiaries amounted to over 656,000 by the end of 1981. Total expenditures amounted to about Dfl. 17.6 billion in 1981, of which Dfl. 8.6 billion was chargeable to the DSA fund and Dfl. 9.0 billion to the GDA fund, and Dfl. 0.6 to the government.

Disability Coverage under the General Public Pension Act and Related Programs

The DSA only covers those who are privately employed. Civil servants, military personnel, those working under a permanent contract with public enterprises, and those working in public or private educational institutions and in a number of other nonprofit institutions financed from general or social security taxes are covered by the General Public Pension Act (GPPA; in Dutch: Algemeen Burgerlijke Pensioenwet, or ABP). This program provides for disability benefits and provisions in kind (as well as for old age, widows, and orphan pensions). Benefits—payable until the pensionable age of 65, once awarded—are paid after 1.5 to 2.5 years of inability to perform one's previous work (during which period salaries continue to be paid). The period is not fixed. Benefits are granted only in case of permanent disability, which otherwise is defined in the same manner as in the DSA and GDA programs. As in the case of DSA benefits, GPPA benefits are related to previous earnings (indexed to the general wage level) and to the degree of disability (minimum of 15 percent).

Policy with regard to provisions in kind is more or less geared to that of the GDA. Since October 1976 a part of the salaries of the publicly employed who have been on sick leave for a year and of the new GPPA benefits, equal to the GDA benefit, as well as the costs of provisions in kind, can be claimed by the GPPA administration from the GDA fund, as public sector employees are covered by that program.

Although GPPA criteria for eligibility are more strict than DSA and GDA criteria, the program has encountered similar problems of rapid increase in the number of applicants.

Provisions in Kind to the Disabled

An important feature of the disability benefit programs is the provisions in kind that they offer, started in October 1976 under the GDA. In fact, the law provides in-kind benefits during the SBA year as well.

The law distinguishes between two broad categories of benefits in kind: (1) provisions to maintain or restore ability to be gainfully employed; (2) provisions to facilitate a handicapped person's general adaption to life, even without work. The specific benefits in the two categories are similar, for example means of transportation (wheelchairs, adapted or normal cars, reimbursement or prepayment of cost of public or private transportation), adaptations within the house, and assistance for activities of daily life. But included in the first category are adaptations of place of work (e.g., to improve accessibility), of tools and machinery, retraining and occupational resettlement, and physiotherapy; included in the second category are household assistance and provision of or payment for hobby equipment. The cost of these in-kind benefits has been expanding rapidly, reaching a level of Dfl. 350 million in 1979, partly due to the fact that these provisions supplement other programs in the medical and social field. In order to gain better control over this expansion, a regulation was issued with the introduction of the GDA which tried to define more precise borderlines between the different programs in this field. This regulation has since been refined, setting income ceilings for eligibility and gradually leaving, for example, the adaptions within the house of a handicapped person to a program under the Ministry of Housing, the rapidly growing number of cases of psychotherapy (from January 1, 1980 onward) to the General Act for Special Cost of Medical Care, and the costs of household assistance to the Ministry of Welfare, Health and Culture.

All applications for provisions in kind have to be submitted to the JMS. In fact, this organization often generates such applications itself when assessing people's degree of disability. Trade associations are less equipped for this as they do not employ work experts, and, in the case of self-administering trade associations, do not even employ many physicians. A point of dispute is that this assessment is deficient for the period when it is considered by many to be the most urgent (especially with a view to maintaining or restoring ability to resume work), namely during the first year of sickness. To facilitate early assessment, the DSA provides two legal instruments:

1. Spontaneous reporting of the case to JMS for assessment of the need of such provisions in kind; this kind of reporting has never occurred to any large extent, however, and has even declined between 1975 and 1979.

2. Reporting of all cases to JMS in which an individual has been ill for 13 weeks; this was stopped in 1970, however, as it required so much inconsequential paperwork.

Discussions have been reopened about these instruments with the introduction of the GDA program. The Minister refused to abolish the obligatory reporting after the thirteenth week as requested by the Federation of Trade Associations requested, and even introduced it into the GDA, accepting that for the time being that it would not be put into practice. Recently the Federation and the JMS introduced, with the consent of the Social Security Council and the Minister, a new system of reporting based on the following: (1) systematic reassessment by the medical advisor of the trade associations and the JAO of sickness beneficiaries after 3 months of illness in view of the appropriateness of spontaneous reporting; (2) second reassessment of cases of 6 months duration, with the possibility of initiating deliberation about the case with JMS experts; (3) advancement of assessment for DSA cash benefits to the point at which sickness has lasted 9 months instead of 10.

The Minister and the supervising Social Security Council have stated that they have sympathy for these measures and are willing to accept them for a period of experimentation provided that they are reformulated in such a way that the prime responsibility of JMS for all assessments is maintained—for example, through inspection of samples of cases and the power to suggest changes in the rules—and provided the experiment is properly evaluated. At present further intensification of the procedure is under discussion.

The Social Employment Program

A formalized social employment program was set up in 1950 under two separate pieces of ministerial decrees for manual workers (Gemeentelijke Sociale Werkvoorzieningsregeling voor Handarbeiders, or GSW) and for white collar workers (Sociale Werkvoorzieningsregeling Hoofdarbeiders, or SWH).[14] This followed voluntary activities to help handicapped persons to become involved in productive activity by a number of municipalities, going far back into the nineteenth century. The new schemes, however—under the impetus of the Atlantic Charter, the Beveridge Report, and the proposals of the van Rhijn Commission of The Netherlands government in exile in London during the war—were the first to bring job provisions for the handicapped entirely under government finance.

Most important was that they introduced a consistent wage system, in which wage levels of those employed in social workshops under these decrees were related to (at 105 to 140 percent) payments under the social assistance scheme (Dutch: Sociale Bijstandregeling), the predecessor of the General Public Assistance Act (Dutch: Algemene Bijstandswet, or ABW of 1963). In addition, criteria for admission into the program were specified. Also, the 1952 decrees gave handicapped workers employed in sheltered workshops employee status, and therefore coverage by social insurance, primarily the SBA and the two predecessors of DSA—the Work Accident and Occupational Disease Insurance Act (Ongevallenwet), and the Invalid Insurance Act (Invaliditeitswet). Also important was that the government recognized the right to work of handicapped people and its obligation to make such work available. For this purpose use was also made of the law regulating employment of the handicapped (a quota system) and of specialized sections for handicapped workers of the Regional Employment Services, set up for this purpose.

During the sixties many sheltered workshops were developed in the form of industrial centers, administrative centers, and open-air worksites. The two decrees were replaced in 1969 by the Social Employment Act (Dutch: Wet Sociale Werkvoorziening, or WSW), which has the following components: (1) sets standards and guidelines for the manner in which employment is provided; (2) establishes requirements which operating staff in the programs should fulfill; (3) provides regulations for the program's organization; (4) stipulates subsidy arrangements to the municipalities responsible for the execution of the law; (5) defines eligibility for participating in the program; (6) regulates renumeration of those socially employed.

State participation in finance is not always 100 percent for all cost and deficit elements, and this may influence the organizational form chosen. Wages of the handicapped were first related to the public assistance benefit plus a bonus based on merit rating. In August 1976 the latter was abolished (after criticism from Parliament) and replaced by a wage system in which people were put in one of ten wage categories, depending on their degree of training, skill, and experience, and could follow a career line of stepwise annual wage increases (of which the maximum number varied with the level of training) within that category.

The Social Employment Act attracted many handicapped (64,000 in 1976, 75,000 in 1980), partly due to the fact that it enabled workshops to employ people with social deficiencies but no clear medically determinable handicap. An interesting feature of the program is that those employed under it receive a normal wage and, in principle, no disability benefit, even though they are often considered to be disabled. The savings thus obtained by the social security administrations are transferred to the Ministry of Social Affairs and Employment, which finances the sheltered workshops. Quite often those socially employed still obtain an additional disability benefit because these are calculated not according to actual (preceding) wages but to a ''standard'' wage within the appropriate interval.

Temporary Social Assistance Program for the Less Able (TRM)

This program (Dutch: Tijdelijke Groepsregeling Minder Validen, or TRM) was introduced in 1965 as part of the General Public Assistance Program (GPA; in Dutch: Algemene Bijstandswet, or ABW) to replace and improve on a number of programs oriented to aid specific categories of handicapped. Its aim was to anticipate the further development of social security, and to provide financial assistance to the less able, excluding married women aged 18-65 years, in case no benefits could be claimed from other social security or welfare programs. The new program extended benefits only to the early handicapped and the self-employed. In addition, it included provisions to improve living conditions (mobility, etc.), and to improve or maintain the working capabilities of the handicapped. Since 1974 benefits net of taxes for primary earners have been equal to the legal minimum wage net of taxes, and those for others equal to 70 percent of that amount. On October 1, 1976, the 22,000 beneficiaries of the program were transferred to the new GDA program.

Quota Legislation

The first piece of legislation after the Second World War to help the disabled was the Act to Place Less Abled Workers (Dutch: Wet Plaatsing Minder Valide Arbeidskrachten), which obliges every employer with a work force of 20 or more to hire at least one disabled person for each 50 employed. To be recognized as disabled, people could be registered as such at the regional Public Employment Office. The act explicitly states the right of disabled people thus employed to earn the wage usually paid for that type of work unless it can be shown that their productivity does not warrant such high payment. Employers not complying with the requirements of this act can be fined a maximum of Dfl. 1,000, with public notice of the penalty.

Since no organization is charged with inspection, however, compliance has not been enforced. In fact, registration and publication of statistical data on the number of disabled workers employed was discontinued a few years after introduction of this legislation. In recent years discussions have taken place to strengthen legislation in this field and to increase its effectiveness, and a draft act has been put before parliament. Discussion of it has not yet been concluded.

Size and Characteristics of the Disability Beneficiary Population

Here we discuss the number of disabled by program, and for each program, the breakdown of the beneficiaries by certain characteristics. The comparison over time of the number of beneficiaries within each program is somewhat affected by change in programs. In particular some extensions of coverage are relevant. Yet it appears that the growth rate of the number of DSA beneficiaries was by far the most important (except for the less important GPPA disability program), and also that this is the largest of the programs concerned, as measured in man-years of beneficiaries (see Table 13.7). For this reason, and because of gaps in statistical data concerning the other programs, we will focus on the characteristics of DSA beneficiaries.

The DSA Program

Since the data with respect to the first full year after the introduction of DSA are still influenced by the incorporation of the beneficiaries of the disability programs preceding the DSA program, figures are given from 1969 onwards.

As Table 13.8 shows, the flow of beneficiaries into the program steadily increased—both in absolute numbers and in comparison to the number of insured—until 1975. As the number of terminations remains substantially lower, the number of beneficiaries continues to rise. Only in recent years has stabilization taken place. Its causes will be discussed in our section on economic issues.

It is remarkable that although the proportion of women in the insured population has risen slightly but constantly over the period considered, their share in the number of new beneficiaries rose about 9 percent in 9 years. Hence the ratio of inflow to the insured population has risen much more for women than for men. Table 13.9 shows the ratios of beneficiaries of the DSA program to the insured population, by age group and sex. Within

Table 13.7. Number of Recipients of Disability Benefits, by Program (in thousands of man-years)

Programs[a]	1963[b]	1968	1971	1974	1976	1978	1980	Average Annual Growth Rate, 1963-80
SBA	136	191	235	273	285	299	304	4.8
DSA	116	143	210	280	338	368	412	7.7
GDA					15	109	12	
GPPA:[c]								
Sickness	32	40	50	60	70	75	77	5.3
Disability	16	24	30	39	45	52	59	8.0
SEA	23	34	44	52	61	69	74	7.1
TRM[e]	0	15	20	23	22	—	—	—
Total	323	447	589	727	836	972	1038	7.1

Source: Based on statistical material from the Social Economic Council, the Central Bank of The Netherlands, and the Social Security Council.

[a]DSA, GDA, GPPA, and TRM are in equivalent numbers of fully disabled, taking into account the degree of disability; DSA insured having a GDSA benefit counted as DSA beneficiary; persons working in sheltered workshops are included in SEA, even if they are eligible for reimbursement from another program. Figures for SBA include estimates for self-insured enterprises.

[b]Figures for DSA and SEA in 1963 relate to the programs preceding the DSA program (author estimates derived from data published by the Social Insurance Bank and Central Bureau of Statistics).

[c]Includes pensions to railway personnel and professional military staff.

[d]First-year estimates.

[e]Previously self-employed disabled, transferred to GDA in 1976.

most age brackets these ratios have risen more for men than for women. However, the share of women beneficiaries has steadily risen for all age brackets. Hence the increase of the share of women under DSA is not due to a changed age composition of the insured female population.

The average age of those awarded a DSA benefit has been steadily declining. As can be seen from Table 13.9, this is partly due to the fact that in the higher age groups so many insured have already been awarded a benefit that relatively few insured are still working, and partly due to the fact that among the younger age groups invalidity ratios continue to increase. The latter may reflect the deterioration of labor market conditions.

The rise in 1973 in the average degree of disability (Table 13.8) may reflect a changed interpretation of the disability criterion authorized at the beginning of 1973. The law takes into account, when assessing the degree of disability, the decreased possibility of a partly disabled person getting a job. At the end of 1972 it was decided that without further proof it would be assumed that *any* lack of possibility could be attributed to an individual's disability. Putting aside the legal interpretations of this change, during the whole period concerned there was a slight increase in the average degree of disability. Possible factors behind this trend will be discussed in our section on economic issues.

As the last column in Table 13.8 shows, there was a considerable increase

Table 13.8. Key Figures for the DSA Program

Year	Beneficiaries at End of Year (000)	Benefits Awarded During Year (000 and % of insured)		Benefits Awarded to Women (% of award)	Average Age Benefit Awarded (years)	Average Degree of Disability New Beneficiaries (%)	Average Annual Benefit per Man-Year of Benefits Awarded[a] (1976 prices, Dfl. 000)
1970	215	50	1.5	17.2	49.2	89.7	15.7
1971	237	52	1.5	18.5	48.7	89.8	16.9
1972	261	54	1.7	19.9	48.4	89.9	17.4
1973	287	57	1.7	20.1	48.3	90.4	17.7
1974	313	61	1.9	19.5	47.9	90.8	18.4
1975	349	73	2.1	21.9	47.7	91.2	18.9
1976[b]	374	70	2.1	24.4	44.7	91.1	20.0
1977	404	71	2.1	24.6	46.5	91.4	20.9
1978	435	77	2.2	25.1	45.2	91.3	22.0
1979[c]	461	76	2.1	25.5	44.7	90.6	22.0
1980[c]	486	75	2.1	26.1	44.3	90.2	21.6

Source: Social Security Council and Joint Medical Service.

[a]Man-years adjusted for differences in the degree of disability; includes holiday allowances.

[b]Figures for 1976, 1977, and 1978 exclusive of DSA insured disabled, socially employed under the SEA program (ca. 30,000 at end of 1978).

[c]Preliminary figures.

Table 13.9. Number of DSA Beneficiaries per 1,000 Insured, by Age and Sex, 1974-1980[a]

Age	1974	1975	1976	1977	1978	1979	1980
Men							
15-19	4	4	3	5	5	5	5
20-24	12	13	13	15	17	16	15
25-29	19	21	23	27	31	32	32
30-34	34	38	43	46	50	52	54
35-39	54	60	64	72	80	84	84
40-44	84	93	97	108	122	127	133
45-49	130	139	143	157	172	185	193
50-54	182	199	204	222	242	258	273
55-59	302	305	311	320	343	353	355
60-64	397	433	444	488	507	526	571
Subtotal	94	102	110	120	132	137	142
Women							
15-19	2	2	2	3	3	3	3
20-24	9	12	11	13	14	14	14
25-29	30	32	33	38	43	44	44
30-34	45	54	64	65	67	67	70
35-39	60	66	73	79	89	90	91
40-44	83	94	100	106	119	125	126
45-49	126	142	145	158	176	185	193
50-54	200	214	214	218	229	233	240
55-59	319	343	333	353	366	430	455
60-64	536	585	541	567	579	593	645
Subtotal	68	76	83	89	97	100	102
Both							
15-19	3	3	2	3	4	4	4
20-24	11	12	12	14	15	15	14
25-29	21	24	25	30	34	36	36
30-34	36	41	47	49	54	56	58
35-39	55	61	66	74	82	85	85
40-44	84	93	98	108	121	127	131
45-49	129	139	144	158	173	185	193
50-54	186	202	206	221	239	252	265
55-59	305	312	315	326	353	367	373
60-64	417	457	460	497	519	538	585
Total	87	95	103	112	122	126	130

Source: Joint Medical Services (1978, p. 46, 1980, p. 60).
[a]End of year estimates.

in the average benefit per man-year (expressed in constant prices) from 1970 to 1980. It should be noted that these rates are calculated on the basis of individual benefits that are adjusted for differences in the degree of disability; that is, they are averages of benefits at the highest rate of disability. The main reason for the increase in average DSA benefits over the period 1969-1976 was the general rise in real wages. Because of the relationship between the collectively bargained wage increases and the level of social security benefits, this accounted for an average annual increase in DSA benefits of 33 percent.[15]

Another factor has been the structural increases of the minimum benefit during the seventies. This policy has had considerable influence on benefits for those carried over into the DSA program from preceding programs. Finally, the gradual substitution of beneficiaries with a low benefit by persons whose previous wage earnings, and consequently benefits awarded, were higher had some effect in the same direction. But because of the structural increase in minimum benefits, the comparison between the distribution of former wages of the DSA beneficiaries on the one hand, and of the wages of the insured population on the other, may be distorted. Yet it seems possible to draw some tentative conclusions from data provided by the Social Security Council. When the distribution of previous earnings of DSA beneficiaries admitted over the period October 1976 (the date at which the GDA program was introduced) to the end of 1977 is compared with the distribution of earnings of the insured, the shares of the lowest income class in both distributions are equal, namely 14 percent. The shares of the highest income class also are approximately equal. Only the shares of the middle income range (Dfl. 421-600) show a remarkable difference. In particular, the relative overrepresentation among beneficiaries of those with previous earnings of Dfl. 421-450 per week is remarkable. Perhaps this is partly due to the overrepresentation of the aged and to the heightening effect on their earnings of past careers. Average annual benefits decreased in 1980 due to decreasing real wages.

The GDA Program

The GDA program, which allows flat-rate disability benefits to all disabled persons between 18 and 65 years of age, regardless of their previous activity (excluding married women until January 1, 1980, when married women in paid work were included), was introduced on October 1, 1976. Table 13.10 shows the number of awards, by category, separating cases of disability already in existence at the date of introduction from new

Table 13.10. GDA Awards, 1976-80 (in thousands)

Category of Insured	Disability Cases in Existence Oct. 1, 1976[a]	1976 last quarter	1977	1978	1979	1980
DSA insured	33.5	11.5	53.6	60.3	61.0	74.3
GPPA insured[b]		1.0	8.0	13.3	14.6	19.2
Self-employed	37.4	0.4	3.3	4.8	5.5	6.1
Others financed from GDA	13.1	—	0.4	1.6	1.8	1.3
Subtotal	84.0	12.9	65.3	80.0	82.9	100.1
Early handicapped[c]	39.8	0.1	0.9	2.1	2.2	2.4
Total	123.8	13.0	66.2	82.1	85.1	103.3

Source: Social Security Council.
[a]Including those accepted only during 1977-1979.
[b]Including those insured with the military and railroad pension funds.
[c]Financed from general revenue.

cases after that date. Table 13.11 shows the number of GDA beneficiaries, by category. Although over 100,000 existing cases of disability were automatically covered by the new program, growth in the years after 1976 increased. The total number of new cases grew from 13,000 in the final quarter of 1976 to over 270,000 at the end of 1980, some of whom received a basic GDA benefit and an additional DSA benefit.

Table 13.11. Number of GDA Beneficiaries by Category of Insurance, 1976-1980 (in thousands)

Category of Insured	1976	1977	1978	1979	1980
Existing cases admitted to GDA on Oct. 1, 1976					
DSA insured	30	29	29	28	25
Self-employed	33	30	30	28	25
Others financed from GDA	11	8	9	9	8
Subtotal	74	67	68	65	59
Early handicapped[a]	38	37	37	35	35
Total existing cases	112	104	105	101	95
Disability cases admitted after introduction of GDA					
DSA insured	12	60	107	156	207
GPPA insured[b]	1	7	17	26	37
Self-employed	—	4	8	13	17
Others financed from GDA	—	—	2	3	4
Subtotal	13	71	133	197	265
Early handicapped	—	1	3	5	7
Total new cases	13	72	136	202	272
Total all cases	125	174	242	303	366

Source: Social Security Council.
[a]Financed from general revenue.
[b]Includes those insured with the military and railroad pension funds.

The GPPA and SEA Programs

On the whole, figures concerning the General Public Pension Act and the Social Employment Act that are presented in Tables 13.12 and 13.13 show the same features as those for the DSA program, that is, an overall upward trend over time of the number of beneficiaries, average degree of disability, and average real benefits, and a downward trend in numbers returning to work and in average age. There are, however, some striking differences.

First of all, the rate of flow into the GPPA program seems moderate compared to that of the DSA program, although the two figures are not fully comparable: In the DSA program an individual is entitled to a benefit after one year of sick leave, whereas in the GPPA program one is entitled to a benefit only after two to three years sick leave in most cases.

Table 13.12. Key Figures for the GPPA Program

Year	Beneficiaries at End of Year (000)	Benefits Awarded During Year (000 and %)		Benefits Awarded to Women (%)	Average Age Benefit Awarded (years)	Average Degree of Disability of New Beneficiaries (%)	Average Annual Benefit (1976 prices, Dfl. 000)
1970	15.6	3.9	0.6	34	54.9	91	20.2
1971	17.7	4.3	0.7	33	55.0	90	22.1
1972	20.5	5.3	0.8	33	55.3	94	24.1
1973	24.6	6.9	0.9	34	54.8	91	26.0
1974	28.4	7.1	1.0	33	55.1	92	27.1
1975	32.2	7.5	1.0	33	55.3	93	26.3
1976	35.6	8.0	1.0	31	55.1	92	25.5
1977	38.5	8.6	1.1	29	55.5	93	25.2
1978	42.7	9.4	1.1	31	55.2	94	

Source: General Public Pension Fund.
[a]The effect on benefits of the degree of disability has been eliminated; includes holiday allowance.

Table 13.13. Key Figures for the SEA Programs

Year	Employed at End of Year (000)	Dismissals: Return to Open Labor Market (000)	Women Employed (%)	Average Age of Employed (years)	Average Annual Benefit (1976 prices, Dfl. 000)	Employed without Medical Indication (%)
1968	34.3	3.2	15.8	42	—	11.5
1969	40.3	3.4	16.7	42	—	11.3
1970	43.8	3.2	17.5	42	—	10.7
1971	44.4	2.1	18.0	42	—	10.3
1972	46.0	1.8	18.1	41	—	11.7
1973	48.8	2.1	18.6	41	—	11.7
1974	52.2	1.3	19.2	40	16.6	12.6
1975	56.2	1.0	19.3	40	18.2	14.6
1976	61.4	1.0	19.3	39	17.9	15.5
1977	65.6	1.0	19.3	39	18.9	13.9
1978	69.3	1.0	19.2	39	19.3	13.2
1979	72.3	1.0	19.5	39	19.9	12.3
1980	75.1	0.7	19.7	39	20.4	10.5

Source: Central Bureau of Statistics and Ministry of Social Affairs.
[a]Includes holiday allowances.

Additionally, the DSA benefit can be temporary, whereas the granting of a GPPA benefit always means final loss of employment. However, even after adjustment for these legal discrepancies (see van den Bosch and Petersen, 1980), DSA inflow rates are more than 1.5 times those of the GPPA.

Presumably this disparity is due to a large extent to the different type of work in the government sector, mainly administration, for in the private administrative sector the DSA inflow rates are also low. A second reason could be expanding employment in the public sector versus decreasing employment opportunities in many parts of the private sector.

The share of women, among new beneficiaries, that has grown over time in the DSA program is stable in the GPPA program, and has increased slightly in the SEA program. On average, in the GPPA program this share surpasses the share of women in the insured population, about 26 percent, and is somewhat lower in the SEA program. In both the DSA and the SEA programs the average age has slightly declined over time, whereas the average age for the GPPA has been roughly constant over time. The average real benefit at full disability in the DSA and SEA programs differs considerably from that of the GPPA program (in 1976, a difference of Dfl. 6,500 a year). Previous earnings of beneficiaries of the GPPA program are much higher than for those in the DSA and SEA programs.

Effects of the Application of the Disability Criterion

With the introduction of the Interim Invalidity Insurance Act in 1963, the executive organization—the Social Security Bank, along with regional

Labor Boards—encountered problems. It was unable to cope with the greatly increased number of applications in 1963, in addition to a reassessment of some 80,000 cases already receiving benefits under the Invalidity Insurance Act. As the increased benefit attracted a completely different kind of applicant and a distinction had to be made between different degrees of disability, the social insurance physicians were faced with an impossible task. The work-expert, who as an agent of the accidents insurance administration had already gained experience in this field, entered the wider field of disability insurance. A department of work-expertise was set up in 1964. The need for a team of such work-experts had also arisen among the Trade Associations, charged with the administration of the Sickness Benefits Act, to assess and rehabilitate cases of long-term illness or impairment (various branches of industry had agreed, on a voluntary basis, to extend the Sickness Benefit Act term beyond one year). For this purpose, lay inspectors were employed. These functionaries, who had frequent contacts with insured and employers, were often better equipped than social insurance physicians to judge the requirements of work performed in the past or of available suitable alternative jobs.

Nevertheless assessment remained difficult in many respects. Even if a diagnosis could be made with certainty (which is doubtful in, e.g., the case of many mental complaints, lower back pains, etc.), it was still far from simple to assess its significance for incapacity to work. To what extent had the cause of the disability arisen after the insurance had commenced so that there was a legitimate basis for entitlement to benefits? To what extent was the disability attributable to disease or impairment if the latter had occurred after a change of job (even within a firm or department)? And who is the "similar" healthy person with whom the subject is to be compared? In that situation the physicians and work-experts were strongly inclined to put the subject in the highest category of incapacity. This is in particular true for the physicians, who are trained to regard people as patients who have to be helped.

These problems, caused by the joint effect of nonobjective criteria and relatively high benefit rates, were multiplied by the advent of the Disability Security Act. An extra complication was that the implementation of the new act was not entrusted to the Social Security Bank and the Councils of Labor, but to the Industrial Associations, which to that end set up a Joint Medical Service to judge cases and make recommendations. The staffing of the JMS, especially the medical component, remained a problem for years. Even though it was possible to take over staff from the Bank and the Councils, rough and ready methods had to be used to get through the overwhelming amount of cases.

In spite of early recognition—by Jacques Weyel[16] among others—of the fact that the one-year waiting period imposed by the Sickness Benefit Act had an iatrogenic effect, and that cutting the bond with the subject's own job and employer greatly reduced his chances of reintegration into employment (making early rehabilitation efforts important), the possibility of spontaneous reporting during the sickness year of cases suitable for rehabilitation efforts, the purpose of incorporating this instrument in the law, has been used only to a limited extent.

As early as 1979 the first "cooperation agreements" were made between the JMS and the Trade Associations to relieve the former of dealing with many clear-cut and routine cases (an agreement regarded by many as contrary to the exclusive statutory assignment to judge applications for benefits or provisions, given by section 22a of the Social Insurance Organization Act to the JMS). Under this agreement a large portion of the applicants (the "evidently" temporary, so-called extended Sickness Benefit Act cases, and the "evidently" terminal cases without further reassessment, rehabilitation, or other aspects requiring investigation) were left to the Trade Associations. There can be little doubt that this practice, since then several times revised and still continuing, has resulted in many permanent or provisional classifications in the highest disability category on the basis of very summary or categorical assessment. The introduction of the General Disability Act in 1976 strongly, though temporarily, increased this trend. During that year the JMS itself dealt only with about 24,000 cases out of approximately 70,000 reported during or at the end of the waiting period (i.e., the Sickness Benefit Act year). Out of these 24,000 cases, some 16,500 were medically examined and the rest dealt with on the basis of documentary evidence. Work-expertise examinations—still a JMS monopoly—occurred in approximately 8,900 cases.

A factor in the problem of work-capacity limitation confronting the JMS is that work-expert examinations may be greatly complicated by a complex institutional structure often requiring consultation with many other bodies. On the medical side, consultations are often required with general practitioners and specialists. The supply of social insurance doctors is permanently insufficient. Although capacity problems have hardly diminished in the course of time, the JMS organization has improved and its staff increased; but the rapid growth in the number of beneficiaries has caused a steady rise in the share of reexaminations and adjustments of recipients' benefits in the total workload of the JMS.

Implementation of the act has also become more complicated in a technical legal sense. The main contributing factor may have been the peculiar role of the Court of Appeal (or, in the second instance, the Central Court of Appeal), whose rulings establish precedents and thereby often have legislative effect. A relatively large portion of the decisions based on JMS recommendations have been contested in the courts (over 6,000 cases in 1975, virtually the same number as under the Sickness Benefit Act, with some 5.5 million applicants, and nearly 50 percent more than under the Unemployment Insurance Act, with some 48,000 applicants) and quite a number of them (16 percent, the same as for the Sickness Benefit Act and below the 22 percent for the Unemployment Insurance Act) have been quashed. This may have helped to establish the need for a corps of legal experts to support and guide the judgments made by the physicians.

In conclusion, we note that the DSA program is carried out by administrations controlled by trade union and employer association representatives. Since the legislation has established criteria which allow many interpretations, the philosophy of the administrations has affected implementation of the law. In wage bargaining, too, it has been found that employers' and workers' representatives do not adopt positions which permit a weighing of social and economic interests within the macroeconomic framework. Since responsibilities for the award and financing of benefits (there is a uniform DSA payroll tax for the whole country, controlled by the Ministry of Social Affairs and Employment) have been so clearly separated, and since it is usual for the members of the governing boards of the administrations to be closely involved in the assessment of cases (through the institution of a so-called "small-committee"), humanitarian reasons unavoidably came to play a substantial role in the assessment and handling of cases. It is not certain, moreover, whether the legal obligation to maintain the existing work contract for two years after commencement of sickness or impairment is strictly observed.

Expenditures on the Disability Programs

As shown in Table 13.1, the ratio of disability expenditures to gross domestic product (at market prices) has increased from 2.7 percent in 1963 to 8.2 percent in 1980. Expressed in 1976 prices, disability expenditures rose from Dfl. 3.2 billion in 1963 to Dfl. 20.6 billion in 1980, roughly six times as much, implying an average annual growth rate in constant price of 11.6 percent. These figures indicate the relative significance, fast growth, and hence the economic importance of the disability programs taken as a group.

One important cause of the tremendous rise of disability expenditures has been the spectacular growth of the number of recipients. Of the total growth in real expenditures, 540 percent over the period considered, the growth in the number of recipients was responsible for about 210 percent (see Table 13.7). Consequently, about 160 percent of the total growth of 540 percent is due to the rise of the average expenditure per beneficiary. As the costs of administration are relatively small (e.g., for the DSA program about 3 percent), the rise of the average expenditure per beneficiary must be attributed to the growth of benefits in cash or in kind.

In the period 1963-68, when the average growth of expenditure per beneficiary was the highest, Dfl. 1,200 a year (in 1976 prices), one of the obvious reasons for the increase was the introduction of the DSA program in 1967. The programs preceding the DSA offered a benefit that was independent of the former wage and substantially lower than the minimum DSA benefit. The maximum obtainable benefit (in January 1967) in the programs preceding the DSA amounted to about Dfl. 2,000 per year less in 1976 prices than the minimum obtainable benefit in the DSA program as of July 1967 (about Dfl. 32,600, nearly three times the former maximum benefit). Furthermore, the DSA benefit, up to a certain limit, is dependent on former wage earnings. Another important reason for the growth of the average expenditure per beneficiary has been the abolition of the wage limit in the SBA in 1967.

As the social security system was not essentially changed from 1967 until October 1976, the date of the introduction of the GDA program, the growth of the average real expenditure per beneficiary per year in the period 1968-78 was less than half of that in the period 1963-68, namely about Dfl. 550. It would have been even less if not for the structural increases in minimum benefit level in the DSA program, introduced in 1971 and 1972, in order to bring that level up to that of the legal minimum wage (both net of taxes). This affected the benefit level of many beneficiaries inherited from preceding programs.

The most important conclusion that can be drawn from the above is, somewhat surprisingly, that the tremendous rise in benefits in the whole period 1963-76 was caused in large part, about 43 percent, by the rise of *real benefit* per beneficiary. In the period 1963-68 this share reached a level of 64 percent. After 1968 the contribution of the growth of real benefit per beneficiary to the total real growth rate of total disability expenditures fell to about 28 percent. It follows that after 1968 the growth of real disability expenditures was caused mainly by the growth in the number of recipients.

Although relatively less important financially, in-kind provisions are granted both to reintegrate the disabled at their workplace and to improve their living conditions. In the DSA program about 75 percent of in-kind provisions are to improve living conditions, more than half of that being devoted to the improvement of mobility, indoor or outdoor. Of the provisions aimed at reintegration, about two-thirds relate to medical treatment. In the DSA program the costs of such provisions rose from Dfl. 6.6 million (in 1976 prices) in 1968 up to Dfl. 140 million in 1976. Per beneficiary these figures are respectively Dfl. 47 and Dfl. 448. Including the GDA program, the cost of in-kind provisions amounted (in 1976 prices) to Dfl. 320 million in 1980. This rapid growth is undoubtedly related to the lack of experience at the beginning of the operation of the DSA program, which offered a much wider range of provisions than the programs preceding it. From the figures given above it follows that reintegration, both at the workplace and in society, has received more attention over time. Unfortunately, little is known about the results of these increased efforts.

Apart from the real outlays mentioned, there has also been a tax reduction for the disabled (abolished in 1983). The regulation exempted a fixed amount of annual income from income tax. Consequently the net income of disabled persons used to be higher than that of people living on comparable wages. These tax expenditures can be roughly estimated at about Dfl. 300 million in 1980.

Somewhat connected with this issue is the problem that the benefits presented are on a gross basis. In order to trace the real burden of the income transfers we have to consider net amounts. The difference can be roughly put at 20-25 percent of gross disability expenditures. This would bring the share of such expenditures in the gross domestic product to roughly 6 percent in 1978.

Economic Issues Related to Disability Security and Employment Programs

There are a number of economic issues that have been raised over the past 5 to 10 years in relation to the disability security and employment programs. What factors caused the unexpectedly rapid growth in the number of beneficiaries of DSA? How much of the growth has been caused by unemployment in the guise of being "partly" disabled? What are the implications of the accepted policy to raise the legal minimum wage to an "acceptable" level (in 1971 and 1972) and keep it there by indexation, and to tie minimum social benefits (now by law) to this same level (after taxes)? To what extent can regulation compensate for the disincentives built into disability security programs? What steps can be taken towards integration of unemployment and disability security programs?

Growth of the Number of DSA Beneficiaries

Very little research has been undertaken in The Netherlands to explain the dramatic rise in expenditures, requiring a payroll tax increase from 4.2 percent in 1967 to 14.1 percent in 1980, and in the number of beneficiaries (75 percent annually between 1963 and 1980) of the DSA program and its immediate predecessors.[17] Naturally, observers of this startling phenomenon did not believe that the health situation of the working population was deteriorating at such a rate. Two main streams of thinking developed. One, supported both by economists and administrators, pointed out that, as one of the articles of the law explicitly stated, program regulations made it possible, when establishing the degree of disability, to take into account the degree to which access to the labor market had been diminished by the handicap. This, together with the deteriorating employment situation from 1972 onwards, led to the belief that program growth was related to economic fluctuations, reflected in the level of unemployment.

The other school of thought, supported by medical and legal experts both inside and outside the administration, stressed that it was impossible for medical and work-expert adjudicators to apply the disability criterion in any objective way and that they tended toward judgments in the best interests of the patient rather than in the best interests of the economy (see, e.g., Hibbeln, 1974). This line of argument does not necessarily conflict with the first one; nevertheless, economists have not been able to prove their point firmly and to incorporate such a relationship in econometric time series work. This task has been difficult because of the brevity of such series, which start after the introduction of DSA in 1967. This situation has not been improved by the widened interpretation of lack of employment opportunities at the beginning of 1973 and the introduction of GDA in 1976 (no complete statistics have been produced since). In fact, macroeconomic models, for example those developed recently by the Central Planning Bureau of the government (see den Hartog, van de Klundert, and Tjan, 1975), take the number of DSA beneficiaries as an exogenous rather than endogenous variable explaining the supply of labor.

One of the reasons why econometricians have found little evidence so far for the assumed relationship between the growth in DSA beneficiaries or awards and the general economic situation may be that this growth has been very much dominated by the weakening of legal constraints (in 1963, 1965, 1967, and 1973) on the application of the disability criterion together with the increase in 1963, 1967, and 1971/72 in the minimum benefit level. Actually, acceleration in the number of awards was apparent as early as 1964, well before the introduction of DSA (see Emanuel, 1979). Nevertheless, in recent years some studies have been published which tried, in various ways and with some success, to establish a relationship between the demand for labor and the increase in the number of disabled with a DSA benefit. It may be useful to spell out in some detail the theories and facts underlying the assumptions on which this research is based.

There is, so the argument goes, reason to believe that the impact of a declining demand for labor makes people who are threatened by (structural) unemployment seek income safety under the partial or full disguise of disability. The opportunity to do so under the conditions of the disability program increase with age, since aging is accompanied by diminishing faculties and increasing ill health. At the individual level such behavior is stimulated—irrespective of the general economic situation—by the negative relationship, presumably influencing the supply of labor, between the level of social benefits relative to that of previous earnings and the potential recipients' willingness to work (Tables 13.14 and 13.15).

Would-be GDA and (before October 1, 1976) TRM beneficiaries, however, are practically the only ones faced with considerable decline in income, due to the fixed amounts, independent of previous income, of these benefits. People who would be solely dependent on these benefits, when

Table 13.14. Gross (before Taxes) and Net (after Taxes) Replacement Rates (in percentages)

Predisability Earnings	Year	Disability Security Act		General Disability Act		General Public Pension Act	
		Gross	Net	Gross	Net	Gross	Net
Minimum legal wage[a]	1968	92	100	92	100	ca. 97	100
	1978	92					
Average of private sector[b]	1968	80	92	67	77	80	ca. 85
	1978	80					
Twice the average[c]	1968	55	85	33	41	80	ca. 85
	1978	76					
Three times the average[d]	1968	37	62	22	31	80	ca. 85
	1978	51					

Source: von Eije and Siegers (1977).

Note: Assume the disabled person is of prime working age, the head of a two-person family, and 80-100 percent disabled; all earnings and benefits are taken, including holiday allowances.

[a]1968—Dfl. 7,500 a year; 1978—Dfl. 21,800 a year.

[b]1968—Dfl. 11,000 a year; 1978—Dfl. 30,000 a year.

[c]1968—Dfl. 22,000 a year; 1978—60,000 a year.

[d]1968—Dfl. 33,000 a year; 1978—Dfl. 90,000 a year.

accepted as disabled, would be much more hesitant to apply for them than those entitled to DSA and/or GPPA benefits, unless their earnings are at or near the legal minimum wage level. This effect of GDA is mainly limited to the self-employed, as DSA and GPPA recipients also covered by this program rely on it only as a basic provision, and the early handicapped (transferred in 1976 from the TRM to the GDA program) have usually no alternative of gainful employment. Moreover, if the self-employed

Table 13.15. Net Replacement Rates (after taxes) of Disability Security, Unemployment Security, and Welfare Programs, by Level of Earnings before Taxes, July 1, 1977

Annual Gross Earnings (incl. 8% holiday allowances (000 Dfl.)	Ratio of Net Earnings to Gross	Ratio of Net Benefits[a] to Net Earnings				
				Unemployment Security Programs		
		SBA[b]	DSA	0-6 months (WW)	>6 months (WWV)	>30 months (RWW)[c]
20.6[d]	.83	.91	1.00	.99	.99	.89
28.6[e]	.75	.95	.91	.86	.82	.70
42.0[f]	.73	.88	.89	.85	.81	.49
51.3	.70	.88	.88	.85	.80	.42
100.0	.56	.58	.58	.55	.53	.27

Source: von Eije and Siegers (1977).

[a]For married men with two dependent children (entitled to tax-free child allowances of Dfl. 1.931 annually), including holiday allowances.

[b]In practice, net SBA benefits are usually supplemented to 100.

[c]Part of the General Public Assistance Program administered by the local authorities; basic benefits are equal to those of the GDA, old age benefit, widow's benefit, and the legal minimum wage, all after taxes.

[d]Equal to the minimum legal wage.

[e]People to 21 years or more; equal to average earnings in private sector.

[f]Equal to the maximum to which wages are submitted to payroll taxation.

(shopkeepers, etc.), become disabled, because of the nature of their activities and their ownership relationship they are often forced to continue using their residual working capacity.

A decline in gross income in the case of income-related benefits can vary from 0 to 20 percent. It should be noted that previous wages on which DSA (contrary to GPPA) and SBA benefits are calculated have a maximum. This means that recipients with a higher previous income than the maximum suffer a greater loss of income than indicated in the table. In the case of SBA, however, this maximum is seldom effective, as employers usually grant a supplement up to 100 percent of actual wages. Social employment workers usually have little chance to acquire a higher income in private industry. Their financial incentive to enter the open labor market can therefore be safely estimated to be zero in most cases. Minimum-wage workers experience little if any decrease in income when they become social security benefit recipients, as the net minimum benefit (for married workers) is equal to the net minimum wage.

Information on replacement rates, both gross and net of taxes, for different income levels is provided in Table 13.14. In the case of DSA beneficiaries, replacement rates only drop considerably with increasing income from a certain (relatively high) income level onwards (that at which the benefit reaches its maximum). At these income levels people may often have supplementary private insurance. GPPA benefits do not show this relative decline. Those depending on GDA benefits experience decline over nearly the full income range. Not only the high and, over time, increasing replacement rates of the major disability security programs are relevant in this context, however. The replacement rates shown up by employment security and welfare programs should also be taken into account, as is demonstrated for 1977 in Table 13.15.

Disability benefits for wage earners, net of taxes, have long been somewhat better than unemployment benefits in the early months. (Only recently were the tax schedules changed to eliminate this). Moreover, the latter drops after 6 months (from 80 percent to 75 percent of previous wages) when another program, financed from general revenue and administered by the local authorities, takes over the role of the Unemployment Insurance, financed by payroll taxes. Unemployment benefits drop again, this time drastically relative to the previous wage, net of taxes, when after another 2 years (and also from the age of 60 to 65) they are set at the level of the net legal minimum wage, regardless of previous earnings, and become means tested as a part of the General Public Assistance, administered by the local authorities. DSA benefits, on the other hand, remain at the same relative level (all benefits are wage indexed) until the age of 65 and are earnings tested only. Only those with earnings at or only slightly above the minimum wage have disability and unemployment benefits which are and remain roughly equal, a category to which 14 percent of the insured population belongs. For the others, to become disabled is financially more attractive in the longer run than to become unemployed. Also, the social stigma attached to unemployment of long duration is usually much more unfavorable than that attached to a lifelong disability status.

There are therefore enough reasons to assume that the threat of unemployment from a deteriorating of the economic situation in the firm in which one works will cause wage earners to seek protection under the guise of ill health and disability.

Hidden Unemployment among the Disabled

In his paper, Hilverink (1978) tried to explain the development of the number of new DSA beneficiaries by the annual relative changes in the employment situation—that is, in the demand for labor—and the relative level of unemployment security beneficiaries (covering the first 6 months of unemployment only), which indicates the imbalance between supply and demand for labor. He studied the period between 1968 and 1974 for both the whole private sector and for Trade Associations. The unemployment variable was introduced with a lag of one year to account for the year of SBA benefits which precedes the award of a DSA benefit; the author thus assumed simultaneity between the unemployment situation and the onset of disability. Using a simple regression analysis, his results were rather modest in terms of correlation and significance of coefficients.

A second attempt in the same direction was undertaken by Bax, de Boer, and Sterrenburg (1979). They found that in cases of near 100 percent identity of those working in a statistically defined sector of industry and those insured with a Trade Association (textile industry, ready-made tailoring, the painting and building trades) there was a strong correlation between the number employed according to official statistics and the aggregated wages of those insured deflated by the average daily wage. They used the latter statistic for each of the 26 Trade Associations as a proxy for the demand for labor in a simple linear regression analysis. As a variable to be explained, the authors used the number of days for which a DSA benefit was paid (divided by 261, the normal annual number of working days for an employed person; this therefore equals the number of man-years of DSA beneficiaries), weighted for degree of disability. A constant trend term (with zero average) was added as an explanatory variable to account for trend movements in the other two variables. The hypothesis of a negative relationship between the number of weighted benefit days and deflated aggregated wages, *when the latter contracted*, was thus tested over the time period 1969-75 (eliminating the disturbances which occurred during the introductory years of the DSA program, 1967 and 1968).

It was found that the expected relationship under the condition of diminishing real total wages did exist to a significant degree only for a number of Trade Associations dealing with manufacturing industries and the mercantile marine (see Table 13.16). In two cases a positive relationship showed up, although the condition of a contracting demand for labor did not exist: under conditions of increasing employment, this happened in the Trade Associations of the retail trades and the crafts, and in one Trade Association catering to a mixed bag of those insured in public service. For Trade Associations of the very capital-intensive chemical industry and of the small tobacco industry, as well as of the important services of banking insurance, wholesale trade, and the liberal professions, the relation was negative under conditions of increasing employment. For 12 Trade Associations, including such manufacturing industries as food and beverages, dairy products, electrotechnical and metal appliances, and readymade

Table 13.16. Trade Associations with a Significant Negative Relationship between Employment (Aggregated Insured Wages) and Number of Days DSA Benefits Were Paid (Weighted for Degree of Disability), 1969-1975

	Regression Coefficient of Aggregated Real Wages Insured		Regression Coefficient of Trend Term	
Trade Association	Size	Standard Deviation	Size	Standard Deviation
Under condition of decreasing employment				
Textile industry	−4.34	0.73	31.85	29.05
Steel industry	−3.01	0.93	494.64	15.35
Mining	−2.26	0.64	110.09	23.75
Leather and leather fabrics	−2.14	0.90	17.72	13.40
Printing industry	−1.31	0.24	127.00	2.39
Building trade	−1.04	0.41	130.00	24.45
Timber processing and furniture	−0.82	0.11	156.43	1.00
Stone, brick, and glass manufacturing, ceramic industry	−0.80	0.16	138.47	1.68
Mercantile marine	−0.18	0.07	26.67	1.49
Under condition of increasing employment				
Chemical industry	−2.51	0.63	202.00	2.58
Banking, insurance, wholesale trade, and liberal professions	−2.29	0.95	1201.62	160.72
Tobacco industry	−0.68	0.23	32.48	0.42
Retailing and crafts	4.28	0.86	504.95	12.14
Public services	0.82	0.18	443.82	16.02

Source: Bax, de Boer, and Sterrenburg (1979).

[a]Mainly those in social employment, those being retrained in government to run centers for professional schooling while retaining an unemployment benefit, and those in temporary public service.

clothing, but also including agriculture and fisheries, transportation, bakers, butchers, the hotel and catering industry, and hospital and social services, no significant relationship between the two main variables could be found. Finally, no cases were found with decreasing demand for labor (aggregated deflated wages) and decreasing (weighted) number of days over which DSA benefits were paid.

The condition of decreasing employment added by the authors stems from their assumption that the relationship is not reversible in the short run. This may not be true for sectors like the capital-intensive chemical industry and banking and insurance, which can afford to pay high wages or to provide attractive secondary working conditions if business conditions create a strong demand for labor. Generally, though, the results of the exercise tend to show that the negative relationship exists for that part of the private sector which is vulnerable to domestic and international adverse cyclical or structural (competitive) movements in demand. This may explain why agricultural products and food and beverages—for which domestic demand is rather stable in growth and in which The Netherlands has a strong position on the international market—do not follow this pattern. Electrotechnical and metal products and retailing and crafts are the major exceptions.

Another recent attempt to establish and even estimate the size of hidden unemployment among DSA beneficiaries was undertaken by van den Bosch and Petersen (1983a). Their thinking is analogous to the main result quoted from the study by Bax, de Boer, and Sterrenburg (1979). There it appeared that the expected negative relationship between the level of disability incidence and the development of employment could be demonstrated only for a large part of the manufacturing industry and the building trade, that is, that part of the economy which is vulnerable to cyclical and structural movements in demands of international and domestic origin. Van den Bosch and Petersen compare disability benefit data for the DSA and GPPA programs, that is, data for the private and public sector. They assume that the growth in the number of GPPA disability beneficiaries—after correction for changes in the (growing) number of insured—only reflects the development in psychomedical causes and in general ideas about ill health, and that these developments affect the number of DSA beneficiaries in the same way.

If this is true, the difference between DSA and GPPA incidence figures —corrected for difference in age, sex, and crude socioeconomic class composition (type of work), and after a 20 percent upward adjustment, the GPPA data to account for the fact that GPPA benefits are not awarded automatically after one year of sick leave—may be fully attributed to economic causes. In this way it is estimated that hidden unemployment among DSA beneficiaries amounted to 141,000 in 1978, or 34 percent of their total number, which, added to officially registered unemployment, would bring the unemployment rate from 5.2 percent to 8.8 percent.

Although these estimates are partly based on rather strong assumptions and crude adjustments, they were the first attempt to produce a figure for the phenomenon of hidden unemployment, or the component of unemployment within the DSA program. Their macroeconomic analysis was supported by analysis at a more specific level in van den Bosch and Petersen (1983b). And their results were roughly corroborated by Leo Aarts (1984), using much more sophisticated survey data.

Social Benefits and Minimum Wage: Economic Implications

Pivotal in the Dutch social security and welfare system is the level chosen for the legal minimum wage and the way social security and welfare benefits are linked to it. As mentioned, labor market legislation includes a compulsory legal minimum wage, which is relatively high compared to other countries. It was introduced in 1968, but since 1964 a minimum wage had been established by agreement between the government and social partners within the context of a postwar belief in a more or less stringent public wage policy. Its level is changed regularly (in recent years, twice a year, on January 1 and July 1) in accordance with the development of the Index of Collectively Bargained Wage Agreements (published monthly by the Central Bureau of Statistics), lagged 6 months. As of January 1, 1980 the legal minimum wage was Dfl. 1,826.50 a month for all adults aged 23 or over (excluding the holiday allowance of 7.5 percent of the annual wage). For those who are younger,[18] this amount is reduced by Dfl. 137 for each year younger; 16-year-olds are entitled to a minimum of Dfl. 867.50 a month (Dfl. 520.56 if working 3 days a week and being trained for 2 days under a part-time training program, which, with some exceptions, is compulsory at that age). In addition, a holiday allowance must be paid each year, consisting of 8 percent of the indexed wage over the preceding 12 months. In certain cases it is possible to obtain dispensation from the legal minimum wage if the economic circumstances of the trade demand it, for example, for small shopkeepers employing young people part time, or in individual cases of poor health. Those socially employed also are entitled to earn at least the legal minimum wage.

The legal minimum wage was put at a level which was considered to be a "social minimum." Although some empirical studies were undertaken over the years to try to establish a minimum household budget (which then could be interpreted in a normative way), the foundations of the concept remained arbitrary, and in fact the level was raised in 1973 and 1974 (above indexation). Nevertheless, it was widely accepted and is now firmly embedded in social policy thinking and legislation. Apparently the belief that income differences contain an institutional component which cannot be justified as the natural outcome of the market mechanism and is amenable to social engineering has—within rather broad limits—been stronger or more widespread than the fear that such legal tinkering with wage levels at the bottom may push wage costs of the unskilled and inexperienced well above the marginal productivity of their labor, and therefore have an adverse effect on the demand for such labor. This belief has remained firm since, notwithstanding the fact that unemployment among the young (usually those with little skill and experience) has increased in recent recessionary years much more rapidly, in relative terms, than among those 25 years or older. This is also more true for women (who usually have a weak labor market position) than for men.

The concept of a social minimum also led to the policy of ensuring that income replacing social benefits, after taxes, should at least be equal to the legal minimum wage, also after taxes. This has in fact been realized since January 1973 for the old age and survivor benefits and since July 1974 for the (means-tested) general public assistance benefits and the (earnings-tested) unemployment and disability benefits. Equality has been realized for married people (or those considered to be in a similar position of need, e.g., in the unemployment security programs those unmarried and aged 35 years or older).

This policy has led to a number of technical problems. First, it is the gross legal minimum wage before taxes which is indexed. As the minimum wage and the different social benefits did not carry the same (payroll) tax burden, the effect of lowering taxes on wages may, through the linkage net of taxes, induce an increase in minimum social benefits (both before and after taxes). Also, social benefits are indexed on a before tax basis. This means that to maintain the linkage for minimum benefits, a special calculation has to be done each time. For a number of years the government tried to maintain the linkage by ad hoc measures. New legislation, effective 1980, equalized the tax burdens on the different benefits and the minimum wage by levying of a special tax on social benefits for new beneficiaries. This eliminated direct interaction between changes in the levels of the minimum wage and the different social benefits, including disability benefits, caused by changes in tax levels.

Given the level of the legal minimum wage, its indexation to general wages, and its linkage with flat and minimum social benefits, the adequacy of minimum social benefits can hardly be contested: they are the highest (minima) in the world. Only child allowances in countries like France and Belgium are somewhat higher. In fact the minima are such that any income incentive to go back to work is taken away for a fairly large, lower-income segment of the population of working age. To take an example: in 1977, of both the working population and those receiving a DSA benefit, 14 percent received the net social minimum. With structural increases in the legal minimum wage during the 1970s, this percentage has slowly but steadily been increasing. This disincentive has probably been increased by the widespread possibility of obtaining work illegally (and untaxed) while receiving benefits. This of course is not restricted to those obtaining the minimum benefit.

Direct Regulation

In Dutch political discussions, policy proposals, and measures for policy change, much emphasis is put on direct regulation as the primary means of controlling the growth of disability benefit programs. In general the level of minimum or flat-rate social benefits, net of taxes, relative to the legal minimum wage, again net of taxes, has so far been considered to be politically untouchable and has been embraced by all coalition governments in the past decade.

Direct regulation can take many forms: (1) preventive and rehabilitative policy measures directed against factors assumed to be causal for the conditions entitling people to benefits; (2) (re)training and (re)schooling, preventive medical care, rehabilitation, special labor market intervention for the disabled, etc.; (3) policy measures to restrict uses of disability programs for purposes unintended but made possible by the wording of the law; (4) policy measures to detect and punish cases of fraud; (5) improvements in programs aimed at faster detection of conditions containing disabling factors or at opportunities for reintegrating the disabled into society and work.

Although the importance of the regulatory approach is apparent, it has severe limitations and drawbacks:

1. To make a real dent, direct regulation needs to be substantial and therefore will be costly; if the aim is to diminish the burden on society of disability benefits, a lot of imaginative and good, as yet unavailable, cost-benefit studies are needed to induce policymakers to accept expenditure and program changes.
2. Very often measures of direct control imply coordination between executives of different programs and/or changes in the distribution of responsibilities between them, which are difficult to obtain.
3. In addition, large-scale measures of direct intervention may easily bring about increased bureaucracy, arbitrariness in decisions, and red tape, which diminish the effectiveness of the efforts and increase frustration, irritation, and resistance with the public.
4. The effectiveness of direct regulation will be limited if labor market conditions are unfavorable, and, moreover, effectiveness is not always easy to demonstrate.
5. Finally, with replacement ratios remaining as high as they are in The

Netherlands, the effectiveness of reintegration efforts by direct regulation may be limited by the lack of sufficient economic incentives.

Notwithstanding these limitations, direct regulation has been an important issue in recent Dutch policy debate with regard to the control of income transfer expenditures since 1976. This arose because of the political constraints on changing the benefit levels. In the area of disability programs, measures of direct control that were discussed, proposed, or introduced concerned improving quota legislation, increasing and improving labor market services for the disabled, general activities to reintegrate them in the labor force, early reporting of those disabled having possibilities for reintegration and improving facilities for retraining the disabled.

Moving toward Integration of Programs

One other issue to be mentioned plays an important role in the Dutch public debate. A proposal by the trade unions to integrate the unemployment security programs and the disability security programs for the private sector into one single program has been the subject of a government study. The reasoning behind this proposal has been that those becoming unemployed before the age of 57.5 years eventually (when they become Public Assistance beneficiaries) undergo a substantial decline in income (unless their previous earnings were at the legal minimum wage level or only slightly above that level), whereas those who become disabled remain at a level net of taxes of 80-100 percent of their previous earnings. In practice many disabled can be considered as partly unemployed. The proposal is to make benefits for both groups equal. Administratively, the proposal may also be attractive. The government has decided to start tackling this problem by a study of the feasibility of integrating the different unemployment security programs.

Notes

1. Excluding an average of about 300,000 persons on sick leave for less than one year.
2. This yardstick is used since it figures in the OECD publication we used as a reference.
3. Programs cover assistance in kind to the disabled (wheelchairs, adapted cars, professional retraining, etc.); age limits do not exist for the employed.
4. Until January 1, 1980, the self-employed were not insured for child allowances with regard to the first and second child. The publicly employed had their own scheme.
5. Up to a rather high maximum, as of October 1, 1982, of Dfl. 253.00 per working day; indexed twice a year to the average of collectively bargained wages.
6. For variation according to marital status, earnings of spouse, and degree of disability, see the section on disability among the privately employed.

7. But the old age programs distinguishes between a high benefit for a married couple and a low one for single people; the GDA program relates the benefit level to marital status and to the contribution of the partner in earnings.

8. Young people can only work at age 15. However, between the ages of 15 and 18 part-time participation in daytime educational programs is obligatory. Most people within this age group fulfill this obligation.

9. One percent of wages is the maximum which can be withheld from the wage earner where benefits are kept to the legally prescribed minimum level of 80 percent.

10. The exemption was introduced after 1976 to take into account the fact that, henceforth, DSA-insured individuals would get a GDA benefit if they became disabled and profit only modestly from the supplementary DSA benefit. If eventually all DSA beneficiaries get a GDA benefit, the exemption will be set at the income level (minimum wage) at which the supplementary DSA benefit would become zero. As this situation will only be reached when payments to all who became disabled before the GDA came into existence are terminated, the exemption will gradually rise from zero to the level mentioned over a fairly long period of time.

11. This is the category of early handicapped, for which costs to GDA for benefits, in-kind provisions, and administration are charged to the government. It also includes individuals with no previous gainful employment who were still in school.

12. Until January 1, 1980, it excluded gainfully employed married women, and those living on other income (like capital income, old age pension, survivor's pension) or working without compensation in the household or private enterprise of a relative. Those accepted under the first title for DSA benefit have continued to receive a DSA benefit since January 1, 1980.

13. Before October 1, 1976, provided by the DSA for those insured under that law.

14. This section relies heavily on Haveman (1977); see also Haveman (1978, pp. 241-275).

15. For the years since 1976, this includes GDA benefits to DSA beneficiaries.

16. Professor of social psychiatry at the University of Amsterdam and head of the Scientific Bureau of the JMS before his death in 1977.

17. As shown in Table 13.7, the growth rate of the number of beneficiaries has been even steeper for the GPPA program (the part dealing with the disabled), which covers civil servants.

18. The legal minimum wages for this category were introduced in 1974.

References

Aarts, Leo. 1984. Work-capacity of the disabled. In Han Emanuel, Eric H. de Gier, and Peter A. B. Kalber Konijn, eds., *Disability benefits: Factors determining applications and awards.* Greenwich, Conn.: JAI Press.

Bax, E. H., de Boer, T. W., and Sterrenburg, K. 1979. Arbeidsmarkt en arbeidsongeschiktheid: De toesting van een hypothese (Labor market and disability: The testing of a hypothesis). *Economisch-Statistische Berichten, 64,* no. 3208, 580-586.

Central Bureau of Statistics. 1974-76. *Gehandicapten welgeteld 1971/1972* (Counting the physically handicapped). 3 vols. The Hague.

Central Bureau of Statistics. 1975. *Statistical yearbook of the Netherlands.* The Hague.

Central Planning Bureau. 1979. *Central economic plan 1979.* March.

den Hartog, H., van de Klundert, T. C. M. J., and Tjan, H. S. 1975. De structurele ontwikkeling von de werkgelegenheid in macroeconomisch perspectief (The structural development of the demand for labor in macroeconomic perspective). In *Werkloosheid: aard, omvang, structurele oorzaken en beleidsad viezen* (Unemployment: character, size, structural causes and policy recommendations). Recommendations to the Vereniging voor Staathuishoudkunde (Association for Political Economy). Leiden and Antwerp: H. E. Stenfert Kroese.

Emanuel, Han. 1979. Achtergronden van het Arbeidsongeschiktheidsverschijnsel in Nederland (Factors behind the disability phenomenon in the Netherlands). In J. J. Klant, W. Driehuis, H. J. Bierens, and A. J. Butler, eds., *Samenleving en onderzoek* (Society and research). Foundation of Economic Research of the University of Amsterdam. Leiden/Antwerp: H.E. Stenfert Kroese.

Halberstadt, Victor; Haveman, Robert H.; Wolfe, Barbara L.; and Goudswaard, Kees P. 1981. *The economics of disability policy in selected European Community countries: A preliminary study and a proposal for further research.* Center for Research in Public Economics, Report 81.20. Leiden.

Haveman, R. H. 1977. *A benefit-cost and policy analysis of the Netherlands' Social Employment Program.* University of Leyden. March.

Haveman, R. H. 1978. The Dutch Social Employment Program. In John L. Palmer, ed., *Creating jobs: Public employment programs and wage subsidies.* Washington, D.C.: The Brookings Institution.

Hibbeln, J. G. 1974. De W.A.O. een misstap? (DSA, a false step?). In A. T. E. Kastein, ed., *Balans en Perspectief* (Balance and perspective). JMS: Amsterdam.

Hilverink, H.G. 1978. Arbeidsongeschikt of arbeid ongeschikt? (Unsuitable to work or work unsuitable?) Rpt. in F. A. J. van den Bosch and C. Petersen, eds., *Arbeidsongeschiktheid: Een multidisciplinaire benadering* (Disability: A multidisciplinary approach). Kluwer: Deventer, 1981.

Joint Medical Services. 1978, 1980. *Annual report.* JMS: Amsterdam.

Kastein, A. T. E., ed. *Balans en Perspectief* (Balance and perspective). JMS: Amsterdam.

Lamers, Leo. 1978. Volumebeleid in de sociale zekerheid (Policies to restrain growth in real terms of social security expenditure), No. 1. *Openbare Uitgaven.* Kluwer Deventer.

OECD. 1979. *Public expenditure on income maintenance programmes.* Studies in Resource Allocation, no. 3. Paris. July.

van den Bosch, Frans A. J., and Petersen, Carel. 1983a. Disability as an economic phenomenon: A first approach to estimating hidden unemployment among disability beneficiaries. In L. Söderström, ed., *Social insurance.* Amsterdam: North-Holland.

van den Bosch, Frans, A. J., and Petersen, Carel. 1983b. An explanation of the growth of social security disability transfers. *De Economist,* vol. 113:1.

von Eije, J. H., and Siegers, J. J. 1977. De invloed van de sociale zekerheid op de relatieve inkomens-verschillen tussen actieve en inactiere werknemers (The influence of social security on relative income differences between active and nonactive wage-earners). *Economische-Statistische Berichten, 62,* no. 3133, 1221-1224.

Chapter 14

Disability Policy in Sweden

Eskil Wadensjö

This chapter deals with Swedish disability policy toward those of working age. The first section describes the number, demographic composition, economic circumstances, and labor market situation of the disabled in Sweden. Our information is taken from a work-up of the Living Conditions Survey for 1978, conducted by the Central Bureau of Statistics. Unfortunately, we lack longer time series concerning the number of disabled in Sweden, since the census listed the number of disabled only on two occasions between the First and Second World Wars.

The second section surveys Swedish disability policy, focusing on the two dominant programs: pensioning, and employment programs. Disability pensioning per se consists of many different programs, but since decisions are made simultaneously or follow directly from one another, the pensioning system must be described in its entirety. The labor market programs are also viewed as an integral system. Other aspects covered are employment injury insurance (workers' compensation) and labor market legislation that concerns the disabled. Certain disability programs—institutional care, medical rehabilitation, and domestic help for the disabled—are excluded from our discussion.

The third section deals with several economic aspects of disability policy:

Eskil Wadensjö is Professor of Labor Economics, Swedish Institute for Social Research, University of Stockholm. Among those who read earlier versions of this study are Bengt Jönsson, Agneta Kruse, and Ann-Charlotte Ståhlberg, of the Department on Economics, University of Lund; Robert Erikson and Walter Korpi of the Swedish Institute for Social Research, University of Stockholm; Lars Ettarp, Swedish Ministry of Labor, Stockholm; Helen Ginsburg, Brooklyn College, City University of New York; Jack Habib, Brookdale Institute, Jerusalem; and Robert Haveman, Department of Economics, University of Wisconsin. I am very grateful for their comments, which have made it possible to improve the study in several respects. The remaining errors are my own. The computations that appear in the first and third sections were made possible by a grant from the Expert Group for Labor Market Research at the Swedish Ministry of Labor.

the rapid increase in costs, effects of the programs on labor supply, policy effectiveness in placing people on the open labor market, program efficiency in terms of cost-benefit analyses, and the effects of the policy on income distribution. This section utilizes the few studies of Swedish disability policy which exist. Its intent is not so much to give a complete account of the effects of Swedish disability policy as to indicate important directions for future research.

In Sweden, disability policy has not been subject to intense controversy. The great expansion of disability programs has been accompanied by only limited discussion. In the last section we take up some of the issues that have been the subject of debate: employment versus income support, whether or not disability policy disguises unemployment figures, and measures to adapt facilities to the special needs of the disabled.

The Disabled in Sweden

In order to judge a country's disability policy, it is obviously necessary first to determine the number and categories of the disabled. That task is extremely difficult, for both conceptual and statistical reasons. We will first discuss the basic problems, and then offer some statistics.

The Concept of Disability

A fundamental problem in discussing disability is that two different concepts exist, and they are not always differentiated. The first defines disability as impairment of some function (physical or mental) through injury, deterioration, or illness. The second defines it as the reduced ability to carry out fully one's job or, more often, a reduced ability to manage work within the particular occupational area where the person is or has been employed.

These two approaches naturally produce different results. Impairment causing insurmountable handicaps in one occupation does not necessarily imply any disability at all in another occupation. Impairment that creates a work disability for a construction worker (for example, different types of back injuries) is not necessarily a disability for someone employed in chemical works, while something that causes a work disability for a person employed in chemical works (for example, an allergy) does not always constitute a handicap for a construction worker. It is possible to have severely limited mobility without having reduced working capacity. In fact, statistics from the national Living Conditions Survey for 1978 show that a majority of those with reduced working capacity do not have reduced mobility. Reduced working capacity is of course in some cases a result of other types of functional limitation (e.g., loss of sight or hearing), but in many cases it has no such relationship, being caused instead, for instance, by mental disorders or problems with drugs and alcohol. Naturally, there are certain types of impairments which create work disability in all occupations. There are also certain occupations in which almost any impairment creates work disability—for example, an Air Force pilot.

Besides the need to differentiate disability concepts, other critical points exist. One is the time dimension. A person with a temporary impairment (say a broken leg from a skiing accident) is not usually considered "disabled." A certain longevity of impairment is required for one to be thought of as disabled. In many cases, it is not known if a particular injury or illness will lead to a permanent impairment or not. In field surveys there are always many people for whom it is uncertain whether injury or illness will lead to permanent damage.

Disability is even more uncertain if its definition is based on work disability. In addition to medical rehabilitation, there can be occupational rehabilitation—changing conditions at the place of employment (for example, altering it for wheelchairs), or retraining for another occupation—which will permit a person to return to work without being disabled. This makes the time dimension important, and it becomes more important when employment programs are offered to the disabled. This means that today's statistics concerning the number of disabled people ought to be supplemented with information about the flow to, and especially from, the stock of disabled; and it is also important to distinguish between the different flows *from* (rehabilitation, death).

Another problem is how to treat that reduced working capacity which comes with age. As one gets older, one's capacity declines in various ways, and at different rates for different functions. A current tendency is to view aging as a symptom of disease and (incorrectly) to treat it medically. Impairment as a result of aging occurs at different rates in different ways: for those in some occupations, a decline in work capacity occurs at a relatively young age; in others, the decline starts relatively late; and in all cases the decline can vary in speed. We do not count teenagers, who generally have a lower working capacity than adults, as disabled. One should therefore be cautious when interpreting the very high percentage of people with impairments and disability in the oldest age groups.

Size and Characteristics of the Disabled Population

It is desirable to have a long time series on the number of disabled that can be compared with the development of disability policy. Unfortunately, no satisfactory series exist for Sweden. The statistical series which cover longer periods of time are various administrative ones containing information about number of disability pension cases, number who have received help in various ways, and number of those seeking rehabilitation at public employment offices. This information is not applicable in the present context, because it indicates chiefly how disability policy has developed, rather than how the number of disabled has changed.

The existing alternatives are two groups of larger field surveys: the Level of Living Investigations of 1968 and 1974, and the Living Conditions Survey, conducted annually by the Central Bureau of Statistics since 1974. Only two censuses asked questions about occupational disability. The 1930 census listed 69,000 persons aged 15-67 with no working capacity and 39,000 with partially reduced working capacity. The partial census of 1936 indicated that 102,000 people aged 16-66 lacked working capacity and 209,000 had a partially reduced working capacity. The most likely explanation for these increases between 1930 and 1936 is the rise in unemployment. In both censuses vague definitions of disability were used (see SOU, 1946), and later censuses have not included any questions about disability.

The 1968 and 1974 Level of Living Investigations are the most thorough and comprehensive in this area, containing a variety of data about different types of ailments and illnesses, but they lack an all-inclusive criterion for handicap or work disability, instead simply listing problems of mobility, eyesight, hearing, etc. That leaves us with the Living Conditions Survey, which started in 1974 with approximately 6,000 subjects. Since 1975, about 12,000 interviews have been conducted annually.

Questions in the survey include, "Do you have any long-standing illness, ailment caused by an accident, handicap or other weakness?" and "Do you regularly take medication for anything (else)?" Anyone who answers positively to at least one of these questions is considered to have a long-standing illness, and is asked detailed questions in order to determine the type and the degree of severity of the problem. Included is "Do/does the illness(es) you have cause a reduction in your working capacity?" answered by "(a) to a large extent, (b) somewhat, or (c) not at all." This method does not guarantee that all cases of long-standing illness and reduced working capacity are reported. Mental disorders are probably underestimated in comparison with other causes of reduced working capacity.

I shall report here some of the findings from the 1978 survey, given in most of the following tables in relative numbers, to facilitate comparison with results from other countries.

The percentage of people with long-standing illnesses is higher in the older than in the younger age groups: in the group aged 55-64, it was near 60 percent in 1978, while the corresponding figure for those in the 16-19 age group was just below 15 percent. Women have a higher frequency of long-standing illness than men: in 1978, 31.7 percent of all persons aged 16-64 had a long-standing illness; for women, the percentage was 32.7, for men, 30.8. The difference between women and men was most pronounced in the oldest age groups.

As defined in the Living Conditions Survey, "long-standing illness" is a very broad concept. In 1978, 45 percent of those so classified nevertheless considered themselves in good health. We therefore need a more restrictive definition: one possibility is to employ a definition of disability that is based on whether working capacity is reduced among those with long-standing illness. According to this measure (illness plus reduced work capacity), 18.7 percent of the population was disabled in 1978—7.9 percent with severely reduced working capacity, and 9.8 percent with reduced working capacity. Tables 14.1 - 14.3 describe the survey results for that year in terms of population characteristics and working capacity.[1]

Table 14.1. Characteristics of the Disabled and the Nondisabled Working-Age Population (16-64 years), 1978 (numbers in thousands)

Characteristic	Total (1)	Severely Reduced Working Capacity (2)	Reduced Working Capacity (not severely) (3)	Reduced Working Capacity (4)=(2)+(3)	No Reduced Working Capacity (5)
Total working-age population	5,158	406	505	911	4,225
Sex					
Men	2,595	198	229	427	2,157
Women	2,563	208	276	484	2,068
Nationality					
Swedish citizens	4,888	386	475	861	4,009
Danish, Norwegian, Icelandic	33	1	4	5	27
Finnish	116	9	12	21	95
Southern European	36	5	6	11	24
Other non-Swedish	51	3	5	8	43
Age					
16-19	433	5	24	29	403
20-34	1,772	40	110	150	1,615
35-44	1,033	54	105	159	869
45-54	918	92	113	205	708
55-64	1,004	216	153	369	630
Marital Status					
Single	1,694	157	142	299	1,386
Married	2,881	221	315	536	2,334
Cohabiting	583	28	47	75	506
Education					
9 years or less	2,344	269	291	560	1,773
High school	1,965	117	173	290	1,671
University	840	20	39	59	776
Residence					
Stockholm	957	76	79	155	795
Gothenburg and Malmö	758	55	69	124	631
Major towns	1,654	125	163	288	1,360
Southern areas	1,081	79	111	190	887
Northern population centers	385	35	39	74	309
Northern sparsely populated areas	324	36	43	79	244

Source: Computations from the Living Conditions Survey of 1978, made for this study by the Swedish Central Bureau of Statistics.

Note: The difference between the total and the sum of different subgroups is due to lack of answers for different questions.

Table 14.2. Percentage Distribution of Population Characteristics, by Working Capacity, 1978

Characteristic	Severely Reduced Working Capacity	Reduced Working Capacity (not severely)	Reduced Working Capacity (Cols. 1 & 2)	No Reduced Working Capacity
Sex				
Men	48.8	45.3	46.9	51.1
Women	51.2	54.7	53.1	48.9
Nationality				
Swedish citizens	95.5	94.6	95.0	95.5
Danish, Norwegian, Icelandic	0.2	0.8	0.6	0.6
Finnish	2.2	2.4	2.3	2.3
Southern European	1.2	1.2	1.2	0.6
Other non-Swedish	0.7	1.0	0.9	1.0
Age				
16-19	1.2	4.8	3.2	9.5
20-34	9.8	21.8	16.4	38.2
35-44	13.3	20.8	17.4	20.6
45-54	22.6	22.4	22.5	16.8
55-64	53.1	30.3	40.5	14.9
Marital Status				
Single	38.7	28.2	32.9	32.8
Married	54.4	62.5	58.9	55.2
Cohabiting	6.9	9.3	8.2	12.0
Education				
9 years or less	66.3	57.9	61.6	42.0
High school	28.8	34.4	31.9	39.6
University	4.9	7.8	6.5	18.4
Residence				
Stockholm	18.7	15.7	17.0	18.8
Gothenburg and Malmö	13.5	13.7	13.6	14.9
Major towns	30.8	32.3	31.6	32.2
Southern areas	19.5	22.0	20.9	21.0
Northern population centers	8.6	7.7	8.1	7.3
Northern sparsely populated areas	8.9	8.5	8.7	5.8

Source: See Table 14.1.
Note: Population includes all of working age, 16-64 years. Missing answers are deleted before the calculation of percentages.

Table 14.3. Percentage Distribution of Population's Working Capacity, by Characteristics, 1978

Characteristic	Severely Reduced Working Capacity	Reduced Working Capacity (not severely)	Reduced Working Capacity (Cols. 1 & 2)	No Reduced Working Capacity
Total working-age population	7.9	9.8	17.7	82.3
Sex				
Men	7.7	8.9	16.5	83.5
Women	8.2	10.8	19.0	81.0
Nationality				
Swedish citizens	7.9	9.8	17.7	82.3
Danish, Norwegian, Icelandic	3.1	12.5	15.6	84.4
Finnish	7.8	10.3	18.1	81.9
Southern European	14.3	17.1	31.4	68.6
Other non-Swedish	5.9	9.8	15.7	84.3
Age				
16-19	1.2	5.6	6.7	93.3
20-34	2.3	6.2	8.5	91.5
35-44	5.3	10.2	15.5	84.5
45-54	10.1	12.4	22.5	77.5
55-64	21.6	15.3	36.9	63.1
Marital Status				
Single	9.3	8.4	17.7	82.3
Married	7.7	11.0	18.7	81.3
Cohabiting	4.8	8.1	12.9	87.1
Education				
9 years or less	11.5	12.5	24.0	76.0
High school	6.0	8.8	14.8	85.2
University	2.4	4.7	7.1	92.9
Residence				
Stockholm	8.0	8.3	16.3	83.7
Gothenburg and Malmö	7.3	9.1	16.4	83.6
Major towns	7.6	9.9	17.5	82.5
Southern areas	7.3	10.3	17.6	82.4
Northern population centers	9.1	10.2	19.3	80.7
Northern sparsely populated areas	11.1	13.3	24.5	75.5

Source: See Table 14.1.
Note: Missing answers are deleted before the calculations of percentages.

When comparing this definition of disability with the concept "long-standing illness," one important difference can be noted: men in the oldest age group have a somewhat higher frequency of severely reduced working capacity than women. This difference may be attributed to the fact that men have had a longer working life than women, especially among the older age groups.

A greater share of the older than of the younger age groups have a reduced working capacity. Of youths 16-19 years old, 93.3 percent did not report any reduced working capacity in 1978, as opposed to 63.1 percent of those aged 55-64 years. The percentage with severely reduced working capacity increases much more strongly with age than the percentage with not severely reduced working capacity.

Foreign citizens have about the same frequency of disability as Swedish citizens. The frequency varies, however, among the different groups of foreigners. According to the survey, 82.3 percent of the Swedish citizens were not disabled, compared with 86.6-84.4 percent for the different groups of foreign citizens; and Southern Europeans were the group with the least favorable percentage. This comparison underestimates, however, the difference between Swedish and foreign citizens' incidences of disability. The immigrants are on the average much younger than the Swedes and the percentage of disabled varies very strongly with age, as mentioned above. If we standardize the different nationalities for differences in age and sex distribution, we find that foreign citizens have a much higher frequency of disability than Swedish citizens. Those who come from Finland and from Southern Europe—areas from which most immigrant manual workers have come to Sweden—have particularly high frequencies.[2]

There are probably several factors contributing to the high frequencies of these groups. First, immigration is to a very large extent one of manual workers, and the frequency of disability for these occupational groups is higher. Second, immigrants often are employed in jobs which are physically demanding, with irregular working hours and relatively high accident risks.[3] Third, the situation of immigrants per se can be a strain and can lead to different types of difficulties, illnesses, and other kinds of ailments (Haavio and Johansson, 1974; Leiniö, 1979a).

Those with higher education have a lower incidence of disability than those with little schooling. There are different explanations for this discrepancy. One is that the average level of education is higher the lower the age group, due to the expansion of the Swedish school system during the last decades. Even if we keep age constant, however, most of the differences remain. This may be attributed to several factors: (1) that some groups of the disabled (e.g., mentally retarded) have little or no possibility of completing high school or university studies; (2) that the incidence of occupational injuries is low in the occupations held by most persons with higher education; and (3) that blue collar occupations require in general a better physical capacity than do white collar occupations (usually held by those with higher education).

The comparison of regions indicates certain differences. The northern part of the country shows higher frequencies of disabilities; and in that region the frequencies are higher primarily among men between the ages of 45 and 64, probably as a result of the industrial structure of the area (forestry, mining, steel industry), where a high percentage of men in those ages have had physically demanding jobs and layoffs have been frequent.

Medical Causes of Disability

Another question in the Living Conditions Survey was what illness, injury, etc. those who had a "long-standing illness" had experienced. Table 14.4 shows the distribution of illnesses among men and women. Illnesses of the circulatory system (heart diseases, high blood pressure) and musculoskeletal diseases are predominant. Women have a frequency as high or higher than men for almost all illnesses, but men have more injuries due to accidents. It is important to note that one person may have several kinds of diseases. Long-standing illness was reported by 308 per 1,000 men, but the number of reported diseases was 414 per 1,000 men. On the average, men with diseases reported 1.34 kinds of diseases. The same figures for women were 327, 462, and 1.41.

Table 14.4. Diseases among Persons Aged 16-64 Who Had Long-standing Illness, 1978 (number of diseases per 1,000 persons)

Disease	Per 1,000 Persons	
	Men	Women
Infectious	8	9
Neoplasms	3	9
Endocrine	20	30
Of blood and bloodforming organs	3	10
Mental disorders	22	33
Of nervous system	47	40
Of circulatory system	67	79
Respiratory	26	29
Of digestive system	39	28
Urogenital	7	28
Cutaneous	21	28
Musculoskeletal	84	81
Congenital malformations	3	2
Others	22	35
Injuries (accidents, poisonings, violence)	42	21
Kinds of diseases per 1,000 persons	414	462
Persons with long-standing illness per 1,000 persons	308	327

Source: See Table 14.1.

Note: A person may be recorded with more than one disease, but not within the same category—e.g., for both infectious disease and neoplasm but not for two infectious diseases.

The frequency of illness for the majority of diseases rises continuously with age. An exception to this is respiratory diseases, where the lowest frequency is in the age group 35-44. The frequency of the most common diseases, those of the circulatory system and musculoskeletal diseases, rises sharply with age.

We must remember that "long-standing illness" is defined in such a way that many less serious illnesses are included. One way to try to isolate the more serious illness is to look only at the group which has reduced working capacity and see which illnesses that group suffers from, as in Table 14.5. Multiple conditions are more common in this group (1.46 on average for men, and 1.59 on average for women). Comparing Tables 14.4 and 14.5, we find differences in the relative frequencies for the various illnesses. Mental disorders and diseases of musculature and skeleton are relatively overrepresented among those with reduced working capacity.

Economic Status of the Disabled

Earnings constitute the main source of income for most persons of working age. For the severely disabled, however, less than half were in the labor force and only 44 percent were employed at the time of interview, as compared with 81 percent of those who did not report any reduction of their working capacity. Of those with reduced, but not severely reduced, working capacity, 75 percent were employed. The labor market participation pattern of this group is more similar to that of the nondisabled than that of the severely disabled. See Table 14.6.

Table 14.5. Diseases among Persons Aged 16-64 Who Had Reduced Working Capacity, 1978

Disease	Per 1,000 Persons	
	Men	Women
Infectious	23	29
Neoplasms	9	27
Endocrine	40	81
Of blood and bloodforming organs	5	29
Mental disorders	103	130
Of nervous system	155	145
Of circulatory system	218	236
Respiratory	103	93
Of digestive system	115	95
Urogenital	23	70
Cutaneous	54	89
Musculoskeletal	347	343
Congenital malformations	16	8
Others	84	136
Injuries (accidents, poisonings, violence)	169	76
Kinds of diseases per 1,000 persons	1,464	1,587

Source: See Table 14.1.

Note: According to the definition of reduced working capacity, all reported at least one kind of disease. See also note to Table 14.4.

Table 14.6. Labor Force Characteristics of the Disabled and Nondisabled, Working-Age Population (16-64 years), 1978 (percentage distributions)

Characteristic	Total Population[a]	Severely Reduced Working Capacity	Reduced Working Capacity (not severely)	No Reduced Working Capacity
Labor Force Status				
Not in labor force	19.4	53.0	20.4	16.1
Employed	77.6	44.1	74.8	81.2
Unemployed	3.0	3.0	4.8	2.7
Working Hours per Week				
1-19	5.2	5.0	5.2	5.2
20-34	17.4	24.0	19.0	16.9
35-	66.7	52.0	60.2	68.1
Employers and self-employed, incl. farmers	10.7	19.0	15.6	9.8
Occupation				
Blue collar	49.4	53.8	56.6	48.3
Unskilled	13.5	14.1	17.3	12.9
Semi-skilled	19.7	22.6	23.5	19.2
Skilled	16.2	17.1	15.8	16.2
White collar	40.2	29.6	28.4	42.2
Unskilled	16.3	15.1	16.5	16.4
Skilled	23.9	14.6	11.9	25.8
Employers and self-employed, incl. farmers	10.4	16.6	15.0	9.5
Yearly Employment Earnings (full year, full time)[b]				
0-39 thousand crowns	5.5	4.9	7.8	5.3
40-49	16.2	26.3	20.6	15.4
50-59	28.0	37.3	32.9	27.1
60-79	33.5	22.8	32.5	33.9
80-	16.8	8.7	6.2	18.1
Mean Annual Earnings (full-year, full-time workers)	65,420 crowns	56,510 crowns	58,210 crowns	66,470 crowns
Median Annual Earnings (full-year, full-time workers)	59,464 crowns	53,704 crowns	56,211 crowns	59,981 crowns

Note: See Table 14.1. Missing answers are deleted before calculation of percentages.

[a]In entire Swedish population.

[b]Sickness benefits are included in earnings from employment.

The unemployment rates are somewhat higher for the disabled if calculated using the working-age population for each work-capacity group as the base; this gives rates of 3.0 percent for the severely disabled, 4.8 percent for the not severely disabled, and 2.7 percent for those not disabled. Calculations using only those of working age who are in the labor force as the base (the normal way of calculating the unemployment rate) lead to more striking differences: 6.2 percent of the severely disabled in the labor force are unemployed, compared with 6.0 percent of the not severely disabled and 3.3 percent of the nondisabled.[4]

The disabled more often work part time than do the nondisabled. One reason is that a proportionally higher number of women are disabled. It is common in Sweden for women, especially those with preschool children, to work part time, but it is unusual for men to do so. Disabled women also work part time more than nondisabled women. Among disabled and nondisabled men, only a small percentage work part time. The frequency of part-time work is, however, higher among disabled than among nondisabled men.

A high proportion of those with reduced and severely reduced working capacity have blue collar occupations or are business owners (mainly farmers). Several factors probably contribute to this condition—e.g., differences in age distribution in various occupations, differences in injury risks, and differences in physical capacity requirements.

Earnings differ also according to degree of disability. Among those employed full time, full year, we find that a low proportion of the disabled belong to the group with the highest earnings, and a high proportion of them are in the 40-59,000 crowns a year group. The average yearly earnings are 11 percent lower for the not severely disabled and 14 percent lower for the severely disabled in comparison with those of the total population.

Earnings are only a part of total household income; other sources are spouse's earnings and income-maintenance payments. Household income is then reduced by income taxes. Table 14.7 shows the distribution of disposable income for households of the severely disabled, of the not severely disabled, and of the nondisabled. A relatively lower number of the disabled are in the highest income brackets, and a relative high number are in the middle of the income range (20-59,000 crowns).[5] There is no clear pattern, however, for those with low disposable household incomes. The nondisabled are more numerous proportionally among those up to 10,000 crowns a year, and those with severe disability are more numerous among those with an annual income of 10-20,000 crowns. The explanation for this lies mostly in the definition of "household" used by the Living Conditions Survey. Only the interviewed person (16-64 years), his/her spouse, and children under 16 are included in the family. This means that, e.g., youths 16-19 years old (the normal high school age) living at home with their parents constitute separate households. They often have, of course, very

Table 14.7. Annual Disposable Household Income of the Disabled and Nondisabled Working-Age Population (16-64 years), 1978 (percentage distributions)

	Total Population[a]	Severely Reduced Working Capacity	Reduced Working Capacity (not severely)	No Reduced Working Capacity
Household income				
0- 9,999 crowns	6.1	1.6	4.0	6.8
10,000-19,999	6.3	8.6	5.8	6.1
20,000-29,999	8.4	17.3	10.3	7.3
30,000-39,999	14.0	18.0	15.8	13.4
40,000-49,999	13.1	14.7	16.2	12.6
50,000-59,999	14.9	15.2	15.3	14.8
60,000-79,999	27.7	20.9	25.7	28.7
80,000-99,999	7.8	3.0	5.8	8.6
100,000-	1.5	0.6	1.0	1.7
	100.0	100.0	100.0	100.0
Mean household income (crowns)	49,810	44,170	48,190	50,590
Average number in household[b]	2.35	1.94	2.34	2.39
Mean household income (crowns)[c] (respondent is aged 20-64)	53,110	44,390	49,760	54,500
Average number in household[c]	2.47	1.95	2.40	2.53

Source: See Table 14.1.
[a]In entire Swedish population 16-64 years old.
[b]Including husband/wife (or consensual unions) and children under 16.
[c]Excludes household in which respondent is aged 16-19.

low incomes. A calculation of the disposable income for those aged 20-64 causes no change in the share with 0-9,999 crowns for the severely disabled. It reduces the share in this income interval from 4.0 percent to 2.4 percent for the not severely disabled, and from 6.8 percent to 2.3 percent for those not disabled. The corresponding shares for those with 10,000-19,999 crowns changes from 8.6 percent to 8.2 percent, from 5.8 percent to 4.7 percent, and from 6.1 percent to 4.2 percent. If we exclude youths 16-19 years old, we find that the household of the nondisabled on the average has a 15 percent higher disposable household income than the household of the disabled (54,500 and 47,320 crowns, respectively).

The Swedish Model of Disability Policy

When personal illness or injury occurs, the basic principle in Sweden is to provide medical rehabilitation, regardless of the cause of illness or injury and regardless of ability to pay. Medical care is handled by the county council and is financed almost exclusively through a proportional income tax paid to that council. It is available to anyone who resides in Sweden.

Similarly, everyone between 16 years and retirement age is insured through sickness benefits against loss of income due to illness. If a worker misses work due to illness or injury, he or she receives 90 percent of earned income. Technically, sickness benefits are limited to a maximum of 90 percent of 7.5 times an index-tied base amount; this amount, however, is sufficiently high to allow the majority (about 94 percent of those of working age in 1977) to receive 90 percent of any income lost from illness or injury.[6] A single base amount is defined as

$$4000 \times \frac{\text{current value of Consumer Price Index}}{\text{value of Consumer Price Index in September 1957}},$$

rounded off to hundreds of crowns. Since October 1980, oil prices are excluded when calculating the price index. Until 1982, the base amount was revised each month if the CPI changed by at least 3 percent since the last revision. The base amount changed in February 1978 from 11,800 crowns to 12,200 crowns, and in April changed for the remainder of 1978 to 12,600 crowns. The maximum allowable sickness benefits were therefore 93,000 crowns on the average in 1978, an amount 8 percent higher than the average annual salary for a male white collar industrial worker and 54 percent higher than the average annual earnings of male blue collar industrial workers.[7] Since 1982 the base amount is revised only in January each year.

Thus, if a disability begins with an acute illness or injury, compensation consists of sickness benefits. If for some reason the sickness benefits are so low that the person is unable to maintain a minimal standard of living, he may receive in addition assistance from the municipal social welfare office; this is the social assistance paid in general to persons with low income.

It is important to emphasize that compensation is given regardless of the cause of illness or injury and regardless of short-term, long-term, or permanent nature. Additional measures—beyond sickness benefits and medical care—are not taken until the existence and extent of permanent impairment can be established with a fair degree of certainty. If a person has been ill for more than 90 days, it is the obligation of the local social insurance office to investigate to see if he needs rehabilitation. Additional measures can be of three types: (1) various types of disability pensions, (2) annuities from employment injury insurance, and (3) special employment programs. Disability pensioning implies that the applicant has left the labor force (even if not entirely), while employment programs imply an effort to preserve the connection to the labor market, if in a different way.

The regional social insurance offices (under the supervision of the National Social Insurance Board) are in charge of disability pensions and the employment injury insurance, while the National Labor Market Board directs the labor market programs for the disabled. It is important to note that the regional social insurance offices, which formally are independent insurance benefit societies, are also in charge of health insurance in general. It is compulsory for all Swedish citizens as well as foreigners residing in Sweden to be members of the insurance benefit society of the county where they live. These societies must all follow the same rules and have the same levels of compensation. In practice they belong to a national social insurance organization headed by the National Social Insurance Board.[8]

Figure 14.1 shows the major components of the formal organization for disability policy. The important contacts occur on a local level, often through rehabilitation groups. In 1975 the National Social Insurance Board recommended to the regional social insurance offices that they form rehabilitation groups; this was made compulsory from January 1, 1979 (Eriksen, 1980, pp. 23-24). The rehabilitation groups discuss whether employment or disability pensioning is the appropriate measure. Not all cases are taken up in the rehabilitation groups. The local social insurance offices take, without referral, cases when employment programs are not considered a possible solution.

Not reflected in the figure is one important avenue for the disabled to make contact with the public employment offices: past surveys have shown that about 50 percent of the occupationally disabled who come to those offices do so directly, without referral from some other social organization. Statistics for the occupationally disabled who were referred to the public employment office in Malmö during 1978 show that 44 percent were referred from medical care institutions, 16 percent from local social insurance offices, 24 percent from prisons, 6 percent from welfare offices, 5 percent from alcoholic-care institutions, and 6 percent from other authorities or organizations.

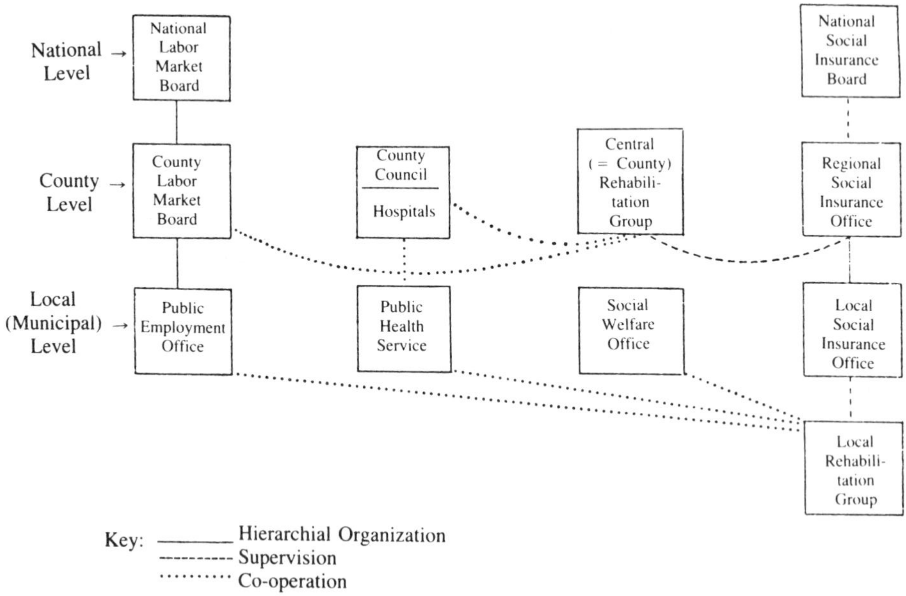

Figure 14.1. Governmental and Local Governmental Organizations Involved in Disability Policy in Sweden.

Disability programs are thus of two types: income support and employment. The main income support programs are described in this survey. Two programs that could be used as income support for the disabled are unemployment insurance and cash labor market support (designed for unemployed who are not insured). Technically, both are only for the nondisabled, but they can in some cases be used for the disabled.

Two other programs, sickness benefits and social assistance, will not be discussed further here. We will concentrate upon the disability pension system and the labor market programs, which together are the most important programs and are rather complicated, offering several alternatives in particular for the disabled aged 60 years or more.

The Disability Pension System

During the period 1946-63, there were only two types of disability pensions: temporary (for a limited period) and regular (until retirement). Compensation consisted of a fixed, low base and a supplementary, income-tested part. The maximum was equal to the old age pension. In addition, the disabled received a housing allowance, which up to 1954 was national but then became municipal, though partly financed with governmental grants. By 1963 all municipalities had established housing supplements, whose amounts vary greatly. During this entire period, the number of disability pensions remained at approximately 145,000.

Since 1963, the pension system has been altered in several ways. First, the income-tested supplementary payment was replaced in the national system by one of three fixed amounts: full pension if 5/6 of working capacity was lost; a two-thirds pension if 2/3 capacity was lost, or a one-third pension if working capacity was reduced by one half.

Also in 1963, the first pensions of the new national supplementary pension scheme were paid out. This supplementary pension system was established only after a long political debate in the 1950s, and it won by a majority in the Riksdag (the Swedish Parliament) of only one vote. It has elements of both a premium reserve system and a pay-as-you-go system. The first payments to it were made in 1960, and the first (small) pensions were paid out in 1963. Its amount in conjunction with old age pensions depends on the number of years worked and the income during those years. When a disability pension is granted, in most cases year with "assumption points" are added to calculate the amount of the supplementary pension (a more detailed account is given below). Then the supplement is paid out like the usual disability pension—full, 2/3, and 1/3 of the calculated amount of supplementary pension. The adoption of supplementary pensioning meant gradual improvements in the economic situation of the disabled.

Several important changes were introduced in 1970. To decrease the difference in economic standards of persons with and without national supplementary pensions, a special bonus supplement was created for those with low or no national supplement. These bonus supplements have successively been raised. A second change was that those with one-third pension were raised to half-pension; a third was that the minimum requirement of a half-year's disability before getting a temporary disability pension was abolished. The fourth and perhaps most significant change in 1970 was that older workers could receive disability pensions more readily: labor market considerations were weighed with medical ones for older persons (usually those over 63, lowered in 1976 to 60), and they no longer had to meet the same requirements regarding occupational and/or geographical mobility as younger persons.

The regulations were further altered in 1972. Medical considerations were no longer applicable to long-term unemployed persons 63 years and older (changed to 60 in 1974). The new alternative requirement for a regular disability pension is that one must have exhausted entitlement to compensation from the unemployment benefit society (or have had a cash unemployment allowance for a minimum of 450 days) and be unable to support oneself with the same type of previously held job or another suitable type of work. In 1977 alcoholism was accepted as grounds for granting a pension—i.e., the law was changed so that disablement alone, and not its cause, figures in the pension decision.

Besides the two national pension systems, most persons are covered by negotiated pension plans. Earlier, only white collar workers had such plans, but in the 1970s the blue collar trade unions also gained them. The negotiated plans are briefly described later.

The Disability Pension

A pension can be applied for by an individual, or the initiative can come from the local social insurance office. Self-initiated applications can be on medical grounds, on medical and labor market grounds, or on labor market grounds alone (no benefits left from the unemployment benefit society, or cash unemployment allowances for more than 450 days for a worker over 60 years). The local offices can take the initiative on behalf of those receiving cash benefits from health insurance or employment injury insurance, and for those receiving a national or local government disability pension under a negotiated pension plan (see below) following a report from Statens pensionsverk (the Government Pensions Institute) or Kommunernas pensionsanstalt (the Municipal Pension Institute) (Hedström, 1980, p. 38).

Most applications for a disability pension receive approval from the Pension Committee of the regional social insurance society. In 1978 only 4.6 percent of the applications (not including applications for labor market reasons alone) were rejected. The rate varied between 4 and 6 percent during the 1970s. In cases initiated by the local social insurance office, in general only 1 to 2 percent of the applications are not approved (information based on monthly reports from the National Social Insurance Board[9]).

The National Social Insurance Board made a study of those granted disability pensions from September through November 1974. It included all except those who had been enrolled in the sickness allowance insurance program for less than 12 months, which means those excluded were mainly youths who were pensioned upon reaching the age of 16—i.e., youths with severe handicaps. The study analyzed the relation of previous illness to disability. The results showed that relatively few, 7.8 percent, of those pensioned only for labor market reasons, but all who were pensioned on the initiative of the local social insurance offices, had been ill immediately prior to pensioning. In both cases, this is what one would expect from the structure of the regulations. More surprising, however, is that only about two-thirds of those who applied themselves, excluding labor market cases, had been ill and received sickness benefits immediately before disability pensioning. This is partly explained by the fact that persons with low sickness benefits (for example, housewives) did not report illness, and partly that many go directly from the labor force (employed or unemployed) to disability pensioning without a sickness benefit period.

Among those ill before pensioning, age differences are clear, as shown in Table 14.8. Older people have much shorter sickness benefit periods than the younger. This is true of both self-initiated and office-initiated cases, but the differences are relatively greater for the former. The explanation for these differences probably lies both in the rule allowing labor market

Table 14.8. Age and Previous Sickness of Temporary and Regular Disability Pensioners, September-November 1974

	Average Number of Sickness Benefit Days Immediately before Pension[a]		Average Number of Sickness Cash Benefit Days during Last Five Years	
Age	Self-Initiated Cases (excl. labor market cases)	Office-Initiated Cases	Self-Initiated Cases (excl. labor market cases)	Office-Initiated Cases
16-44	380.3	666.8	623.9	1,034.5
45-59	336.5	597.7	529.0	845.2
60	265.0	523.3	401.6	730.5
61	245.5	522.8	353.6	702.8
62	240.2	500.4	346.8	681.7
63	232.9	480.7	316.9	656.7
64	225.6	496.8	295.0	636.0
65	225.5	498.5	279.4	644.2
66	211.8	504.5	263.7	618.2
Average	295.4	551.8	439.9	764.2

Source: National Social Insurance Board (1977b).
Note: The mandatory retirement age was 67 in 1974.
[a]Only those who drew sickness benefits are included in calculations.

(unemployment) reasons as grounds for older people and in the different interpretations of current regulations for different age groups. For young groups the traditional work principle is valid, while the cash support principle in its various forms is accepted for the older.

The study also showed that the number of cases initiated by a local social insurance office as opposed to self-initiated cases (excluding those based solely on unemployment) is approximately the same, whereas the labor market cases constitute a relatively small share. This is also the case for those age groups for whom pensioning solely for labor market reasons is possible. During the entire time that this possibility has existed, few have been so pensioned—in 1978 there were only 2,050 cases. Nevertheless, various studies have demonstrated that labor market conditions probably play a part in disability pensioning. For example, more are pensioned in regions of the country with high unemployment;[10] one explanation is that for most workers, unemployment compensation yields lower benefits than either sickness compensation or disability pensioning. Two years' unemployment compensation followed by disability pensioning gives, in many cases, less economic compensation than an immediate disability pension with no unemployment-benefit period. There is therefore an economic motive to be pensioned for medical reasons.

The three most common medical diagnoses for which disability pensions are granted are mental disorders, diseases of the circulatory system, and musculoskeletal diseases; the last is the most frequent. If, however, we study the expected total number of years on disability pension resulting from different diagnoses (frequency times expected number of years on disability pension, on average for each diagnosis), mental disorders become the most important (see Table 14.9). The reason is that those pensioned because of mental disorders are on the average much younger than those with other diagnoses.[11]

Earlier we mentioned that disability pensions can be either temporary or regular. A temporary one is granted when the chances of recovery are considered good. However, the majority of those who receive a temporary

Table 14.9. New Disability Pensions in 1976 and Expected Years on Disability Pensions (percentage distribution for the three most frequent diagnoses)

Diagnosis	Percentage of Total New Disability Pensions	Percentage of Total Number of Expected Disability Pension Years
Mental disorders	18.0	33.3
Circulatory diseases	20.9	12.0
Musculoskeletal diseases	36.1	27.6
Total	75.0	72.9

Source: Eriksen (1980, p. 48).

Note: In calculating the expected number of disability pension years, information about the mortality rates of the disability pensionists has been used.

pension eventually receive a regular pension. For most people, a temporary pension is a provisional solution while waiting for permanent pensioning, although most of those who have regular disability pensions have not had a temporary pension. This is especially true of older people, who rarely go through the temporary stage.

Table 14.10 shows the growth in both types of pensions over the last twenty years, and the ratio of pensioners to employed persons. It is important to remember that one need not have been employed to get a disability pension.

Temporary pensions have increased in comparison with regular pensions; see Table 14.11. At the end of the 1950s, temporary pensions accounted for 10 percent of the total number; twenty years later, they made up 18 percent. This rise is particularly striking for women, for whom the increase was from 8 percent to 20 percent. One reason for the increase in temporary pensions is an overall rise in disability pensioning; temporary disability pensions increase more because they often are the first step toward permanent pensions. Another reason is that a disabled person now more often starts out as a temporary pensioner, which may also explain the fact that a decreased percentage of those with temporary pensions leave them for something other than disability pensioning.

The disabled can receive full, two-thirds, and one-half pensions, depending on their reduction in earnings capacity. There are no other fixed limits. Usually, 2/3 and 5/6 reduction of working (earnings) capacity is the limit for two-thirds and full pensions, respectively.

From the beginning of the pension system, full pensions have been the dominant type. Even though their percentage of all pensions has decreased somewhat, they still account for around 90 percent (see Table 14.11). Two-thirds and one-half pensions occur most often, relatively, among middle-aged people. Two-thirds and one-half pensions can be combined with work on the labor market, with work in one's own firm, and also with different types of sheltered work under the auspices of the National Labor Market Board. Those pensions are more common among women (15 percent of the female pensioners) than among men (10 percent), probably because disabled housewives in many cases have been considered able to continue with household work to some extent. In 1970 the law was changed to exclude household tasks in measuring work capacity in most instances, so the difference will probably disappear gradually. See Särnmark (1974, pp. 23-26).

Tables 14.10 and 14.12 show the age and sex distribution of disability pensioners. Until the end of the 1960s, the number of disability-pensioned men and women was approximately equal. The number of men then increased, and by the mid-1970s they exceeded women by almost 20,000. With the lowering of the retirement age from 67 to 65 in 1976, however, the difference diminished sharply, since most of the disability pensioners 65 or

Table 14.10. Annual Number of Disability Pensioners since 1959 and Ratio to Those Employed

Year (January)	Regular Disability Pensioners			Temporary Disability Pensioners			Both Types			Ratio of Disability Pensioners (both types) to Those Employed[a]		
	Men	Women	All	Men	Women	All	Men	Women	All	Men	Women	All
1959	60,990	65,992	126,982	7,540	5,904	13,444	68,530	71,895	140,426	—	—	—
1960	62,231	66,334	128,565	8,093	6,301	14,394	70,324	72,635	142,959	—	—	—
1961	63,677	66,226	129,903	8,490	6,643	15,133	72,167	72,869	145,036	—	—	—
1962	64,598	65,770	130,368	8,690	6,912	15,602	73,288	72,682	145,970	—	—	—
1963	67,127	66,862	133,989	9,306	7,584	16,890	76,433	74,445	150,879	0.034	0.056	0.042
1964	64,526	65,862	130,388	8,486	7,624	16,110	73,012	73,486	146,498	0.032	0.055	0.041
1965	66,903	67,022	133,925	8,435	8,265	16,700	75,338	75,287	150,625	0.033	0.056	0.042
1966	71,466	70,410	141,876	9,304	9,705	19,009	80,770	80,115	160,885	0.035	0.059	0.044
1967	74,429	71,872	146,301	10,092	10,755	20,847	84,521	82,627	167,148	0.037	0.061	0.046
1968	77,496	73,296	150,792	10,404	11,003	21,407	87,900	84,299	172,199	0.039	0.060	0.047
1969	80,988	74,650	155,638	11,284	11,367	22,651	92,272	86,017	178,289	0.041	0.059	0.048
1970	86,188	76,243	162,431	12,934	12,520	25,454	99,122	88,763	187,885	0.043	0.059	0.050
1971	98,375	85,201	183,576	14,679	14,219	28,898	113,054	99,420	212,474	0.050	0.065	0.056
1972	110,062	92,446	202,508	16,714	17,008	33,722	126,776	109,454	236,230	0.056	0.070	0.062
1973	121,816	100,373	222,189	18,839	19,301	38,140	140,655	119,674	260,329	0.062	0.076	0.068
1974	130,494	107,819	238,313	19,390	20,414	39,804	149,884	128,233	278,117	0.066	0.078	0.071
1975	134,529	112,895	247,424	19,790	21,670	41,460	154,319	134,564	288,884	0.067	0.079	0.072
1976	137,549	116,555	254,104	19,955	22,587	42,542	157,504	139,142	296,646	0.068	0.080	0.073
1977[b]	111,551	101,467	213,018	21,038	24,037	45,075	132,589	125,504	258,093	0.059	0.071	0.064
1978	117,242	106,834	224,076	22,715	26,004	48,719	139,957	132,838	272,795	0.062	0.074	0.067
1979	121,132	110,851	231,983	24,238	27,911	52,149	145,370	138,762	284,132	0.064	0.075	0.069

Source: Statistical Abstract of Sweden, various issues; annual Labor Force Surveys; information from the National Social Insurance Board.

[a]The employment figures are for the age group 16-66 from 1963 to 1976, and 16-64 in 1977-78—i.e., in the period after the lowering of the retirement age from 67 to 65. Labor force surveys exist only since 1963.

[b]The retirement age for old age pensions was changed from 67 to 65 in July 1976.

Table 14.11. Percentage Distribution of the Various Forms of Disability Pensions, 1959-1979

Year (January)	Full Pension	Two-Thirds Pension	Half-Pension[a]	Percentage Temporary Pensions
1959				10
1960				10
1961				10
1962				11
1963	98	1	0.5	11
1964	96	3	1	11
1965	93	5	2	11
1966	91	6	3	12
1967	90	7	3	12
1968	89	8	4	12
1969	87	8	4	13
1970	87	9	4	14
1971	90	6	4	14
1972	91	6	4	14
1973	91	5	4	15
1974	91	5	4	14
1975	91	5	4	14
1976	90	5	5	14
1977	89	5	6	17
1978	88	5	7	18
1979	87	5	9	18

Source: See Table 14.10.
[a]Until July 1970 this was a one-third pension.

66 years old were men. In the age distribution, the oldest age groups are greatly overrepresented; among them the number of disability pensions sharply increased in the 1970s, particularly among older men. On the other hand, the number of pensions is low in the 16-29 age group, and their number has not tended to rise. Temporary disability pensions are more common among the young than among the old. In 1976 it was more

Table 14.12. Age and Sex Distribution of Disability Pensioners, 1964, 1970, 1975, 1977-80 (temporary and regular pensioners in January of each year)

	1964	1970	1975	1977	1978	1979	1980
Men							
16-29	6,476	8,404	9,351	8,942	9,023	8,968	8,767
30-44	10,643	10,841	13,642	14,694	15,652	16,628	17,576
45-59	26,703	35,121	50,086	53,969	57,242	60,258	62,508
60-64	19,326	30,175	51,464	54,986	58,040	59,516	60,675
65-66[a]	9,864	14,581	29,776	—	—	—	—
Women							
16-29	5,261	6,704	7,626	7,260	7,264	7,121	7,063
30-34	8,724	10,986	13,924	15,337	16,479	17,675	18,552
45-59	29,586	36,476	52,499	57,829	61,218	64,281	67,092
60-64	19,450	24,365	40,774	45,078	47,877	49,675	51,101
65-66[a]	9,005	10,232	19,740	—	—	—	—

Source: Statistical Abstract of Sweden, 1981.
[a]Retirement age was lowered from 67 to 65 in July 1976.

common up to the age of 23 to have a temporary disability pension than a disability pension. See, e.g., National Social Insurance Board (1979).

Kindlund (1978) has studied the two Level of Living surveys for 1968 and 1974 to examine the factors that influence disability pensioning. Among those who responded in both surveys and who were employed in 1968, she found that the most important factors were age and occupation. Older persons (60-64 years in 1974) and manual laborers in 1968 were more likely to be pensioned in 1974. The percentage of men aged 60-64 with a disability pension in 1974 was also much higher if they had reported in 1968: (1) either mental or physical exhaustion at the end of the working day, or (2) working at a job in which they had to lift 60 kilos or more and had back ailments. A closer analysis of the causes for the increase in disability pensions is given in the next section, concerning the economic effects of the pensions.

From the early 1950s, disability pensions have been tied to the Consumer Price Index. Since 1963, the pension has been structured so that size is calculated in a certain number of base amounts, which are indexed: as soon as the Index rises at least 3 percent from the last previous change in base amount, the amount is raised by the same percentage as the Index. (This indexation is similar to that for sickness benefits, discussed earlier.)

Indexation means that the real value of the pensions is held constant. On two occasions, however, their real value was raised—first in connection with the large revision of the pension system in 1963, and again in 1970, when a bonus pension supplement was established for those who had no or low supplementary pensions. In 1970 the bonus was 0.03 of one base amount if the pensioners were on full pension (if they had 2/3 or 1/2 it was reduced correspondingly); by January 1978, it had risen gradually to 0.58 of one base amount, and an increase to 0.90 of base amount was obtained in July 1981. Another modification occurred in 1975, when a full pension was raised from 0.90 to 0.95 of base amount for a person not married to another person with old age or disability pension. The total disability pension for a person not married to another pensioner with full disability pension and a nonreduced bonus pension supplement was, in 1978, 1.53 of base amounts, or about 18,000 crowns.

Other Forms of Support in the Disability Pension System

In addition to temporary and regular disability pensions, there are four types of assistance to the disabled in the disability pension system: a municipal housing supplement, a wife supplement, a child supplement, and a handicap allowance.

Municipal housing supplements were discussed earlier. They vary from municipality to municipality—some provide fixed amounts independent of dwelling costs; others provide amounts related to dwelling costs; still others provide amounts based in part on fixed rates and in part on dwelling costs. The third variety is the most common. Since 1963 all municipalities have had some form of housing supplement, which since 1975 has been partly financed by the state. By law the supplements are income-tested, as follows:

$$M = M_{max} - 1/3\,(I - A),$$

where

M = municipal housing supplement (yearly amount),

M_{max} = maximum municipal housing supplement (can depend on the dwelling cost),

I = yearly income (excluding national disability pension, bonus pension supplement, and the national supplementary pension up to the level that makes the bonus pension supplement disappear),

A = 1,500 crowns for married people,
= 2,000 crowns for single people.

Neither the national pension nor a part of the national supplementary disability pension is considered here as income. The value 1/3 before the parenthesis in the formula implies an implicit tax rate of 1/3 in the income interval from that part of the pensions not reckoned as income plus 1,500 (or 2,000) up to the maximum allowable income permitting a municipal housing supplement. It is important to note that this support is paid in cash and not in kind, and that in some municipalities it is not related to dwelling costs at all (12 percent of the municipalities in 1974) and in most other municipalities only to a minor extent (62 percent in 1974). In 1974 the maximum figure in the municipality with the highest amount was ten times that of the one with the lowest amount (Kommunförbundet, 1975).

Since 1978 it has been possible to receive national housing supplements in those cases where they provide higher benefits than municipal ones—if so, the national government pays the difference between the higher amount and the municipal housing supplement. Since January 1980 (government proposition 1978/79:95), the government has paid 43 percent of the costs of the municipal housing supplement, but only for those municipalities which calculate the maximum municipal housing supplement according to certain rules (at least 80 percent of the dwelling cost up to 700 crowns a month for a single pensioner and 800 for a couple). It is expected that most municipalities will change their rules so that they will be eligible for government subsidies. As a result the differences among rules of the different municipalities will diminish drastically.

The wife supplement can be paid to the wife of a disability pensioner if she has no pensions herself. With certain exceptions, she must be at least 60 and the couple must have been married at least five years. The wife supplement is composed of the differences between the disability pension for a couple and that for a single person. It is earnings-tested, and together with the municipal housing supplement is derived from the formula given above. If a decrease occurs, it is made first in the municipal housing supplement, then in the wife supplement.

The child supplement consists of 25 percent of a base amount per child for disability-pensioned parents with children under 16. If the child already has a pension, the amount of supplement is reduced to 10 percent of a base amount. The child supplement is not earnings-tested, but is reduced by half of the amount that the supplementary disability pension exceeds half of the base amount.

In July 1975, the handicap allowance replaced two earlier forms of compensation: disability supplements and disability allowance. The disability supplement could be paid to those who had a pension and needed extra help of some sort, while the disability allowance was paid to those who did not have a pension and needed aid. The handicap allowance consolidates both of these forms of assistance. It can be paid to anyone 16 and older. Its purpose is to provide economic compensation for the additional expenses that a handicapped person incurs. It is not related to the recipient's employment situation, but only to the additional expenses of daily activities. It can be dispensed both to those who receive a disability pension and as an independent benefit, and consists of 60 percent, 45 percent, or 30 percent of the base amount; the choice of percentage depends on the extent and costs of the assistance needed. It is indexed, being calculated according to base amount. The blind, the deaf, and those with grave hearing impairments always receive a handicap allowance.

In January 1978, 8,856 persons received a handicap allowance without simultaneously having disability pensions (or old age pensions). Of these, 3,420 received 60 percent, 768 received 45 percent, and 4,668 received 30 percent of a base amount (so few received 45 percent because only 60 percent and 30 percent existed as alternatives in the earlier compensation forms). In the same year, 19,112 had a handicap allowance as well as a disability pension; in this group, 8,781 received 30 percent, 3,798 45 percent, and 6,533 60 percent of a base amount. The handicap allowance is neither earnings-tested nor taxable.

Supplementary Disability Pension

The national supplementary pension system was established in 1960. Participation in it is mandatory for wage earners; self-employed persons may choose whether to participate or not. Most who receive a supplementary pension do so through the old age pension, but it can also be added to disability pensions (temporary as well as regular). The rules for these pensions can best be described by starting with the criteria for the old age pension within the national supplementary disability system. The equation for old age pensions is the following:

$$P = 0.60 \frac{t}{N} \bar{p} B \qquad 3 \leqslant t \leqslant 49: \qquad \frac{t}{N} = 1 \text{ for all } t \geqslant N,$$

where

t = the number of pension point-carrying years;
N = 30 (for persons born 1896-1923, a figure lower than 30 is used);
$\bar{p}$ = average number of pension points; if more than 15 years with pension points, the 15 best years are counted; pension points for one year are calculated by dividing that part of the income which lies between 1 and 7.5 base amount by the base amount, that is, $\bar{p}$ can reach a maximum of 6.5. Not only earnings from employment but also most transfer incomes as sickness cash benefit and unemployment insurance compensation and also partial pension are reckoned as income (see the next section);
B = the size of the base amount the year the pension is paid out (the base amount, as mentioned earlier, is tied to the consumer price index).

As can be seen from the equation, supplementary pensioning is indexed, the amount depending on number of years worked and income during these years.

The same calculations can be applied to disability pensions, resulting in lower pensions for those with few pension-point years. Another calculation exists, however, if one of two requirements is fulfilled: (1) the person's insurance for sickness benefits is based on an income equivalent to at least a single base amount, or (2) the person has received pension points in two of the last four years prior to pensioning (till July 1979, the rule was three of the last four years). If the person fulfills one or both of these requirements, the disability pension is calculated with the help of assumption pension points for each year up to age 65. Assumption points are calculated from the more favorable of the two alternatives: (1) the average of the two highest pension-point amounts during the last four years; or (2) the average amount of pension points during that half of all the years from age 16 up to the year prior to pensioning that the pensioned person had the highest pension points. With the assumption points and pension points from earlier years, the average number of pension points ($\bar{p}$ in equation (1)) and the number of pension-point-carrying years (t) are calculated. The assumption points are maximized to 6.5 a year. Just as for the old age pension, the pensioner must have received pension points for three years.

The structure of the pension system is such that a very large number of pensioners receive supplementary disability pensions. Tables 14.13 and 14.14 show that their number has greatly increased; in 1979, 69 percent of

Table 14.13. Number of Regular and Temporary Supplementary Disability Pensions, 1963-1979

Year (January)	Regular Supplementary Disability Pensions			Temporary Supplementary Disability Pensions			Both Forms of Supplementary Disability Pensions		
	Men	Women	All	Men	Women	All	Men	Women	All
1963	2,869	452	3,321	932	217	1,149	3,801	669	4,470
1964	5,657	1,152	6,809	1,956	560	2,516	7,613	1,712	9,325
1965	10,715	2,474	13,189	3,151	1,231	4,382	13,866	3,705	17,571
1966	17,189	4,368	21,557	4,543	2,150	6,693	21,732	6,518	28,250
1967	22,931	6,297	29,228	5,791	3,065	8,856	28,722	9,362	38,084
1968	27,877	8,423	36,300	6,206	3,532	9,738	34,083	11,955	46,038
1969	34,791	10,931	45,722	7,417	4,317	11,734	42,208	15,248	57,456
1970	42,231	13,668	55,899	9,096	5,259	14,355	51,327	18,927	70,254
1971	55,903	19,530	75,433	10,762	6,522	17,284	66,665	26,052	92,712
1972	69,430	25,536	94,966	12,611	8,321	20,932	82,041	33,857	115,898
1973	82,877	32,555	115,432	14,446	10,103	24,549	97,323	42,658	139,987
1974	93,470	40,054	133,524	15,091	11,341	26,432	108,561	51,395	159,956
1975	99,431	46,091	145,522	15,560	12,731	28,291	114,991	58,822	173,813
1976	104,436	51,946	156,382	15,864	13,888	29,752	120,300	65,834	186,134
1977	83,591	47,478	131,069	17,038	15,504	32,542	100,629	62,982	163,611
1978	90,539	54,122	144,661	18,692	17,797	36,489	109,231	71,919	181,150
1979	95,589	59,821	155,410	20,288	20,179	40,467	115,877	80,000	195,877

Source: See Table 14.10.

Table 14.14. Percentages of Supplementary Disability Pensioners among All Disability Pensioners, 1963-1979

Year (January)	Men	Women	All
1963	5	1	3
1964	10	2	6
1965	18	5	12
1966	27	8	18
1967	34	11	23
1968	39	14	27
1969	46	18	32
1970	52	21	37
1971	59	26	44
1972	65	31	49
1973	69	36	54
1974	72	40	58
1975	75	44	60
1976	76	47	63
1977	76	50	63
1978	78	54	66
1979	80	58	69

Source: Calculated from Tables 14.10 and 14.13.

those with disability pensions had a supplementary disability pension. The percentage is calculated on the assumption that all persons with supplementary disability pensions have disability pensions. There are, however, a few foreign citizens who have qualified only for a supplementary disability pension (1,568 persons in January 1978). The differences between men and women are great. Only 58 percent of the women, but 80 percent of the men, had a supplementary disability pension.[12] The men's pensions on average were considerably higher than the women's—19,673 crowns as compared to 9,577 crowns in January 1978. The reasons for the difference lie partly in the fact that the men have higher incomes, partly in the regulations for qualification. If housewives have disability pensions, it is in many cases on the basis of the rules for old age pensions.

New pensions grew gradually larger during the 1960s and 1970s. Many persons also meet the criteria for calculating the pensions from assumption points, as different types of transfer payments have gradually come to be considered as pension-point-giving income. Two examples are unemployment compensation and sickness benefits.

Alternative Pension Schemes for Older Persons

For persons 60 to 65 years of age, there are several options for retirement. A disability pension is only one of them. Until July 1976 it was possible to receive an early old age pension from the age of 63, or to delay the pension up to the age of 70. In the former case, the pension amount was reduced by 0.6 percent times the number of months taken (maximum 48) prior to the mandatory pension age of 67, that is, up to 28.8 percent monthly for the duration of the pension; for each month of delay, the total pension was augmented by 0.6 percent. In 1976, when the mandatory retirement age was lowered to 65, the rules were changed, making it possible to take early retirement at 60 with a pension reduced only by 0.5 percent a month. Pensioning can still be delayed up to age 70 with an increase of 0.6 percent a month. If one elects early or delayed retirement, one may also take a half pension at the reduced (augmented) rate, receiving the other half at the age of 65. If a person takes whole or half pension at a reduced rate, the reduction remains in force after 65. In January 1978, 78,359 persons received old age pensions whose amounts were reduced due to early retirement. Of these, 10,484 were below the mandatory retirement age of 65 (246 had half pension). In the same month, 9,702 had augmented amounts due to delayed pensioning.

In July 1976, a partial pension system was introduced. A separate system, it is financed by a payroll levy and is administered by the National Social Insurance Board and the regional social insurance societies in the same way as the other pension schemes. It is possible to receive a partial pension under the following conditions: (1) The person must be between 60 and 65 years old; (2) work time must be reduced by at least 5 hours a week; (3) the remaining work time must be at least 17 hours a week; (4) the person must have worked at least 10 years since the age of 45; (5) the remaining income, after reduction of work time, may not exceed 7.5 times the base amount; (6) the person must reside in Sweden.

The partial pension compensates 65 percent of the income loss. A person's disposable income with partial pension will in most cases be 80 to 90 percent of income before pensioning. It is not possible to combine partial pension with an old age or disability pension.

The number of partial pensioners has increased rapidly. In January 1978, one and a half years after the system began, 33,424 had this type of pension; by September 1979 the number had increased to 47,713. The majority are men (69.1 percent in September 1979). The most frequent form of reduction of working hours, for both men and women, is from full time to half time.

It is possible to compare the economic results of the different schemes for the pensioners. A full early retirement pension is up to 30 percent lower than a full disability pension when everything else except the cause of retirement is kept constant.

It is also possible to compare an early retirement half pension, a disability half pension, and a partial pension covering reduction of working hours from full to half time. The difference between an early retirement pension and a disability pension is proportionally the same as in the full pension case. The partial pension in most cases gives less reduction of income than does the disability pension. This difference may, however, in some cases be reversed by negotiated pension plans (see below, "Negotiated Pension Plans"). The partial pension is also considered as income by the National Insurance Act, which means that it may lead to higher supplementary old age pensions than a disability pension.

Costs and Financing of Disability Pensions

The costs of disability pensioning have increased because their number has risen and because the terms for the pensioners have been improved. In nominal terms, the amount has of course also gone up due to inflation. Table 14.15 shows the range of cost increase during the last two decades. The costs of the supplementary disability pensions have increased sharply since their inception, and in the long run will probably exceed the costs for the national disability pension, unless the regulations change; e.g., the disability pension expressed in numbers of base amount increases.

Financing of the regular and temporary disability pensions is the same as for old age and widows' pensions. On the other hand, the supplementary pensions (old age, widows', and disability) are financed differently from the

Table 14.15. Expenditures for Disability Pensions, 1959-1979 (millions of Swedish crowns)

	Disability Pensions[a]		Supplementary Disability Pensions		
Year	Regular	Temporary	Regular	Temporary	Total
1959	319	35			354
1960	325	37			362
1961	361	43			404
1962	374	45			419
1963	435	54	4	2	495
1964	428	50	10	6	494
1965	493	57	25	12	587
1966	569	71	50	23	713
1967	643	85	80	35	843
1968	695	92	116	43	946
1969	753	103	168	56	1,080
1970	814	119	236	75	1,244
1971	994	150	370	106	1,620
1972	1,213	195	568	150	2,125
1973	1,363	227	777	189	2,556
1974	1,962	314	1,086	229	3,591
1975	2,409	390	1,416	277	4,492
1976	2,709	440	1,752	321	5,222
1977	2,869	579	1,794	400	5,642
1978	3,400	703	2,309	528	6,940
1979	3,954	829	2,877	690	8,350

Source: Statistical Abstracts of Sweden, various issues; and information from the National Social Insurance Board.

[a]Including the following programs when they supplement disability pensions: bonus pension supplement, municipal housing supplement, national housing supplement, child supplement, disability supplement (up to July 1975), handicap allowance; wife supplement not included.

national pensions (old age, widows', disability, municipal housing supplement, wife supplement, child supplement, handicap allowance). We include here a short review of the two systems of financing.

The national pension (including partial pensions) at present is financed primarily through the government budget and a payroll levy. The latter in January 1978 was 8.6 percent of paid wages. It is important to note that the levy finances national old age, widows', and partial pensions as well as national disability pensions. Up to and including 1974, there was a special national pension fee, structured in such a way that it most resembled a part of the income tax. The municipal housing supplements are paid primarily by the municipality from its budget. There is a national pension fund whose proceeds go to the financing of the national pensions. The size of the fund has been constant in nominal terms for a long time, and its importance for financing has therefore decreased continuously. The distribution among the various financing methods is displayed in Table 14.16.

The supplementary pensions are financed by payroll levies, which in 1978 constituted 11.75 percent of wages paid by firms. Wages exceeding 7.5 times the base amount (93,000 crowns in 1978) for an employee were not counted in the calculation of the levy up to 1982, nor is there a levy on employees over 65. From 1982 the total wage amount is included in the calculation of the levy. The payroll levy has steadily risen since 1960 and must continue to increase to cover the augmented pensions costs (see National Social Insurance Board, 1977a). Self-employed persons who belong to the supplementary pension system pay the corresponding fees themselves. Four different funds have been created within the supplementary pension system. The proceeds from them currently cover about one-third of the costs of pensioning.

Negotiated Pension Plans

For most disability pensioners, the national and the national supplementary disability pensions are probably augmented by other pension schemes (see Erikson, 1978; Folksams Sociala råd, 1977). Those employed in the governmental sector have a supplementary pension system for both the old and the disabled. The general rule is that the old age pensioner receives 65 percent of his last salary (the average of the salaries of the last five years calculated at the price level of the last year), plus 3.1 percent of one base amount a month if 65 years or older. The percentage is not calculated on the total salary for those with the highest salaries. The supplementary pension plan for governmental employees pays the difference between this level and the pensions from the national and the national supplementary pensions. For disability pensioners the percentage is still higher: 90 percent of the salary plus 3.1 percent of one base amount a month.

Persons employed by municipalities and county councils have a pension

Table 14.16. Souces of Financing National Pensions and National Supplementary Pensions (Old Age, Widows, Child, and Disability), 1959-1979 (percentage distribution)

	1959	1960	1961	1962	1963	1964	1965	1966	1967	1968	1969	1970	1971	1972	1973	1974	1975	1976	1977	1978	1979
National Pensions																					
Government grants	56.1	43.3	46.0	47.3	52.9	52.4	54.7	64.2	63.7	61.0	57.5	59.4	59.6	56.9	58.5	63.1	59.6	39.1	26.7	25.1	27.5
Municipal grants	14.3	14.4	14.1	14.9	12.8	15.3	15.1	8.3	8.9	9.3	10.7	10.7	10.8	10.6	10.2	9.7	9.6	9.1	8.7	8.5	8.5
Employers' contributions	—	—	—	—	—	—	—	—	—	—	—	—	—	—	—	—	30.4	49.5	61.9	62.9	60.8
Contributions from the insured	27.3	40.1	38.0	36.1	32.7	30.9	28.9	26.4	26.4	28.7	30.8	29.0	28.9	31.8	30.7	26.7	—	1.9	2.4	3.1	2.9
Interest, funds, etc.	2.3	2.2	1.9	1.7	1.6	1.4	1.3	1.1	1.0	1.0	1.0	0.9	0.8	0.7	0.6	0.5	0.4	0.4	0.3	0.3	0.3
National Supplementary Pensions[a]																					
Government grants		—	—	—	—	—	—	—	—	—	—	—	—	—	—	—	—	—	—	—	—
Municipal grants		—	—	—	—	—	—	—	—	—	—	—	—	—	—	—	—	—	—	—	—
Employers' contributions		97.3	93.7	92.0	84.6	83.0	79.7	76.8	74.9	74.7	71.7	68.9	68.2	68.0	65.9	64.1	62.9	64.4	63.7	63.1	60.6
Contributions from the insured		—	—	—	5.6	5.2	5.5	5.8	5.1	4.6	4.5	4.1	3.6	3.4	2.9	2.7	2.5	2.7	2.6	2.1	2.2
Interest, funds, etc.		2.7	6.3	8.0	9.8	11.8	14.8	17.4	20.0	20.7	23.8	27.0	28.2	28.6	31.2	33.2	34.6	32.9	33.7	34.7	37.2
Both National and National Supplementary Pensions																					
Government grants	56.1	36.6	37.0	32.7	33.8	31.2	31.6	35.8	33.9	30.2	27.9	28.9	28.9	26.7	27.7	31.0	29.3	18.6	12.8	12.1	13.3
Municipal grants	14.3	12.2	11.3	10.3	8.2	9.1	8.7	4.6	4.8	4.6	5.2	5.2	5.2	5.0	4.8	4.8	4.7	4.3	4.1	4.1	4.1
Employers' contributions	—	15.1	19.0	28.9	32.6	33.5	33.7	33.9	35.0	37.7	36.9	35.4	35.1	36.1	34.7	32.6	46.9	57.3	62.9	63.1	60.7
Contributions from the insured	27.3	33.9	30.5	25.0	20.9	20.5	19.0	17.3	16.4	16.5	17.3	16.2	15.9	16.8	16.0	14.5	1.3	2.3	2.5	2.6	2.6
Interest, funds, etc.	2.3	2.3	2.4	3.1	4.6	5.6	7.0	8.3	9.9	10.9	12.7	14.3	14.9	15.5	16.7	17.1	17.8	17.5	17.7	18.2	19.3

Source: See Table 14.15. Central Bureau of Statistics, Official Statistics of Sweden, *Social Welfare 1961*, Statistical Reports, Subgroup R 1964:12, 65:9, 66:12, 67:10, 68:15, Subgroup S 69:3, 70:4, 71:8, 72:7, 73:8, 74:10, 75:3, 76:9, 77:13, 78:2, 79:17, 80:12, 81:13.

[a]The system originated in 1960.

plan which differs only in minor details from that of the government sector. In general, 90 percent of the final salary is guaranteed, plus 3.6 percent of a base amount a month.

Most salaried employees in industry get supplementary pensions according to the industrial supplementary pension scheme, which gives disability pensioners 80 percent of the portion of the final salary which is below 7.5 times the base amount, 65 percent of the portion between 7.5 and 20 times base amount, and 32.5 percent of the portion between 20 and 30 times base amount. This pension scheme has been followed by other parts of the private sector.

These three supplementary pensions have existed since the national supplementary pension system started at the beginning of the 1960s. Since the early 1970s, the Swedish Trade Union Confederation (of blue collar workers), also has had an agreement concerning supplements to the national disability pension schemes. This system guarantees a total disability pension of about 95 percent of that part of the final wage which is below 7.5 times the base amount.

Employment Injury Insurance

In 1977 a new employment injury insurance law went into effect, replacing the industrial injury insurance that had existed since 1955. All wage earners, including employers and the self-employed, are covered, as well as certain groups of students. The previous system did not include employers and self-employed. "Industrial Injury" includes occupational accidents, occupational diseases, and accidents on the way to or from the place of work. Compensation during the first 90 days after an accident comes through health insurance, in the form of sickness benefits. Medical costs in the first 90 days are paid just as they are for nonoccupational injuries or illnesses: primarily through county income taxes. The only costs that employment injury insurance itself covers during these initial 90 days are medical care outside the country, dental care not covered by the dental care insurance, and special assistance not covered by health insurance. In 1975, 90.5 percent of the persons occupationally injured got support solely from health insurance.

Employment injury insurance covers expenses after the first 90 days. Prior to determination of a permanent reduced working capacity, sickness benefits continue to be paid, but are financed by employment injury insurance. Medical care is given in the same hospitals that other sick or injured persons go to; the only difference is that the insurance reimburses the county for the medical care. If working capacity is permanently reduced by at least 1/15, the injured party has the right to an annuity corresponding to the loss of income; the calculated loss must, however, be at least 0.25 times one base amount. The income upon which the annuity is calculated is maximized to 7.5 times base amount. The annuity is figured in number of base amounts and is indexed in this way. As is true of disability pensions, terms are more lenient for older persons, who are subject to fewer requirements for geographic or occupational mobility in the labor market.

If a person with an annuity becomes disability pensioned, only that part of the annuity which exceeds the pension is paid. Under the earlier industrial injury insurance, the relation of disability pension to annuity was formulated differently and the annuity was paid out according to different rules.

Industrial injuries resulting in invalidism have numbered between two and three thousand cases annually since 1955. From 1969 to 1970 the number increased markedly, from 2,280 cases to 2,545, because of a change in the rules for older wage earners, applying particularly to occupational diseases. The number of cases of invalidism due to occupational diseases climbed sharply during the 1970s (159 cases in 1969, 686 cases by 1974). Furthermore, many occupational diseases suffered previously have been reassessed as invalidism, and annuities have been granted. In 1969, 2,280 cases of invalidism were reported. That number increased by 995 through reassessment up to September 1979.

The insurance is financed through a payroll levy, which from 1975 to 1979 was 0.25 percent. The levy has been increased to 0.60 percent for the period 1980-84.

Employment Policy for the Disabled

The official policy concerning persons who have some form of injury or longstanding illness is to provide medical and vocational rehabilitation. An injury is not sufficient in itself to warrant an annuity or disability pension—the determining factor is whether the injury prevents the person from carrying out his job. In many cases that judgment is not self-evident and is difficult for the social insurance offices to make. The decision is often left to the labor market authorities, who can more easily evaluate a person's capabilities on the labor market. Those authorities also control the different labor market programs for the disabled. The Labor Market Administration in many ways holds a central position in disability policy.

Labor market policy toward the disabled has steadily expanded since the end of the 1950s. In the late 1950s about 3 percent of the Labor Market Administration's budget was for disability; twenty years later, it was 13 percent. During this period, labor market programs as a whole grew from 2 percent of the national budget and 0.5 percent of GNP to 9 percent of the budget and 3 percent of GNP. The increase has occurred primarily in such traditional areas as sheltered work and archive work (described below); new programs, such as semi-sheltered work, have played a smaller role.

The Labor Market Administration has three organizational levels: (1)

the National Labor Market Board, (2) the county labor market boards, and (3) the district labor market boards and local public employment offices. In addition to labor market policy decisions made by Parliament and the national government, decisions are also made by the National Labor Market Board, which formulates rules and interprets the laws passed by Parliament. When decisions on particular programs are to be made, decision-making can take various forms. In some cases the National Labor Market Board alone decides, as in vocational training courses for the unemployed. In other cases, the Board decides on some projects, and the county labor market boards on others, as in public relief work. In still other cases, the Board delegates all decisions to the county boards.

The assignment of individuals to the various programs takes place at the employment office level. This applies to all programs involving individuals (subsidies to firms that are not related to placement of persons into the firms are handled on different levels). This is also true for those cases where the county labor market boards are formally the decision-makers.

Earlier, the employment offices' efforts for the disabled that were classified as rehabilitation were distinct from their other efforts—a separate file was kept for all those seeking rehabilitation. In the mid-1970s, rehabilitation was integrated into the other functions of the offices and the special file disappeared, taking with it the possibility of getting statistical information concerning the number of rehabilitation cases. New statistics were introduced, however, concerning those seeking work at the offices, and the existence of a handicap is recorded, which makes it possible to estimate the number of disabled persons who contact the employment office in any given year. About 65,000 disabled persons did so at least once a year in 1977 and 1978.

The employment offices can classify an applicant as disabled either by referral from another authority, by a medical report, or on their own authority (if the last, the applicant must concur). The offices' criterion is that due to illness or injury the applicant will encounter difficulty in working on the open labor market. Most special programs are open only for persons classified as disabled. Under the new statistical system fewer persons are classified as disabled in comparison with the previous system. The number has sunk from 90,000-100,000 per year during the first half of the 1970s to 65,000 since 1976. There are three main reasons: (1) the old statistical series includes those in vocational rehabilitation; (2) disability is defined more narrowly in the new statistical series; and (3) the data of the new statistical series is continuously revised (see Andersson, 1977).

Employment Programs for the Disabled

As is true for all others seeking work at the public employment offices, placement on the open labor market has priority for the disabled. All labor market programs—e.g., labor market training, public relief work, and moving-cost allowances—which are available for nondisabled persons are of course also available for the disabled, who have long constituted a relatively large percentage within those programs. According to rehabilitation statistics, one-third of those participating in labor market training in the early 1970s were disabled. Of those who completed vocational training courses in 1975, 18 percent were occupationally disabled, as were 30 percent of those completing non-job-oriented training courses.

In addition to the general labor market programs, certain programs are geared especially to the disabled or to the disabled and certain other groups. These programs are of four types: (1) vocational rehabilitation, (2) programs to place the disabled in special or subsidized places of employment, (3) occupational assistance for the disabled, and (4) help in starting and sustaining a private business.

Vocational Rehabilitation

When a disabled person contacts the employment office, the first step is to assess his working capacity. Medical and psychological examinations are often given, and in a fair number of cases, more extensive examinations are conducted. Each county has special centers for vocational rehabilitation and guidance. Until 1980 they were operated by the county councils but financed by the government through the National Labor Market Board. Since 1980 they have been operated by the National Labor Market Board, through the county labor market boards. The rehabilitation centers were renamed labor market institutes, and some of the training centers were also reorganized as labor market institutes. The total cost of the new organization of the rehabilitation centers is calculated to be 490 million crowns for the first year. The rehabilitation centers provide more careful examination to determine a disabled person's capacity to manage different aspects (physical, mental, and social) of work, and they also provide work training, which means developing the physical, mental, and/or social capacities to enable a disabled person to carry out a job. Specific occupational training is in most cases performed *not* at the rehabilitation centers but at the same places as, and together with, the nondisabled.

Special Relief Work

In addition to public relief work, whose primary aim is to act as a business-cycle stabilizer, there are various kinds of special relief work. The most important is for older workers. Another is industrial relief work, established in 1967 to employ older industrial workers affected by structural changes in certain industries. These two programs accounted for about 60 percent of those engaged in special relief work in 1976. Since 1980 industrial relief work has been a part of the new organization for sheltered work (see below). A third type is for those with psychological or sociomedical occupational disabilities (about 14 percent of all those in special relief work). Other types are for persons with reduced working capacity (25 percent) and work in certain mental hospitals (2 percent). Thus, a large share of special relief work is geared to the variously disabled.

It is difficult to trace the development of special relief work because the statistics have been reorganized several times. Also, the distinction between general and special relief work has been vague in the northern parts of the country. The problem was "solved" in 1978 by making no statistical distinction between general and special relief work, so that it is no longer possible from 1979 on to determine what percentage of relief work is intended for disabled and older workers.

Sheltered Work

Until 1980, municipalities and county councils were eligible for national support to operate sheltered workshops for the disabled. The establishment must be approved by the National Labor Market Board and the workers must be referred by employment offices. Support was given in three ways: (1) an allowance covering some of the rent costs, (2) an allowance to purchase machines (half or sometimes two-thirds of the costs), and (3) an allowance toward running expenses (related to number of work hours).

The wages paid in the workshops were decided by agreement between the Association of Local Authorities and the Federation of County Councils on the one hand and the relevant labor unions on the other.

Since January 1980 the sheltered workshops have become parts of an organization, Samhällsföretag (Swedish Communal Industries), with a central administration and regional offices in each county. It will include about 27,000 employees (22,500 disabled) in 370 sheltered workshops (which include the previous sheltered workshops, office work centers, industrial relief work, and home work). The costs during fiscal year 1981-82 are estimated at 3.049 billion crowns, of which 2.126 billion will be paid by government subsidies. The wages are decided through negotiations between SFO (the negotiating body for state companies) and the trade unions. The subsidies are estimated to be 1.7 times the wage costs for disabled persons employed in 1981-82 (see Samhällsföretag, 1980).

Work with Wage Subsidy

This program was introduced in 1980. It combined two earlier programs, archive work and semi-sheltered work, described as follows.

Archive work consisted of office tasks of various kinds performed for the state or municipalities, paid completely or in part by the National Labor Market Board. It was established during the 1930s to assist unemployed clerks and other white collar groups for whom traditional public relief work was not considered suitable. During the Second World War, the number so employed rose from 200-300 annually at the end of the 1930s to 1,400 in

1945. The increase was composed mainly of refugees with a higher education who could not be directly employed in Sweden (for example, those with legal training). Of an average number of 1,385 archive workers during 1945, 1,008 were refugees (Inrikesdepartementet, 1968). After the war, archive work was used more and more for the disabled; by 1980 nearly 90 percent were disabled workers. A significant part of the nondisabled were the wartime or later refugees.

Archive work was performed either for governmental bodies and nonprofit organizations, in which case the National Labor Market Board paid the entire cost, or for municipal authorities, for which the Board paid 33 percent of the wages. There were five different wage groups. Those who were in archive work for five years or more could obtain an individual appointment, in which case wages did not fall into any of the five categories but instead were calculated according to type of work. At the end of 1977, 700 persons had individual appointments. An archive worker had a forty-hour week, or the normal work week for his occupation. In addition to full-time workers there were also three-quarter and half-time jobs with corresponding wage reductions.

A special type of archive work was in sheltered office work—printing houses and typewriting agencies—where up to one hundred were employed. This form of archive work became a part of the new sheltered work organization in January 1980. The other forms of archive work were incorporated in July 1980 into "work with wage subsidy."

Semi-sheltered employment was established in 1950 and was extended in 1968 in an attempt to give employment to the disabled on the regular labor market. Semi-sheltered employment meant that a disabled person was normally employed and the National Labor Market Board subsidized a part of the wages. It was intended primarily for new employees, but could also apply to those already employed, subject to certain requirements (as a rule, that the firm employed another disabled person).

In 1968 the subsidy was 2,500 crowns per six months per job. In 1972, compensation was raised to 40 percent of wage costs; in 1977, this was increased to 75 percent of the wage costs the first year, 50 percent the second, and 25 percent the third and fourth. For later years the compensation is to be determined by negotiations between the employer and the Labor Market Board. (The percentage is higher for severely disabled youths under 25 years of age.) The 1977 change was intended to give firms a stronger incentive to train the disabled in normal jobs.

In January 1977, 76 percent of those with semi-sheltered employment were employed by private firms, 21 percent by municipalities and county councils, and 3 percent by government-owned firms (SOU, 1978:14, p. 172). The wages for employees in semi-sheltered employment were the same as for other employees with corresponding work. Those with semi-sheltered work, however, could not take piecework employment. The terms of employment were the same as for other employees.

In July 1980, semi-sheltered work and archive work were combined into one "work with wage subsidy." The rules are generally those of semi-sheltered work. The terms of employment are the same as for other employees. The wage subsidy is 100 percent for government work, 90 percent for nonprofit organizations, and the same as for the earlier semi-sheltered employment for other employers.

The growth of the various labor market programs is shown in Table 14.17. It is important to keep in mind that a large part of those in special relief work, and a small part of those in archive work, are not disabled. None of these programs is intended as a permanent placement—the long-range goal is to place the disabled worker outside of the sheltered sector.

The age and sex distribution differs among the various forms of sheltered work, as shown in Table 14.18. For obvious reasons, few older people are placed in vocational rehabilitation. Men predominate in sheltered work, whereas more women are in archive work: sheltered employment implies

Table 14.17. Number of Participants in Labor Market Programs for the Disabled, 1961-1979 (yearly average)

	Archive Work[a]	Sheltered Work	Semi-Sheltered Work	Vocational Rehabilitation	Special Relief Work[b]
1961	1,590	1,893[c]			
1962	1,791	2,168			
1963	2,077	2,581			2,100
1964	2,392	3,641			2,600
1965	2,718	4,658			3,800
1966	3,068	5,695			4,500
1967	3,617	6,809			8,300
1968	4,922	7,801	286[c]		13,500
1969	6,629	9,254	713	1,789[c]	11,300
1970	8,239	10,788	1,274	1,881	11,400
1971	9,563	11,877	1,682	1,964	14,300
1972	10,048	12,819	2,163	2,108	13,600
1973	12,436	13,796	4,021	2,427	19,800
1974	13,900	15,057	6,326	2,716	15,600
1975	14,663	15,996	8,302	2,559	13,000
1976	14,953	16,410	9,828	2,546	13,500
1977	15,097	16,792	10,786	2,682	14,100
1978	15,362	17,175	11,687	2,794	14,900
1979	15,465	17,952	13,288	2,733	. . .[d]

Sources: National Labor Market Board, *Labor Market Statistics* (various issues).

[a]The figures for July 1974-April 1975 include only the disabled; all other figures include both disabled and other persons. The figures from 1974 and 1975 are therefore too low compared to those from other years.

[b]Some forms of special relief work are available only for disabled workers, but others are also available for other categories, e.g., older workers.

[c]Eleven-month average; figures from January not available.

[d]Not available; not possible to distinguish general from special relief work after 1978.

Table 14.18. Age and Sex Distribution of Participants in Labor Market Programs for the Disabled, June 1978

	Semi-Sheltered Work		Sheltered Work		Archive Work		Vocational Rehabilitation (work training)		Total	
Age	Men	Women	Men	Women	Men	Women	Men	Women	Men	Women
-17	47	6	25	13	—	—	7	8	79	27
18-19	124	41	64	33	14	11	50	37	252	122
20-24	734	379	581	324	129	166	213	167	1,657	1,036
25-34	1,563	718	2,002	1,114	877	853	519	305	4,961	2,990
35-44	1,284	630	2,050	1,202	1,156	1,060	425	294	4,915	3,186
45-49	806	427	1,307	823	889	914	242	169	3,244	2,333
50-54	1,002	546	1,612	975	1,241	1,462	136	99	3,991	3,082
55-59	1,262	600	1,926	1,024	1,619	1,920	70	39	4,877	3,583
60-64	1,010	324	1,292	609	1,331	1,514	3	2	3,636	2,449
65-	186	46	121	55	111	137	—	—	418	238
Total	8,018	3,717	10,980	6,172	7,367	8,037	1,665	1,120	28,030	19,046

Source: Information from the National Labor Market Board.

manual labor, and archive work implies office work; consequently the sex distribution in the sheltered sector reflects that of the open labor market. Semi-sheltered work has come to mean above all industrial work, which explains why this program contains a significantly larger number of men.

Comparing the distribution of various types of disabilities across programs (Table 14.19), one finds that, for example, the mentally retarded are greatly underrepresented in archive work as compared to semi-sheltered and sheltered work. The table shows only a part of the picture, since not all the labor market programs are included. Table 14.20 provides a general view of the differences in placement of the disabled in normal labor market jobs and in special employment. Clear differences exist. A higher proportion of the sociomedically handicapped relative to other handicapped are placed in public relief work. Those with visual handicaps are more numerous in labor market training (which for this group includes mostly non-job-oriented adjustment courses). The mentally retarded have proportionally more placements within sheltered and semi-sheltered work.

If factors such as age, sex, occupation, region, and nationality are held constant, one finds that unemployed disabled persons registered at the employment offices are placed in the special programs significantly more often than unemployed nondisabled persons registered there. This is so for all groups of handicapped (Wadensjö, 1978).

In addition to direct placement in forms of sheltered work, support exists in the form of assistance of financial aid. These allowances can be paid to employees, business owners, and the self-employed. There are four types of support: grants and loans for motor vehicles, grants for tools and equipment, grants for special arrangements at place of work, and grants for assistants. The amounts given below were valid in 1980.

Table 14.19. Distribution of Disability Types among Labor Market Programs for the Disabled, June 1978

Disability	Semi-Sheltered Work		Sheltered Work		Archive Work		Vocational Rehabilitation (work training)		Total	
	No.	%	No.	%	No.	%	No.	%	No.	%
Heart or lung disease	809	30	854	32	946	35	71	3	2,680	100
Hearing impairment	358	40	239	27	276	31	21	2	894	100
Visual impairment	361	40	244	27	268	30	35	4	908	100
Motor handicap	4,619	31	4,688	32	4,575	31	984	7	14,866	100
Other physical handicaps	1,733	25	2,512	36	2,412	34	366	5	7,023	100
Mental handicap	1,583	18	3,691	41	2,985	33	696	8	8,955	100
Mentally retarded	1,218	29	2,556	62	242	6	135	3	4,151	100
Sociomedical handicap	1,054	19	2,368	43	1,638	30	477	9	5,537	100
None	—	—	—	—	2,062	100	—	—	2,062	100
Total	11,735	25	17,152	36	15,404	33	2,785	6	47,076	100
Excluding nondisabled	11,735	26	17,152	38	13,342	30	2,785	6	45,014	100

Source: Information from the National Labor Market Board.

Table 14.20. Number and Percentage of the Disabled Placed through Employment Offices, 1978 (percentages in parentheses)

Disability	Placed in Normal Job	Semi-Sheltered Work	Sheltered Work	Archive Work	Public Relief Work	Vocational Rehabilitation	Labor Market Training	No Longer in Contact with Employment Office (reasons unknown)	No Longer in Contact with Employment Office (reasons unknown)
Heart or lung disease	211 (6.5)	77 (2.4)	75 (2.3)	65 (2.0)	304 (9.3)	192 (5.9)	575 (17.6)	1,351 (41.4)	532 (16.3)
Hearing impairment	105 (8.3)	57 (4.5)	22 (1.7)	20 (1.6)	118 (9.3)	41 (3.2)	349 (27.5)	402 (31.6)	165 (13.0)
Visual impairment	64 (5.0)	43 (3.4)	22 (1.7)	28 (2.2)	86 (6.7)	69 (5.4)	487 (38.2)	212 (16.6)	229 (18.0)
Motor handicap	1,652 (7.1)	593 (2.5)	582 (2.5)	440 (1.9)	1,016 (4.4)	2,104 (9.0)	5,743 (24.7)	4,589 (19.7)	4,708 (20.2)
Other somatic handicaps	756 (7.6)	293 (3.0)	263 (2.7)	220 (2.2)	846 (8.5)	655 (6.6)	2,976 (30.0)	2,064 (20.8)	1,532 (15.5)
Psychiatric handicap	644 (6.1)	219 (2.1)	383 (3.6)	262 (2.5)	1,145 (10.8)	1,159 (10.9)	2,533 (23.9)	2,349 (22.1)	1,940 (18.3)
Mentally retarded	86 (4.0)	177 (8.1)	193 (8.9)	31 (1.4)	332 (15.3)	208 (9.6)	446 (20.5)	392 (18.0)	314 (14.4)
Sociomedical handicap	619 (4.5)	224 (1.6)	372 (2.7)	139 (1.0)	5,010 (36.1)	1,051 (7.6)	3,019 (21.8)	4,687 (33.8)	2,324 (16.8)
Total	4,137 (6.3)	1,683 (2.6)	1,912 (2.9)	1,205 (1.8)	8,857 (13.5)	5,479 (8.3)	16,128 (24.6)	16,046 (24.4)	11,744 (17.9)

Source: Information from the National Labor Market Board.
Note: The same person may appear in several programs; the sum of the percentages in a row may therefore exceed 100.

Grants and Loans for Motor Vehicles

Disabled persons who need a car or special vehicle to get to work can receive an allowance of up to 30,000 crowns plus the expense of converting a car to handicap needs. The allowance is income-tested: the entire cost is paid for persons with a pre-tax income under 34,000 crowns per year; the allowance disappears completely with an income of over 50,000 crowns. The amount paid out to persons with incomes between these two sums is reduced proportionally. Those who receive a reduced amount may in certain cases borrow an interest-free sum toward the rest of the cost. A new allowance cannot be paid out until at least five years have passed. In fiscal year 1978-79, 1,255 persons received this type of allowance, for a total sum of 14.1 million crowns.

Grants for Tools and Equipment

These grants cannot exceed 50,000 crowns for new purchases and 6,000 crowns for repairs up to a maximum of half the replacement cost. In fiscal year 1978-79, 1,715 such grants were made, for a total of 6.2 million crowns.

Grants for Special Arrangements at Place of Work

Grants for special elevators, widening doors, etc. are available up to a maximum of 50,000 crowns per disabled person. If the arrangement is of value to someone other than the disabled person, the amount can be reduced to half the cost. In fiscal year 1978-79, 827 such allowances were given to 957 persons for a total cost of 13 million crowns.

Grants for Assistants

A firm is entitled to a maximum of 10,000 crowns per disabled person each half year toward the expenses of an assistant for that person. This support cannot be given if the person has work with wage subsidy or sheltered work, or is in relief work, with the exception of disabled youths. In fiscal year 1978-79, 480 received support for a work assistant.

All four types of support described here have increased rapidly in the last few years.

Grants for Resettlement in Independent Work

Most of the labor market programs are geared toward helping people obtain or maintain employment. There are also aids to facilitate the starting or running of a business. This form of support is available to small business owners and the self-employed, and is called "grants for resettlement in independent work." Up to 15,000 crowns can be given as an allowance or interest-free loan for the purchase of machine equipment so that an older disabled person can start, or a disabled person can continue, a small-enterprise or self-employment activity. To start up a firm, an additional 60,000 crowns can be granted as a loan.

Resettlement in independent work is the oldest labor market program for the disabled, having been established in 1915. Until 1962, the National Pensions Board (predecessor of the National Social Insurance Board) was in charge of it. Activity was modest, but increased after the National Labor Market Board took over the program in 1962. The number of applications granted since then has varied from 400 to 800 per year. During the 1970s the number of granted requests diminished; in fiscal year 1977-78 only 383 grants were given out, for a total of 8.4 million crowns.

Costs and Financing of Employment Programs for the Disabled

The government share of the labor market program is financed mainly through the national budget rather than through special taxes or fees. The only exception is labor market training, which is financed in part through a proportional payroll tax equal to 0.4 percent of wages. Thus, all the special labor market programs for the disabled are financed through the general budget. The municipal and county council costs are financed through their proportional income taxes, but those costs have been very small since the reorganization of sheltered workshops and vocational rehabilitation in 1980.

The growth of expenditures for labor market programs for the disabled has been rapid during the last twenty years, as can be seen in Table 14.21.

Expenditures for special relief work are usually not included among labor market programs for the disabled. During the last few years, these costs exceeded one billion crowns, and a large part was for the disabled. Government payments for labor market programs for the disabled during the budget year 1976-77 were as follows: archive work, 703 million crowns; sheltered work, 155 million; semi-sheltered employment, 126 million; vocational rehabilitation, 42 million; grants and loans for work aids for the disabled, 30 million; and grants for resettlement in independent work, 8 million. In addition, of course, there are administrative and other expenses.

Municipal and county council net expenditures for labor market measures for the occupationally handicapped were 533 million crowns in 1976. Of this amount, 77 million went to vocational rehabilitation and 456 to sheltered workshops. The rise has been rapid in the last decade—in 1970, municipal and county council expenditures for both of these programs were 115 million crowns.[13]

Labor Market Legislation

Until the 1970s, the labor market in Sweden was regulated mainly through various agreements between the trade unions and the employers'

Table 14.21. Government Expenditures for Labor Market Programs for the Disabled through the National Labor Market Board, 1959-1978 (million of Swedish crowns)

	Programs Excluding Special Public Relief Jobs					Programs Including Special Public Relief Jobs[a]			
Year	In Current Prices	In 1968 Prices	Real Growth Rate (%)	% of GNP	Special Public Relief Jobs,[a] Current Prices[b]	In Current Prices	In 1968 Prices	Real Growth Rate (%)	% of GNP
1959	14	20	—	0.02	—	—	—	—	—
1960	14	19	−4.1	0.02	—	—	—	—	—
1961	17	22	18.8	0.02	—	—	—	—	—
1962	23	29	29.1	0.03	—	—	—	—	—
1963	31	38	31.0	0.03	—	—	—	—	—
1964	45	53	40.4	0.04	78	123	146	—	0.11
1965	63	71	33.3	0.06	86	149	169	15.8	0.13
1966	75	80	11.9	0.07	133	208	221	30.8	0.17
1966/67[c]	86	89	—	0.07	151	237	247	—	0.18
1967/68	109	110	23.0	0.08	249	358	362	46.6	0.26
1968/69	152	150	35.0	0.10	334	486	480	32.6	0.33
1969/70	212	199	33.0	0.13	303	515	485	1.0	0.32
1970/71	295	259	29.7	0.17	284	579	508	4.7	0.33
1971/72	346	285	10.0	0.18	455	801	659	29.7	0.42
1972/73	388	300	5.4	0.19	635	1,023	791	20.0	0.49
1973/74	472	337	12.2	0.20	771	1,243	886	12.0	0.53
1974/75	693	450	33.7	0.26	670	1,363	885	−0.1	0.51
1975/76	921	544	20.8	0.30	771	1,692	998	12.8	0.55
1976/77	1,159	617	13.5	0.34	991	2,150	1,144	14.6	0.64
1977/78	1,358	653	5.9	0.36	1,393	2,751	1,323	15.6	0.74
1978/79	1,466	650	−0.4	0.34	1,068	2,534	1,097	−17.1	0.58

Sources: National Labor Market Board, Annual Reports; information from the National Labor Market Board; Statistical Reports N 1975:98, Appendix 4, N 1979:7.4, P 1980:8. Konjunkturläget Hösten 1981:3.

[a]Note that special public relief work is also for older workers.

[b]Values are deflated by the consumer price index.

[c]July 1 through June 30.

associations. This policy has changed, and the labor market is now regulated to a great degree by legislation. The trade unions have been the prime supporters of the new laws, whose primary goal is better job security.

The legislation has both directly, through special provisions for the disabled, as well as indirectly, influenced the labor market position of the disabled. Two laws in particular, both passed in 1974, are of interest—the Job Security Law and the Law for Promotion of Employment. The first regulates, among other things, rules for layoffs, which may be made for individual reasons or because of redundancies.[14] Age, illness, or reduced working capacity are not sufficient individual reasons for layoffs; only if the employee cannot perform any work at all is dismissal permitted, but in that case a disability pension is recommended as a better alternative. Until 1980, persons who were disability pensioned could be laid off; now only those who receive a regular, not a temporary, disability pension can be let go.

Seniority is the main principle when a firm must reduce its labor force.[15] Employees 45 years or older may, however, count each month employed in the firm (but no more than 60 months) after they have reached the age of 45 as two months. Other exceptions to the general rule are that persons who are employed under the Law for Promotion of Employment (old or disabled workers) and workers in semi-sheltered employment as a rule may not be dismissed.

The Law for Promotion of Employment permits a county labor market board to obtain information from a firm about its work force—for example, the number of workers with reduced working capacity. The board may compel a firm to negotiate an agreement to retain or hire disabled workers; if no such agreement is reached, the board may request the firm to increase the share of disabled (or aged) hired. This section of the law was applied very infrequently until the National Labor Market Board carried on a campaign for job placement under it in the last months of 1979 and the first half of 1980.[16] The number of disabled persons placed by the employment offices in normal jobs increased by 50 percent between two periods, November 1978-April 1979 and November 1979-April 1980. Some of the increase may, however, be explained by changes in the general labor market situation (National Labor Market Board, 1980).

The Economic Effects of Disability Policy

In this section we address the central questions concerning disability policy, confining ourselves as before to the disabled of working age. The questions are these:

1. The preceding discussion clearly shows the marked increase both in the number of programs for the disabled and in costs. What factors account for the increase?

2. Improved pension benefits can contribute to reduction of the labor supply, yet the goal of labor market policy is to increase the labor supply of the handicapped. How have these different measures together affected labor supply?

3. The aim behind programs for the disabled is to keep them in the open, not just the sheltered, labor market. Temporary disability pensions are based on the belief that possibilities other than pensioning exist, and reentry into the labor market is not considered impossible even for those with regular pensions. What success has been achieved by this labor-market-oriented policy?

4. The costs of labor market programs for the disabled have increased rapidly during the last two decades, and the economic efficiency of the programs has therefore become a question of great importance. What do the few existing cost-benefit analyses indicate?

5. One of the major objectives of disability policy is to ameliorate the economic situation of the disabled relative to other groups. How has their economic situation changed in this respect?

Causes of the Growth of Disability Programs

The number of disability pensions remained unchanged during the 1950s and the beginning of the 1960s. The number began to increase in the middle of the 1960s; the growth accelerated rapidly from 1970 to 1976. In 1976 the age for retirement pensions was lowered from 67 to 65, resulting in a sharply reduced number of disability pensions that year, but the number of disability pensions has continued to increase from that new, lower number. If the rates of new disability pensions granted, and of old pensions terminated through rehabilitation, were to continue at the 1974 level for each age group, the number of disability pensions among those aged 16-64 will continue to increase to the point that in 1985 there will be 282,000 pensions as compared with 231,000 in 1974 (see National Social Insurance Board, 1978).

In the previous pages we have described various aspects of the increase in numbers of disability pensions. That growth is shown even more clearly in Tables 14.22 and 14.23, displaying the flows into, between, and out of temporary and regular disability pensions, and the age structure of new disability pensioners. The tables show that the upswing began in 1970 and continued to the mid-1970s.

Flows out of disability because of rehabilitation are small, as seen in Table 14.22, and they have decreased during the last decade. A study by the National Social Insurance Board (1978a, pp. 30-31) of the average yearly percentage rehabilitated in different age groups 1971-74 shows that the percentage decreases with age: it was 4.9 percent for men aged 20, 2.3 percent for women of that age, 1.5 percent and 1.3 percent for those aged 30, 1.4 percent and 1.0 percent for those aged 40, 0.6 percent and 0.8 percent for those aged 50, and 0.2 percent and 0.6 percent for those aged 60.

If we examine changes in the demographic composition of disability pensions during the sharp upswing in the 1970s, we find that the rise in the youngest age groups, 16-29 and 30-44, is slight. Table 14.23 shows that the number of new disability pensions among those aged 16-19 decreased sharply during the 1970s. On the other hand, the number in that period rose in the age group 45-59, and even more in the group 60-64. It is also quite clear that the number of disability-pensioned men increased much faster than the number of women in the oldest age group, whereas the differences in the younger age groups were very slight.

The number granted annuities through employment injury insurance also rose in the early 1970s, although they are considerably fewer than those granted disability pensions. A large part of this increase stems from the fact

Table 14.22. Net Flows Into and Out of Temporary Disability Pensions (TDP) and Disability Pensions (DP), 1968-1978

Year	New TDPs	Outflow from TDP (other than to DP)		New Flow from TDP to DP	New DPs (not from TDP)	Outflow from DP		Net Outflow from TDP and DP to Other pensions[a]	Net Inflow to DP and TDP
		Deaths	Withdrawals			Deaths	Withdrawals		
1968	8,942	499	2,617	4,781	17,116	5,272	285	11,834	5,551
1969	9,270	547	1,281	4,702	18,355	5,199	259	12,118	8,221
1970	9,619	508	1,402	5,606	22,088	5,237	412	11,695	12,453
1971	12,318	603	1,192	6,162	35,267	5,641	338	13,053	26,758
1972	13,019	719	1,042	7,427	33,894	6,271	255	17,245	21,381
1973	13,593	721	1,072	8,479[b]	36,569	6,451	309	20,118	21,491
1974	12,952	773	933	9,413	34,930	6,780	405	21,982	17,009
1975	12,079	795	933[c]	9,464	30,817	7,047	377	24,610	9,134
1976 (1st half)	6,127	357	930	4,634[b]	14,219	3,630	203	12,837	2,389
1976 (2nd half)	8,124	394	809	4,555[b]	15,578	2,796	140	60,454[d]	−40,891[d]
1977	19,021	842	1,155	8,752	30,558	5,449	258	21,817	20,058
1978	16,748	952	1,029	10,282	26,910	5,421	217	22,814	13,225

Source: Månadsstatistik för allmän försäkring (Monthly Statistics for Social Insurance), Riksförsäkringsverket (National Social Insurance Board).

[a]Flow to old age pensions is the most important.

[b]The numbers for 1973 and 1976 (1st half and 2nd half) are calculated on the assumption that there are no transitions from other pensions to DP and TDP and no transitions from DP to TDP. The actual value for 1976 is 9,296. The method used in the table underestimates this year by 107.

[c]The published figure is 6,345. It includes, however, short-term withdrawals, which are not included in any other year. We have assumed that withdrawals excluding short-term ones were the same in 1975 as in 1974.

[d]In July 1976, 49,200 disability pensions were converted to old age pensions when the mandatory retirement age was lowered from 67 to 65. An adjusted value of net outflow from TDP and DP to other pensions in the 2nd half of 1976 is 11,254 and the adjusted net inflow to DP and TDP 8,309. The adjusted value for the net inflow for the entire year 1976 will be 10,698.

Table 14.23. New Temporary and Regular Disability Pensions by Age Groups, 1970-1979

Year	Age 16-19	Age 20-24	Age 25-29	Age 30-34	Age 35-39	Age 40-44	Age 45-49	Age 50-54	Age 55-59	Age 60-64	Age 16-64	Age 65-66	Age 16-66
1970	1,057	482	462	499	648	1,189	2,048	3,481	6,153	10,814	26,833	5,887	32,720
1971	642	456	545	615	807	1,369	2,643	4,753	8,685	16,774	37,289	6,129	43,418
1972	813	489	648	750	1,028	1,740	3,286	5,502	10,101	19,978	44,335	7,508	51,843
1973	700	463	674	740	1,029	1,679	3,192	5,967	10,307	19,808	44,559	7,058	51,617
1974	578	363	579	673	917	1,470	2,795	5,262	8,876	17,926	39,439	6,014	45,453
1975	660	352	544	693	900	1,403	2,813	5,490	9,589	17,058	39,502	5,496	44,998
1976	525	319	566	833	1,033	1,581	3,015	5,887	11,110	18,322	43,191	1,576	44,767
1977	543	410	680	1,013	1,250	1,885	3,385	6,498	12,129	17,940	45,733	—	—
1978	430	321	638	984	1,289	1,971	3,344	6,316	12,087	17,114	44,494	—	—
1979	479	307	594	980	1,291	1,770	3,176	5,962	12,623	16,501	43,683	—	—

Source: Information from the National Social Insurance Board.

Notes: Table 14.22 dates a pension in year it is granted; this table dates it in year pensioner made application. Several months may elapse between application and decision; the pension is then paid retroactively.

The transfers from widow pension and wife supplement are included in this table but not in Table 14.22

The mandatory retirement age was lowered from 67 to 65 in July 1976.

that the National Social Insurance Board took over 25,100 annuities from private insurance companies in 1974. The greatest increment occurred in the same group as for disability pensions: older men. It is important to note that annuities in the majority of the cases are granted to persons whose working capacity is reduced by less than half of total capacity.

The rise of labor market (employment) programs shown in Table 14.24 has been more continuous. Regardless of the condition of the economy, the number of persons employed in archive, sheltered, and semi-sheltered work and the costs for those programs have risen each year. The age distribution of those in the labor market programs is completely different from that of disabiity pensioners. This is true even of archive work, which is aimed at older and middle-aged white collar workers.

In summary, measures for the disabled have expanded rapidly during the last decade, but the expansion has taken different forms for different age groups: the increase has occurred for older persons mainly in disability pensions, and for the younger mainly in labor market programs. Three explanations can be considered: (1) an increase in the actual number of persons with disabilities has occurred, (2) the labor market has changed in such a way that a particular impairment results more and more in occupational disability, and (3) it has become easier or more attractive for a person with a given disability to receive a disability pension or to work in one of the special programs for the disabled.

Increase in the Number of Disabled

The first is the most obvious explanation. The number of disabled could have risen, for example, through a change in age composition of the population, resulting in augmentation of the number of disability pensioners, even if all other things remained equal. Such a change could account only for a very limited increase in disability pensioning, however, and it cannot explain the upswing of labor market programs, which are aimed primarily at those in younger age groups. Table 14.25 shows a sharp rise in the percentage of disability pensioners in the highest age groups, whereas the increase among those up to age 40 is quite limited.

Of course we cannot rule out the possibility that there are increasingly more people who are disabled from illness, injury, or abuse of alcohol or narcotics. As mentioned earlier, we lack a time series for the number of disabled. Annual labor force surveys report a pronounced rise since 1963 in the number of persons who say that they do not work because they are unable to do so. That rise occurred only in the older age groups—for those aged 45-54, the number rose from 16,800 in 1963 to 22,900 in 1978; and for those aged 55-64, it rose from 39,200 in 1963 to 76,300 in 1978. Caution must be used in interpreting this information, however. The increase accompanied the rise in number of disability pensions, and the direction of causality is more likely to go *from* disability pensioning to a respondent's

Table 14.24. Government Expenditures for Employment Programs for the Disabled, 1969-1979 (in millions of Swedish crowns)

Year	Vocational Rehabilitation[a]	Special Relief Jobs[b]	Sheltered Work[a]	Archive Work[c]	Semi-Sheltered Work	Grants and Loans for Motor Vehicles	Grants for Tools and Equipment	Grants for Special Arrangements at the Workplace	Grants for Work Assistants	Grants for Resettlement in Independent Work
1969/70	—	303	59	101	4	11	0.2	0.04		8
1970/71	—	284	84	138	7	15	0.3	0.1		9
1971/72	—	455	103	196	8	15	0.3	0.2	0.4	11
1972/73	23	635	80	241	16	13	0.4	1.3	0.5	10
1973/74	26	771	84	292	39	12	1.1	2.1	0.8	9
1974/75	33	670	125	395	66	11	1.1	2.5	1.0	7
1975/76	33	771	135	557	96	12	2.4	4.2	1.6	8
1976/77	41	991	155	703	125	16	3.0	8.4	2.2	8
1977/78	51	1,393	188	826	154	14	3.7	8.4	2.9	8
1978/79	57	1,068	182	850	222	19	5.3	11.0	3.7	9

Source: National Labor Market Board, Annual Reports and Information from the National Labor Market Board.
[a]Sheltered work included vocational rehabilitation up to 1972-73.
[b]Also for groups other than the disabled; e.g., for some groups of aged workers.
[c]A few in archive work are not disabled.

Table 14.25. Temporary and Regular Disability Pensioners as a Percentage of Total Population, by Sex and Age Groups, Selected Years

	Men					Women				
Age Group	1967	1970	1973	1976	1979	1967	1970	1973	1976	1979
16-19	0.9	1.1	1.2	1.1	0.9	0.7	0.8	0.9	0.8	0.7
20-29	0.9	0.9	1.1	1.1	1.1	0.8	0.8	0.9	1.0	0.9
30-39	1.3	1.3	1.4	1.4	1.6	1.3	1.3	1.5	1.5	1.7
40-49	2.1	2.4	2.9	3.2	3.5	2.3	2.6	3.2	3.6	3.5
50-59	4.7	5.4	7.3	8.5	10.4	5.2	5.5	7.3	8.7	10.7
60-64	11.2	13.0	19.2	22.6	26.0	9.5	10.0	14.2	17.3	20.7

Source: SOU (1978:14, p. 45) and National Social Insurance Board, Official Statistics of Sweden, *National Insurance 1979.*

statement that he or she does not work because of physical incapacity, rather than vice versa. The rise in both areas is so rapid that it is hard to believe that the actual number of disabled would have increased so quickly.[17] However, the number reporting they are unable to work has decreased in the oldest age groups (45-54 and 55-64) during the last few years, and at the same time the number of disability pensioners in those age groups has increased.

One must use other information to determine if the percentage of disabled persons has increased. A possible reason could be a rise in occupational injuries—yet the number both of occupational accidents and of resultant deaths has declined during the last few decades.[18] The decline in accidents can be explained primarily by changes in the occupational structure rather than by a decrease in the frequency of injuries in the various occupations. The number of cases of invalidism resulting from occupational injuries rose in the beginning of the 1970s, but was probably due to altered ways of dealing with older persons so injured.

The upswing cannot be explained by an increase in the number of traffic accidents (which have not increased in the last ten years; see Andreasson, 1978), nor by increased frequency of disability resulting from physical illnesses. The disease which formerly crippled so many, polio, has been eliminated. There is probably no great increase in the number of cases of mental illness during this period, and improved treatment methods, mainly through tranquilizers, have shortened treatment time and have reduced the number of people in institutions. These circumstances may have contributed to a rise in the number of persons in labor market programs for the disabled, but not to a rise in the number with disability pensions.[19]

Consumption of alcohol has risen in Sweden during the last two decades. A contributing factor was the elimination in the mid-1950s of the rationing system that made it necessary to show a permit when buying spirits and wine and which limited the quantity that could be bought each month. The elimination of the system was accompanied by higher duties on spirits. The result was a fairly constant level of consumption of spirits but increased wine consumption.[20] According to Lassenius (1974), who studied the effects of abolishing the rationing system in the municipality of Sundsvall (51,000 inhabitants in 1955) the main effect was that the alcoholics drank more and their medical, social, and employment problems increased, but the number of alcoholics did not rise. Increased alcohol abuse probably has in fact contributed to the number of persons with disabilities, and also to the number of disability pensioners and participants in disability employment programs, but it can explain only a part of the increase. The number of disability pensioners has increased primarily in the northern parts of Sweden,[21] whereas alcoholism is concentrated primarily in the larger cities.

It is difficult to determine from disability pension statistics how many persons were pensioned because of alcoholism. Until 1946, it was impossible for a person with alcohol problems in the two years preceding pensioning to get a disability or old age pension, and a pensioner who developed alcohol problems could lose his pension.[22] According to the 1946 law, alcoholics could receive an old age pension, but only in exceptional cases was it possible for them to be awarded a disability pension. That practice gradually changed, and alternative diagnoses (mainly back injuries) were used as a disguise for alcoholism. A study of disability-pensioned men in Uppsala (Bernhardsson, 1977) shows that in 30 percent of the cases, alcoholism was a contributing factor but was not the main diagnosis and was therefore not included in the statistics. (On average, 50 percent of disability pensioners have one or more secondary diagnoses; Eriksen, 1980, p. 174.) In 1977 the law was changed so that only the existence of disability, not its cause, could be considered. It is therefore now easier to get a pension when the diagnosis is alcoholism, drug addiction, or sociopathology. The number of new disability pensions based on a diagnosis of alcoholism increased from 1,059 in 1976 to 1,805 in 1977,[23] but it is not clear whether this means more new pensions or only that the diagnoses changed. Even after 1977, the social stigma connected with alcoholism probably makes statistics unreliable. Similarly, in the classification of the occupationally disabled by the public employment offices, alcohol abuse (sociomedical reasons) is probably underrepresented in the statistics.

In sum, despite the increase of alcoholism, in all probability only a small part of the rise in disability programs can be attributed to an actual increase of disabled persons, nor does a general rise in their number explain why the upswing is largely concentrated in a short period at the beginning of the 1970s.

Increase in Occupational Disability

The second possible explanation for the increase of disability programs is that occupational disability has become more common. Several different arguments can be pursued. During the 1960s the Swedish economy underwent considerable structural change. Forestry was rationalized and mechanized, causing a great reduction in employment. Certain branches of industry, for example textiles, suffered heavy losses leading to structural transformation. More firms went out of business than in the 1950s, especially during the recession of 1967-68. These changes may have in part been caused by the solidarity wage policy pursued by the labor unions, which led to diminished wage differences across industries and firms in the 1960s.[24]

Each time a firm folds, a certain number of employees will have difficulty in getting a new job or will not get one at all. They may be people whose work was not meaningful; more often, perhaps, they are people who were barely able to perform their job but who, because of physical, mental, or other problems, would be difficult to place in other types of work. A study of employees at the Volvo works in Skövde indicated that 25 percent of the blue collar workers and 21 percent of the white collar workers were only "conditionally fit for work."[25] The percentage was much higher among older than younger employees.

The solidarity wage policy has come to mean an equalizing of wage levels not only across industries and firms, but also across groups of workers within a firm. This means that the wage differences between persons with different productivity levels have gradually decreased, and that persons with lower productivity—due to a disability, for example—have had a more difficult time in getting a job.

Even with the greater employment security of the 1970s, the disabled could have encountered increased difficulties in the labor market. Reduced possibilities for layoffs, thus creating an increased economic commitment for every employment decision, make employers less willing to hire the disabled, especially the older ones, who have the strongest employment protection.

Structural changes, wage equalization, and increased employment protection for those already employed no doubt contributed to participation in disability programs, but they cannot explain why the rise was so concentrated in time, nor are they really sufficient to explain the overall rise.

More Generous Pensions and Programs

The economic situation of disability-pensioned persons has improved in successive stages. The three most important steps are the raising of pensions in 1963, the addition of bonus supplements since 1970, and, especially, the introduction of the supplementary pension system. The first supplementary pensions were paid out in 1963, but the transition regulations have been such that, as described in more detail earlier, the pensions have gradually become larger.

Another important factor is the liberalization of rules for granting pensions, especially in 1970 and 1972, when pensioning for labor market and medical reasons together, and for labor market reasons alone, was established. These changes were introduced after great pressure from the trade unions, who wanted older persons exempted from the selective labor market policy, which required geographic mobility by many of the older unemployed persons in the northern part of the country. An indirect test of this liberalization is that a much higher percentage of employees 60-64 years old reported physical exhaustion at the end of the work day in 1968 than in 1974, according to the Living Conditions Survey; this decline is probably a consequence of the liberalization in 1970. For the age group 15-59 years old, there was on the contrary a slight increase in percentage (Kindlund, 1978). Liberalization of the rules also made it easier, as we have just seen, for those with alcohol problems to benefit from disability programs.

The increased opportunities for those over 60 to receive disability pensions can be seen as one part of a policy of general reduction of, and increased flexibility in, retirement age. In the 1970s the retirement age was lowered to 65, a partial pension was provided for those aged 60-65 who reduced their weekly work hours (subject to employer approval), and more generous terms were offered for those retiring early (at 60) or late (up to 70). It should be noted, however, that benefits for those with a disability pension are greater than for those with an early retirement pension.

Older employees, as mentioned above, have received much greater employment security than they had before. In practice they cannot be forced to leave even if the employer, for economic reasons, wants to release them. At the same time, their benefits from disability pensions are as a rule very good, especially when boosted by supplementary and negotiated pensions. If older employees are disability pensioned, the younger employees have greater chances for continued employment; as a consequence, strong moral pressure may be placed on older employees to apply for disability pensions. The local labor union and employer often share an interest in bringing about this result (see Nilsson and Stenkula, 1978). Various contractual pensions and benefits can be added to disability and supplementary disability pensions, which means that the economic terms connected with a pension can be very favorable. This is especially true for the white collar groups.

Special Studies of Disability Increase

Few studies have dealt with the expansion of disability programs, and all have focused on the increase of disability pensions in the 1970s. Hedström (1980) used the Level of Living surveys from 1968 and 1974 to study the increase in disability pensioning. He relates different individual characteristics as explanatory variables to the (binary) variable of disability pensioning in 1969-72 and in 1975-78. The explanatory variables include demographic characteristics, variables related to individual employment situations, and health factors. His main finding is that the coefficients of most of the health variables are significantly higher in the latter period than in the former, but that there are no corresponding changes for the other variables. He concludes that the change in the law in 1970 making medical criteria less stringent for older persons is the main reason for the increase of disability pensions.

His results can, however, be interpreted in different ways. The change in the law may have been a necessary but not a sufficient condition for the rapid increase in disability pensions (see, e.g., Eriksen, 1980, pp. 186-187). Possibly, changes in the structure of the labor market and relatively high unemployment rates combined with a higher level of compensation to explain an increase in the demand for disability pensions, and the legal change was a necessary but not in itself a sufficient change on the supply side.

Berglind (1977) tries to explain the regional variations in disability pensions. He uses 1974 data for Sweden's 278 municipalities. He has stocks and flows of disability pensioners in relation to the population of the same age as dependent variables in different regression estimates. The explanatory variables are those representing demographic structure, employment conditions, industrial structure, and health conditions in the different municipalities. The regressions indicate that the unemployment rate is the most important factor in explaining differences between different municipalities in disability pensioning for men, and that the unemployment rate and health conditions (sickness benefit days) are the most important ones for women.

The conclusions we can draw are that expansion of expenditures on the disabled during the last decade can be attributed to changes in the Swedish labor market and changes in the rules and conditions for the different disability programs. These factors are interdependent in many ways—more ways than mentioned above. The increasingly difficult labor market conditions for older persons contributed to changes in disability pensioning in 1970 and 1972, and in turn the improved terms of disability pensions have had some connection with layoffs. In the same way, for the disabled there is a relation between changes in the labor market, changes in labor market policy, and changes in the policy of firms. More research in this area is greatly needed, however, before stronger conclusions can be drawn.

Effects on Labor Supply

In analyzing the effects of programs for the disabled on the labor supply, one must make a clear division between the effects on older and on younger persons.

For older persons (primarily those 60 and over), measures consist mainly of disability pensioning (or other forms of cash support); only to a limited extent do they include employment programs. For older persons with unemployment insurance who have exhausted their eligibility for benefits, it is possible to receive a disability pension with no medical reasons at all. It is clear that changes in disability pensioning have contributed to reducing the labor supply of older people, and it is equally clear that this is a conscious policy aimed at attaining a lower and more flexible retirement age.

Changes in the disability pension regulations could thus explain some of the decrease in labor force participation rates for older men during the last decade. The effects of this decrease should not, however, be exaggerated. Some of these pensioners had already been unemployed for a long time and had minimal chances of getting a job on the open labor market: for them, the change often consisted of receiving a disability pension in place of unemployment compensation, cash labor market support, or social welfare assistance; they had already ceased to be job seekers. Needless to say, many other pensioners were previously employed, but they had reported ill over a long period of time. In the beginning of the 1970s, absence from work because of long-term illness decreased (according to labor force surveys) at the same time that disability pensioning increased. The average sickness benefit period also decreased. Even for this group of employed persons, disability pensioning implies no real reduction of the labor supply.

On the other hand, disability pensioning as a rule implies a decrease in the labor supply for those older persons who, when pensioned, leave an employment that they could actually have maintained.

Yet disability pensioning per se does not necessarily mean that a person is removed from the labor market. When half and two-thirds pensions are granted, it is expected that the person retains the possibility of gainful employment, and a disability pensioner with a full-time pension does not automatically lose all or part of it if he starts to work again on a limited basis. Pensioning should, however, limit the labor supply of these groups through both the income effect and the substitution effect. The wage per hour after taxes decreases if one receives a pension for a given hourly wage before taxes; moreover, there is always the chance that the pension will be withdrawn if one is gainfully employed. There is also a direct income test for the municipal housing and wife supplements.

Table 14.26 shows that the replacement rate, especially after taxes, is very high for a person with disability and supplementary disability pensions. In most cases it is probably even higher. Negotiated pension schemes fill in some of the gaps between pre-pension income and income from the national pension systems. The economic arguments for continuing work are in many cases very small. For those with little or no supplementary disability pension (mostly young persons who never have been employed or persons with part-time work, the benefit level is, however, still low. See Table 14.27.

It is not clear exactly how the labor supply of younger persons has been affected by expansion of disability policy. They are affected less by

Table 14.26. Replacement Rates (Percentages) of Different Income Support Programs for a Household with One Disabled Person, 1968 and 1978[a]

		Level of Earnings before Displacement					
		One Half thc Average[b]		Average		Twice the Average[c]	
Program		before tax	after tax	before tax	after tax	before tax	after tax
Disability (Incl. Supplements) and Supplementary Disability Pension	1968	92	105	65	73	45	55
	1978	104	117	73	88	42	66
Employment Injury Insurance	1968	87	110	58	83	29	49
	1978	92	93	92	95	59	78
	1968	89	114	45	64	22	38
Social Assistance	1978	86	109	43	69	22	50

Sources: Statistical Reports Bo 1970:25 (Survey of Housing and Rents, 1969; Part 1: Dwellings) and Bo 1979:10 (Survey of Housing and Rents, 1978; Part 1: Data concerning dwellings in multi-dwelling buildings), Official Statistics of Sweden, *Income and Wealth Statistics 1967 and 1968*; Statistical Reports 1980:9, *Distribution of Income and Assets in 1978*.

Note: Most blue collar workers in 1978 belonged to negotiated disability pension schemes. For them a national disability pension is complemented by a negotiated disability pension.

[a]Household characteristics: husband and wife both 50 years old; no children at home; husband totally disabled since January 1 of 1968 and 1978, respectively; wife is a housewife; household is in Stockholm, where dwelling costs were 424 crowns a month in 1968, 997 crowns in 1978.

[b]Level of earnings is underestimated for those with half of the average because households with low earnings may get transfers to cover all or part of their dwelling costs. The replacement rates therefore are overestimated in 1978 for those with disability pension or social assistance. For those with employment injury insurance, both the numerator and the denominator are underestimated, for the same reason.

[c]Twice the average means a white collar worker. Almost all white collar workers in 1968 and 1978 belonged to negotiated disability pension schemes, complementing the national and the supplementary disability pensions. The real replacement rates of a disability pension are therefore underestimated.

disability pensioning than by disability employment programs. If those in some type of sheltered work (semi-sheltered jobs, sheltered workshops, or archive work) are counted as part of the labor force (which they are, according to the definitions in the labor force surveys), then the expansion of the programs for the disabled has probably increased the labor supply and even more the employment of these groups. The number of those of younger age groups who are outside the labor force due to institutionalization has diminished, and the number without work because they are incapable of it has been about the same during the 1960s and 1970s.

The probability that a disabled person will stay listed as unemployed at the public employment offices in any given month, given age, sex, region and occupation, is lower than for a nondisabled person, because of the large percentage of the disabled who are placed in employment programs. Disability pensioning in the youngest groups is granted only when the disability is severe, and should therefore have very limited effect on their labor supply.

Table 14.27. The Level of Disability Pensions (Excluding Supplementary Pensions) Compared with Salaries for White Collar Workers, 1963-1979

Year	Disability Pension Rate[a] (% of base amount)	Bonus Pension Supplement Rate[b] (% of base amount)	Total Pension (% of base amount	Base Amount (Swedish crowns; January)	Total Pension (Swedish crowns; January)	Average Salary, Male White Collar Worker; Manufacturing Industry (Swedish crowns)	Pension as Percentage of Salary
1963	90		90	4,700	4,230	24,984	17
1964	90		90	4,800	4,320	26,592	16
1965	90		90	5,000	4,500	28,452	16
1966	90		90	5,300	4,770	31,068	15
1967	90		90	5,500	4,950	33,228	15
1968	90		90	5,700	5,130	35,184	15
1969	90		90	5,800	5,220	36,984	14
1970	90	3	93	6,000	5,580	39,996	14
1971	90	6	96	6,400	6,144	43,212	14
1972	90	9	99	7,100	7,029	47,268	15
1973	90	12	02	7,300	7,446	51,192	15
1974	90	15	05	8,100	8,505	57,432	15
1975	95	18	13	9,000	10,170	67,944	15
1976	95	21	16	9,700	11,252	74,352	15
1977	95	50	45	10,400	15,080	81,312	19
1978	95	58	53	11,800	18,054	86,040	21
1979	95	66	161	13.100	21,091	92,280	23

Sources: Central Bureau of Statistics, Official Statistics of Sweden, Wages, Part 1, various issues; National Social Insurance Board, Official Statistics of Sweden, *National Insurance*, various issues.

[a]For a person not married to another person with old-age or disability pensions.

[b]Paid to persons with little or no supplementary disability pension.

In sum, although the basic data are too limited to permit us to say anything more definite concerning effects of various disability programs on labor supply, the indications are that changes in disability pension regulations have decreased the labor supply of the oldest age groups, whereas disability employment programs have had an opposite effect on the youngest age groups.

Labor Market Rehabilitation

The explicit aim of the labor market programs is to return the disabled to the open labor market under normal terms—that is, without special, subsidized work. Temporary disability pensions are granted only for a limited term (often one year), and after that they can be extended, but one of the goals of the term limit is that during the period other solutions will be sought. Rehabilitation and resulting pension termination is the desired outcome, but it has not been achieved.

Table 14.22, above, showed that only a small percentage of those with temporary disability pensions leave the pension system. More often, the temporary disability pensioner moves to a regular disability pension. In general, the number of withdrawals is very low compared with the number of pensions; withdrawals have remained at approximately the same level for a long time, despite the fact that the number of pensions has risen sharply. The normal pattern has become movement from temporary disability pension to regular pension and ultimately to old age pension.

Table 14.28 shows that the employment programs have tended to become permanent placements. (One exception is vocational rehabilitation, where the average and the longest participation terms are relatively short.) The number who withdraw from archive, sheltered, and semi-sheltered work programs is low. Note, when examining the table, that all of the programs have grown in the last few years, which prevents calculating the length of an average period of program participation directly from the table. Remember also that the recent reorganization of semi-sheltered work means that the transition to nonsubsidized work may increase, and that 1978 was a year of relatively high unemployment by Swedish standards. Table 14.28 unfortunately demonstrates that the statistics for those who leave the various employment programs are unsatisfactory. In many cases the reasons for leaving are unknown. A possible cause could be that participants found work on the open market but did not report it. This is, however, not very plausible. Disability pensioning is a relatively common reason for withdrawal, especially in the sheltered work program.

The most important conclusion to be drawn from these statistics is that employment programs for the disabled at present result chiefly in long-term placement in the sheltered sector, and that temporary disability pensions as a rule lead to regular pensions.

Table 14.28. Participation and Withdrawal in Employment Programs for the Disabled, 1978

	Semi-Sheltered Work		Sheltered Work		Archive Work		Vocational Rehabilitation	
	No.	%	No.	%	No.	%	No.	%
Participants during 1978	13,740		19,580		17,260		9,390	
Participants not in program at end of 1978	1,500	100.0	2,063	100.0	1,785	100.0	6,396	100.0
Reasons for leaving program:								
Job in the open labor market	171	11.4	148	7.2	249	14.0	553	8.6
Semi-sheltered work	10[a]	0.7	24	1.2	107	6.0	282	4.4
Sheltered work	31	2.1	20[a]	1.0	2	0.1	852	13.3
Archive work	18	1.2	20	1.0	1[a]	0.1	305	4.8
Labor market training	33	2.2	37	1.8	44	2.5	741	11.6
Disability pension	155	10.3	484	23.5	267	15.0	576	9.0
Old age pension	253	16.9	359	17.4	452	25.3	20	0.3
Other reasons	829	55.3	971	47.1	663	37.1	3,067	48.0

Source: National Labor Market Board (1979).
[a]Reflects move to another job in the same program.

Cost-Benefit Analysis of Employment Programs for the Disabled

To my knowledge only three cost-benefit analyses have been conducted for employment programs for the disabled in Sweden. Two are of the sheltered workshops, and one is of vocational rehabilitation.

SOU (1968:61, Chap. 11.9-11) contains a cost-benefit analysis of eleven sheltered workshops for 1963, 1964, and 1965. In each year, five workshops show higher costs than benefits, and six show the opposite. The value of reduced leisure for the disabled through placement in a sheltered workshop is set equal to zero. The difference between benefits and costs per disabled employee in 1965 varied from 9,750 to -2,200 crowns. The results are least favorable for workshops for the severely disabled and workshops in the big cities.

The second analysis of sheltered workshops was by Bexelius and Kjellén for the period 1970-74. A government report extended their analysis to 1975 (see SOU, 1978:14). The study shows that total costs for all sheltered workshops were greater than benefits in every year except 1970, and the divergence between costs and benefits increased steadily. The most likely explanation is that sheltered workshops have increasingly employed severely disabled persons, primarily because time spent in the workshops is considered more "meaningful" for the severely disabled than time entirely outside the labor force. An interview survey by Bexelius and Kjellén also shows that most disabled persons prefer sheltered (or semi-sheltered) work to a disability pension if they get the same remuneration. A central assumption in the study is that none of the disabled would have gotten a job in the open labor market if the sheltered workshops had not existed.

Johansson (1974) conducted a cost-benefit analysis of vocational rehabilitation in the county of Blekinge. One hundred persons who in 1971 left the center for vocational rehabilitation in Blekinge were followed for two years. Johansson's results are very positive regarding vocational rehabilitation: its present value for one person shows net benefits in the range 34,500 to 165,000 crowns. The method used to estimate benefits (increase in production) is, however, based on comparisons of employment earnings before and after rehabilitation. Earnings are generally very low in the period (month or year) before vocational rehabilitation, but one should not assume that they would necessarily have remained at the same low level without the intervention of vocational rehabilitation.

Disability Policy and Equity

Perhaps the main purpose of government policy toward the disabled is to improve their economic situation. As noted earlier, no general survey has yet been made of the economic condition of the disabled. Using the information from the various programs, we can at least get a picture of their general income. We will look at each program individually.

Those in the various types of sheltered employment receive a wage. The principles for setting wages vary according to the different types of work. In work with wage subsidy (earlier semi-sheltered work), the wage agreement is the same as for work in a private firm. Since piecework is prohibited, wages are required to be identical to time wages for the nondisabled.

Those in sheltered workshops have special wage agreements, and wages are comparable to those for nondisabled persons in the same occupation in the open labor market. Wages for a metal worker, for example, in a sheltered workshop are comparable to those of a metalworker in the open labor market. On the other hand, a metalworker in a sheltered workshop is not entitled to the types of supplements tied to piecework, shift work, etc.

The wage range for archive workers was larger, since those with individual appointments received wages under the terms of the agreement that applied to nondisabled workers doing the same work, while others had a special archive workers' wage schedule. Wages in this area were relatively low. Since July 1980, the wages for archive work have been set in the same way as for semi-sheltered work, with the exception of those employed in special sheltered office work, who, since January 1980, fall under the same rules as other sheltered workshops.

Sickness benefits are paid to those in sheltered work on the same basis as to other wage earners. Some of those who work less than full time in sheltered workshops and in archive work have partial disability pensions.

The wages for those in the sheltered sector are about the same as for those for other workers in the same occupations. Disability policy for these sheltered groups has contributed to an equalization of incomes.

Disability pensioning affects the largest number of disabled persons. As shown earlier, the amounts that different persons receive from disabibility pensioning vary greatly. We can make a rough estimate by treating separately the groups with and without supplementary pensions.

The economic standard of those without pension supplements has improved lately, due mainly to the bonus pension supplements. Municipal housing supplements have also increased, but vary widely by municipality.

Disability pensioners without supplementary pensions fall into the truly low income groups in Sweden. However, among those receiving only a disability pension are the institutionalized, whose standard of living is determined by that of the institution itself, not by the size of the pension.

The amounts of the supplementary pensions vary greatly among different groups. The pension may be large, for example, for those with assumption points and with high incomes for some prior years. A large part of the disability pensioners now are older men, many of whom have had occupations and incomes that make the pension high, and in this age group disability and supplementary disability pensions are often combined with different contractual pensions and other compensation.

There are disabled persons who do not receive compensation either through disability pensioning or from wages in the sheltered sector—many work on the open labor market; others get various types of cash compensation, the most important types being sickness benefits, social welfare assistance, unemployment insurance benefits, and cash labor market support (for those without unemployment insurance). Of these, sickness benefits most often provide the highest compensation; cash labor market support, the lowest. None of these types of support is intended primarily for the disabled, and the number of disabled who collect them is not known.

Household incomes in 1978, based on the Living Conditions Survey, are given in Table 14.29. It shows that disabled households on the average have somewhat lower incomes that do the nondisabled. The difference in standard of living may, however, be overestimated by this measure. Households of the disabled have fewer members (see table), and the differences disappear if we adjust for the number of household members.

We can sum up by stating that the disability programs result in considerable income increase for the disabled, but that the distribution of the contributions by various programs is uneven.

Leading Issues in Disability Policy

The costs of disability programs in Sweden have grown rapidly in recent years, both in income support programs and labor market programs. The rapid expansion has not yet led to extensive discussions or suggestions for reducing expenditures on disability policy. On the contrary, political

Table 14.29. Mean Household Income and Average Household Size of the Disabled and Non-disabled, 1978[a]

Level of Disability	Men: Mean household income	Men: Average household members	Women: Mean household income	Women: Average household members	Men and Women: Mean household income	Men and Women: Average household members
Severely disabled						
With disability pension	38,400	1.70	42,250	1.69	40,390	1.70
With another pension	51,890	1.85	32,500	1.32	39,370	1.51
Without pension	47,900	2.27	51,740	2.27	49,740	2.27
Total	43,200	1.96	45,540	1.91	44,390	1.94
Disabled (not severely)						
With disability pension	36,600	1.32	46,090	2.00	40.870	1.64
With another pension	59,660	2.16	39,710	1.64	42,310	1.71
Without pension	48,870	2.42	52,050	2.39	50,570	2.40
Total	48,390	2.36	50,880	2.33	49,760	2.34
Disabled (both severely and not severely)						
With disability pension	38,220	1.66	42,550	1.72	40,430	1.69
With another pension	54,210	1.94	36,890	1.52	40,940	1.62
Without pension	48,570	2.37	51,970	2.36	50,340	2.37
Total	45,930	2.18	48,540	2.15	47,320	2.16
Not Disabled						
With disability pension	38,020	1.56	40,510	1.53	39,280	1.55
With another pension	47,900	1.76	40,450	1.50	42,480	1.57
Without pension	53,840	2.32	56,070	2.52	54,910	2.42
Total	53,700	2.31	55,340	2.48	54,500	2.39

Source: Computations from the Living Conditions Survey of 1978 made for this study by the Central Bureau of Statistics.

[a]The income figures exclude households for which the respondent was 16-19 years old. Household members include household head, spouse (if any), and children under 16.

unanimity prevails on increasing resources in this area. The sole issue of contention is the size of that increase.

Common agreement concerning enlargement of disability programs does not, however, prohibit discussion of the content of disability policy. This discussion revolves around a particular theme: the work principle versus the cash support principle. I will discuss first this fundamental theme and then some of its variations—namely, disability policy as a way of disguising unemployment, and measures to increase access of the disabled to the workplace and to society at large.

Employment versus Income Support

Throughout this century, Swedish labor market and social policies have been built upon the work principle—income support should be only a temporary measure; steps should be taken to find some sort of employment for those in need of assistance. In the interwar period, the preferred form of support for the unemployed was public works, and the government attempted in various ways to decrease income support for those out of work. Not until 1934 did the government begin to support unemployment benefit societies, and even then it enforced such stringent conditions that most of the societies preferred to go without such assistance. Disability pensions were small and income-tested, and were granted only after a thorough medical examination.

After World War II, labor market policy and social policy changed, but emphasis on the work principle remained. A new and major addition to labor market policy has involved programs for regional and occupational mobility, but the goal is unchanged: to avoid income support and find employment for both disabled and nondisabled persons. Disability pension policy did not alter in the 1940s and 1950s: a stringent medical examination was required and benefits were low.

This strong emphasis on employment weakened somewhat in the 1960s and 1970s. Income support for older people of still active age has received increased importance. Since its inception in 1963, the national supplementary pension has meant that economic conditions for older people with disability pensions have gradually improved. The rules concerning older persons of active age were also in effect altered when the definition of disability was changed in 1963.[26] In 1970 and again in 1972, the formal rules governing disability pensions for older working-age people were changed, and it became relatively easy for people 63 years and older to receive them (later changed to 60 years and older). Also in that period, the maximum terms of unemployment compensation insurance were lengthened for older workers, and special forms of support were introduced for those who did not qualify for unemployment insurance. This development can be described as a shift from the work principle to that of the cash support principle for older people of working age.

The same trend, from employment to income support, has affected another group. Until 1977 alcoholism per se was not, except in extreme cases, sufficient cause for disability pensioning. In practice, however, physical illness was often given as the cause for pensioning when alcoholism was the underlying reason. Since 1977, disability pensions can be granted solely on the basis of decreased working capacity. The number of disability pensions for those diagnosed as alcoholics increased sharply that year, but it is not certain that the real increase was as large.

The extent of disability pensioning has been criticized in recent years—criticism covering the pensioning of older persons and alcoholics as well as of young people. The major argument against the disability pensioning of older working-age people is not an economic one; it instead is that as a result of pensioning, they lose contact with others and become socially isolated, and also that the members of this group, usually pensioned for medical reasons, will feel sicker and perhaps even will worsen physically and mentally. It was partly to curtail disability pensioning of older persons that the half (reduced) old age pension and the partial pension at age 60 were introduced. These pension forms make contact with working life easier to maintain, and the recipient can avoid being stigmatized as disabled. The benefits from a half old age pension are too little to compete with the other pension forms, whereas benefits under a partial pension are very favorable. The number of partial pensions has increased rapidly since their introduction in 1976. It is not certain, however, that partial pensioners are recruited from the same groups as disability pensioners and that disability pensioning will therefore decrease as a result of partial pensioning.

Alcoholism and alcohol policy are issues that are receiving intense discussion at present. The incidence of alcoholism is rising in Sweden, as it is in other western European countries. Disability pensioning of alcoholics has played a definite, if not yet decisive, role in this rise. Disability-pensioned alcoholics have more money to buy alcohol, a factor that hastens the development of their alcoholism (e.g., Kristensson, 1979), and perhaps shortens their life expectancy. A more restrictive pensioning of alcoholics has, however, its own problems. In the 1940s and 1950s, an alcoholic had a relatively good chance of finding temporary employment; among the groups of disabled, they were the easiest to place on the open labor market. By the beginning the the 1970s, just the opposite was true: alcoholics were the hardest to place, a change accounted for primarily by alterations in the Swedish labor market (many temporary jobs, such as on the docks, which alcoholics could manage, have gradually disappeared). Decreased disability pensioning of alcoholics would perhaps lead to an increase in the number of persons requiring social welfare.

The sharpest controversy has surrounded the disability pensioning of young people. Criticism has been colored in part by the misconception that disability pensioning for young people has increased. The opposite is the case, as we have seen in this text. The essence of the criticism is that disability pensioning sets young people apart, isolating them socially; regardless of the expense and the degree of their disability, young people should be given some form of work rather than be pensioned.

A return to the work principle at least for those under 60, and an opportunity to choose different combinations of work and pension for those over 60, are currently the chief elements in the Swedish disability debate. Some of the new measures can be seen as steps leading in this direction: e.g., the founding of Stiftelsen Samhällsföretag (the trust in charge of all sheltered workshops), the consolidation of archive work with semi-sheltered work, and the National Labor Market Board's campaign to place the disabled on the open labor market through the Law for Promotion of Employment.

Disability Policy—a Way of Hiding Unemployment?

Since World War II, low unemployment has been a major goal of Swedish economic policy. Unemployment has in fact been low throughout the postwar period, as compared both with other periods in Sweden and with most other western European countries. Even during the two recessions of the 1970s, the unemployment rate did not exceed 3 percent, according to labor force surveys.

Low unemployment figures have been regarded as the result of Sweden's selective labor market policy. Opponents of this policy charge, however, that the success has not lain in *decreasing* unemployment but in *disguising* it. According to the critics, the labor force surveys should include among the unemployed the disability pensioners, those participating in various labor market programs, groups of part-time workers, etc. Defining them as unemployed would naturally lead to higher unemployment rates—at least 5-6 percent for the recession years 1977 and 1978.

There are, however, problems with that concept of unemployment. A broadened definition leads to distinctions which are not always meaningful. People employed by the National Road Administration for road work, paid by the National Labor Market Board, would have to be considered unemployed, while those doing the same job but paid through the National Road Administration's regular budget would not be so counted. People who are disability pensioned at 60 would be considered unemployed, but not people of the same age and with the same prospects on the labor market who have opted for an early old age pension. Many such examples could be cited.

Another problem with this definition is that, for the disabled, the main alternative to the disability programs is not unemployment (or gainful employment), but rather being (remaining) outside the labor force, possibly with other forms of income support.

Although the programs for the disabled reduce unemployment (as currently defined) within that group, it is uncertain how large the reduction is. The borderline between, on the one hand, programs for the disabled and, on the other, other public employment programs is often vague. For these and other reasons, it is difficult to create a satisfactory unemployment time series in which hidden unemployment could be revealed. A better solution would be to complement the unemployment statistics with statistics for the number of people participating in different programs without summarizing the different time series.

Measures to Increase the Access to Facilities for the Disabled

In many cases, special programs are necessary to permit application of the work principle to those suffering from impaired mobility. One is work at home, a form of sheltered work in which the disabled person subcontracts with a sheltered workshop. Not all types of work can be performed that way, however, and working at home is in any case socially isolating, which defeats the goal of integrating the disabled into society.

The preferred alternative is to increase access to the workplace. To enlarge opportunities for the disabled to work (as well as to perform other activities), stipulations have gradually been introduced into the design of dwellings, transportation, and places of work. Construction legislation now has design regulations concerning access for the physically handicapped. Exceptions exist for single-family houses, and exemptions are available in some cases. A central demand by the disability organizations has been intensification and stricter application of these rules.

A major effort has been made to improve the mobility of the disabled through transportation assistance. Existing programs include grants or loans for the purchase of specially equipped cars (mentioned earlier) and subsidized public transport. The latter exists in all of the municipalities in Sweden, mostly through subsidized taxi rides. In one county (Stockholm), the county council covers the costs; in all other cases, the municipality does so. The majority of those eligible for the service are old age pensioners, but in 1978 50,000 persons under 65 were also covered. In the majority of the country's municipalities (246 out of 277 in 1978), public transport fares are subsidized for travel to and from work. Eleven municipalities in 1978 had free transportation to and from work, 49 had a fixed fare for all such trips regardless of their length, and 186 had reduced fares depending upon the length of the ride (Statistical Reports, 1979).

Another way to increase the mobility of the disabled is to improve their physical ability to use transportation, an issue that has been stressed in recent years by the disability organizations. One result was that the Swedish State Railroads had to alter the design of a new railroad car to make it better adapted to the disabled.

Measures have been taken to increase access of the disabled to the workplace, as we noted above. There have also been increasing demands that new construction incorporate adaptations to the needs of the disabled.

The greater emphasis in Sweden on disability programs that encompass employment, dwelling, and transportation needs can be regarded as a continuation of the traditional work principle. That principle means that the disabled will be able to participate on an equal footing in working life (and in society in general), and that a policy whose main component is economic support will be avoided.

Notes

1. Comparing the results from 1975, 1976, 1977, and 1978 shows that the 1977 survey has somewhat higher frequencies of long-standing illness and of reduced, but

not severely reduced, working capacity. The questions are the same in all surveys except that health condition was a main area of study in the 1977 survey and covered several extra questions. This may have resulted in a higher tendency to report illnesses and reduction of working capacity.

2. According to Central Bureau of Statistics (1978), persons of Finnish nationality and citizens from Southern European countries had 39 percent and 29 percent higher frequencies of severely reduced working capacity, respectively, than the average population in 1975. If sex and age distribution are kept constant, the differences increase to 165 percent and 104 percent, respectively.

3. See, e.g., Wadensjö (1976), Central Bureau of Statistics (1977), and Leiniö (1979b). Wadensjö uses the census of 1970 combined with statistics of occupational injuries, the Central Bureau of Statistics uses the Living Conditions Survey of 1975, and Leiniö uses the Level of Living Investigation of 1974.

4. The survey's definition of unemployment differs somewhat from that used in the labor force surveys. The unemployment rates are generally higher according to the Living Conditions Survey than according to the labor force surveys.

5. According to Central Bureau of Statistics (1979b), the severely disabled were slightly overrepresented among those under the poverty line (the subsistence level according to the tax authorities), but were highly underrepresented among those with high incomes (the highest 20 percent) in 1975-76.

6. Those employed by the government and those with government-regulated wages (mostly teachers employed by the municipalities) receive a reduced salary when absent due to illness or injury. The salary is reduced by 8 percent for the first 30 days, then by 6 percent. The social insurance offices pay the sickness benefits to the government instead. Most salaried employees in the private sector have negotiated supplements to their sickness benefits. For the first 90 days of sick leave, the employer pays the difference between the normal salary and the sickness benefits. After that a special insurance supplements the sickness benefit up to 95 percent of the salary, with a maximum salary of 7.5 times the base amount.

Blue collar workers employed in the private sector or by municipalities receive a supplement if sick for more than 30 days; if so, their sickness benefit is supplemented retroactively from the eighth day of illness with 3 crowns a day. The supplement makes total compensation about 95 percent of the normal wage. See Erikson (1978).

7. The salary figure is from Central Bureau of Statistics (1979c); the wage figure is calculated from Central Bureau of Statistics (1979a, 1979d).

8. Elmér (1978, pp. 82-83) gives a brief overview of the structure of the social insurance system.

9. A flow chart of the decision process for disability pension is given by Helander (1972). The last two steps in the decision process have been changed in recent years.

10. Berglind (1977) analyzes the differences in the numbers of disability pensions as well as differences in the incidence of new disability pensions among different municipalities. His main finding is that the local unemployment rate is the variable which explains most of the differences.

11. Ten years earlier, in 1966, mental disorder was the most frequent diagnosis—26.1 percent of all new pensions, compared with 21.5 percent for musculoskeletal diseases (Eriksen, 1980, App. 7, p. 179).

12. The difference is decreasing, and will continue to do so according to a

forecast by the National Social Insurance Board (1978a); in the year 2000, the difference will be 4.8 percent (87.1 percent for men, 82.3 percent for women).

13. No statistical series exist for these municipal and county council expenditures. The figures given are from SOU (1978:14, p. 173).

14. An employee may also be dismissed for misconduct, etc.

15. The trade unions may, however, make an agreement with a firm permitting rules other than seniority to be followed.

16. Letter from the National Labor Market Board to the county and district labor market boards of October 11, 1979.

17. The rapid rise starts in the third quarter of 1970. From the second to the third quarter of 1970, the number of men aged 55-64 who stated they were not in the labor force because they were not able to work increased from 19,500 to 31,100, and the corresponding rise for women was from 12,000 to 15,800, according to the labor force surveys.

18. The number of deaths from occupational accidents has diminished at least since 1918; for earlier years no reliable time series exists. See Jarl and Thorsson (1978).

19. The number of persons institutionalized has declined continuously in the period for which we have reliable statistics—from 42,500 in 1963 to 20,400 in 1978 (among those aged 16 to 64).

20. See Nilsson and Rydberg (1979) for a more thorough analysis.

21. For an account and an analysis of the regional differences in disability pensioning, see Berglind (1977).

22. Strandberg (1967) describes the rules for alcoholics according to the national pension laws of 1935 and 1946 and surveys the interpretation of the law of 1946 in the 1950s and 1960s.

23. Unpublished statistics from the National Social Insurance Board.

24. For a general discussion of this problem, see Östlind (1975).

25. This study is reported in SOU (1977:89) and Heijbel (1978, 1979).

26. See Carlsson (1976) for a discussion of the effects of changes in the definition of disability, and the effects of coordination of the sickness benefits and the disability pension in 1963.

References

Andersson, E. 1977. Statistik över sökande med arbetshandikapp (Statistics on the occupationally disabled registered at the Employment offices). Stockholm: National Labor Market Board, mimeo.

Andreasson, R. 1978. Traffic accidents. In *Health and Society, I: Accidents and Violent Death.* Stockholm: Committee for Future-Oriented Research.

Berglind, H. 1977. Förtidspension eller arbete? (Disability pension or employment?). In SOU, 1977:88, *Förtidspensionering* (Disability Pensioning).

Bernhardsson, G. 1977. *Sysselsättning och förtidspension bland män i Uppsala* (Employment and disability pensions among men in Uppsala). Stockholm: Sysselsättningsutredningen (The Employment Committee).

Carlsson, G. 1976. Socialförsäkringens utveckling (The development of the Social Insurance System). *Socialmedicinsk tidskrift, 53,* 223-230.

Central Bureau of Statistics. 1977. *Living conditions*. Report no. 9: Living conditions of Swedish immigrants, 1975. Official Statistics of Sweden. Stockholm: Liber Förlag.

Central Bureau of Statistics. 1978. *Living conditions*. Report no. 11: Health and medical care utilization, 1975. Official Statistics of Sweden. Stockholm: Liber Förlag.

Central Bureau of Statistics. 1979a. Comparison of wages and salaries, 1973-1977. Working paper 1979-05-07.

Central Bureau of Statistics. 1979b. *Living conditions*. Report no 16: Low-income families: Who they are and how they live in 1975/76. Official Statistics of Sweden. Stockholm: Liber Förlag.

Central Bureau of Statistics. 1979c. Wages 1978: Part 1. Official Statistics of Sweden. Stockholm: Liber Förlag.

Central Bureau of Statistics. 1979d. Wages 1978: Part 2. Official Statistics of Sweden. Stockholm: Liber Förlag.

Elmér, A. 1978. *Svensk socialpolitik* (Swedish Social Policy). Lund: Liber Förlag.

Eriksen, T.E. 1980. *Den ökade sjukfrånvaron: En statistisk analys* (Rising sickness absences: A statistical analysis). Delegationen för Social Forskning, Rapport 1980:1 (Delegation for Social Research, Report 1980:1).

Erikson, H. 1978. Kompletterande pensionering inom enskild och offentlig tjänst (Supplementary pensions in the private and public sector). In C. Ström and Y. Zotterman, eds., *Våra pensionssystem i dag och i framtiden* (Our pension systems today and in the future). Stockholm: Liber Förlag.

Folksams Sociala Råd. 1977. *Försäkringar genom anställning* (Employment-related insurance). Stockholm: Folksam.

Haavio, E. and Johansson, S. 1974. Finska utvandrares levnadsnivå i Sverige (The level of living of Finnish immigrants in Sweden). *Sosiologia, 17*, 192-205.

Hedström, P. 1980. *Förtidspension: välfärd eller ofärd*? (The disability pension: welfare or misfortune?) 1980 års levnadsnivåprojekt, No. 2. Stockholm: Swedish Institute for Social Research.

Heijbel, C.A. 1978. Occurrence of personal handicaps in an industrial population: Survey and appraisal. *Scandinavian Journal of Rehabilitation Medicine*, Supplement, 182-192.

Heijbel, C.A. 1979. Betingat arbetsföra: Erfarenheter från Volvo Skövdeverken (The partially disabled: Experiences from the Volvo Works in Skövde). *Socialmedicinsk tidskrift, 56*, 103-108.

Helander, E. 1972. Har vi fått fri förtidspension? (Is everyone eligible for a disability pension?). *Läkartidningen, 69*, 3577-3582.

Inrikesdepartementet. 1968. *PM om arkivarbete och musikerhjälp* (Memorandum on archive work and aid to musicians). Stockholm: In, 1968:3.

Jarl, T., and Thorsson, J. 1978. Occupational accidents in Sweden. In *Health and Society, I: Accidents and Violent Death*. Stockholm: Committee for Future-Oriented Research.

Johansson, O. 1974. Ekonomisk studie om verkningar av arbetsprövning/träning (An economic analysis of the effects of work testing/work training). Umeå: Department of Economics, mimeo.

Kindlund, H. 1978. *Arbetsmiljö och hälsa: En preliminär studie av vissa riskgrupper på arbetsmarknaden* (Working conditions and health: A preliminary study of certain risk groups in the labor market). Stockholm: Sysselsättningsutredningen (The Employment Committee).

Kommunförbundet (Swedish Association of Local Authorities). 1975. Kommunala bostadstillägg för pensionärer (Municipal housing supplements for pensioners). Mimeo.

Kristensson, H. 1979. Förtidspension av missbrukare (Disability pensioning of alcoholics), *Nykterhetsvården*, No. 6, pp. 27-30.

Lassenius, B. 1974. Motboksreformens effekt på alkoholism (The effect on alcoholism of abolishing the rationing system for spirits). *Nordisk Psykiatrisk Tidskrift, 28* (supplement), 1-122.

Leiniö, T.-L. 1979a. Finländska invandrares hälsotillstånd och utnyttjande av sjukvården (The health of Finnish immigrants and their utilization of medical care). *Nordisk Medicin, 94*, 44-46.

Leiniö, T.-L. 1979b. *Finska invandrare i Sverige 1974.* (Finnish immigrants in Sweden, 1974). Stockholm: Swedish Institute for Social Research.

National Labor Market Board. 1979. Vid arbetsförmedlingen aktuella sökande med arbetshandikapp under 1978 (Handicapped persons seeking employment through the public employment offices in 1978). *Labor Market Statistics*, no. 3B.

National Labor Market Board. 1980. Platsförmedling för äldre och arbetshandikappade (Job placement for older and disabled persons). Report 1980-06-09.

National Social Insurance Board. 1977a. Angående avgiftsuttag för allmän tilläggspension för åren 1980-1984 (About payroll levies for the National Supplementary Pension 1980-1984). Letter to the government.

National Social Insurance Board. 1977b. Sjukskrivning före förtidspensionering (Sickness cash benefit periods before disability pensioning). Statistisk Rapport No. 1977:3.

National Social Insurance Board. 1978a. En antalsprognos 1977-2020 avseende ATP-systemet (A forcast of the number of persons with support from the supplementary pension system, 1977-2020). Statistisk Rapport No. 1978:1.

National Social Insurance Board. 1978b. *National Insurance 1976.* Official Statistics of Sweden. Stockholm: Liber Förlag.

National Social Insurance Board. 1979. Förtidspensionering av ungdomar har minskat under 70-talet (Disability pensioning of youths has decreased in the 70's). Mimeo.

Nilsson, C., and Stenkula, P. 1978. Förundersökning av förtidspensionering utanför det offentligrättsliga systemet (A pilot study of disability pensions separate from the National Insurance Act.) Rapport till Arbetsmarknadsdepartementet (Report to the Ministry of Labor). Stockholm.

Nilsson, T., and Rydberg, U. 1979. The Impact of Alcohol on Health. In *Health and society, IV: The use of tobacco and alcohol and its influence on health.* Stockholm: Committee for Future-Oriented Research.

Olson-Frick, H. 1977. Förtidspensionärens situation (The conditions of the disability pensioners). In SOU, 1977:88, *Förtidspensionering* (Disability pensioning).

Östlind, A. 1975. *Arbetsmarknadspolitik och löneutjämning åren 1964-1974* (Labor market policy and reduction of the wage differences, 1964-1974). Stockholm: Riksdagens rivisorers kansli.

Samhällsföretag. 1980. Anslagsframställning för budgetåret 1981/82 (Budget requests for fiscal year 1981/82). August.

Särnmark, O. 1974. Förtidspension, sjukbidrag och livräntor: Riktlinjer och tillämpning (Regular disability pensions, temporary disability pensions and annuities: Guidelines and application). Stockholm: National Social Insurance Board, mimeo.

Sociallagarna (The Social Laws). 1978. Stockholm: Kommunförbundets Förlag.

SOU (Statens Offentliga Utredninga). 1946:24. *Förslag till effektiviserad kurators- och arbetsförmedlingsverksamhet för partiellt arbetsföra m.m.* (A proposal for more efficient advisory and employment service for partially disabled persons, etc.). Kommittén för partiellt arbetsföra: Betänkande 1 (Committee for Partially Disabled Persons: Report 1.).

SOU. 1968:61. *Arbetsmarknadsverket och arbetsmarknadspolitiken 2* (Swedish National Labor Market Administration and Manpower Policy, Part 2).

SOU. 1977:10. *Pensionär '75* (Pensioner 1975).

SOU. 1977:89. *Betingat arbetsföra: Rapport om försöksverksamhet vid två Volvoenheter* (The partially disabled: Report on experimental work in two divisions of Volvo). Rapport till Sysselsättningsutredningen (Report to the Employment Committee).

SOU. 1978:14. *Arbete åt handikappade* (Full employment for the handicapped). Delbetänkände från Sysselsättningsutredningen (Report of the Employment Committee).

Statistical Reports. 1979. Transport service on October 1st 1978, S 1979:15.

Strandberg, S.E. 1967. Invaliditetsbedömningen inom den allmänna pensioneringen (Determination of disability in the national pension system). *Tidskrift för allmän försäkring, 60,* 209-219.

Wadensjö, E. 1976. Occupational segregation of migrant workers in Sweden. *Växjö Migration Studies, 5.*

Wadensjö, E. 1978. *Selection of applicants for labor market programs.* Lund: Meddelande från Nationalekonomiska institutionen, 1978:49.

Chapter 15

Disability Policy in the United Kingdom

M. J. McCrostie and Alan Peacock

This chapter is an account of the characteristics of the disabled population in the United Kingdom and of how those characteristics govern the nature and extent of disability policy. Even in the discussion of policy issues, we have been content largely to summarize the current debate in the United Kingdom about how disability policy might be changed, rather than to offer views of our own. This is deliberate, for to have embarked on a full discussion of a plan of our own would have meant writing a disquisition on our own philosophy of the welfare state, of which disability policy is only a part.

The reader will note that the amount of information on disability in the United Kingdom is extremely sparse in comparison with other countries. Indeed, one of the problems encountered in preparing this study has been the wide variety of sources that have had to be consulted. There is information on particular kinds of disability, though even specialized studies are hard to come by, but the last complete study of the characteristics of disability carried out in official quarters was based on the 1966 Census of Population and was published as long ago as 1968. The only way in which we could provide a general picture of the present dimensions of the disability problem was by assuming that in 1978 (the last year for which we have useful comparative data) the incidence of disability had remained constant, after adjusting for changes in population composition, age distribution, and regional population distribution.

The lack of such basic information may seem to imply a lack of concern over the condition of the disabled, possibly because the incidence of

M. J. McCrostie is Lecturer in Economics, University of Buckingham; Alan Peacock is Vice Chancellor and Professor of Economics, University of Buckingham.

disability among those of working age may appear to be comparatively low. This is in fact not the case, for when one unravels the complicated skein of disability provision in the United Kingdom, it is apparent that the quantum of benefits for major categories of disabled persons is not ungenerous. Moreover, the real value of benefits has not suffered through a period of rapid inflation in relation to other major social security benefits and real incomes generally.

However, it soon becomes clear that there are two major problems with the British system. Broadly speaking, the system developed out of the activities of a considerable number of voluntary bodies concerned with disablement generally in terms of some medical category such as blindness, deafness, or mental handicap. The concentration on the medical aspects of the problem of disability brought with it a tendency to help the disabled by provision of specific goods and services designed to ameliorate their physical condition. Matters were further complicated when government became the main source of support for disabled persons, for those government departments concerned with health, education, and employment were themselves going through periods of large-scale reorganization.

The result has been that horizontal economic inequities between different categories of disablement were bound to arise, though the extent of these inequities is very difficult to measure, given the problem of attributing the different benefit entitlements to particular categories of disabled, and of evaluating the services provided to them at zero cost. Naturally, the various pressure groups who have derived their cohesion from support of particular forms of disability have been quick to point this out. Rectifying the disparity between levels of benefit, though adjusted for such factors as the degree of impairment, and reducing the costs of access to benefits is now becoming a major issue of social policy within the United Kingdom.

A second problem resulting from the growth of provision based on medical categories has been the emphasis placed on help in kind rather than in money, though the proportions between the two modes of provision has varied according to the type and degree of impairment. Opinions are divided on this issue. The argument for benefits in money rests on the liberal philosophical principle that disabled persons should be free to spend their incomes as they consider fit and should be encouraged to be independent. It is believed that the best way to give this principle is to introduce some form of negative income tax scheme for disabled and nondisabled alike, with supplementation in the form of real benefits restricted to those, such as the mentally handicapped, who cannot handle their own affairs.

A consolidation of benefits, so that a greater proportion of what amounts to a social security payment could be in the form of money, would probably command wide support. However, a liberal principle applied to the employment of the disabled suggests, as argued by Wiseman and Cullis

(1974), a move away from the use of quotas, designated employments for the disabled, and sheltered employment arrangements. Public policy would then be concentrated more on investment in the education and training of the disabled and on the removal of labor market imperfections which discriminate against the employment of the disabled. Granted that removal of imperfections would encounter strong trade union opposition: This "second best" solution would entail working for the acceptance of financial incentives to employers (rather than compelling them to accept disabled pensions) "designed to neutralize the difference between the value (marginal product) of a disabled worker to an employer, and the value to him of other workers" (Wiseman and Cullis, 1974, p. 160). Though such ideas are fully familiar to officials and others in the United Kingdom concerned with the design of disabled policy, their adoption in principle is still in question and their implementation would involve practical difficulties, as their supporters would be the first to admit. This report is not designed, as we have made clear, to resolve such issues, but to offer essential background to all concerned.

Characteristics and Economic Status of the Disabled Population

Population Size

The exact size of the disabled population in the United Kingdom is impossible to measure and estimates are liable to a wide margin of error. Two reasons for this problem are the variety of definitions that can be adopted and the lack of information available. For purposes of registering as a disabled person in order to attain the associated benefits, a person is regarded as being disabled if "he/she is one who on account of injury, disease or congenital deformity is substantially handicapped in obtaining or keeping employment, or in undertaking work on his own account of a kind which, apart from that injury, disease or deformity, would be suited to his age, experience and qualifications" (Disabled Persons [Employment] Act, 1944). The disablement must be expected to last at least 12 months. However, as registration is voluntary and the benefits of registering may often be perceived as negligible, a large and increasing proportion of disabled eligible to register fail to do so. According to figures from the *Department of Employment Gazette* (various issues), the number of disabled people actually registered as such has been consistently dropping over the last 30 years —from 936,000 in 1950 to 495,000 in 1980. The Department of Employment (1972) estimates that about half of those eligible actually do register; for instance, in 1971, when there were 625,000 registered, it was estimated that 1.2 million (including those already registered) were actually eligible for registration, although this figure is "necessarily speculative." The Manpower Services Commission (1978) which has recently taken over the responsibility of providing employment services for the disabled from the Department of Employment, appears to accept this view of registration as well. Another estimate (House of Commons, 1974) suggests that "the number of impaired earners might be expected to lie between 1,440,000 and 1,780,000, and that the number of disabled earners (i.e., those whose impairment involved some work handicap measureable in financial terms) could be estimated at about 650,000."

None of these estimates can be viewed as having a high degree of accuracy and none give a demographic breakdown in any detail of the characteristics of the disabled population in the United Kingdom. Fortunately, however, a national survey was carried out between October 1968 and February 1969 by the Social Survey Division of the Office of Population Censuses and Surveys (OPCS Survey) covering impaired persons aged 16 or over living at home (Harris, Cox and Smith, 1971; Buckle, 1971). The survey resulted in over 82,000 households containing one or more impaired person being directly interviewed. However, the figures relied mainly on self-assessment and should be treated with caution.

The survey was more concerned with impairment generally rather than disability in particular, following those definitions suggested by Jefferys (1969, p. 2): impairment—"lacking part or all of a limb or having a defective limb, organ or mechanism of the body"; disablement—"the loss or reduction of functional ability"; handicap—"the disadvantage or restriction of activity caused by disability." Eight main categories were used in the OPCS Survey for defining the impaired, although they are really different stages of a continuum rather than discrete categories; there is little difference between the bottom of one category and the top of the one below it, categories 1-3 being defined as very severe, 4-5 as severe, 6 as appreciable, and 7 and 8 as minor. The categories are repeated here as they are quite frequently referred to in our discussion.

Category 1: Contains people who need help going to or using the W.C. practically every night. In addition, most of those in this group need to be fed and dressed or, if they can feed and/or dress themselves, need tangible help during the day with washing, using the W.C., or coping with incontinence.

Category 2: Contains people who need help with the W.C. during the night but not quite so much help with feeding, washing, dressing, or who, while not needing night-time help with the W.C., need a great deal of day-time help with feeding and/or washing and the W.C.

Category 3: Contains those who are permanently bedfast or confined to a chair and need help to get in and out, who are senile or mentally impaired, or who though unable to care for themselves as far as normal everyday functions are concerned do not need as much help as categories 1 and 2.

Category 4: Contains people who either have difficulty performing all everyday tasks or find most tasks difficult and some impossible.

Category 5: Contains people who find most tasks difficult or three or four items difficult and some impossible.

Category 6: Contains people who can do a fair amount for themselves but have difficulty with some items, or have to have help with one or two minor items.

Category 7: Contains people who can do everything themselves, but have difficulty with one or two items.

Category 8a: Contains people to whom physical impairment presents no difficulty in taking care of themselves, but whose main impairment is mental, endocrinal, sensory, etc.

Category 8b: Contains people to whom impairment presents no special difficulty in taking care of themselves.

Although the survey was carried out in 1968 and based partly on population figures obtained from the 1966 Census, we have, where possible, attempted to update the figures to 1978 by assuming that the incidence of disability has remained constant after allowing for changes in population composition and with reference to geographical and age distribution in the last decade. We estimate that the size of the impaired population of working age (16-64) is about 1.25 million, of whom the majority suffer from only minor impairment. Table 15.1 shows a breakdown of impairment by age and degree of severity, and Table 15.2 shows the estimated incidence of impairment for various age groups. As may be noted, about 1

Table 15.1. Estimated Disabled Population of Working Age in Great Britain, by Degree of Severity of Handicap, 1978 (in thousands)

	Degree of Handicap				
Age Group	Very Severe	Severe	Appreciable	Minor	Total
16-29	5	5	11	76	97
30-49	13	30	55	270	368
50-64	25	87	152	519	783
Total	43	122	218	865	1,248

Source: OPCS Survey (1971); survey figures here and in following tables extrapolated to 1978.

Table 15.2. Estimated Population per 1,000 of Men and Women in Different Age Groups with Some Impairment, 1978

Age Group	Men	Women	All
16-29	10.0	7.9	8.9
30-49	30.2	25.6	27.9
50-64	85.6	84.6	85.0
65-74	211.4	227.1	220.7
75 & over	316.2	409.0	378.0
All Ages	66.7	88.2	78.0

Source: OPCS Survey (1971).

in 13 people aged 16 and over has some physical, mental, or sensory impairment, the ratio of men being approximately 1 in 15, and women 1 in 11. About 1 in 100 men aged 16-29 and 3 in 100 men aged 30-49 are impaired, the proportions for women being slightly lower in each of the two age groups. One in 12 men and women aged 50 to 64 has some impairment, the proportions rising to just over 1 in 5 men and women aged 65 to 74, and about 1 in 3 men and 2 in 5 women aged 75 and over.

Demographic Composition

As one would expect on a priori grounds, and as can be observed in Tables 15.1 and 15.2, disability increases with age in absolute terms and by degree of severity. Tables 15.3 and 15.4 further emphasize this fact. While Table 15.3 might lead one to conclude that the incidence of impairment among women overtakes that of men above the age of 50, Table 15.4 shows that this is not the case, for the incidence of impairment is slightly higher in men than women throughout (although this trend is sharply reversed in people above working age). This apparent discrepancy is explained by the population sex distribution of the Second World War.

Table 15.3. Estimated Numbers of Impaired Persons of Working Age by Age Group, 1978 (in thousands)

Age Group	Men	Women	All
16-29	55	42	97
30-49	199	169	368
50-64	380	403	783
Total	634	614	1,248

Source: OPCS Survey (1971).

When one considers marital status, however, there are marked differences between the sexes, as Table 15.5 indicates. The incidence of marriage among disabled men of working age is considerably above the average 0.79 as compared with 0.71, whereas for disabled women the incidence is well below the average at 0.65.

Table 15.4. Estimated Numbers of Impaired Persons of Working Age as a Percentage of the Working-Age Population, 1978

Age Group	Men	Women	All
16-29	0.9	0.7	0.8
30-49	3.0	2.6	2.8
50-64	8.5	8.4	8.4
Weighted Average	3.7	3.6	3.6

Source: OPCS Survey (1971).

Table 15.5. Marital Status of the Disabled Working-Age Population, 1968 (in percentages)

Category of Handicap	Men			Women			All		
	Married	Single	Previously Married	Married	Single	Previously Married	Married	Single	Previously Married
1-3	70	29	1	57	32	11	62.1	31.0	6.9
4	80	16	4	64	19	17	69.6	18.1	12.3
5	87	11	2	72	13	15	77.3	12.3	10.4
6	80	14	6	67	13	20	72.5	13.5	14.0
Weighted average for categories 1-6	81	15	4	67	16	17	72.2	15.5	12.3
7	82	13	5	67	14	19	74.6	13.7	11.7
8a	76	18	6	59	21	20	68.4	19.5	12.0
8b	83	14	3	65	16	19	74.2	14.9	10.9
Weighted average for all categories 1-8	79	16	5	65	17	18	72.1	16.4	11.5
Average for working population as a whole	71	27	2	71	22	7	71.2	24.4	4.4

Source: OPCS Survey (1971).
Note: Previously married includes widowed, legally separated, and divorced.

Table 15.6. Estimated Numbers of Impaired Men and Women Aged 16 and over Living in Different Areas, 1978 (in thousands)

Area	Men	Women	All
Northern	77	122	199
Yorkshire & Humberside	136	179	315
North Western	166	251	417
East Midland	154	203	357
West Midland	124	158	282
East Anglia	47	63	110
South Eastern (excl. Greater London)	195	308	503
Greater London	148	247	395
South Western	110	172	282
England	1,157	1,703	2,860
Wales	58	67	125
Scotland	111	164	275
Great Britain	1,326	1,934	3,260

Source: OPCS Survey (1971).
Note: Areas referred to are the standard regions of England (as defined in the 1966 Census), Wales, and Scotland.

Table 15.6 shows the estimated number of impaired persons aged 16 and over living in different areas of Great Britain. It is regrettable that similar figures for the working-age population (aged 16-65) are not available. Since the populations of Scotland, Wales, and the regions of England vary in size, it is to be expected that the actual numbers of impaired will vary accordingly. If, however, the proportions of impaired per 1,000 of the population aged 16 and over are considered it becomes apparent that there are considerable regional differences, as is shown in Table 15.7.

The South Western region has a far higher proportion of impaired people than any other area, whereas the South Eastern region has the

Table 15.7. Estimated Proportion per 1,000 Population of Impaired Men and Women Aged 16 and over Living in Different Areas, 1968

Area	Men	Women	All
Northern	67.1	97.1	82.7
Yorkshire & Humberside	80.7	97.1	89.3
North Western	71.4	96.3	84.6
East Midland	62.2	77.7	70.2
West Midland	66.8	81.0	74.1
East Anglia	69.4	91.2	80.6
South Eastern (excl. Greater London)	55.2	77.6	67.0
Greater London	58.7	86.4	73.4
South Western	79.2	109.2	95.1
England	65.9	88.8	77.9
Wales	85.4	91.6	88.7
Scotland	63.1	81.5	72.9
Great Britain	66.7	88.2	78.0

Source: OPCS Survey (1971).

Table 15.8. Proportion of Men and Women Aged 65 and Over in the Population in Different Areas, 1966 (in percentages)

Area	Men	Women	All
Northern	13.2	18.1	15.7
Yorkshire & Humberside	12.9	19.1	16.1
North Western	12.8	19.6	16.4
East Midland	12.9	18.4	15.7
West Midland	11.1	16.8	14.0
East Anglia	15.0	20.7	17.9
South Eastern (excl. Greater London)	14.3	20.9	17.7
Greater London	11.9	18.7	15.5
South Western	15.6	21.9	19.0
England	13.1	19.4	16.4
Wales	14.2	19.7	17.1
Scotland	12.7	18.0	15.5
Great Britain	13.1	19.3	16.3

Source: 1966 Census

smallest proportion. As has already been indicated, the proportion of impaired people rises with age so it is necessary to take into account the proportion of elderly people (65 and over) in the population when comparing regions (see Table 15.8). The 1966 Census shows that, of the population aged 16 and over, the South Western region has a far greater proportion of both men and women aged 65 and over than any other region. It may be, then, that the high proportion of impaired in the South West, and the comparatively lower proportion in the South East are partly due to the proportion of elderly in these areas. However, Yorkshire and Humberside, with average proportion of elderly men and women, has a high proportion of impaired, particularly among men, true also of Wales. Clearly age distribution is by no means the only factor. The high concentration of heavy industry, principally steel and coal-mining, in both these areas may be a consideration as well; the South East, with the lowest proportion of impaired and an above average proportion of elderly, has little heavy industry.

Tables 15.9 and 15.10 show the estimated numbers of impaired people with different degrees of handicap in different regions of Great Britain, and the proportion per 1,000 of men and women in each area who are very severely, severely, or appreciably handicapped respectively. Comparing this table with Table 15.7, which shows the proportion of impaired men and women, it can be seen that the South Western region not only has a very high proportion of impaired men and women, but also the highest proportion of very severely, severely, or appreciably handicapped. This is mainly due to the high proportion of elderly impaired and handicapped. Wales, the Northern and Yorkshire and Humberside regions have a higher than average proportion of more handicapped men, possibly reflecting

Table 15.9. Estimated Numbers of Impaired Persons Aged 16 and Over in Different Areas with Varying Degrees of Handicap, 1978 (in thousands)

Area	Degree of Severity				All Impaired
	Very Severe	Severe	Appreciable	Minor	
Northern	10	24	44	121	199
Yorkshire & Humberside	13	34	66	202	315
North Western	20	48	78	271	417
East Midland	11	22	33	291	357
West Midland	14	31	60	177	282
East Anglia	5	13	19	73	110
South Eastern (excl. Greater London)	27	62	96	318	503
Greater London	17	39	85	254	395
South Western	16	39	64	163	282
England	133	312	545	1,870	2,860
Wales	13	17	29	66	125
Scotland	16	35	57	166	274
Great Britain	162	364	631	2,102	3,259

Source: OPCS Survey (1971).

industrial accidents and illnesses; while East Anglia, the South Eastern, East Midland and Greater London areas have the lowest proportions of more handicapped men.

Educational and Occupational Status

As many of the disabled are elderly and the statutory provisions of education has changed more than once during this century, it is necessary to break down the education of the disbled by age. Although Table 15.11 does this, it should be pointed out that the numbers in some categories are based

Table 15.10. Proportion per 1,000 of Men and Women Aged 16 and Over in Each Area Who Are Very Severely, Severely, or Appreciably Handicapped, 1968

Area	Men	Women	All
Northern	22.1	41.7	32.3
Yorkshire & Humberside	24.3	39.1	32.0
North Western	19.3	38.0	29.2
East Midland	16.6	33.9	25.5
West Midland	17.7	36.9	27.5
East Anglia	13.2	40.4	27.2
South Eastern (excl. Greater London)	15.8	32.6	24.7
Greater London	17.0	34.2	26.1
South Western	30.4	48.7	40.1
England	19.2	37.2	28.6
Wales	24.9	31.8	28.5
Scotland	19.7	36.9	28.8
Great Britain	19.5	36.9	28.6

Source: OPCS Survey (1971).

Table 15.11. Age at Which Impaired Men and Women of Different Ages Left Full-Time Education, 1968 (in percentages)

Age Left Full-Time Education	Age Groups					
	16-29	30-49	50-64	65-74	75+	All Ages
Never went	4	1	1	—	1	1
Still in education	2	—	—	—	—	—
9 years or younger	1	1	—	—	1	1
10-13 years	2	3	14	30	44	25
14 years	5	59	64	53	35	50
15 years	49	18	7	6	6	9
16-17 years	30	13	10	8	9	10
18-20 years	5	3	3	2	3	3
21 years +	2	2	1	1	1	1
	100	100	100	100	100	100

Source: OPCS Survey (1971).

on a rather small sample and may therefore be somewhat unrepresentative. The estimates, however, have been included as they are the only ones available. The differences between men and women are not significant and thus are not included, but there are differences due to age because of the fact that the statutory school age has not remained constant. Disabled people tend to leave school at an earlier age than the general population; this in turn limits their chances of being qualified and subsequently affects their chances of employment.

Table 15.12 shows the highest qualification obtained by impaired men and women in comparision with that of the general population. Although the impaired population is less well qualified than the general population, the distributions are not as dissimilar as one may have been led to expect. This is reinforced by Table 15.13 which indicates the occupational status of

Table 15.12. Highest Qualification Obtained by Impaired Persons Age 16 and Over Compared with the General Population, 1968 (in percentages)

Highest Qualification Obtained	Impaired Persons			General Population		
	Men	Women	All	Men	Women	All
Degree	2	1	1	2	1	1
Diploma/professional body	1	—	1	3	1	2
Minor profession (Nurse, etc.)	1	3	2	1	4	3
GCE A level[a]	—	—	—	1	1	1
GCE O level[b]	2	2	2	8	6	7
Minor technical	1	—	1	4	1	2
Commercial	4	5	4	7	5	6
Served apprenticeship	18	6	11	15	5	10
Serving apprenticeship	—	—	—	2	—	1
Skilled, not apprenticed	24	14	18	23	18	20
No qualifications or skills	7	69	60	34	58	47

Source: OPCS Survey (1971).
[a]General Certificate of Education Advanced Level certificates, generally taken at age 18.
[b]General Certificate of Education Ordinary Level certificates, generally taken at age 16.

Table 15.13. Occupational Status of Working-Age Impaired Persons Compared with Economically Active Persons in the General Population, 1968 (in percentages)

Occupational Status	Impaired Persons	General Population
Employers and managers	11	12
Professional workers	2	3
Intermediate nonmanual workers	5	6
Junior nonmanual workers	20	22
Personal service workers	5	5
Foremen and supervisors	4	3
Skilled manual workers	21	23
Semiskilled manual and agricultural workers	20	16
Unskilled manual workers	12	8
Members of armed forces	—	1
Others	—	1

Source: OPCS Survey (1971).

the impaired population in comparison with the general population of Great Britain. The impaired may expect only a marginally lower occupational status than the general population, with just over 20 percent skilled manual workers, 20 percent junior nonmanual workers, and 20 percent semi-skilled manual workers and agricultural workers. Just over 10 percent are employers and managers and 2 percent are professional workers.

It should be pointed out that these classifications are primarily based on self-assessment and the table does not show whether the individuals are employed or not. Indeed 70 percent of the impaired felt that their disability had limited their choices of job, but this feeling was expressed by a higher proportion of those with fewest qualifications. Of the impaired with qualifications, 42 percent had been forced to take jobs where their qualifications or skills were not used due to their disability.

Medical Characteristics

Table 15.14 shows a breakdown of the disabled population by cause of impairment following the International Classification of Diseases, 1959. It can be seen that by far the greatest cause is diseases of bones and organs of movement, particularly among women. The other main causes of impairment are diseases of the circulatory, central nervous, and respiratory systems. The total figure of 3.3 million is higher than the previous estimates of 3.25 million because of some doublecounting; that is, if two separate conditions were thought to be incapacitating then they were both included.

Economic Status

Problems arise when dealing with the economic status of the disabled in the United Kingdom and trying to compare it with the disabled in other countries. Whereas in many countries disability incomes are paid on a sliding scale according to the degree of disability, in Britain such incomes are generally paid only to a distinct category of people. The disabled in Great Britain are in a Catch 22 situation. If they are disabled they cannot work because if they can work they are, by definition, not disabled. Most of the benefits to which the disabled may be entitled, such as invalidity benefits, disappear as soon as employment begins. There are exceptions to this, such as the family income supplement (q.v.), however these tend to be universal benefits rather than specifically designed for the disabled.

While not giving any information on actual earnings levels of the disabled, the OPCS Survey did throw some light on their economic status through their employment status and how this might be influenced by their disability. As was shown in Table 15.13, a slightly higher proportion of the impaired, in comparison with the general population, are unskilled manual workers. This perhaps reflects educational disadvantage, particularly among those disabled at birth or during childhood. The effect upon job mobility and promotional prospects may also be quite large.

As well as dictating the jobs open to the impaired, disability can affect the extent to which any job is pursued. The OPCS Survey showed that 44

Table 15.14. Main Cause of Impairment of Disabled Population Aged 16 and Over, 1968 (in thousands; percentages in parentheses)

Main Cause of Impairment	Estimated Numbers		
	Men	Women	All
Infective & parasitic diseases	17(1.3)	12(0.6)	30(0.9)
Neoplasms	13(1.0)	15(0.7)	27(0.8)
Allergic, endocrine, metabolic & nutritional diseases	16(1.2)	35(1.7)	51(1.5)
Diseases of blood & blood-forming organs	4(0.3)	24(1.2)	28(0.8)
Mental, psychoneurotic & personality disorders	38(2.8)	60(3.0)	98(2.9)
Diseases of central nervous system	163(12.1)	197(9.8)	360(10.7)
Diseases of circulatory system	199(14.8)	292(14.6)	492(14.7)
Diseases of respiratory system	179(13.3)	104(5.2)	284(8.5)
Diseases of digestive system	35(2.6)	47(2.3)	82(2.4)
Diseases of genito-urinary system	9(0.7)	26(1.3)	35(1.0)
Diseases of sense organs (including blindness)	92(6.8)	186(9.3)	277(8.3)
Diseases of skin & cellular tissues	9(0.7)	11(0.5)	20(0.6)
Diseases of bones & organs of movement	351(26.0)	836(9.3)	1,187(35.4)
Congenital malformations	5(0.4)	10(0.5)	16(0.5)
Injuries	73(5.4)	41(2.0)	114(3.4)
Amputations	105(7.8)	24(1.2)	129(3.8)
Senility & ill-defined conditions	40(3.0)	82(4.1)	122(3.6)
Total	1,348(100)	2,002(100)	3,352(100)

Source: OPCS Survey (1971).
Note: Totals sometimes do not add up or tally exactly because of rounding off of estimates.

Table 15.15. Remploy Basic Weekly Wage Rates, 1973-1977

Year	Basic Wage	As Percentage of Average Weekly Earnings	
		Manual Workers	All Workers
1973	£18.12	47.6	43.2
1975	£30.00	53.9	49.3
1976	£38.50	53.8	49.0
1977	£42.70	52.9	47.6

Source: Jordan (1979).

percent of impaired workers felt that the number of hours that they worked was affected by their disability. A shortfall in the number of hours worked in comparison with the average worker is bound to have an effect upon relative wage levels, particularly in Britain where it was estimated that 14.3 percent of total male manual workers' wages were attributed to overtime payments and 57 percent of all male manual employees received some overtime pay (DOE, 1978b).

The disabled have also been trapped in relatively low-paid jobs, particularly in sheltered workshops and other government or local authority institutions. As Table 15.15 shows, the basic wage paid by Remploy (a government subsidized organization specifically designed to help the disabled) has been significantly below that paid in open employment, although this differential has been slightly eroded in recent years following an offical report on sheltered employment (DOE, 1973).

As well as receiving lower earnings when in employment, the disabled face a greater probability of being unemployed. The unemployment rate among the registered disabled has generally been about three times the

Table 15.16. Unemployment Rate of Registered Disabled Compared with Total Work Force, 1965-1978

Year	Registered Disabled	Total Work Force
1965	7.3	1.5
1966	6.9	1.5
1967	8.9	2.3
1968	10.0	2.5
1969	10.6	2.5
1970	11.3	2.6
1971	13.0	3.4
1972	14.9	3.8
1973	12.4	2.7
1974	10.4	2.6
1975	12.7	4.2
1976	14.0	5.4
1977	14.1	6.1
1978	14.3	6.5

Source: Department of Employment *Gazette* (various issues).

average for the general population and, as Table 15.16 indicates, the special provisions for the employment of the disabled has failed to shelter them against the worsening employment situation that has affected the British economy in recent years. The disabled also face the possibility of being unemployed for a longer time than the average worker, as indicated in Table 15.17.

Table 15.17. Unemployment, by Time, of Disabled and General Work Forces as of January 1978 (in percentages)

Length of Time Unemployed	Disabled Unemployed	General Unemployed
Up to 2 weeks	2.7	7.8
2-4 weeks	2.0	5.5
4-8 weeks	5.6	12.0
8-12 weeks	6.8	12.8
13-26 weeks	13.1	20.7
26-52 weeks	15.8	18.6
1 year plus	54.0	22.5

Source: Hansard (1978).

The OPCS Survey also gave some indication of working status and the effect upon it of age, sex, and severity of impairment. Table 15.18 shows that permanent disability and inability to work correlates with age, while Table 15.19 shows that a similar relationship exists with respect to degree of severity.

Summary and Conclusions

It must be said that any conclusions drawn about the available information have to be of a tentative nature. It would appear that there are in excess of 3 million people in the United Kingdom who suffer from some degree of impairment, of whom about 40 percent (about 1.25 million) are of working age. The incidence and severity of impairment increases with age, particularly for those over retirement age. There appear to be marked regional differences which are only partly explained by differing age distributions, although other determinants such as industrial concentration may be important. Unfortunately, however, information on this and other relevant factors is sadly lacking.

Educationally and occupationally the disabled do not appear to be as badly off as one might have imagined. However, their economic status is well below the average as they occupy less well paid jobs and also are unable to work as many hours as their ablebodied counterparts. Finally, it should be observed that the disabled have a greater chance of being unemployed and remaining unemployed for longer than the general population.

Table 15.18. The Working Status of Impaired Persons in Different Age Groups, 1968 (in percentages)

Working Status	Men Aged			Women Aged			All Men Aged		
	16-29	30-49	50-64	16-29	30-49	50-64	16-29	30-49	50-64
Working	61	68	48	36	31	17	50	51	32
Attending an occupation center	9	1	—	7	1	—	9	9	—
Unemployed (although available for work)	10	7	5	8	2	1	9	5	3
Temporarily sick	7	11	12	3	6	2	5	8	7
Housewife	—	—	—	19	36	47	8	17	24
Retired[a]	—	—	—	—	—	17	—	—	9
Permanently disabled and unable to work again	13	13	34	27	24	16	19	18	25

Source: OPCS Survey (1971).
[a]The retirement age for women in Britain is 60.

Table 15.19. Working Status of Impaired Persons (Excluding Housewives and Retirees) by Degree of Handicap, 1968 (in percentages)

	Category of Handicap							
	Very Severe	Severe		Appreciable		Minor		All
Working Status	1-3	4	5	6	7	8a	8b	1-8
Working	6	10	38	48	57	54	74	55
Attending an occupation center	4	3	1	2	1	2	1	1
Unemployed (although available for work)	1	3	2	5	4	7	5	5
Temporarily sick	4	10	10	9	10	10	8	9
Permanently disabled & unable to work again	85	74	49	36	28	27	12	30

Source: OPCS Survey (1971).

Economic Aspects of Disability Policies

In this section the major public programs designed to help the disabled will be presented and described, as well as those more general benefits to which the disabled may also be entitled. In order to appreciate the British system it will be necessary to explain briefly how the current system, which is characterized by a plethora of overlapping benefits, has arisen. A clearer view of the British system can be obtained if we split the history of the system into two periods, before and after 1970.

The Period before 1970

The cornerstone of the British Social Security System is the so-called "insurance principle"; that is, payments are made out of earned income in order for benefits to be provided in the event of sickness, unemployment, or retirement.[1] This, of course, affects the disabled person directly. Those disabled from birth or suffering from recurrent disabilities find that they may have inadequate contributions to enable them to receive comparable benefits to those which other members of society who have made the required number of contributions receive.

The main developments in the United Kingdom welfare system have occurred since the Second World War, and particularly following the Beveridge Report in 1942. Some of the main Beveridge recommendations were implemented, but in a watered-down and amended form. The major changes were the government's acceptance of and responsibility for the maintenance of full employment (1944), the introduction of family allowances (1946), the National Insurance and Industrial Injuries Acts (1948) and the creation of the National Health Service (1948).

One of Beveridge's main themes was that the social welfare system should be "first and foremost a plan of insurance—of giving in return for contributions benefits up to subsistence levels, as of right and without means test so that individuals may build freely upon it'' (Beveridge Report, 1942, Part I). A principal aim, therefore, was ''adequacy of benefit'' which would remove the need for supplementary means-tested benefits. The main National Insurance contributory benefits are unemployment and sickness benefits and industrial injuries benefits. The intended role of National Assistance, as introduced by the National Assistance Act of 1948 to replace Public Assistance, was as a safety net to provide support for the ''limited number of cases of need not covered by Social Insurance.'' It was expected that a large and growing proportion of the population would be kept above the ''poverty line'' by the National Insurance benefits and that the role of fall-back benefits would gradually diminish. This had patently not been the case as the total numbers dependent to a greater or lesser extent upon National Assistance, or Supplementary Benefit as it was called after 1966, grew from 1 million recipients in 1948 to almost 3 million in 1976.

One reason why this situation arose was because of government decisions not to implement Beveridge's recommendations in full. Pension levels when introduced were set at a lower level than that recommended by Beveridge. The proposed provisions for dependent children were also diluted. Family allowances were set at only two-thirds of their intended rate. It was argued that free school meals and welfare milk and food would be introduced for all children to compensate for this, and although this was never done family allowances were not increased to take this into account.

During the 1950s and up to the mid-1960s no major legislation affecting disabled people was introduced. The level of benefits was periodically changed, although it can be argued that this was due more to political pressure than to any long-term objective. In 1966, when the Supplementary Benefit Act replaced the National Assistance Act of 1948, one of the main elements contained within the scheme was that of ''discretion'' which, so it was claimed, would give ''flexibility of response to varying situations of human need'' (Supplementary Benefits Commission, 1975, p. 1). As the cost of the scheme and the need to guard against its abuse increased, this discretion became used as a way of rationing benefits.

The reaction to this policy was the formation of a considerable number of voluntary organizations to help the economic and social positions of underprivileged groups of society. In Parliament several attempts were made in the late 1960s to have legislation introduced to help the disabled. However, it was not until 1970 that any significant change occurred.

The Period after 1970

In 1970 the Chronically Sick and Disabled Persons Act was passed through Parliament. The main points of this Act can be summarized as follows:

1. Local authorities had to discover how many people within their area were in need of the various services for the handicapped.

2. It became the responsibility of local authorities to provide a wide range of services for the disabled. These included opportunities for intellectual, physical and social recreations, and education, as well as assistance with transport.

3. Local authorities were required to increase their responsibilities toward housing the chronically sick and disabled.

4. Buildings to which the public were admitted and educational facilities were legally required to provide access for members of the public who were disabled.

5. Disabled people were to be represented on a wide range of central advisory bodies and local authority committees.

6. Provision was made for the hospitalization of the chronically sick and disabled.

7. Schemes were introduced with respect to powered invalid carriages and wheelchairs and the provision of special parking regulations.

It can be argued that the high standards implied in the 1970 Act have not been reached. There are a number of reasons for this: notably, the unexpected economic crisis in the 1970s and the delays associated with the major simulataneous reorganization in the system of local government. Also, rather than offering universal and comprehensive benefits, as are central government benefits, local authorities have been given considerable discretion. This has led to a large degree of variability in how the 1970 Act has been implemented in different local authority areas.

A number of benefits that affect the disabled to a greater or lesser extent have also been introduced since 1970, as will be evident from the next section. Although one would have expected these changes to have improved the lot of the handicapped person, the result, in fact, is a "volume of instructions ... so long, so complex and so frequently amended that officials themselves often find them very difficult to understand" (Supplementary Benefits Commission, 1975, p. 45).

Contributory Benefits

Sickness Benefits

These are paid to men aged 16 to 70 and women aged 16 to 65 years who are incapacitated for work due to illness for up to 28 weeks. Apart from the age criteria the incapacity has to be supported by medical evidence and the claimant has to satisfy the contribution conditions—for 1979/80 these were that he/she had to have earned and paid contributions on at least £875 in the tax year 1978/79 to qualify for the full benefit. Increases in benefits are payable for one dependent adult and dependent children. For example, a married man with two dependent children would receive £35.90 weekly in 1980; this compares with £10.30 in 1970 and £5.10 in 1960.

The number of people receiving sickness benefits has remained remarkably constant throughout the years 1966 to 1977, varying between only 922,000 and 995,000. After 28 weeks those receiving sickness benefits who are still incapacitated for work transfers to invalidity benefits.

Invalidity Benefits

This was introduced in 1971 to replace the long-term sickness benefit and consists of two parts, pension and allowance. The invalidity pension is paid to those previously receiving sickness benefits for 28 weeks. The invalidity allowance is an additional payment to the pension paid at one of three rates, depending upon the age of the recipient when the incapacity began: (1) under 40—higher rate; (2) at least 40 but under 50—middle rate; (3) over 60 (55 for women)—no allowance is payable. A married man with two dependent children eligible for an invalidity pension and allowance at the higher rate would receive £56.40 in 1980 (£51.50 pension plus £4.90 allowance); this compares with £15.70 in 1971 (£14.70 pension plus £1 allowance).

The number of people receiving invalidity benefits has risen steadily since its introduction, from 415,000 in 1972 to 610,000 in 1979. Of these 610,000 recipients 504,000 (83 percent) also received an invalidity allowance. Invalidity benefits cannot be paid if the claimant is already receiving any other national insurance benefit (except attendance allowance, mobility allowance, maternity grant, or war disablement pension).

Recipients of invalidity benefits are allowed to earn a small amount (£13 a week in 1980) in the form of "therapeutic" earnings, although this has to be sanctioned by a General Practitioner. The level of a spouse's earnings may also affect the size of benefit received. Currently, if he/she earns under £45.09 net per week then invalidity benefit is unaffected, but it is reduced by 50 percent of what he/she earns between £45 and £49, and by 100 percent of the amount over £49 up to £61 when benefit is paid for her/him as a dependent. For example, the amount received for a working wife will be as follows, depending on her net weekly income (net income means the amount after all deductions and all expenses incurred in working; benefit cannot be claimed for any dependent adult if they earn more than £14 per week):

Weekly Net Income	Benefit Received
£45.10	£14
£47.00	£13
£50.00	£11
£55.00	£ 6
£65.00	£ 0

Industrial Injury Benefits

These are paid to individuals who are incapable of work because of personal injury suffered in an industrial accident or due to a prescribed industrial disease. Payable as an alternative to sickness benefits, it is available to all persons, including those not entitled to sickness benefits because they have not paid full contributions, providing they satisfy conditions of insurability and presence. Benefits are payable for a maximum of 26 weeks.

A man who is eligible for industrial injury benefits would receive considerably more than if he were entitled to only sickness benefits. The benefits for dependents are the same under both schemes, but the personal benefit under the two schemes is different. The personal benefit under the industrial injury is currently about 18 percent higher than under sickness benefits. When the industrial injury scheme was introduced in 1948 the personal benefit was 73 percent higher than sickness benefit rates.

The number of people receiving industrial injury benefits has been constantly falling in recent years, from 41,000 in May 1979 to 75,000 in 1966. The reasons for this are not clear; however, these factors may have contributed to the decline:

1. Although the average population at risk had only fallen from 22,600,000 in 1965 to 22,183,000 in 1975, the size of the male population at risk, which has a higher incidence of industrial accidents than women, had fallen from 14,378,000 to 13,510,000 during the same period.

2. The distribution of jobs has been changing away from relatively dangerous manufacturing and heavy industries toward safer service industries and office jobs.

3. The availability of alternative benefits may have led less people to apply for industrial benefits, for which the eligibility criteria require examinations by a medical board.

Industrial Disablement Pensions

Disablement benefits are paid after 26 weeks and replace injury benefits. If there is a loss of faculty it will be paid even after a return to work. The loss of faculty is expressed as a percentage of disablement and is assessed by a medical board. If the disablement is assessed at under 20 percent, it is normal for a lump sum to be paid. If the assessment is 20 percent or more, then the individual would receive a weekly pension. The size of the pension is related to the degree of disablement assessed by the medical board. At about 60 percent (associated with the loss of one hand) the pension is of comparable value to the invalidity pension.

The number of pensions has stayed remarkably constant, only varying between 201,000 and 208,000 for the period 1964 to 1979. As well as the basic disablement pension 70 percent (about 140,000) of recipients also receive one or more of the following allowances:

1. *Special hardship allowance.* This is paid to individuals who are unable to work in their regular (pre-accident) occupation or in work of an equivalent standard as a result of an industrial accident or a prescribed disease. The amount of the allowance is related to loss of earnings up to a weekly maximum rate, subject to the condition that the basic pension plus the allowance does not exceed 100 percent of the disablement rate.

2. *Hospital treatment allowance.* Payable to individuals assessed at less than 100 percent disabled in addition to normal pension for any period in the hospital for treatment of the injury for which they were awarded the pension.

3. *Unemployability pension.* This is normally payable only as an increase of the disablement pension if the individual is permanently incapable of work or unable to earn more than a limited amount in a year because of the result of an industrial accident.

4. *Constant attendance allowance.* Payable to individuals in receipt of 100 percent industrial disablement pension who require constant attendance.

5. *Exceptionally severe disablement allowance.* This is paid to individuals who qualify for a rate of constant attendance allowance of more than the normal maximum.

Non-Contributory Benefits

Family Income Supplement

Family Income Supplement (FIS) is a means-tested benefit introduced in 1971, payable to families with dependent children where the head of the family is in remunerative full-time work (at least 30 hours per week), where the gross weekly income falls below a prescribed amount determined by the number of children in the family. The size of the award is half the difference between the family's total gross income and the prescribed amount for that size of family. Recipients of FIS are automatically entitled to free prescriptions and dental treatment as well as free school meals, where applicable.

The number of awards of FIS has increased slightly, from 80,000 in 1971 to 86,000 in 1977; however, in each year since its introduction there have been somewhere in the region of 50,000 claims that have been rejected. It should also be noted that about a quarter of those who are entitled to FIS do not claim it.

Non-Contributory Invalidity Pensions

Non-contributory invalidity pensions (NCIP) were introduced in November 1975 for individuals between 16 years and pension age incapable of work for over 28 weeks. This is primarily intended for people who fail to qualify for the invalidity pension due to an insufficient contributions record. Unfortunately NCIP is paid at only 60 percent of the rate of invalidity benefits. As with invalidity benefits, claimants are allowed to earn up to £13 per week therapeutic earnings. It was estimated that of about 130,000 persons who were in receipt of NCIP in 1976, about 60,000 were in psychiatric hospitals.

Non-Contributory Invalidity Pensions for Married Women

Housewives' non-contributory invalidity pensions (HNCIP) were introduced in 1977 for married women and common-law wives who are incapable of both paid work and of carrying out normal household duties. The rates of payments are the same as for NCIP, i.e., 60 percent of the rate of invalidity benefits. As with invalidity benefits and NCIP, recipients may earn up to £13 a week therapeutic earnings.

Attendance Allowance

The attendance allowance was introduced in 1971 for individuals aged 2 years and over who need substantial care by day and night, with a lower rate introduced in 1973 for those requiring attendance *either* by day or by night. This benefit is unique in that it is payable by right irrespective of means, contribution record, and source of the incapacity. The main drawback, however, is that it is set at an unrealistically low level. The current rates (1980) are £18.60 per week at the higher rate and £12.40 at the lower rate of allowance.

The total number of people receiving the attendance allowance has been steadily increasing. The total number receiving the allowance at the higher rate in 1977 was 152,508, of whom 38,928 (26 percent) were of working age (16-64); the total receiving the allowance at the lower rate was 147,473, of whom 45,759 (31 percent) were of working age. In 1972 85,201 received the allowance at the higher rate, of whom 25,461 (30 percent) were of working age; in 1973 44,625 received the allowance at the lower rate, of whom 17,763 (40 percent) were of working age.

Invalid Care Allowance

Invalid care allowance (ICA) was introduced in 1976 for people of working age who are prevented from working by the need to care for a severely disabled relative. Unfortunately, married women cannot qualify for the allowance as they are regarded as "being at home in any event."

The allowance is not means-tested and does not depend on national insurance contributions, but is different from all the previously mentioned benefits in that it is taxable. Claimants may earn up to £6 per week without affecting their benefit. It was estimated that the number of people receiving ICA was 6,348 by the end of 1979.

Mobility and Other Travel Allowances

The *mobility allowance* is a non-means-tested, noncontributory cash benefit, which is currently (1980) £12 a week, designed to help severely disabled people to be more mobile. As with ICA it is taxable. The benefit began in January 1976 and has been phased in over 3 years. It is available to individuals between the ages of 5 and 65. In order to qualify, an individual has to be unable or virtually unable to walk because of physical disablement. When assessing walking ability artificial aids are taken into account. The individual also has to be able to make use of enhanced facilities for locomotion, although in practice this only bars those who cannot be moved for medical reason or those in a coma. About 110,000 people received this benefit in 1979.

The introduction of the mobility allowance replaced the *old vehicle service* for new applicants under pensionable age, and extended help with mobility to disabled passengers, including children. However, new applicants over pensionable age are not entitled to the mobility allowance from the old scheme. The old scheme involved issuing the disabled with either invalid tricycles, small cars, or a private car allowance. We need not explain the old scheme in detail as it is expected to be totally phased out over the next 5-7 years. This situation has created many anamalies which will persist for some time, since those who benefited under the old vehicle scheme will, in most cases, continue to receive pre-1976 benefits, whereas the majority of new applicants can only apply for the mobility allowance, which currently stops at pensionable age.

The Manpower Services Commission can assist severely disabled people with the *cost of fares to and from work*. In order to qualify for help a person has to be registered under the Disabled Persons (Employment) Act (1944), and be unable to use public transport for all or part of his/her journey to and from work because of disability as well as the cost. Financial help is normally given for taxi fares at a rate of three-quarters of the total cost, and is subject to a maximum weekly amount of £36 for 5 day week workers. The average amount given in 1977 was £9.38 when the maximum amount was £25.

Numerous *other benefits associated with travel* are available to disabled people. These include rate relief on garages, assistance with purchasing cars, concessions on cars and wheelchairs, exemptions from vehicle excise duty (currently £60 per year), and special privileges in relation to parking.

War Disablement

War pensions. This is a scheme for people whose disability is a result of, or was aggravated by, military service during the First or Second World War or following the Second World War, including Merchant Seamen injured in either World War and civilians injured in the Second World War.

The principles of this scheme are similar to those of the industrial injuries scheme. There is a basic disablement pension, the amount of which is conditional upon two factors: the degree of disablement due to service, and the rank held in the forces. The current pension for a private at the 100 percent rate is £38, the 20 percent rate being therefore £7.60.

As would be expected, the numbers receiving war disablement pensions have been continuously falling from 725,000 in 1950 to 276,000 in 1979, of whom 164,000 (60 percent) were of working age. The distribution of disablement is heavily weighted to the lesser end, with 75 percent of recipients being assessed at 40 percent or less disabled.

War disablement pensions are payable whether the recipient is working or not and there is no overlap with other main benefits. For example, recipients of war pensions are still eligible, assuming that they satisfy the qualifying criteria, for a whole range of other benefits such as invalidity benefits, industrial injury benefits, and ICA.

Unemployability supplement. This is paid to individuals so seriously disabled as to be unemployable or able to earn more than a small amount of "therapeutic earnings." There were 11,320 recipients in 1977 when the supplement was £18.60 per week. In 1980 the supplement was £24.70 plus £14.00 for a dependent adult relative.

Constant attendance allowance. Paid to individuals whose disablement is 80 percent or more and who require regular attendance of a personal nature, this allowance is payable at four different rates, ranging from £7.60 to £30.40 in 1980. In 1977 there were 6,460 recipients, the majority being at the lower rates. This allowance is not payable in addition to any other attendance allowance.

Exceptionally severe disablement allowance. As with the similar allowance in the industrial injuries scheme, this is for the most severely disabled group of those receiving the constant attendance allowance. The weekly payment in 1980 was £15.20, there were 596 recipients in 1977.

Allowance for lowered standard of occupation. This is payable where there is an earnings loss because pensionable disablement permanently prevents the recipient of a pension from following his regular occupation or work of an equivalent standard. Allowance and pension together cannot exceed the 100 percent pension rate. The 1980 weekly maximum was £15.20. There were 15,180 recipients in 1977.

Comforts allowance. This is payable in addition to unemployability supplement and/or the constant attendance allowance. It is paid at a higher rate (£6.60 per week in 1980) or lower rate (£3.30 per week in 1980). There were 13,889 recipients in 1977, the majority at the lower rate.

Other benefits. There is still a plethora of other benefits payable to beneficiaries under the war disablement scheme. Benefits include a treatment allowance, a severe disablement occupational allowance, a clothing allowance, free prescriptions, refunds for dental and optical treatment, assistance with children's education, house adaptions, and assistance with travel.

Supplementary Benefits

Supplementary benefits (SB) replaced National Assistance in 1966, which, as the state's "safety net," provided a basic minimum income for those who have no claim on national insurance benefits due to insufficient contributions, and those who receive some contribution benefits but little or nothing else. Many disabled people receive SB, often as a small amount on top of their invalidity or sickness benefit. However, there are estimated to be over 100,000 disabled people who could receive SB but who are not claiming it.

Basic Allowance

Anyone over the age of 16 who lives in Great Britain and is not in full-time work is eligible for SB. Benefits do not depend on having paid national insurance contributions. The weekly benefit is the amount by which an individual's "resources" fall short of his "requirements."

A recipient's first £4 net plus the first £4 net of a wife's earnings are not counted if they are not registered for work, but if registered for work, i.e., unemployed, only the first £2 is ignored. "Net" means after tax and insurance and all expenses connected with work have been deducted.

Table 15.20 shows the weekly requirement rates for 1980. In addition to the basic requirements is the full rent (or weekly mortgage interest) repayment and possible allowance for any special expenses (these are dealt with in the next part of this section). According to *Social Security Statistics*, the numbers of sick and disabled claiming SB who receive no contributory benefits has been gradually rising (from 142,000 in 1966 to 158,000 in 1977), although by no means as fast as the total number of recipients (from approximately 2.5 million to 3 million between 1966 and 1977). The decline in numbers of sick and disabled claiming SB in addition to contributory benefits (from 156,000 in 1966 to 71,000 in 1977) is probably due to the introduction of new benefits for disabled people during the 1970s, so reducing the necessity and/or eligibility for SB. *Social Security Statistics* further shows that the average amount of SB received by the sick and disabled did not rise as fast as the average for all recipients; however, as has been pointed out, this is probably explained by the new benefits introduced for the disabled since 1970.

There are many anomalies associated with SB; a typical one illustrates the complexity of the system which the disabled are expected to cope with. Young people under 18 who are unlikely to be able to work because of disability will find that claiming SB at 16 or 17 instead of NCIP will result in

Table 15.20. Weekly Supplementary Benefit Requirement Rates, 1980

Weekly Rates	Ordinary Rate	Long-Term Rate[a]
Married couple	£29.70	£37.65
Single householder	18.30	23.70
Any other person		
18 and over	14.65	18.95
16-17	11.25	11.25
Dependent Child		
13-15	9.35	9.35
11-12	7.70	7.70
5-10	6.25	6.25
under 5	5.20	5.20
Blind Scale		
Married couple (one blind)	30.95	38.90
Married couple (both blind)	31.75	39.70
Single person 18 or over	19.55	24.95
16-17	12.15	12.15

Source: Department of Health and Social Security (1980).
[a]Assumes claimant and wife are under 80.

the long-run maximization of benefits. Choosing SB between 16 and 18, however, will mean that they are marginally worse off for these 2 years, assuming that they are not in receipt of any extra allowances. However, in 2 years time they would then be eligible for long-term SB, which will assist their pension rights, and receive the balance of their weekly income as SB, which may also entitle them to extra allowances.

Extra Allowances and Grants

Disabled people receiving supplementary benefits may also be entitled to extra grants and allowances in addition to the basic weekly allowance. There are two types of extra payments: exceptional circumstances additions (ECA's) and exceptional needs payments (ENP's).

ECA's are weekly allowances for essential expenses which lie outside those supposed to be met by the basic allowance. An ECA can be for any amount, though in practice fixed rates are usually paid for the more common types of extra expenses. The most common ECA's are for heating, special diets, and laundry expenses. In 1979 the average weekly amount of ECA received by the sick and disabled was £2.40 for those with contributory benefits and £1.85 for those without. This compares with an average weekly amount of ECA for all recipients of £1.66, which is probably explained by the extra day-to-day expenses incurred through disablement.

ENP's cover expenses such as clothing, bedding, and household equipment. The number of ENP's made per year has risen from 560,000 in 1970 to 1,130,000 in 1979, with the average payment rising from £6.86 to £33.59 respectively.

Recipients of SB, however little they receive, are automatically entitled to other benefits such as free prescriptions, fares to hospital, free legal advice, and free school meals for children.

Other Benefits and Services

There are still other benefits to which the disabled are entitled. The most obvious one is, of course, retirement pensions, but since we are primarily concerned with people of working age this will be ignored. Other benefits that the working-age disabled may be entitled to include housing grants and allowances, as well as rent rebates and allowances. The disabled can also get assistance with heating and services to help with incontinence.

In addition, a large number of local authorities provide a considerable range of welfare services following The Chronically Sick & Disabled Persons Act, 1970. These include assistance with housing, parking, day care, home helps, meals, telephones, holidays, etc. As has already been noted, there is a large degree of variance in the adherence to the Act by local authorities.

Summary of Benefits and Services

As may be readily concluded, the benefits and services available that the disabled may be entitled to are many and varied. This has resulted in a confusing overlapping of benefits that has led to many disabled people being unwilling to claim benefits even though they are entitled to them. Many more are not claiming benefits through ignorance of even their existence.

Financing of and Expenditure on Disability Policies

Sickness and invalidity benefits are financed out of a National Insurance Fund, as are (since 1975) industrial injuries benefits following the Social Security Act of 1973. This fund is financed by a general payroll tax on both employers and employed and is collected in a rather complex manner. There are four main classes of contribution: (1) paid by employed earners and their employers—this is earnings related; (2) paid in respect of self-employment (flat rate); (3) paid voluntarily by nonemployed persons and others (flat rate); (4) paid mainly by certain self-employed people along with Schedule D income tax.

For the tax year 1980/81 Class 1 earnings-related contributions consisted of two elements: primary Class 1 contributions paid by employed earners and secondary contributions paid by their employers. Liability for Class 1 contributions depends on whether earnings reach the lower earnings level of £23 per week. If they reach this level the contribution is a percentage of *all* earnings up to the upper earnings level of £165. The primary contribution is at the rate of 6.75 percent, with the secondary contribution at the rate of 13.7 percent. The latter includes 3.5 percent which is payable under the National Insurance Surcharge Act of 1976; the money raised goes to the government's general tax revenue and not the National Insurance Fund.

Flat rate Class 2 contributions are payable in respect of self-employment at a rate of £2.50 per week, although exemption from liability may be granted if expected earnings are less than £1250 per annum. Class 3 contributions are flat rate and voluntary and can be paid only to help a person qualify for certain benefits if, in any tax year, their Class 1 or 2 contributions are insufficient for that purpose. The weekly rate of contribution is £2.40. Class 4 contributions are payable by self-employed earners on profits or gains chargeable to income tax. The contributions are at the rate of 5 percent of profits between £2,650 and £8,300.

The picture is further complicated by the fact that not only is the National Insurance Fund responsible for retirement pensions, death grants, maternity grants, and other benefits that do not necessarily affect the disabled, but that these contributions also include amounts collected on behalf of the National Health Service, and in the case of the secondary Class 1 contribution, the redundancy payments scheme.

As Table 15.21 shows, for 1977 receipts exceeded payments by £928

Table 15.21. Receipts and Payments of the National Insurance Fund, 1976 and 1977

	£ millions			
Receipts	*1976*	*1977*	*1978*	*1979*
Contributions from employers and employees	6,184	7,729	8,559	8,991
Supplement from consolidated fund	1,333	1,387	1,537	1,976
Net income from investments	193	281	387	443
Total receipts	7,509	9,398	10,484	11,410
Payments				
Benefits				
Unemployment	454	559	629	632
Sickness	425	496	585	632
Invalidity	448	563	701	847
Maternity	55	81	92	121
Widows	393	434	466	505
Guardian's Allowance	2	2	2	2
Retirement Pension	4,791	5,651	6,592	7,593
Death Grant	15	15	15	16
Industrial Injury	39	46	50	51
Industrial Disablement	145	167	191	216
Industrial Death	22	25	29	32
Other Industrial Benefits	4	4	4	5
Total benefits	6,793	8,044	9,357	10,652
Administrative expenses	395	426	449	493
Total payments	7,190	8,467	9,805	11,144
Excess of receipts over payments	319	928	678	265

Source: Social Security Statistics (Department of Health and Social Security, 1976-79).
Note: Numbers do not always tally due to rounding to nearest million.

Table 15.22. Expenditures on Noncontributory Benefits

Consolidated Fund Payment in Respect of	1966	1970	1976	1977	1978	1979
Attendance allowances & ICA	N/A[a]	N/A	96	129	170	171
Old persons' retirement pensions	N/A	7	34	36	36	37
Family allowances	146	339	532	544	873	1,798
Family income supplement	N/A	N/A	12	18	25	24
Supplementary pensions & allowances	246	524	1,187	1,526	1,945	2,017
War pensions & allowances	121	128	258	283	310	340
Administration	39	69	214	270	326	365
Total	552	1,067	2,333	2,806	3,685	4,752
Administration as percentage of total	7.1	6.5	9.2	9.6	8.8	7.6

Source: Social Security Statistics (various issues).
[a]N/A = not applicable, as benefit not introduced then.

million, and in 1976 by £319 million, as has generally been the case since 1948. Table 15.22 shows that the level of expenditure on all benefits has been rising, as one would expect, to take account of inflation. Administrative costs as a percentage of total expenditures have also risen, which is probably explained by the number of new benefits introduced between 1971 and 1977.

Table 15.23 records money expenditure levels of the industrial injury scheme, deflated by the Retail Price Index. Expenditures in real terms on the disablement pension are then revealed as being remarkably constant, as are administrative costs. Industrial injury benefits, in contrast, have been falling in real terms, which is explained by the declining number of recipients.

Table 15.23. Expenditures and Administrative Costs of the Industrial Injuries Scheme, 1964-1975

Year	Industrial Injury Benefit (£m.)	Real Terms	Industrial Disablement Pension (£m.)	Real Terms	Administrative Costs (£m.)	Real Terms
1965	28	100	42	100	9	100
1966	35	121	50	113	9	101
1967	32	110	51	114	10	108
1968	35	113	54	115	10	106
1969	34	105	58	118	11	109
1970	33	97	61	115	12	112
1971	33	87	65	112	12	101
1972	31	76	71	115	14	115
1973	32	73	78	116	15	110
1974	34	66	81	112	15	97
1975	35	55	110	114	22	110

Source: Social Security Statistics (various issues).

Table 15.24. Expenditures on Sickness and Invalidity Benefits and Social Security Administrative Costs, 1965-1975

Year	Sickness and Invalidity Benefit Expenditures		Social Security Administrative Costs	
	£m.	Real Terms	£m.	Real Terms
1965	£201	100	£54	100
1966	248	119	59	113
1967	262	122	62	116
1968	323	144	71	127
1969	348	147	74	126
1970	383	152	85	136
1971	374	136	98	143
1972	414	141	115	156
1973	487	151	125	155
1974	548	147	143	154
1975	665	144	201	175

Source: Social Security Statistics (various issues).

When one considers sickness and invalidity benefits (see Table 15.24), one can see that expenditures have been growing consistently; however, it should be noted that in real terms expenditures have remained reasonably constant since 1968. Adminstrative costs for social security as a whole have been constantly rising, although this includes the administration of other benefits, notably unemployment benefits, which have been increasing at a faster rate in recent years.

Unfortunately, figures are not available for the administrative costs of the benefits individually; however, estimates have been made by the Economist Intelligence Unit (EIU) which relate to fiscal year 1975/76. These are reproduced in Table 15.25. As can be seen, administration costs on cash benefits are in the region of 4-12 percent of total expenditure on benefits. However, as Table 15.26 indicates, when one considers services for the disabled the administrative costs are about 10-15 percent of total expenditure costs, and in the case of aids and adaptations over 40 percent of total expenditure costs.

Table 15.25. Estimated Administrative Costs of Benefits for the Disabled, 1975/76

Benefit	Total Administrative Costs (£m.)	Administrative Costs of Benefits Received by the Disabled (£m.)	Administrative Costs as % of Total Net Expenditure on Benefits
National Insurance	£270-290	£22-25	£4.0
Industrial Injury	22-25	22-25	10.3
War Disablement	6-7.5	6-7.5	4.2
Family Income Supplement	1	0.07	7.1[a]
Supplementary Benefits	190	15-35 (minimum) 45-60 (probably)	11.8

Source: Economist Intelligence Unit (1978).
[a]Does not include estimated £100,000 spent on advertising.

Table 15.26. Estimated Administrative Costs of Services for the Disabled, 1975/76

	Total Administrative Costs (£m.)	Administrative Costs of Benefits Received by the Disabled (£m.)	Administrative Costs as % of Total Net Expenditure on Benefits
Adaptations	£0.14-0.15	£0.14-0.15	£45.0
Holidays	0.31-0.32	0.11-0.12	11.0
Day care centers	1.18-1.20	1.18-1.20	12.8
Meals-on-wheels	N/A	N/A	17.5
Home help service	9.85-1.00	8.88-9.50	10.5
Residential accommodation for handicapped adults	1.61-1.65	1.61-1.65	13.1
Aids	0.94-0.95	0.94-0.95	43.9

Source: Economist Intelligence Unit (1978).
Note: This table applies to England and Wales only.

The Chartered Institute of Public Finance and Accountancy (CIPFA) provides estimates on expenditures by local authorities in England and Wales on social services for adults with disabilities, as is shown in Table 15.27. The EIU used the CIPFA figures to estimate that the administrative costs for 1975/76 for local authority Social Services Departments were in the region of £135-140 million. If this is added to the administrative costs for central government benefits then the total costs for the administration of benefits for disabled people for 1975/76 was in the region of £300 million. If one accepts the estimates of 3.5 million disabled in the United Kingdom, then this represents an administrative cost of about £90 per disabled person per annum (at 1975 prices).

Obviously, to people on limited incomes, as most of the disabled are, this represents a substantial amount. It is also one further reason for a rationalization of a system that has become topheavy with bureaucracy.

Table 15.27. Expenditures of Local Authorities in England and Wales on Personal Social Services for Adults with Disabilities, 1975/76 (in thousands of pounds)

Service	Expenditure
Residential care of the elderly	£156,700
Residential care for the younger physically handicapped	12,320
Residential care for mentally handicapped adults	12,502
Day care centers/clubs for:	
elderly	9,339
younger physically handicapped	9,216
mentally handicapped	836
multipurpose (18-64)	3,509
Home help service	93,987
Meals services for pensioners	8,555
Sheltered housing	4,338
Telephones	3,055
Aids and adaptations	5,186
Holidays	2,850
Travel concessions	5,639

Source: Chartered Institute of Public Finance and Accountany (1976).

Services Connected with the Employment of the Disabled

In the United Kingdom, in addition to income maintenance programs there are a variety of services available for the disabled designed to assist them with employment. Most of these services stem either directly or indirectly from the Disabled Persons (Employment) Acts of 1944 and 1958. The services provided for the disabled in Britain discussed here are the quota system, designated employment, sheltered employment, special aids, and rehabilitation and training.

The Quota System

This requires every employer of 20 or more to fill 3 percent of all jobs with registered disabled persons. It is not an offense under the 1944 Act for an employer to be below the quota level, but it is an offense for an employer who is below quota to engage any ablebodied person or unregistered disabled person when the business is already below quota or would become so after the engagement. These requirements and regulations have never been rigorously enforced. The maximum fine for an offense was set at £100 in 1944 and has stayed at this level ever since. Indeed, only nine prosecutions have been brought against employers under the Act since 1947, of which only two have received the maximum fine. This should be seen against the background of the percentage of firms failing to fulfill their quota requirements, rising from 38.2 percent in 1960 to 63.2 percent in 1978.

It should also be pointed out that universal compliance with the quota is currently impossible. If all unemployed registered disabled persons were recruited by firms, only an average of about 2.1 percent of the requisite quota obligation would be filled. The fact is that quota obligations are commonly not met, and this is true of the government as an employer as well as the private sector. Indeed, in June 1978, 27 of the 29 government departments failed to meet their quota obligation, including the Department of Employment. That the number of disabled persons registered as such has fallen from 936,000 in 1950 to 495,000 in 1980 partly emphasizes that the quota system has not significantly improved the lot of the disabled person. The quota system is itself currently under review and a more thorough examination of it is carried out further in this chapter.

Designated Employment

Under the 1944 Act certain types of employment are "designated," in the sense that an ablebodied person may only be employed in that occupation if no disabled person is available. Currently the only designated jobs are those of electric passenger lift attendant and car park attendant. The number of disabled people affected by this program, therefore, is small, rising from 4,080 in 1953 to only 4,435 in 1964. This scheme has attracted a great deal of criticism on the grounds that it encourages the view that disabled people are fit for only inferior types of employment requiring only limited mental ability.

Sheltered Employment

This is normally reserved for registered disabled persons whose disability is so severe as to render the probability of their employment under normal market conditions very small. Sheltered employment can range from the general character of charity-supported occupational therapy to a close approximation of open working conditions. Sheltered employment is provided by Remploy Ltd. (a nonprofit company set up in 1945 through which the government channels subsidies toward the cost of employing severely disabled workers), and in workshops for sighted and blind people run by local authorities and voluntary organizations wholly or partly subsidized by the government via the Employment Services Agency. In 1975/76 the subsidies totaled about £24 million, of which Remploy received about £15 million, local authorities about £5.5 million, and the remaining £3.5 million went to voluntary organizations.

Remploy, although a nonprofit organization, operates as an ordinary commercial concern. It is a national organization, with around 8,000 sighted disabled workers employed in 87 factories and at home, primarily engaged in the production of basic utility furniture. Remploy has facilities similar to normal commercial enterprises, such as a head office, area offices, warehouses, and showrooms.

There are 52 workshops for the blind, run by both local authorities and voluntary bodies, employing about 3,000 disabled workers. There are also 66 workshops for sighted disabled people which employ just over 2,000 workers. (All figures relate to the financial year 1974/75.)

A cost-benefit analysis of sheltered employment is discussed in detail further in this chapter.

Special Aids

The arrangements so far described have been concerned with the provision of job opportunities. There are also policies whose purpose is to improve the potential contributions of disabled workers to the economy. The Department of Employment has about 550 full-time disablement resettlement officers and 35 blind persons' training officers, who are authorized under the 1944 Act to provide special aids for disabled persons who have a reasonable prospect of "satisfactory settlement." Most of the aids take the form of special tools and equipment, but some focus on adjustments in the work environment. The aids are provided free, unless the applicant can provide them himself without suffering financial hardship, and are issued on a permanent loan basis. About 9 percent of the aids go to blind people.

The scheme is limited in scope for two main reasons. First, it concentrates on the individual worker to improve his economic contribution rather than on the work environment itself, which would raise the economic contributions of a larger number of workers. Second, there is no financial incentive, indeed there may well be disincentives, for employers to accept such workers. Generally, the program results in about 350-400 items or modifications annually, but this must be seen against a background of almost 70,000 registered disabled unemployed.

Rehabilitation and Retraining

Apart from special aids, there are also arrangements for improving the technical potential of disabled persons themselves. The first of these are Industrial Rehabilitation Units (IRU's), which are provided to facilitate the recovery of those who have been affected by mental or physical illness. There are currently 27 such centers, offering about 2,760 places on courses lasting from 4 weeks to 6 months. In 1977 13,906 disabled took courses at IRU's, 86 percent of whom completed their courses. Of those who enrolled in IRU courses in 1977, 6,371 (46 percent) were recommended directly by medical authorities, and 2,600 (19 percent) were recently discharged from hospitals or had completed a course of medical treatment and were identified at job centers or employment offices. Local disablement resettlement officers recommended 3,963 (28 percent) registered disabled persons, while 972 (7 percent) were people without apparent disability or people referred by skill because of their inability to cope with a particular training course. Unfortunately, only about half of the people completing IRU courses obtain employment within 6 months of completion.

Second, vocational training courses are provided for disabled persons, fitted by age, experience, general qualifications, and capacities. The disabled are often given easier access to general training schemes by being exempted from some of the requirements which have to be met by other workers, and by being allowed to "jump the queue" when, as is often the case, there is a waiting list for training. Disabled persons competent to do so are often given special facilities to work for professional qualifications or degrees. For example, the Open University accepted 608 (88 percent) of the 697 disabled and disadvantaged people who applied to study for degrees in 1978.

Third, the job introduction scheme, introduced in 1977, is a program whereby disabled people who, in the opinion of the resettlement officer, require a period of adjustment in a job to demonstrate their capabilities to a new employer, are subsidized for an initial period. The Manpower Services Commission will currently pay £30 a week to a firm that gives a 6-week trial period to a disabled person; this can be extended to 13 weeks in exceptional circumstances. It its first year of operation 80 percent of those given a trial period remained in employment.

Summary and Conclusions

The piecemeal approach that has been adopted by successive governments since the Second World War to the social and economic problems concerning the disabled population in the United Kingdom has resulted in the current complex position characterized by a large number of overlapping benefits such that very few disabled people are in a position whereby any one benefit is likely to prove financially sufficient. The main benefits—sickness and industrial injury benefits (short-term), and invalidity benefits and industrial disablement pensions (long-term)—are contributory. Of the long-term benefits about half a million claim invalidity benefits, while 200,000 receive the industrial disablement pension. Unfortunately, many disabled people have made insufficient contributions, due to their disability, and so are ineligible for these benefits. Other non-contributory benefits have been introduced since 1970 to which disabled people are entitled: NCIP and HNCIP, set at 60 percent of the contributory invalidity benefit, a family income supplement, an attendance allowance, ICA, travel allowances, and a war disablement scheme.

Even with this large number of benefits potentially available many disabled people find that their "resources" fall short of their "requirements" in the state's opinion, and therefore have to rely on supplementary benefits. Although the number of disabled relying on SB has fallen slightly since the introduction of the non-contributory benefits, in 1976 about 250,000 disabled people received some element of SB as part of their weekly income, while it is estimated that at least 100,000 more disabled are eligible for SB but fail to claim it.

As well as income maintenance programs, there exist a number of services connected with the employment of the disabled: the quota scheme, sheltered and designated employment, and special training and rehabilitation schemes. Unfortunately, these have not had any great degree of success in achieving their objectives.

What is obviously needed is a complete rationalization and overhaul of the current system and its replacement by a more equitable and efficient way of tackling the problems faced by the disabled. A number of alternatives are considered further in this chapter.

The Economic Impact of Disability Policy

Labor Supply Effects

It is natural to inquire about what effects the previously described policies have had on the labor supply by removing the incentives for the disabled to work. Unfortunately, there is little empirical evidence available for the United Kingdom. Although unemployment among disabled persons has risen in recent years, this is partly explained by the fact that the concentration of the disabled among the unskilled increases their vulnerability to economic recessions. As Table 15.16 indicated, although unemployment among the registered disabled has been considerably higher than the general level, it has also moved in the same direction. The special provisions for the unemployment of the disabled have failed to protect them from the economic recession of the 1970s.

It would appear likely that the increase in unemployment among the disabled is explained more by general economic pressures than by changes in supply availability or adequacy of benefits for the disabled. However, one would imagine that there are severe disincentives faced by the disabled. Unless they can earn a relatively high wage they will be facing exceedingly high marginal tax rates, in the sense that for every unit of income earned only a small increase is achieved in net resources. This is because even if they do not earn enough to be eligible for income tax their income may render them ineligible for certain benefits.

For example, consider a married man with two dependent children who suffers from some disabling disease of a relapsing nature, such as multiple sclerosis or epilepsy, and who tries to work during his "good" periods. During his "bad" periods he will be eligible for some form of benefit. If we assume invalidity benefits, then in 1980 he would have received £56.40 per week, which is tax free. If he starts a job during his "good" period then he will be ineligible for invalidity benefits as, by definition, his invalidity has disappeared. Also, if his disablement recurs, causing him to lose his job, he would not be entitled to the long-term benefits (if he had been employed for 13 weeks or more) and would have to start on sickness benefits and so would only receive £35.90 per week.

Although certain benefits, such as the attendance allowance, are independent of an individual's income, most are not. This has resulted in the majority of the disabled population of the United Kingdom being caught quite firmly in the "poverty trap." Many of the disabled face very high marginal tax rates. For example, an increase of £1 could lead to 30 percent being paid in income tax, a 6.75 percent National Insurance contribution, together with a 50 percent loss of family income supplement. As well as this, the individual may well lose entitlement to a number of other benefits such as rent and rates rebates, etc.

This situation has become progressively worse over time with the erosion of tax thresholds through inflation and the failure of successive governments to maintain the real value of these thresholds. For example, whereas in 1950 a single man did not pay income tax unless he was earning at least 50 percent of average gross earnings, by 1976 this had fallen to only 21 percent. A married man with two children in 1950 did not pay taxes unless earning *more* than the average; in 1976 he became liable for taxes at earnings of only 44 percent of the average. Indeed, in recent years the absurd position has been reached where an individual can be paying income tax while at the same time receiving a family income supplement, which is designed to assist low-income families.

This position may lead one to conclude that financially there is little incentive for the disabled to work, or at least to increase their individual supply of labor. Psychologically, however, one could advance strong reasons why the disabled may wish to work. Having gainful employment may have strong therapeutic effects by enabling a disabled person to become a "normal" member of society. Also, working for a living would go a long way toward removing the stigma which may be attached to being disabled.

It should again be emphasized that there is little place for the partially disabled in the British scheme of things. Generally, if an individual is disabled then he is unable to work because if he is able to work he is no longer disabled. If an individual suffering from some minor form of handicap is deemed "fit to work" by an insurance officer then he would not be entitled to sickness or invalidity benefits, etc., but only to unemployment or supplementary benefits, as the case may be.

This situation leads to disincentives for those who are handicapped but not sick to be treated as such. A person in general good health but who might be handicapped by, say, cerebral palsy, may be advised to register as sick rather than as unemployed. He would be entitled to a higher level of benefit, particularly if this condition was expected to persist for an indefinite period; it would require fewer visits to register as unemployed or to see an employment officer.

Unfortunately, there are a number of disadvantages with taking this "easy way out" in regard to the long-term employment prospects. First, if someone is registered as sick as opposed to unemployed they may be overlooked for job opportunities. Second, by falsifying their own health record they are reducing their chance of future employment, since employers are not keen to take on someone who is likely to be off sick a large amount of the time.

The level of benefits will also of course determine the incentives faced by the disabled to return to the work force. To illustrate this we will consider the replacement rates for certain individuals receiving benefits and how they have fared in relation to the general worker. By "replacement rates" we mean the level of benefits after taxes, if any are applicable, after disablement as a percentage of gross and net earnings (gross earnings minus income tax and national insurance contributions), and before disablement. The levels of earnings are average industrial earnings, half this level and twice the average. To consider how various benefits compare, we will look at three hypothetical individuals: each (A, B, and C) is married and 100 percent disabled. Although our individuals are disabled to the same extent, their circumstances are different.

Individual A was disabled in an industrial accident while at work. He is entitled to industrial disability pension at 100 percent, the unemployment supplement, and the constant attendance allowance. Individual B was disabled by an inherited illness, but before the onset of the illness had been in employment long enough to have paid sufficient contributions to entitle him to receive an invalidity pension, invalidity allowance at the middle rate, attendance allowance at the higher rate, and supplementary benefits, where applicable. Individual C was disabled through a nonindustrial accident which was later heightened by the onset of an inherited illness. Unfortunately, the accident happened when he was young and had paid insufficient contributions to entitle him to the same benefits as individual B. Individual C is therefore entitled to the noncontributory invalidity pension, the attendance allowance at the higher rate, and again supplementary benefits, where applicable. To make a comparision over time we will consider the replacement rates at 1968 and 1978 levels (Table 15.28).

As can be seen, individual A has fared consistently better than B and C although it can be seen that all three were better off in 1978 than in 1968 in terms of industrial earnings. Individual B's position has improved the most since in 1968 the only benefits to which he would have been entitled would have been long-term sickness benefits (replaced by invalidity benefits in 1971) and supplementary benefits. Individual C is still the worst off; this is because although NCIP was introduced in 1975, it was at such a low level that it failed to meet the "requirement" as set out by the Supplementary Benefits Commission, so that the majority of recipients were still in receipt of SB. The government estimated that only 7 percent of disabled people receiving SB would be relieved of the need to claim it by the introduction of NCIP (Hansard, 1975).

It is impossible to say to what extent the apparent increase in the level of benefits has caused people to drop out of the workforce. It is interesting that the numbers claiming industrial injury benefits have fallen, and, although it is paid at a higher rate than sickness benefits as has been pointed out, this differential has been steadily reduced over time.

The Effectiveness of Rehabiliation and Employment Programs

There has been little or no empirical work carried out in the United Kingdom on the effectiveness of rehabilitation or retraining scheme, though the Department of Employment (1978a) has recently carried out a study into sheltered employment, provided by Remploy Ltd. as well as by blind and sighted workshops run by both local authorities and voluntary organizations. Central government subsidizes to a large extent the financial losses of these organizations. On the face of it the benefits received and the costs incurred are obvious—the costs being the subsidies provided,

Table 15.28. Replacement Rates (Total Benefits Received as a Percentage of Former Gross and Net Income Levels), 1968 and 1978

	Average Earnings				Half Average Earnings				Twice Average Earnings			
	Gross		Net		Gross		Net		Gross		Net	
	1968	1978	1968	1978	1968	1978	1968	1978	1968	1978	1968	1978
Individual A	72	83	102	107	144	166	176	178	36	42	56	60
Individual B	48	74	69	96	97	149	118	160	24	37	38	54
Individual C	48	56	69	72	97	111	118	119	24	28	38	40

amounting to £14 million in the financial year 1974/75, and the benefits being the advantages gained by disabled people in terms of income and psychological well-being in employment.

The DOE study shows how consideration of the costs and benefits in these simple terms can be misleading, and that the costs and benefits of sheltered employment can be viewed in a variety of ways. The analysis considers the costs and benefits from the point of view of the economy as a whole and the Exchequer. Data for the financial year 1974/75 for Remploy, and for a sample of blind and sighted workshops, were used. Some comparisons are drawn with a previous (unpublished) study of sheltered employment in 1968/69, and included is an updated financial analysis for Remploy for the financial year 1976/77.

The economic analysis examines the question of how the real resources consumed in the provision of sheltered employment compare with the real resources produced, such as the goods manufactured or processed. The term "real" resources refers to resources whose use in one particular activity (such as sheltered employment) is a real cost to the economy in the sense that it is then precluded from use in other activities—the opportunity cost. The importance of this concept is that there may be some resourses whose market prices do not adequately reflect their real resource cost; the prime example in this analysis is the labor of disabled workers who would be unemployed if they were not working in sheltered conditions and whose real resource cost to the economy (that is the alternative cost) is zero.

There are other inputs whose real resource costs are undervalued in the financial costings used on workshop accounts, such as the economic rents for land, buildings occupied and capital wage; allowance was made for these to reflect resource cost. In addition, allowance was made for the cost of central government services provided free of charge to the workshops, such as the Workshop Inspectorate. The various adjustments are made so as to arrive at an estimate of the cost of the real resources used in the operation of sheltered employment.

The primary resource benefits of sheltered employment are the value of the output produced and the sales of this output on the open market. There are also resource benefits which are produced but for which no market price is paid; these constitute the psychological benefit derived by disabled people from being in employment and the value of the rehabilitative services that sheltered employment provides. Both are important considerations but accurate quantification is very difficult. Because of this fact the analysis decided not to make any specific monetary allowances for these benefits since to apply arbitrary assumptions in order to quantify their value might be misleading. Hence, the estimates of resource benefits in the analysis are minimal estimates.

Therefore, in the analysis, resource costs are measured by adjusting total financial costs so as to reflect the real market value of land and capital used and by subtracting from these costs and gross wages of severely disabled workers, while resource benefits are measured by the value of sales made. The estimates of resource costs and benefits can be compared to show the net effect of sheltered employment on real resources in the economy. The results are expressed in terms of net benefits per disabled worker per annum in Table 15.29 which also compares the results for 1969/70 with those of 1974/75.

The comparison between 1974/75 and 1969/70 shows that there has been a significant real improvement in the performance of Remploy and the sighted workshops, while the blind workshops have incurred higher costs. The economic analysis showed that in 1974/75 Remploy produced net resource benefits of just over £400,000 (£54 per disabled worker), while the sighted workshops produced net resource benefits of £374,000 (£169 per disabled worker). Blind workshops incurred net resource costs of just over £2 million (£750 per disabled worker), which meant that overall net resource costs of about £1.2 million (£95 per disabled worker) were incurred under conditions of sheltered employment. However, as has already been pointed out, the estimates of net resource benefits which have been made may be considered as minima while the net resource costs may be considered as maxima.

The financial analysis examines the question: How does the cost to public funds of providing sheltered employment compare with the cost of providing the social benefits to which the disabled workers would have been entitled if they had been unemployed? This is essentially an accounting exercise from the Exchequer's viewpoint which goes beyond that of the apparent public expenditure costs. It looks at the net effect on the public sector borrowing requirement by taking account of offsets in saved expenditure and increased revenue. The analysis takes account of flows of public funds which occur at present as a result of the existence of sheltered employment, and contrasts them with the net flows that would have occurred had sheltered employment not existed.

A number of simplifying assumptions have to be made to quantify the net flows. It is assumed that if sheltered unemployment had not existed, then (1) all of the severely disabled employees would have been unable to secure employment and hence would receive state benefits; (2) all of the less severely disabled workers and ablebodied workers would have been able to

Table 15.29. Net Resource Benefits of Sheltered Employment (per Disabled Workers per Annum)

	1969/70	1974/75
Remploy	£ −91	£ +54
Sighted Workshops	+101	+169
Blind Workshops	−215	−750

Source: DOE (1978a).

secure alternative employment; (3) the demand for the output currently produced under sheltered employment would have been distributed throughout the economy, needing only a marginally greater output from a large number of firms to meet consumer demand without needing any direct increase in employment.

Under the assumptions made, the net cost to public funds essentially comprises the following: (1) the current and capital subsidies paid by the Exchequer; (2) the income tax and national insurance contributions presently made by severely disabled workers; (3) the state benefits that would otherwise be paid to these severely disabled workers; *minus* (4) the net loss of indirect tax revenue (resulting from the fact that the consumption expenditure of the severely disabled would be less when they are unemployed than employed, as their income would be lower).

No account is taken of value added tax (VAT) or indirect tax payments made on goods produced in sheltered employment, since it is assumed that in the absence of sheltered employment consumer demand is reallocated throughout the economy and indirect tax revenue would still be received. A number of further assumptions were necessary to estimate the state benefits that would have been received by the severely disabled workers had they been unemployed. The results are summarized in Table 15.30.

Again it can be seen that when comparing 1974/75 with 1969/70 both Remploy and sighted workshops have improved their performance. The results for 1974/75 show that the net saving to public funds by sighted workshops was £234,000 (£105 per disabled worker). Remploy's net financial cost to public funds was estimated to be just over £1 million (£133 per disabled worker) while blind workshops were estimated to have incurred a net financial cost of about £2 million (£716 per disabled worker). The provision of sheltered employment as a whole was estimated to have resulted in a net cost to public funds of about £2.8 million (E215 per disabled worker) in 1974/75.

The distinction between the economic and financial analysis is important, since they consider essentially different policy questions. The consideration of sheltered employment from the point of view of resource allocation is likely to be more pertinent under near-full employment conditions, whereas the financial question of the net burden on public funds is likely to be of more relevance when the size of the public sector borrowing requirement is of concern. Although the two analyses are interrelated, with

Table 15.30. Net Financial Benefits of Sheltered Employment (per Disabled Workers per Year)

	1969/70	1974/75
Remploy	£ − 203	£ − 133
Sighted Workshops	+ 30	+ 105
Blind Workshops	− 143	− 716

Source: DOE (1978a).

various items appearing either directly or indirectly in both, it does not necessarily follow that they will provide similar results.

It is clear from the detailed analysis that there are wide variations, in both economic and financial terms, in the performance of individual blind and sighted workshops. For example, in the economic analysis the net resource benefits for blind workshops per disabled worker per annum ranged from £1,069 to -£1,586 (average -£750), and in sighted workshops from £1,420 to -£1,109 (average £169). In the financial analysis the net financial cost per disabled worker per year in blind workshops ranged from £1,364 to -£957 (average £716), and in sighted workshops from £785 to -£1,147 (average -£105).

These differences are partly explained by the nature of the trades pursued, the degree of mechanization and the extent of modernization of the workshop premises and capital stock. Factors that are historically determined and specific to individual workshops were not investigated in the analysis, which was primarily concerned with the overall effects of the existence of sheltered employment.

The results of the analysis are clearly based on a number of strong assumptions at various points, but the study also examines how sensitive the estimates are to change in key assumptions. The results of the economic analysis are sound and are only marginally affected by alterations in the key assumptions; the financial analysis is sensitive if one particular assumption is not accepted—that in place of private industry, sheltered employment output leads directly to an increase in employment and a reduction in unemployment (causing reduced social security payments).

Table 15.31 shows an updating of the financial analysis of Remploy for 1976/77. The net financial costs of Remploy have increased, partly as a result of inflation and partly because of increased real wages paid to severely disabled workers. The updated results also permit some comparisons to be drawn with the particular cases covered by Gennard and Wright

Tablew 15.31. Financial Costs and Benefits of Remploy, 1974/75 and 1976/77

	1974/75 (£)	1976/77 (£)
Costs (−)		
Subsidy on current account	8,992,967	16,042,000
Capital grant	941,641	2,334,000
Regional employment premium	430,598	—
Benefits (+)		
National insurance and income tax	2,824,070	4,788,624
Cost of state benefits	6,276,362	8,755,344
Cost of indirect tax revenue	170,834	288,627
Miscellaneous necessary expenditure	1,335	6,831
Net benefits	−1,092,605	−4,601,574
Net benefits per capita	−133	−565

Source: DOE (1978a).

for 1978. From their twelve cases, they estimated that if the workers were unemployed, the Exchequer would lose an average £13 a week in revenue in the form of income tax and national insurance contributions and have to pay out an average of £22 a week in the form of welfare benefits—a net cost to the Exchequer of £468 per annum per disabled worker. This suggests that the results of the two studies, as far as Exchequer offsets are concerned, are consistent.

Of the 13,000 or so people who annually take courses at employment rehabilitation centers, about 80 percent complete these courses, as is indicated in Table 15.32. The total proportion resettled 3 months after completion of a course (which could last from 4 weeks to 6 months) was about 60 percent for 1972-1974, but in 1975 only 47.4 percent of those who completed courses had secured employment or a training position within 3 months. This fell to 43.9 percent in 1977 when unemployment among the registered disabled had increased to over 14 percent. These figures compare with a resettlement rate of over 80 percent for people undertaking a vocational course at a skill center.

Table 15.32. Number of Entrants Resettled Within 3 Months of Completing Courses at Employment Rehabilitation Centers, 1972-1977

Year	Number Starting	Number Completing	Completion Rate (%)	In Employment[a] (%)	Training Course[a] (%)	Total Resettled[a] (%)
1972	13,781	11,491	83	36.8	18.7	57.3
1973	12,682	10,284	81	46.2	18.7	64.9
1974	12,026	9,519	79	41.2	19.4	60.6
1975	13,339	10,800	81	25.5	21.9	47.4
1976	13,395	11,233	84	23.3	21.6	44.9
1977	13,906	11,936	86	25.0	18.9	43.9

Source: Department of Employment *Gazette* (various issues).
[a]As a percentage of those completing.

The general decline of the British economy and accompanying rising unemployment throughout the 1970s only partly explains the increasing failure of IRU resettlement courses. Even from 1972-1974, when general unemployment was about 3 percent, 40 percent of those completing courses were unemployed 6 months later. Clearly, although these courses may achieve their aim "to improve a client's physical capacity, restore his confidence, and produce a considered and practical recommendation about the type of work most likely to lead to permanent resettlement," they are to a large degree failing to achieve resettlement. Unfortunately, no studies appear to have been carried out into the costs and benefits of employment rehabilitation centers, so any conclusion reached will have to be of a general nature.

Take-Up Rates of Benefits

Having earlier looked at the main benefits which affect the disabled we now examine the effectiveness of this large array of schemes in guaranteeing a stipulated income level. This must be judged mainly by the extent to which those who are intended to benefit actually do so. The estimates, all of which are liable to error, are normally presented as "take-up rates," that is, percentages related to the total number of people estimated eligible for a given benefit to those who actually receive it.

As has already been said, these estimates, are based on a number of surveys that have been carried out, some at the national level but others at a local level, involving only a small number of people. The majority of studies have been concerned primarily with the take-up of Supplementary Benefits. The national estimate is of a 75 percent take-up rate, but local estimates have consistently shown a lower rate. However, the estimates of take-up by the sick and disabled tend to be lower than the average. For example, in November 1974, it was estimated that 260,000 sick and disabled people were receiving Supplementary Benefits out of a provision for 385,000, i.e., a 67.5 percent take-up.

Knowledge, and accordingly take-up, of additional Supplementary Benefit allowances has been low in the past, partly because they have not been widely publicized by the Supplementary Benefits Commission. A 1972 study showed that 42 percent of the chronically sick and disabled sample were eligible for conditional allowances and knew of them, but that only 12.8 percent had applied. Another 1972 survey found that 75 percent of respondents had not heard of Exceptional Circumstances Additions and 95 percent had not heard of Exceptional Needs Payments. Table 15.33 shows the official estimates of the take-up rates and those obtained from local surveys of certain benefits to which disabled people may be entitled.

There have been a number of reasons advanced as to why the take-up of certain benefits has been low. The following are the most common reasons given: ignorance; complexity of the schemes; stigma; fear of the reaction of employers, landlords or even the authorities administering the benefits;

Table 15.33. Estimates of Take-up Rates of Benefits (in percentages)

	Official National Estimate	Local Survey Estimate
Family Income Supplement	75%	40%
Supplementary Benefit	75	50
Rent Rebates	70	60
Rate Rebates	62	35
Rent Allowances (unfurnished)	30	20
Rent Allowances (furnished)	10	5

Source: National Consumer Council (1976).

lack of incentive due to the scant nature of the benefits; difficulties of access to the benefits; invasion of privacy.

While it is admitted that the estimates of take-up rates are open to a large degree of error, it is clear that a large number of benefits are not being received by those for whom they were designed, and this is true for the disabled as well as the general population. In our concluding section we consider ways whereby the system could be reformed so that take-up rates are improved and those in need receive the benefits to which they are entitled.

Adequacy and Coverage of Benefits

The concept of "adequacy" is a very hard one to define, let alone measure. With reference to Table 15.29, we can see that individuals A, B, and C have fared reasonably well in the 1969-78 period in comparison to the general levels of earnings, and after deductions and additions. To conclude, however, that this is adequate is to propound a somewhat erroneous argument. Although the disabled are generally in a relatively better position than those of a decade ago in comparison with ablebodied workers, this does not reflect the costs of being disabled, so no real measure of adequacy can be made or conclusions drawn.

With reference to coverage, the disabled are in a much more favorable position than a decade ago. This is mainly due to the introduction of the non-contributory invalidity pension introduced in 1975 for people who had paid insufficient contributions to be eligible for the general invalidity benefit. It was found, however, that this was still discriminatory against married women, and so in 1977 the housewives' non-contributory invalidity pension was introduced.

As has already been indicated, the British system of programs for the disabled is very complex. The majority of recipients of benefits are claimants to more than one single benefit. Indeed, it is rare to find an individual whose sole source of income is limited to one particular benefit. In 1977, 229,000 sick and disabled people received Supplementary Benefits in addition to other benefits. The number of people whose income is "topped up" by some amount of SB has increased for those who do not receive contributory benefits, although the size of the top-up has fallen in real terms. For example, it was estimated that the introduction of NCIP would relieve only about 7 percent of recipients of the need to claim SB as well (Hansard, 1975).

The benefits themselves are often related in a very complex manner. Receiving one benefit may make one ineligible for another. For example, neither of the invalidity benefits, NCIP and HNCIP, can be paid at the same time as any other maintenance benefit of an equal or higher amount.

The attendance allowance is normally paid in full in addition to all other benefits from Social Security. However, if a constant attendance allowance is being paid under the industrial injuries scheme, or with a war pension, the attendance allowance will be affected. Supplementary benefits are not affected unless they include a special payment to meet attendance needs.

The majority of benefits to which the disabled may be entitled are not taxed, although there is some political discussion about this at the moment. The question of taxation would only really affect those who are temporarily sick and who will soon be returning to the work force rather than the long-term disabled. The mobility allowance, invalid care allowance, and retirement pensions are the main benefits that are currently taxable.

Although coverage for the disabled is more universal now, the current system of welfare has led to numerous anomalies which still exist. Disabled people in the United Kingdom are entitled to a wide spectrum of benefits, depending on a number of diverse criteria such as the number of national insurance contributions made in the past and where the disablement took place, irrespective of the disability itself. For example, people injured at work are treated more favorably than those whose disability cannot be directly attributed to their work. Some of these are not entitled to any benefit (unless they qualify for the attendance allowance) without undergoing a means test.

The industrial injuries scheme grants a disablement pension which may be on top of benefits obtained through National Insurance. Thus, it is possible for these recipients to receive considerably more than people under the general scheme, even though the severity of their disablement may be less.

Due to these anomalies and inconsistencies, as well as to other factors such as the level of adequacy, growing dissatisfaction has arisen with the present system and a number of alternative approaches to the question of disablement have been advocated. These range from modifications to the present system to encourage a higher level of take-up benefits in general to more radical changes whereby the disabled are dealt with in a more satisfactory manner than at present. These schemes are considered in our next section.

Leading Issues in Disability Policy

The piecemeal approach that has been adopted by successive governments over the past 30 years or so has resulted in a fragmentary system for assisting disabled people in the United Kingdom that does not conform to any clear set of principles. This has led to a large number of groups being formed with the intention of applying pressure on the government of the day to introduce a more equitable system for the treatment of the disabled.

As a result of this both principal political parties in Britain recognize the inequities inherent in the existing system and have promised reforms. For the May 1979 general election the Labour Party Manifesto proposed to "introduce a new disablement allowance ... varying according to the severity of disablement." The Conservatives, who won the election, stated in their Manifesto, "Much has been done in recent years to help the disabled, but there is still a long way to go. Our aim is to provide a coherent system of cash benefits to meet the costs of disability, so that more disabled people can support themselves and live normal lives. We shall work toward this as swiftly as the strength of the economy allows." Unfortunately, little progress has been made due to the current decline of the British economy.

Numerous suggestions have been made that go some way toward removing the inconsistencies, anomalies, and inadequacies that currently exist. These range from modifications to the present system to its replacement by alternative approaches which, hopefully, would lead to a more equitable and efficient approach toward the problem of the disabled person within society.

Rationalization of the Present Welfare System

The National Consumer Council has outlined three main modifications to the present system which would lead to administrative simplifications as well as a higher take-up rate of the benefits to which disabled people are entitled. *The passport principle* is an extension of that used by family income supplements and supplementary benefits to allow automatic entitlement to a range of other benefits. *Benefit harmonization*, which overlaps to some extent with the passport principle, embraces two possible changes: (1) a common income definition—the standardization of income and expenses; and (2) a common income threshhold—the standardization of the levels at which one becomes eligible for benefits. *Combined assessment* does not alter the rules of benefits but instead combines the application procedures (although in some cases it might involve some harmonization of local benefits).

Other measures have been suggested as well. Take-up rates would certainly increase if people realized to which benefits they were entitled. To this end it has been suggested that the Department of Health and Social Security (DHSS) should review its system for publicizing benefits. Take-up rates would also improve if application forms were of a more comprehensive nature. For example, in a survey into rent allowances forms, 62 percent of interviewees found the instructions and answer space provided unacceptable.

In recent years the simplification approach has gathered a number of advocates with hopes of increasing take-up, particularly through combined assessment. As Taylor-Goodby (1976) has said: "Combined assessment is simply a logical approach to the problem of reducing administrative and publicity costs and increasing take-up at the same time .... if the right information is gathered all benefits to which the family is entitled can be allocated on the basis of a single form. The result is higher take-up yet less administrative hassle for the family and the state and no extra publicity costs."

The passport principle is illustrated by the following example. Claimants of family income supplement (FIS) are automatically entitled to free prescriptions, free dental and optical treatment, free milk, free hospital fares and free school meals. The FIS book acts as their "passport" to these benefits. Only one means test takes place—the application for FIS—but the claimant still has to go through the formality of applying for each benefit separately. As Table 15.34 indicates, this can lead to a dramatic increase in take-up rates.

It would be highly likely that a FIS or SB claimant would also be entitled to a rent and rate rebate. However, as rent and rate rebates are varied according to rent and rate levels, they cannot follow automatically and therefore cannot be included in the passport. Claimants could, however, have the assessment for FIS, the passport benefits, and the rent and rate rebates carried out simultaneously, and this would be a combined assessment. As can be seen, the two principles are not the same. Combined assessment combines the procedure for applying for various benefits while the passport scheme combines rules of eligibility as well as much of the procedure of application.

The Economic Intelligence Unit also favors amendment of the present system by the more widespread introduction of combined assessment. In common with many other authors they favor a "back to Beveridge" approach. This would involve a thorough reappraisal of the current system with the raising of basic benefits to a more adequate level. Unfortunately, they fail to consider what implications this may have for the incentive for partially disabled workers to stay in employment.

Alternative Systems of Income Maintenance

Certain more radical reforms of the present system in the United Kingdom have also been put forward in recent years. One of these is a

Table 15.34. Benefits Claimed on Direct Means-Test or by FIS or SB Passport, Wandsworth 1972 (in percentages)

	Take-Up Rates	
	Direct	Passport
Free school meals	52	79
Free welfare milk	10	83
Free prescription	4	77
Free dental/optical treatment	4	85

Source: Purnell (1973).

disability income, proposed by the Disablement Income Group (DIG). A similar scheme has been proposed by the Disability Alliance. Consisting of over 60 organizations, the Disability Alliance came into being in 1974 to press the government to introduce a comprehensive disablement allowance for disabled people. Some of the organizations have a membership consisting entirely or mainly of disabled people. These include the National Federation of the Blind, the National Union of the Deaf, the Multiple Sclerosis Action Group, the Disablement Motorists Federation, and DIG.

They view the long-term policy objectives as being threefold: to eliminate poverty, to bring the incomes of the disabled up to the levels of the nondisabled, and to redistribute resources among the disabled so that people with equally severe disablement, irrespective of the cause or place of disablement are entitled to similar weekly allowances of pensions. They recommend that the construction of policy should take the following form.

Disablement Allowance

An allowance should be paid to compensate people for the degree to which they are restricted from following ordinary activities. The disablement allowance would only come into operation after 6 months if there were no early prospect of recovery. There would be provisional and long-term allowances, depending on the expectations of an assessment board about the long-term nature of the degree of disablement. It is suggested that the assessment should be based on three criteria: capacity to undertake household activities, and capacities for social communication and participation.

The Disability Alliance further suggests that the allowance would be tax-free and payable to, or on behalf of, persons of both sexes and all ages, including children. In principle, parents of handicapped children of under 2 years of age would be eligible for allowances, but in practice few could be assessed with any degree of accuracy during this early period of life.

Like war and industrial disablement pensions, these allowances would be payable whether or not people had earnings, and whether or not they received retirement pensions or other social security benefits. They would not be reduced against other forms of income but payable in addition to such incomes. The Disability Alliance envisages that in amount the allowances would correspond with war and disablement pensions. That is, allowances would be paid on a sliding scale according to the degree of severity of disablement. One can infer from the OPCS survey that the majority of recipients would be eligible only for the 20 percent to 40 percent rate of benefits.

The disablement allowance is not intended to be sufficient without other resources on which to live, but to represent in income form the various financial disadvantages which the disabled experience by comparison with the nondisabled, and to try to help make good these disadvantages. Thus, a man who earned a relatively low wage because of disablement would have that wage augmented by the allowance. The allowance would help raise his wage to the level he might have reached if he had not been disabled, or it might be thought of as meeting extra expenses or compensating him (in so far as any weekly payment can so compensate) for the general disadvantages of disablement.

A retirement pensioner would also have his pension augmented by the allowances. By comparison with a nondisabled contemporary, the allowance would compensate him in at least three respects: for some of the general extra expenses of disablement in old age, to enable certain comforts or services to be purchased to compensate for activities foregone, and to make up in some measure for previous inability to earn enough to qualify for an average or substantial earnings-related pension in addition to a flat-rate pension.

Invalidity or Disablement Pension

A basic invalidity pension at the full rate of the contributory invalidity pension would be paid to all those of working age who cannot earn at all because of disablement. The Disability Alliance suggests that this invalidity payment should also be paid to disabled people employed in low-income jobs, but that the amount paid should be progressively reduced for those earning above half the national average wage.

They believe that it would be wrong for any income maintenance scheme to be based primarily or mainly on the principle of income relationship to earnings, or compensation for loss of earnings. The reason for this is that disablement may take many years to develop and its onset may be imperceptible. As a result some people may be forced to take a succession of increasingly low-paid jobs before they are forced to stop working. It would therefore be unfair to relate benefits to their last previous employment.

Special Allowances

The Disability Alliance further recommends the development of special allowances to meet the expenses of specific disabilities. Certain specific impairments make special calls for cash, such as the need for special diet on the part of diabetics, the maintenance of guide dogs and the provision of writing and reading aids for the blind. Therefore, whatever the general argument for degree of disablement or for severity of restriction of personal, household, and social activities, and whatever the arguments for replacement pensions, there will be people with specific impairments or disabilities which result in particular expenses.

Although many of these needs are currently met by local authorities and voluntary organizations, the Disability Alliance advocates that to get a more uniform provision it should be paid for from a supplement to the general allowance.

Accommodation Allowance

A flat-rate accommodation allowance would be payable to those receiving a disablement allowance who experience difficulty with self-care, mobility, and participation in household management. The allowance is intended to meet the extra housing costs of those who have difficulty with ordinary personal and household activities. Eligibility for the allowance would be determined during assessment for the disablement allowance and would be paid at three rates: full, two-thirds, and one-third, depending on the degree of restriction of activities for self-care and household management. It is proposed that the full rate would be fixed in relation to mean national housing expenses in order that values could be maintained during times of inflation.

The Disability Alliance envisages that this scheme would in part replace rent and rate rebates (as well as Supplementary Benefits and tax relief on mortgage interest) for the disabled. Hopefully, it would result in a much higher take-up rate than currently exists for such benefits. They also advocate the indexing of benefits, but linked to changes in earnings rather than prices.

Using the estimates obtained in the OPCS Survey, the Disability Alliance estimates that in 1975 the net extra cost in benefits paid out would be in the region of £417 million or about £5 per week per disabled person. The costs are net in the sense of the extra costs incurred in paying these new benefits less the savings made by not paying previously paid benefits. For example, it was estimated that these proposals would free about 200,000 disabled people from applying for supplementary benefits. The estimate fails to make any allowance for any extra costs, or savings, that may be incurred with regard to administrative expenses.

One reason why we have looked in detail at alternative systems of income support for the disabled in the United Kingdom is that both major political parties are pledged to reform of the current system. Unfortunately, little more than lipservice has been paid to it. In 1972 Sir Keith Joseph, the then Conservative Secretary of State for Health and Social Security, said, "The introduction of a disability income to compensate for loss of earnings and extra expenses is only a matter of time." A policy statement made by the Labour party in 1973 states that "disabled people have long been denied the help they need. The aim of a Socialist policy for this group must be to provide financial support as of right, even for those with no insurance qualification. The *cause* of disability must cease to be the main consideration in determining the benefit. We must make the *degree* of handicap the basic factor." While these remain fine words they have not so far served as anything more than placatory statements of good intentions.

Changes in the Quota System

As has already been noted, the quota system has to a large extent failed to achieve its objectives in providing employment for the disabled. The reform of the current system has recently been advocated, with a large number of alternative schemes being discussed. As much of the current debate is still in its infancy we will only cast a cursory glance at the main proposals that have been put forward.

Jordan (1979) has suggested that the present quota system be enhanced and improved and that the policing of it should be much more rigorously enforced. He recommends that a scheme similar to that in force in the Federal Republic of Germany should be considered whereby employers fulfilling or exceeding the quota should receive subsidies out of a levy raised from firms failing to meet their quota. He further suggests that sheltered and enclave employment should be rapidly expanded, as should the rehabilitation and retraining schemes. The latter should also expand their scope to offer a fuller range of job possibilities as currently they are too heavily biased toward unskilled and semiskilled workers.

In 1976 the responsibility for operating the quota system was transferred from the Department of Employment to the Manpower Services Commission (MSC). The MSC hoped to review thoroughly the situation and report on it later in 1980. As a prelude they have recently published a discussion document containing several alternatives to the present system (MSC, 1979). They consider four main types of measures involving statutory measures which could be used: quota systems, antidiscrimination legislation, specific statutory obligations, and provision of special rights.

Summary and Conclusions

By far the leading issue relating to disability in the United Kingdom is the reform of the current welfare system. As has already been indicated, the present scheme is complex, inequitable, and inefficient. To improve this a number of suggestions for reform have been put forward. These range from a simplification of the current scheme to a major reform incorporating the introduction of a disability allowance.

The simplifications suggested include an extension to the passport system, whereby the receiving of one benefit automatically entitled the recipient to a number of other benefits without the need for separate means tests for each one. This is similar to combined assessment where an individual is assessed for several benefits at the same time. It is believed that these changes would lead to a much higher take-up rate of benefits. It is also suggested that there should be a harmonization of benefits, including a common income definition and a common income threshold. It is believed that this would remove some of the complexity involved, with individuals having a much clearer idea as to which benefits they were entitled and how any earnings would affect the level of benefit received.

Although these suggestions would undoubtedly improve the present system, it has been argued by many that the system at the moment is so fragmentary that much more than "tinkering" is required. Many pressure groups have suggested that a comprehensive system of income maintenance for the disabled should be introduced. The most widely propounded scheme in recent years has been that put forward by the Disability Alliance, who sees the introduction of a comprehensive income scheme for the disabled people as attaining three objectives: eliminating poverty, raising the incomes of the disabled to those of the nondisabled, and redistributing resources among the disabled so that those with comparable disabilities receive comparable benefits.

Suggestions have been put forward with regard to the services available to assist the employment of the disabled. These have primarily involved changes in the quota system, which the Manpower Services Commission is currently reviewing. MSC suggests four areas which could be developed to assist the employment of the disabled: the present system could be modified and improved, antidiscrimination legislation could be introduced, there could be specific statutory obligations imposed on employers, and disabled employees could be afforded special rights. It is clear that the current quota system is not working as it was intended to and it is to be hoped that MSC's review will conclude with a more efficient system. Hopefully, this will include the abolition of designated employment which only serves to reinforce the stigma associated with disablement by associating disability with inferior types of work.

Our study of research on sheltered employment leads to the conclusion that, generally, the benefits outweigh the costs, and it is to be hoped that this area, at least, is expanded in the future. The role of rehabilitation and resettlement courses is far less clear. The success rate of reintegrating people into the work force has not been great and the reasons for its failure are not clear. It is to be hoped that a study into its costs and effectiveness is carried out as speedily as possible as it is one area of great potential for assisting disabled people to become "normal" members of society, and it would be tragic if it failed to achieve this potential.

Note

1. It has been well said that the "adoption of the term 'insurance' was a stroke of promotional genius" (Merrian, 1950). For a detailed criticism of the principle as enunciated in the Beveridge report, see Peacock (1952).

References

Beveridge Report. See *Inter-departmental Committee on Social Insurance and Allied Services.*

Buckle, J.R. 1971. *Work and housing of impaired persons in Great Britain.* Part II of *Handicapped and impaired in Great Britain* (see Harris, Cox, and Smith, 1971). London: HMSO.

Chartered Institute of Public Finance and Accountancy, 1976. *Personal social services statistics.* London.

Department of Employment. 1972. *Resettlement policy and services for disabled people.* Discussion Paper. London.

Department of Employment. 1973. *Sheltered employment for disabled people: A consultative document.* London.

Department of Employment. 1978a. *Economic and financial analysis of sheltered employment research.* Paper No. 5. London.

Department of Employment. 1978b. *New earnings survey.* London.

Department of Health and Social Security. 1980. Leaflets SB8 and SB9. London.

Department of Health and Social Security. Various issues. *Social Security statistics.* London: HMSO.

DOE. See Department of Employment.

Economist Intelligence Unit. 1978. *Whose benefit?* London.

Gennard, J., and M. Wright. 1978. A sheltcred workshop. *Department of Employment Gazette,* Vol. 86. London: HMSO.

Hansard. 1975. Written answers, May 12. London: HMSO.

Hansard. 1978. Written answers, June 19. HMSO.

Harris, J.A., E. Cox, and C.R.W. Smith. 1971. *Handicapped and impaired in Great Britain: Part I* (OPCS Survey). London: HMSO.

House of Commons. 1974. *Social Security provision for chronically sick and disabled people.* A report to Parliament by the Secretary of State, July 31.

Inter-departmental Committee on Social Insurance and Allied Services: Report. 1942 (Beveridge Report). Cmnd 6404. London: HMSO.

Jefferys, M. 1969. A set of tests for measuring motor impairment in prevalence studies. *Journal of Chronic Diseases,* Vol. 22.

Jordan, D. 1979. *A new employment programme wanted for disabled people.* Low Pay Unit, London.

Manpower Services Commission. 1978. *Developing employment and training services for disabled people.* London: HMSO.

Manpower Services Commission. 1979. *The quota scheme for the employment of disabled people.* Discussion Document. London.

Merrian, C. 1950. *The costs of financing of Social Security.* Washington, D.C.: Brookings Institution.

National Consumer Council. 1976. *Means tested benefits.* Discussion Paper. London.

OPCS Survey. See Harris, Cox, and Smith, 1971; Buckle, 1971.

Peacock, A. 1952. *Economics of national insurance.* London.

Purnell, C. 1973. *The prospects for rent allowances.* Wandsworth Peoples Rights. London.

Report of the Committee of Inquiry on the rehabilitation, training and resettlement of disabled persons (Piercy Committee). 1956. Cmnd 9883. London: HMSO.

Report of the Inter-departmental Committee on the rehabilitation and resettlement of disabled persons (Tomlinson Committee). 1943. Cmnd 6415. London: HMSO.

Supplementary Benefits Commission. 1975. *Annual report.* London.

Supplementary Benefits Commission. 1977. *Supplementary benefits handbook.* London.

Taylor-Goodby, P. 1976. *Poverty,* No. 34. CPAG. London.

Wiseman, J., and J. Cullis. 1974. Social policy towards disabled workers. In A.J. Culyer, ed., *Economic policies and social goals: Aspects of public choice.* York Studies in Economics. Oxford: Martin Robertson.

Index

Note: Subject entries referring to policies in specific countries are indexed under the country name.

Library of Congress Cataloging in Publication Data

Haveman, Robert H.
Public policy toward disabled workers.

Includes bibliographical references and index.
1. Vocational rehabilitation—Government policy—United States. 2. Insurance, Disability—Government policy—United States. 3. Vocational rehabilitation—Government policy. 4. Insurance, Disability—Government policy. I. Halberstadt, Victor. II. Burkhauser, Richard V. III. Title.
HD7256.U5H39 1984 362.8'5'0973 83-73115
ISBN 0-8014-1626-4 (alk. paper)